COOK'S ILLUSTRATED

1993

$29.95

Published by
Boston Common Press Limited Partnership
17 Station Street
Brookline, MA 02445

ISBN: 0-9640179-0-3
ISSN: 1068-2821

To get home delivery of future issues of *Cook's Illustrated*, call 800-526-8442 inside the U.S., or 515-247-7571 if calling from outside the U.S.

In addition to the Annual Hardbound editions, *Cook's Illustrated* offers the following publications:

The *How to Cook* series of single topic cookbooks
Titles include *How to Make A Pie, How to Make An American Layer Cake, How to Stir-Fry, How to Make Ice Cream, How to Make Pizza, How to Make Holiday Desserts, How to Make Pasta Sauces, How to Make Salad, How to Grill, How to Make Simple Fruit Desserts, How to Make Cookie Jar Favorites, How to Cook Holiday Roasts & Birds, How to Make Stew, How to Cook Shrimp & Other Shellfish, How to Barbecue & Roast On The Grill, How to Cook Garden Vegetables, How to Make Pot Pies & Casseroles, How to Make Soup, How to Sauté, How to Cook Potatoes,* and *How to Make Quick Appetizers.* A boxed set of the first 11 titles in the series is available in an attractive, protective slip case. New releases are published every two months, so give us a call for our complete list of available titles.

The Best Recipe
This 560-page book is a collection of over 700 recipes and 200 illustrations from the past seven years of *Cook's*. We've included basics, such as how to make chicken stock, as well as recipes for quick weeknight meals and special entertaining. Let *The Best Recipe* become your indispensable kitchen companion.

Multi-Year Master Index
Quickly find every article and recipe *Cook's Illustrated* has published from the Charter Issue in 1992 through the most recent year-end issue. Recipe names, authors, article titles, subject matter, equipment testings, food tastings, cookbook reviews, wine tastings, and ingredients are all now instantly at your fingertips.

The Cook's Bible* and *The Yellow Farmhouse Cookbook
Written by Christopher Kimball and published by Little, Brown and Company.

To order any of the books listed above, call 800-611-0759 inside the U.S., or 515-246-6911 if calling from outside the U.S.

You can order subscriptions, gift subscriptions, and any of our books by visiting our online store at **www.cooksillustrated.com**

BC=Back Cover

COOK'S ILLUSTRATED INDEX 1993

A

Acorn squash, field guide .... Nov/Dec 93 **14**
  Prosciutto, and Parmesan Filling for Pasta .... Sep/Oct 93 **18**
Ancho chiles .... May/Jun 93 **23**
Anderson, Jean (*The New German Cookbook*) .... Sep/Oct 93 **31**
Angel food cake .... Charter Issue **10–12**
  Best .... Charter Issue **12**
  cake pans for .... Charter Issue **12**
Appetizers and first courses
  Artichoke Cups with Seafood Salad and Herb Vinaigrette .... May/Jun 93 **BC**
  Grilled Bread with Roasted Garlic and Fresh Tomato Sauce .... Sep/Oct 93 **19**
  pizza
    with Grilled Shrimp Topping with Roasted Tomatoes and Farmer's Cheese .... May/Jun 93 **9**
    with Roasted Tomato Topping with Fennel and Asiago .... May/Jun 93 **9**
  soups
    Broth of Black Bass and Minced Vegetables .... Charter Issue **9**
    Gazpacho .... May/Jun 93 **28**
    Puree of Broccoli, with Garlic and Hot Red Pepper .... Charter Issue **29**
    Puree of Cauliflower, with Cardamom and Mace .... Charter Issue **29**
  White Bean and Tomato Casserole .... Charter Issue **9**
Apple(s)
  crisps and betties .... Sep/Oct 93 **26**
  Mashed Potatoes and, with Bacon and Browned Onions .... Nov/Dec 93 **11**
  Pancake, Reuben's Legendary .... Charter Issue **19**
  poaching .... May/Jun 93 **26**
Apple parers, "mobile" .... Sep/Oct 93 **2**
Appliances
  deep-fryers, electric, rating of .... Charter Issue **20–21**
  espresso machines
    rating of .... Sep/Oct 93 **27–29**
    sources for .... Sep/Oct 93 **32**
    working of .... Sep/Oct 93 **27**
  food processors, kneading pasta dough in .... Sep/Oct 93 **15**
  ice cream makers
    rating of .... Jul/Aug 93 **28–29**
    sources for .... Jul/Aug 93 **32**
  immersion blenders
    rating of .... May/Jun 93 **27–29**
    recipes for .... Sep/Oct 93 **28**
    sources for .... May/Jun 93 **32**
    using .... May/Jun 93 **27–28**
  microwave, baking angel food in .... Charter Issue **11**
  pasta machines
    making breadsticks with .... Charter Issue **24**
    rolling out dough with .... Sep/Oct 93 **16**
    sources for .... Sep/Oct 93 **32**
  replacement parts for .... Sep/Oct 93 **32**
  rice steamers .... Charter Issue **7**
  waffle irons
    rating of .... Nov/Dec 93 **29**
    sources for .... Nov/Dec 93 **32**
Apricot(s)
  crisps and betties .... Sep/Oct 93 **26**
  poaching .... May/Jun 93 **26**
Artichoke(s)
  Cups with Seafood Salad and Herb Vinaigrette .... May/Jun 93 **BC**
  trimming and coring .... May/Jun 93 **5**
Asiago, Roasted Tomato Topping with Fennel and (for pizza) .... May/Jun 93 **9**
Asian (cuisines). *See also* Chinese
  marinades
    Indian .... Jul/Aug 93 **12**
    Master Recipe for .... Jul/Aug 93 **12**
  Sweet and Sour Pan Sauce .... Sep/Oct 93 **11**
  Thai-Style Asparagus with Chiles, Garlic, and Basil .... May/Jun 93 **7**
Asparagus
  cooking .... May/Jun 93 **6–7**
  Grilled .... May/Jun 93 **7**
  Jumbo, Salad with Parma Ham, Parmesan, and Lemon Vinaigrette .... May/Jun 93 **7**
  selecting .... May/Jun 93 **7**
  Steamed, Master Recipe for .... May/Jun 93 **7**
  Thai-Style, with Chiles, Garlic, and Basil .... May/Jun 93 **7**
Avocado(s)
  Basil Dressing .... Charter Issue **30**
  pitting .... Sep/Oct 93 **5**

B

Bacon
  Balsamic Vinegar Sauce with, Warm .... Jul/Aug 93 **25**
  Mashed Potatoes and Apples with Browned Onions and .... Nov/Dec 93 **11**
Bakeware and baking supplies
  cookie cutters, sources for .... Nov/Dec 93 **32**
  muffin tins, commercial, sources for .... Sep/Oct 93 **32**
  parchment paper
    commercial, sources for .... Nov/Dec 93 **32**
    liners, sizing .... May/Jun 93 **4**
  tube pans .... Charter Issue **12**
    lining with parchment paper .... May/Jun 93 **4**
Baking powder
  making your own .... May/Jun 93 **12**
  science of .... Nov/Dec 93 **28**
Balsamic Vinegar Sauce with Bacon, Warm .... Jul/Aug 93 **25**
Banana Berry Popover .... Charter Issue **18**
Basil, field guide .... Jul/Aug 93 **13**
  Avocado Dressing .... Charter Issue **30**
  and Garlic Roast Chicken with Lemon Pan Sauce .... Sep/Oct 93 **20**
  Meat and Ricotta Filling with, for Pasta .... Sep/Oct 93 **18**
  Pesto, Grilled Bread with Roasted Garlic, Fresh Tomato Sauce and .... Sep/Oct 93 **19**
  Tomato Sauce with Capers and .... Sep/Oct 93 **11**
Bavarian, Raspberry Orange .... Charter Issue **BC**
Bean(s)
  black (Chinese fermented)
    Marinade .... Jul/Aug 93 **12**
    Sauce, Chinese .... May/Jun 93 **19**
  Tuscan, with Sage .... Charter Issue **2**
  White, and Tomato Casserole .... Charter Issue **9**
Beard, James (*James Beard's Simple Foods*) .... Sep/Oct 93 **31**
Beef
  Flank Steak, Spicy Southwestern .... Jul/Aug 93 **12**
  marinating for flavor .... Jul/Aug 93 **11**
  rib roast, carving .... Nov/Dec 93 **5**
  roast, flavoring with garlic .... Nov/Dec 93 **5**
  Tenderloin, Grill-Roasted .... Jul/Aug 93 **20**
Berry(ies). *See also* specific berries
  Banana Popover .... Charter Issue **18**
  crisps and betties .... Sep/Oct 93 **26**
Betties .... Sep/Oct 93 **26**
  Basic, Master Recipe for .... Sep/Oct 93 **26**
  preparing fruits for (chart) .... Sep/Oct 93 **26**
Beurre Blanc, Ginger .... May/Jun 93 **28**
Biscuits .... May/Jun 93 **10–12**

baking ....May/Jun 93 11–12
Cheddar ....May/Jun 93 12
Cream, with Herbs ....Nov/Dec 93 13
Flaky ....May/Jun 93 12
shaping ....May/Jun 93 11
Fluffy ....May/Jun 93 12
shaping ....May/Jun 93 10
Herb ....May/Jun 93 12
key ingredients in ....May/Jun 93 10
mixing technique for ....May/Jun 93 10
Strawberry Shortcake ....May/Jun 93 12
Black Bass, Broth of Minced Vegetables and ....Charter Issue 9
Black bean(s) (Chinese fermented)
Marinade ....Jul/Aug 93 12
Sauce, Chinese ....May/Jun 93 19
Black Trumpet mushrooms, field guide ....Sep/Oct 93 14
Blenders. *See* Immersion blenders
Blind tastings. *See also* Wine—blind tastings of
caviar ....Nov/Dec 93 24–26
olive oils ....Charter Issue 13–15
red wine vinegars ....Sep/Oct 93 24–25
soy sauce and tamari ....May/Jun 93 13–15
sparkling waters ....Jul/Aug 93 21–22
Bok choy ....Charter Issue 6
Hot and Sour ....Charter Issue 7
Shanghai, Stir-Fried with Crabmeat ....Charter Issue 7
Bookman, Ken *(Fifty Ways to Cook Most Everything)* ....Charter Issue 31
Book of Feasts, A (Goldstein and Nelson) ....Jul/Aug 93 31
Book reviews
A Book of Feasts (Goldstein and Nelson) ....Jul/Aug 93 31
China Moon Cookbook (Tropp) ....Charter Issue 31
Classic Cuisine of Provence (Holuigue) ....Nov/Dec 93 31
Cooking Under Wraps (Routhier) ....May/Jun 93 30
Emeril's New New Orleans Cooking (Lagasse and Tirsch) ....May/Jun 93 30
Fifty Ways to Cook Most Everything (Schloss and Bookman) .Charter Issue 31
The Foods of Greece (Kremezi) ....Nov/Dec 93 31
Great Good Food (Rosso) ....Jul/Aug 93 31
James Beard's Simple Foods (Beard) ....Sep/Oct 93 31
Michel Richard's Home Cooking with a French Accent (Richard and Zeidler) ....Sep/Oct 93 31
The New German Cookbook (Anderson and Würz) ....Sep/Oct 93 31
New York Cookbook (O'Neill) ....Charter Issue 31
Provence the Beautiful Cookbook (Olney) ....Nov/Dec 93 31
A Treasury of Southern Baking (Hilburn) ....May/Jun 93 30
Bouquet garni ....Sep/Oct 93 2
Bourbon Chocolate Glaze ....Jul/Aug 93 3
Brandied Whipped Cream ....Nov/Dec 93 23
Bran muffins ....Sep/Oct 93 8
with Raisins and Dates, Big ....Sep/Oct 93 7
Bread(s). *See also* Biscuits; Muffins
Banana Berry Popover ....Charter Issue 18
Basic, Master Recipe for ....Charter Issue 24
basic techniques for ....Charter Issue 22–25
crusts on ....Charter Issue 23–24
Deep-Fried Devils ....Jul/Aug 93 2
dinner rolls ....Nov/Dec 93 15–17
Master Recipe for ....Nov/Dec 93 15
preparing dough for ....Nov/Dec 93 15
shaping ....Nov/Dec 93 16–17
flours for ....Charter Issue 22–23
specialty, substituting ....Charter Issue 24
Grilled, with Roasted Garlic and Fresh Tomato Sauce ....Sep/Oct 93 19
kneading ....Charter Issue 23
microwave ....Charter Issue 23
proofing, shortcuts for ....Charter Issue 23
Pudding, Raspberry Summer ....Jul/Aug 93 BC
shaping
cylindrical loaf ....Charter Issue 25
ear-of-wheat shapes ....Charter Issue 25
rectangular loaf ....Charter Issue 25
round loaf ....Charter Issue 25
shortcuts for ....Charter Issue 23
slashing dough before baking ....Charter Issue 23
slow-rise ....Charter Issue 22;
....Nov/Dec 93 2
testing for doneness ....Charter Issue 22
yeasts for ....Charter Issue 22
Breadsticks, making with pasta machine ....Charter Issue 24
Breakfast. *See also* Muffins
Banana Berry Popover ....Charter Issue 18
waffles ....Nov/Dec 93 27–28
Almost-as-Good-as-Buttermilk ....Nov/Dec 93 28
Buttermilk, Best ....Nov/Dec 93 28
Raised ....Charter Issue 2
Brining
science of ....Nov/Dec 93 19
turkey ....Nov/Dec 93 19
Broccoli
keeping green ....Nov/Dec 93 2
Puree of, Soup with Garlic and Hot Red Pepper ....Charter Issue 29
Broth
of Black Bass and Minced Vegetables ....Charter Issue 9
Quick ....Charter Issue 28
Salmon, Quick ....Jul/Aug 93 25
stock vs. ....Charter Issue 28
Brown rice vinegar ....Charter Issue 30
Burgundy wines (Pinot Noir), blind tasting of ....Sep/Oct 93 30
Butter
Brown, and Pine Nut Sauce (for pasta) ....Sep/Oct 93 18
cookies ....Nov/Dec 93 6–9
See also Cookies—butter
Ginger Beurre Blanc ....May/Jun 93 28
health concerns and ....Charter Issue 20
science of ....Charter Issue 2
Buttermilk
Fried Chicken, Spicy ....Charter Issue 21
science of ....Jul/Aug 93 1
Waffles, Best ....Nov/Dec 93 28
Butternut squash, field guide ....Nov/Dec 93 14

C

Cabbage(s)
bok choy
Hot and Sour ....Charter Issue 7
Shanghai, Stir-Fried with Crabmeat ....Charter Issue 7
Chinese ....Charter Issue 6–7
growing your own ....Charter Issue 7
Seafood Casserole ....Charter Issue 6
Stir-Fried ....Charter Issue 7
Café Latte ....Sep/Oct 93 28
Café Mocha ....Sep/Oct 93 28
Cake flour, unbleached, substitute for ....Nov/Dec 93 9
Cake mixers or cake whisks, English ....Nov/Dec 93 3
sources for ....Nov/Dec 93 32
Cakes
angel food ....Charter Issue 10–12
Best ....Charter Issue 12

cake pans for . . . . Charter Issue **12**
Mississippi Mud . . . . Jul/Aug 93 **3**
Orange, Neopolitan . . . . Charter Issue **15**
California wines, blind tastings of
Chablis . . . . Jul/Aug 93 **30**
Pinot Noirs . . . . Sep/Oct 93 **30**
rosés . . . . May/Jun 93 **31**
sparklers . . . . Nov/Dec 93 **30**
Campylobacter, temperature and . . . . Nov/Dec 93 **21**
Canola oil, health concerns and . . . . Charter Issue **20**
Caper(s)
Lemon Sauce . . . . Sep/Oct 93 **10**
Tomato-Basil Sauce with . . . . Sep/Oct 93 **11**
Cappuccino . . . . Sep/Oct 93 **28**
Carrots, Roasted Parsley Roots and . . . . Jul/Aug 93 **25**
Carving
beef rib roast . . . . Nov/Dec 93 **5**
chicken . . . . Charter Issue **26**
ham . . . . Charter Issue **5**
Casseroles
Seafood Cabbage . . . . Charter Issue **6**
White Bean and Tomato . . . . Charter Issue **9**
Cauliflower
breaking into florets . . . . Sep/Oct 93 **5**
Puree of, Soup with Cardamom and Mace . . . . Charter Issue **29**
Caviar
blind tasting of . . . . Nov/Dec 93 **24–26**
fresh, buying and serving . . . . Nov/Dec 93 **24**
lesser types of . . . . Nov/Dec 93 **24**
mail-order sources for . . . . Nov/Dec 93 **32**
transforming fish eggs into . . . . Nov/Dec 93 **25**
Celery, Braised . . . . Jul/Aug 93 **25**
Celery cabbage, Chinese **6**
Seafood Casserole . . . . Charter Issue **6**
Chablis, blind tasting of . . . . Jul/Aug 93 **30**
Champagnes, blind tasting of . . . . Nov/Dec 93 **30**
Chanterelles, field guide . . . . Sep/Oct 93 **14**
Charcoal grills, grill-roasting on . . . . Jul/Aug 93 **18–19**
Cheddar Biscuits . . . . May/Jun 93 **12**
Cheese(s)
Asiago, Roasted Tomato Topping with Fennel and (for pizza) . . . . May/Jun 93 **9**
Farmer's, Grilled Shrimp Topping with Roasted Tomatoes and (for pizza) . . . . May/Jun 93 **9**
Omelet . . . . Sep/Oct 93 **22**
Parmesan
Jumbo Asparagus Salad with Parma Ham, Lemon Vinaigrette and . . . . May/Jun 93 **7**
Mashed Potatoes with Lemon and . . . . Nov/Dec 93 **11**
pregrated vs. freshly grated . . . . Nov/Dec 93 **3**
Squash, and Prosciutto Filling for Pasta . . . . Nov/Dec 93 **18**
ricotta
and Meat Filling with Basil for Pasta . . . . Sep/Oct 93 **18**
and Spinach Filling for Pasta . . . . Sep/Oct 93 **18**
Two, Broiled Eggplant Slices with . . . . Jul/Aug 93 **7**
Cherry(ies)
and Peaches Poached in Spiced Red Wine . . . . May/Jun 93 **26**
poaching . . . . May/Jun 93 **26**
Cherry pitters . . . . Jul/Aug 93 **32**
Chervil, field guide . . . . Jul/Aug 93 **13**
Chianti, blind tasting of . . . . Charter Issue **32**
Chicken
breast(s)
Cutlets, Sautéed, Master Recipe for . . . . Sep/Oct 93 **10**
fanning . . . . Sep/Oct 93 **11**
flouring . . . . Sep/Oct 93 **11**
judging doneness of . . . . Sep/Oct 93 **9**
preparing for sautéing . . . . Sep/Oct 93 **10**
removing boneless meat from . . . . May/Jun 93 **17**
sautéing . . . . Sep/Oct 93 **9–11**
breasts, sauces for
Asian-Style Sweet and Sour Pan . . . . Sep/Oct 93 **11**
Lemon-Caper . . . . Sep/Oct 93 **10**
Oaxacan-Style, with Cloves and Cinnamon . . . . Sep/Oct 93 **10**
Peach Salsa . . . . Sep/Oct 93 **11**
Sherry-Cream, with Mushrooms . . . . Sep/Oct 93 **10**
Tomato-Basil, with Capers . . . . Sep/Oct 93 **11**
butterflying . . . . May/Jun 93 **17**
carving . . . . Charter Issue **26**
cutting
into uniform pieces for stir-fry . . . . May/Jun 93 **20**
whole birds . . . . May/Jun 93 **16–17**
Fried, Spicy Buttermilk . . . . Charter Issue **21**
Grilled, with Olives, Rosemary, and Garlic . . . . Jul/Aug 93 **12**
Grill-Roasted Hickory . . . . Jul/Aug 93 **20**
judging doneness of . . . . Charter Issue **27**
"lollipops" for hors d'oeuvres . . . . May/Jun 93 **17**
marinating for flavor . . . . Jul/Aug 93 **11**
roast . . . . Charter Issue **26–27**
Basic Recipe for . . . . Charter Issue **27**
customizing roasting pan for . . . . Charter Issue **27**
with Dijon Mustard–Thyme Sauce . . . . May/Jun 93 **28**
Garlic and Basil, with Lemon Pan Sauce . . . . Sep/Oct 93 **20**
reader's comments on . . . . May/Jun 93 **3**
"stuffing" skin before . . . . May/Jun 93 **17**
Roasted in Red Peppers . . . . Sep/Oct 93 **BC**
thighs, boning . . . . May/Jun 93 **17**
trussing . . . . May/Jun 93 **3**
Chile(s)
Corn and Zucchini Sauté with . . . . Jul/Aug 93 **9**
dried
cutting and seeding . . . . Sep/Oct 93 **4**
sources for . . . . May/Jun 93 **32**
Jalapeño Preserves . . . . May/Jun 93 **23**
Red, Marinade . . . . May/Jun 93 **22**
varieties of . . . . May/Jun 93 **23**
Chili Sauce, Szechwan . . . . May/Jun 93 **19**
Chimney starters . . . . Jul/Aug 93 **32**
China Moon Cookbook (Tropp) . . . . Charter Issue **31**
Chinese (cuisine)
cabbage . . . . Charter Issue **6–7**
Hot and Sour Bok Choy . . . . Charter Issue **7**
Seafood Casserole . . . . Charter Issue **6**
Shanghai Bok Choy Stir-Fried with Crabmeat . . . . Charter Issue **7**
Stir-Fried . . . . Charter Issue **7**
cookbooks
China Moon Cookbook (Tropp) . . . . Charter Issue **31**
short list of . . . . May/Jun 93 **21**
Deep-Fried Devils . . . . Jul/Aug 93 **2**
Duck, Peking . . . . Sep/Oct 93 **12**
flavoring sauces, for stir-fry . . . . May/Jun 93 **19**
Chinese oil vegetable . . . . Charter Issue **6**
Stir-Fried . . . . Charter Issue **7**
Chipotle(s) . . . . May/Jun 93 **23**
Chives, field guide . . . . Jul/Aug 93 **13**
Chocolate
Cake, Mississippi Mud . . . . Jul/Aug 93 **3**
cookie(s)
Butter, Dough . . . . Nov/Dec 93 **7**

Linzer .... Nov/Dec 93 9
Glaze, Bourbon .... Jul/Aug 93 3
Ice Cream .... Jul/Aug 93 28
Parfaits, Trinity .... Nov/Dec 93 BC
Chowder, Corn and Clam, with Roasted Parsnips .... Jul/Aug 93 9
Cilantro, field guide .... Jul/Aug 93 13
Pesto .... May/Jun 93 22
Citrus. *See also* specific citrus fruits
Butter Cookie Dough .... Nov/Dec 93 7
oils, sources for .... Nov/Dec 93 32
Spirals .... Nov/Dec 93 8
Clam and Corn Chowder with Roasted Parsnips .... Jul/Aug 93 9
Classic Cuisine of Provence (Holuigue) .... Nov/Dec 93 31
Coconut curry sauce
Chinese .... May/Jun 93 19
Seared Snapper with Pea Shoots and, Lynne Aronson's .... May/Jun 93 2
Coffee
beans .... Sep/Oct 93 28–29
espresso .... Sep/Oct 93 27–29
drinks .... Sep/Oct 93 28
information sources on .... Sep/Oct 93 32
espresso machines
rating of .... Sep/Oct 93 27–29
sources for for .... Sep/Oct 93 32
working of .... Sep/Oct 93 27
Ice Cream .... Jul/Aug 93 28
Compotes, Strawberry and Rhubarb, with
Sugared Pecans .... May/Jun 93 25
Condiments. *See also* Marinades; Salad dressings; Salsas; Sauces
exotic tropical jams, mail-order sources for .... Sep/Oct 93 32
Garlic, Roasted, Puree, Master Recipe for .... Sep/Oct 93 19
Jalapeño Preserves .... May/Jun 93 23
"Margarine" .... May/Jun 93 28
Mayonnaise, Raspberry .... May/Jun 93 28
vanilla extract, homemade .... Nov/Dec 93 2
Cookbooks. *See also* Book reviews
Chinese, short list of .... May/Jun 93 21
Cookie(s)
butter .... Nov/Dec 93 6–9
Chocolate, Dough .... Nov/Dec 93 7
Citrus, Dough .... Nov/Dec 93 7
Citrus Spirals .... Nov/Dec 93 8
Classic Cut-Outs .... Nov/Dec 93 8
cornstarch in .... Nov/Dec 93 9
Decorative Icing for .... Nov/Dec 93 9
Dough, Master Recipe for .... Nov/Dec 93 7
Jam Pinwheels .... Nov/Dec 93 9
Mincemeat or Jam Turnovers .... Nov/Dec 93 8
Mock Thumbprints .... Nov/Dec 93 8
Nut, Dough .... Nov/Dec 93 7
Petticoat Tails .... Nov/Dec 93 9
Pinwheels .... Nov/Dec 93 8
shaping .... Nov/Dec 93 8
Spice, Dough .... Nov/Dec 93 7
tender, "short" dough for .... Nov/Dec 93 7
Viennese Crescents .... Nov/Dec 93 9
Linzer .... Nov/Dec 93 9
Chocolate .... Nov/Dec 93 9
shaping .... Nov/Dec 93 8
Spice .... Nov/Dec 93 9
Walnut Wafers .... Charter Issue 15
Cookie cutters, sources for .... Nov/Dec 93 32
Cooking schools .... May/Jun 93 32
Cooking Under Wraps (Routhier) .... May/Jun 93 30
Corn
and Clam Chowder with Roasted Parsnips .... Jul/Aug 93 9
on cob, removing corn from .... Jul/Aug 93 8–9
"Indian Corn of the Americas" poster .... Jul/Aug 93 32
muffins .... Sep/Oct 93 8
Double .... Sep/Oct 93 7
Pudding, Shaker-Style Creamy .... Jul/Aug 93 9
Roasted, Salsa .... Jul/Aug 93 8
and Zucchini Sauté with Chiles .... Jul/Aug 93 9
Corn-kernel cutters .... Jul/Aug 93 32
Corn oil, health concerns and .... Charter Issue 20
Cornstarch, in cookies .... Nov/Dec 93 9
Crabmeat
Artichoke Cups with Seafood Salad and Herb Vinaigrette .... May/Jun 93 BC
Stir-Fried Shanghai Bok Choy with .... Charter Issue 7
Cream
Biscuits with Herbs .... Nov/Dec 93 13
Sauce, Sherry, with Mushrooms .... Sep/Oct 93 10
Whipped, Brandied .... Nov/Dec 93 23
Cream of tartar .... Charter Issue 10
Crème Caramel .... Charter Issue 3
Crescents, Viennese .... Nov/Dec 93 9
shaping .... Nov/Dec 93 8
Crimini, field guide .... Sep/Oct 93 14
Crisps, fruit .... Sep/Oct 93 26
Master Recipe for .... Sep/Oct 93 26
preparing fruits for (chart) .... Sep/Oct 93 26
Cucumber(s)
dicing .... Charter Issue 8
seeding .... Jul/Aug 93 4
Curry coconut sauce
Chinese .... May/Jun 93 16
Seared Snapper with Pea Shoots and, Lynne Aronson's .... May/Jun 93 2
Custard
Prune, Pudding (Far Breton) .... Charter Issue 19
scalding milk for .... Charter Issue 2
Cut-Outs, Classic .... Nov/Dec 93 8
Cutting. *See also* Dicing
julienning greens .... Nov/Dec 93 4
mincing ginger .... May/Jun 93 21
Cutting boards, safety concerns and .... Sep/Oct 93 2

D

Dates, Big Bran Muffins with Raisins and .... Sep/Oct 93 7
Decorating
disposable piping cones for .... Nov/Dec 93 5
Icing (for cookies) .... Nov/Dec 93 9
scallion brushes .... Sep/Oct 93 4
Deep-fryers, electric, rating of .... Charter Issue 20–21
Delicata squash, field guide .... Nov/Dec 93 14
Desserts. *See also* Cookie(s); Ice cream; Puddings
angel food cake .... Charter Issue 10–12
Best .... Charter Issue 12
Apple Pancake, Reuben's Legendary .... Charter Issue 19
Banana Berry Popover .... Charter Issue 19
Basic Batter (Master Recipe for Dessert Pancakes and Puddings) .... Charter Issue 18
Betties, Basic, Master Recipe for .... Sep/Oct 93 26
Chocolate Trinity Parfaits .... Nov/Dec 93 BC
Crème Caramel .... Charter Issue 3
crisps, fruit .... Sep/Oct 93 26
Master Recipe for .... Sep/Oct 93 26
preparing fruits for (chart) .... Sep/Oct 93 26
Mississippi Mud Cake .... Jul/Aug 93 3
Orange Cake, Neopolitan .... Charter Issue 15

pie pastry .... Charter Issue **16–17**
Flaky Shell .... Nov/Dec 93 **23**
poached fruit .... May/Jun 93 **24–26**
Peaches and Cherries, in Spiced Red Wine .... May/Jun 93 **26**
Pears, with Star Anise .... May/Jun 93 **25**
pumpkin pie .... Nov/Dec 93 **22–23**
Best .... Nov/Dec 93 **22**
Raspberry Orange Bavarian .... Charter Issue **BC**
sauces and toppings for
Brandied Whipped Cream .... Nov/Dec 93 **23**
using immersion blender for .... May/Jun 93 **28**
strawberry
and Rhubarb Compotes with Sugared Pecans .... May/Jun 93 **25**
Shortcake .... May/Jun 93 **12**
Dicing
cucumbers .... Charter Issue **8**
onions .... Charter Issue **5**
tomatoes .... Jul/Aug 93 **15**
Dill, field guide .... Jul/Aug 93 **13**
Dinner rolls .... Nov/Dec 93 **15–17**
Master Recipe for .... Nov/Dec 93 **15**
preparing dough for .... Nov/Dec 93 **15**
shaping .... Nov/Dec 93 **16–17**
Dressings. *See* Salad dressings
Duck
Peking .... Sep/Oct 93 **12**
preparing for air-drying .... Sep/Oct 93 **13**

E

Egg(s)
omelets .... Sep/Oct 93 **21–22**
See also Omelets
separating .... Jul/Aug 93 **5**
whites
cream of tartar and .... Charter Issue **10**
science of .... Charter Issue **11**
Eggplant
cooking .... Jul/Aug 93 **6–7**
number of seeds in .... Nov/Dec 93 **2**
male vs. female .... May/Jun 93 **5**
salting and pressing .... Jul/Aug 93 **6–7**
sautéed
with Crisped Bread Crumbs .... Jul/Aug 93 **7**
Master Recipe for .... Jul/Aug 93 **7**
in Spicy Garlic Sauce .... Jul/Aug 93 **7**
in Tomato Sauce with Basil .... Jul/Aug 93 **7**
slices, broiled
Master Recipe for .... Jul/Aug 93 **7**
with Two Cheeses .... Jul/Aug 93 **7**
Emeril's New New Orleans Cooking (Lagasse and Tirsch) .... May/Jun 93 **30**
English cake whisks .... Nov/Dec 93 **3**
sources for .... Nov/Dec 93 **32**
Equipment. *See also* Appliances; Bakeware and baking supplies; Gadgets and utensils
grilling
charcoal grills, grill roasting on .... Jul/Aug 93 **18–19**
chimney starters .... Jul/Aug 93 **32**
gas grills, grill roasting on .... Jul/Aug 93 **19, 20**
ratings of
deep-fryers, electric .... Charter Issue **20–21**
espresso machines .... Sep/Oct 93 **27–29**
ice cream makers .... Jul/Aug 93 **28–29**
immersion blenders .... May/Jun 93 **27–29**
waffle irons .... Nov/Dec 93 **29**
Espresso
coffee beans for .... Sep/Oct 93 **28–29**
drinks .... Sep/Oct 93 **28**
information sources on .... Sep/Oct 93 **32**
Espresso machines
rating of .... Sep/Oct 93 **27–29**
sources for .... Sep/Oct 93 **32**
working of .... Sep/Oct 93 **27**
Exotic produce, mail-order sources for .... Nov/Dec 93 **32**

F

Far Breton (Prune Custard Pudding) .... Charter Issue **19**
Farmer's Cheese, Grilled Shrimp Topping with Roasted Tomatoes and (for pizza) .... May/Jun 93 **9**
Fennel
Roasted Tomato Topping with Asiago and (for pizza) .... May/Jun 93 **9**
trimming and slicing .... Sep/Oct 93 **5**
Field guides
autumn and winter squashes .... Nov/Dec 93 **14**
herbs .... Jul/Aug 93 **13**
mushrooms .... Sep/Oct 93 **14**
Fifty Ways to Cook Most Everything (Schloss and Bookman) .... Charter Issue **31**
Figs, poaching .... May/Jun 93 **26**
Fines Herbes Omelet .... Sep/Oct 93 **22**
First courses. *See* Appetizers and first courses
Fish. *See also* Seafood
Black Bass, Broth of Minced Vegetables and .... Charter Issue **9**
marinating for flavor .... Jul/Aug 93 **11**
monkfish, preparing .... Sep/Oct 93 **4**
roundfish, filleting .... Charter Issue **3**
salmon
Broth, quick .... Jul/Aug 93 **25**
Grill-Roasted, with Alderwood .... Jul/Aug 93 **20**
Roasted, with Kasha and Leek Stuffing .... Jul/Aug 93 **23**
whole, boning .... Jul/Aug 93 **24–25**
Snapper, Seared, with Pea Shoots and Coconut Curry Sauce, Lynne Aronson's .... May/Jun 93 **2**
Tuna, Grilled, with Ginger and Garlic .... Jul/Aug 93 **12**
Fish Sauce (nuoc mam) Lemon Marinade .... Jul/Aug 93 **12**
Flank Steak, Spicy Southwestern .... Jul/Aug 93 **12**
Flay, Bobby, master class with (Roast Leg of Lamb with Red Chile Crust and Jalapeño Preserves) .... May/Jun 93 **22**
Flour
cake, unbleached, substitute for .... Nov/Dec 93 **9**
measuring .... Sep/Oct 93 **6**
protein content of .... May/Jun 93 **10**
specialty, substituting .... Charter Issue **24**
Food processors, kneading pasta dough in .... Sep/Oct 93 **15**
Foods of Greece, The (Kremezi) .... Nov/Dec 93 **31**
French (cuisine)
book reviews
Classic Cuisine of Provence (Holuigue) .... Nov/Dec 93 **31**
Michel Richard's Home Cooking with a French Accent (Richard and Zeidler) .... Sep/Oct 93 **31**
Provence the Beautiful Cookbook (Olney) .... Nov/Dec 93 **31**
Prune Custard Pudding (Far Breton) .... Charter Issue **19**
wines, blind tastings of
Chablis .... Jul/Aug 93 **30**
Champagnes .... Nov/Dec 93 **30**
Pinot Noirs .... Sep/Oct 93 **30**
rosés .... May/Jun 93 **31**
Fruit(s). *See also* specific fruits
crisps .... Sep/Oct 93 **26**
Master Recipe for .... Sep/Oct 93 **26**

preparing fruits for (chart) . . . Sep/Oct 93 **26**
Muffins, Any-Fruit-Will-Do, with Streusel Topping (Master Recipe) . . . Sep/Oct 93 **8**
poaching . . . May/Jun 93 **24–26**
seasonings for . . . May/Jun 93 **25**
syrups for . . . May/Jun 93 **24–25**
various fresh fruits (chart) . . . May/Jun 93 **26**

G

Gadgets and utensils
apple parers, "mobile" . . . Sep/Oct 93 **2**
cake mixers or cake whisks, English . . . Nov/Dec 93 **3**
sources for . . . Nov/Dec 93 **32**
cherry pitters . . . Jul/Aug 93 **32**
corn-kernel cutters . . . Jul/Aug 93 **32**
cutting boards, safety concerns and . . . Sep/Oct 93 **2**
ice-cream scoops, professional, sources for . . . Sep/Oct 93 **32**
marinating needles . . . Jul/Aug 93 **3**
sources for . . . Jul/Aug 93 **32**
piping cones, disposable . . . Nov/Dec 93 **5**
pop-up timers . . . Nov/Dec 93 **21**
potato mashers, Italian . . . Nov/Dec 93 **10**
sources for . . . Nov/Dec 93 **32**
ravioli cutters . . . Sep/Oct 93 **32**
rolling pins, types of . . . Sep/Oct 93 **3**
salamanders . . . Charter Issue **2**
spaetzle machines . . . May/Jun 93 **2**
sources for . . . May/Jun 93 **32**
thermometers, testing bread's doneness with . . . Charter Issue **32**
vegetable peelers . . . Nov/Dec 93 **32**
V-racks . . . Nov/Dec 93 **20**
sources for . . . Nov/Dec 93 **32**
Garlic
and Basil Roast Chicken with Lemon Pan Sauce . . . Sep/Oct 93 **20**
Cream Sauce, Linguine with . . . Sep/Oct 93 **20**
flavoring roasts with . . . Nov/Dec 93 **5**
Ginger Marinade . . . Sep/Oct 93 **12**
Herb Pizza Crust, Master Recipe for . . . May/Jun 93 **8**
roasted . . . Sep/Oct 93 **19–20**
Grilled Bread with Fresh Tomato Sauce and . . . Sep/Oct 93 **19**
Puree, Master Recipe for . . . Sep/Oct 93 **19**
tips and techniques for . . . Sep/Oct 93 **20**
Sauce, Spicy, Sautéed Eggplant in . . . Jul/Aug 93 **7**
Sesame Dressing . . . Charter Issue **30**
Gazpacho . . . May/Jun 93 **28**
German (cuisine): *The New German Cookbook* (Anderson and Würz) . . . Sep/Oct 93 **31**
Ginger
Beurre Blanc . . . May/Jun 93 **28**
Garlic Marinade . . . Sep/Oct 93 **12**
juice, extracting . . . Jul/Aug 93 **5**
mincing . . . May/Jun 93 **21**
Walnut Miso Dressing . . . Charter Issue **30**
Glazes
Brown Sugar and Honey Mustard . . . Nov/Dec 93 **12**
Chocolate-Bourbon . . . Jul/Aug 93 **3**
Golden Nugget squash, field guide . . . Nov/Dec 93 **14**
Goldstein, Kay *(A Book of Feasts)* . . . Jul/Aug 93 **31**
Grapeseed oil, health concerns and . . . Charter Issue **20**
Great Good Food (Rosso) . . . Jul/Aug 93 **31**
Greek (cuisine): *The Foods of Greece* (Kremezi) . . . Nov/Dec 93 **31**
Greens
julienning . . . Nov/Dec 93 **4**
Stuffing, Spicy . . . Nov/Dec 93 **12**
Grilled dishes
Asparagus . . . May/Jun 93 **7**
Bread with Roasted Garlic and Fresh Tomato Sauce . . . Sep/Oct 93 **19**
Chicken with Olives, Rosemary, and Garlic . . . Jul/Aug 93 **12**
Lamb, Skewered, with Yogurt, Curry, and Mint . . . Jul/Aug 93 **12**
pizza . . . May/Jun 93 **8–9**
with Grilled Shrimp Topping with Roasted Tomatoes and Farmer's Cheese . . . May/Jun 93 **9**
with Roasted Tomato Topping with Fennel and Asiago . . . May/Jun 93 **9**
Shrimp Topping with Roasted Tomatoes and Farmer's Cheese (for pizza) . . . May/Jun 93 **9**
Tuna with Ginger and Garlic . . . Jul/Aug 93 **12**
Grilling equipment
charcoal grills, grill roasting on . . . Jul/Aug 93 **18–19**
chimney starters . . . Jul/Aug 93 **32**
gas grills, grill roasting on . . . Jul/Aug 93 **19, 20**
Grill roasting . . . Jul/Aug 93 **18–20**
Beef Tenderloin . . . Jul/Aug 93 **20**
Chicken, Hickory . . . Jul/Aug 93 **20**
Salmon with Alderwood . . . Jul/Aug 93 **20**
setting up charcoal grill for . . . Jul/Aug 93 **19**
setting up gas grill for . . . Jul/Aug 93 **20**
Spareribs with Barbecue Sauce . . . Jul/Aug 93 **20**
Turkey, Best . . . Nov/Dec 93 **21**

H

Ham
carving . . . Charter Issue **5**
country
sources for . . . Nov/Dec 93 **32**
Stuffed with Spicy Southern Greens . . . Nov/Dec 93 **12**
trimming and stuffing . . . Nov/Dec 93 **13**
Potato, and Parsley Omelet . . . Sep/Oct 93 **22**
prosciutto
Jumbo Asparagus Salad with Parma Ham, Parmesan, and Lemon Vinaigrette . . . May/Jun 93 **7**
Squash, and Parmesan Filling for Pasta . . . Sep/Oct 93 **18**
Harp Peeler . . . Nov/Dec 93 **32**
Hazelnuts, skinning . . . Jul/Aug 93 **3**
Herb(s). *See also* specific herbs
Biscuits . . . May/Jun 93 **12**
bouquet garni . . . Sep/Oct 93 **2**
Cream Biscuits with . . . Nov/Dec 93 **13**
field guide to . . . Jul/Aug 93 **13**
Fines Herbes Omelet . . . Sep/Oct 93 **22**
Garlic Pizza Crust, Master Recipe for . . . May/Jun 93 **8**
Tomato Sauce, Master Recipe for . . . Jul/Aug 93 **14**
Hilburn, Prudence *(A Treasury of Southern Baking)* . . . May/Jun 93 **30**
Holuigue, Diane *(Classic Cuisine of Provence)* . . . Nov/Dec 93 **31**
Honey
Mustard and Brown Sugar Glaze . . . Nov/Dec 93 **12**
Pepper Vinaigrette . . . May/Jun 93 **28**
Hot and Sour Bok Choy . . . Charter Issue **7**
Hubbard squash, field guide . . . Nov/Dec 93 **14**

I

Ice cream . . . Jul/Aug 93 **26–28**
Chocolate . . . Jul/Aug 93 **28**
Coffee . . . Jul/Aug 93 **28**
cream and sugar in . . . Jul/Aug 93 **26–27**
"diet" . . . Jul/Aug 93 **27**
egg yolks in . . . Jul/Aug 93 **26**
storing . . . Jul/Aug 93 **27**
Strawberry . . . Jul/Aug 93 **28**

Vanilla, Master Recipe for .Jul/Aug 93 **27**
Ice cream makers
rating of .Jul/Aug 93 **28–29**
sources for .Jul/Aug 93 **32**
Ice-cream scoops, professional, sources for .Sep/Oct 93 **32**
Icing, Decorative (for cookies) .Nov/Dec 93 **9**
Immersion blenders .May/Jun 93 **27–29**
rating of .May/Jun 93 **27, 29**
recipes for .May/Jun 93 **28**
sources for .May/Jun 93 **32**
using .May/Jun 93 **27–28**
Indian Marinade .Jul/Aug 93 **12**
Ingredients, ratings of. *See* Blind tastings
Italian (cuisine). *See also* Pasta; Pizza
Beans with Sage, Tuscan .Charter Issue **2**
Chianti, blind tasting of .Charter Issue **32**
Orange Cake, Neopolitan .Charter Issue **15**
potato mashers .Nov/Dec 93 **10**
sources for .Nov/Dec 93 **32**

J

Jalapeño(s) .May/Jun 93 **23**
Preserves .May/Jun 93 **23**
Jam(s)
exotic tropical, mail-order sources for .Sep/Oct 93 **32**
Pinwheels .Nov/Dec 93 **9**
Turnovers .Nov/Dec 93 **8**
James Beard's Simple Foods (Beard) .Sep/Oct 93 **31**
Julienning greens .Nov/Dec 93 **4**

K

Kaffir lime .Charter Issue **9**
Kale, julienning .Nov/Dec 93 **4**
Kasha and Leek Stuffing .Jul/Aug 93 **23**
Kremezi, Aglaia *(The Foods of Greece)* .Nov/Dec 93 **31**
Kunz, Gray, master class with (Broth of Black Bass and Minced Vegetables) .Charter Issue **8**

L

Lagasse, Emeril *(Emeril's New New Orleans Cooking)* .May/Jun 93 **30**
Lamb
Grilled, Skewered, with Yogurt, Curry, and Mint .Jul/Aug 93 **12**
leg of
flavoring with garlic .Nov/Dec 93 **5**
Roast, with Red Chile Crust and Jalapeño Preserves .May/Jun 93 **22**
tying .May/Jun 93 **23**
Latte Macchiato .Sep/Oct 93 **28**
Leek(s)
cleaning .Jul/Aug 93 **4**
cutting .Charter Issue **8**
and Kasha Stuffing .Jul/Aug 93 **23**
Lemon(s)
Caper Sauce .Sep/Oct 93 **10**
Fish Sauce Marinade .Jul/Aug 93 **12**
oil, sources for .Nov/Dec 93 **32**
peel
Candied .Charter Issue **3**
grating .May/Jun 93 **5**
Sauce, Chinese .May/Jun 93 **19**
Vinaigrette .May/Jun 93 **7**
Lemongrass, preparing .Nov/Dec 93 **4**
Lime, kaffir .Charter Issue **9**
Lindeborg, Susan McCreight, master class with (Country Ham Stuffed with Greens) .Nov/Dec 93 **12–13**
Linguine with Garlic Cream Sauce .Sep/Oct 93 **20**
Linzer Cookies .Nov/Dec 93 **9**
Chocolate .Nov/Dec 93 **9**
shaping .Nov/Dec 93 **8**
Spice .Nov/Dec 93 **9**
Lobster
boiled, eating .Jul/Aug 93 **17**
male vs. female .Jul/Aug 93 **16**
preparing
for grilling or broiling .Jul/Aug 93 **16–17**
for sautéing or stir-frying .Jul/Aug 93 **17**

M

Main dishes. *See also* Pasta
Artichoke Cups with Seafood Salad and Herb Vinaigrette .May/Jun 93 **BC**
beef
Flank Steak, Spicy Southwestern .Jul/Aug 93 **12**
Tenderloin, Grill-Roasted .Jul/Aug 93 **20**
Black Bass, Broth of Minced Vegetables and .Charter Issue **9**
bok choy
Hot and Sour .Charter Issue **7**
Shanghai, Stir-Fried with Crabmeat .Charter Issue **7**
Cabbage, Stir-Fried .Charter Issue **7**
chicken
Breast Cutlets, Sautéed, Master Recipe for .Sep/Oct 93 **10**
Fried, Spicy Buttermilk .Charter Issue **21**
Garlic and Basil Roast, with Lemon Pan Sauce .Sep/Oct 93 **20**
Grilled, with Olives, Rosemary, and Garlic .Jul/Aug 93 **12**
Grill-Roasted Hickory .Jul/Aug 93 **20**
Roast, Basic Recipe for .Charter Issue **27**
Roast, with Dijon Mustard–Thyme Sauce .May/Jun 93 **28**
Roasted in Red Peppers .Sep/Oct 93 **BC**
Duck, Peking .Sep/Oct 93 **12**
Eggplant Slices, Broiled, with Two Cheeses .Jul/Aug 93 **7**
Ham, Country, Stuffed with Spicy Southern Greens .Nov/Dec 93 **12**
lamb
Grilled Skewered, with Yogurt, Curry, and Mint .Jul/Aug 93 **12**
Leg of, Roast, with Red Chile Crust and Jalapeño Preserves .May/Jun 93 **22**
omelets .Sep/Oct 93 **21–22**
Asparagus .Sep/Oct 93 **22**
Basic, Master Recipe for .Sep/Oct 93 **22**
Cheese .Sep/Oct 93 **22**
Fines Herbes .Sep/Oct 93 **22**
Potato, Ham, and Parsley .Sep/Oct 93 **22**
Smoked Salmon .Sep/Oct 93 **22**
pizza
with Grilled Shrimp Topping with Roasted Tomatoes and Farmer's Cheese .May/Jun 93 **9**
with Roasted Tomato Topping with Fennel and Asiago .May/Jun 93 **9**
salmon
Grill-Roasted, with Alderwood .Jul/Aug 93 **20**
Roasted, with Kasha and Leek Stuffing .Jul/Aug 93 **23**
Seafood Cabbage Casserole .Charter Issue **6**
Snapper, Seared, with Pea Shoots and Coconut Curry Sauce, Lynne Aronson's .May/Jun 93 **2**
soups
Corn and Clam Chowder with Roasted Parsnips .Jul/Aug 93 **9**
Spring Vegetable, with Egg Noodles and Mint .Charter Issue **28**
Summer Harvest, with Basil .Charter Issue **29**
Spareribs, Grill-Roasted, with Barbecue Sauce .Jul/Aug 93 **20**
Stir-Fry, Master Recipe for .May/Jun 93 **19**
Tuna, Grilled, with Ginger and Garlic .Jul/Aug 93 **12**
turkey
Grill-Roasted, Best .Nov/Dec 93 **21**

Oven-Roasted, Best, with Giblet Pan Sauce ....Nov/Dec 93 **21**
Veal Breast, Braised, with Sausage, Olive, and Swiss Chard Stuffing Sep/Oct 93 **3**
Mango(es), cutting ....Jul/Aug 93 **4**
"Margarine" ....May/Jun 93 **28**
Marinades ....Jul/Aug 93 **10–12**
Asian, Master Recipe for ....Jul/Aug 93 **12**
flavoring with ....Jul/Aug 93 **11–12**
Garlic-Ginger ....Sep/Oct 93 **12**
Mediterranean, Master Recipe for ....Jul/Aug 93 **12**
Red Chile ....May/Jun 93 **22**
Marinating needles ....Jul/Aug 93 **3**
sources for ....Jul/Aug 93 **32**
Marjoram, field guide ....Jul/Aug 93 **13**
Master classes
Broth of Black Bass and Minced Vegetables ....Charter Issue **8–9**
Country Ham Stuffed with Greens ....Nov/Dec 93 **12–13**
Peking Duck ....Sep/Oct 93 **12–13**
Roasted Salmon with Kasha and Leek Stuffing ....Jul/Aug 93 **23–25**
Roast Leg of Lamb with Red Chile Crust and Jalapeño Preserves .May/Jun 93 **22–23**
Mayonnaise
Raspberry ....May/Jun 93 **28**
whole-egg ....Nov/Dec 93 **3**
Meat(s). *See also* specific meats
organic, sources for ....May/Jun 93 **32**
and Ricotta Filling with Basil for Pasta ....Sep/Oct 93 **18**
Mediterranean (cuisines). *See also* French; Italian
Marinade, Master Recipe for ....Jul/Aug 93 **12**
Mexican (cuisine)
Oaxacan-Style Sauce with Cloves and Cinnamon ....Sep/Oct 93 **10**
Salsa Cruda ....Jul/Aug 93 **14**
Michel Richard's Home Cooking with a French Accent
(Richard and Zeidler) ....Sep/Oct 93 **31**
Microwave, baking angel food in ....Charter Issue **11**
Milk
frothing ....Sep/Oct 93 **27, 28**
scalding for custard ....Charter Issue **2**
Mincemeat Turnovers ....Nov/Dec 93 **8**
Mincing ginger ....May/Jun 93 **21**
Miso ....Charter Issue **30**
Dressing, Ginger Walnut ....Charter Issue **30**
Mississippi Mud Cake ....Jul/Aug 93 **3**
Mocha Latte ....Sep/Oct 93 **28**
Mock Thumbprints ....Nov/Dec 93 **8**
shaping ....Nov/Dec 93 **8**
Monkfish, preparing ....Sep/Oct 93 **4**
Morels, field guide ....Sep/Oct 93 **14**
Muffins ....Sep/Oct 93 **6–8**
Any-Fruit-Will-Do, with Streusel Topping (Master Recipe) .....Sep/Oct 93 **8**
Bran, with Raisins and Dates, Big ....Sep/Oct 93 **7**
Corn, Double ....Sep/Oct 93 **7**
high-capped, technique for ....Sep/Oct 93 **7**
ingredients for ....Sep/Oct 93 **6**
soured-milk vs. buttermilk ....Sep/Oct 93 **7**
whisking ....Sep/Oct 93 **6**
whole grains in ....Sep/Oct 93 **8**
Muffin tins, commercial, sources for ....Sep/Oct 93 **32**
Mushroom(s)
field guide to ....Sep/Oct 93 **14**
mail-order sources for ....Sep/Oct 93 **32**
Sherry-Cream Sauce with ....Sep/Oct 93 **10**
Wild, Filling for Pasta ....Sep/Oct 93 **18**
Mustard
Honey, and Brown Sugar Glaze ....Nov/Dec 93 **12**
Two-, Dressing with Chives ....Charter Issue **30**
Mustard greens, in Spicy Greens Stuffing ....Nov/Dec 93 **12**

N

Napa cabbage ....Charter Issue **6**
Seafood Casserole ....Charter Issue **6**
Natural foods, glossary of ....Charter Issue **30**
Nectarine crisps and betties ....Sep/Oct 93 **26**
Nelson, Liza *(A Book of Feasts)* ....Jul/Aug 93 **31**
Neopolitan Orange Cake ....Charter Issue **15**
New German Cookbook, The (Anderson and Würz) ....Sep/Oct 93 **31**
New Orleans (cuisine): *Emeril's New New Orleans Cooking*
(Lagasse and Tirsch) ....May/Jun 93 **30**
New York Cookbook (O'Neill) ....Charter Issue **31**
Notecards, culinary ....May/Jun 93 **32**
Nuoc mam, in Lemon Fish Sauce Marinade ....Jul/Aug 93 **12**
Nut(s). *See also* specific nuts
Butter Cookie Dough ....Nov/Dec 93 **7**

O

Oaxacan-Style Sauce with Cloves and Cinnamon ....Sep/Oct 93 **10**
Oils. *See also* Olive oils
best for health ....Charter Issue **20**
citrus, sources for ....Nov/Dec 93 **32**
peanut, cold-pressed, sources for ....May/Jun 93 **32**
sesame ....Charter Issue **30**
Olive(s)
pitting ....Sep/Oct 93 **5**
Sausage, and Swiss Chard Stuffing ....Sep/Oct 93 **3**
Olive oils
blind tasting of ....Charter Issue **13–15**
choosing, based on usage ....Charter Issue **13**
extracting ....Charter Issue **13**
grading ....Charter Issue **13**
health concerns and ....Charter Issue **15, 20**
light ....May/Jun 93 **2**
sources for ....Charter Issue **15**
Olney, Richard *(Provence the Beautiful Cookbook)* ....Nov/Dec 93 **31**
Omelets ....Sep/Oct 93 **21–22**
Asparagus ....Sep/Oct 93 **22**
Basic, Master Recipe for ....Sep/Oct 93 **22**
Cheese ....Sep/Oct 93 **22**
fillings for ....Sep/Oct 93 **22**
Fines Herbes ....Sep/Oct 93 **22**
low-cholesterol ....Sep/Oct 93 **22**
perfect, four steps to ....Sep/Oct 93 **21**
Potato, Ham, and Parsley ....Sep/Oct 93 **22**
Smoked Salmon ....Sep/Oct 93 **22**
O'Neill, Molly *(New York Cookbook)* ....Charter Issue **31**
Onion(s)
Browned, Mashed Potatoes and Apples with Bacon and ....Nov/Dec 93 **11**
dicing ....Charter Issue **5**
Orange(s)
Cake, Neopolitan ....Charter Issue **15**
oil, sources for ....Nov/Dec 93 **32**
poaching ....May/Jun 93 **26**
Raspberry Bavarian ....Charter Issue **BC**
segmenting ....Charter Issue **4**
Oregon Pinot Noirs, blind tasting of ....Sep/Oct 93 **30**
Oyster(s)
Flavored Sauce, Chinese ....May/Jun 93 **19**
shucking ....Charter Issue **4**
varieties of ....Nov/Dec 93 **2**
Oyster mushrooms, field guide ....Sep/Oct 93 **14**

P

Pancake(s)
- Apple, Reuben's Legendary . . . Charter Issue **19**
- Basic Batter (Master Recipe for Dessert Pancakes and Puddings) . . Charter Issue **18**
- batter, resting . . . Charter Issue **19**

Paprika, sweet vs. hot . . . Charter Issue **3**

Parchment paper
- commercial, sources for . . . Nov/Dec 93 **32**
- liners, sizing . . . May/Jun 93 **4**

Parfaits, Chocolate Trinity . . . Nov/Dec 93 **BC**

Parmesan
- Jumbo Asparagus Salad with Parma Ham, Lemon Vinaigrette and . May/Jun 93 **7**
- Mashed Potatoes with Lemon and . . . Nov/Dec 93 **11**
- pregrated vs. freshly grated . . . Nov/Dec 93 **3**
- Squash, and Prosciutto Filling for Pasta . . . Sep/Oct 93 **18**

Parnsips, Roasted, Corn and Clam Chowder with . . . Jul/Aug 93 **9**

Parsley Roots, Roasted Carrots and . . . Jul/Aug 93 **25**

Pasilla chile(s) . . . May/Jun 93 **23**

Pasta
- dough
  - kneading in food processor . . . Sep/Oct 93 **15**
  - Master Recipe for . . . Sep/Oct 93 **15**
  - rolling out with manual machine . . . Sep/Oct 93 **16**
- filled . . . Sep/Oct 93 **15–18**
  - Meat and Ricotta, with Basil . . . Sep/Oct 93 **18**
  - shaping . . . Sep/Oct 93 **16–17**
  - Spinach and Ricotta . . . Sep/Oct 93 **18**
  - Squash, Prosciutto, and Parmesan . . . Sep/Oct 93 **18**
  - Wild Mushroom . . . Sep/Oct 93 **18**
- Linguine with Garlic Cream Sauce . . . Sep/Oct 93 **20**
- sauces for
  - Brown Butter and Pine Nut . . . Sep/Oct 93 **18**
  - Garlic Cream . . . Sep/Oct 93 **20**
  - Tomato, Garden . . . Sep/Oct 93 **18**

Pasta machines
- making breadsticks with . . . Charter Issue **24**
- rolling out dough with . . . Sep/Oct 93 **16**
- sources for . . . Sep/Oct 93 **32**

Pea shoots . . . May/Jun 93 **2**
- Seared Snapper with, and Coconut Curry Sauce, Lynne Aronson's . . . May/Jun 93 **2**
- sources for . . . May/Jun 93 **32**

Peach(es)
- and Cherries Poached in Spiced Red Wine . . . May/Jun 93 **26**
- crisps and betties . . . Sep/Oct 93 **26**
- poaching . . . May/Jun 93 **26**
- Salsa . . . Sep/Oct 93 **11**
- Spiced . . . Nov/Dec 93 **13**

Peanut oil
- cold-pressed, sources for . . . May/Jun 93 **32**
- health concerns and . . . Charter Issue **20**

Pear(s)
- coring . . . May/Jun 93 **25**
- crisps and betties . . . Sep/Oct 93 **26**
- poached . . . May/Jun 93 **26**
  - with Star Anise . . . May/Jun 93 **25**
- Pudding, Baked . . . Charter Issue **18**

Pecans, Sugared . . . May/Jun 93 **25**

Peking Duck . . . Sep/Oct 93 **12**

Pepper(s), bell
- reader's tip for . . . Nov/Dec 93 **3**
- Red, Chicken Roasted in . . . Sep/Oct 93 **BC**
- roasted, peeling and seeding . . . Jul/Aug 93 **5**
- trimming . . . May/Jun 93 **4**

Pepper(s), chile. *See* Chile(s)

Pepper-Honey Vinaigrette . . . May/Jun 93 **28**

Pesto
- Basil, Grilled Bread with Roasted Garlic, Fresh Tomato Sauce and Sep/Oct 93 **19**
- Cilantro . . . May/Jun 93 **22**

Petticoat tails (cookies) . . . Nov/Dec 93 **9**
- shaping . . . Nov/Dec 93 **8**

Pie pastry . . . Charter Issue **16–17**
- edging techniques . . . Charter Issue **17**
- fitting dough to pan . . . Charter Issue **17**
- Flaky Shell . . . Nov/Dec 93 **23**
- lattice top . . . Charter Issue **16**
- rolling out dough . . . Charter Issue **16**
- two basic variations . . . Charter Issue **16**

Pie, pumpkin . . . Nov/Dec 93 **22–23**
- Best . . . Nov/Dec 93 **22**
- fresh pumpkin in . . . Nov/Dec 93 **23**

Pineapple
- poaching . . . May/Jun 93 **26**
- slicing . . . May/Jun 93 **25**

Pine Nut and Brown Butter Sauce (for pasta) . . . Sep/Oct 93 **18**

Pinot Noirs, blind tasting of . . . Sep/Oct 93 **30**

Pinwheels . . . Nov/Dec 93 **8**
- Jam . . . Nov/Dec 93 **9**
- shaping . . . Nov/Dec 93 **8**

Piping cones, disposable . . . Nov/Dec 93 **5**

Pizza
- Crust, Garlic-Herb, Master Recipe for . . . May/Jun 93 **8**
- grilled . . . May/Jun 93 **8–9**
- toppings
  - Grilled Shrimp, with Roasted Tomatoes and Farmer's Cheese . May/Jun 93 **9**
  - Roasted Tomato, with Fennel and Asiago . . . May/Jun 93 **9**
  - simple . . . May/Jun 93 **9**

Plum(s)
- crisps and betties . . . Sep/Oct 93 **26**
- poaching . . . May/Jun 93 **26**

Pomegranates, extracting seeds from . . . Nov/Dec 93 **4**

Popovers, Banana Berry . . . Charter Issue **18**

Pop-up timers . . . Nov/Dec 93 **21**

Porcini, field guide . . . Sep/Oct 93 **14**

Pork. *See also* Bacon; Ham
- roast, flavoring with garlic . . . Nov/Dec 93 **5**
- sausage(s)
  - Olive, and Swiss Chard Stuffing . . . Sep/Oct 93 **3**
  - sources for . . . Jul/Aug 93 **32**
- Spareribs, Grill-Roasted, with Barbecue Sauce . . . Jul/Aug 93 **20**

Portobello, field guide . . . Sep/Oct 93 **14**

Potato(es)
- Ham, and Parsley Omelet . . . Sep/Oct 93 **22**
- mashed . . . Nov/Dec 93 **10–11**
  - and Apples with Bacon and Browned Onions . . . Nov/Dec 93 **11**
  - best potatoes for . . . Nov/Dec 93 **10**
  - Master Recipe for . . . Nov/Dec 93 **11**
  - with Parmesan Cheese and Lemon . . . Nov/Dec 93 **11**
  - peeling and cooking potatoes for . . . Nov/Dec 93 **10**
  - with Poached Garlic and Olive Oil . . . Nov/Dec 93 **11**
  - tools for . . . Nov/Dec 93 **10–11**
  - variations in . . . Nov/Dec 93 **11**

Potato mashers, Italian . . . Nov/Dec 93 **10**
- sources for . . . Nov/Dec 93 **32**

Poultry. *See also* Chicken; Duck; Turkey
- cutting up . . . May/Jun 93 **16–17**

pop-up timers in . . . . . Nov/Dec 93 **21**
Preserves, Jalapeño . . . . . May/Jun 93 **23**
Prosciutto
Jumbo Asparagus Salad with Parma Ham, Parmesan, and Lemon Vinaigrette . . . . . May/Jun 93 **7**
Squash, and Parmesan Filling for Pasta . . . . . Sep/Oct 93 **18**
Provence the Beautiful Cookbook (Olney) . . . . . Nov/Dec 93 **31**
Prune Custard Pudding (Far Breton) . . . . . Charter Issue **19**
Puddings
Basic Batter for (Master Recipe for Dessert Pancakes and Puddings) . . . . . Charter Issue **18**
Bread, Raspberry Summer . . . . . Jul/Aug 93 **BC**
Corn, Shaker-Style Creamy . . . . . Jul/Aug 93 **9**
Pear, Baked . . . . . Charter Issue **18**
Prune Custard (Far Breton) . . . . . Charter Issue **19**
Souffléed Batter for . . . . . Charter Issue **18**
Pumpkin pie . . . . . Nov/Dec 93 **22–23**
Best . . . . . Nov/Dec 93 **22**
fresh pumpkin in . . . . . Nov/Dec 93 **23**

R

Raisins, Big Bran Muffins with Dates and . . . . . Sep/Oct 93 **7**
Raspberry(ies)
Mayonnaise . . . . . May/Jun 93 **28**
Orange Bavarian . . . . . Charter Issue **BC**
Summer Bread Pudding . . . . . Jul/Aug 93 **BC**
Ravioli . . . . . Sep/Oct 93 **15–18**
See also Pasta—filled
Master Recipe for . . . . . Sep/Oct 93 **16**
shaping . . . . . Sep/Oct 93 **17**
Ravioli cutters . . . . . Sep/Oct 93 **32**
Replacement parts for appliances . . . . . Sep/Oct 93 **32**
Reuben's Legendary Apple Pancake . . . . . Charter Issue **19**
Rhubarb
poaching . . . . . May/Jun 93 **26**
and Strawberry Compotes with Sugared Pecans . . . . . May/Jun 93 **25**
stringing . . . . . May/Jun 93 **4**
Rice
converted . . . . . Nov/Dec 93 **3**
and Summer Vegetable Stuffing . . . . . Jul/Aug 93 **25**
Rice steamers . . . . . Charter Issue **7**
Rice syrup . . . . . Charter Issue **30**
Richard, Michel *(Michel Richard's Home Cooking with a French Accent)* . . . . . Sep/Oct 93 **31**
Ricotta
and Meat Filling with Basil for Pasta . . . . . Sep/Oct 93 **18**
and Spinach Filling for Pasta . . . . . Sep/Oct 93 **18**
Ring molds, lining with parchment paper . . . . . May/Jun 93 **4**
Roasting racks, V-shaped . . . . . Nov/Dec 93 **20**
sources for . . . . . Nov/Dec 93 **32**
Roberts, Michael, master class with (Roasted Salmon with Kasha and Leek Stuffing) . . . . . Jul/Aug 93 **23**
Rolling pins, types of . . . . . Sep/Oct 93 **3**
Rolls
dinner . . . . . Nov/Dec 93 **15–17**
Master Recipe for . . . . . Nov/Dec 93 **15**
preparing dough for . . . . . Nov/Dec 93 **15**
shaping . . . . . Nov/Dec 93 **16–17**
shaping . . . . . Charter Issue **25**
Rosemary, field guide . . . . . Jul/Aug 93 **13**
Rosés, blind tasting of . . . . . May/Jun 93 **31**
Rosso, Julee *(Great Good Food)* . . . . . Jul/Aug 93 **31**
Routhier, Nicole *(Cooking Under Wraps)* . . . . . May/Jun 93 **30**

S

Safflower oil, health concerns and . . . . . Charter Issue **20**
Sage, field guide . . . . . Jul/Aug 93 **13**
Tuscan Beans with . . . . . Charter Issue **2**
Salad dressings
Avocado Basil . . . . . Charter Issue **30**
Ginger Walnut Miso . . . . . Charter Issue **30**
Honey-Pepper Vinaigrette . . . . . May/Jun 93 **28**
Sesame Garlic . . . . . Charter Issue **30**
Two-Mustard, with Chives . . . . . Charter Issue **30**
Salads
Asparagus, Jumbo, with Parma Ham, Parmesan, and Lemon Vinaigrette . . . . . May/Jun 93 **7**
Seafood, Artichoke Cups with, and Herb Vinaigrette . . . . . May/Jun 93 **BC**
Salamanders . . . . . Charter Issue **2**
Salmon
Broth, Quick . . . . . Jul/Aug 93 **25**
Grill-Roasted, with Alderwood . . . . . Jul/Aug 93 **20**
Roasted, with Kasha and Leek Stuffing . . . . . Jul/Aug 93 **23**
Smoked, Omelet . . . . . Sep/Oct 93 **22**
whole, boning . . . . . Jul/Aug 93 **24–25**
Salmonella, temperature and . . . . . Nov/Dec 93 **21**
Salsas
Corn, Roasted . . . . . Jul/Aug 93 **8**
Cruda, Mexican-Style . . . . . Jul/Aug 93 **14**
Peach . . . . . Sep/Oct 93 **11**
Sauces. *See also* Marinades
Balsamic Vinegar, with Bacon, Warm . . . . . Jul/Aug 93 **25**
Black Bean, Chinese . . . . . May/Jun 93 **19**
Brown Sugar and Honey Mustard Glaze . . . . . Nov/Dec 93 **12**
Chili, Szechwan . . . . . May/Jun 93 **19**
Chinese flavoring (for stir-fry) . . . . . May/Jun 93 **19**
Chocolate-Bourbon Glaze . . . . . Jul/Aug 93 **3**
Coconut Curry, Chinese . . . . . May/Jun 93 **19**
Ginger Beurre Blanc . . . . . May/Jun 93 **28**
immersion blenders and . . . . . May/Jun 93 **28**
lemon
Caper . . . . . Sep/Oct 93 **10**
Chinese . . . . . May/Jun 93 **19**
Oaxacan-Style, with Cloves and Cinnamon . . . . . Sep/Oct 93 **10**
Oyster Flavored, Chinese . . . . . May/Jun 93 **19**
for pasta
Brown Butter and Pine Nut . . . . . Sep/Oct 93 **18**
Garlic Cream . . . . . Sep/Oct 93 **20**
Tomato, Garden . . . . . Sep/Oct 93 **18**
Raspberry Mayonnaise . . . . . May/Jun 93 **28**
Sherry-Cream, with Mushrooms . . . . . Sep/Oct 93 **10**
Sweet and Sour . . . . . May/Jun 93 **19**
Asian-Style . . . . . Sep/Oct 93 **11**
Tangerine, Chinese Spicy . . . . . May/Jun 93 **19**
Sausage(s)
Olive, and Swiss Chard Stuffing . . . . . Sep/Oct 93 **3**
sources for . . . . . Jul/Aug 93 **32**
Scallion brushes, decorative . . . . . Sep/Oct 93 **4**
Scallops, in Seafood Cabbage Casserole . . . . . Charter Issue **6**
Schiacciapatate . . . . . Nov/Dec 93 **10**
sources for . . . . . Nov/Dec 93 **32**
Schloss, Andrew *(Fifty Ways to Cook Most Everything)* . . . . . Charter Issue **31**
Science of cooking
baking powder . . . . . Nov/Dec 93 **28**
brining . . . . . Nov/Dec 93 **19**
butter . . . . . Charter Issue **2**
buttermilk . . . . . Jul/Aug 93 **1**
egg whites . . . . . Charter Issue **11**

pancake batter . . . . Charter Issue 19
Seafood. *See also* Caviar; Fish; Lobster
Cabbage Casserole . . . . Charter Issue 6
Clam and Corn Chowder with Roasted Parsnips . . . . Jul/Aug 93 9
Crabmeat, Shanghai Bok Choy Stir-Fried with . . . . Charter Issue 7
oyster(s)
shucking . . . . Charter Issue 4
varieties of . . . . Nov/Dec 93 2
Salad, Artichoke Cups with, and Herb Vinaigrette . . . . May/Jun 93 BC
Shrimp, Grilled, Topping with Roasted Tomatoes and
Farmer's Cheese (for pizza) . . . . May/Jun 93 9
Sesame
Garlic Dressing . . . . Charter Issue 30
oil . . . . Charter Issue 30
Shaker-Style Corn Pudding, Creamy . . . . Jul/Aug 93 9
Sherry Cream Sauce with Mushrooms . . . . Sep/Oct 93 10
Shiitake, field guide . . . . Sep/Oct 93 14
Shortcake, Strawberry . . . . May/Jun 93 12
Shrimp
Artichoke Cups with Seafood Salad and Herb Vinaigrette . . . . May/Jun 93 BC
Grilled, Topping with Roasted Tomatoes and Farmer's
Cheese (for pizza) . . . . May/Jun 93 9
Seafood Cabbage Casserole . . . . Charter Issue 6
Side dishes. *See also* Biscuits; Breads
asparagus
Grilled . . . . May/Jun 93 7
Jumbo, Salad with Parma Ham, Parmesan, and
Lemon Vinaigrette . . . . May/Jun 93 7
Steamed, Master Recipe for . . . . May/Jun 93 7
Thai-Style, with Chiles, Garlic, and Basil . . . . May/Jun 93 7
bean(s)
with Sage, Tuscan . . . . Charter Issue 2
White, and Tomato Casserole . . . . Charter Issue 9
Carrots, Roasted Parsley Roots and . . . . Jul/Aug 93 25
Celery, Braised . . . . Jul/Aug 93 25
corn
Pudding, Shaker-Style Creamy . . . . Jul/Aug 93 9
Roasted, Salsa . . . . Jul/Aug 93 8
and Zucchini Sauté with Chiles . . . . Jul/Aug 93 9
dinner rolls . . . . Nov/Dec 93 15–17
Master Recipe for . . . . Nov/Dec 93 15
preparing dough for . . . . Nov/Dec 93 15
shaping . . . . Nov/Dec 93 16–17
eggplant
Sautéed, Master Recipe for . . . . Jul/Aug 93 7
Sautéed, with Crisped Bread Crumbs . . . . Jul/Aug 93 7
Sautéed, with Spicy Garlic Sauce . . . . Jul/Aug 93 7
Sautéed, with Tomato Sauce with Basil . . . . Jul/Aug 93 7
Slices, Broiled, Master Recipe for . . . . Jul/Aug 93 7
Slices, Broiled, with Two Cheeses . . . . Jul/Aug 93 7
Gazpacho . . . . May/Jun 93 28
peach(es)
Salsa . . . . Sep/Oct 93 11
Spiced . . . . Nov/Dec 93 13
potato(es), mashed
and Apples with Bacon and Browned Onions . . . . Nov/Dec 93 11
Master Recipe for . . . . Nov/Dec 93 11
with Parmesan Cheese and Lemon . . . . Nov/Dec 93 11
with Poached Garlic and Olive Oil . . . . Nov/Dec 93 11
Salsa Cruda, Mexican-Style . . . . Jul/Aug 93 14
Spaetzle, Buttered . . . . May/Jun 93 2
stuffings
Greens, Spicy . . . . Nov/Dec 93 12
Kasha and Leek . . . . Jul/Aug 93 23
Sausage, Olive, and Swiss Chard . . . . Sep/Oct 93 3
Summer Vegetable and Rice . . . . Jul/Aug 93 25
Snapper, Seared, with Pea Shoots and Coconut Curry
Sauce, Lynne Aronson's . . . . May/Jun 93 2
SooHoo, David, master class with (Peking Duck) . . . . Sep/Oct 93 12
Souffléed Batter Pudding . . . . Charter Issue 18
Soups
Corn and Clam Chowder with Roasted Parsnips . . . . Jul/Aug 93 9
Gazpacho . . . . May/Jun 93 28
stock for . . . . Charter Issue 29
vegetable . . . . Charter Issue 28–29
Base (Master Recipe for Chunky and Pureed Soup) . . . . Charter Issue 28
Broth, Quick . . . . Charter Issue 28
Spring, with Egg Noodles and Mint . . . . Charter Issue 29
Summer Harvest, with Basil . . . . Charter Issue 29
Southern (cuisine): *A Treasury of Southern Baking* (Hilburn) . . . . May/Jun 93 30
Southwestern (cuisine)
Flank Steak, Spicy . . . . Jul/Aug 93 12
Lamb, Roast Leg of, with Red Chile Crust and Jalapeño Preserves May/Jun 93 22
Marinade . . . . Jul/Aug 93 12
Soybean oil, health concerns and . . . . Charter Issue 20
Soy milk . . . . Charter Issue 30
Soy sauce
blind tasting of . . . . May/Jun 93 13–15
history of . . . . May/Jun 93 13
as low-sodium alternative . . . . May/Jun 93 15
making of . . . . May/Jun 93 15
sources for . . . . May/Jun 93 32
storing . . . . May/Jun 93 15
tamari vs. . . . . May/Jun 93 13–15
types of . . . . May/Jun 93 15
Spaetzle, Buttered . . . . May/Jun 93 2
Spaetzle machines . . . . May/Jun 93 2
sources for . . . . May/Jun 93 32
Spaghetti squash, field guide . . . . Nov/Dec 93 14
Spanish wines
rosés . . . . May/Jun 93 31
sparklers . . . . Nov/Dec 93 30
Spareribs, Grill-Roasted, with Barbecue Sauce . . . . Jul/Aug 93 20
Sparkling waters, blind tasting of . . . . Jul/Aug 93 21–22
Sparkling wines, blind tasting of . . . . Nov/Dec 93 30
Spice(s)
bouquet garni . . . . Sep/Oct 93 2
Butter Cookie Dough . . . . Nov/Dec 93 7
Linzer Cookies . . . . Nov/Dec 93 9
Spicy foods, mail-order sources for . . . . Jul/Aug 93 32
Spinach
julienning . . . . Nov/Dec 93 4
and Ricotta Filling for Pasta . . . . Sep/Oct 93 18
Spicy Greens Stuffing . . . . Nov/Dec 93 12
Spirals, Citrus . . . . Nov/Dec 93 8
Spring Vegetable Soup with Egg Noodles and Mint . . . . Charter Issue 29
Squash
Acorn, Prosciutto, and Parmesan Filling for Pasta . . . . Sep/Oct 93 18
autumn and winter, field guide to . . . . Nov/Dec 93 14
Zucchini and Corn Sauté . . . . Jul/Aug 93 9
Stir-fries . . . . May/Jun 93 18–21
Chinese Cabbage . . . . Charter Issue 7
Chinese flavoring sauces for . . . . May/Jun 93 19
cutting ingredients for . . . . May/Jun 93 20–21
marinades in . . . . May/Jun 93 18–19
Master Recipe for . . . . May/Jun 93 19
Shanghai Bok Choy with Crabmeat . . . . Charter Issue 7
in skillet . . . . Sep/Oct 93 2

Stock
- broth vs. .... Charter Issue **28**
- for soup .... Charter Issue **29**
- Veal, Simple .... Sep/Oct 93 **3**

Strawberry(ies)
- Ice Cream .... Jul/Aug 93 **28**
- poaching .... May/Jun 93 **26**
- and Rhubarb Compotes with Sugared Pecans .... May/Jun 93 **25**
- Shortcake .... May/Jun 93 **12**

Streusel Topping .... Sep/Oct 93 **8**

Stuffings
- Greens, Spicy .... Nov/Dec 93 **12**
- Kasha and Leek .... Jul/Aug 93 **23**
- Sausage, Olive, and Swiss Chard .... Sep/Oct 93 **3**
- Summer Vegetable and Rice .... Jul/Aug 93 **25**

Sugar
- Brown, and Honey Mustard Glaze .... Nov/Dec 93 **12**
- superfine .... Jul/Aug 93 **3**

Summer
- Bread Pudding, Fresh Raspberry .... Jul/Aug 93 **BC**
- Harvest Soup with Basil .... Charter Issue **29**
- Vegetable and Rice Stuffing .... Jul/Aug 93 **25**

Sunflower oil, health concerns and .... Charter Issue **20**

Sweet and sour sauces
- Chinese .... May/Jun 93 **19**
- Pan, Asian-Style .... Sep/Oct 93 **11**

Sweet Dumpling squash, field guide .... Nov/Dec 93 **14**

Swiss chard
- julienning .... Nov/Dec 93 **4**
- Sausage, and Olive Stuffing .... Sep/Oct 93 **3**

Syrups, poaching .... May/Jun 93 **24–25**
- seasonings for .... May/Jun 93 **25**

Szechwan Chili Sauce .... May/Jun 93 **19**

T

Tamari
- blind tasting of .... May/Jun 93 **13–15**
- soy sauce vs., ... **13–15**

Tangerine Sauce, Spicy Chinese .... May/Jun 93 **19**

Tarragon, field guide .... Jul/Aug 93 **13**

Thai-Style Asparagus with Chiles, Garlic, and Basil .... May/Jun 93 **7**

Thermometers, testing bread's doneness with .... Charter Issue **22**

Thyme, field guide .... Jul/Aug 93 **13**

Tirsch, Jessie *(Emeril's New New Orleans Cooking)* .... May/Jun 93 **30**

Tofu .... Charter Issue **30**

Tomato(es)
- dicing .... Jul/Aug 93 **15**
- peeling .... Charter Issue **4;**
  - .... Jul/Aug 93 **15**
- roasted
  - Grilled Shrimp Topping with Farmer's Cheese and (for pizza) .May/Jun 93 **9**
  - Topping with Fennel and Asiago (for pizza) .... May/Jun 93 **9**
- seeding .... Charter Issue **4**
- and White Bean Casserole .... Charter Issue **9**

Tomato sauces
- basil
  - with Capers .... Sep/Oct 93 **11**
  - Sautéed Eggplant in .... Jul/Aug 93 **7**
- Fireworks .... May/Jun 93 **19**
- Garden (for pasta) .... Sep/Oct 93 **18**
- Grilled Bread with Roasted Garlic and .... Sep/Oct 93 **19**
- raw .... Jul/Aug 93 **14**
  - Herb, Master Recipe for .... Jul/Aug 93 **14**
- Salsa Cruda, Mexican-Style .... Jul/Aug 93 **14**
- Yogurt .... Jul/Aug 93 **14**

Tortelli .... Sep/Oct 93 **15–18**
- *See also* Pasta—filled
- shaping .... Sep/Oct 93 **17**
- Twisted .... Sep/Oct 93 **16**

Tortellini .... Sep/Oct 93 **15–18**
- *See also* Pasta—filled
- recipe for .... Sep/Oct 93 **16**
- shaping .... Sep/Oct 93 **17**

Treasury of Southern Baking, A (Hilburn) .... May/Jun 93 **30**

Tropp, Barbara *(China Moon Cookbook)* .... Charter Issue **31**

Tube pans .... Charter Issue **12**
- lining with parchment paper .... May/Jun 93 **4**

Tuna, Grilled, with Ginger and Garlic .... Jul/Aug 93 **12**

Turban squash, field guide .... Nov/Dec 93 **14**

Turkey
- brining .... Nov/Dec 93 **19**
- Grill-Roasted, Best .... Nov/Dec 93 **21**
- internal temperature of .... Nov/Dec 93 **21**
- pop-up timers in .... Nov/Dec 93 **21**
- real weight of .... Nov/Dec 93 **20**
- roast .... Nov/Dec 93 **18–21**
  - Oven-, with Giblet Pan Sauce, Best .... Nov/Dec 93 **20**
- trussing .... Nov/Dec 93 **18**

Turnovers
- Jam .... Nov/Dec 93 **8**
- shaping .... Nov/Dec 93 **8**

Tuscan Beans with Sage .... Charter Issue **2**

U

Utensils. *See* Gadgets and utensils

V

Vanilla
- beans .... Jul/Aug 93 **27**
- extract, homemade .... Nov/Dec 93 **2**
- Ice Cream, Master Recipe for .... Jul/Aug 93 **27**

Veal
- Breast, Braised, with Sausage, Olive, and Swiss Chard Stuffing . . .Sep/Oct 93 **3**
- Stock, Simple .... Sep/Oct 93 **3**

Vegetable(s). *See also* specific vegetables
- cutting into uniform pieces for stir-fry .... May/Jun 93 **20**
- marinating for flavor .... Jul/Aug 93 **11**
- Minced, Broth of Black Bass and .... Charter Issue **9**
- soaking before cooking .... May/Jun 93 **3**
- soups .... Charter Issue **28–29**
  - *See also* Soups—vegetable
- Summer, and Rice Stuffing .... Jul/Aug 93 **25**

Vegetable peelers .... Nov/Dec 93 **32**

Vegetable shortening, health concerns and .... Charter Issue **20**

Viennese Crescents .... Nov/Dec 93 **9**
- shaping .... Nov/Dec 93 **8**

Vinaigrette, Honey-Pepper .... May/Jun 93 **28**

Vinegar(s)
- Balsamic, Sauce with Bacon, Warm .... Jul/Aug 93 **25**
- brown rice .... Charter Issue **30**
- equipment sources for .... Sep/Oct 93 **32**
- glass flasks for .... Sep/Oct 93 **32**
- making your own .... Sep/Oct 93 **23**
- red wine, blind tasting of .... Sep/Oct 93 **24–25**
- wine, commercial production of .... Sep/Oct 93 **24**

V-racks
- roasting turkey on .... Nov/Dec 93 **20**
- sources for .... Nov/Dec 93 **32**

W

Wafers, Walnut .... Charter Issue **15**
Waffle irons
rating of .... Nov/Dec 93 **29**
sources for .... Nov/Dec 93 **32**
Waffles .... Nov/Dec 93 **27–28**
Almost-as-Good-as-Buttermilk .... Nov/Dec 93 **28**
baking powder and .... Nov/Dec 93 **28**
Buttermilk, Best .... Nov/Dec 93 **28**
ingredients in .... Nov/Dec 93 **27**
Raised .... Charter Issue **2**
Walnut(s)
Ginger Miso Dressing .... Charter Issue **30**
Wafers .... Charter Issue **15**
Waters, sparkling, blind tasting of .... Jul/Aug 93 **21–22**
Whipped Cream, Brandied .... Nov/Dec 93 **23**
White bean(s)
and Tomato Casserole .... Charter Issue **9**
Tuscan, with Sage .... Charter Issue **2**
Wine
blind tastings of
Chablis .... Jul/Aug 93 **30**
Champagnes .... Nov/Dec 93 **30**
Chianti .... Charter Issue **32**
American Pinot Noirs and French Burgundies .... Sep/Oct 93 **30**
rosés .... May/Jun 93 **31**
Red, Spiced, Peaches and Cherries Poached in .... May/Jun 93 **26**
vinegars
commercial production of .... Sep/Oct 93 **24**
red, blind tasting of .... Sep/Oct 93 **24–25**
Würz, Hedy *(The New German Cookbook)* .... Sep/Oct 93 **31**

Y

Yogurt Tomato Sauce .... Jul/Aug 93 **14**

Z

Zucchini and Corn Sauté with Chiles .... Jul/Aug 93 **9**

NUMBER ONE ◆ CHARTER ISSUE

FOUR DOLLARS

COOK'S ILLUSTRATED

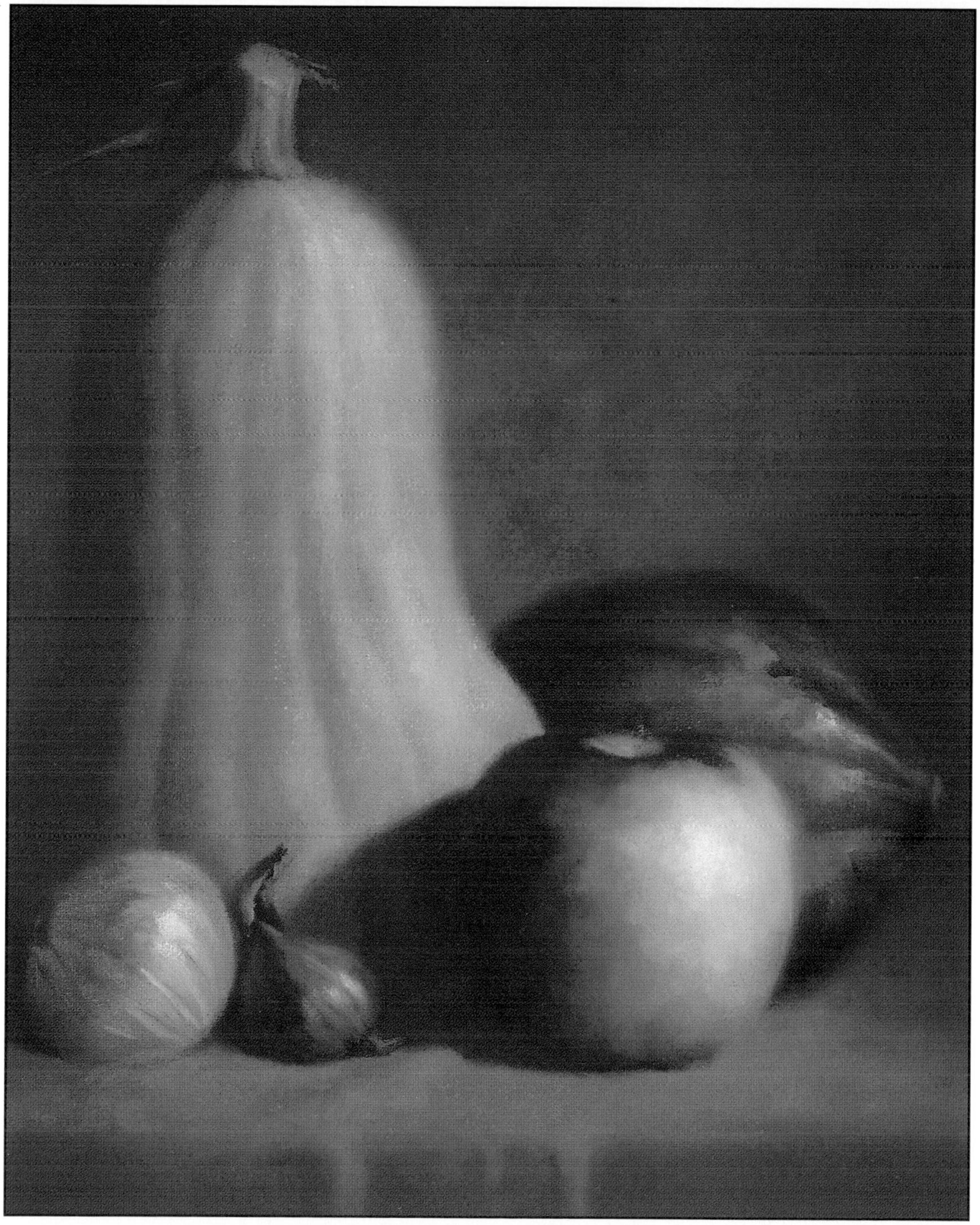

Improvising Soups

Learn to Improvise Vegetable Soups Using Two Master Recipes

Perfect Angel Food

The Perfect Balance of Six Ingredients Makes Perfect Cake

How To Make Bread

A New Master Recipe Requires No Hands-On Kneading

Quick Techniques

Shucking Oysters, Seeding Tomatoes, Dicing Onions, and Carving Ham

RATING ELECTRIC FRYERS

•

HOW TO ROAST A CHICKEN

•

TASTE-TESTING OLIVE OILS

•

NATURAL SALAD DRESSINGS

•

BLIND TASTING: CHIANTI

CHARTER ISSUE 1992

TABLE OF CONTENTS

VOLUME ONE • NUMBER ONE

2
Notes From Readers
Beans cooked in a bottle, Tuscan-style; the ultimate crème caramel; candied citrus peel; and old-fashioned raised waffles.

4
Quick Tips
How to shuck oysters, peel and seed tomatoes, segment oranges, dice onions, and carve two kinds of ham.

6
Five Chinese Cabbages
Discover the crunchy, creamy texture and mildly sweet flavor of five varieties of Chinese cabbage. *By Nina Simonds*

8
Master Class: Broth of Black Bass and Minced Vegetables
Learn classic brunoise cuts; make a quick, low-fat sauce with an immersion blendor; and add exotic flavor to a simple stock. Gray Kunz, chef at New York's Lespinasse, provides a private cooking class. *By Dorie Greenspan*

10
The Perfect Angel Food Cake
The perfect angel food cake is a delicate balance of six ingredients. Our test kitchen delivers a foolproof master recipe for this deceptively simple classic. *By Brooke Dojny and Melanie Barnard*

13
Taste-Testing Olive Oils
A blind tasting of 17 different oils proves that price has very little to do with quality. Find out why and discover new uses for this essential kitchen staple.

16
The Secrets of Pie Pastry
This illustrated guide to perfect pie pastry includes how to roll out and fit dough to a pie plate or tart pan, making a lattice top, basic crust variations, and four edging techniques. *By Nick Malgieri*

Spring Vegetable Soup page 29

Electric Fryers page 20

Gray Kunz's Master Class page 8

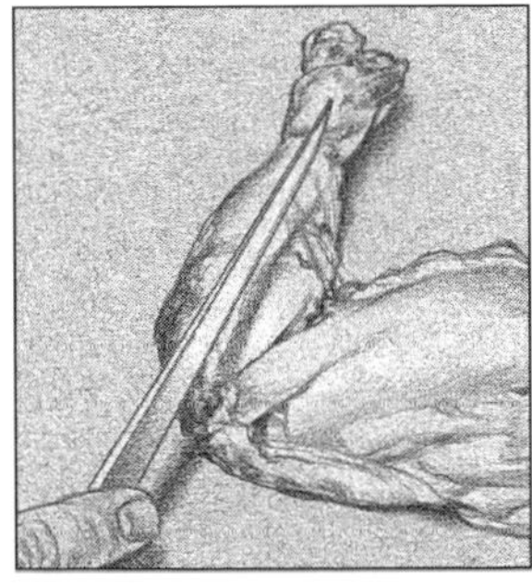

Carving Roast Chicken page 26

18
One Batter, Many Desserts
Simple variations on a basic pancake batter create baked puddings, souffléed skillet pancakes, popovers, and more. *By Richard Sax*

20
Choosing the Right Electric Deep-Fryer
The perfect fryer costs $150 but less expensive models (under $50) also get the job done. *By Jack Bishop*

22
How To Make Bread
Should you use rapid-rise yeast? Are there benefits to kneading by hand? How can you produce a crispy crust? Two weeks of kitchen testing results in a master recipe that you can use every day. *By Pam Anderson*

26
The Way To Roast Chicken
Can legs finish cooking before breasts become dry? Our kitchen scientist roasted 15 chickens to find out. *By Harold McGee*

28
Improvising Vegetable Soups
Two master recipes that yield hundreds of variations; stocks versus broths; and good stock from scratch in 60 minutes.

30
Natural Salad Dressings
Tofu, miso, and other health food staples make creamy, rich salad dressings with less fat. *By Laurel Vukovic*

31
Book Reviews
Can you cook Barbara Tropp's food in your kitchen? Do you need 2,500 new ideas for dinner? Where can you find New York's secret (and best) recipes?

32
Inexpensive Chianti Wins Blind Tasting
Food-lovers and professional wine tasters look for different characteristics when rating wines. *By Mark Bittman*

FRONT AND BACK COVER ILLUSTRATIONS BY BRENT WATKINSON

Publisher and Editor
Christopher Kimball

Executive Editor
Mark Bittman

Food Editor
Pam Anderson

Senior Writer
Jack Bishop

Copy Editor
David Travers

Art Director
Meg Birnbaum

Associate Art Director
Robin Record

Director of Photography
Richard Felber

Photography Consultant
Sara Barbaris

Circulation Director
Adrienne Kimball

Circulation Manager
Mary Taintor

Production Director
James McCormack

Treasurer
Janet Carlson

About Cook's Illustrated
Web Site The *Cook's* Web site features original editorial content, searchable databases for recipes, equipment ratings, food tastings, buying advice, cookbook reviews, and quick tips. It also has our online bookstore, e-mail newsletter, and a message board. Visit **www.cooksillustrated.com**.
Magazine-Related Items *Cook's Illustrated* is available in annual hardbound editions for $26.95 each plus shipping and handling; each edition is fully indexed. Discounts are available if more than one year is ordered at a time. Individual back issues are available for $5 each. *Cook's* also offers an annually updated comprehensive index of the magazine for $12.95.
Books *The Best Recipe*, which features 700 of our favorite recipes from *Cook's*, is available for $24.95. We also publish a series of single-subject books on a wide range of cooking topics for $14.95 each; visit our Web site to learn about them.
To Order call 800-611-0759 inside the U.S. or 515-246-6911 from outside the U.S., or visit our Web site, **www.cooksillustrated.com**.

EDITORIAL

Bringing It All Back Home

Back in 1979 I was working on the launch of *Cook's* magazine when I was introduced to James Beard. I asked him to define American cooking. He said, "That's simple. It's what your neighbor down the street is making for dinner." To Jim, American cooking was his mother's cream of tomato soup, potato pancakes made by second-generation German immigrants, and osso bucco from the Italian-American family next door. In the 1980s, however, American home cooking took its lead from restaurant fare, from classic French haute cuisine and nouvelle cuisine, from California and Cajun and anything with Asian ingredients. American food became global, and amid the changes we lost a cohesiveness of food and place and culture. We lost traditions that had connected us, and in which food played an important role: the social vitality of a meal, for example, as an occasion for families to talk, argue, persuade, or even shout.

Christopher Kimball

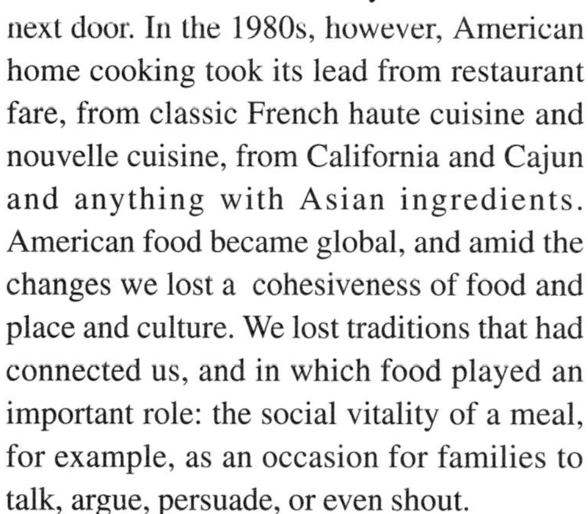

Two years after the original *Cook's* magazine ceased publication, I have decided to relaunch the magazine as *Cook's Illustrated,* a new format that is dedicated to the pleasures of home cooking, with first-hand accounts of how to cook from the best cooks and chefs in America. *Cook's Illustrated* is a cookbook, a reference library, a resource, a cooking school, a consumer's guide, and a source of original, well-illustrated cooking instruction. We do it for you, the reader, without advertising so that we may bring you honest, no-nonsense editorial that you can depend on.

Why relaunch *Cook's* now? Because we need to cook. Less than half of all Americans have their main meal together with the rest of the family. Forty-two percent find it difficult to make time to prepare meals (up from 30 percent in the 1970s). Yet 30 percent of Americans now say they are making more meals from scratch. All of us at *Cook's Illustrated* sense that, at long last and once again, Americans are hungry for home cooking. And given the quality of our fast-paced and veneer-deep life-styles, we should be. If it's true that life is in the little things, then how we fry an egg matters.

The food in our pages must meet the criteria of modern times — sensible, fresh, reasonable in preparation time, yet satisfying and mostly from scratch. *Cook's Illustrated* is about what our neighbors are making (or should be making) for dinner. Although never stated explicitly, *Cook's* is also about the choice between convenience and quality. The choice is up to you.

American cooking wasn't an abstract concept to Jim Beard. It was plain folks cooking for their families. The spirit of good food lies in neighbors and in family, in local farmers and in holiday get-togethers. It can be Gray Kunz's Black Sea Bass in Broth (page 9) or a simple roast chicken (page 27). But it has to be homemade, that is, made for a group of people who share a sense of community.

America's home has always been in the kitchen. It's time to roll up our sleeves and get busy. ■

NOTES FROM READERS

Cooking Beans in Tuscany

I just returned from Tuscany where I visited an old farmhouse that had a fireplace with large andirons fitted with circular holders of some sort. Were these used for cooking?

Traditionally, Tuscans cooked dried beans in a fireplace, often in a fiasco, the straw-covered bottle used for Chianti (obviously, they removed the straw first). The beans were heavily scented with sage and garlic and allowed to rest in the embers overnight. You can try this yourself at home, using the heaviest glass bottle you can find, topping the beans and flavorings with water, loosely capping the bottle with cotton or aluminum foil, and warming it before nestling it in not-too-hot embers. You'll get more reliable if somewhat less romantic results using this recipe atop the stove:

TUSCAN BEANS WITH SAGE

Makes 8 small servings

1 cup dried cannelini, navy, or pea beans
20 fresh sage leaves
Ground black pepper
1 garlic clove, minced
Salt
2 tablespoons extra virgin olive oil

Cover beans with 3 inches of water and soak overnight. Drain beans and transfer to a pot and cover with water; add sage and pepper and bring to a boil. Simmer until tender, about 45 minutes. When soft but not mushy (drain cooking liquid if necessary), add garlic and salt to taste. Return to heat and cook over low heat a few minutes to meld flavors. Sprinkle with olive oil and serve.

Is Scalding Milk Necessary?

When making a custard, is it really necessary to scald the milk before mixing it with the eggs?

No. Custards are thoroughly cooked, so scalding isn't essential for safety. (Although I have seen custard recipes that call for the eggs to be mixed with cold or warm milk, they're definitely in the minority.) But scalding is useful. It's necessary to extract flavor from a vanilla bean or citrus peel. Sugar dissolves rapidly and eggs disperse more evenly in hot milk, so scalding makes it easier to mix the custard ingredients. And because it instantly raises the temperature of the mix to 140 degrees or more, scalded milk shortens baking time considerably. — *Harold McGee*

The Science of Butter

I have noticed that certain brands of butter are sometimes watery, and don't melt as evenly as usual. Do brands vary in moisture content? Does this affect quality?

Butter shouldn't vary much in its water content, which is defined by regulation as no more than 16 percent of its weight. However, the consistency of butter can vary a great deal according to the physical state of its fat. Butterfat takes three very different forms: the original fat globules in which it came from the milk; highly organized fat crystals; and unstructured or "free" fat. The relative proportions of these three forms are determined by production methods and subsequent cooling and storage conditions. The higher the proportion of free fat, the more the butter will suffer from "oiling off," or the premature separation of easily melted free fat from the more stable crystals and globules. In addition, summer butter is usually softer than winter butter, due to changes in the cows' feed which affect the composition of their milkfat. Oiling off could compromise the flakiness of puff pastries that depend on solid butter to separate the sheets of dough. Otherwise, it's mainly an annoyance.

— *Harold McGee*

What Is It?

I found this odd-looking object in a local antique store. The shop owner thought it was some sort of kitchen device. Can you tell me the name of this implement and how it was used?

When cooking was accomplished in large kitchen fireplaces, this two-legged salamander was used to brown foods, especially pies and roasts. Named for the mythical creature able to withstand fire without harm, the salamander's head (right) was placed directly in the hearth until very hot. The handle (left) was used to pull the salamander out of the flames. The hot salamander head was then gently placed over a pastry crust or roast in need of browning.

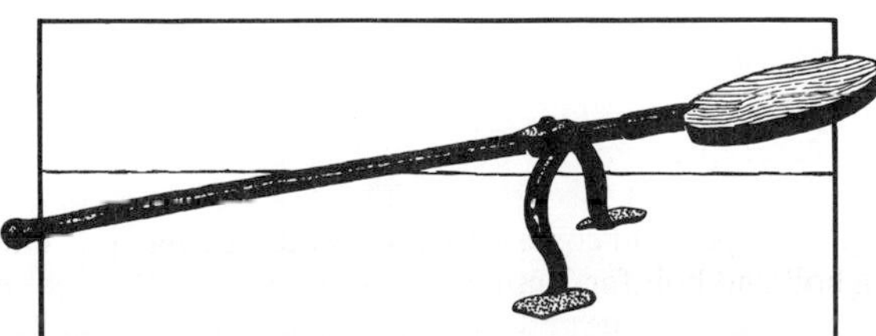

— *Jack Bishop*

Old-Fashioned Raised Waffles

When I was a kid, my mother used to make waffles that had yeast in them. They were crisp on the outside yet delicate on the inside. I've lost the recipe. Can you help?

Marion Cunningham, author of *The Breakfast Book* (Knopf, 1987), includes a recipe for Raised Waffles which comes from an early Fannie Farmer cookbook. Do yourself a favor and buy a copy of Marion's book. It's terrific.

RAISED WAFFLES

Serves 8

½ cup warm water
1 package dry yeast
2 cups milk, warmed
½ cup (1 stick) butter, melted
1 teaspoon salt
1 teaspoon sugar
2 cups all-purpose flour
2 eggs
¼ teaspoon baking soda

1. Use a large mixing bowl — the batter will rise to double its original volume. Put water in the mixing bowl and sprinkle in yeast. Let stand to dissolve for 5 minutes.

2. Add milk, butter, salt, sugar, and flour to yeast mixture and beat until smooth and blended (You can use a hand-rotary beater to get rid of

ILLUSTRATIONS THIS PAGE BY DAN KROVATIN/PHOTOGRAPHY BY G.K. HART

How to Fillet a Roundfish

Filleting a roundfish (as opposed to a flatfish such as flounder or sole) involves no more than a sharp filleting knife (a boning knife also works well) and the basic knowledge that most roundfish have a straight backbone with ribs coming off it. Practice, if you like, on mackerel, which is not only cheap but nicely shaped. In time, you'll cut down on waste, save money, and have loads of lovely bones for fish stock.

1. If you're starting with a whole fish, make a cut from the top to the bottom of the fish, right behind the gill cover.

2. Cut on one side of the dorsal fin(s), straight into the fish. Feel with the blade of the knife for the central backbone, and keep the knife right on top of it as you move down the length of the fish.

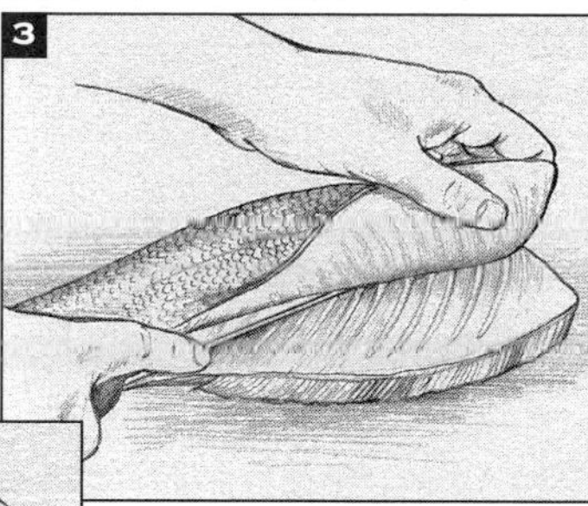

3. Peel back the meat so you can see the ribs beneath the backbone, keeping the knife on top of them. Turn the fish over and repeat the technique on the other side.

the lumps). Cover the bowl with plastic wrap and let stand overnight at room temperature.

3. Just before cooking the waffles, beat in eggs, add baking soda, and stir until well mixed. The batter will be very thin. Pour ½ to ¾ cup batter into a very hot waffle iron. Bake the waffles until golden and crisp.

This batter will keep well for several days in the refrigerator.

The Best Creme Caramel

I was in Boston recently and had dinner at Azita, located in the South End. Their crème caramel was the best I have ever had. Could you get the recipe?

This is our favorite dessert in the Boston area. The secret is long slow cooking at 300 degrees. You will need eight, one-half-cup custard cups.

CREME CARAMEL

Serves 8

- 1½ cups sugar
- 2 cups milk
- 2 cups heavy cream
- 1 vanilla bean, split lengthwise
- 1 strip lemon peel (2" x ½")
- 5 egg yolks

1. Heat oven to 300 degrees and butter custard cups. Mix first 5 ingredients in a saucepan reserving 1 cup sugar; bring mixture to a simmer then remove from heat. Cool for 10 minutes. Remove and discard vanilla bean and lemon peel.

2. Whisk egg yolks in a large bowl and then whisk liquid mixture into yolks.

3. Bring 1 cup sugar and ½ cup water to a boil over low heat in a small saucepan. *Do not stir.* Cover and boil until mixture turns light brown and thickens, about 15 minutes.

4. Pour equal portions of sugar syrup into prepared custard cups; chill for 15 minutes.

5. Pour equal portions of custard mixture into each custard cup. Bake until a knife inserted in the center comes out clean, about 80 minutes.

Citrus Peel for Dessert

I love the kind of sweet, thick lemon peel they serve with cookies in some restaurants. How can I make it at home?

This is a recipe for a thick, sugar-coated lemon peel that you can munch on like candy or have with espresso. If you store it in a covered container with wax paper separating the layers it will keep for about a week at room temperature.

CANDIED LEMON PEEL

Makes 48 candied peels

- 4 bright-skinned lemons
- 3 cups sugar
- 2½ tablespoons light corn syrup
- 1 cup cold water

1. With a sharp paring knife, score the skin of the fruit into quarters; peel off each quarter of rind, reserving fruit for another use. Cut each quarter into 3 strips lengthwise. Place peels in a large saucepan and cover with cold water. Bring to a boil and boil for 2 minutes. Drain peels and rinse with cold water; repeat boiling and rinsing process. Drain peels and set aside while you make the syrup.

2. In a medium saucepan, bring 2 cups of sugar, the corn syrup, and cold water to a boil. Boil for 20 minutes, washing down any crystals that may form on the sides of the pan with a brush dipped in cold water. Add peels and bring syrup back to boil. Lower heat to medium and simmer peels for 25 minutes, stirring occasionally.

3. Put remaining sugar in a baking pan or bowl. When peels are cooked, lift them out one by one with chopsticks or tongs; hold each peel over the pot for a few seconds to let excess syrup drip back, then drop peel into sugar. Using a spoon or your hands, mix peels and sugar until pieces are coated. Shake or gently rub off excess sugar from each peel. Transfer peels to a rack, arranging them in a single layer. Allow peels to dry for a few hours or overnight.

— *Dorie Greenspan*

Paprika Pepper

What is the difference between sweet and hot paprika?

Although we now associate paprika with Hungarian cooking, this bright red spice is native to the New World and was first brought to Europe by Columbus. The dried and powdered form of a red pepper called *Capsicum annum,* paprika was introduced in Hungary during the sixteenth century. Until the nineteenth century, the spice was always hot. At that time, Hungarian spice millers developed a process to remove the seeds and veins of the fiery red peppers. Since most of a pepper's heat is concentrated in the seeds and veins, the resulting paprika was "sweet." The intensity of the paprika could be controlled by removing some or all of the veins and seeds.

In recent years, much sweet paprika has been made from a mild red pepper hybrid that can be ground whole with the seeds and veins. Most of the sweet paprika sold in this country comes from this new pepper grown in Spain and California. However, for paprika — either sweet or hot — with superior flavor and character, look for brands imported from Hungary. ■

This traditional Hungarian sweet chile pepper is used to make 'sweet' paprika.

ILLUSTRATIONS THIS PAGE BY ELAINE SEARS

Quick Tips

To Shuck an Oyster

To shuck oysters you need an oyster knife. A common can opener can also be used to open up the shell. Start by preparing a plate filled with rock salt or seaweed to hold the opened oysters. Brush the oysters as clean as possible under running water to avoid the possibility of contamination from bacteria on the shell. Using a folded kitchen towel to protect your hand, hold the oyster with its convex shell down to catch the liquor.

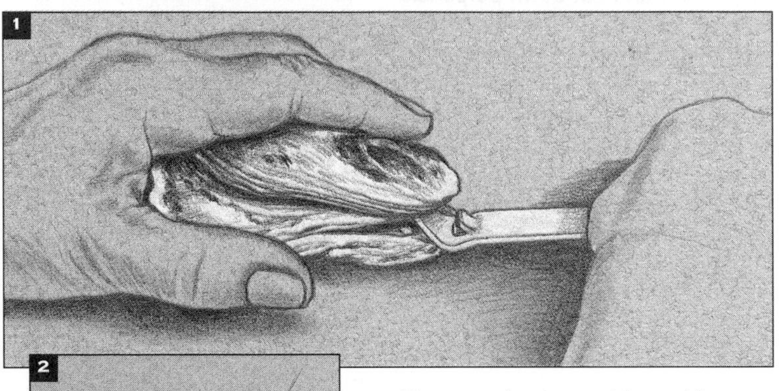

1. Every oyster has a hinge. You can use a can opener in much the same way as you would to open a soda bottle, but hold it upside down.

2. If you use an oyster knife, wedge the tip of the knife into the hinge. Push and turn until the hinge pops.

3. When the top shell loosens, run the knife along the inside of the top shell to sever the oyster from it. Lift off the top shell.

4. Now run the knife under the oyster, severing it from the bottom shell. Keep as much of the liquid in the shell as you can, and lay the oyster on rock salt or seaweed.

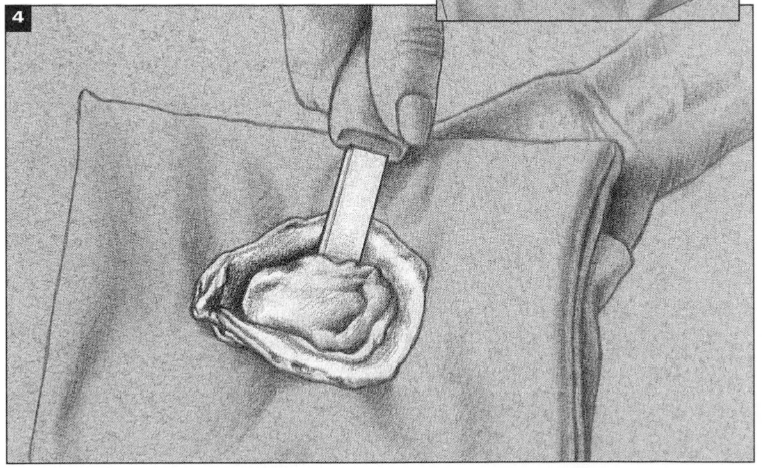

Peeling & Seeding Tomatoes

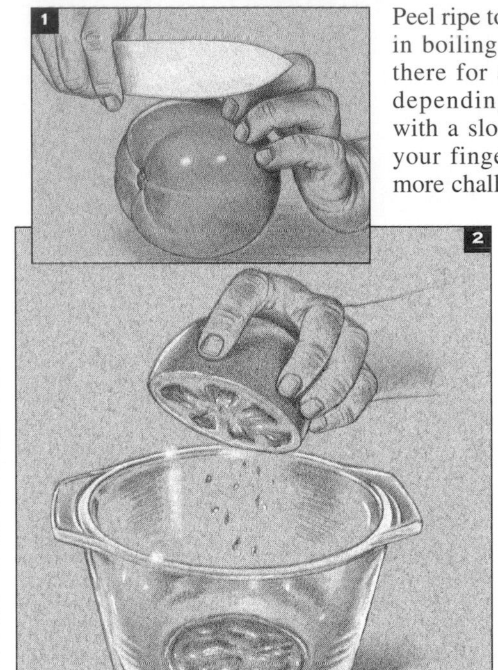

Peel ripe tomatoes by dropping them in boiling water and leaving them there for about 15 to 30 seconds, depending on ripeness. Remove with a slotted spoon and peel with your fingers. Unripe tomatoes are more challenging — if boiled to the point of loosening the skin, the flesh cooks. It's easier to peel them, raw, with a sharp paring knife.

1. To seed tomatoes, cut them in half through their equator, as shown.

2. Gently squeeze out the juice and seeds while giving the tomato a sharp downward shake. Use your finger to remove any remaining seeds.

Segmenting Oranges

Removing the bitter membrane from citrus fruit is an essential step in many tarts, and also produces a more pleasant fruit salad. The task is made easier if you start by sharpening a medium-size paring or vegetable knife (the latter has a very thin blade).

1. Cut the ends from the fruit and sit it on a flat surface. Trim all the peel and white pith using a large chef's knife, making a series of vertical cuts.

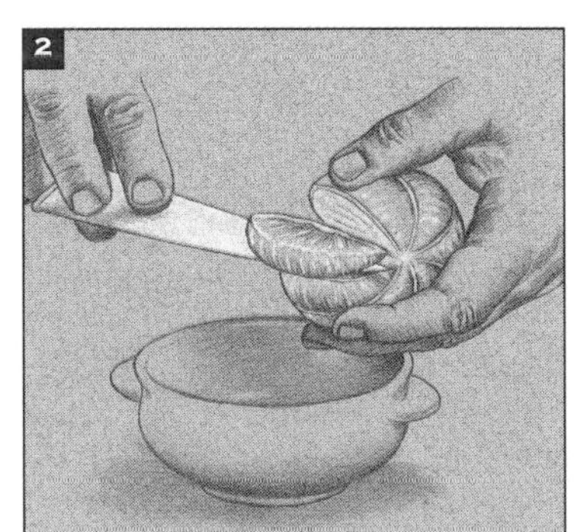

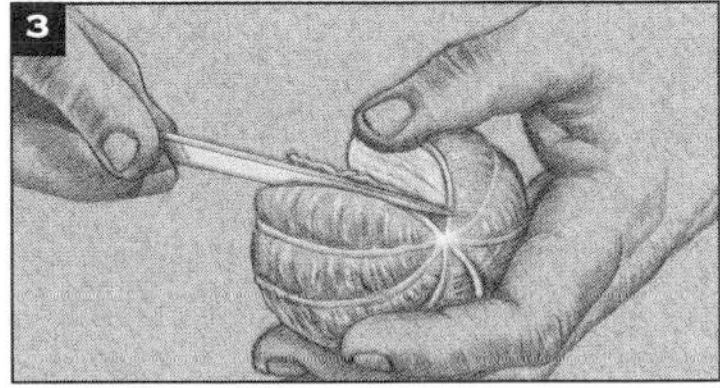

2. Insert the blade of a paring knife between the membrane and the pulp of each segment, and cut towards the center.

3. Flip the cutting edge away from you so that the blade is now parallel to the next membrane. Push out to remove segment.

Illustrations by Alan Witschonke

Dicing Onions

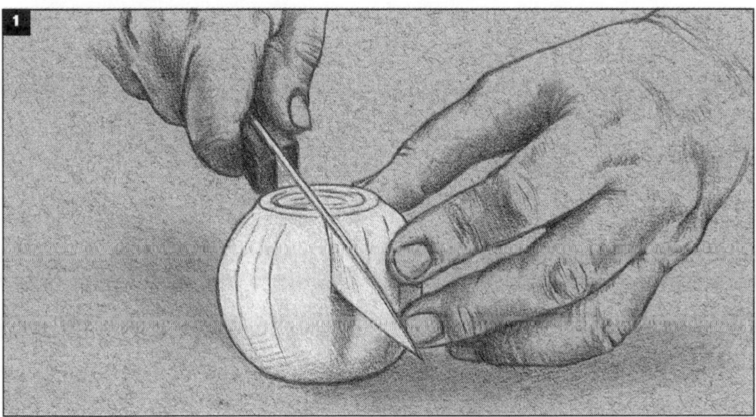

A large, well-sharpened chef's knife is the best tool for this task. (We recommend the Chef's Choice electric knife sharpener.) Cut off the ends of the onion and then peel it. Be careful not to remove too much of the onion, although you should remove dried-up outer layers.

1. Cut the onion in half, pole to pole (from one end to the other).

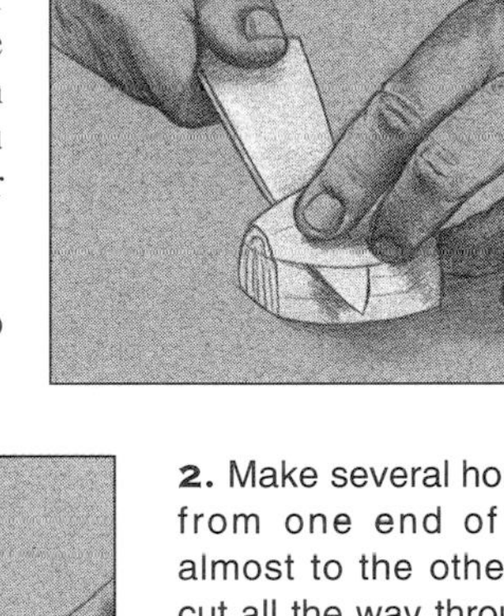

2. Make several horizontal cuts from one end of the onion almost to the other, but don't cut all the way through the root end. The exact number of cuts will depend on the size of the onion and the desired size of the dice.

3. Now make several vertical cuts, pole to pole. Cut all the way through the onion.

4. Finally, chop across the lengthwise cuts from the last step. Use your knuckles as a guide for the knife while holding the onions with your fingertips. Always pull your fingertips in towards your palm, extending the knuckles outward when doing this sort of dicing. It provides more control and eliminates the possibility of an accident.

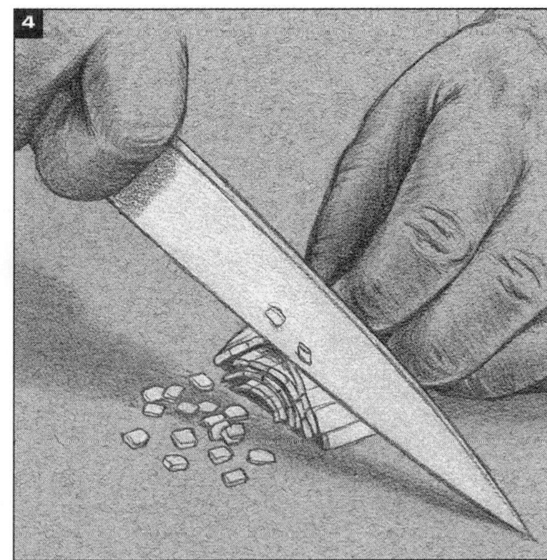

To Carve a Whole Ham

Most country hams are sold whole and require a special carving technique. You can follow any recipe for a country ham, but since they remain very salty even after cooking try to keep the slices as thin as possible.

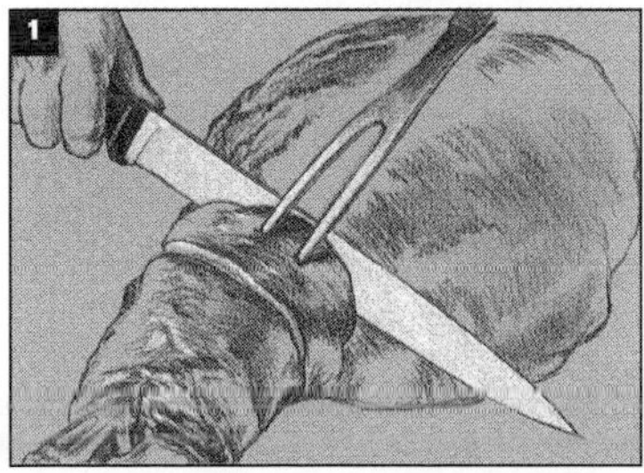

1. Use a thin-bladed, flexible carving knife, and cut down perpendicular to the bone. Remove a wedge-shaped piece at a 45-degree angle.

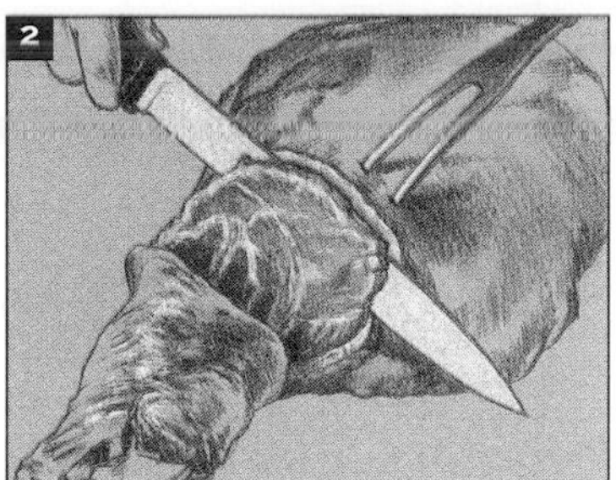

2. Carve thin slices right down to the bone. Twist the knife slightly when it hits the bone to release each slice.

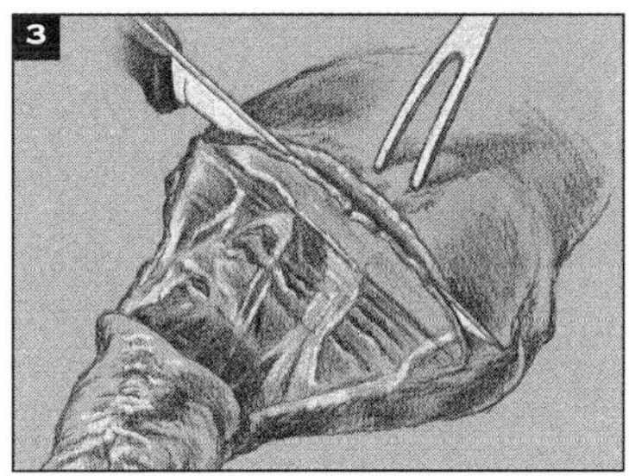

3. Decrease the carving angle in order to obtain slices of uniform thickness.

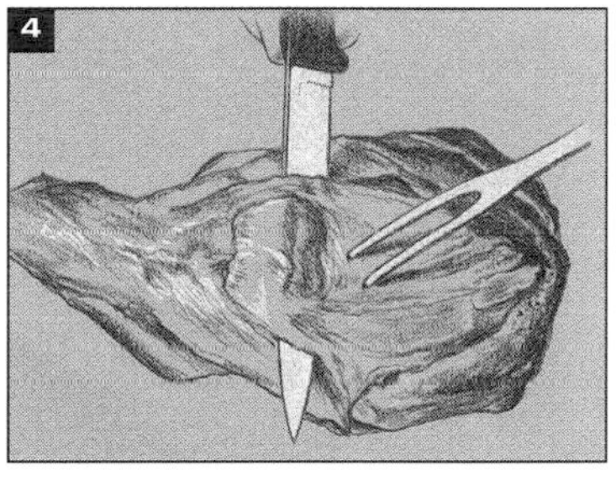

4. Turn the ham over and carve lengthwise now, thinly slicing the remaining meat.

To Carve a Half-Ham

Wet-cured hams — such as those sold in supermarkets — are usually only a portion of the leg, and are easy to slice. Generally speaking, slices should be about one-quarter-inch thick. Again, use a sharp, thin-bladed, flexible carving knife.

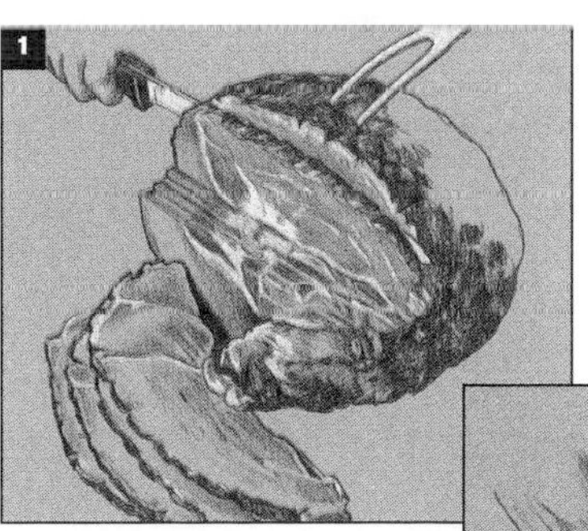

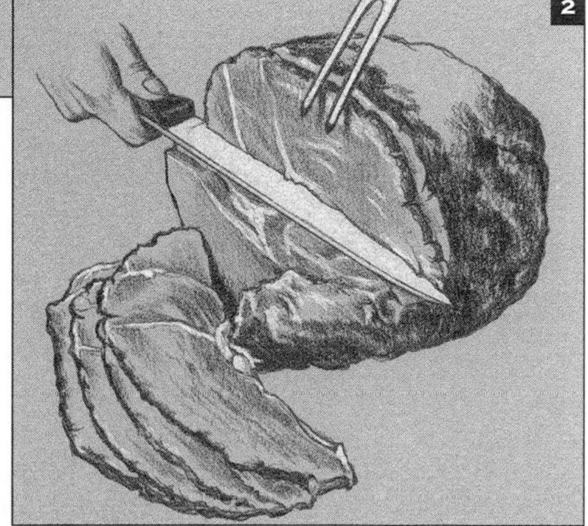

1. Holding the knife perpendicular to the bone, carve full slices until you reach the bone. Then cut half-slices.

2. Cut parallel to the leg bone to release the slices. Turn the ham over and carve half-slices in the same fashion. ■

Five Chinese Cabbages

Discover the crunchy, creamy texture and mildly sweet flavor of five varieties of Chinese cabbage.

BY NINA SIMONDS

Chinese cabbages are now widely available and come in two varieties: heading cabbages such as Napa, and the non-heading varieties such as bok choy.

As members of the much-touted genus *Brassica,* Chinese cabbages have all the health benefits of their somewhat better-known relatives such as broccoli and cauliflower. Cold-hardy and pest-resistant, these cabbages enjoy a long growing season and are well suited to the northern United States. And, as gardeners know, there are literally scores of varieties of Chinese cabbages.

What all of these vegetables have in common is texture that can be both crunchy and creamy, and a sweet, juicy, mild flavor that blends well with other foods. Yes, there are differences among the Chinese cabbages; but most of them are essentially interchangeable. And they can easily be distinguished, once you divide them into heading and non-heading varieties.

Of the heading cabbages, **Chinese celery cabbage,** also known as Peking cabbage (*wong nga baak* in Cantonese), is widely available in two forms: Napa, with full leaves and an oval head; and Tientsin, also known as Michihili, which has a long, cylindrical shape.

Of the non-heading, leafy cabbages, **bok choy** is the most widely available. It typically has dark green leaves and ivory stalks, and is traditionally used in soups, stir-fried dishes with meats and seafood, and in pickled salads. Like broccoli, this is really two vegetables in one: the stalks have a sweet, cabbage-like flavor, the leaves a mildly bitter bite.

Flowering bok choy (*choy sum*), an immature plant, is found sporadically throughout the year. It looks like bok choy with narrow stalks and yellow flowers. Also used in stir-fries, flowering bok choy is sometimes arranged around the outside of a dish as an edible garnish.

Shanghai bok choy, Shanghai cabbage, or baby hearts of cabbage (*seut choy*), another member of the bok choy family, has spoon-shaped, vivid green stalks and flat, full leaves. So small that many markets bundle five or six plants together, Shanghai bok choy is sweeter (and considerably more expensive) than ordinary bok choy, and is used, whole or split, in stir-fries or as an edible garnish.

Chinese oil vegetable, or flowering cabbage (*yow choy*), is the treasured cabbage of Hong Kong and was traditionally grown for its oil. Look for it year-round in Chinese and other specialty markets. With slim, tender stalks, oval leaves, and bright yellow flowers, this slightly bitter plant is often simply stir-fried in smoking hot oil with rice wine and a pinch of salt, as in the delicious stir-fry on the following page. As with Shanghai bok choy and flowering bok choy, it can also be arranged around a platter as an edible garnish.

SEAFOOD CABBAGE CASSEROLE

Serves 6

When buying Napa cabbage, peel back several layers of leaves and sneak a peek into the center; reject the head if you see black spots. When cutting the cabbage into pieces, keep thicker stem pieces separate from the thinner leafy pieces. The stem pieces will need to cook longer and need to be added to the casserole first.

- 3½ tablespoons soy sauce
- 3 tablespoons rice wine
- 2 tablespoons minced scallions
- 2 tablespoons minced ginger
- 1½ tablespoons Chinese black vinegar or Worcestershire sauce
- 1 teaspoon sesame oil
- ½ pound medium shrimp, peeled and butterflied
- ½ pound scallops, sliced horizontally in half
- 1 quart Quick Broth (page 28)
- 1 piece ginger root (2 inches long), sliced thin
- 10 dried Chinese black mushrooms, softened in hot water, stems removed and caps cut into quarters
- ½ cup rice wine or sake
- Salt
- 1 tablespoon vegetable or peanut oil
- 8 cloves garlic, smashed and skins removed
- 1 medium-sized Napa or celery cabbage, about 2½ pounds, halved lengthwise and cored, leaves cut into 2-inch squares
- ⅓ pound snow peas, ends snapped and strings removed

1. Combine first 6 ingredients; add shrimp and scallops and toss to coat. Cover with plastic wrap and marinate 30 minutes.

2. Bring chicken broth and ginger root to boil; simmer to blend flavors, about 10 minutes. Remove ginger root with a slotted spoon. Add mushrooms and rice wine and salt to taste; simmer 5 minutes longer. Set aside.

3. Heat oven to 375 degrees. Heat vegetable oil in a 4-quart casserole or Dutch oven (which can later be covered) until smoking. Add garlic cloves and cabbage stem pieces and toss lightly over high heat for about 1 minute, adding several tablespoons of broth if pan is

ILLUSTRATION BY ALAN WITSCHONKE

The Secret to Perfect Rice

All of these cabbage recipes are best served with long-grain rice. To make this, Asian restaurants have long depended on huge electric steamers to produce rice in quantity, and many Asians have smaller versions of the same appliances in their homes. In recent years, several manufacturers have expanded the market, and rice steamers are now widely available. Usually costing less than $50 (and sometimes less than $30), they make perfect long- or short-grained rice and keep it warm for an hour or more—with little effort on your part. Just add rice and water, cover, turn on the electric steamer, and the rice will be cooked in simmering liquid. When mostly cooked, the machine automically reduces the heat, thus steaming, rather than boiling, the rice in the last few minutes. Rice steamers are also good for reheating cold rice.

DAN KROVATIN

Rice steamers cost from $30 to $50 and can also reheat cold rice through gentle steaming.

dry. Add cabbage leaves and several more tablespoons of broth; cover and simmer for 2 minutes. Uncover, add remaining broth with mushrooms and bring to boil. Cover, transfer casserole to oven and bake until cabbage is tender, about 45 minutes.

4. Arrange shrimp, scallops, and snow peas in separate piles atop cabbage; cover and bake for 10 minutes longer. Using a spoon, toss seafood and baste it with broth. Taste for seasoning, adding more salt if necessary. Serve directly from casserole.

Variation: Substitute 1 pound center-cut pork loin for the seafood, cutting it into thin slices about ¼-inch thick and 1½-inches square. Omit the Chinese black vinegar or Worcestershire sauce in the marinade and prepare as directed.

HOT AND SOUR BOK CHOY

Serves 6

Bok choy keeps for 4 to 5 days, loosely wrapped in plastic, although the leaves may become a bit limp. Remove tough outer leaves before using. This dish is very spicy. For a milder version, reduce the number of chile peppers to 2.

- 1½ pounds bok choy, rinsed thoroughly, stems and leaves separated; stems trimmed and cut diagonally into 2-inch pieces, leaves torn into large pieces
- 1 tablespoon vegetable or peanut oil
- 4 small dried chile peppers, cut into ¼-inch lengths and seeds removed
- 2 tablespoons ginger, finely shredded
- 1½ tablespoons rice wine or sake

Sauce

- 1½ tablespoons soy sauce
- ¾ teaspoon salt
- 1 tablespoon sugar
- 2¼ teaspoons Chinese black vinegar or Worcestershire sauce
- 1 teaspoon cornstarch

1. Heat 1 gallon water to boiling and add bok choy stems. Boil until nearly tender, 1 to 2 minutes; drain. Place under cold running water until cool and drain again. Mix together sauce ingredients.

2. Heat a wok or skillet until very hot; add oil and heat until smoking. Add the chile peppers and stir-fry over high heat for about 20 seconds. Remove peppers with a slotted spoon and discard. Add ginger shreds and stir-fry until fragrant, about 15 seconds. Add cabbage stems and leaves; stir-fry over high heat until leaves wilt, about 1 minute. Add rice wine and stir-fry for 45 seconds longer. Add the sauce and, stirring to prevent lumps, cook until the sauce thickens, about 1 minute. Transfer to a serving platter and serve hot, at room temperature, or cold.

Variation: Substitute Napa cabbage for the bok choy. Omit the parboiling; instead, cook the cabbage stalks for about 1 minute with the seasonings, then add the leafy sections and proceed with the recipe.

STIR-FRIED SHANGHAI BOK CHOY WITH CRABMEAT

Serves 6

Always strip away the tough outer leaves of Shanghai bok choy and trim tough sections of all the leaves before cooking.

- 6 baby hearts of cabbage or Shanghai bok choy, (1½ pounds), stems trimmed, hearts halved or quartered lengthwise (depending on size)
- 1 tablespoon vegetable or peanut oil
- 3 tablespoons minced scallions, white part only
- 1½ tablespoons minced ginger
- ½ pound lump crabmeat, picked through to remove any cartilage
- 2 tablespoons rice wine or sake

Sauce

- ½ cup chicken broth, simmered briefly with one or two slices of ginger
- ¾ teaspoon salt
- 1 teaspoon sesame oil
- 1½ teaspoons cornstarch

1. Heat 1 gallon water to boiling. Add hearts and cook until tender, about 3½ minutes. Drain, place under cold, running water, and drain again. Mix sauce ingredients.

2. Heat a wok or skillet until very hot; add oil and heat until smoking. Add scallions and ginger and stir-fry until fragrant, about 15 seconds. Add crabmeat and rice wine; cook over high heat for 15 seconds, then add sauce. Stir continuously over high heat until sauce thickens, about 1 minute. Add cabbage hearts, toss lightly to coat, and cook until heated through, 1 to 1½ minutes. Transfer to a serving platter and serve immediately with rice.

Variation: Substitute ½ pound of medium, raw, shelled shrimp for the crabmeat. Halve the shrimp lengthwise and cook for about 2 minutes in the rice wine until opaque, and proceed with the recipe.

STIR-FRIED CABBAGE

Serves 6

Although this recipe calls for oil vegetable (*yow choy*), any cabbage may be substituted with the changes noted below.

- 1½ pounds Chinese oil vegetable, leaves separated, and stalks trimmed and cut into 2-inch pieces
- ½ tablespoon vegetable or peanut oil
- 1 tablespoon minced garlic
- 2 tablespoons rice wine
- ½ teaspoon salt, or to taste

1. Heat 4 quarts of water until boiling; boil stalks until tender, about 1½ minutes. Drain, place under cold running water, and drain again.

2. Heat wok or skillet until very hot; add oil and heat until smoking. Add cabbage and stir-fry until leaves wilt, about 45 seconds. Add cabbage stems, garlic, rice wine, and salt. Stir-fry until hot, about 45 seconds. Transfer to a serving platter. Serve hot or at room temperature.

Variations: Substitute broccoli for the oil vegetable. Parboil stalky sections for about 2½ minutes, or until nearly tender. Add broccoli florets to the hot oil; stir-fry for 45 seconds before adding stems, garlic, rice wine, and salt. For celery cabbage, omit precooking and add the stalkier sections to the hot oil; stir-fry 45 seconds until hot. Add leafier sections, garlic, rice wine, and salt; stir-fry until done. ■

Nina Simonds is the author of *China's Food* (HarperPerennial, 1991).

Grow Your Own

If you're interested in planting Chinese cabbages, *"Grow Your Own Chinese Vegetables"* by Geri Harrington (Garden Way, 1978) is an excellent source. Although many catalogs offer a wide selection of seeds for Chinese cabbages, the following companies specialize in Asian plants: **Kitasawa Seed Company** (1111 Chapman, San Jose, CA 95126; telephone 408-243-1330) and **Shepherd's Garden Seeds** (6116 Highway 9, Felton, CA 95018; telephone 408-335-5400).

MASTER CLASS

Gray Kunz's Broth of Black Bass and Minced Vegetables

BY DORIE GREENSPAN

Just off Fifth Avenue, beyond the luxe of the banquettes, brocade, and chandeliers of Lespinasse's dining room, is Gray Kunz's stainless steel kitchen, as polished as a cherished roadster's trim and as well organized as a strategic command center. Trained in precision and excellence by Swiss master chef Fredy Girardet, and steeped in the style of the East after a three-year stint in Hong Kong's famed Regent Hotel, Kunz's intense, sophisticated cuisine is multicultural.

Gray Kunz's New York restaurant, Lespinasse, is located in the St. Regis Hotel. The food is light and aromatic, featuring subtle flavorings such as kaffir lime leaves.

Now cooking in New York, Kunz has found an international clientele who appreciates his unusual selection of dishes. The frequently changing menu includes a four-course vegetable-and-spice tasting menu; lamb and eggplant tart flavored with curry-carrot juice; fricassee of mushrooms in risotto flavored with truffles and herbs; and the knockout dish presented here, Broth of Black Bass and Minced Vegetables.

This deceptively simple blend of broth, fish, vegetables, and aromatics — served with a casserole of white beans and tomatoes — is a dish that elegantly showcases the East-West mix in Kunz's style, combining rich, French-style broth and brunoise-cut vegetables with the heady kaffir lime of Southeast Asia. The result is both exotic and harmonious.

But this elaborate, chef-style dish can be prepared at home. As Kunz says, "This is very easy to cook. In fact, the entire assembly and cooking take less than five minutes. It's the mise-en-scene, the advance preparation, that demands planning, time, attention, and some precise knifework."

There are no tricks, and the techniques involved require no more specialized equipment than a couple of sharp knives, although an immersion blender helps enormously. Following the step-by-step directions here, you'll learn how to evenly cut food for quick cooking and how to prepare food in advance for last-minute assembly. You'll also see why so many top chefs have begun to rely on the immersion blender, which emulsifies ingredients almost instantly.

At Lespinasse, Kunz serves this dish in reduced portions as part of his six-course tasting menu. We have reworked it to serve four, either as an impressive appetizer or as a light main course. You can double the ingredients to make larger portions or serve more people without doing much more work.

To reduce time demands on the day you wish to serve the dish, consider preparing the following ingredients in advance:

White beans can be cooked up to three days ahead and refrigerated. Kunz cooks these in stock, but you may substitute water seasoned with a bouquet garni, two celery ribs, and two carrots.

Bread crumbs can be made up to two weeks ahead.

Chopped vegetables can be prepared up to one day ahead and stored in the refrigerator in tightly covered containers.

Chicken stock can be prepared several days ahead and refrigerated, or one month ahead and frozen. Use the Long-Cooked Stock recipe (*see sidebar, page 29*). You could use the Quick Broth recipe, but the richer and more full-flavored the stock, the better.

Cutting Techniques for Vegetables and Aromatics

These must be cut into extremely small pieces, less than one-eighth-inch square; they will be cooked for just an instant, and they must all be the same size so that they will cook evenly. The cutting, slicing and dicing needed to achieve these traditional brunoise cuts (very small cubes, used in many preparations) is the most time-consuming part of this recipe and also the most important. The garlic and kaffir lime leaf can be preserved in oil and kept covered in the refrigerator for up to one week, but the other vegetables should be refrigerated no longer than one day, and preferably less.

Shallots and garlic: Use the same cutting technique for each, but keep the vegetables separate. Slice very thinly, lengthwise. Keeping the slices together, cut the slices horizontally into very small dice. Work with a large chef's knife and use a rocking motion (one hand holding the handle, the other held on the top of the blade to direct it) to finely mince them (they should be so finely minced they seem almost pureed). If you're working ahead, place the garlic in a small container and pour vegetable or corn oil over it

COOKING TIPS FROM GRAY KUNZ

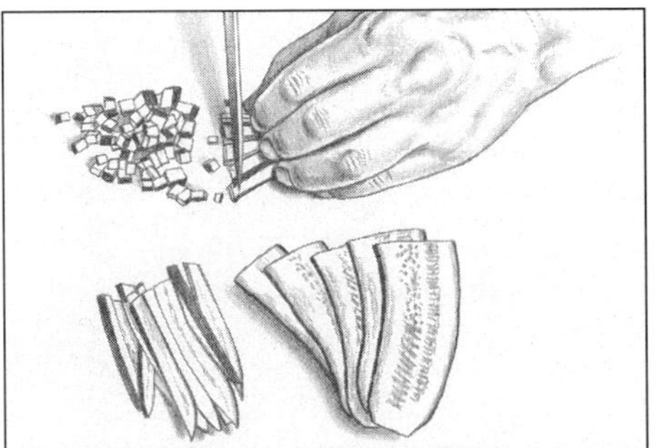

To dice the cucumber, use a slicer or knife to remove one long slice. Then cut even, thin slices, lengthwise. Cut the slices into strips, line up the strips, and evenly and finely dice them.

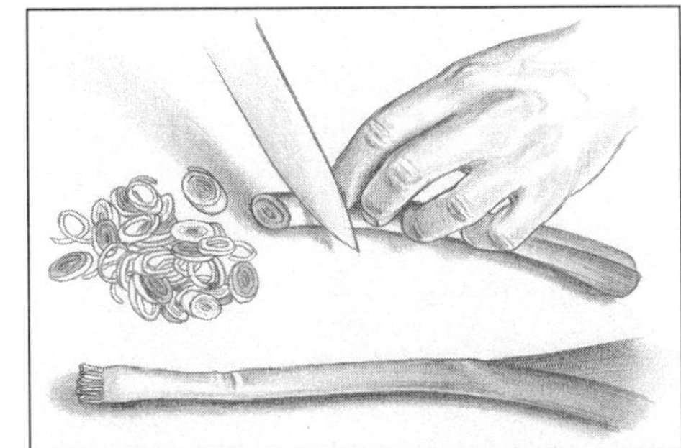

Note that thin, baby leeks are used in this recipe. If they are unavailable, cut small leeks into quarters or substitute scallions. In either case, cut them on the bias into thin oval rounds.

ILLUSTRATIONS BY ALAN WITSCHONKE/PHOTOGRAPH BY RICHARD FELBER

to cover. You can store it this way for a week or so. The shallots may be stored in the refrigerator, covered, for a few hours.

Orange and lemon zests: Again, use the same cutting technique for each, but keep the ingredients separate. Use a vegetable peeler or paring knife to remove strips of zest from the orange and lemon. You want just the thin, colored peel; cut or scrape off any white, bitter pith that adheres to the underside. Stack several strips of peel together and julienne them, cutting lengthwise into long, very thin strands. Gather the julienne together and cut crosswise into very fine dice.

Kaffir lime leaf: To finely dice the kaffir lime leaf, stack five or six leaves together and julienne, then dice as you did for the zests. If you are working ahead, you can place the diced leaves in a small container, cover them with vegetable or corn oil, and store, refrigerated, for two days.

Thyme: Remove the leaves from six or eight sprigs, gather them together and finely mince, using a large chef's knife and a rocking motion.

Tomato: First skin and seed the tomatoes (*see* page 4). Slice the halves crosswise into one-eighth-inch thick slices, then cut the slices into one eighth-inch cubes.

Leek: Cut off almost all the green and remove the roots. Wash well to remove all sand; dry thoroughly. Cut two or three baby leeks on the bias into thin ovals, or cut one small leek into quarters, then cut each quarter into thin slices.

Fennel: Cut the top branches from a fennel bulb into very thin rounds, the same size as the leeks.

Red pepper: Cut the pepper in half lengthwise. Remove the stem, seeds, and veins. Cut the pepper halves into very thin julienne, line up the strips of pepper side-by-side on the cutting board, then cut crosswise into very fine dice.

Cucumber: If possible, use a vegetable slicer to remove a long, thin strip from the length of the cucumber in order to "square" it. Cut the cucumber in half crosswise. Working with one half at a time, place the squared side against the slicer fitted with a medium julienne blade; julienne the cucumber. Then line the julienne up on a cutting board and, using a chef's knife, cut into very fine dice. Without a slicer: cut thin, flat, lengthwise cuts of cucumber, cut these into julienne, and dice the julienne.

WHITE BEAN AND TOMATO CASSEROLE

Serves 4

- 1¼ cups dried navy beans, picked over
- 1 clove
- 1 small onion, peeled
- 1 bay leaf
- 8½ cups chicken stock or broth
- 2 ½-inch thick slices French bread, crusts trimmed and discarded, for bread crumbs
- 1 tablespoon olive oil
- 2½ teaspoons minced fresh thyme leaves
- 3 tablespoons butter
- 1 small shallot, minced
- 1 small garlic clove, minced
- 5 medium tomatoes, peeled, seeded and diced very fine (1½ cups)
- Salt

BROTH OF BLACK BASS AND MINCED VEGETABLES

Serves 4

- 1 pound black sea bass, fluke, flounder, or sole fillet, cut into ½-inch dice
- Salt and ground white pepper
- 3 tablespoons butter
- 4 medium shallots, minced very fine
- 4 large garlic cloves, minced very fine
- 3 cups chicken stock or broth
- 4–6 kaffir lime leaves, diced very fine (1½ tablespoons)
- 1 small lemon, enough zest removed and diced very fine to yield 1 tablespoon
- 1 small orange, enough zest removed and diced very fine to yield 1 tablespoon
- 1 teaspoon minced fresh thyme leaves
- 1 small leek, quartered lengthwise, rinsed thoroughly and sliced very thin (3 tablespoons)
- 1 small fennel bulb, top branches removed and sliced very thin (3 tablespoons), bulb reserved for another use
- ¼ small red bell pepper, seeded and diced very fine (3 tablespoons)
- ¼ small seedless cucumber, diced very thin (3 tablespoons)

1. *For the casserole,* soak beans in cold water to cover by 3 inches at least 4 hours or overnight; drain and rinse. Stick clove in onion; make a shallow slit on the onion's side and insert bay leaf. Place rehydrated beans and prepared onion into Dutch oven or soup kettle; add 2 quarts of stock and bring to a simmer. Simmer until beans are tender but not mushy, 45 to 60 minutes. Drain, cool, then refrigerate beans; reserve stock for another use.

2. Heat oven to 350 degrees. Brush both sides of bread slices with oil and sprinkle with ½ teaspoon thyme. Bake in oven, turning occasionally, until bread has dried out and is golden, about 10 to 15 minutes. Cool toasted bread then pulverize in food processor or blender. Store in airtight container.

3. Heat butter in a 12-inch skillet. Add shallots and garlic; sauté until vegetables are tender, 2 to 3 minutes. Add remaining 2 teaspoons thyme, sauté until fragrant, about 30 seconds. Add tomatoes; cook over medium-high heat until tomatoes have released their juices, about 3 to 5 minutes; season to taste with salt. Stir in cooked beans and remaining ½ cup stock; bring to boil, then simmer until liquid reduces slightly, about 3 to 5 minutes. Spoon beans into each of 4 buttered ramekins and keep warm. Adjust oven rack 3 inches from the heating element and preheat broiler.

4. *For the broth,* season fish with salt and pepper; set aside. Heat butter in a large saucepan. Add shallots and garlic; sauté until softened, 3 to 5 minutes. Stir in stock and bring to boil; simmer until stock reduces by one-third, about 10 minutes. Stir in kaffir lime leaves. Off heat, use an immersion blender to emulsify the liquid, or process liquid in a blender until emulsified. Pour liquid back into pan and return pan to high heat. Add fish and all remaining ingredients. Cook until fish turns opaque, about 1 minute. Adjust seasoning with salt and white pepper. Meanwhile, sprinkle an equal portion of breadcrumbs over each ramekin of beans; broil bean casseroles until breadcrumbs are golden brown, about 3 minutes.

5. Ladle a portion of fish and vegetable broth among each of 4 soup plates. Set each ramekin on a small plate and serve both fish broth and bean casserole together as a first course or light main course. ■

New Yorker **Dorie Greenspan** is the author of *Sweet Times — Simple Desserts for Every Occasion* (Morrow, 1991).

Kaffir lime (*Citrus hystrix*), a native of Southeast Asia, has an intense citrus aroma that cannot be duplicated. Other citrus leaves, or even rind, can be substituted, but you can also order kaffir lime leaves, fresh or dried, from Adriana's Bazaar (2152 Broadway, New York, NY 10023; telephone 212-877-5757).

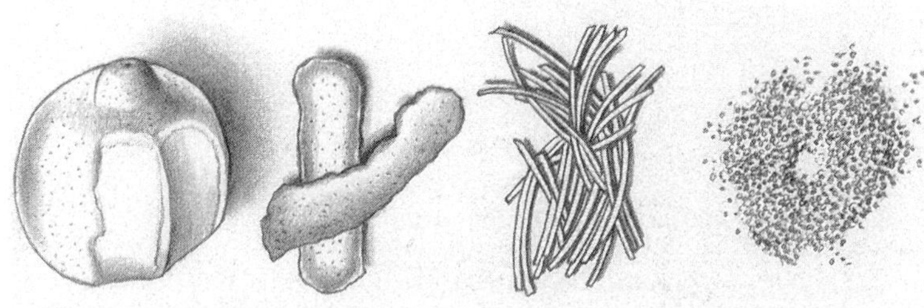

All citrus rinds are minced the same way. Using a vegetable peeler or sharp paring knife, remove thin strips of zest, leaving behind the bitter white pith or trimming it from the zest. Cut the slices into thin shreds, then line up the shreds and mince them as finely as possible.

The Perfect Angel Food Cake

With only six ingredients, angel food is the ultimate test of finesse and timing.

BY BROOKE DOJNY AND MELANIE BARNARD

At its heavenly best, an angel food cake should be tall and perfectly shaped, have a snowy-white, tender crumb, and be encased in a thin, delicate, golden crust. Although most angel food cakes contain no more than six ingredients, there are literally hundreds of variations on this basic theme. The type of flour used, baking temperature, type of sugar, proportions, mixing and folding methods, and even the use of baking powder — a serious transgression for most experts — are all in dispute. What is not in dispute is that angel food requires a delicate balance of ingredients and proper cooking techniques. Like a good pie crust, a perfect angel food cake is the mark of the seasoned cook.

An angel food cake is distinguished by its lack of egg yolks, chemical leaveners, and fat. Other cakes also use beaten egg whites for leaveners, but there are differences. Chiffon cake is similar to angel food cake, with the addition of egg yolks, which make for a slightly heavier, moister cake. Sponge cake also includes whole or separated eggs; it, too, is denser and more yellow than angel food. The classic Génoise cakes use butter, although their preparation is quite similar to the American sponge cake. Génoise are often soaked in a sweet syrup after baking, but can also be used as a regular cake in layers.

The perfect angel food cake is light yet firm with an even, biscuit-colored crust. Angel food cake batter can also be used to make cake rolls which can be filled with flavored creams.

The six ingredients found in every angel food cake are egg whites, sugar, flour, cream of tartar, salt, and flavorings. Most recipes begin by separating the eggs. (Some still stress the fact that two- or three-day-old eggs are easier to separate than fresh ones. Unless you live on or near a farm this is a moot point — all supermarket eggs are "old". If you do live on or near a farm, eggs should be at least three days old.) Since eggs are *the* critical ingredient in angel food cake, it is important to use the right quantity. Our recipe calls for large eggs. If you happen to have another size, you may substitute: 15 medium eggs = 12 large eggs = 9 jumbo eggs.

We tested frozen and thawed egg whites in our cakes, with excellent results. (We suggest you freeze egg whites in ice trays.) We also tested powdered egg whites (available at baking supply stores) and found them to be satisfactory. But they offer no real advantage over fresh eggs.

Beating Egg Whites

Since an angel food cake is leavened only by the beaten egg whites, it is critical that you whip them correctly. Although most cookbooks call for eggs at room temperature, we found no discernible difference in volume between egg whites beaten at 72 degrees and those taken straight from the refrigerator (48 degrees). And if you separate cold eggs, you'll find that the whites cling together better, making this chore easier. You can then let the whites stand until you're ready to beat them.

Mixer speed is important for well-beaten whites. Starting at high speed will produce quick, but inconsistent, results. To create the most stable foam, beat the whites at low speed just to break them up into a froth. Add the cream of tartar and the salt, increase the speed to medium, and beat until the whites form very soft, billowy mounds. When large bubbles stop appearing around the edges, and with the mixer

WHAT IS CREAM OF TARTAR?

Cream of tartar was once known as the secret ingredient in angel food cakes. A common solid salt of tartaric acid, it was first used by a Mr. Sides of St. Louis, Missouri, one of the many reported inventors of angel food cake. The substance acts as a stabilizer when beaten with egg whites, making for a higher, lighter cake. The acidity in cream of tartar also acts as a bleach, helping to make cakes snowy-white (lemon juice works in much the same way). Cream of tartar does not produce greater volume in beaten whites. It does, however, make the foam less prone to overcoagulation during beating by slightly lowering the pH of the egg whites from about 9 to about 8. Chemically, the cream of tartar adds hydrogen ions, creating a more stable molecular structure.

PHOTOGRAPH BY RICHARD FELBER

still on medium, begin adding the sugar, a tablespoon at a time, until all the sugar is incorporated and the whites are shiny and form soft peaks when the beater is lifted. The mass should still flow slightly when the bowl is tilted. Do not beat until the peaks are stiff — this makes it difficult to fold in the flour, deflating the whites and therefore reducing volume.

Which Sugar? Which Flour?

Sugar is critical to the taste and texture of the cake. And because there is no fat in angel food cakes the sugar also performs a stabilizing function. Fully half the sugar is beaten into the whites to form a meringue, which is a far more substantial mixture than beaten whites alone. Be sure to add the sugar slowly — about a tablespoon at a time — to make certain that it dissolves fully and is completely incorporated.

The type of sugar is also important. Confectioner's sugar cannot be used because it comes with a small amount of cornstarch added, and its texture is too dense for angel food. Superfine sugar, made from granulated sugar in a food processor, is simply too fine, and produces a soft cake with little substance. Ordinary granulated sugar is best; be sure to sift it to break down clumps and remove unusually large granules.

Flour is the starch that sets the cake batter. But since it also adds weight, the flour you use should be as light and airy as possible. Start with cake flour, which is finer and lighter than all-purpose. It also has a lower gluten content and a lower pH, which contributes to a more delicate structure and therefore more tender crumb. (Cake flour generally produces more delicate baked products.)

If you are using a recipe that calls for all-purpose flour, you can substitute cake flour at the rate of seven-eighths cup cake flour for each cup of all-purpose. Then sift the cake flour twice before measuring and once more before you add it to the batter; this contributes to a light, white, tender cake.

Adding Flavor

The ingredients discussed to this point would give you a sweet but bland cake. That's why most angel food recipes add flavorings. Salt, of course, is the most basic, and has the added advantage of further stabilizing the beaten egg whites. Other common additions are extracts of vanilla or almond, especially appealing because they give loads of flavor without changing the basic chemistry of the batter. You can also flavor angel food by adding grated citrus zests to some of the flour before incorporating it. But high-fat flavorings such as chocolate and nuts should be avoided, because they can greatly alter the cake's texture.

Further Tests

We tried using baking powder for added leavening and stability, but found that the resulting cake was not as white as the more pure variety; it also had a coarser crumb. Although the flavor and texture were acceptable, baking powder offers no clear benefits. If you make the meringue properly and use cake flour, you will have no need of this crutch.

Our most intriguing experiment involved oven temperatures. We baked the same recipe in the same pan at 300 degrees, 325 degrees, 350 degrees, and 375 degrees — baking all of them until the cake tested done with a skewer and "bounced" back when the top was depressed with a finger. Surprisingly, all the cakes cooked evenly, but the 350 and 375 degree versions had a thicker, darker crust while the 300 and 325 degree cakes had a more desirable, delicate, evenly pale golden crust. After many tastings we decided that 325 degrees was the ideal temperature.

Unmolding Angel Food Cake

The ideal tool to remove angel food cake from the pan is a thin, flexible, non-serrated knife

Microwave Angel Food?

Although we noted that microwave cookbooks do *not* carry recipes for angel food cakes (now we know why), we decided to give this method a shot simply out of curiosity. Using our standard batter in a microwave-safe tube pan, we used the highest power setting in a large oven for 18 minutes, rotating the cake twice during the baking time. The cake was not a success. The exterior was pure white, the egg proteins had been toughened by the oven, and the texture was gluey because flour absorbs liquid quickly in a microwave oven. The result was a damp white tubular sponge with an uneven texture (dense and treacly in spots, lighter in others) that was almost completely lacking in taste.

The microwave cake was pure white and tasteless.

The Science of Egg Whites

When egg whites are beaten, they produce a foam much like the head on a beer, or soap bubbles. Like most other foams, egg whites, which are liquid, create a lattice-work structure through agitation. This traps pockets of air or gas which in turn form a series of bubbles. Stable foams (egg whites are particularly stable) have two things in common: the bubbles are very small and the liquid that traps the gas is very strong. Albumen, the protein in egg whites, is particularly well-suited to producing stable foam. It's thick and viscous which gives it long life. In addition, the whites are made of several type of protein. One of these proteins acts as a "quick-setting cement" and another, called ovalbumin, does its work later, in the heat of the oven, helping to further set the structure of the foam. Of course heat also causes the trapped air to expand (gases expand when heated), causing the entire structure to rise.

These proteins have another interesting physical property. One end (these proteins are curled up before beating and have "ends") is attracted to liquid, the other is repelled by it. This dual action is the force behind the creation of a lattice-work structure as the protein unfolds in different directions, either seeking out liquid or air.

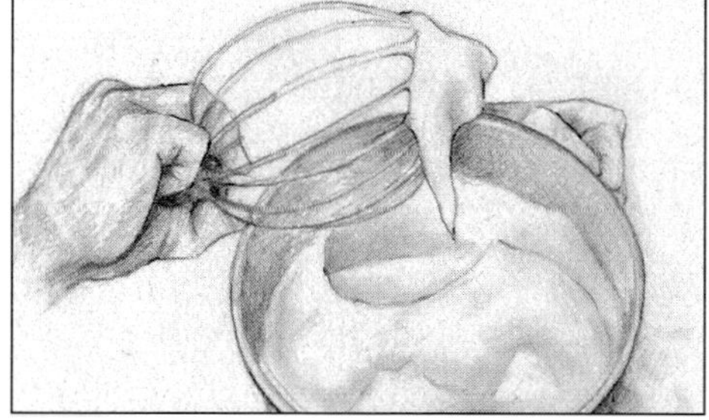

Correctly beaten whites are smooth, glossy, and moist and will flow slightly when the bowl is tilted.

For cooks, it's important to remember that small bubbles are more stable and therefore preferable to large bubbles. Consequently, start beating whites at low speed, then increase the speed to medium. This encourages the development of smaller and more stable bubbles.

Overbeaten egg whites produce a flatter cake.

Overbeaten whites clump and cling to bowl.

ILLUSTRATIONS BY KATHY BRAY

that is at least five inches long. Tilt the pan at a right angle to the counter to make it easy to work the knife around the sides. Insert the knife between the crust and the pan, pressing hard against the side of the pan, and work your way all the way around the cake. To cut around the central core, use a long thin skewer. Invert the pan so the cake slides out, then peel off parchment or wax paper; if using a pan with a removable bottom, slide the knife blade between the cake and the pan to release it. Present the cake bottom side up, sitting on its wider, crustier top, with the delicate and more easily sliced crust facing up.

Cutting the Cake

To cut the cake, use a long, serrated knife, and pull it back and forth with a gentle sawing motion. (When we tried using the specially made tool for cutting angel food — a row of prongs attached to a bar — it did little more than mash and squash the tender cake.) If you want to cut off the top of a cake in order to fill it, use a taut thread or piece of dental floss.

DO YOU REALLY NEED A TUBE PAN?

To find out if a tube pan is really necessary to successfully make angel food cake, we tested our recipe in a 9-by-1½-inch cake pan and in an 8-by-3-inch cake pan. As the cakes baked, neither batter rose more than flush with the pan top. When we took the cakes out of the oven to cool, we had to place them top side down on a cooling rack; there was no center hole to balance them. The rack left its mark on each of the cake tops. The cake in the 9-by-1½-inch pan baked and cooled successfully, but its squatty height created problems — how attractively or practically would the cake serve up? You would need to serve a huge slice to make up for the height. The big surprise came as we unmolded the 8-by 3-inch cake. The cake bottom had dramatically fallen in the center while cooling upside down. We were so surprised by this test that we tested each cake again, with the same results. It appears that you cannot successfully make angel food — at least a tall version of it — without the specially designed pan. The batter needs the center surface area to cling to as it bakes and cools.

THE BEST ANGEL FOOD CAKE

- 1 cup sifted cake flour
- 1½ cups sifted granulated sugar
- 12 large egg whites
- 1 teaspoon cream of tartar
- ¼ teaspoon salt
- 1½ teaspoons vanilla extract
- 1½ teaspoons lemon juice
- ½ teaspoon almond extract

1. Heat oven to 325 degrees. Have ready an ungreased 9¾-inch angel food cake pan, preferably with a removable bottom, or use parchment or wax paper to line bottom of pan with nonremovable bottom.
2. In a small bowl, combine flour with ¾ cup sugar. Place remaining ¾ cup sugar next to the mixer. Use a whisk to completely combine and aerate flour/sugar mixture.
3. In a large, grease-free mixing bowl, beat egg whites at low speed until just broken up and beginning to froth. Add cream of tartar and salt and beat at medium speed until whites form very soft, billowy mounds. With the mixer still at medium speed, beat in ¾ cup sugar, 1 tablespoon at a time, until all sugar is added and whites are shiny and form soft peaks. Add vanilla, lemon juice, and almond extract and beat until just blended.
4. Place flour/sugar mixture in a sifter set over waxed paper. Sift flour mixture over egg whites about 3 tablespoons at a time, and gently fold it in, using a large rubber spatula, a large flat whisk, or your hand.
5. Gently scrape batter into pan, smooth the top, and give pan a couple of raps on the counter to release any large air bubbles.
6. Bake in lower third of oven for 50 to 60 minutes until cake is golden brown and the top springs back when pressed firmly.
7. If cake pan has feet, invert pan onto them. If not, invert pan over the neck of a bottle so that air can circulate all around it. Allow to cool completely for 2 to 3 hours before removing from pan.

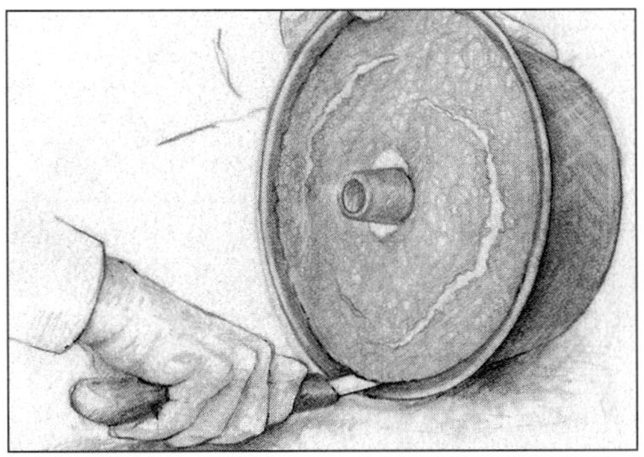

To unmold, insert knife between the crust and the cake, pressing hard against the side of the pan.

8. To unmold, run a knife around edges, being careful not to dislodge the golden crust (*see* illustration, left). Pull cake out of pan and cut the same way around removable bottom to release, or peel off parchment or wax paper, if used.
9. Cool cake completely, bottom side up. When completely cold, cut slices by sawing gently with a serrated knife or pulling with a taut thread through the cake. Serve cake the same day or freeze overnight if serving the next day. (Cake may be frozen for up to 2 weeks, but will compress slightly.) ■

Brooke Dojny and **Melanie Barnard** are regular columnists for *Bon Appetit* magazine and jointly authored *Parties!* (HarperCollins, 1992).

THE RIGHT CAKE PAN

The traditional pan for angel food cake is a tall tube pan with a central column.The central tube exposes more batter to the heat, helps the center of the cake to rise, dries out the cake evenly, and, as an important bonus, creates more of the lightly caramelized macaroon-like outer crust. Most older recipes call for an old-fashioned 10-inch tube pan, which in reality usually measured about 9¾ inches across the wide top and had a four and one-half-quart capacity. Many newer pans call themselves 9¾ inch, but measure 9¼ inches, with a four-quart capacity. We have scaled down our recipe to fit the newer, smaller pans. The older pans will also work, although the cake will not be quite as high.

We recommend using a pan with a removable bottom if possible. An angel food cake pan is *never* greased — you want the batter to climb up the sides, which will not happen with a greased surface. The cake must be cut out of its pan. Removable bottoms allow the cook to slide a thin knife between the bottom of the cake and the pan, a task that is impossible with a regular cake pan. We suggest using parchment or wax paper to line the bottom of a pan with a nonremovable bottom. The newer nonstick pans are of no real benefit to angel food cakes. Although the cake will rise properly, it will in fact stick to the sides, and must be removed in the traditional manner.

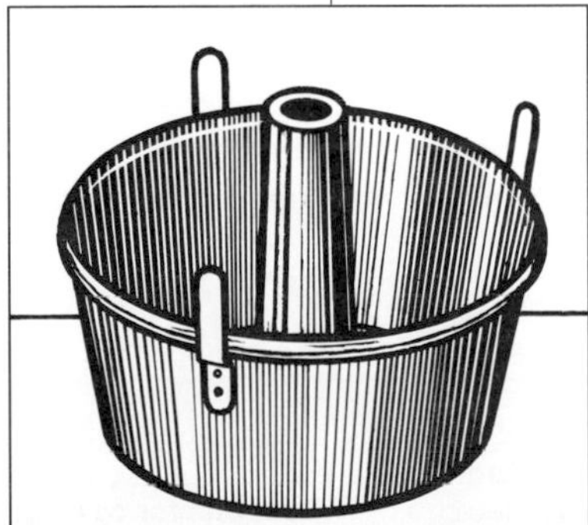

Left: The inner tube of an ungreased angel food pan helps the fragile batter to rise. Below: This angel food cake cutting tool doesn't work; use a serrated knife instead.

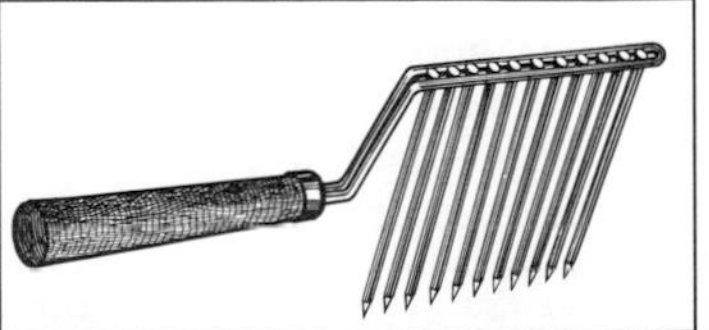

ILLUSTRATIONS BY ELAINE SEARS AND DAN KROVATIN

Taste-Testing Olive Oils

Four tasters find that price, color, and country of origin have little to do with quality.

The key to buying oil, like any other food or wine, is in the price–value relationship. The questions to ask are not, "Where is it from?" or "Is it extra virgin?" but "How does it taste?" and "How much does it cost?"

There is no doubt that these questions are worth asking — olive oil is experiencing a tremendous boom and consequently the choices have become more complex. Sales of olive oil have tripled in the past eight years, and doubled since 1989; olive oil has become the third-best-selling oil in the country, after corn oil and blended vegetable oil. In today's supermarket or specialty store, $20 can buy anything from a liter of trendy oil to a gallon of "regular."

Olives used in Italian olive oils aren't necessarily from Italy. Greece, Spain, and Italy trade olives frequently and there have been years in which Greece has sold 80 percent of its crop to Italy. However, the larger Italian producers do in fact produce a consistent product by carefully blending olive varieties.

Extracting Olive Oil

The olive easily renders its oil. When you squeeze it (this is traditionally done with a mechanical screw or press, although it was often done with the feet, and you can even do it with your hands if you're strong enough) you get a mixture of oil and water. Skim off the water and you've got oil. This cannot be done with corn, flax, or almost any other seed or vegetable that must be refined either to extract the oil or to remove any poisonous substances accompanying it.

A relatively small percentage of all olive oil is now made by the old method, although extra virgin oil is often still traditionally made. After picking and sorting, the olives are quickly moved to the pressing area. Fermentation can begin within hours, so there is some urgency. The olives are crushed, using a stone or steel mill. The paste is then spread on round straw mats, which are in turn layered, dozens high, on the press, with a steel plate between every few mats. The press is usually turned by machine, sometimes by whatever beast of burden is available, and the water is siphoned off the resultant extract. The modern method is similar, but uses extrusion devices and centrifuges, mimicking the old style but doing it more efficiently.

Grading Olive Oil

The oil that comes from this pressing either qualifies as extra virgin or virgin or it does not. To qualify as virgin oil it must contain less than 2 percent acidity; to qualify as extra virgin it must contain less than 1 percent acidity. Acidity is the only objective measure of oil; of course, both these grades naturally look, smell, and taste good. Neither grade may be further treated except for filtering.

Oil that does not meet these standards is destined for refining, to remove acidity. Refining leaves the oil virtually tasteless, so a percentage (the amount is unregulated) of extra virgin or virgin oil is added to restore color and taste. The oil now contains less than 1½ percent acidity and is labeled either pure or, as of 1 January 1992, simply olive oil. ("Light" olive oils are pure oils that contain little flavorful virgin oil.) Further refining can extract more oil from the paste (or pomace) that remains after the initial pressing. This oil is labeled pomace, and should be avoided; it is not worth the lower cost.

All of these labels are backed by law in the European Community. Since there are no such standards in the United States, we must rely on the honesty of exporters and importers. The recently formed American Olive Oil Association has instituted voluntary testing of randomly selected oils in an attempt to limit fraud. More significantly, the group has petitioned the Food and Drug Association to duplicate and enforce the European standards in this country.

Does Color or Country of Origin Matter?

If our tasting of more than 20 oils demonstrated nothing else, it clearly showed that country of ori-

Choosing an Oil Based on Usage

Best all-purpose oils: Colavita Extra Virgin; Carthage Extra Virgin

Best sprinkling oils (strong-tasting foods): Saifan Extra Virgin; Tipico Calabrese Extra Virgin; Carthage Extra Virgin

Best sprinkling oils (mild foods): Olio Santo Extra Virgin; Italica Pure; Lorenza de Medici Extra Virgin

Best oils for sautéing/frying: Filippo Berio Special Selection Extra Virgin; Carthage Extra Virgin

Best oils for vinaigrette: Olio Santo Extra Virgin; Tipico Calabrese Extra Virgin; Carthage Extra Virgin

Best oils for baking: Bertolli Extra Light; Filippo Berio Pure

PHOTOGRAPH COURTESY OF THE INTERNATIONAL OLIVE OIL COUNCIL

Olive Oil Blind Tasting: Does Price Make a Difference?

Tasters on this panel — two representatives of the olive oil industry and two food writers — judged these oils based on aroma, flavor, and projected usefulness. Oils were downgraded for obvious flaws such as lack of flavor or complexity, acrid aromas or tastes, or excessive harshness. Color, which ranges from pale straw to almost bright green, was noted but not graded, since there is no intrinsic value in color, nor is color indicative of anything else. Oils were tasted blind, poured from identical, numbered bottles. They are presented here in rough overall order of preference; when two oils were judged to be more or less equal, we have listed the less expensive one first. Note that prices are per bottle, but that bottles vary greatly in size; all oils were purchased in New Jersey, Connecticut, New York City, or by telephone as noted; prices vary nationally, by as much as 20 percent. Many of these oils are available in other sizes as well.

Olive Oils Listed in Order of Preference

1 **Colavita Extra Virgin** *(Italy)*, $5.29 per half-liter (approximately 17 ounces). Pretty yellow oil, with hints of green. Very assertive aroma: big, bright, and fruity. Taste is nutty, fruity, and rich, with some pepper in the finish. Nicely balanced, warm, and inviting, fine for sprinkling, dressings and — at this price — even sautéing. Good buy. *Widely available.*

2 **Olio Santo Extra Virgin** *(Napa Valley)*, $12 per half-liter. Proof that the Californians are catching up. Lovely, clear green with light tinge of yellow. Fresh, fruity, pleasant aroma. Taste is big up-front, very complex and appealing, with a slight peppery finish. Use for sprinkling; the most wonderful tasting oil we sampled. (To order, call De Medici Imports at 914-651-4400.)

3 **Saifan Extra Virgin** *(Lebanon)*, $17.50 per gallon. On the green side. Fresh, light aroma. Heavy oil with good flavor, nutty and fairly complex with just a hint of pepper in the throat. Good for drizzling on beans, bread, bitter greens; too strong for fish. The surprise of the tasting. Terrific buy, enjoyable oil. *Limited availablility.*

4 **Tipico Calabrese Extra Virgin** *(Italy)*, $5.75 per liter. Dark yellow with a lot of green. Big, rich, forward aroma, smells "like a warm summer day." Peppery, perfumed flavor; not harsh. Nice for drizzling (not on fish); the warm flavor of this oil would be lost in sautéing or even in a vinaigrette sauce. *Limited availablility.*

5 **Filippo Berio Special Selection Extra Virgin** *(Italy)*, $13 per three-quarter-liter (about 25 ounces). Top of the line from best-known producer. Light green, with bright, clean, lightly flowery aroma. Taste is long, lingering, and smooth, with slightly peppery, "fun" finish. *Limited availability.*

6 **Carthage Extra Virgin** *(Tunisia)*, $15 per gallon. Dark yellow oil with intense, very fruity aroma. Rich and warm flavor, fruity and very olivey. Finish is unexceptional. Note price; this is an excellent all-purpose oil. *Limited availability.*

7 **Italica Pure** *(Spain)*, $4.19 per liter. Light golden color, tending towards yellow. Clean, open, lovely nose. Flavor is flowery, spicy, complex and very appealing. Not especially strong — you can sprinkle this on anything, although it might get lost if blended with strong flavors. *Widely available.*

8 **Lorenza de Medici Extra Virgin** *(Italy)*, $25 per three-quarter-liter. Lovely, yellow oil with subtle but nicely perfumed aroma. Flavor is complex, finish mild. (To order, call De Medici Imports at 914-651-4400.)

9 **Filippo Berio Extra Virgin** *(Italy)*, $5.29 per half-liter. Deep yellow oil with hints of green. Pleasant, straightforward aroma, good, rich flavor; some bite in the finish. Simple but enjoyable. *Widely available.*

10 **Bertolli Extra Light** *(Italy)*, $7.59 per liter. Straw-colored and very light but perfumey, flowery aroma, light, ripe olive flavor, with some pepper in the finish. You wouldn't use this for sprinkling — or give it as a gift — but it's fine for light dressings or sautéing. *Widely available.*

11 **Old Monk Extra Virgin** *(France)*, $3.99 per 10 ounces. Bright greenish tan, with some yellow; odd but pleasant color. Very perfumey aroma. Mild, not especially assertive oil, with some pepper in the finish. Useful but not distinctive. *Widely available.*

12 **Lungarotti Extra Virgin** *(Italy)*, $34.00 per liter. Deep, pretty green oil with light, olive-straw aroma. Flavor is not especially assertive — downright bland, in fact — but pleasant, with some kick in the finish. Probably best for cooking. Price a definite drawback. *Limited availability.*

13 **Filippo Berio Pure** *(Italy)*, $4.59 per half-liter. Very light, pale yellow oil. Simple, olivey aroma; smooth, simple, pleasant flavor. No intensity or complexity. *Widely available.*

14 **Louis de Regis Extra Virgin** *(France)*, $9.00 per liter. Dark yellow oil, tinged with green and slightly cloudy. Flowery nose, but taste is extremely mild; peppery finish. Decent oil. *Limited availablility.*

15 **Carapelli Extra Virgin** *(Italy)*, $8.87 per three-quarter-liter. Golden yellow, very clear; lovely oil. Flowers and perfume in nose, but flavor is quite flat and not especially appealing. Strong peppery finish might make this good with harsh or acidic foods such as bitter greens or tomatoes. *Widely available.*

16 **Rienzi Pure Oil** *(Italy)*, $3.29 per half-liter. Light golden and very clear. Not much nose; flavor is fruity but simple, and slightly muddy. Inoffensive; would be good for sautéing or combining with vinegar. *Widely available.*

17 **Peloponnese Extra Virgin Oil** *(Greece)*, $10.99 per three-quarter-liter. Almost orange; not very appealing. Aroma is oily, not much else; flat and neutral in mouth, with acrid finish. *Widely available.*

gin matters little. Oils from Lebanon and California were more delicious than any of the boutique oils from Italy, generally considered the world's best. The tasting also showed that price is not an obstacle to good flavor. The widely distributed and relatively inexpensive Colavita (which can be bought by the gallon for $20 or so) was the surprise of the tasting.

It would make things simpler if we could judge olive oil by its color — but we cannot. Although the mild-flavored pure and extra-light oils were also the lightest in color, the darkest, greenest oil of the tasting was milder than many yellow oils. Olive oils are made from green olives, black olives, and both. There are hundreds of varieties of olives, and each produces a slightly different color of oil. Also, underripe (green) olives tend to make greener oil and ripe (dark) olives produce a yellow oil. Deep green oil can be light-flavored and sweet, pale yellow oil peppery and full. Like grapes and almost everything else that is grown, the flavor and quality of olives are affected by variety, climate, soil, cultivation and irrigation, pests and diseases, and the given vintage. The oil, of course, is further affected by processing. Ultimately, color means little.

In fact, generalizations about olive oil are hard to come by. It is true that certain regions have distinct characteristics; many Tuscan oils, for example, have such a harsh finish that tasters frequently coughed. (This is not necessarily a flaw: Tuscans use such oil for sprinkling on beans, vegetables, or grilled meats, where their strong character shows nicely.) But statements such as "The Californians have a long way to go in making good oil," or "The French make the best oil," or even "Italian oil is different from any other," appear to be out-and-out nonsense. This is especially true when you consider that Greece, Spain (the largest producer of olive oil), and Italy (the largest consumer of olive oil) all trade olives frequently, and that there have been years in which Greece sold 80 percent of its crop to Italy. This means that the fancy extra virgin Tuscan oil you just bought could have been made with Greek olives. Again, the point is to judge oil by what's in the bottle and what it costs.

Matching Oils and Palates

Having found a favorite oil or two, you might wonder whether it will remain consistent from one bottle to the next. With the oils of the larger Italian producers, the answer seems to be "yes." Subsequent to our group tasting, we sampled bottles of Colavita from three different sources and could not distinguish among them. "Although olives vary from year to year, like wines," says Thomas Mueller, president of Filippo Berio, "and the quality of oil that can be obtained from them also varies, our tasters sample and sample and sample, blending oils to produce a flavor that is consistent from one year to the next."

Such consistency may not be possible when the number of olives to choose from is more limited, as in the case of Napa Valley's Olio Santo. "We've contracted with local growers," says Kevin Cronin, one of the oil's producers, "but it's still a pretty small group." Cronin and his partner in the project, Tra Vigne chef Michael Chiarello, are not after a stable product. This fall they're making "vineyard designated" oils, small batches produced from olive trees scattered on private property — often in vineyards — throughout Napa Valley.

The beauty of olive oil lies in its versatility, and in the differences among oils; this is not sterile stuff, nor do we want it to be. Aside from the oils we rejected because of off-flavors or -aromas, every oil in our tasting could be put to good use, and you may want to keep several olive oils in your pantry (always dark and cool, please, and never for more than a year). Full-flavored extra virgin oil should be thought of as a seasoning, one that can be used to anoint foods; it should not be used for sautéing, or even heated more than gently, because much of its character will dissipate. Less expensive pure oils, however, are great for sautéing, frying (with a smoking point of over 400 degrees, olive oil compares favorably to all oils commonly used for frying), and even baking. The key is to match the flavor of the oil to the flavors of the finished preparation.

If You Have Trouble Finding an Oil . . .

Those oils with limited availability often may be found at ethnic stores catering to foodstuffs from the Mediterranean area, including Italian, Middle Eastern, Portuguese, Greek, and Spanish retailers. You can also purchase many of these oils from Sahadi Importing Company (187 Atlantic Avenue, Brooklyn, NY 11201; telephone 718-624-4550). ■

The Fat the Doctor Ordered?

If you aren't already eating olive oil for its taste, you might be eating it for your health. Many people are, which explains the proliferation of the virtually tasteless extra-light olive oils that now account for 15 percent of all olive oil sales. Most of the olive oil sold in the U.S. is pure, the blend of refined and virgin oils; extra virgin oil makes up about one-fifth of sales.

The biggest health benefit of olive oil is that nearly three-quarters of its fat content is monounsaturated fats, which lower bad cholesterol (LDL) while leaving the good cholesterol (HDL) undisturbed. This is in contrast to polyunsaturated fats, which are now thought to be carcinogenic and which lower HDL, thereby increasing the possible risk of heart disease. Oils high in polyunsaturates (e.g., corn oils) are also implicated in increased activity of free radicals, thought to be a precursor of cancer.

There are some other benefits of olive oil. It contains a high proportion of linoleic acid, an essential nutrient which the body cannot synthesize; common cooking oils contain only a trace. Linoleic acid helps, among other things, to metabolize cholesterol properly. Olive oil also contains Vitamin E and other antioxidants that are now thought to be anticarcinogenic. And olive oil is said to facilitate the functioning of the gall bladder and to decrease the incidence of gallstones. While it is true that fewer Mediterranean people than Americans have gallstones, there are few direct studies about this.

Finally, the radical fringe of olive oil advocates also say it slows aging, especially in the brain. The jury is still out on that one; but it would come as no surprise.

For a comparison of the fat content of common oils, see page 20.

Recipes for Desserts Using Olive Oil

Walnut Wafers

Makes 5 dozen

- 6 tablespoons mild-flavored olive oil
- ¾ cup light brown sugar, tightly packed
- 2 egg whites
- ¼ teaspoon salt
- 1 teaspoon vanilla extract
- 2 cups unbleached all-purpose flour
- ½ cup chopped walnuts

Beat oil and sugar to combine. Beat in remaining ingredients to form a stiff dough. Halve dough and roll into 2 cylinders 1½ inches in diameter. Wrap in foil and refrigerate until firm, at least 1 hour. Heat oven to 400 degrees. Cut dough into ¼-inch rounds and place on a nonstick or greased cookie sheet. Bake until golden brown, 8 to 10 minutes. Remove from sheet and cool on wire rack before serving.

Neopolitan Orange Cake

- 1 cup sugar
- 1¾ cup flour
- 2 teaspoons baking soda
- 1 scant teaspoon salt
- 6 tablespoons mild-flavored olive oil
- ½ cup milk
- ¼ cup Grand Marnier

Heat oven to 350 degrees. Lightly oil and flour an 8- or 9-inch cake pan. Combine dry ingredients in a bowl and stir to blend. Add wet ingredients and beat until smooth. Batter will be very thick; pour it into cake pan. Bake until a toothpick inserted in the middle comes out clean, about 40 minutes. Cool on a wire rack, in the pan, for 30 minutes. Run a knife around the rim of the cake, and invert it back onto the rack to cool completely before serving.

The Secrets of Pie Pastry

BY NICK MALGIERI

ROLLING OUT DOUGH

1. Flour work surface very lightly. Excess flour will toughen pastry dough. Add additional flour sparingly, as needed.

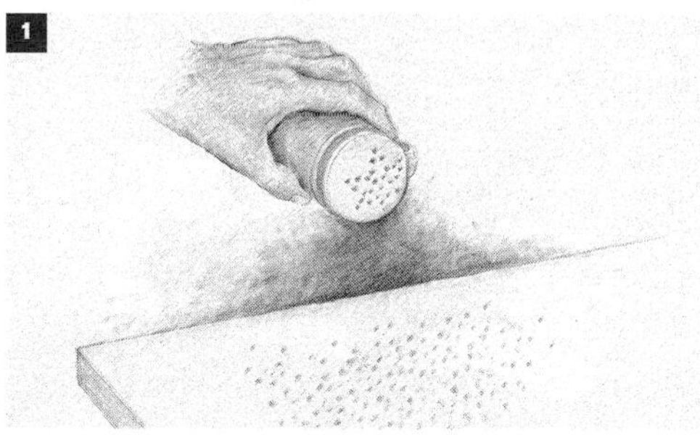

2. Roll out dough from the center to avoid overworking. A straight rolling pin, rather than the tapered pin shown here, is preferable for beginners (straight pins more easily produce doughs of even thickness).

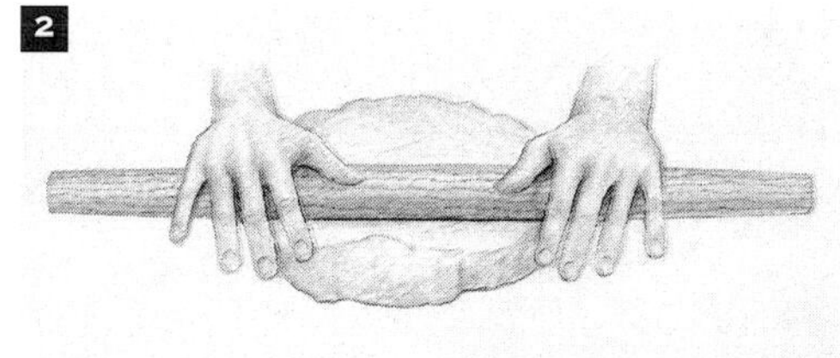

3. Dough can be easily moved on a rolling pin to flour the work surface or to fit dough into a pie plate.

4. To size the dough, place a pie plate upside down on the rolled-out dough and measure an additional one inch around the perimeter of the plate.

TWO BASIC CRUST VARIATIONS

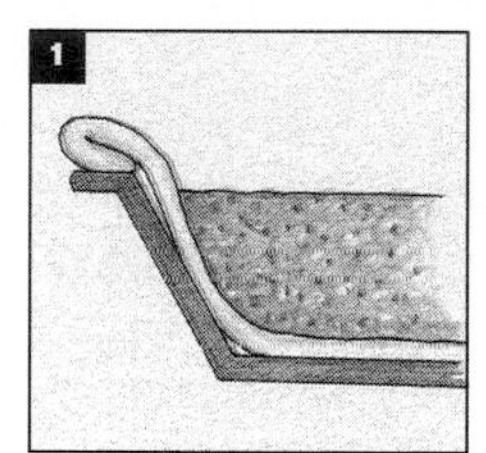

1. For a simple single-crust pie, fold a half-inch of excess dough back under itself.

2. For a double-crust pie, fold the top crust over and under the bottom crust. The bottom crust should be trimmed even with the edge of the pie plate.

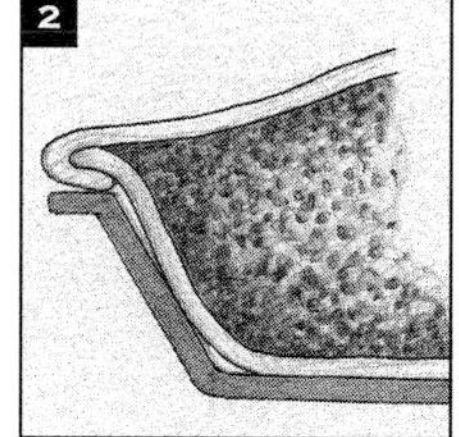

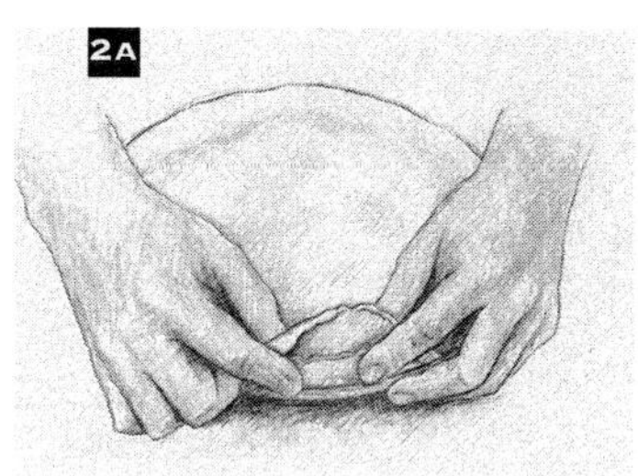

2A. Use both hands to fold the top crust under the bottom crust.

HOW TO MAKE A LATTICE TOP

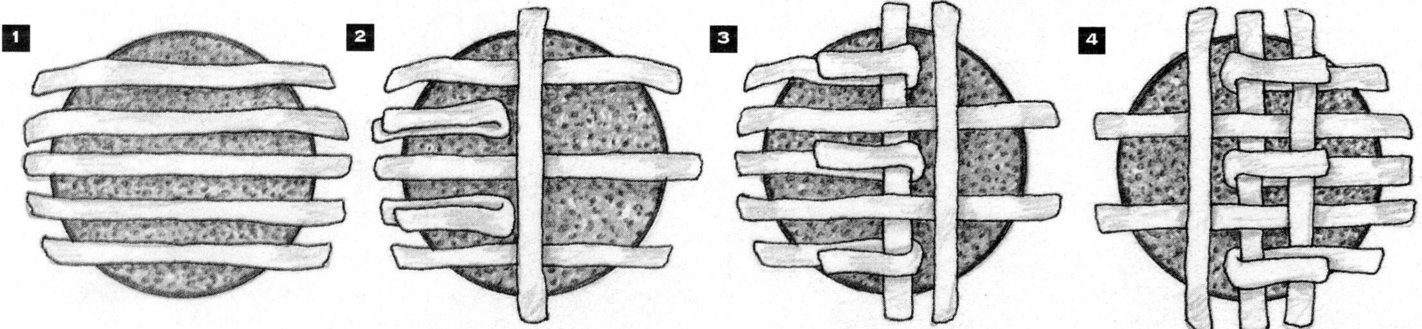

1. Start with five strips of dough.

2. Pull back two strips and add center strip.

3. Pull back other three strips and add right strip.

4. Repeat last step on other side.

Nick Malgieri directs the baking program at Peter Kump's New York Cooking School. He is the author of *Perfect Pastry* (Macmillan, 1989) and *Great Italian Desserts* (Little, Brown, 1990) and is currently at work on a complete baking guide to be published by HarperCollins.

ILLUSTRATIONS BY KATHERINE BRAY

Fitting Dough to Pan

1. You can use a rolling pin to transfer dough to a pie plate or tart pan.

1

2. You can also fold the dough in half, and place it into a plate or tart pan. Now unfold it and fit it as shown below.

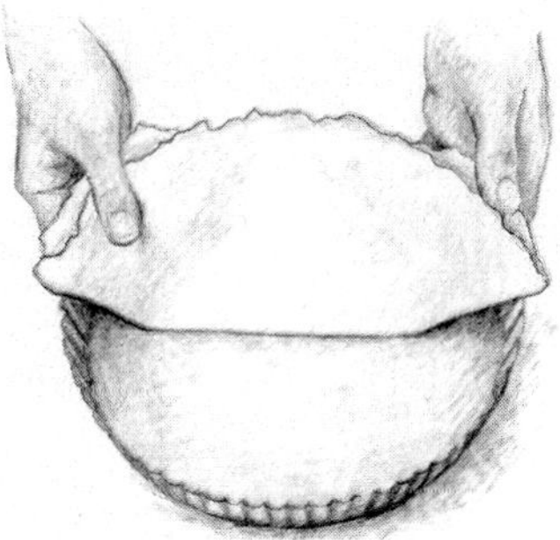

3. To fit dough into a pie plate or tart pan, gently push dough down into edges of pan with one hand while holding outer edge of dough with the other.

4. The back of a small paring knife can be used to trim excess dough for a two-crust pie.

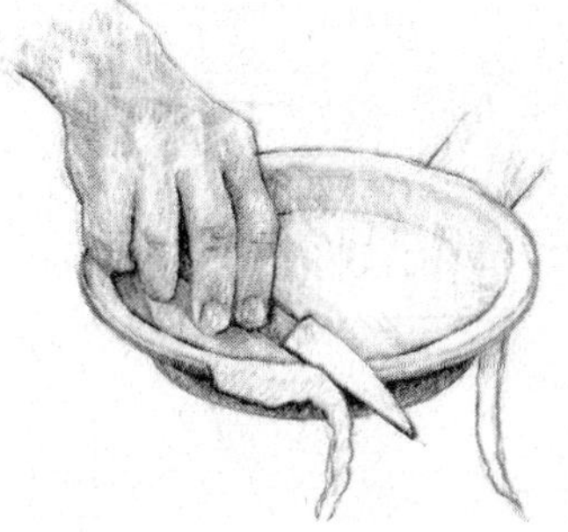

5. Once the dough is carefully fitted into the edges of a tart pan and then pressed down into the sides, trim the excess dough with a rolling pin. This will create a perfectly neat edge.

6. For a thicker, more durable edge, trim a half-inch of dough around the edge of a tart pan using a knife or scissors.

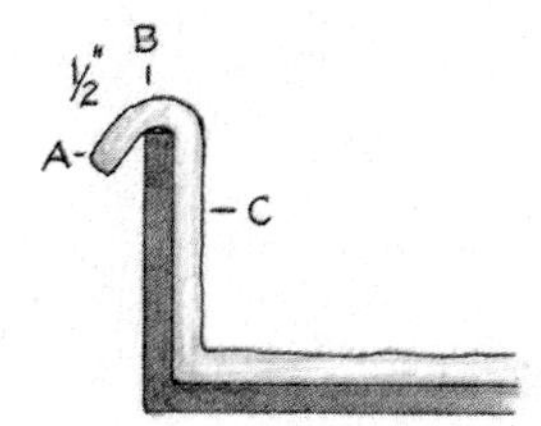

6A. Now fold the extra half-inch of dough back over the edge of the pan.

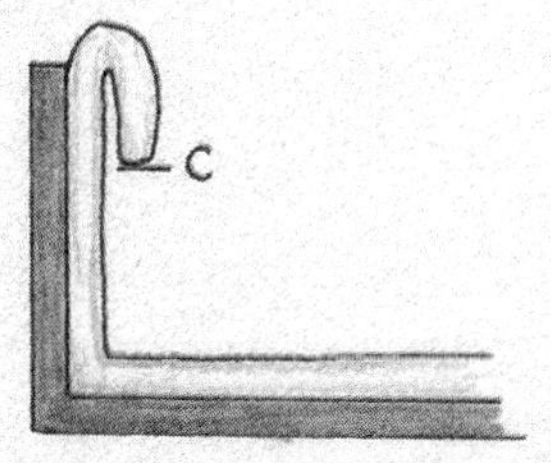

6B. Finally, press the dough against the edge of the pan with your thumb while pressing down with your forefinger. This will create a smooth top edge while creating a thicker side to the tart.

6B

Four Techniques for Edging

1

1. A simple fork-fluted edge.

2

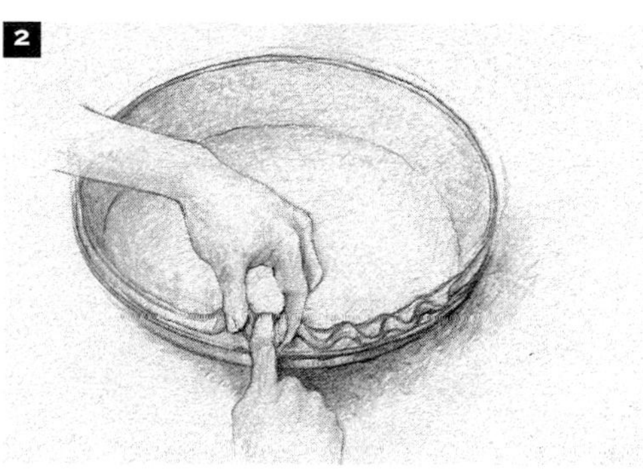

2. For a ruffle edge, hold the dough with thumb and forefinger of one hand while pulling gently with the forefinger of the other hand.

3

3. A rope edge is formed by gently squeezing dough between the thumb and forefinger.

4

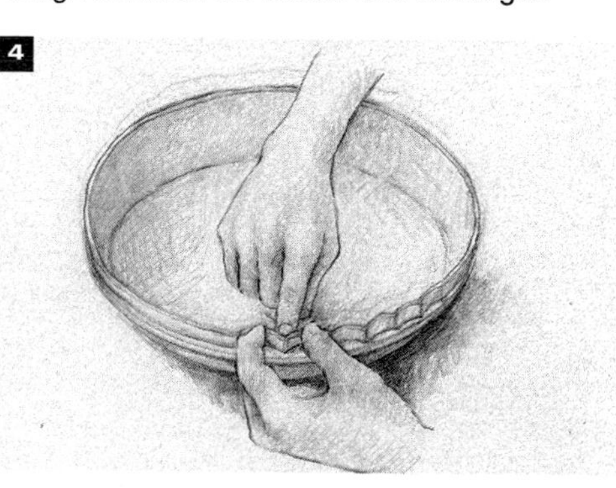

4. For a pinched edge, push the dough with the fingertip while holding it with the thumb and forefinger of the other hand. ■

One Batter, Many Desserts

Simple variations on a basic pancake batter create baked puddings, souffléed skillet pancakes, and popovers.

BY RICHARD SAX

What do puddings, popovers, clafouti, and breakfast pancakes all have in common? They share the same basic recipe for batter, one that can be made thicker or thinner, lighter or richer, to produce a surprising range of desserts, from a custardy prune pudding from France to crepes and skillet pancakes.

The master recipe I've developed resembles a thin pancake batter, with three important differences. First, most batters for griddle cakes include baking powder, whose leavening power is not needed for fruit pancakes and batter puddings, where you want a smoother, less cakelike texture. However, for a lighter texture, you can beat the egg whites separately, then fold them into the batter.

"American pancakes are descendants of European dishes including the fraze, moise, and tansy," notes Richard Sax, shown here in his New York apartment. "The fraze is a French dish dating back to the 1300s which was made from fried apple slices and an egg batter."

Most pancake batters also contain melted butter or oil, which adds flavor and tenderness. To keep the fat content down, I've eliminated butter from the Basic Batter. For richer results, you can add a tablespoon or two of melted butter to any of these batters. To further cut back on fat, use 2 percent milk instead of whole milk.

Finally, I use a combination of cake and all-purpose flour in the batter. Although this is not essential, the lower protein of cake flour translates to less gluten in the dough, and a low-gluten dough is a tender dough.

While it isn't absolutely necessary, pancake batters do benefit from a brief rest — up to an hour — before cooking (*see* sidebar, page 19). Never overmix any pancake batter; the few lumps you leave will dissolve, especially if you allow the batter to sit.

BASIC BATTER
A Master Recipe for Dessert Pancakes and Puddings

Do not make this batter in a blender or food processor. The best results come from gently blending the ingredients by hand and then allowing the batter to sit for 1 hour. Lumps in the batter will disappear by themselves. Substitute ½ cup seltzer for ½ cup of milk in this recipe to make 8 to 12, 9-inch crepes. Add 2 teaspoons baking powder and 2 tablespoons butter to yield 12 to 16 small pancakes.

- ⅔ cup sifted all-purpose flour
- ⅓ cup sifted cake flour (not self-rising)
- ½ cup sugar
- ¼ teaspoon salt
- 1 cup milk
- 2 large eggs, lightly beaten
- 1 teaspoon vanilla extract

1. Mix flours, sugar, and salt in a medium bowl, until free of lumps.
2. Whisk milk, eggs, and vanilla in a smaller bowl until smooth.
3. Make a well in dry ingredients and add liquid mixture. Whisk gently until just blended. A few lumps are fine.

BAKED PEAR PUDDING
Serves 6

This recipe uses a higher proportion of liquid to flour, resulting in a more custardlike texture. You can substitute an equal amount of apples for the pears. Peel and cut as you would the pears, but sauté the apples in 2 tablespoons of butter in a large skillet to evaporate some of the apple moisture.

- ⅓ cup raisins
- 2 tablespoons cognac or whiskey
- 1 tablespoon Amaretto or other liqueur
- ½ recipe Basic Batter
- 1 cup milk
- 2 eggs
- 2 teaspoons vanilla extract
- 4 large pears (about 1 pound), peeled, quartered, cored, and sliced thin
- ½ lemon, juiced
- 1½ tablespoons unsalted butter, cut into small bits
- Confectioner's sugar
- Warm maple syrup, for serving (optional)

1. Soak raisins in cognac and Amaretto for at least 30 minutes.
2. Adjust rack to upper third of oven and heat oven to 375 degrees
3. Prepare ½ recipe Basic Batter; whisk extra milk, eggs, and vanilla into batter.
4. Butter a 9½- to 11-inch baking dish. (You can use a gratin dish measuring 9½ to 11 inches in length, a pie dish, or a ceramic casserole. If using Pyrex, heat oven to 350 degrees.) Toss fruit with lemon juice and raisins (with their soaking liquid), then distribute fruit evenly in prepared dish. Pour batter over fruit. Dot the surface with butter.
5. Bake pudding until batter has just set, about 35 minutes (the timing can vary based on depth of dish — do not overbake). Remove pudding from oven. Adjust oven rack to approximately 3 inches from heat source. Sift and heat confectioner's sugar over the pudding surface and broil, watching carefully to prevent burning, until glazed and golden, usually under 1 minute. Cool pudding on a wire rack. Serve warm. Drizzle with optional warm maple syrup.

SOUFFLÉED BATTER PUDDING
A Variation on Baked Pear Pudding

This is not a true soufflé, but a lighter, puffier pudding. Separate the egg called for in the ½ recipe Basic Batter and do not add it to the other ingredients. Also separate the 2 eggs called for in the Baked Pear Pudding. Add all 3 egg yolks when recipe directs to "whisk in eggs." Beat all 3 whites to fairly stiff peaks and fold into batter just before pouring it over the fruit. Dot with butter and bake as above. This version usually browns as it bakes, and therefore doesn't need to be run under a broiler. Cool briefly, then serve warm.

BANANA BERRY POPOVER
Serves 6

A pie-size, not-too-sweet popover with fruit, this dessert puffs up crisp and golden on the surface, soft and eggy within. By baking the Basic

PHOTOGRAPH BY RICHARD FELBER

Batter in a hot oven, not on a griddle, you wind up with a popover instead of a pancake. Not only a dessert, this popover can stand in for a muffin at brunch or breakfast.

- Pinch grated nutmeg
- 1 recipe Basic Batter
- ½ cup blackberries or raspberries (sprinkle with sugar if tart)
- 1 small banana, halved lengthwise, then sliced into ¼-inch pieces
- 1½ tablespoons light or dark brown sugar
- ¼ teaspoon cinnamon

1. Heat oven to 425 degrees. Generously butter a 9-inch metal pie plate or other shallow baking dish, including the rim; set aside.
2. Gently stir nutmeg into Basic Batter. Leaving a 1-inch border around the edge, distribute fruit evenly in prepared pan. Gently pour batter over fruit. Mix brown sugar and cinnamon. Sprinkle over batter.
3. Bake 20 minutes. Lower heat to 350 degrees. Without opening oven door, continue to bake until popover is puffed and golden, 15 to 20 minutes longer. Cut into wedges and serve immediately.

PRUNE CUSTARD PUDDING

Far Breton — A Dessert from Brittany

Serves 6

Far Breton is a traditional regional dessert from Brittany, on France's Atlantic coast (*far* means "pudding" in Breton). This is a thick custard with marinated prunes, similar to a clafouti, but more custardy due to the addition of milk and eggs to the Basic Batter recipe. Try baking this with prunes from The Prune Tree (12393 Smithfield Road, Dallas, Oregon 97338; telephone 503-623-3779). They are incredibly moist; when baked they emerge almost jamlike.

- 12–16 moist prunes (about 4 ounces), pitted
- 2 tablespoons rum, brandy, or whiskey
- 1 recipe Basic Batter
- ¼ cup sugar
- 1 cup milk
- 1 egg

1. Soak the prunes in rum for at least ½ hour, stirring occasionally.
2. Heat oven to 350 degrees. Generously butter a 9-inch pie pan, or other shallow baking dish, or a gratin dish measuring 9 inches in length. (If baking dish is Pyrex, bake at 325 degrees.) Leaving an opening at the center, arrange prunes in prepared dish. Spoon any soaking liquid over prunes; set aside.
3. Prepare Basic Batter. Gently whisk in extra sugar, milk, and egg. Pour batter over prunes.
4. Bake until pudding surface is spotted with gold and custard has just set, 50 to 60 minutes. Cool on a wire rack to lukewarm or room temperature. Cut into wedges and serve.

REUBEN'S LEGENDARY APPLE PANCAKE

Serves 2

Generations of New Yorkers tucked into Reuben's 12-inch apple pancake as an after-theater snack. Food writer Marian Burros, who first tasted this 30 years ago, sleuthed out its source, after rejecting several impostors. I've streamlined the recipe by cooking the eggy batter in a nonstick skillet, cutting back on butter and sugar, and by inverting the pancake rather than flipping it, daredevil fashion.This is a variation on the Basic Batter recipe but has 2 additional eggs.

- 1 large Granny Smith apple, peeled, quartered, cored, and sliced ¼-inch thick
- 2 tablespoons raisins
- ½ teaspoon cinnamon
- 1½ tablespoons sugar, plus ½ cup sugar
- ½ recipe Basic Batter
- 2 eggs
- 3 tablespoons unsalted butter, or more as needed

1. Mix apples, raisins, cinnamon, and 1½ tablespoons of sugar in a small bowl. Cover and let stand; stir occasionally if time allows.
2. Prepare ½ recipe Basic Batter. Gently whisk in extra eggs. Heat oven to 400 degrees. Heat 1 tablespoon butter in an 8-inch nonstick sauté pan over medium heat until it sizzles. Add apple mixture; cook, stirring occasionally, until apples soften, about 5 minutes.
3. Increase heat to medium high; add another tablespoon of butter to apples. When butter has melted, pour batter evenly into pan, cook batter, pulling the more set sides away from edges, allowing batter to flow under and cook. Shake pan occasionally as you work, to prevent sticking. When pancake begins to firm up, about 3 minutes, sprinkle about 2 tablespoons sugar evenly over top.
4. Invert pancake decisively onto a plate. Heat another tablespoon of butter in empty pan, sprinkle with 1½ tablespoons sugar, and slide pancake back in. Cook the other side, lowering heat slightly if it sizzles too insistently, and allowing sugar to caramelize on the bottom. When it begins to brown, about 3 minutes, sprinkle top with another 1½ tablespoons of sugar. If pancake seems to stick, slip a little more butter underneath it. Invert pancake again (without adding more butter and sugar this time), and allow sugar to caramelize on the bottom, about 4 minutes.
5. Sprinkle another 2 tablespoons sugar on top. (Add more butter to pan if needed.) Invert pancake once again and continue to caramelize, shaking pan occasionally, about 4 minutes longer. Sprinkle top lightly with remaining 1 tablespoon sugar and place in oven for 10 to 15 minutes, or until surface is golden brown. Halve pancake in the pan, transfer each half to a plate and serve immediately. ■

Richard Sax, a regular contributor to several food publications, has recently completed a new book on old-fashioned desserts from around the world.

SHOULD PANCAKE BATTER REST?

Food science writer Shirley Corriher explains: "Different flours vary in their content of glutenin and gliadin, the proteins that form gluten." When you knead bread dough, you are developing the strands of gluten in the flour. This is the "muscle" in the dough, the structure that traps the bubbles of gas produced by the yeast. The less protein, the less gluten. "Protein can range from 14 grams per cup in Pillsbury bread flour, to 11 to 13 grams in most national brands of all-purpose flour, down to only 8 or 9 grams in White Lily all-purpose flour from Tennessee," says Corriher. "For tender pancakes, you should be using a low-protein flour."

The mix of flours I use in the basic batter recipe is a good compromise. If you mix gently to develop as little gluten as possible, and then allow the batter to rest for an hour or so — both to complete the blending of ingredients and allow any gluten that has developed to relax — you will produce tender pancakes. Resting the batter makes no discernible difference in the baked puddings, however. *—R.S.*

THREE STEPS TO REUBEN'S APPLE PANCAKE

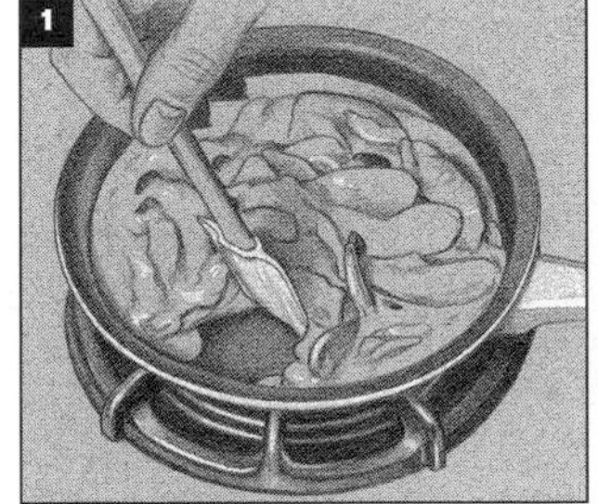

1. Pull sides of pancake away from edges, allowing batter to flow underneath pancake and cook.

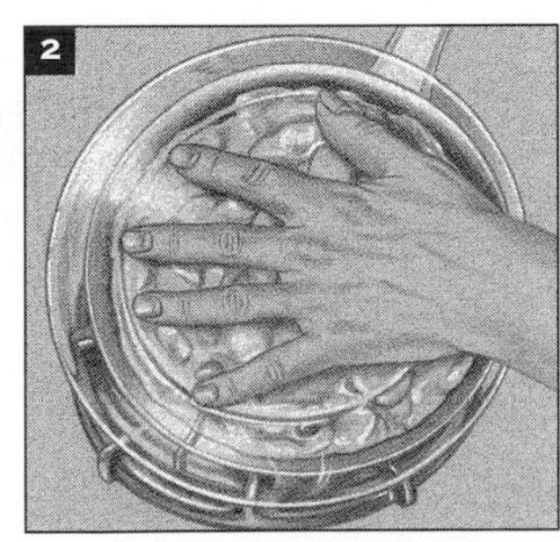

2. Place plate over top of pancake and invert pan decisively to flip.

3. Slide pancake back into pan.

ILLUSTRATIONS BY ALAN WITSCHONKE

Choosing the Right Electric Deep-Fryer

Watch out for escaping steam, scorching lids, and large drops in temperature when food is added.

BY JACK BISHOP

The most important consideration when deep-frying is safety. With bubbling hot oil often reaching 400 degrees, grease fires are a very real concern. Electric deep-fryers greatly reduce that risk by separating hot oil from pilot lights and burners. In addition, covered models protect the hands and face from splattering oil. Covered fryers also use charcoal filters to screen out some of the obnoxious odors that otherwise linger in your house for days.

We tested four different fryers. The winner — the DeLonghi Roto Fryer — was also the most expensive. It costs about $150 (when discounted, as is often the case) but is worth every penny. The frying basket rotates within the covered chamber, thus reducing the amount of oil required by half; four cups is enough to fry a full batch of potatoes or chicken. The rotating action also promotes even cooking. The DeLonghi preheats faster than other machines (about five minutes to reach 320 degrees) and it produced crisp fries and perfect fried chicken in tests. The seamless interior was a breeze to clean.

Although not our first choice, the Tefal Super Deep Fryer is also an excellent machine. Test results with fries and chicken were perfect. Unfortunately, several design flaws make this machine somewhat difficult to use. To open the lid after frying it is necessary to put one's hand in the path of escaping steam. We were forced to wear a clumsy oven mitt to open the lid. (The DeLonghi fryer has a button on the side of the lid, so that one's hand is not scorched by escaping steam.) The Tefal lid also became dangerously hot. While the front and back locks remained warm to the touch, the rest of the lid (which looks deceptively like the locks) was scorching.

The Tefal has a small viewing window. However, the panel is useless during cooking since steam immediately hides the chamber from view. The manufacturers of the DeLonghi fryer solved this problem by installing a simple but effective wiping mechanism to keep the surface free of steam. One final flaw in the Tefal design is in the heating element, which protrudes into the cooking chamber; pieces of food can become trapped here and are difficult to extract when cleaning up. Despite these problems, the overall design of the machine is excellent and results are equal to that achieved in the DeLonghi. Often discounted at $80 to $90, the Tefal is an excellent choice if cost is an important concern.

The two remaining fryers we tested are both open kettles with plugs that fit into wall sockets and the machines. The Presto FryDaddy is a bargain at $25. However, its smallish chamber holds just four cups of oil and consequently can fry only small quantities of food. Although the manual says four cups of food can be fried at one time, three cups is a more realistic limit. When cold food is added to hot oil, splattering is expected. What we did not anticipate was the quickly rising oil level, which came perilously close to the top on one occasion. If you use this machine improperly, the possibility of hot oil boiling over onto the counter is quite real.

Unlike all the other machines, the FryDaddy does not have a basket to hold foods while they fry. A slotted scoop is provided, but without a basket twice-cooking foods (such as french fries) is difficult at best. In addition, the cook must

Which Oils Are Best For Your Health?

Oils low in saturated fat but high in monounsaturated fat are desirable.

Content	Saturated Fat	Monounsaturated Fat
Canola	6%	62%
Grapeseed	7%	79%
Safflower	9%	12%
Sunflower	11%	20%
Peanut	13%	49%
Corn	13%	25%
Olive	14%	77%
Soybean	15%	24%
Vegetable shortening	26%	43%
Butter	54%	30%

How They Tested and What They Cost

Fryers Listed in Order of Preference

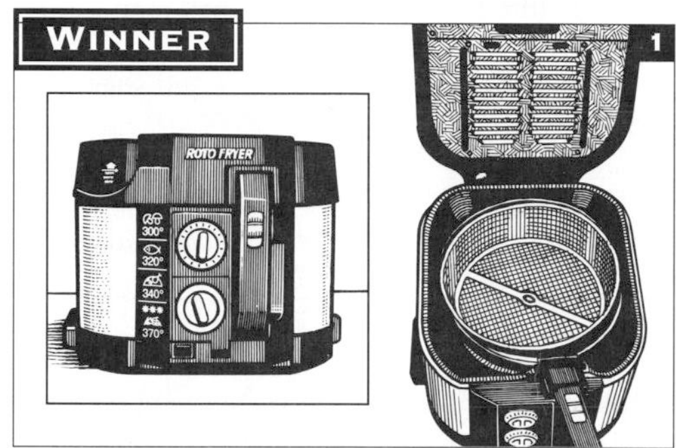

1. DeLonghi Roto-Fryer, *Model D 10:* $130–$160

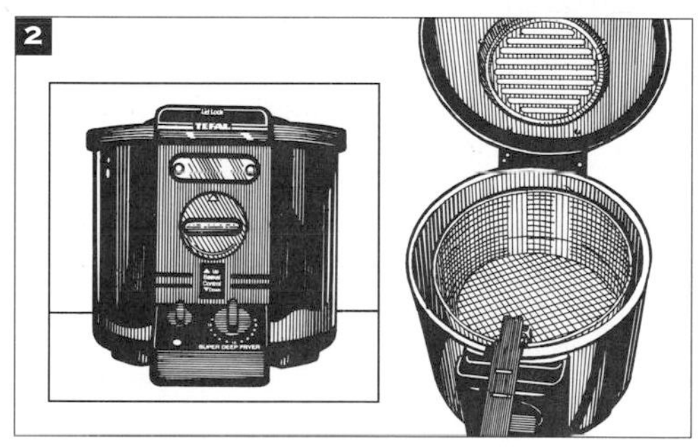

2. Tefal Super Deep Fryer, *Model 8215 M:* $80–$100

3. Dazey Chef's Pot, *Model DCP-6* $30–$40

4. Presto FryDaddy, *Model 21-146:* $25–$35

ILLUSTRATIONS BY DAN KROVATIN

Electric Deep-Fryers: Performance and Features

	DeLonghi	Tefal
Wattage	1500	1600
Thermostat	Yes	Yes
Temperature settings	300–370 degrees	338 or 374 degrees
Fry basket	Yes	Yes
Covered	Yes	Yes
View panel	Yes, with wiper	Yes, no wiper
Preheat time[1]	6 minutes	8 minutes
Oil capacity	4 cups	8–10 cups
Food capacity[2]	1 pound	1 pound
Drop in temperature[3]	35 degrees	20 degrees
Time to recover[3]	4 minutes	3 minutes
Ease of cleaning	Excellent	Fair

	Chef's Pot	FryDaddy
Wattage	1400	1200
Thermostat	Yes	No
Temperature settings	0–400	None
Fry basket	Yes	No
Covered	No	No
View panel	No	No
Preheat time[1]	11 minutes	8 minutes
Oil capacity	7½ cups	4 cups
Food capacity[2]	¾ pound	½ pound
Drop in temperature[3]	50 degrees	60 degrees
Time to recover[3]	6 minutes	7 minutes
Ease of cleaning	Excellent	Excellent

1. Time it took oil to reach 335 degrees.
2. Amount of potatoes that can be easily fried at one time.
3. Drop in temperature when one-half pound of potatoes was added to oil at 335 degrees, and time it took to regain original frying temperature.

supply a thermometer since the FryDaddy doesn't have one built in. On the plus side, the FryDaddy is lined with a nonstick surface that makes cleaning easy.

If you want an electric fryer but are not prepared to spend over $50, the Chef's Pot by Dazey is your best bet. Priced around $35, the Chef's Pot is a combination steamer, roaster, slow-cooker, and fryer. The open chamber comes with a useful frying basket that rests in what the company calls the "Drip-Grip." Despite the corny name, this little gadget really works. While the basket rests on the handle of the Drip-Grip, grease falls back into the cooking chamber. This feature is great when twice-frying potatoes or waiting for foods to cool before eating. Heatproof handles (something the FryDaddy lacks) are another welcome feature. On the downside, the Chef's Pot takes almost twice as long as the DeLonghi to preheat and the heat regulator attached to the plug was inaccurate in our testing, often by 25 or 30 degrees.

One final note about the Chef's Pot and the FryDaddy. Both machines yielded fries that were greasier than those cooked in the covered fryers. Without a lid, oil temperatures dropped 50 to 60 degrees when food was added and took at least six minutes to recover in both fryers.

Choosing an Oil

While most Americans would never fry in olive oil, Europeans have been doing so for centuries. The reasons we shy away from olive and peanut oils for frying are simple — we think smoking points for these oils are too low and that they will impart an odd flavor to foods. The question of smoking points is moot when working with electric deep-fryers. The DeLonghi and Tefal machines don't exceed 375 degrees, while the two other fryers have 400 degrees as their maximum setting. Oils that are properly processed won't break down until the temperature reaches 440 degrees. Even when the FryDaddy and Chef's Pot were left heating for 30 minutes, the oil never reached the danger limit.

The concern about oil flavoring the fried foods is correct. Any strong oil, a good peanut oil for example, will flavor fried foods. While this may not be desirable when frying jelly doughnuts, strongly flavored oils can give squid, potatoes, and even chicken a delicious boost. In general, reserve olive oil for bland foods, like potatoes, where the flavor of the oil can really come through. For most savory items (everything from chicken to seafood), use peanut oil when cost is not a factor. For sweets, like doughnuts and fritters, choose neutral-tasting canola or corn oil. If you fry often and would like to use a cheaper oil, corn and canola oils are also fine for savory items. Generally speaking, saturated fats are dangerous to your health while monounsaturated fats may actually provide some health benefits (*see* sidebars, pages 15 and 20).

The Chemistry of Frying

When oil is heated to frying temperature several chemical reactions take place that can degrade or break down its structure. As boiling oil comes into contact with oxygen in the air, decomposition of the fat begins. The process, known as oxidation, can be slowed by using a tall, narrow pan that minimizes the amount of oil in direct contact with the air. Of course, covered fryers also reduce oxidation.

In addition to oxidation, particles of food that remain in the oil can cause it to degrade. To minimize this effect, strain cooled oil through a coffee filter before reusing. As long as tiny food particles are removed, the same oil can be used for about five fryings. However, oil that has been used to fry strongly flavored foods, such as fish, will impart off-flavors to subsequently fried foods.

If at any point during frying the oil begins to smoke, turn off the heat source immediately. Since smoking is a sign of degradation, discard oil once it has cooled. The smoking point, which varies from one oil to the next, is the temperature at which a fat breaks down into visible gaseous elements. Cheaper oils that are not properly processed may fall below these average values, as will oils that have been used several times.

Smoking Points	
Safflower	510 degrees
Soybean	495 degrees
Corn	475 degrees
Olive	450 degrees
Canola	450 degrees
Peanut	440 degrees
Sunflower	440 degrees

SPICY BUTTERMILK FRIED CHICKEN

Serves 4

Stan Frankenthaler, chef at the Blue Room in Cambridge, Massachusetts, prepares this extra-spicy, extra-crisp fried chicken. You can substitute boneless thighs if you like. In either case, serve with a green salad and baked sweet potatoes or sweet-potato fries. The restaurant bottles its own thunderous hot sauce called Inner Beauty, which is sold by Mo Hotta Mo Betta, a mail-order business specializing in spicy foods. (For a catalog, call 800-462-3220.)

- 1 cup buttermilk
- 1 tablespoon Inner Beauty, tabasco, or other hot sauce
- 2 pounds boneless, skinless chicken breasts, tendons and excess fat removed, chicken cut into 2-inch wide strips
- 1 quart oil for frying
- 1 cup flour
- Salt and ground black pepper
- 2 tablespoons fresh herbs such as parsley, oregano, and/or thyme

1. Mix buttermilk and hot sauce in large bowl; add chicken and refrigerate overnight.

2. Heat oil to 360 degrees in a fryer or large kettle. Mix flour, 2 teaspoons salt, 2 teaspoons pepper, and herbs in a shallow bowl. Take chicken pieces from marinade and dredge in seasoned flour. Fry chicken, in batches if necessary, until golden, about 4 minutes. Keep chicken warm in 200-degree oven until serving. ■

Jack Bishop, former Associate Editor of *Cook's* magazine, is a freelance writer living in Fairfield, Connecticut.

How To Make Bread

This simple master recipe eliminates hands-on kneading and can be shaped into everything from French baguettes to round dinner rolls.

BY PAM ANDERSON

Flour, water, yeast, and salt; ingredients so basic that even the most casual cook could make a loaf of bread without running to the grocery store. But breadmaking is still like many of life's disciplines, such as exercising or reading the daily newspaper: either it's important — you make time for it and perform the task faithfully — or it's not.

I was determined to bake bread at least once a week, and to find my own way of doing it — the best flour, the best yeast, whether to oil the bowl, how to get a crisp crust, whether to let the dough rise twice. Cookbooks are filled with hundreds of master recipes and variations. This was to be a search for the mother recipe, the one that can be kneaded into any shape with the least amount of fuss or variation.

TESTING FOR DONENESS WITH A THERMOMETER

I've never understood how even a seasoned farmer could identify a juicy, ripe watermelon with just a thump. And for the same reason I'd rather test a bread's doneness with a meat thermometer than with a thump on its bottom. Bread is ready for the cooling rack when a meat thermometer plunged into the center of the loaf registers between 190 degrees and 200 degrees.

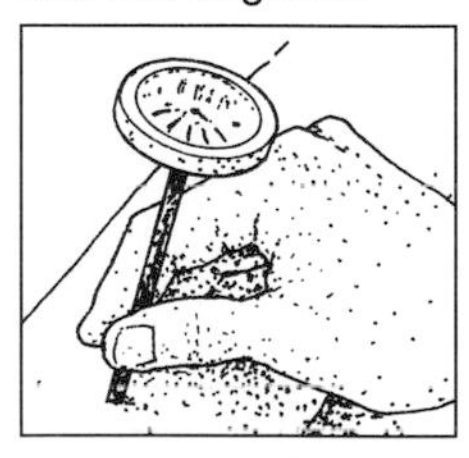

Fast-Acting, Cake, and Dry Yeasts

I set out to make three loaves of bread: one with cake yeast, one with active dry yeast, and another with 50-percent-faster active dry yeast. Because of its yeastier smell and old-fashioned appeal, cake yeast initially had the edge. The rapid-rise seemed like a cheap shortcut — and from all I had read, the slower the dough rises, the better its flavor.

The cake yeast required fork-mashing to dissolve — a minor inconvenience compared to the two snip-and-pour packets of active dry yeasts. The rapid-rise dough won the rising race, coming in at just under two hours. Not far behind, surprisingly, were the other two, completing their rises in about two hours and forty-five minutes. However, I was surprised to find that the doughs all looked the same, baked and tasted the same, and had the same texture.

The master bread recipe developed for this article is prepared in a food processor, eliminating kneading. The resulting dough can make five different types of loaves as well as breadsticks (when run through the fettucine attachment of a manual pasta machine).

Choosing the Best Flour

Depending on its protein content, wheat flour can be hard (high protein), soft (low protein), or an all-purpose combination. When kneaded, hard flour develops a higher percentage of gluten, which strengthens the structure of the dough and gives it a better "chew." I tested the three readily available wheat flours: bread flour, made with hard wheat; all-purpose bleached, a chemically bleached mix of hard and soft wheat flours; and all-purpose unbleached, a mix of the two flours, but bleached by natural aging (a process that apparently affects the bonding characteristics of the gluten so that it forms a stronger, more elastic dough).

The bread flour eked by as the winner in both the dough and bread categories. It kneaded into a firm, elastic ball, rose and proofed into a perky, taut dough round, and baked into a firm, shapely loaf of bread. Compared to the others, the bread-

PHOTOGRAPH BY ERIC ROTH

flour loaf displayed better body and offered a less gummy texture, although the variances in texture were small.

But since making and eating bread were both to become frequent exercises for me, the flour's price and nutritional content were factors as well. Although its price was right (19 cents to 25.8 cents per pound), all-purpose bleached flour has been stripped of much of its vitamin E during the bleaching process. Moderately priced, all-purpose unbleached flour (31.8 cents to 39 cents per pound) turned out to be the best buy; bread flour, available only in two-pound boxes from a boutique-style mill, averaged a whopping 94.5 cents per pound. Many of the major flour companies, however, do package five-pound bags of bread flour, carried at least seasonally by many grocery store chains.

Do You Really Need to Knead?

The biggest surprise for me was that dough kneaded by machine (either food processor or mixer) was no worse than the dough kneaded by hand. The choice is personal. I settled into the food-processor method because it's the fastest; I can satisfy my need to knead by playing with the dough for a few minutes after it comes out of the food processor. Many who favor the food-processor method prefer the plastic blade to the steel. The steel blade, they caution, can overknead and overheat the dough. I obediently followed their instructions and started with the plastic blade, but quickly discovered that my machine overheated, not my dough. (For the record, I have a heavy-duty food processor and this was only a three and one-half cup flour recipe.) I switched to the steel blade, and used Julia Child's technique of proofing the yeast in a bit of warm water, then adding cold water to the bowl to compensate for the heat of the blade. With only 35 seconds of steel-blade kneading, I turned out a batch of dough that was beautifully warm and smooth.

More Kitchen Lore Put to the Test

Two mainstays of breadmaking kitchen lore are the damp towel and the greased bowl. I discovered the following: A damp towel used to cover the bowl in which the dough rises will absorb accumulated moisture from the rising bread. Plastic wrap traps it; beads of water hang on plastic wrap like bats on a cavern ceiling. This condensation will cause plastic wrap to stick to risen ungreased dough. Although I had hoped that greasing the bowl would be unnecessary (I dislike oily dough), I found that dough risen in an ungreased bowl will stick slightly. But I also determined that only a breath of oil is necessary to coat the bowl and the top of the dough. Treat the oil like expensive hand cream: apply sparingly.

Shaping and Proofing Shortcuts

The classic shaping technique for French bread ensures bread that will not lose its characteristic shape when the dough rises and bakes. But is it worth the scores of stretches, pulls, pinches, troughs, and tucks for one supremely cylindrical loaf? I describe a compromise technique on the following pages. If loaves were legs, my results might not win a beauty contest, but they'd look good in stretch pants.

The way the dough is finally risen or proofed also contributes to the French loaf's shape. The most uniformly shaped doughs are those proofed on trough-formed, floured kitchen towels, or in French bread pans. The kitchen-towel technique requires that after proofing the bread be rolled from the towel over onto a cornmeal-coated peel or cookie sheet. This also added extra time and steps so I tried proofing directly on the peel or cookie sheet. I got a respectable-looking loaf of dough, and I was virtually done with the process once the loaves were shaped.

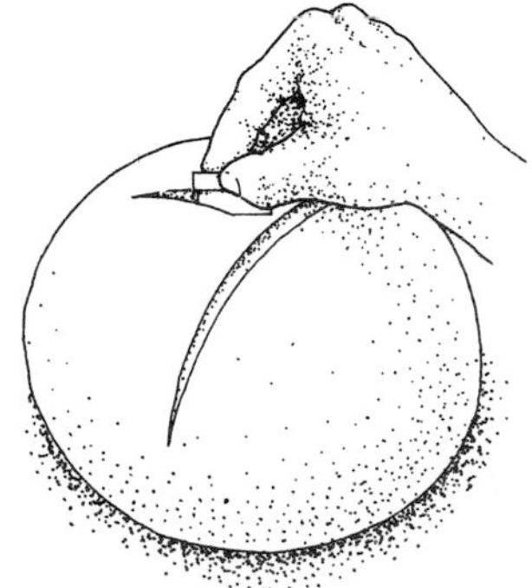

When the loaves have risen, use a single-edged razor blade in firm, decisive strokes to cut slashes one-half-inch deep in the tops of the loaves.

When and How Do You Slash Bread Dough?

Some bakers advocate slashing the dough before proofing; others perform the task right before baking. If you slash before proofing, the marks rise flush with the rest of the dough, and they often become almost invisible unless the dough has been sprinkled beforehand with sesame or poppy seeds. I prefer slashing just before baking. However, slashing is not easy, regardless of when you do it. Successful slashing begins with a razor-sharp blade used with courage (I use an X-Acto knife); for certain dough cuts I found scissors to be successful gougers. If you hesitate as you slash, the dough will stick to your blade like bubble gum to a shoe. Call on your killer instincts — jab and slash, jab and slash, quickly and effortlessly.

How to Bake Cracker-Crisp Crusts

If I hadn't already spent my $15 on quarry tiles, the sine qua non for most bakers, I'm not so sure I would now. After baking bread on three different surfaces (quarry tiles, heavy-duty baking sheets, and French bread pans) I found that preheated baking sheets rivaled quarry tiles, without the investment or the hassle. The breads

Microwave Bread Is Fast but Is it Any Good?

In *Bread in Half the Time,* (Crown Publishers, New York, NY, 1991), authors Linda Eckhardt and Diana Butts suggest another use for the microwave. Set at the right power level, and with the help of a food processor and a heated oven, their "micro-rise" technique promises bread on the table in as little as 60 minutes.

For novices, the authors suggest one of their basic recipes, No Pain Ordinaire. The recipe calls for three cups bread flour, one and one-half tablespoons sugar, one teaspoon salt, four teaspoons 50-percent-faster active dry yeast, one and one-half tablespoons unsalted butter or margarine, and one and one-eighth cup water at 120 degrees. All dry ingredients are mixed in the bowl of a food processor fitted with a steel blade. With the motor running, the hot water is added. Once the dough has formed a ball, kneading takes 60 seconds. This recipe was already making me nervous — using almost two packages of rapid-rise yeast for one loaf of bread; calling for exceptionally hot water; then kneading this hot, super-charged dough with a steel processor blade. Most bakers seem to agree that the steel blade is acceptable for kneading, but caution that while in its clutches the dough can very quickly overheat and overknead. No such warnings in this recipe. I'm starting to hum "Livin' on the Edge."

The next step instructs the baker to remove the dough and steel blade from the food processor, knead the dough a few seconds, form it into a doughnut shape, return it to the food processor bowl, and cover with plastic wrap or a damp towel. After following these directions, I found the dough to be grainy with bits of undissolved yeast. It lacked the smooth, elastic texture and satiny sheen of a well-kneaded dough.

Now the dough is proofed in a microwave oven using the 3-3-6 method. You place the dough (in the proofing bowl) and an eight-ounce glass of water in the oven, turn on the power for 3 minutes, let it rest for 3, turn it on again for 3, and then let it rest for 6. You repeat this sequence before baking in a regular oven.

According to the author's calculations, my 700-watt oven's power setting should be between 10 percent and 35 percent. I started out at the 30 percent setting and then also tried proofing dough at 20 percent. In both cases, the yeast was killed and the dough had to be tossed out. I did manage to get a loaf into the oven using the 10 percent power setting but the cooked bread had a pronounced yeast flavor which left a nasty aftertaste. One sampler aptly commented, "This bread is drunk with yeast." Even though this technique is geared to the busy cook, I find that it produces inferior quality bread, not worth the savings in preparation time.

ILLUSTRATION BY KATHY BRAY

How to Substitute Specialty Flours

Bake bread that looks and tastes completely different from the featured loaf — substitute a specialty flour for a portion of the bread or all-purpose flour. Follow the master recipe ingredient list and instructions and substitute the following proportions of flour:

Whole wheat or rye flour	1¾ cups
All-purpose or bread flour	1¾ cups
Oat flour	¾ cup
All-purpose or bread flour	2¾ cups
Soy, millet, corn, rice, buckwheat, or barley	½ cup
All-purpose or bread flour	3 cups

baked on heavy-duty, hot cookie sheets and quarry tiles all sported thick, cornmeal-textured bottoms worthy of display in a great bakery. The breads baked in the French bread pans sported a gleaming top crust but offered the least impressive bottom crust: barely browned and not very crisp. The curved shape of the pans traps moisture, retarding the browning process. The bottom crusts of breads baked on cold cookie sheets were thin and homemade-looking, but after they cooled I was relatively impressed with their bottom crusts as well: they remained crisp. The other breads' bottom crusts had, upon cooling, become somewhat tough and leathery. However, no bread's crust remains crisp for very long. They all need the oven's warmth to re-crisp.

Quarry tiles seem to give a heated oven a life independent of the thermostat control. It will run hotter and stay hotter than its tileless counterpart. After a few burned loaves I started to rely on an oven thermometer.

Good bakers know that steam tames the oven's scorching heat, allowing the dough to swell a bit longer before its yeast is killed. Moist heat also sets the starch on the dough's surface, giving the dough a satiny sheen which is later transformed into a glazy, crisp crust. Bakers have a variety of tricks to add steam to an oven and I tried them all: ice cubes on the floor of the oven, pans of water placed in a preheating oven, cupfuls of water sprayed into the hot oven.

All of these techniques worked equally well, but the easiest is tossing three-quarters of a cup of water onto the floor of an electric oven (or into a skillet or pan placed on the floor of a gas oven) just after the dough starts baking. Follow up with two or three spritzes of water (use a spray bottle) in the first 10 minutes of baking. Be careful, however. I got spray-happy with the atomizer on my first try and blew out the oven lightbulb.

MASTER RECIPE FOR BASIC BREAD

Yields 2, 12-oz rounds or loaves, or 12 rolls

Bread recipes don't get more basic than this. The 3½-cup flour recipe makes dough that is easily kneaded in a food processor with a 2-quart workbowl. To make a larger quantity, make consecutive batches rather than doubling or tripling the recipe.

- 1 package dry-active yeast
- ⅓ cup warm water (110 degrees)
- 3½ cups bread or all-purpose unbleached flour
- 2 teaspoons salt
- 1 cup water, room temperature
- Cornmeal for pizza paddle surface

1. Sprinkle yeast over warm water; let stand until yeast dissolves and starts to swell, about 5 minutes. Meanwhile, mix flour and salt in the workbowl of a food processor fitted with a steel blade. Add cold water to yeast mixture, and with machine running gradually pour this liquid through feeder tube into dry ingredients; process until a rough ball forms. If dough is too wet to form a ball, add flour, 1 tablespoon at a time, and continue to process until a rough but solid dough ball is formed. Let dough rest for 5 minutes; then continue to process until dough is smooth and elastic, about 35 seconds.

2. Turn dough onto lightly floured work surface; knead by hand for a few seconds to insure that dough is satiny smooth. Form dough into a round and place in a very lightly oiled bowl. Rub dough top around bowl to lightly coat with oil. Turn dough right side up in bowl. Cover with a damp cloth and place in 70-degree draft-free environment until dough doubles in size, 2 to 3 hours.

3. Punch dough down and turn onto work surface. Follow specific instructions to shape bread (*see* below). Cover dough shapes with a lightly floured dish towel and, again, place in a 70-degree draft-free environment until they have almost doubled in size. Follow slashing instructions under specific shape.

4. Place heavy-duty, lipless cookie sheets, or arrange quarry tiles, in oven and heat to 450 degrees. (If oven is gas, place a heavy-duty, oven-safe skillet or roasting pan on oven floor.) Slide risen and slashed dough shapes from peel onto chosen surface. Carefully toss ¾ cup water onto oven floor or into pan, and close oven door. Spritz dough 2 or 3 times during the first half of baking. Bake until crust is brown and interior registers 190 to 200 degrees, about 30 minutes for loaves and about 15 minutes for rolls. Cool breads on a wire rack. (Or wrap in plastic and store at room temperature for 2 days; reheat in 350-degree oven 10 to 15 minutes. Bread can also be wrapped in plastic and frozen; reheat in 300-degree oven 20 to 30 minutes.)

Instructions for Shaping Dough

Round loaves — Halve the dough; set aside one half. Holding the dough in one hand, use the other hand to bring excess dough together at the top. Pinch this unincorporated dough together, then turn ball over, smooth side up. Place dough round on work surface and rotate with both palms. Repeat this pinching and rotating process until the dough forms into a smooth, tight round. Place dough, smooth side up, on cornmeal-coated pizza paddle. Repeat with remaining half of dough. For one large loaf, follow the same procedure, without halving the dough. Slash risen dough rounds in a tic-tac-toe or cross pattern.

Long cylindrical loaves — Halve the dough; set aside one half. Press and stretch dough into a 14-by-6-inch rectangle. With the long edge of the dough facing you, fold the dough lengthwise into thirds. Pinch to seal seam. With the side of your hand, punch a trough lengthwise down the center of the dough. Bring sides of dough in towards the trough and pinch to seal. Pinch and tuck under the dough at each end of the cylinder. Place dough seam side down on cornmeal-coated pizza paddle. Repeat process with remaining half of dough. Make three to four long, diagonal slashes, about one-half-inch deep along the top of each risen dough loaf. Or, to make ear-of-wheat shapes, skip the slashing step and use scissors to make deep V-cuts every three inches down the length of risen dough. Carefully

Making Breadsticks with a Pasta Machine

If you're tired of paying two dollars for an eight-ounce box of those long, slender imported bread sticks, siphon off a portion of bread dough and make your own. With the help of a manual pasta machine you can make about 6-dozen breadsticks with a half-batch of dough from this recipe.

Divide dough into three equal pieces. Working with one piece at a time, press dough into a 6"x4"x¼" rectangle on a well-floured work surface. Make sure that dough is coated with flour or dough will stick together as it comes out of the pasta machine. Use a pasta machine fitted with the fettucine attachment to cut dough into strips. Separate dough strips and place them one-half-inch apart on a heavy-duty, cornmeal-coated cookie sheet. Bake in a 350-degree oven until crisp and golden brown, about 20 minutes. (Will keep in an airtight container for up to one month.)

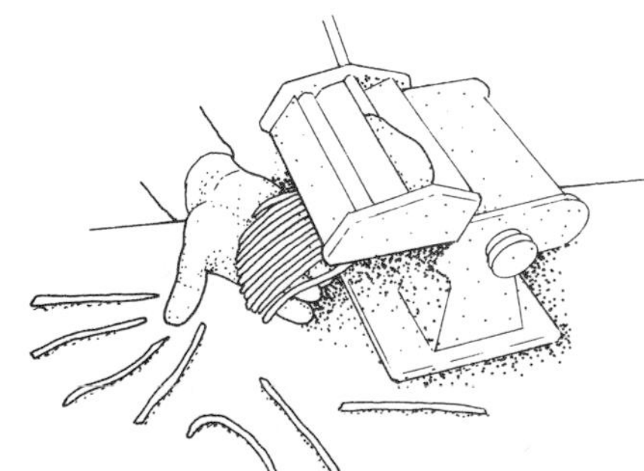

The fastest, easiest way to make breadsticks at home: Run our basic dough through a manual pasta machine, using the fettucine attachment.

lift the first cut section of dough and point the dough to the left; lift the next section to the right. Repeat, alternating left and right to resemble an ear of wheat.

Short cylindrical loaves — Divide dough in half; set aside one half of the dough. Press and stretch dough into a 14-by-6-inch rectangle. With long edge of the dough facing you, fold the dough crosswise so that short ends meet in the middle. Press dough to incorporate folds into dough, making the side farthest from you slightly thicker. Starting with the thicker side, roll the dough towards you to form a tight cylinder. Pinch at seam to seal. Gently roll cylinder on work surface with palms to yield a smooth, even loaf. Place loaf, seam side down, on a cornmeal-coated pizza paddle. Repeat process with remaining half of dough. Starting at one end of the risen dough, make a zig-zag pattern using the scissor technique. (For scissor technique, plunge open scissors into dough, then close them shut.) Repeat these diagonal cuts at about two-inch intervals.

Round rolls — Divide the dough into 12 pieces. Working with one at a time, press on dough to release air bubbles. Form dough into a rough round and place on work surface. With cupped palm, roll dough until it is smooth and perfectly round. Place on cornmeal-coated pizza paddle. Repeat with remaining balls of dough. Cut a cross on each risen roll, using the scissor technique.

Oval-shaped rolls — Follow the above steps to form 12 round, smooth balls. With fingertips, roll dough round back and forth on work surface to form oval shapes. Place on a cornmeal-coated pizza paddle. Make a shallow slash lengthwise down the center of each risen roll. ■

Pam Anderson was Culinary Director of *Cook's* magazine and then served as Food Editor of *Restaurant Business Magazine* until 1991. She now works as a freelance cookbook editor and food writer out of her home in Solebury, Pennsylvania.

Shaping the Dough

1

For the round loaf:
1. Holding dough in one hand, bring excess dough together at the top. Pinch unincorporated dough together.

2

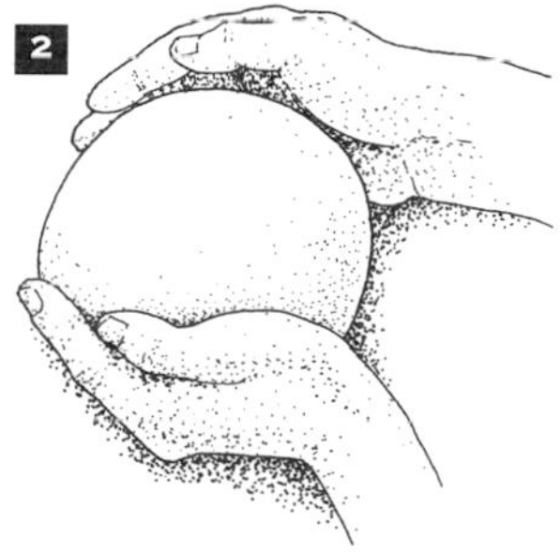

2. Place dough on work surface, rough side down. Pat and rotate the ball with both palms. Alternate pleating with patting the ball until it forms a smooth, round loaf.

For the rectangular loaf:

1

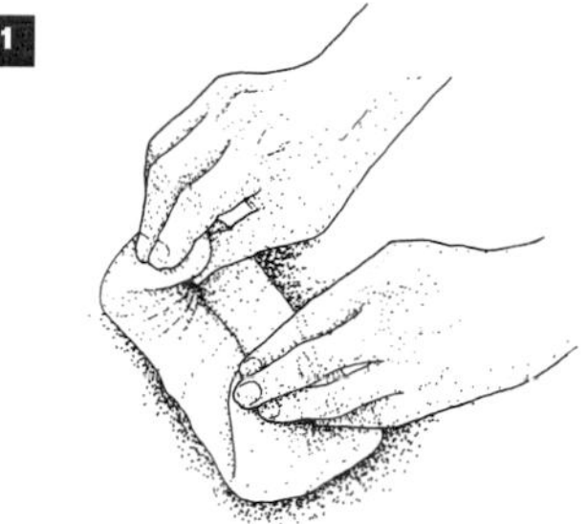

1. Press dough into a rectangle. With the long edge of the dough facing you, fold the dough crosswise so that short ends meet in the middle.

2

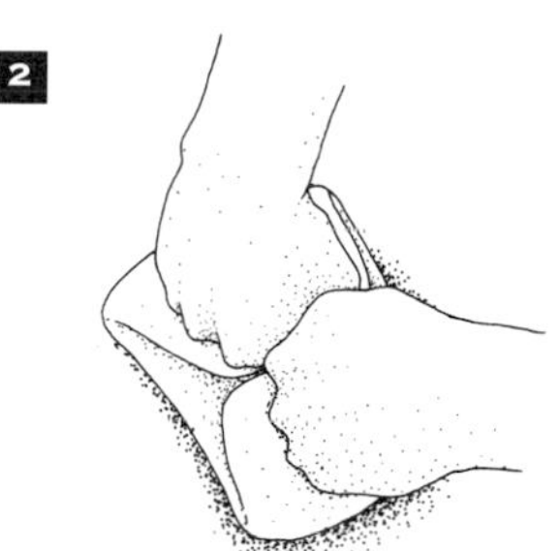

2. Press down firmly on folded dough to form a rectangle that is slightly thicker along the side farthest from you.

3

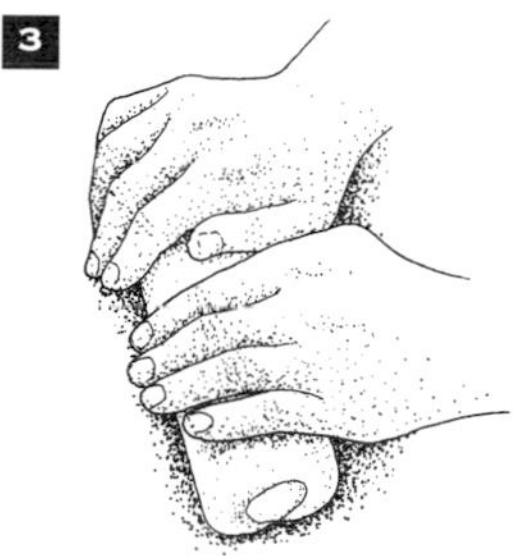

3. Starting with the far side of the dough, roll it towards you to form a tight cylinder.

4

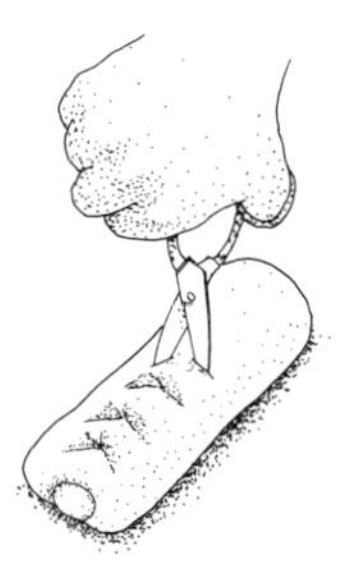

4. Starting at one end of the risen dough, make a zig-zag pattern using the scissor technique. Repeat diagonal cuts at 2-inch intervals.

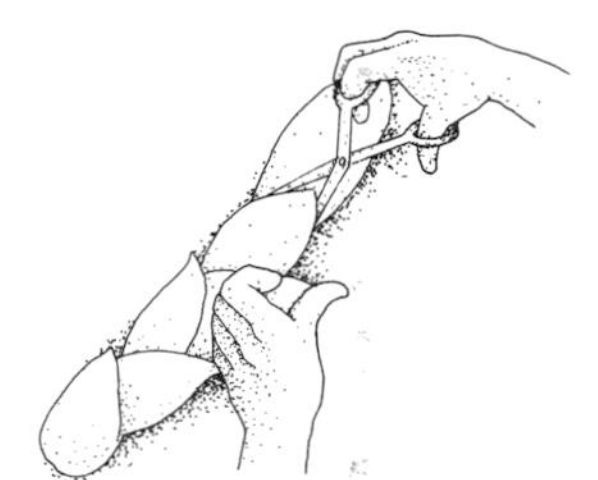

Ear-of-wheat shapes: Use scissors to make deep V-cuts every three inches. Lift first cut section of dough, point the dough to the left, lift the next section to the right.

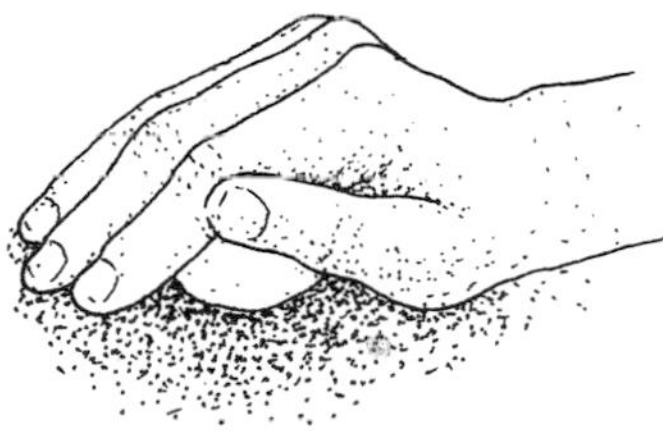

For the round rolls: With cupped palm, roll dough until it is smooth and perfectly round. Cut an "x" on each risen roll.

For the oval rolls: With fingertips, roll dough ball back and forth to create oval shapes.

1

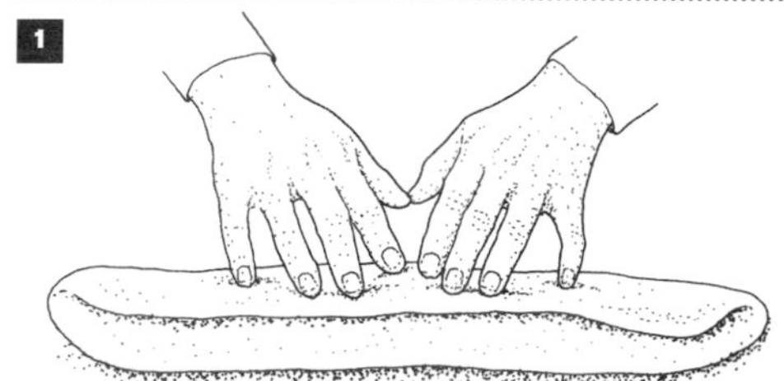

For the cylindrical loaf: 1. Press and stretch dough into a 14-by-6-inch rectangle. With the long edge of the dough facing you, fold the dough in thirds, lengthwise; pinch to seal.

2

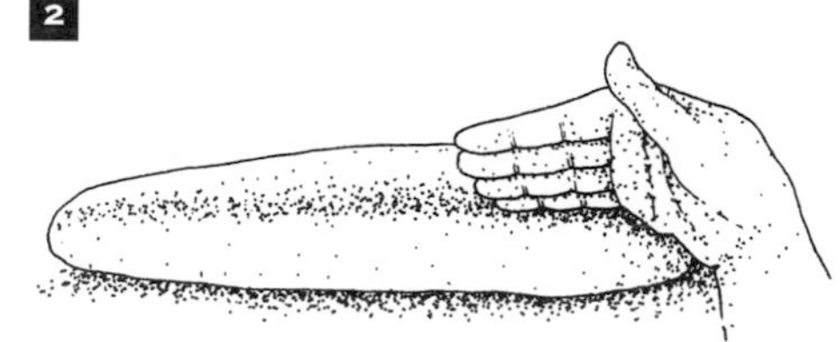

2. With the side of your hand, punch a trough lengthwise down the center of the dough.

3

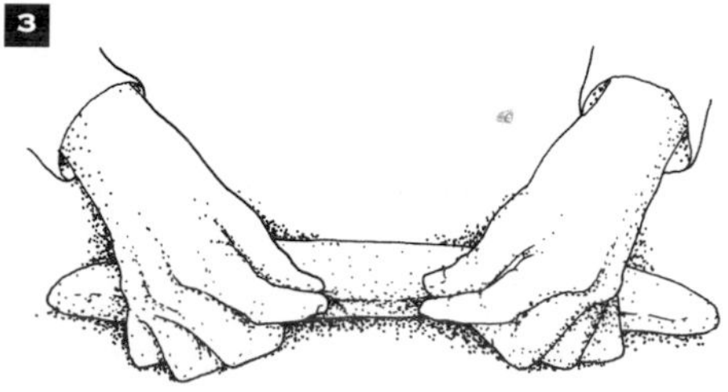

3. Pinch both sides of the trough together to form a tight cylinder.

ILLUSTRATIONS BY KATHY BRAY

The Way to Roast Chicken

Can legs finish cooking before breasts become dry? Our kitchen scientist roasted 15 chickens to find out.

BY HAROLD MCGEE

Why do we refer to a chicken baked in the oven as a "roast"? At least in part because the word "roast" evokes a culinary ideal, a bird cooked to a crisp, golden, juicy, aromatic turn over a live fire. And many traditional oven recipes do in fact mimic spit-roasting to an extent when they call for trussing, basting, and turning the bird.

Modern cooks have streamlined this routine; most of us place the untrussed bird in a very hot oven, close the door, and forget about it until the bird is done. Others, more uncompromising, say that with or without fussing it's basically impossible to make a whole roast chicken come out perfectly, because you cannot cook the legs through while keeping the breast moist.

Is it possible that trussing, basting, and turning chickens help us approximate a true roast? Can we do just as well without all the fuss? I cooked more than a dozen chickens, under a variety of conditions and at several temperatures, in order to find out.

Cooking a whole chicken in the oven *is* a challenge: the breast and leg meats are entirely different in character and deployment. The breast, which lies exposed in a flat, boneless sheet across one side of the bird, is lightly pigmented, lean, and tender. Cook it much past 150 degrees and it becomes dry and chewy. The bony legs, which protrude from the opposite side, sport meat that is deeply colored, fatty, and toughened by connective tissue. Only above 160 degrees does it lose its gristliness and raw, metallic flavor.

How a Chef Carves a Chicken

Jean-Louis Gerin, chef-owner of the eponymous restaurant in Greenwich, Connecticut, shows how to remove the breast before carving, how to easily find the drumstick joint, and how to carve the meat from the thigh.

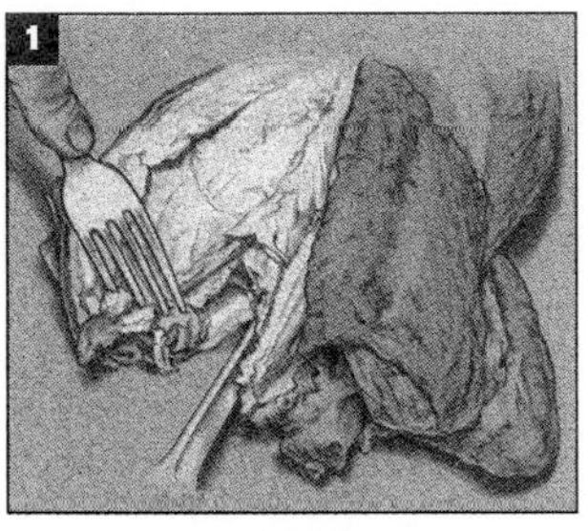

1. To remove the breasts, use a sharp boning knife and, following the contour of the rib cage, cut straight down until you hit the wishbone. Follow the wishbone and cut through the joint where it meets the breastbone.

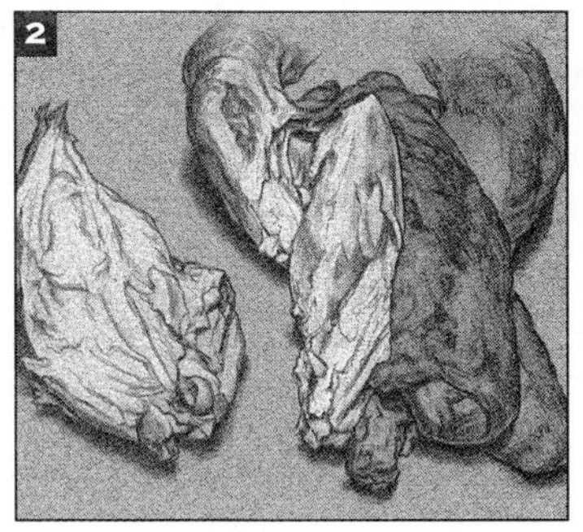

2. The rest of the breast easily separates from the body. Remove it entirely. You can remove the wing where it joins the breast, or leave it attached.

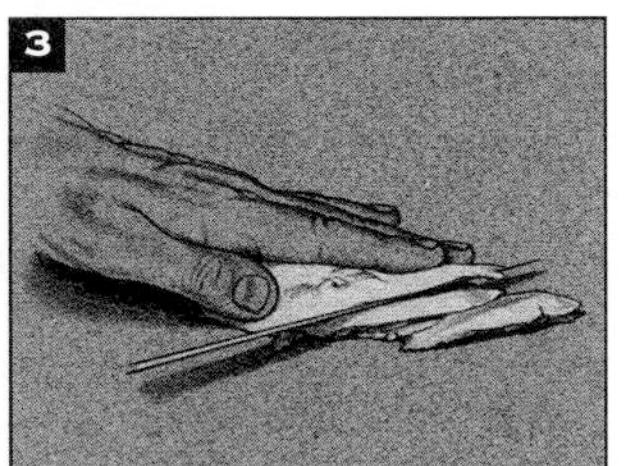

3. Using a carving knife, slice the breast horizontally, making long, thin slices. You should get four or more slices from each breast.

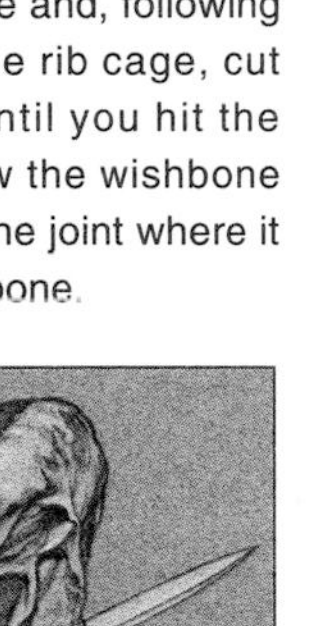

4. You can see the thigh joint as soon as you bend the leg quarter out from the carcass. Any sharp knife can be used to sever the joint.

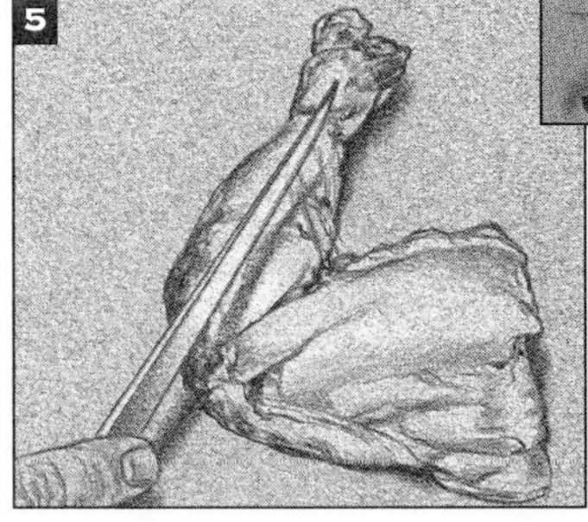

5. A straight line along the leg bone will intersect at the point where the thigh and leg join. **5A.** Shift the angle of the knife and cut; if you meet resistance, just change the knife angle.

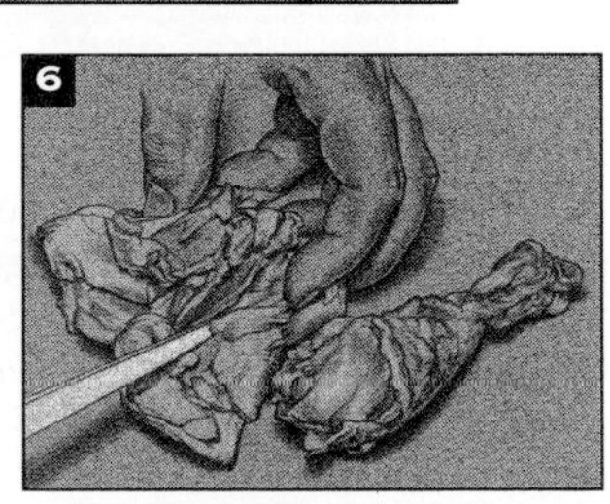

6. Use a boning or paring knife to remove thigh meat from the bone. It's difficult to get neat slices, but you can get nice chunks.

Turning: Essential

This basic asymmetry made me skeptical of any streamlined approach to roast chicken. Cooking the bird breast side up without turning exposes the delicate breast to the most intense heat, and leaves the tougher legs partly shielded between the breast and the roasting pan. When I roasted several birds as simply as possible — no trussing, turning, or basting — I found that the breast did usually end up overdone by the time the thighs were ready. And while the breast skin colored nicely, the leg skin remained unappetizingly pale.

The obvious remedy for this uneven cooking was to turn the bird, as many older recipes recommend. I gave that a try, turning the chickens frequently, without trussing or basting. However, I found these multiple turns awkward to perform and time consuming; furthermore, the partly cooked skin can stick to the rack and tear. I tried cooking the bird with its back up for 20 minutes (30 minutes for larger birds of five pounds or so), then breast up till done. This simple, one-turn routine heated the chicken as evenly as the multiple turns did. (No matter how many times you turn the bird, it's a good idea to oil the rack first.) At the same time, I found that elevating the rack (*see* sidebar, page 27) gave me a crisper bird, and increased the likelihood of breasts and legs being done simultaneously.

If the fast-trackers are wrong to forgo turning, they're right when it comes to oven temper-

ILLUSTRATIONS THIS PAGE BY ALLAN WITSCHONKE

ature: High heat is best. I tried temperatures as low as 325 degrees and as high as 500 degrees. Although gentle heat will yield somewhat moister drumsticks, only a hot oven can give you that desirable nut-brown coloring and roasted aroma. At 500 degrees, this browning will take 20 to 30 minutes per side. So I recommend starting at 500 degrees to develop color and flavor, then turning the heat way down to finish the cooking. (Chickens under four pounds are done so quickly that there's not time for this low-temperature finish. Very large chickens, turkeys, and stuffed birds take long enough to cook through that they brown at lower initial oven temperatures.)

Basting: Desirable

While investigating the temperature question, I was surprised to find that even a 500-degree oven doesn't brown plain leg skin well. Could basting be more than the harmless annoyance I has long assumed it to be? I did the experiment of roasting a single bird two ways, brushing one side every 10 minutes with melted butter while leaving the other side alone. The skin on the plain thigh ended up a dull, pale yellow, while the buttered thigh colored beautifully. Basting, it turns out, is essential for an evenly browned chicken.

Many recipes advise basting with oil, butter, or pan juices. I basted half a chicken with oil and the other half with butter and found that oil alone does very little. Both butter and pan juices work well, thanks to their protein and sugar content, which oven heat transforms into a dark, richly flavored essence. The active ingredient in butter is not fat, as you might imagine, but the traces of milk it contains. You can baste with milk alone, or use butter lightened with extra milk. Lemon butter also works well. And basting liquids that contain sugar, honey, or fruit juice brown faster than butter or pan juices, allowing you to turn down the oven heat earlier.

My experiments with basting every seven or eight minutes turned up a second, rather surprising advantage. Basting prolongs the cooking, and not only because it interrupts it. When I checked the doneness of my half-oil-basted, half-butter-basted bird, the butter side had cooked noticeably more slowly. Apparently the water in the butter cools the chicken skin as it evaporates. This stop-and-go heating may sound inefficient to culinary streamliners, but it does help approximate the effect of true spit-roasting, and gives the cook some useful leeway. How? The ideal temperature for moist chicken breast is 150 degrees. An unbasted breast goes from a perfect 150 to a dry 160 in only three or four minutes, but a basted breast takes five or six.

Trussing: Questionable

I wondered whether trussing could do anything more than make a bird look attractively trim. I discovered that most trussing is counterproductive. By holding the legs against the body, trussing slows their cooking and exacerbates the leg-breast problem. When I trussed birds, I found that the inner drumstick was still underdone when the breast and thigh were ready.

I did notice, however, that unusually extended legs are so exposed that parts of them become overcooked; it is a good idea to tie the drumsticks loosely together if one or both of the legs tends to splay away from the body. But don't bother to truss tightly unless presentation of the whole bird is important.

> **CUSTOMIZING A ROASTING PAN**
>
> You can improve the crisping of the leg skin and the doneness of dark meat by raising the cooking rack to a level slightly above the edge of the pan, where the legs will continue to get direct oven heat even after you turn the bird. Crumple four sheets of aluminum foil into balls of the right diameter and place them underneath the rack. Use another wad of foil to prop up the breast to drumstick level to improve browning.
>
> 

Judging Doneness

The key to a properly done chicken is knowing when to take it out of the oven. If you wait for the "juices to run clear," you risk being misled by the presence of pink juices in the body cavity. To avoid confusion or worry, remove the source of these dark juices, the dark red kidneys ensconced along the backbone.

The best way to judge doneness is to use an instant-read thermometer. At high heat, cooking times range from about 45 minutes for a three-and-one-half-pound bird to 65 or 70 minutes for a five-pound bird. As you approach these times, check the deepest part of the breast with an accurate thermometer. At 150 degrees or a shade under, the breast is done. If it's not, figure that it will gain about three degrees every minute and time your next check accordingly. The leg meat should be at least 160 degrees.

I'm always ready to abandon unnecessary complications in recipes. When it comes to oven-roasted chickens, however, turning and basting do take us closer to the spit-roasted ideal. Uncompromising cooks in pursuit of perfect succulence may still prefer to cook legs and breasts separately. Even turning and basting can't guarantee that dark meat and white will reach their ideal doneness at just the same moment. But I'm not about to abandon the oven-roasting of whole birds. A handsome platter, richly flavored skin, copious pan juices: to me, an elusive perfection is no substitute for these simple pleasures.

BASIC RECIPE FOR ROAST CHICKEN

Serves 4–6

- 1 chicken (3½ to 5 pounds), giblets, kidneys, and excess fat removed; chicken rinsed and dried
- Salt and pepper
- Aromatics (e.g., herbs, citrus peel, onions)
- ¼ cup melted butter

1. Adjust oven rack to middle position; heat oven to 500 degrees. Elevate roasting rack (*see* sidebar) and lightly oil roasting rack.

2. Season cavity with salt and pepper to taste; place aromatics in cavity. Pin flaps of skin at leg end together. If legs splay badly, tie drumstick ends loosely together. Arrange chicken, backside up, on rack.

3. Roast chicken, brushing bird with butter or pan juices every 8 to 10 minutes. (If pan juices begin to spatter loudly, add a few tablespoons of water to pan; repeat whenever necessary).

4. After 20 minutes (for a small chicken) to 30 minutes (for a chicken approaching 5 pounds), season legs and turn chicken, breast side up, pouring juices from body cavity into pan. Prop up the breast end with 1-inch-thick wad of foil under the back. Baste and return to oven.

5. Roast chicken, basting every 7 to 8 minutes, until breast side has browned sufficiently. Turn down oven to 325 degrees and prop oven door open for a minute or two to quickly bring temperature down. After 40 minutes total cooking time (50 minutes for large birds) season breast and legs, then check inner breast temperature by inserting thermometer from neck-end along ribs. When thermometer registers 148 to 150 degrees (145 degrees if you don't mind some slightly pink spots), the breast is done. Figure on breast temperature rising 2 degrees (larger birds) to 3 degrees (small ones) for every additional minute in oven. When breast is done, insert thermometer into thigh meat closest to body; it should read at least 160 degrees.

6. When chicken is done, tip cavity juices into pan and poke skin below thigh to release under-skin juices. Transfer chicken with rack to a plate, let rest for at least 20 minutes before serving. ■

Harold McGee is the author of *On Food and Cooking* and *The Curious Cook* (both published by Macmillan).

ILLUSTRATION BY ELAINE SEARS

Improvising Vegetable Soups

Learn to improvise your own homemade soups using two master recipes and follow our one-hour chicken broth recipe for quick and easy homemade stock.

Endless variations are possible once the basic proportions are understood. A chunky vegetable soup uses one and one-quarter pounds of vegetables per quart of liquid. A pureed soup uses about two pounds of vegetables per quart.

Just as decorators know that even the most beautiful wallpaper can't enhance a bad plaster job, all good cooks learn that what you throw into the pot doesn't matter nearly as much as the stock or broth that you begin with. The cook who values flavor comes to love skimming gray foam and yellow grease from the top of the pot, straining (and spilling) the stock, and hauling the spent bones directly to the garbage. All of this is in pursuit of the hidden foundation — the *fonds de cuisine* — that makes an exceptional vegetable soup.

Here, we describe how to make two distinct styles of vegetable soups: a chunky, main-course soup full of seasonal vegetables, and a pureed first-course soup, featuring one vegetable supported by a mirepoix for flavoring and potato for thickening. Each should be based, of course, on a solid foundation — which need only take one hour. The soups differ basically in the proportion of liquid to vegetables. For a chunky vegetable soup, keep the ratio of vegetables to liquid at about one and one-quarter pounds per quart, and always include some carrots, onions, and celery. For pureed soups, use a one-half pound of the onion-carrot-celery trinity (twice as much onions and carrots as celery), one and one-half pounds of the featured vegetable, and one pound of potatoes to one and one-half quarts of liquid.

Herbs are important in many soups. Try celery root with thyme; scent carrot soup with basil; or add mint to sweet pea. But remember that chilling reduces herbs and spices to dormancy, so use a heavier hand if you are planning a cold soup. (We sprinkled one-half teaspoon hot red pepper flakes into the broccoli soup. When hot, it scorched the palate; chilled, it was perfect.)

QUICK BROTH

Makes 3 quarts

Since the cooking time on this broth is short, cut up the vegetables and chicken first.

- 1 chicken (3½ to 4 pounds), cut into 10 pieces (plus neck and gizzard)
- 1 medium onion, chopped coarse
- 1 medium carrot, chopped coarse
- 1 medium celery stalk, chopped coarse
- 1 bouquet garni
- 1 teaspoon salt
- 13 cups water

1. Bring all ingredients to simmer, skimming foam and fat as it rises to surface. Continue to simmer until chicken is tender, about 40 minutes. Remove and reserve chicken pieces for another use. Simmer broth to blend flavors, about 20 minutes longer.
2. Strain and skim remaining fat from broth and continue with any soup recipe, or cool to room temperature and refrigerate. Remove congealed fat before reheating. You can refrigerate this for up to 5 days (or longer, if you bring it to a boil every few days), or freeze it for several months.

SOUP BASE

A Master Recipe for Chunky and Pureed Soup

Makes about 3 quarts

This is the basis for any soup you wish to make. See the following recipes for some suggestions on how to use it.

- 2 tablespoons olive oil
- 2 medium onions, diced coarse
- 2 medium carrots, diced coarse

WHAT'S THE DIFFERENCE BETWEEN BROTH AND STOCK?

The terms chicken stock and broth appear to have become synonymous — how many recipes call for "homemade chicken stock or canned chicken broth"? Yet although broth and stock share common ingredients — chicken of some sort, onions, carrots, celery, and a bouquet garni (thyme, bay leaf, and parsley sprigs) — the similarities end there.

Broth is made with a whole chicken or chicken parts and simmered until the chicken is done. The chicken is then pulled from the pot and later either joins the vegetables in the soup or finds itself in a salad or casserole. Stock, however, is made from the bird's bones, which, along with the vegetables, give their life to the stock, simmering in the liquid for hours. The differences in taste, texture, time, and economy cannot be overstated. Which is best for you? *See* sidebar, page 29.

PHOTOGRAPH BY RICHARD FELBER

1 celery stalk, diced coarse
2 garlic cloves, minced
3 quarts chicken broth

Heat oil in a large soup kettle. Add onions, carrots, and celery. Sauté until vegetables soften, about 5 minutes. Add garlic and sauté until fragrant, about 1 minute. Add stock and simmer 1 to 2 minutes, then add other vegetables and seasonings as you like.

SUMMER HARVEST SOUP WITH BASIL

Serves 8 as a main course

If you let this soup stand to develop the flavors, do not cook the pasta. When ready to serve, bring the soup back to a simmer, add the pasta, and cook about 10 minutes or until done.

1 recipe Soup Base
4 new potatoes, cut into ½-inch dice
2 large tomatoes, peeled, seeded, and chopped coarse
¼ teaspoon summer savory
Salt
1 medium zucchini, cut into ¼-inch dice
1 medium yellow squash, cut into ¼-inch dice
2 ears corn, kernels cut from cob (1½ cups)
¼ pound green beans, trimmed and cut into l-inch lengths
½ cup elbow macaroni
½ cup chopped fresh parsley
¼ cup julienned fresh basil
Ground black pepper
½ cup basil pesto

Bring Soup Base to simmer. Add potatoes, tomatoes, summer savory; salt to taste and simmer for 30 minutes. Add squashes, corn, and beans and simmer 5 minutes. Add macaroni and simmer until pasta is done, about 10 minutes. Stir in parsley and basil. Season with additional salt, if necessary, and pepper to taste. Serve with basil pesto passed separately.

SPRING VEGETABLE SOUP WITH EGG NOODLES AND MINT

Serves 8 as a main course

1 recipe Soup Base
4 coarsely diced medium new potatoes
1½ cups fresh or frozen green peas (about 8 ounces)
¾ pound thin asparagus spears trimmed and cut into 1-inch pieces
1 cup egg noodles (about 2 ounces)
4 ounces fresh spinach, stemmed, cleaned, and shredded
¼ cup fresh mint, minced

Bring Soup Base to simmer. Add new potatoes, peas, asparagus, and noodles and simmer until vegetables are tender and noodles are done, 8 to 10 minutes. Add spinach and simmer 3 minutes longer. Stir in mint. Let stand 2 hours to let flavors blend before serving.

PUREE OF CAULIFLOWER SOUP WITH CARDAMOM AND MACE

Serves 8 as a first course

To use as a master recipe, simply substitute 1½ pounds of another vegetable for the cauliflower and eliminate the cardamom and mace, using other appropriate herbs and/or spices.

½ recipe Soup Base
1 large head cauliflower, trimmed and cut into florets (or 1½ pounds other vegetable)
1 pound potatoes, peeled and cut into 1-inch dice
¼ teaspoon cardamom
⅛ teaspoon mace
Salt and ground black pepper
¼ cup light cream (optional)

Bring Soup Base to simmer. Add cauliflower, potatoes, cardamom, mace, and salt to taste; simmer until vegetables are very tender, about 20 minutes. Season with additional salt, if necessary, and pepper to taste. Puree in batches in a food processor or blender. Return to kettle. Stir in optional cream and reheat, or cool and refrigerate. Serve chilled.

PUREE OF BROCCOLI SOUP WITH GARLIC AND HOT RED PEPPER

Serves 8 as a first course

Follow the above recipe, adding 3 garlic cloves to the sautéing Soup Base vegetables. Substitute ¼ teaspoon hot red pepper flakes for the cardamom and mace. Add 1½ pounds broccoli, trimmed and cut into ½-inch pieces or florets, to the simmering broth, along with the potatoes. Cook and puree, stirring in an optional 2 tablespoons extra virgin olive oil in place of the cream. Serve hot or chilled. ■

STOCK FOR SOUP: A KITCHEN TEST

Most cooks agree on stock ingredients, give or take a garlic clove; it's cooking times that differ dramatically. Some simmer broth for forty minutes; others cook stock all day. To see how time and ingredients affect stock and broth, we tried six variations; all contained a one-pound mirepoix of celery, carrots, and onions, a bouquet garni of thyme, bay leaf, and parsley, and a teaspoon of salt. After cooking, we strained the liquids, refrigerated them, removed the fat layer, and reheated them for tasting.

With the exception of the Vegetable Broth, which was thin, bland, and without character, all of the stocks and broths were acceptable. But the Long-Cooked Stock was a clear victor in terms of body and flavor, with a rich flavor that lingered in the mouth. The Quick Broth produced a strong chicken flavor, but, in the words of one taster, "The chicken flavor hits you, then it's gone." The Slow-Cooked Broth was no better.

There was no mistaking Roasted Stock. It was mild, but in no way meek. In fact, it was distinctive, and provides a splendid opportunity to use bones that normally get tossed.

Unless you have plenty of time as well as access to lots of chicken bones, use the Quick Broth for most soup making. Clearly the Long-Cooked Stock is preferable if you're looking for the best flavor possible. And, unless you have moral convictions or dietary restrictions, steer clear of vegetable stock altogether.

Quick Broth *Ingredients:* One 3½-pound chicken, cut into 10 pieces; 13 cups of water; mirepoix, bouquet garni, salt. *Technique:* Bring ingredients to simmer, skim, simmer for 40 minutes. Remove chicken, simmer 20 more minutes.

Slow-Cooked Broth *Ingredients:* As above, but with slightly more water to compensate for longer cooking time. *Technique:* Bring ingredients to simmer, skim, simmer for 1¼ hours. Remove chicken, simmer for 2 more hours.

Short-Cooked Stock *Ingredients:* Four pounds of chicken bones (backs, wings, and gizzards), 12 cups water, mirepoix, bouquet garni, salt. *Technique:* Bring ingredients to simmer, skim, simmer for 2½ hours.

Long-Cooked Stock *Ingredients:* Same as Short-Cooked Stock, plus ½ quart additional water. *Technique:* Bring bones and stock to a simmer, skim, and simmer for 3 hours. Add mirepoix, bouquet garni, and salt, simmer another 2 hours. Total cooking time: 5 hours.

Roasted Stock *Ingredients:* Same as Short-Cooked Stock but with 3 pounds of roasted chicken bones. *Technique:* Bring ingredients to simmer, skim, and simmer for 2½ hours.

Vegetable Broth *Ingredients:* Onions, leeks, celery, carrots, cabbage, garlic, tomato, salt. *Technique:* Saute onions, leeks, celery, and cabbage until very soft. Add water along with cabbage, garlic, tomato, and salt; simmer 1 hour.

Natural Salad Dressings

Tofu, miso, and other health food staples make creamy, rich salad dressings with less fat.

BY LAUREL VUKOVIC

The Vegan movement advocates nutritious foods with a rich variety of flavors and textures, while avoiding consumption of any animal foods or dairy products. As ingredients from the East were introduced in the West, throughout the 1970s and much of the 1980s, they were often used primarily as substitutes for traditional Western foods. Today, however, tofu, miso, rice vinegar, sesame oil, and soy milk are all part of a new style of cooking that is neither Asian nor Western, but that simply uses each ingredient to its best advantage. Rich textures; clean, sharp flavors; and deep, subtle accents make these salad dressings very appealing for home cooks. Unused portions will keep, refrigerated, for a week. Ingredients can be found at many supermarkets and at all health food stores.

Laurel Vukovic, Assistant Editor at **Natural Health** *magazine, and her husband Dragomir run a Boston-based catering company that specializes in natural food cooking.*

AVOCADO BASIL DRESSING

Refresh your tofu by simmering or steaming it for 2 minutes. (Unused tofu will keep, refrigerated, for a week; cover in water and change water daily.) Serve this rich dressing over mixed greens or on a salad of basmati rice, corn, and red peppers.

- ⅓ pound soft tofu
- 1 ripe avocado, peeled and pitted
- ½ cup water
- ¼ cup extra virgin olive oil
- ¼ cup light miso
- 2 tablespoons brown rice or other vinegar
- 1 tablespoon lemon juice
- ½ small onion, minced (2 tablespoons)
- 1 small garlic clove, minced
- ¼ cup minced fresh basil

Bring 2 cups of water to simmer; add tofu and simmer for 2 minutes. Drain and cool tofu to room temperature in cold water; drain again. Puree tofu with next 8 ingredients in blender or food processor. Stir in basil. Use immediately or refrigerate until serving.

GINGER WALNUT MISO DRESSING

Walnuts give this dressing a slightly rosy hue. Try it over a combination of watercress, apples, and cucumbers, or on lightly steamed spinach or bitter greens.

- ¼ cup soy or whole milk
- ¼ cup light, toasted sesame oil
- 2 tablespoons white miso
- 2 tablespoons minced onion
- 1 tablespoon rice syrup or honey
- 3 tablespoons brown rice or other vinegar
- 2 tablespoons fresh ginger juice, made by grating a 2-inch piece of ginger root and squeezing through cheesecloth
- ½ cup walnuts, toasted
- 2 tablespoons minced parsley

Put first 7 ingredients plus ¼ cup walnuts in a food processor or blender and puree until smooth. Coarsely chop remaining walnuts and stir into dressing along with the parsley. Serve or refrigerate until serving.

SESAME GARLIC DRESSING

This dressing is great over blanched fresh vegetables or pasta served at room temperature.

- ⅓ pound soft tofu
- ¼ cup light, toasted sesame oil
- 3 tablespoons apple cider or other vinegar
- 3 tablespoons white miso
- 1 small garlic clove, minced
- 1 tablespoon rice syrup or honey
- 1½ tablespoons sesame seeds, toasted
- 2 tablespoons minced parsley

Bring 2 cups of water to simmer; add tofu and simmer for 2 minutes. Drain and cool tofu to room temperature in cold water; drain again. Put tofu with next 5 ingredients in blender or food processor and puree until smooth. Stir in sesame seeds and parsley; cover and refrigerate until chilled and serve.

TWO-MUSTARD DRESSING WITH CHIVES

Try this on a salad of new potatoes, green peas, and sweet onions, or with a combination of chilled green beans and chickpeas.

- ¼ cup soy or whole milk
- ¼ cup extra virgin olive oil
- 1 tablespoon Dijon-style mustard
- 1 tablespoon whole-grain mustard
- 2 tablespoons brown rice or other vinegar
- 1 tablespoon rice syrup or honey
- 2 tablespoons minced chives

Process first 6 ingredients in a blender or food processor until smooth; stir in chives. Serve or refrigerate until serving. ■

NATURAL FOODS GLOSSARY

TOFU First produced more than two thousand years ago, tofu is essentially a cheese made from the "milk" of soybeans; it has traditionally been a staple in China, Japan, and Indonesia. The firmness of tofu is determined by the amount of water left in the curd after pressing. Firm and extra-firm tofu are similar to the tofu produced in China; silken and soft tofu are like those of Japan. Generally speaking, use silken and soft tofu interchangeably in sauces, pudding, dips, and dressings. Firm and extra-firm tofu retain their shape in cooking. (To substitute firm tofu for soft in the dressings above, increase the amount of liquid in the recipe by a tablespoon or so.)

RICE SYRUP A mild sweetener made from rice and malted grain; similar in consistency to honey, it is metabolized slowly by the body, eliminating the rush one may feel after eating refined sugars.

BROWN RICE VINEGAR The delicate, sweet taste of this naturally brewed vinegar makes it an interesting alternative to balsamic or other vinegars.

MISO A fermented soybean paste made with salt and often with rice or barley. The lighter varieties generally tend to be milder, the darker colors more full-flavored.

SOY MILK The liquid strained from cooked, pureed soybeans; used in cooking and baking, in sauces, with cereals, and as a beverage.

SESAME OIL Made from sesame seeds, often cold-pressed and unrefined; also made in light and dark varieties from toasted seeds.

PHOTOGRAPH BY BOB KRAMER

BOOK REVIEWS

New York Cookbook
By Molly O'Neill
Workman, $27.95 cloth; $17.95 paper.

New York Times food writer Molly O'Neill has hand-picked and distilled the choicest culinary treasures from one of the world's greatest food towns and presented them for use in your kitchen. O'Neill spent five years culling recipes from Manhattan's chefs and celebrities, from Brooklyn grandmothers and Bronx bakers. Here is an invitation to Bronx Jerk-Style Chicken, Brooklyn Blackout Cake, Queens Potato Pancakes, and Staten Island Roast Pork.

The best part is that this is no cultural sideshow. The food is not just good, it's superb. Fashion designer Adolfo shares his family's recipe for Cuban Roast Chicken, with a stuffing of rice, sausage, olives, raisins, and pine nuts that perfectly matches the spicy exterior of the bird. Mohamed's Marvelous Marrakesh Carrots comes from a Moroccan native who works as a private chef on Park Avenue and, yes, they're marvelous. If you thought you were through with brownie recipes, just wait; Katharine Hepburn's Brownies are so fudgy and delicious that you will change your mind. And the recipe for Eli's Bread (a sourdough *ficelle*) is worth the cover price all by itself.

O'Neill is a pro. In addition to great recipes, she brings New York's special culinary history to life in well-researched, well-written essays. She also provides information on street festivals and walking tours of the city's food landmarks. In short, regardless of where you live — even if you hope to never venture east of the Hudson — ya gotta check this one out.

Fifty Ways to Cook Most Everything
By Andrew Schloss and Ken Bookman
Simon & Schuster, $25

The subtitle of *Fifty Ways to Cook Most Everything: 2,500 creative solutions to the daily dilemma of what to cook* is only partly accurate. Technically speaking, there are 2,500 recipes here. But they're not recipes in the sense that they provide precise instructions and practical suggestions for serving, storage, and cooking in advance. Rather, they are "creative solutions," good ideas accompanied by enough information to get many home cooks well on his or her way to executing a dish. What is sometimes lost in this mammoth project, however, are the nuances and details that can make or break a recipe.

The book grew out of a newspaper article, "50 Ways to Love Your Liver." Here is that theme writ large, 50 paragraph-long recipes for each of 50 topics. There are chapters about foods — tomatoes, fish, and chicken breasts, for example — and some about themes — fighting fat, cleaning out the fridge, topping a pizza.

Schloss is a creative cook; Bookman, former editor of the *Philadelphia Inquirer,* is a wordsmith. Most of the ideas here are both inspired and simple, an unusual combination. We had excellent results with Grilled Oriental Chicken Salad, Spicy Red Bean Peanut Soup, and Best-Ever Chocolate Pudding, which fully lived up to its name.

When we made these recipes, we didn't miss the details that have been omitted to save space. But novice cooks might. Pancetta, Hazelnut, and Garlic Sauce makes a tasty pasta topping. Although the recipe calls for skinned hazelnuts, however, it fails to provide instructions. And since the procedure for this is not immediately obvious (the nuts must be toasted in a warm oven for 10 minutes, wrapped in a dish towel, and then rubbed vigorously), many cooks — including our mothers, our spouses, and most of our friends — would have to consult another source before proceeding.

Furthermore, time guidelines are not always given. At first glance, Eggplant with Garlic Jam might seem like a nice quick fix. But with directions to "simmer until most of the liquid evaporates," it's hard to know whether to allow 20 minutes or an hour for this recipe (indeed, it took us an hour).

Fifty Ways to Cook Most Everything is a valuable resource for experienced cooks looking for loads of fresh, uncomplicated ideas. And those ideas, in the right hands, can produce lovely food. But for many people, good ideas are not enough. If you're after precise directions, you'll have to look elsewhere.

China Moon Cookbook
By Barbara Tropp
Workman, $24.95 cloth; $14.95 paper

Barbara Tropp's reputation as one of this country's most serious cooks of Chinese food is well deserved. Her *Modern Art of Chinese Cooking,* now 10 years old, is still in print and still worth buying. Her San Francisco restaurant, China Moon Cafe, where authentic technique meets California style, is a must stop on any culinary tour.

Her new book allows us to duplicate Tropp's personal, creative cuisine at home. But it also reminds us why we usually steer clear of chef's books — like so many of her colleagues, Tropp gives us complex recipes better suited to a staff of five than a lone home cook. Cooking from *China Moon Cookbook* requires a commitment of time and effort that few but the most devoted cooks will make.

Many recipes require trendy produce that may be easy to find in California but is far less common elsewhere. Stir-Fried Spicy Pork Ribbons with Summer Beans and Baby Squash calls for fresh baby corn, Blue Lake string beans, baby pattypan squash, and baby green or yellow squash (with blossoms, of course). Tropp suggests alternatives for the corn and beans (fresh corn kernels and any tender beans) but not for either squash.

Even more frustrating is Tropp's reliance on her own pantry staples, which are included in nearly every recipe. She insists that readers make her oils, vinegars, and sauces before embarking on more ambitious recipes. For instance, before tackling the pork stir-fry we had to make China Moon Hot Chili Oil and Oven-Dried Plum Tomatoes. Both were superior in quality to store-bought equivalents, but each took the same amount of time we usually devote to preparing an entire meal. Since the pork stir-fry and accompanying Pot-Browned Noodle Pillow took two hours to prepare, this deceptively simple dish wound up taking all day.

Of course our pantry is now at least partly stocked with the requisite ingredients. And if we were to cook solely from this book, eventually things would become simpler. But it would take a commitment akin to learning tai-chi.

However, such a commitment might be warranted. Although Tropp virtually ignores the realities of home cooking, she does give us clearly written recipes that yield delicious results. Serious afficionados of uncommonly good Chinese food will consider this book a treasure. Just don't plan to open your China Moon Cafe at five o'clock and hope to get dinner on the table much before bedtime. ■

Inexpensive Chianti Wins Blind Tasting

BEST WINE

BY MARK BITTMAN

BEST BUY

Food-lovers and professional wine tasters look for different characteristics when rating wines. One man's "lovely nose" may be "too much" for another.

One rather welcome conclusion you might draw from a recent tasting of 14 Tuscan red wines (mostly Chiantis) is that wine-drinking food-lovers prefer inexpensive wines. The wines we tasted ranged in price from about $7 to about $33 (with an average price of about $18), and in reputation from nonexistent to exalted. The top finisher was a $13 bottle, and the third-place wine was the least expensive tasted.

The wines were selected by Bob Feinn, a highly regarded wine retailer whose Hamden, Connecticut store, Mt. Carmel Wine and Spirits, is one of the best-stocked in the country. He assembled a group of wines that represented a range of styles, prices, and maturity levels. There were 10 tasters. In addition to Feinn, who tastes and rates wines on a daily basis, the group included three food writers, a chef, and five accomplished home cooks. All enjoy drinking wine with meals, either nightly or a few times a week, but some admitted that, in a blind tasting, they wouldn't know a Chianti from a Barolo. This range of expertise was purposeful. Would an accomplished home cook agree with the tastes and preferences of an experienced wine or food professional?

The tasting was blind. Bottles were foil-wrapped and randomly numbered. Each taster was asked to judge the wines based on enjoyment, with or without food (food was available). No discussion of the wines was allowed during the tasting. Participants wrote down comments, and followed a relative scoring system that enabled them to rank their top seven wines in order.

Villa Antinori's Chianti Classico Riserva 1987 received three first-place votes and three second-place votes; eight tasters named it as one of the top seven wines. Melini's Borghi D'Elsa Chianti, 1990 — a fruity wine that few experienced tasters would peg as a Chianti — also received three first-place votes and was hailed by eight tasters. Of the remaining wines finishing in the top seven, four were pricey, ranging from $25 to $33 a bottle. None, however, garnered more than one first-place vote.

It would be a mistake to attribute these results to a lack of sophistication on the part of the tasters. That their palates were finely honed was evident by their comments. Rather, it was a case of real preferences. Feinn's top-ranked wine, of which he wrote "excellent appearance . . . lovely nose, complex on the palate . . . Medoc-like," finished 12th. One other taster wrote, of the same wine: "I know I should like this wine, but it's too much for me." And two of the mature, expensive wines were described by tasters with terms such as "over the hill" or "too old."

In two instances, a producer's less expensive wines finished ahead of its glamour wines. The top-ranked Antinori overshadowed its $25 cousin, and the straightforward Lamole di Lamole, at $17, finished five places higher than its wood-aged counterpart, which cost $27. ■

Mark Bittman writes about wine for the *Hartford Courant.*

ARE WINE PROFESSIONALS THE BEST JUDGES OF WINE?

Wine, traditionally, was locally produced. The fortunate few chose between red and white; the rest just drank what was around. Today, however, we choose between tens of thousands of wines. Wine professionals seek to judge dozens, sometimes hundreds, of wines at once, based on merits which typically include color, bouquet, flavor, and finish as well as structure, balance, aging potential, and links to tradition.

When we're lucky, professional wine tastings recommend affordable wines that are fun to drink with whatever we are cooking tonight. More often than not, however, they overlook the important question, "What tastes good, won't kill my food, and doesn't cost too much?" As we prepare lighter, cleaner-tasting foods at home, perhaps our tastes in wine are also changing. Seasoned home cooks now seem to prefer simpler, less complex wines, passing over the fuller, more robust varieties that demand a style of cooking less in evidence today in America's kitchens than it was even a decade ago.

BLIND TASTING RESULTS

Wines are listed in overall order of preference. Comments were drawn from the tasters' written notes.

1. Villa Antinori Chianti Classico Riserva 1987 ($13): *pleasant, nice taste, smooth, fruity*
2. Monsanto Il Poggio Chianti Classico Riserva 1982 ($27): *rich color, mellow, dark, old, delicious*
3. Melini Borghi D'Elsa Chianti 1990 ($6.99): *smooth and buttery, most alive and complex*
4. Monsanto Il Poggio Chianti Classico Riserva 1985 ($31): *delicious, substantial, well-balanced, mature*
5. Badia a Coltibuono Chianti Classico Riserva 1978 ($33): *woody and complex, round*
6. Tenute Marchese Antinori Riserva Chianti Classico 1987 ($25): *light, pleasant, straight but no complexity*
7. Lamole di Lamole Chianti Classico Riserva 1988 ($17): *super-pleasant but a lightweight*
8. Gattavecchi Rossi di Montepulciano 1990 ($10): *pleasant but not distinctive*
9. Castello dei Rampolla Chianti Classico 1988 ($16.99): *thin, little fruit*
10. Ruffino Ducale Chianti Classico Gold Label Riserva 1986 ($24): *flat, unsubstantial*
11. Coltibuono Cetamura Chianti 1988 ($7.99): *light, lacks fruit, acidic*
12. Lamole di Lamole Chianti Classico Riserva, 1985 (barrique aged) ($27): *not real flavorful, tart finish*
13. Antinori Santa Christina Tuscan Red Wine 1990 ($7.69): *thin, boring*
14. Capezzana Chianti Montalbano 1990 ($10): *thin and very acidic*

RECIPE INDEX

BROTH OF BLACK BASS AND MINCED VEGETABLES page 9

THE BEST ANGEL FOOD CAKE page 12

BREAKFAST
Raised Waffles...2

SOUPS
Puree of Broccoli Soup with Garlic and Hot Red Pepper.........................29
Puree of Cauliflower Soup with Cardamom and Mace 29
Quick Broth 28
Soup Base...28
Spring Vegetable Soup.............................29
Summer Harvest Soup with Basil.................29

MAIN COURSES
Broth of Black Bass and Minced Vegetables.............................9
Hot and Sour Bok Choy.............................. 7
Roast Chicken..27
Seafood Cabbage Casserole.........................6
Spicy Buttermilk Fried Chicken....................21
Stir-Fried Cabbage....................................7
Stir-Fried Shanghai Bok Choy with Crabmeat...7

SIDE DISHES
Tuscan Beans with Sage...............................2
White Bean and Tomato Casserole................9

BREADS
Master Recipe for Basic Bread.....................24

SALAD DRESSINGS
Avocado Basil Dressing..............................30
Ginger Walnut Miso Dressing.....................30
Sesame Garlic Dressing.............................30
Two-Mustard Dressing with Chives..............30

DESSERTS
Baked Pear Pudding.................................18
Banana Berry Popover...............................18
Best Angel Food Cake................................12
Candied Lemon Peel.................................3
Creme Caramel..3
Neopolitan Orange Cake............................15
Prune Custard Pudding..............................19
Raspberry Orange Bavarian............back cover
Reuben's Legendary Apple Pancake............19
Souffléed Batter Pudding...........................18
Walnut Wafers...15

REUBEN'S LEGENDARY APPLE PANCAKE page 19

SUMMER HARVEST SOUP WITH BASIL page 29

SEAFOOD CABBAGE CASSEROLE page 6

MASTER RECIPE FOR BASIC BREAD page 24

Raspberry Orange Bavarian

Puree 1 pint of raspberries and strain out seeds. Stir 2 tablespoons Grand Marnier into the puree, and set ¼ cup aside to flavor the Bavarian; reserve remaining puree for sauce. Stir ½ tablespoon Grand Marnier into ¼ cup fresh-squeezed orange juice. Sprinkle 1 packet unflavored gelatin over ¼ cup cold water in a small saucepan; let stand until softened (5 minutes). Stir in ⅓ cup honey and 2 teaspoons minced orange zest; heat gently until mixture just simmers. Cool mixture slightly in a medium bowl, and stir in 1 cup whipping cream and ¾ cup sour cream. Halve this cream mixture. Stir berry puree into one-half of mixture and orange juice into the other. Spoon 2 tablespoons of the berry cream into each of 4, 6-ounce custard cups. Refrigerate until set (15 minutes). Divide orange cream among the cups and refrigerate until set (30 minutes). Top each with an equal portion of remaining berry cream; refrigerate at least 2 hours. Stir 3 tablespoons confectioner's sugar into ¼ cup fresh-squeezed orange juice and reserved berry puree. Cover and refrigerate. To serve, divide puree among 4 dessert plates. Run a knife around each custard cup and unmold Bavarian onto the puree. Garnish with raspberries and mint sprigs.

NUMBER TWO ◆ PREMIER ISSUE

FOUR DOLLARS

COOK'S ILLUSTRATED

Stir-Frying Comes Home

How to Stir-Fry at Home Without a High-Heat Wok

Grilling Pizza

The Best and Simplest Pizza Is Made on a Backyard Grill

Poaching Fruit

Three Basic Syrups Yield Hundreds of Recipes

The Art of Biscuits

How to Make Them Fluffy or Flaky

TESTING IMMERSION BLENDERS
•
BONING POULTRY STEP-BY-STEP
•
RATING SOY SAUCES
•
HOW TO COOK ASPARAGUS
•
THE BEST DRY ROSÉS
•
QUICK TECHNIQUES

PREMIER ISSUE, MAY/JUNE 1993

TABLE OF CONTENTS

VOLUME ONE • NUMBER TWO

~2~
Notes from Readers
Light olive oils, pea shoots, Alsatian spatzle, whether to soak vegetables before cooking, and how to truss and roast chicken.

~4~
Quick Tips
How to string rhubarb, grate lemon peel without gumming up the grater, line a mold with parchment paper, stem and core artichokes, and choose a less bitter eggplant by sex.

~6~
How to Cook Asparagus
We compare boiling, steaming, and microwaving to find the best and easiest way to prepare perfectly cooked asparagus. *By Stephanie Lyness*

~8~
Grilling Pizza
Grilling pizza in the backyard produces an extraordinarily crisp dough and makes easy summer appetizers. *By Steve Johnson*

~10~
The Art of Biscuit-Making
Do you prefer your biscuits soft and fluffy, or flaky and high-rising? We show you how to bake the biscuits you want. *By Stephen Schmidt*

~13~
Secrets of Soy Sauce
After discovering the secrets of soy sauces, you can choose smooth, wood-aged brands and avoid those reminiscent of "bicycle lubricant." *By Joni Miller.*

~16~
Cutting Up Poultry, Step-by-Step
Learn how to cut up chicken in different ways for different uses, and how to "stuff" chicken skin without cutting at all.

Front Cover: In this issue, you will learn how to core artichokes (page 4), the best way to cook asparagus (page 6), a recipe for strawberry shortcake (page 12), and a master stir-fry recipe ideal for broccoli (page 19). *Illustration by Brent Watkinson.*

Back Cover: For a spring salad, chef Emeril Lagasse steams and cores artichokes, fills them with a rich mixture of shrimp and crabmeat, then drizzles them with a fragrant herb vinaigrette. Recipe is from Lagasse's cookbook, *Emeril's New New Orleans Cooking*, reviewed on page 30. *Illustration by Edward Martinez.*

~18~
Stir-Frying Comes Home
We discover that, in order to create perfect stir-fry dishes at home — without the benefit of a high-heat restaurant wok — you need to vary the technique. *By Pam Anderson*

~22~
Master Class: Roast Leg of Lamb with Red Chile Crust and Jalapeño Preserves
A New York chef uses classic French techniques to create a dish that's utterly southwestern.

~24~
How to Poach Fruit
Learn how to make hundreds of poached fruit desserts using two basic techniques and syrups of varying densities and flavors. *By Nick Malgieri.*

~27~
Using and Rating Immersion Blenders
Are they just gadgets, or useful kitchen tools? We explore the ways chefs and home cooks are using these hand-held blenders, and find that the criteria for buying the right model are simple: price and attachments. *By Michele Anna Jordan*

~30~
Book Reviews
Wrapped foods are more versatile than you might think, traditional southern baking shines, but does brilliance in a restaurant kitchen translate into a great cookbook?

~31~
French Rosés Are Still the Best — Barely
In a blind tasting of dry pink wines, a classic Tavel wins first prize — but a $4 Spanish rosé races to an upset in third place. *By Mark Bittman*

~32~
Sources and Resources
Where to find products from this issue, plus organic meats, cold-pressed peanut oil, culinary notecards, and the right cooking school.

Cook's Illustrated is published bimonthly by Natural Health Limited Partners, 17 Station Street, Box 1200, Brookline, MA 02147. Application to mail at second class postage rates is pending at Boston, MA and additional mailing offices. Editorial office: 17 Station Street, Box 1200, Brookline, MA 02147 (617) 232-1000, FAX (617) 232-1572. Editorial contributions should be sent to: Editor, *Cook's Illustrated*, 17 Station Street, Brookline, MA 02147. We cannot assume responsibility for manuscripts submitted to us. Submissions will be returned only if accompanied by a large self-addressed stamped envelope. Subscription rates: $24.95 for one year; $45 for two years; $65 for three years. (Canada: add $3 per year; all other foreign add $12 per year.) Postmaster: Send all new orders, subscription inquiries, and change of address notices to *Cook's Illustrated*, P.O. Box 59046, Boulder, CO 80322-9046, or call (303) 447-7330. Single copies: $4 in U.S., $4.95 in Canada and foreign. PRINTED IN THE U.S.A.

EDITORIAL

BREAD IN HALF THE TIME

The history of cooking is also largely the history of convenience. Cooking over open fires was supplanted by the wood stove, which in turn gave way to the gas and electric stoves, complemented by the microwave oven. At each evolutionary stage, cooking has become a little less primitive and a little more a means to an end. But not every convenience wins our heart: when, for example, did you last use an electric knife?

In "How To Make Bread," an article which ran in our charter issue of *Cook's Illustrated,* food editor Pam Anderson reviewed a recipe for No Pain Ordinaire that appears in *Bread In Half the Time* (Crown, 1991). The recipe uses rapid-rise yeast, a food processor, and a microwave oven to make bread in as little as 90 minutes. One of the authors, Linda West Eckhardt, wrote to say that she felt that we were unfairly siding with tradition when in fact this new method was a major-league time-saver that did not sacrifice "quality for convenience." The author pointed to a taste test conducted by Julia Child and her staff, who compared one of Julia's seven-hour French bread recipes with the microwave version and found no discernable difference in texture and taste. As a final commentary, Julia herself invited me over for champagne and caviar and a first-hand demonstration of the No Pain Ordinaire. As she put it, "Some people are so holy about bread. What does it matter as long as it tastes good?"

Following this prodding from Julia, I went home to try it myself. After 90 minutes, I turned out a respectable loaf, with good texture and good flavor. I then made the Master Recipe for Basic Bread (page 24) from our charter issue. Using the food processor for mixing and some kneading, the simple recipe allowed me to turn out an excellent loaf in a little over four hours.

In reality, the No Pain Ordinaire was somewhat more time consuming. It took about 45 minutes of constant attention — the process requires repeated heating and resting in a microwave oven — whereas the more traditional recipe took no more than 20 minutes at the outset; most of the rest of the process was unattended. I will gladly concede the issue of quality — the two loaves were quite similar — but the traditional method was actually more convenient.

Nevertheless, I will add No Pain Ordinaire to my cooking repertoire; there are times when I need a 90-minute bread. Still, when I asked my wife, Adrienne, to comment on the bread-making methods, she dissented, "But I *like* to knead bread." She reminded me of the essential point: quality and convenience are not the only yardsticks for assessing cooking methods.

For many of us, there *is* something "holy" about making bread. The kneading of dough, cooking over an open fire, or spending an afternoon collecting wild blackberries for jam are not always the most "efficient" ways of producing food, but I and many of our readers often choose them. In doing so, we are participating in a kind of modern primitivism that serves as a necessary counterpoint to modern technology. For what is more primitive than preparing food? Although most of us usually have an hour or less to put dinner on the table, the kitchen is a place to which we turn for many other reasons, for a different kind of fulfillment and nourishment. And when we do, we implicitly recognize that cooking is about the process as much as it is about the product. ■

NOTES

FROM READERS

WHAT IS IT?

When I was in my grandmother's house, I found this unusual grater tucked awayin a kitchen cabinet. What is it for?

This device shapes spatzle — thin, pasta-like dumplings common to Alsace, southern Germany, and Switzerland. The name spatzle comes from the German word for "little sparrow" and is thought to refer to the round shape of the noodles, which look somewhat like the small worms birds eat. To use a spatzle machine, set the grater over a pot of simmering salted water and pour the batter (*see* recipe) into the container on top. Slide the container back and forth, forcing small lengths of batter to drop through the holes in the grater and into the water. When the spatzle float (about two to three minutes), the noodles are done and should be retrieved with a slotted spoon. Spatzle can then be sautéed until crisp and used as a garnish for meat or game dishes, or baked au gratin and served as a hearty side dish or even as a simple main course.

BUTTERED SPATZLE

Serves 4

Although a machine cuts more precisely, spatzle batter may be formed by passing it through a ricer or a metal colander.

- 2 eggs, beaten
- ⅓ cup milk or water
- ½ teaspoon salt
- ¼ teaspoon finely ground white pepper
- ⅛ teaspoon grated nutmeg
- 1½ cups flour
- 4 tablespoons room-temperature butter, cut into 6 pieces

1. Beat eggs, milk, and seasonings in a medium bowl. Stir in flour to form a smooth but thick batter; let batter rest for 10 minutes.
2. Meanwhile place 1 tablespoon butter into a bowl that has been rinsed in hot water and dried. Heat water to boil in a kettle or saucepan small enough so that the short ends of the spatzle machine can rest on its rim.
3. Salt boiling water, then spoon a portion of the batter into the the square container that runs along the grater track. With the machine resting on the pan rim, move the metal container quickly back and forth along the grater until about ⅙ of the dough is pressed through the grater into the boiling water.
4. With a slotted spoon transfer spatzle that have floated to the water's surface to the warm bowl. Repeat cooking in batches with remaining batter, adding butter to each batch of cooked spaztle. Toss and serve.

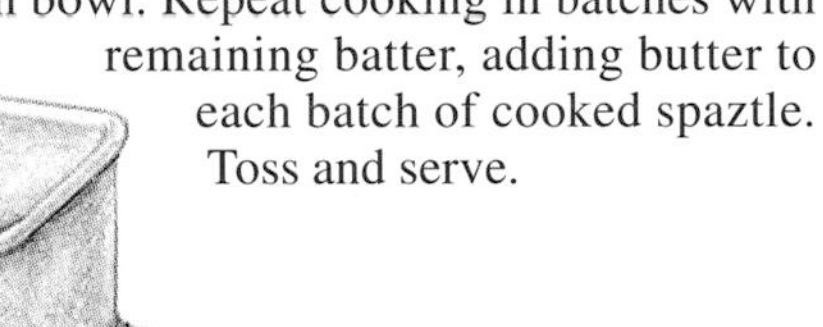

LIGHT OLIVE OIL

I enjoyed reading about olive oils in your charter issue. I was wondering about the light olive oils I see in the supermarket. Do they have fewer calories than other olive oils? How do you rate their taste?

Despite the misleading name, light olive oils are nutritionally equivalent to regular olive oils. Several years ago, in an attempt to overcome the American perception that olive oil is too heavy and too strong for everyday use, several Italian companies began bottling a refined pure olive oil that has been stripped of its flavor. Although not sold in Italy, light olive oils were a hit with American consumers looking for oils high in monounsaturated fat but without much taste. Light olive oils can be used in any recipe that calls for a bland vegetable oil. Note that these olive oils have lost their flavor but not their high cost and often are twice the price of cheaper bland oils like canola which, by current nutritional standards, has a somewhat more desirable ratio of fats.

—Jack Bishop

PEA SHOOTS

I recently saw something called pea shoots at a greengrocer in Chinatown. What are they and how can I prepare them?

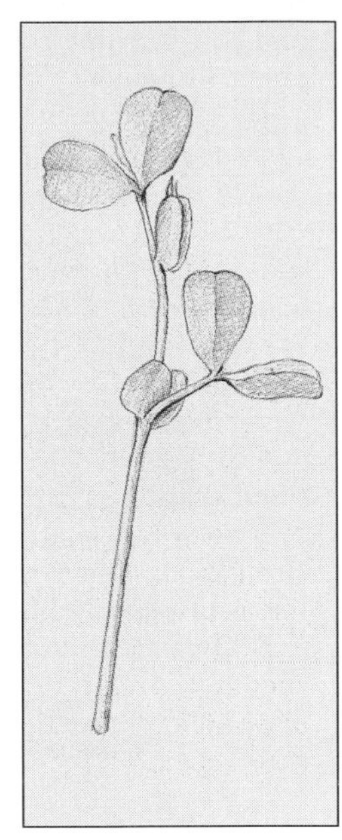

In addition to the peas themselves, the shoots of *Pisum sativum* are edible. Pea shoots (sometimes called pea leaves) are the young crisp stalks and leaves from a snow pea plant. They have a mild pea flavor and can be prepared like other greens. Toss young, tender shoots in salads; sauté, stir-fry, or steep older, crisper shoots in hot liquids. Lynne Aronson, chef/owner at Lola in New York, softens shoots in hot ginger or in a tomato-horseradish broth and uses them as a garnish. She also adds this sproutlike green to seafood dishes (*see* recipe below). Pea shoots occasionally turn up at gourmet markets, but Chinatown (whether in New York, San Francisco, or elsewhere) is a better bet.

—Pam Anderson

LYNNE ARONSON'S SEARED SNAPPER WITH PEA SHOOTS AND COCONUT CURRY SAUCE

Serves 8

Serve this spicy fish with steamed white rice. You can grill the snapper or even sauté it. If you do opt for sautéing and are preparing the full recipe, you'll need at least two pans or you'll have to cook in batches — not an easy last-minute task.

- 3 tablespoons hot chili oil
- 1 tablespoon curry powder
- 3 tablespoons minced ginger (about 1 ounce)
- 2 medium red or green jalapeño chiles, cored, seeded, and minced
- Zest from ½ lime, grated fine
- 1 tomato or ½ cup canned tomatoes, chopped

ILLUSTRATIONS BY KATHY BRAY

- 1 cup unsweetened coconut milk
- ¾ cup chicken stock or low-sodium chicken broth
- 3 tablespoons lime juice from 1 large lime
- Salt and white pepper
- 8 red snapper or other flaky fish fillets (each about 6 ounces)
- 16 long or 1 cup short pea shoots
- ½ cup julienned basil leaves
- ¼ cup snipped chives, plus extra for garnish

1. Heat broiler. Heat 1 tablespoon chili oil in a medium nonreactive saucepan over medium heat. Add curry powder and toast briefly to bring out its flavor. Add ginger, half the chiles, and half the lime zest; sauté to blend flavors, about 1 minute.

2. Add tomatoes, coconut milk, and chicken stock and bring to boil; adjust heat to medium; simmer until sauce is reduced by ⅓ (about 1½ cups), about 10 minutes. Transfer to a blender or food processor; puree until smooth. Strain and return sauce to saucepan. Stir in lime juice and salt and white pepper to taste. Cover and keep warm. (Can refrigerate sauce overnight; warm over low heat before serving.)

4. Place fish fillets, skin side down, on an oiled broiler pan; brush with remaining chili oil and sprinkle with salt and white pepper. Broil about 4 inches from the heat source until fish is just cooked through, 6 to 8 minutes.

5. On each of 8 dinner plates, over an area about the size of the fillets, distribute a portion of pea shoots, basil, and chives, as well as remaining chiles and lime zest.

6. Place a cooked fillet atop each bed of herbs and aromatics. Ladle a portion of sauce (about 3 tablespoons) over each fish fillet. Garnish with additional chives and serve immediately.

Pre-Soaking Vegetables

I have noticed that several Italian cookbooks recommend soaking vegetables before they are cooked. Is this a good idea?

Traditionally, many vegetables — including artichokes, string beans, zucchini, spinach, and carrots — have been soaked by Italian cooks, for two reasons. A generation ago, many vegetables (especially those that grow close to the ground) were covered with dirt when purchased. Today, vegetables are mechanically washed before they reach the supermarket so that a quick rinse under running water at home usually removes any remaining dirt.

Italian cooks also have traditionally soaked vegetables for 20 or 30 minutes to remove harsh mineral flavors imparted by rich soils. It was thought that these minerals hampered digestion and interfered with the vegetables' natural flavors. We now know that water-soluble nutrients like vitamin C and the B vitamins also leech into the water. In order to maximize vitamin intake, skip the soaking step and steam or microwave vegetables instead of blanching them. If you soak or blanch vegetables, reserve the liquid for soups or stocks since it contains more nutrients than plain water.

There are two exceptions to this rule. To prevent discoloration, soak artichokes in acidulated water until ready to be cooked. Also, tubers like potatoes may be briefly soaked in several changes of water to remove excess starch.

—*Jack Bishop*

Roast Chicken Reply

*I have learned virtually everything I know about the science of cooking from Harold McGee's brilliant, eloquent work. Thus I was surprised to find myself taking issue with one aspect of his generally excellent recommendations on the roasting of chicken (*Cook's Illustrated*, no.1).*

It is my view that chicken should be roasted directly on the pan rather than elevated on a rack, as Mr. McGee advises. Assuming that the bird has been tightly trussed and is turned frequently from side to side throughout cooking, roasting directly on the pan ensures that the dark meat, resting on the sizzling-hot pan, will cook at a faster rate than the breast, which, scrunched up in a tight package and partially covered by the wings and legs, will be shielded from the two most intense sources of heat, namely, the pan and the oven roof. I turn the chicken breast side-up only during the last 5 to 10 minutes of cooking, to brown the skin. On all other points Mr. McGee and I are in agreement. I, too, have found that a high oven temperature works best and that frequent basting with butter both helps the skin to brown and keeps the meat moist. To my taste, the chicken is done when the inner part of the thigh, near the joint, reaches a temperature of 170° on an instant-read thermometer; the thickest part of the breast, near the wings, should register around 160° (and not much less, I think, or one runs the risk of lingering salmonella contamination).

As a final note I will add that roasting chicken in a nonstick-coated skillet completely eliminates the problem of sticking skin. A 10-inch skillet will comfortably hold a bird weighing as much as six pounds. And, of course, a skillet proves very convenient to deglaze in the making of an accompanying sauce. ■

— *Stephen Schmidt*

Simple Chicken Trussing

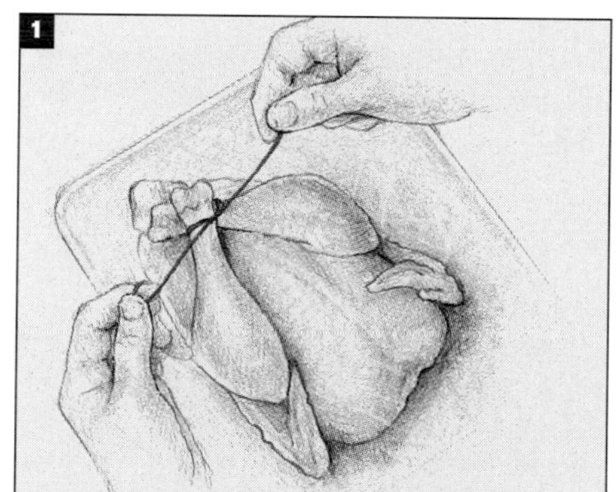

1. With chicken breast up, tie legs together with a 12-inch piece of kitchen twine.

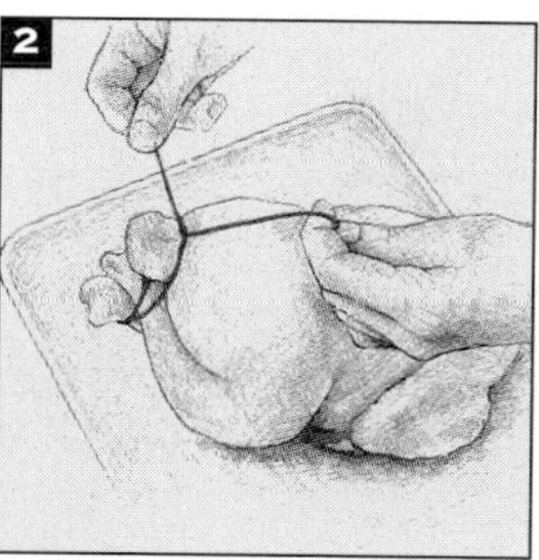

2. Turn chicken back up and tie same piece of twine around pope's nose to secure cavity opening.

3. Run a 24-inch length of twine widthwise around the lower body, pinning wings to body in the process, and twist twine in a cross shape as if tying a gift package.

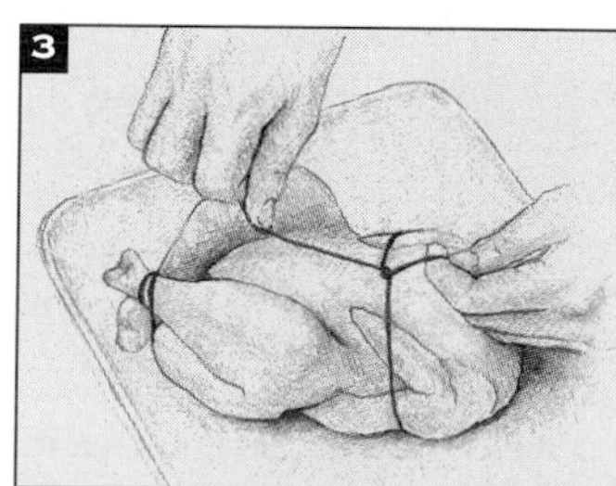

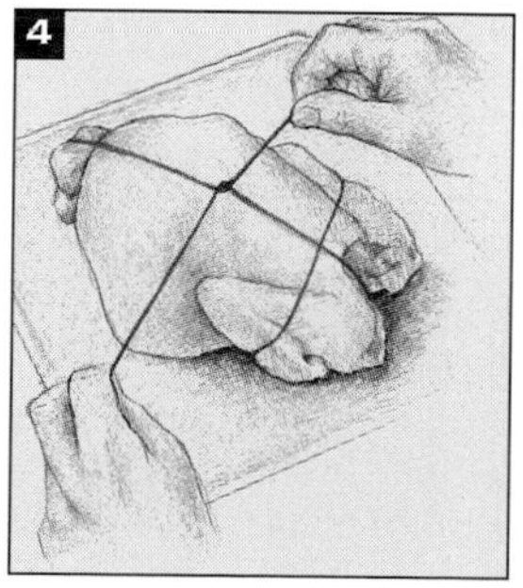

4. Run remaining length of twine completely around chicken body lengthwise, turning bird over during the process, then tie securely.

5. Place trussed chicken on its side in a rackless roasting pan for roasting.

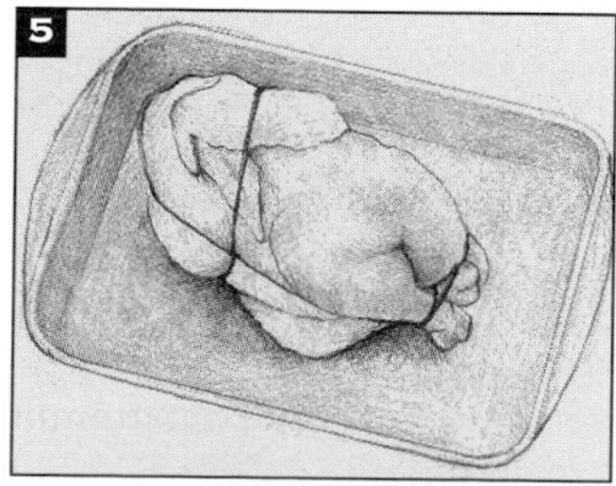

Quick Tips

Sizing a Parchment Paper Liner

Lining a tube pan or ring mold with parchment paper is easy once you know how. To start, cut a square of parchment paper with edges longer than the diameter of the tube pan.

1. Fold the parchment square in half to form a triangle with two equal sides. Make sure that one of the open sides of the triangle faces you. Fold the top right corner of the triangle over to the bottom left corner.

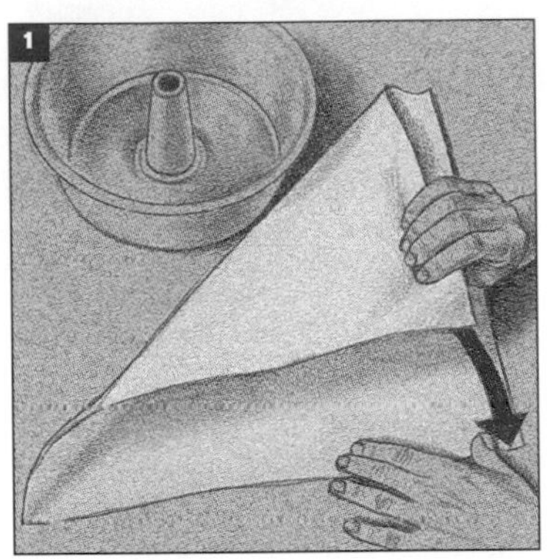

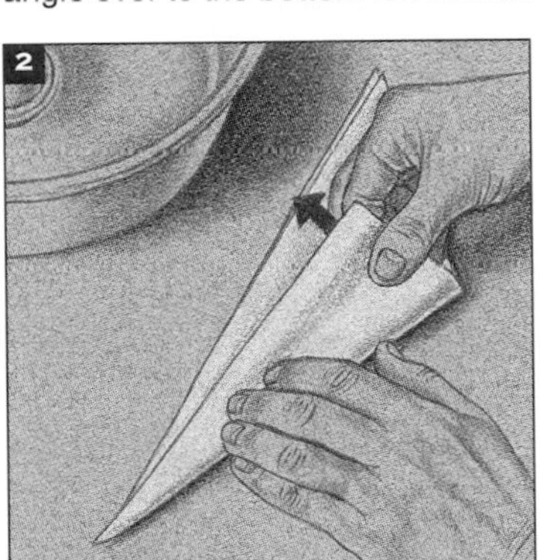

2. Rotate the triangle so that the side with two folded sheets faces you. (The other sides have one fold and four open sheets.) Fold about ½ inch of the bottom side of the triangle towards the top. The left side of the triangle should remain pointed, while the right side is jagged. Fold several more times until the bottom of the triangle reaches the top. The parchment should look like a paper airplane.

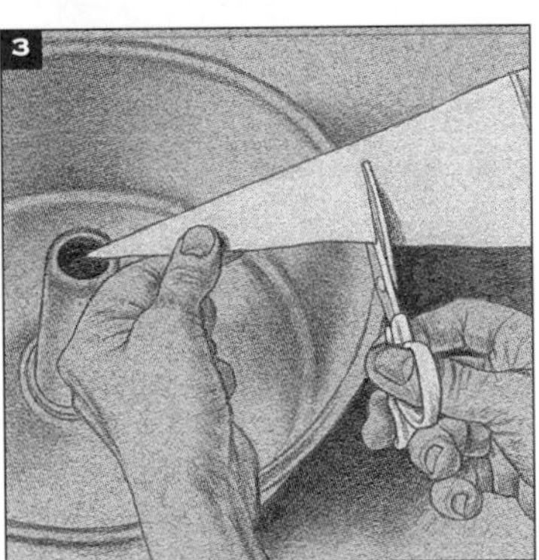

3. Place the narrow point of the folded paper over the middle of the tube. Trim the triangle along the inside edge of the pan.

4. With the base of the triangle flush against the edge of the pan, snip the top of the triangle so that it is even with the outside bottom of the tube.

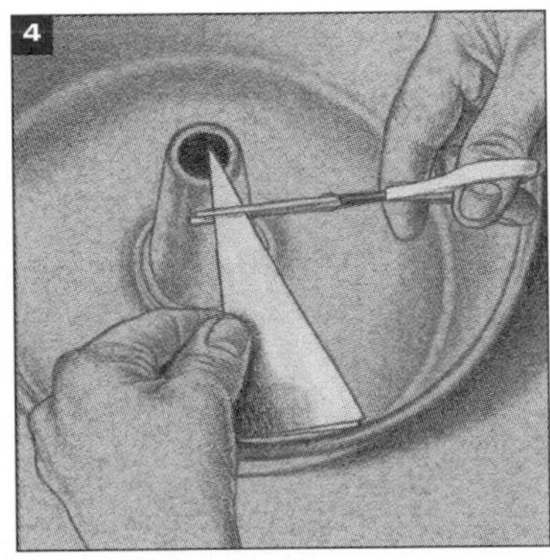

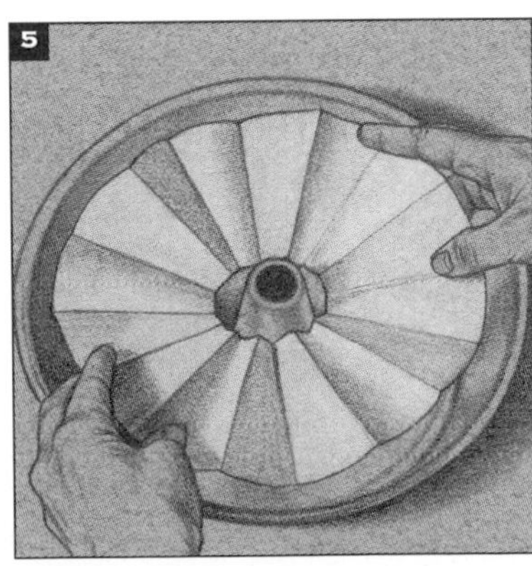

5. Unfold the triangle and lay it over the bottom of the pan.

Stringing Rhubarb

The stringy, outside layer should be removed from a rhubarb stalk before cooking. Start by cutting away and discarding the toxic leaves and trimming both ends of the stalk.

1. Partially slice a thin disk from the bottom of the rhubarb; do not cut all the way through the stalk. Gently pull the partially attached piece of rhubarb away from the stalk.

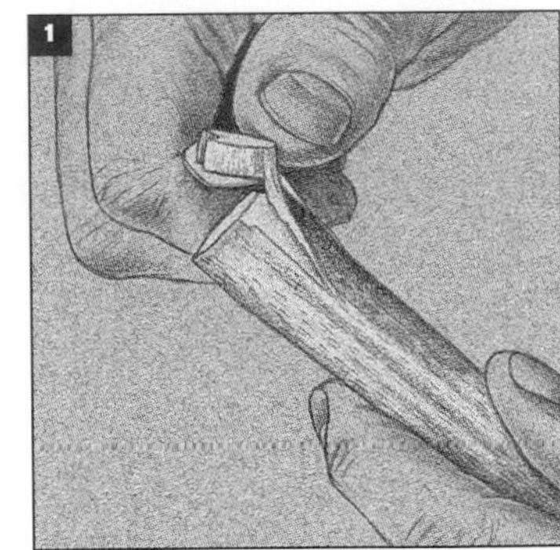

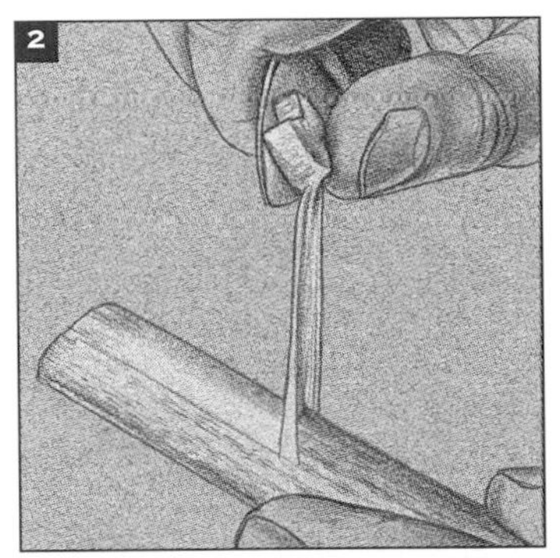

2. Holding tight to the small disk, pull back the outer peel and discard. Make a second cut partially through the bottom of the stalk in the reverse direction. Pull back the peel on the other side of the stalk and discard.

Trimming Bell Peppers

To make bell peppers more attractive, trim away the thin, semi-translucent, almost tasteless layer of flesh that lines the inside. This technique also removes the white pith and the seeds. After it has been cleaned and trimmed, julienne the pepper and use the strips in salads, stir-fries, or sautés.

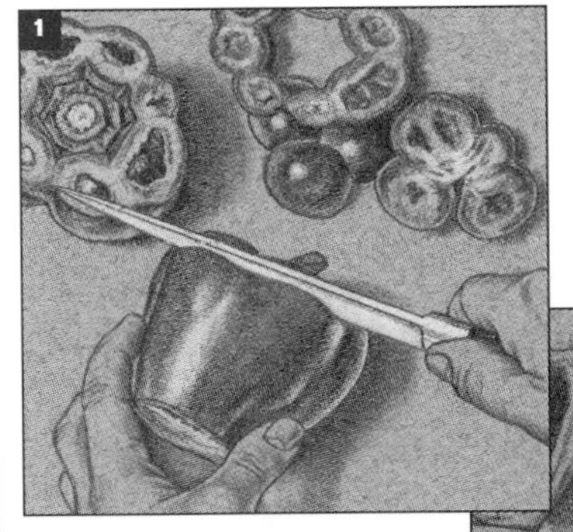

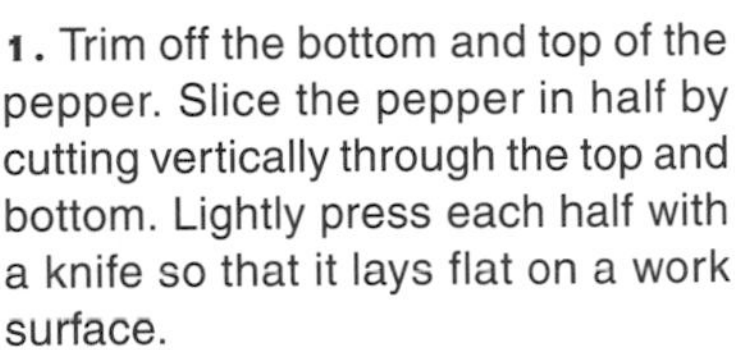

1. Trim off the bottom and top of the pepper. Slice the pepper in half by cutting vertically through the top and bottom. Lightly press each half with a knife so that it lays flat on a work surface.

2. Taking one half at a time, slide knife along the inside of the pepper and cut away the white pith, the seeds, and the top layer of semi-translucent flesh.

ILLUSTRATIONS BY ALAN WITSCHONKE

Trimming and Coring Artichokes

1. Use a paring knife to cut off the stem of each artichoke, then cut off the top third of each leaf with scissors.

2. After the artichokes are cooked and have cooled to room temperature, take hold of the leaves in the center of the artichoke and pull them out as a single clump.

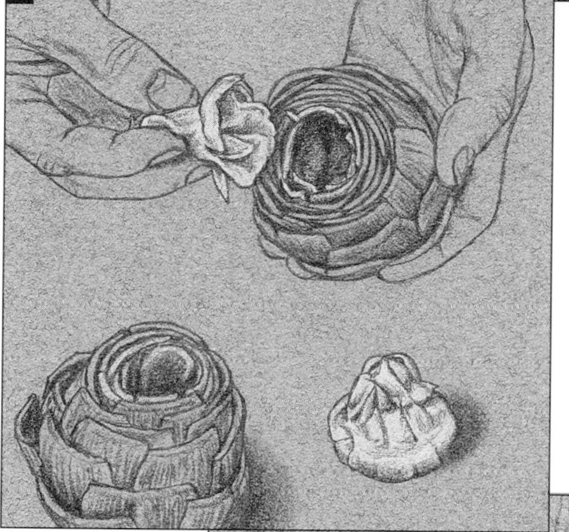

3. Remove the choke (the hairy material at the base of the artichoke) with a spoon.

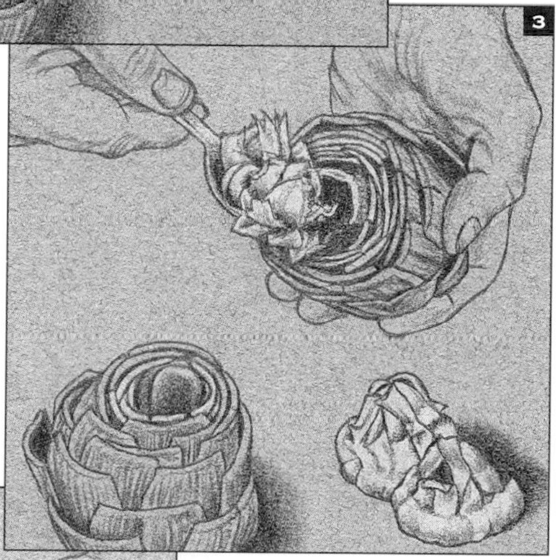

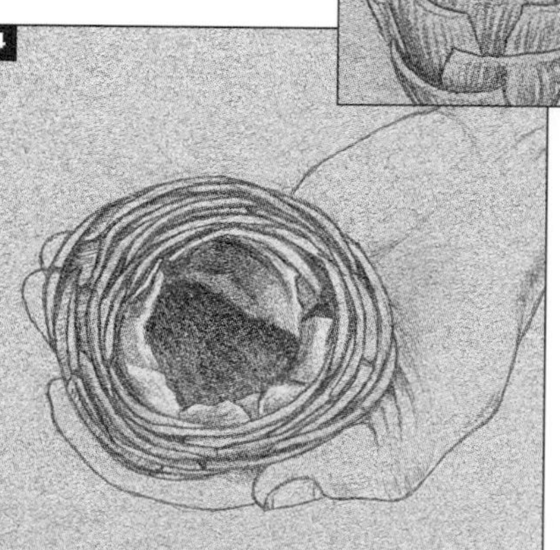

4. This will leave a clean, hollow core which can be easily stuffed.

Male vs. Female Eggplant

Male eggplants have fewer seeds and are less likely to be bitter than female eggplants. Look at the bottom of an eggplant to determine its gender. In specific, examine the small spot where the eggplant was once attached to its flower.

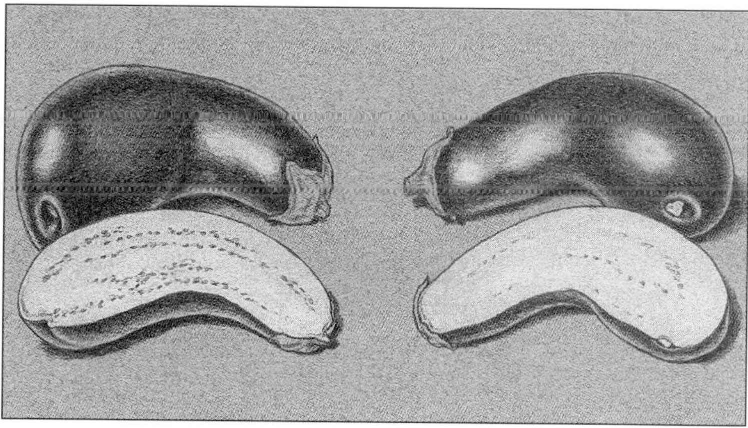

LEFT: A female eggplant has a small indentation on the bottom that looks like a belly button. The female has many seeds inside, especially if it is large and mature. **RIGHT:** The stem spot on a male eggplant is much shallower and in some cases may be flat. It looks more like a scar than a belly button. The male has few if any seeds.

Grating Lemon Peel

When any citrus fruit is scraped across a metal grater, much of the peel ends up stuck between the grater's holes. To avoid this, lay a piece of parchment paper over the grater; the paper acts as a barrier and prevents any peel from becoming lodged between the holes. When grating citrus, do not grate the bitter white pith. ■

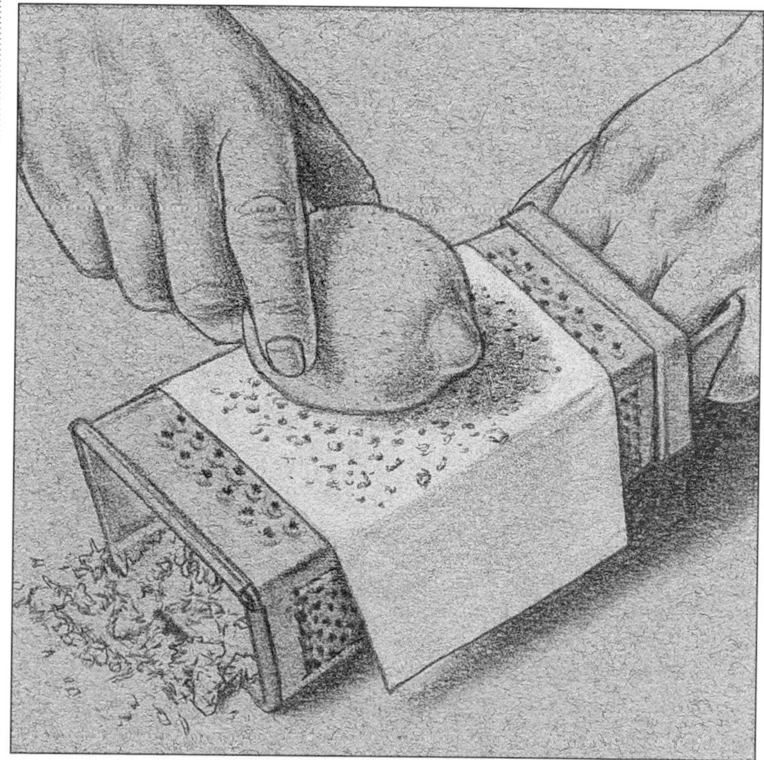

How to Cook Asparagus

Three techniques — boiling, steaming, and microwaving — are compared to determine the best and easiest method of preparing perfectly cooked asparagus.

BY STEPHANIE LYNESS

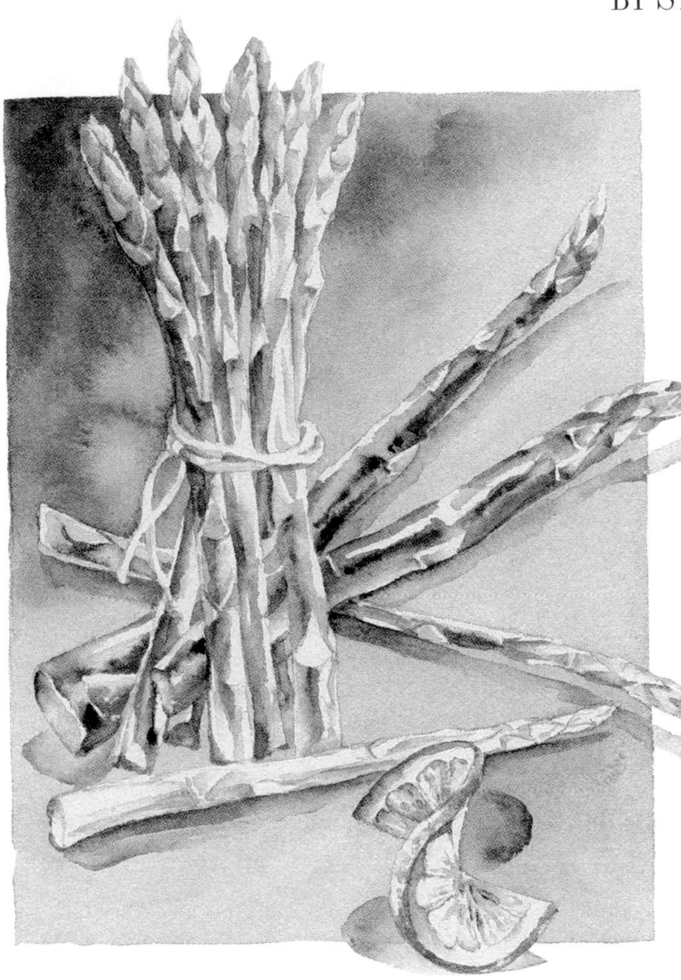

Each asparagus plant produces shoots of various sizes; fat shoots are already large when they emerge from the ground, slender shoots do not grow fatter with age. White asparagus is harvested before it emerges from the ground.

Asparagus provokes a certain fanaticism among chefs and cooks of all persuasions. Everyone, it seems, knows the best way to treat it. I learned to prepare asparagus the French way: break off the ends, peel the spears, tie them into neat bundles with kitchen twine, and cook them in boiling salted water until very tender. As the years went by, I stopped peeling and bundling, but it wasn't until I started teaching at a French cooking school that I began to wonder what is *really* the best way to cook asparagus.

To find out, I ran a number of kitchen tests using the three cooking methods most useful for the home cook — blanching, steaming, and microwaving. Using each method, I cooked both peeled and unpeeled samples of three different sizes of green asparagus — pencil-thin, small-to-medium, and medium-large — and medium-sized white asparagus (harvested before the spear emerges from the ground). In each case, I compared ease of cooking as well as the quality of color, taste, and texture of the cooked asparagus.

Steaming Takes the Lead

I rejected microwave cooking early in the process, because it shriveled and dried out the asparagus. This left blanching and steaming as the competitors. These two methods gave very comparable results for unpeeled asparagus. When I tested peeled asparagus, however, I found that blanching made it watery in both texture and flavor. Steaming is therefore the more desirable technique for peeled asparagus.

There are other advantages to steaming as well: it is faster than blanching because you need to heat less water; fewer nutrients are lost in the cooking; and you need not bundle the asparagus, because you simply remove the entire steaming compartment from the pot. The one advantage to blanching over steaming is that the asparagus is seasoned as it cooks in the salted water.

To Peel or Not to Peel?

My taste comparisons of peeled versus unpeeled asparagus were less conclusive. Even when steamed, peeled asparagus is less flavorful than unpeeled, but it has a more consistently luscious mouth-feel. Unpeeled offers a lovely contrast between tender peel and juicy flesh, but there is less waste with peeled. This results from the fact that, while it is necessary to snap the stalk of unpeeled asparagus to remove the fibrous end, once the asparagus has been peeled a mere half-inch trimmed off the end will suffice.

Since the pros and cons seem about equal, and peeling involves additional effort, I have concluded that it is worth peeling only when the asparagus is large and fibrous, or when you want an especially elegant presentation.

Versatile Serving Styles

Asparagus is a very versatile vegetable — it is delicious served hot, cold, or at room temperature. If you plan to serve it cold, refresh the spears in a bowl of ice water immediately after removing them from the steamer, then drain on a clean towel.

Melted butter, lemon juice, brown butter, or a mustardy, red wine vinegar and olive oil vinaigrette make excellent accompaniments to asparagus served at any temperature. Thinly sliced shallots, or chopped thyme, tarragon, parsley, or chives also make tasty additions to the vinaigrette. Or you might want to drizzle the asparagus with melted butter and sprinkle it with fresh bread crumbs that have been sautéed in butter and seasoned with one of the herbs above. Sieved egg (some cooks use just the yolk), crumbled bacon or pancetta, or thinly sliced ham are also good accompaniments.

Asparagus stems will snap off in just the right spot if you hold them the right way: hold the asparagus about halfway down the stalk; with the other hand, hold the cut end between the thumb and index finger about an inch or so up

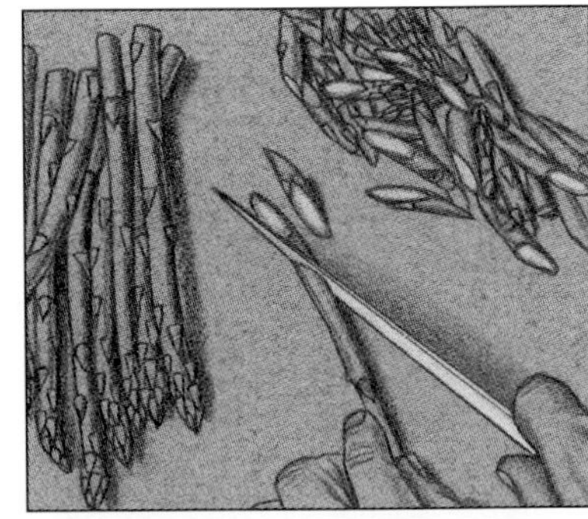

To roll-cut asparagus, roll the spear ¼ turn away from you and cut with blade at 30-degree angle; repeat for entire spear.

ILLUSTRATION (LEFT) BY JOYCE STIGLICH (ABOVE) BY ALAN WITSCHONKE

Selecting the Best Asparagus

Seasonality: Once a seasonal vegetable, asparagus has become a year-round delicacy, with crops from California and the northwestern United States, New Zealand, Mexico, and South America extending the season. Kevin Murphy, owner of Baldor, a specialty food purveyor in the New York area, has found that the quality of California, Washington, and New Zealand asparagus is the best.

Size: Each asparagus plant produces a range of spears of distinct size — fat asparagus shoots are already large when they emerge from the ground, and slender shoots do not increase in size as they age. Cooks' opinions vary wildly as to the most desirable size for green asparagus spears. Alfred Portale, chef at Gotham Bar and Grill and at One Fifth Avenue in New York, buys the biggest ones he can find. Others prefer medium, saying it tastes best and looks most attractive on the plate. Still others believe that the skinny pencil asparagus has the sweetest taste. Throughout my testing, I tasted to determine whether there were differences in taste between sizes. I found no significant differences, although I did find the larger size more luscious.

Age: Age affects the flavor of asparagus enormously. As asparagus becomes older it loses moisture and sweetness, causing it to shrivel, toughen, and become bitter. When buying asparagus, select spears that are bright green, firm, and crisp, with tightly closed tips. Store it either in an unsealed plastic bag (the tips will rot if they are damp) in the crisper, or like flowers, stems trimmed and standing in a bowl of water.

the stalk; bend the stalk until it snaps. Discard stem ends or save them for a kettle of asparagus soup.

MASTER RECIPE FOR STEAMED ASPARAGUS

Serves 4

To steam asparagus, all you need is a collapsible steamer basket (even a wire cooling rack will do, as long as it fits into the steaming vessel) and a pot with a lid — a large sauté pan, a soup kettle, or a roasting pan with a makeshift tinfoil lid are all possibilities. Just keep the asparagus above the water level and keep the pot covered. You may also use a bamboo steamer and a wok, but add a few minutes to the cooking time.

- 1½ pounds medium asparagus, rinsed and ends snapped

1. Bring 1 inch water to boil in a soup kettle. Put asparagus in steamer basket then carefully place steamer basket in kettle; cover and steam over medium-high heat until asparagus spears bend slightly when picked up and flesh at cut end yields when squeezed, 4 to 5 minutes for asparagus under ½ inch in diameter, 5 to 6 minutes for the jumbo size.
2. Drain and serve asparagus immediately with suggested accompaniments or plunge spears immediately into ice water to stop the cooking process. (You may cover and refrigerate cooled and drained asparagus overnight.)

ALFRED PORTALE'S JUMBO ASPARAGUS SALAD WITH PARMA HAM, PARMESAN, AND LEMON VINAIGRETTE

Serves 4

Even though Portale peels, bundles, and cooks his asparagus in boiling water, I still prefer the steaming method, even for the jumbos. After peeling these super spears, just follow the Master Recipe for Steamed Asparagus. Of course, large or even medium asparagus can be substituted.

Vinaigrette:

- 3 tablespoons juice and 2 teaspoons zest from 1 medium lemon
- 1 tablespoon sherry wine vinegar
- Salt and ground white pepper
- ¾ cup extra virgin olive oil

- 2 shallots, minced
- 1 teaspoon minced thyme
- 1 pound jumbo asparagus (about 12 spears), peeled, steamed, and chilled
- 1½ pounds small new potatoes, boiled until tender and sliced thick
- 2 tablespoons minced fresh chives
- 12 very thin slices prosciutto de Parma or other cured ham (about 6 ounces)
- 1 quart mixed baby or regular lettuces, rinsed, dried, and torn into bite-size pieces
- 1 piece Reggiano parmesan cheese for shaving
- 2 hard-boiled eggs, whites and yolks separated and pressed through a fine sieve

1. Mix lemon juice, zest, vinegar, and salt and pepper to taste in a medium bowl. Whisk in olive oil and set aside.
2. In a medium bowl, combine the shallots, thyme, asparagus, sliced potatoes, and 1 tablespoon chives. Add ¼ cup vinaigrette; toss to coat. Season to taste with salt and pepper.
3. Arrange asparagus-potato mixture with the prosciutto alongside it on 4 large serving plates. Dress lettuces with another ¼ cup vinaigrette, and arrange a portion on each plate. Use a vegetable peeler to shave parmesan curls over each salad. Sprinkle each with sieved egg and remaining chives; serve immediately with remaining dressing passed separately.

GRILLED ASPARAGUS

Serves 4

For really great-tasting asparagus you should grill it over charcoal or wood. A gas grill will do in a pinch but, unfortunately, a broiler doesn't do the trick.

- 1½ pounds asparagus, snapped and steamed, but slightly undercooked
- 1 tablespoon olive oil
- Salt and ground black pepper

1. Heat grill. Toss asparagus in oil, sprinkle with salt and pepper.
2. Grill asparagus until marked, about 2 minutes on each side. Serve hot or at room temperature, unadorned or with a vinaigrette.

THAI-STYLE ASPARAGUS WITH CHILES, GARLIC, AND BASIL

Serves 4

Adapted from a recipe by Nancie McDermott (author of *Real Thai*, Chronicle Books, 1992), this Asian-style side dish needs only simple grilled chicken or fish and steamed rice to round out its full flavors.

- 1 tablespoon vegetable oil
- 1 tablespoon minced garlic
- 1 tablespoon minced serrano or jalapeño chile
- 1½ pounds asparagus, snapped and steamed, but slightly undercooked
- 2 tablespoons soy or fish sauce
- 1 teaspoon dark soy sauce (optional)
- 1 tablespoon water
- 1 tablespoon sugar
- 1 cup chopped basil
- 3 large chiles of your choice, sliced on the diagonal into thin ovals, or 9 thin strips cut from a red bell pepper

1. Heat a wok or large, deep skillet over high heat. Add oil and swirl to coat surface.
2. Add garlic and minced chile; toss until garlic begins to turn golden, about 15 seconds.
3. Add the asparagus; stir-fry until coated with oil, about 15 seconds.
4. Add soy sauces and 1 tablespoon water; stir-fry until liquid almost evaporates, about 30 seconds.
5. Add sugar; stir-fry another 30 seconds. Add the basil and sliced chiles; stir-fry until basil wilts. Serve hot or at room temperature. ■

Stephanie Lyness, a freelance food writer and cooking teacher living in New York City, is at work on a translation of a French book about steamed food, to be published by William Morrow.

Grilling Pizza

Grilling pizza in the backyard produces an extraordinarily crisp dough and makes easy summer appetizers.

BY STEVE JOHNSON

I have long believed that, for flavor and texture, the best pizzas are made in wood-fired ovens. However, while a few restaurants are equipped with wood-fired ovens, it's safe to say that few homes are. So I've experimented with a number of restaurant techniques to develop a method for getting the taste of flame-cooked pizza at home using your grill, whether the fuel is charcoal, briquettes, wood, or even gas.

A good pizza can be made in your oven, but cooking over direct flame makes a tremendous difference in taste, and also allows you to get two crisp sides rather than just one. If you're planning to grill anyway, it takes little effort to make a few rounds of pizza for appetizers; once the dough is cooked, these can be finished on the grill or in the oven.

Since dough is the heart and soul of a good pizza, I've developed a dough that is not only easy to make and handle, but is also crunchy and, like a focaccia, has built-in flavor. You can also use the same dough, and essentially the same cooking technique, to make calzones.

Steve Johnson, pictured here in the kitchen of Hammersley's Bistro in Boston, Massachusetts, cites the 'aroma factor' as an important asset of wood grilling.

The Dough

Pizza dough, like bread dough, can be made with four ingredients: water, flour, salt, and yeast. But standard bread dough, which is smooth and silky, didn't give me the crunch I wanted from a pizza crust. So I began experimenting with adding other flours. The best addition turns out to be cornmeal, which is coarse, sweet, and crunchy. But it must be added in small amounts, or it changes the texture of the crust radically, making it much too crumbly.

I also found that adding olive oil not only creates a richer-tasting crust, it also makes the dough more forgiving during handling and less fragile during grilling. Without oil, the crust is too dry, has a tendency to scorch more quickly, and becomes brittle during cooking. Finally, scenting the olive oil with aromatics improves the flavor of the crust, which becomes permeated with garlic, herbs, salt, pepper, or whatever else you choose to add to it. In fact, this dough is delicious with no topping at all.

You can, of course, use store-bought dough, with good results — it's easy to handle and grills well. But the flavor is far inferior to that of homemade dough, even those not accented by olive oil and aromatics. Since dough takes no more than 15 minutes to make by machine or hand, is absolutely foolproof, and can be frozen for weeks with no deterioration in quality, there is little reason to rely on store-bought product.

You can make your dough in the morning or, if the weather is warm, in the late afternoon. I often make a batch while I'm cooking something else, then wrap individual balls of dough in plastic wrap and toss them in the freezer. I like to make small pizzas so I can serve a variety of toppings at a single sitting, and also because they're easier to handle. These little balls of dough will defrost in a couple of hours in warm weather.

How to Grill

Wood-fired grilling is impractical for most of us, so I tested charcoal and gas. I found that hardwood charcoal is best, because it is reliably hot and adds good flavor. But briquettes and gas grills both work well.

You want a medium-hot fire, which toasts the crust quickly, giving you a crisp but still-chewy pizza. When the coals are red hot and there is no flame left, spread them out, clean the grill, and set it in place to heat up. The heat source should be four inches under the grill — if the fire is too hot, your pizzas will burn; if it's too cool, they'll puff up without becoming crisp, and will remain doughy inside. The perfect fire toasts and lightly chars the circles as they cook through. To test the temperature, put your hand five inches above the grill surface: if you can hold it there for three to four seconds, your fire is about the right temperature.

Before grilling each circle, brush it lightly with olive oil and sprinkle it with salt. This is a fast process; the right size fire cooks the dough in less than a minute per side, and you'll probably be able to fit two circles at once on your grill. Plan to stay nearby and keep alert.

When to Top?

This is a question that has been solemnly addressed by the country's pizza-grilling experts. George Germon, chef and owner of the Providence, Rhode Island restaurant Al Forno — a grilled pizza mecca — builds two separate fires on his home grill, dividing them with a line of bricks. Over the hot fire, he grills the circles; over the cooler one, he finishes the pizzas. The lower heat warms the toppings without burning the crust.

There are at least three other ways to tackle this problem. With a gas grill, you can grill the circles over high heat then, when you remove them to add the toppings, lower the heat and complete the cooking.

You can also pre-grill the pizzas over a wood or charcoal fire, let the fire die down as you top the pizzas off the grill, then finish grilling with toppings on.

Perhaps the simplest method combines char-grilled flavor with the convenience of pre-cooking. Grill the pizza circles in advance — as early as 5:00 P.M. for an eight o'clock dinner — then stack the cooked circles in an out-of-the-way spot in the kitchen. When you're ready to cook, turn on the broiler, top the circles one at a time, and run them under the broiler for a minute or so, just long enough to heat the toppings and re-crisp the crust.

MASTER RECIPE FOR GARLIC-HERB PIZZA CRUST

Makes 8 7-inch dough rounds

This dough can be kneaded by any of the usual methods and shaped into rounds as small or as large as you like.

PHOTOGRAPH BY BOB KRAMER

6 tablespoons virgin olive oil
1 tablespoon minced garlic
½ teaspoon *herbes de Provence*
1 teaspoon ground black pepper
1¼ cups water
1 package dry active yeast
1 teaspoon sugar
3 cups bread flour
¼ cup cornmeal
2 teaspoons salt, plus extra for sprinkling

1. Heat 2 tablespoons oil in a small skillet; add next 3 ingredients and cook over low heat until garlic softens, about 5 minutes. Cool.

2. Sprinkle yeast and sugar over ¼ cup warm water and let stand until yeast starts to swell, about 5 minutes. Mix flour, cornmeal, and salt in a food processor. Add 1 cup cool water and herb oil to yeast mixture. With machine on, gradually pour liquid into dry ingredients; process until a rough ball forms. If dough is too sticky or dry, add flour or water, 1 tablespoon at a time. Let dough rest for 5 minutes, then continue to process until dough is smooth, about 35 seconds.

3. Knead dough by hand a few seconds to form smooth, round ball; place in a lightly oiled bowl, cover with a damp cloth and let rise until dough doubles in size, about 2 hours.

4. Punch dough down and divide into 8 equal pieces. Roll each portion to form a smooth, round ball. Place the balls on a lightly floured surface, cover with a damp cloth, and let rest until they puff slightly, about 30 minutes.

5. Heat grill. Roll each dough ball into a 7-inch round, flouring work surface and dough as necessary. Place on a floured cookie sheet; sprinkle top with flour. Stack the rounds in groups of four.

6. Brush tops of 4 dough rounds with some of remaining olive oil, then sprinkle each with salt. Grill oil side down, covered, until dark brown grill marks appear, 1 to 1½ minutes. Burst any bubbles that develop. Brush dough tops with oil, then flip. (If topping pizzas at this point, quickly arrange a portion of toppings over each pizza round; cover and grill until pizza bottoms are crisp and browned, 2 to 3 minutes; serve immediately and repeat process with remaining rounds.) Grill until bottoms are brown, about 2 minutes longer. Repeat with remaining dough circles. (Can cover and store at room temperature up to 6 hours.)

7. If topping pizzas at this point, place pizza rounds on a cookie sheet, arrange a portion of toppings over each round, and broil until toppings sizzle and cheese melts, 1 to 2 minutes. Serve immediately.

ROASTED TOMATO TOPPING WITH FENNEL AND ASIAGO

Serves 4 as a main course or 8 as a first course

3 tablespoons virgin olive oil, plus extra for drizzling
1 large Spanish onion (about 1¼ pounds), halved and sliced thin
1 medium fennel bulb (about 1 pound), sliced thin
4 large garlic cloves, minced
1 tablespoon fresh thyme, or 1 teaspoon dried
1 teaspoon fennel seeds
¼ teaspoon red pepper flakes

Roasted Tomatoes
12 small plum tomatoes, halved lengthwise
3 tablespoons virgin olive oil
Salt and ground black pepper

½ cup grated Asiago cheese (about 1 ounce)
8 7-inch pizza rounds, on the grill and ready for toppings, or fully cooked (*see* Master Recipe for Garlic-Herb Pizza Crust)

1. Heat 3 tablespoons oil in a large sauté pan over medium-high heat. Add onion and fennel; sauté until vegetables soften, about 8 minutes. Add garlic; sauté until garlic softens, about 2 minutes. Stir in thyme, fennel, and red pepper flakes; season to taste with salt and pepper and set aside. (Can cover and refrigerate overnight.)

2. Heat oven to 375° or heat grill. If roasting tomatoes in oven, place tomato halves in a roasting pan, brush with remaining oil and sprinkle with salt and pepper; roast until tomatoes are just tender, 20 to 30 minutes. If grilling, place oiled and seasoned tomatoes, cut side down, on grill; grill until marked, about 5 minutes. Turn tomatoes cut side up; grill until just tender, 7 to 10 minutes. (Can set aside at room temperature up to 6 hours ahead.)

3. Following steps 6 and/or 7 of Master Recipe, spread a portion of onion-fennel mixture over each pizza round. Top each with 3 tomato halves and sprinkle with cheese. Drizzle with olive oil and proceed with cooking.

GRILLED SHRIMP TOPPING WITH ROASTED TOMATOES AND FARMER'S CHEESE

Serves 4 as a main course or 8 as a first course

48 large unpeeled shrimp (about 2 pounds)
3 tablespoons olive oil, plus extra for drizzling
1 teaspoon hot chili powder
¼ teaspoon cayenne pepper
Salt and ground black pepper
1 recipe Roasted Tomatoes (*see* Roasted Tomato Topping with Fennel and Asiago)
8 ounces farmer's cheese, crumbled
⅔ cup packed cilantro leaves, minced
⅔ cup packed parsley leaves, minced
8 7-inch pizza rounds, on the grill and ready for toppings, or fully cooked (*see* Master Recipe for Garlic-Herb Pizza Crust)

1. Heat grill. Toss shrimp with 3 tablespoons oil, chili powder, cayenne, and salt and pepper. Grill over medium-high heat until shrimp just turn opaque, 5 to 7 minutes. Cool slightly, peel, and set aside.

2. Following steps 6 and/or 7 of Master Recipe, arrange a portion of shrimp and tomatoes over pizza rounds. Sprinkle each with a portion of cheese, cilantro, and parsley. Drizzle with oil, sprinkle with salt and pepper, and proceed with cooking. ■

Steve Johnson is sous-chef at Hamersley's Bistro in Boston, Massachusetts.

SIMPLE TOPPINGS

Throughout Italy, you'll find pies served with a minimum of flavorings and toppings — perhaps a couple of pieces of tomato, or a few sliced mushrooms with some olive oil. Americans prefer heftier toppings; therefore I suggest you use an average of about five cups of topping for each batch of six nine-inch pies. Here are some suggestions to get you started:

Sauté sliced onion with portabello mushrooms, garlic, and fresh thyme, finishing the topping with a drizzle of olive oil and a sprinkling of salt and pepper.

Sauté onion, fennel, and garlic, mixed with canned or slow-grilled fresh plum tomatoes. Add salt, pepper, fennel seed, and crushed red pepper at the last minute.

Sauté onion with julienne of sun-dried tomato. Add crumbled goat cheese and fresh marjoram.

Mix pureed white beans with sautéed fennel, chopped anchovy, and fresh basil.

Mix pureed white beans with crisp-cooked pancetta or bacon, fresh sage, and grated pecorino romano.

Mix a fresh tomato sauce with some sausage slices and a couple of grated cheeses, such as fontina and pecorino romano.

Grill shrimp and mix bits of it with your favorite tomatillo salsa and chopped fresh cilantro.

Slice fresh tomatoes and top with basil, olive oil, salt, pepper, and grated parmesan.

The Art of Biscuit-Making

Biscuits can be soft and fluffy or flaky and high-rising. Each type requires surprisingly different ingredients and techniques.

BY STEPHEN SCHMIDT

***The type of flour and fat used, as well as the shaping technique, are key factors in determining whether biscuits turn out fluffy* (left) *or flaky* (right).**

While many people think of "biscuits" as a single category, there are actually two distinct varieties — soft, fluffy mounds and flaky, high-rising cylinders. If you know which type you prefer, it is easy to tailor your ingredients and cooking method to produce it.

Key Ingredients

The *flour* you begin with has a great effect on the biscuit you end up with. The main factor here is the proportion of starch to protein in the flour. Starchy, or "soft," flour encourages a tender, cakelike texture, while high-protein, "strong" flour promotes crisper, chewier results (*see* "How Much Protein Is in My Flour?" below).

This means that, for fluffy biscuits, you should use a soft flour, such as White Lily brand (favored for biscuit-making throughout the South), or a blend of low-protein, all-purpose flour, such as Gold Medal brand, and plain cake flour, which is extremely soft. For flaky biscuits, on the other hand, you need dough with a lot of structure to produce a multilayered, well-defined shape, so strong flour is called for. You can use all-purpose, but for the best results use a high-protein brand, such as Hecker's or King Arthur, or combine relatively soft Gold Medal all-purpose with bread flour, which is very strong.

Fat also plays an important role, since it makes biscuits (and other pastries) more tender, moist, smooth, and tasty. Butter, of course, delivers the best flavor, but lard and shortening make for more tender biscuits, so you have to balance these two factors, again depending on the type of biscuit you want. Since flaky biscuits are handled a fair amount — handling activates gluten and makes a potentially less tender product — I use two parts butter (for flavor) to one part shortening or lard (for texture). For fluffy biscuits, which are handled less during preparation, you can use all butter without too much worry about the texture.

Generally, I have found that a proportion of one-half cup fat to two cups of flour provides the best balance of tenderness and richness to structure. If you use less fat, your biscuits will rise well but will be tough and dry. If you use more, your biscuits will have a lovely texture but they may end up a bit squat.

The Mixing Technique

After mixing flour and leavening, you must "rub" the fat into the dry ingredients, making a dry, coarse mixture akin to large bread crumbs or rolled oats, with some slightly bigger lumps mixed in. This rubbing may seem unimportant, but in fact it is crucial to proper rising of the biscuits. Gas released by the leavening during baking must have a space in which to collect; if the texture of the dough is homogeneous, the gas will simply dissipate. Melting fat particles create convenient spaces in which the gas can collect, form a bubble, and produce rising. Proper rubbing breaks the fat into tiny bits and disperses it throughout the dough. As the fat melts during baking, its place is taken up by gas and steam, which expand and push the dough up. The wider the dispersal of the fat, the more even the rising of the dough.

If, however, the fat softens and binds with the dry ingredients during rubbing, it forms a pasty goo, the spaces collapse, and the biscuits become leaden. To produce light, airy biscuits, the fat must remain cold and firm, which means rubbing must be deft and quick. Traditionally, biscuit-makers pinch the cut-up fat into the dry ingredients, using only their fingertips — never the whole hand, which is too hot — and pinch hard and fast, practically flinging the little bits of flour and fat into the bowl after each pinch. Less experienced cooks turned to using two knives, scraped in opposite directions, or a bow-shaped pastry blender. Now, however, there is no reason not to use the food processor for this task: pulsing the dry ingredients and fat is fast and almost foolproof.

After cutting in the fat, liquid is added and the dough is stirred, just until the ingredients

Fluffy biscuit dough is too soft to roll and cut easily, so it is best formed by gently batting back and forth, then patting lightly with cupped hands.

HOW MUCH PROTEIN IS IN MY FLOUR?

All you have to do to determine the protein content of any flour is read the side panel on the bag or box. Cake flour, the softest kind, has around eight grams of protein in every four ounces of flour; bread flour, the hardest, contains around 20. All-purpose flours generally range from 11 grams of protein per four ounces (though some southern brands have even less) to 14. If you stock plain (not self-rising) cake flour, plus a low-gluten all-purpose flour such as Gold Medal, plus bread flour, you can always make the perfect blend for biscuits or any other recipes requiring specific types of flour.

ILLUSTRATIONS BY KATHY BRAY

are bound, using a light hand so the gluten will not become activated. Flaky biscuits can be challenging at this point: If the dough is even a bit too dry and firm, the biscuits will fail to rise properly and will be dry. If the dough is too wet and soft, the biscuits will spread and lose their shape. Since dough consistency is critical in flaky biscuits, follow my recipe carefully the first few times you make them, paying particular attention to the feel of the dough.

Shaping the Dough

Fluffy biscuits are best formed by gently batting gobs of dough between lightly floured hands. If the work surface, the dough, and the cutter are generously floured, fluffy biscuits can be rolled and cut; but the softness of the dough makes this a tricky procedure, and the extra flour and handling will make the biscuits heavier and somewhat dense.

Flaky biscuits *must* be rolled out and cut for proper appearance and texture. For extra flakiness, I shape the dough into a rectangle, fold it up, and roll it a second time (*see* illustrations at right). This technique, which is also used to make puff pastry, sandwiches the particles of fat between sheets of dough, which separate into layers during baking. Use a light touch with the rolling pin or the biscuits will be small and tough.

When you begin cutting, in order not to flatten the edges of the biscuits and cause a low or lopsided rise, very lightly grease the cutter and dip it in flour; after the first biscuit has been made, the cutter should be floured (though not greased) before each cut. Press into the dough with one decisive punch and cut as close together and as close to the edges as possible in order to generate few scraps. Forming the dough into a neat eight-inch square and cutting it into little squares or triangles with a knife (*see* illustrations at right) eliminates all scraps and thus all the problems of re-rolling.

Baking

It's best to bake both kinds of biscuits on ungreased sheets, to give them a firm foundation from which to rise. Spacing them closely gives them support, which improves the rise, and helps keep them moist. (But don't jam the biscuits right up against each other or the ones in the middle will not bake through.) I brush my biscuits with plenty of butter, which not only promotes browning and improves flavor, but also produces a lovely, tender crust. Brushing with milk gives an even deeper color but leaves a shiny, slightly tough glaze that I find less attractive. Of course, biscuits will also brown, if not quite so well, when not brushed at all.

Since they need quick heat, biscuits are best baked in the middle of the oven. Placed too close to the bottom, they burn on the underside and remain pale on top; set too near the oven roof, they do not rise well, because the outside hardens into a shell before the inside has had a chance to rise properly. As soon as they are a light brown, they are done. Be careful, as over-

Shaping Flaky Biscuits

1. Roll the dough into a rough rectangle using as light a touch as possible on the rolling pin. Proceed directly to cutting, or follow steps 2, 3, and 4.

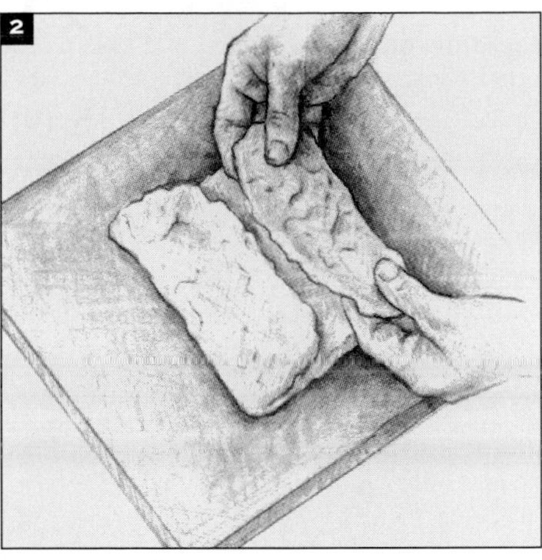

2. For extra-flaky biscuits, after you have rolled the dough into a rectangle, fold in both short ends to meet in the center.

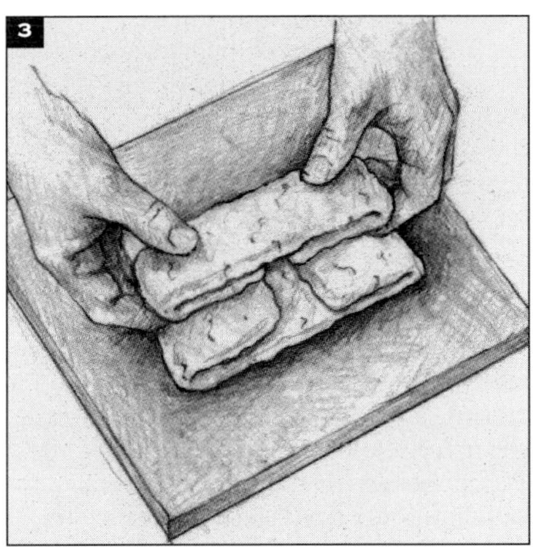

3. Next, fold the dough in half by width, and you are ready to roll again before cutting.

4. For an extra-precise effect, turn the dough onto a lightly floured eight-inch square pan, pat to fill the contours of the pan completely, then unmold.

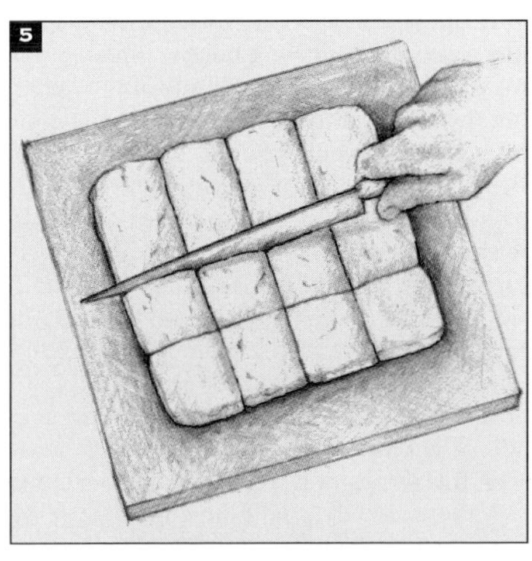

5. To make 16 square biscuits, cut the dough into four strips, then cut each strip into four equal pieces.

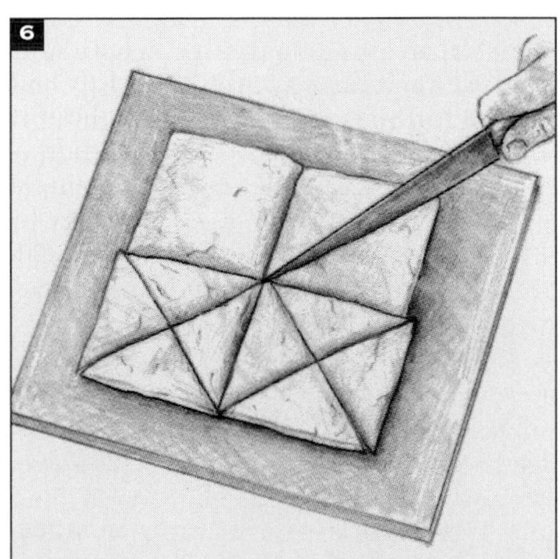

6. To make 16 triangular biscuits, cut the dough into quarters, then cut each quarter diagonally into four.

cooking will dry them out. Biscuits are always at their best when served as soon as they come out of the oven. The dough, however, may be made some hours in advance and baked when needed; they will still rise well.

FLUFFY BISCUITS

Makes 1 dozen

If you are using yogurt instead of buttermilk in this recipe, note that 8 ounces of yogurt equals ¾ cup plus 2 tablespoons (⅞ cup), not 1 cup as you might expect. Make sure that your oven rack is set at the center position. Baked too low, your biscuits will likely end up with burned bottoms. If your oven is accurate, stick with the 450° suggested temperature. If you suspect your oven runs hot, lower the temperature to 425°.

- 1 cup all-purpose flour
- 1 cup plain cake flour
- 2 teaspoons baking powder
- ½ teaspoon baking soda
- 1 teaspoon sugar
- ½ teaspoon salt
- ¼ pound chilled unsalted butter, cut into ¼-inch cubes, plus 2 tablespoons melted
- ¾ cup cold buttermilk or ¾ cup plus 2 tablespoons low-fat or whole-milk plain yogurt
- 2–3 tablespoons additional buttermilk (or milk), if needed

1. Set rack at middle position and heat the oven to 450°.

2. Mix or pulse first 6 ingredients in a large bowl or the workbowl of a food processor fitted with steel blade. With your fingertips, a pastry blender, 2 knives, or steel blade of the food processor, mix, cut, or process butter into the dry ingredients until mixture resembles coarse meal with a few slightly larger butter lumps.

3. If making by hand, stir in buttermilk with a rubber spatula or fork until mixture forms into soft, slightly sticky ball. If dough feels firm and dry bits are not gathering into a ball, sprinkle dough clumps with additional tablespoon of buttermilk (or milk for the yogurt dough). Be careful not to overmix. If using food processor, pulse until dough gathers into moist clumps. Remove from food processor bowl and form into rough ball.

4. With lightly floured hands, divide dough into 12 equal portions. Lightly bat a portion of dough back and forth a few times between floured hands until it begins to form a ball, then pat lightly with cupped hands to form a rough ball (*see* illustration, page 10). Repeat with remaining dough, placing formed dough rounds 1 inch apart on ungreased cookie sheet or pizza pan. Brush dough tops with melted butter or milk. (May be covered with plastic wrap and refrigerated for up to 2 hours.) Bake until biscuit tops are light brown, 10 to 12 minutes. Serve immediately.

FLAKY BISCUITS

Makes 16

After stirring in the milk, this dough should feel very soft and moist, but you should be able to hold it briefly between lightly floured hands without its sticking. If it turns out wet and sticky, return it to the bowl and sprinkle it with 2 to 4 tablespoons additional flour (of any kind) on all sides, gently patting in the flour with your palm. Let the dough rest another half-minute before removing it to your work surface. It is best to discard the dough that is left over from the second cutting, as biscuits made with thrice-recycled dough tend to be tough and flat. These biscuits are best served at once, though leftovers may be wrapped and refrigerated for a day, then reheated for a few minutes in a 350° oven.

- 2 cups "strong" all-purpose flour or 1 cup each "soft" all-purpose flour and bread flour (*see* page 10 for flour descriptions)
- 1 tablespoon baking powder
- ¾ teaspoon salt
- 5 tablespoons chilled unsalted butter, cut into ¼-inch cubes, plus 2 tablespoons melted
- 3 tablespoons chilled vegetable shortening or lard
- ¾ cup cold milk

1. Adjust rack to center position and heat oven to 450°.

2. Mix first 3 ingredients in a large bowl or the workbowl of a food processor fitted with steel blade. Add butter; with your fingertips, a pastry blender, 2 knives, or steel blade of a food processor, mix, cut, or process butter and shortening into dry ingredients, until the mixture resembles dry oatmeal. (Transfer food processor mixture to a large bowl.)

3. Stir in milk with a rubber spatula or fork until dry ingredients are just moistened. Let dough rest for 1 minute, then transfer it to a well-floured work surface.

4. Roll the dough into a rough 6-by-10-inch rectangle. With the long edge of the dough facing you, fold in both short ends of the dough so that they meet in the center (*see* illustration 2, page 11); then fold the dough in half by width, forming a package of dough four layers thick (*see* illustration 3, page 11). Once again, roll the dough into a 6-by-10-inch rectangle ½-inch thick.

5. Using a lightly greased and floured 2-inch cutter, stamp, with one decisive punch per round, 4 rows of 3 dough rounds, cutting them close together to generate as few scraps as possible. Dip cutter into flour before each new cut. Push the scraps of dough together so that their edges join; firmly pinch the edges with fingertips to make a partial seal. Pat the dough into small rectangle, fold it as before, and re-roll ½-inch thick. Cut out 3 or 4 more biscuits.

6. Place dough rounds 1½ inches apart on an ungreased baking sheet; brush dough tops with melted butter or milk. (May be covered with plastic wrap and refrigerated up to 3 hours.)

7. Bake until biscuits are lightly browned, 10 to 12 minutes. Serve immediately.

CHEDDAR BISCUITS

Decrease the butter called for in Fluffy Biscuits to 5 tablespoons or that in Flaky Biscuits to 3. After the fat has been cut or processed into the flour, add 1 cup shredded extra-sharp cheddar cheese (4 ounces); toss lightly, then stir in liquid.

HERB BISCUITS

Make Fluffy Biscuits, adding 3 tablespoons minced parsley or 2 tablespoons parsley and 1 tablespoon of either minced fresh tarragon or dill after the fat has been cut or processed into the flour. Split these and use them as a base for rich scrambled eggs or creamed chicken or seafood, or serve them as biscuits plain and simple.

STRAWBERRY SHORTCAKE

Serves 8

Follow the directions for Flaky Biscuits, but increase the butter to ¼ pound and the shortening to ¼ cup. With a 3-inch cutter, stamp out 8 dough rounds. Brush tops with melted butter and sprinkle with about 1 tablespoon sugar. Toss 1 quart hulled and sliced strawberries with ¼ cup sugar. Let stand at room temperature for about 30 minutes. Split shortcakes in half and spread with a bit of unsalted butter. Arrange bottoms on plates, cover with berries, and replace the tops. Top with 2 to 3 tablespoons of sweet cream. ■

Stephen Schmidt, a caterer and cooking teacher, is the author of *Master Recipes* (Ballantine, 1987) and of the forthcoming *Dessert America* (Morrow).

MAKING YOUR OWN BAKING POWDER

Unlike baking *soda,* which keeps forever, baking *powder* begins to react and lose its potency the instant you open the can and expose the contents to humidity in the air. For maximum leavening power, I recommend buying baking powder in the smallest can available, dating the can when opened, and discarding the contents after three months.

The alternative, uncommon but hardly daunting, is to make your own baking powder. Simply combine one teaspoon of baking soda (an alkaline) and two teaspoons of cream of tartar (an acid) for each tablespoon of baking powder called for. This substitution works very well for biscuits.

Secrets of Soy Sauce

Soy sauce varies remarkably, from smooth, wood-aged brands to those reminiscent of "bicycle lubricant." Here is a guide to sorting out the different varieties and flavors.

BY JONI MILLER

Few condiments are as misunderstood as soy sauce, the pungent, fragrant, fermented flavoring that's a mainstay in Japanese, Chinese, and, now, Pacific-Rim cooking. Its simple, straightforward composition — equal parts soybeans and a roasted grain, usually wheat, plus water and salt — belies the subtle, sophisticated contribution it makes as an all-purpose seasoning, flavor enhancer, tabletop condiment, and dipping sauce.

Soy sauce possesses a complex bouquet of flavors and aromas, the result of fermentation, which adds nuances of taste and brings out the flavor notes of other ingredients without masking a dish's primary flavors. When soy sauce brewers discuss this aspect of the sauce, they describe it as operating "just below the flavor perception level." Used straight or in combination with other ingredients, it is ideal for meat, poultry, and seafood marinades. A few drops enhance the flavors of scrambled eggs, vegetables, meats, and fish as well as soups, casseroles, and stews. Soy sauce's saltiness adds depth and richness. The flavor of soy sauce has a special affinity for cured, dried meats, so it is often used in the manufacture of jerky. In its unobtrusive way, a dash or two of soy sauce has much the same unfathomable yet enlivening effect that a judicious splash of tabasco offers, minus the heat.

This ancient sauce evolved from *shih,* a fermented grain mixture first used as a preservative and flavoring in China more than 2,500 years ago. Shih was introduced in Japan during the seventh century by Buddhist priests who, in an effort to teach their followers vegetarianism, promoted the salty mixture as a replacement for the meat- and fish-based seasonings previously used. Known as "miso-tamari," this by-product of the production of miso (fermented soybean paste) was the precursor of today's soy sauce. Tamari, which means "that which collects," was the name given to the liquid that accumulated at the top of miso barrels.

By 1700, demand for the sauce had grown to the point that commercial tamari breweries began springing up throughout Japan. In the seventeenth century, canny Dutch traders stationed in Nagasaki were the first to export tamari to the West. It was rumored in the court of Louis XV of France that the secret ingredient in the king's kitchen was tamari, and it later became a "mystery" ingredient in countless English condiments, including (probably) Worcestershire sauce. Eventually, wheat was added to the soybean/water recipe, a formulation change which resulted in modern-day soy sauce.

The best soy sauces are fermented and aged up to four years. During this process, more than 285 individual flavor components are created, including 20 flavor-boosting amino acids. The higher the quality of the sauce, the more nuances you can taste.

Defining Soy Sauce and Tamari

In this country, soy sauce has suffered from an identity crisis that is the result of consumers' longstanding confusion over the difference between soy sauce and tamari. For years the terms were interchangeably used to identify what are in fact two distinctly different products; even today some bottles are still incorrectly labeled "tamari shoyu" (shoyu is another name for soy sauce). Not surprisingly, the difference between the two lies in their ingredients.

PHOTOGRAPH BY CHRIS JOHNS/ALLSTOCK

Soy Sauce and Tamari Blind Tasting

Tasters on the panel included two food writers, a representative of a soy sauce manufacturer, a professional natural foods chef, and a sophisticated home cook. They evaluated 14 soy sauces and tamaris based on color, aroma, and flavor. The sauces were tasted in a blind test, poured from numbered bottles into clear glasses. Note that prices are per bottle, but there was some variation in bottle size. All sauces were purchased in New Jersey and New York City; prices vary nationally.

Tasters' evaluations were highly favorable regarding the seven top-ranked sauces, but markedly unenthusiastic — and sometimes militantly negative — about the remaining seven. Chemical synthetic versions prompted particularly negative responses, with participants gasping out loud as they sniffed and sipped.

Soy Sauces and Tamaris Listed in Order of Preference

1 **Mitoku Macrobiotic Johsen Organic Shoyu** (*Japan*), 10 ounces, $3.79. Dark amber-colored brew with a complex, clean-tasting, well-balanced, rich flavor that was mellow and understated. Aged in cedar casks for more than 18 months, this connoisseurs' shoyu is made from cracked whole winter wheat and steamed whole soybeans. In 1988 it received the Japanese Ministry of Agriculture's first-place award for highest-quality soy sauce from a field of 2,000 entries. Also sold under the Emperor's Kitchen, Tree of Life, Koyo,and Westbrae labels. *Health food stores.*

2 **San-J Naturally Brewed Tamari** (*United States*), 10 ounces, $1.99. Deep reddish-brown, with a mild, slightly sweet scent and a clean, richly balanced straightforward flavor; pronounced saltiness. A popular tamari made from soymeal rather than whole soybeans. Aged in fiber-reinforced plastic. San-Jirushi is Japan's largest miso manufacturer. *Health and natural food stores, some chain supermarkets.* Good buy.

3 **Eden Double Brewed Low Sodium Shoyu** (*Japan*), 10 ounces, $4.25. Dark, almost opaque, with deep, intensely fragrant aroma, and mellow flavor with a pleasantly "winey" aftertaste. Aged for three years. *Health and natural food stores.*

4 **Kikkoman Naturally Brewed Soy Sauce** (*United States*), 10 ounces, $1.19. Clear, reddish-brown color with a tart, faintly sweet, pleasantly salty fermented flavor. A reliable all-purpose seasoning; aged in stainless steel. *Widely available.*

5 **Pearl River Bridge Golden Label Superior Soy** (*People's Republic of China*), 21.2 ounces, $1.35. Opaque, almost black color; thick, syrupy consistency; soy or burnt caramel aroma; rich, rounded flavor with molasses or burnt sugar overtones; very salty. *Chinese and Japanese specialty food stores.* Note price.

6 **Ohsawa Nama Shoyu Unpasteurized Organic Soy Sauce** (*Japan*),10 ounces, $4.45. Clear, rich deep mahogany color; complex, predominantly soybean bouquet; slightly sweet, almost woody flavor with a faintly acidic finish; pronounced saltiness. Considered "the Champagne of shoyu" by professional natural foods chefs, this is the original organic sauce introduced to the United States. by George Ohsawa. Made in small batches, aged four years in cedarwood kegs, it is unpasteurized and contains 17 percent less salt than most other sauces. *Health and natural food stores.*

7 **Emperor's Kitchen Organic Mansan Tamari** (*Japan*), 5 ounces, $2.69. Dark brown color; pleasant, fragrant aroma; complex, well-rounded, full taste with hints of caramel. Produced from organically grown soybeans, brewed for more than a year in cedar kegs. A blended sauce containing 4 percent *mirin* (sweet rice wine). *Health and natural food stores.*

8 **Yamasa Soy Sauce** (*Japan*),17 ounces, $2.50. An everyday soy sauce used by many professional chefs in Japan and by some home cooks. *Japanese and Chinese specialty food stores.*

9 **San-J Naturally Brewed Whole Soybean Shoyu** (*United States*),10 ounces, $2.69. Made from whole soybeans and sea salt. Less well-known than this company's tamari (*see* above). *Health and natural food stores, some chain supermarkets.*

10 **Wei-Chuan China Dark Soy Sauce** (*Singapore*), 21.64 ounces, $1.20. Dark, opaque blackish-brown color; rather unpleasant Parmesan-like aroma; faintly cheesy flavor with dense, sweet caramel overtones. A common, garden-variety sauce. *Chinese and Japanese specialty food stores.*

11 **La Choy Soy Sauce** (*United States*),16 ounces, $2.09. Classic example of a chemical synthetic-style sauce. Dark, muddy brown color; harsh, bitter, sharply acidic taste; very salty. Unpleasant. The one we all grew up with. *Widely available.*

12 **Pearl River Bridge Mushroom Soy Sauce** (*People's Republic of China*), 21 ounces, $1.15. Cloudy, medium amber color; bicycle lubricant aroma; burnt caramel taste. Made using extract of soybeans; sugar and mushrooms added for flavor. *Chinese specialty food stores.*

13 **KA-ME Chinese Light Soy Sauce** (*Singapore*), 12 ounces, $1.50. Very dark, clear brown color; repulsive, almost rotten aroma with an overpowering, unrefined taste; extremely salty. A chemical synthetic-style sauce containing sugar and caramel color. *Chinese specialty food stores, some chain supermarkets.*

14 **WY Brand Packet of Takeout Soy Sauce.** Chemical synthetic-style sauce complete with corn syrup and caramel coloring. Molasses-like color; virtually without aroma; weak, slightly nutty salt-water taste. *Widely available at neighborhood Chinese takeout spots.*

For information about finding individual soy sauces, see Sources and Resources, page 32.

Soy sauce is made from equal parts soybeans and wheat, plus water, and salt. Tamari is made from soybeans, water, and salt. To tell the difference, simply read the label. If there's wheat, it's soy sauce; no wheat, it's tamari. As a general rule of thumb for kitchen usage, soy sauce is the more subtle of the two, though it is also saltier. Tamari, which has a more intense, complex taste, a higher concentration of minerals (including sodium), and a darker, thicker consistency, is more appropriate for use as a tabletop condiment (a dipping sauce for sashimi and sushi) than as a cooking seasoning.

The roots of the confusion over the two products date back to the 1960s, when George Ohsawa, the "father of macrobiotics," first introduced authentic, naturally fermented traditional Japanese soy sauce (shoyu) to the West. Ohsawa called it tamari, reasoning that "shoyu" was too difficult a word for Westerners to pronounce. Of course, he could have chosen to identify it as soy sauce, but did not because, at that time, most soy sauces marketed in the West were chemical synthetic versions with Chinese-sounding names, and he was anxious to differentiate between natural, brewed soy sauces and their chemically produced counterparts.

Types of Soy Sauce

Soy sauces fall into three basic categories: natural Japanese, natural Chinese, and chemical synthetic.

The standard, commonly used all-purpose soy sauce favored by Japanese home cooks is a "dark" soy sauce (*koikuchi shoyu*). Deep-brown or amber in color and full-bodied, it is suitable for use in virtually all Japanese recipes. A lighter-colored, thinner, saltier Japanese soy sauce known as "light," (*usukuchi shoyu*), is also produced. Few Westerners would have occasion to buy "light," although it is available in the United States at Japanese specialty food stores and is sometimes specified in Japanese cookbooks. Usukuchi shoyu is used mainly as a tabletop condiment and in the cuisines of the southern and southwestern regions of Japan (Osaka, for example), where cooks prefer it for aesthetic reasons since it does not darken the appearance of food. Both shoyus are slightly sweeter and more refined in flavor than their Chinese counterparts.

Densely flavored and quite salty, Chinese soy sauce comes in a wide variety of types ranging from a thick, very dark reddish-brown to versions as thin and light as Japanese shoyu. Like shoyu, Chinese sauces are categorized as "dark" (also labeled "standard," "superior," "black," or "double dark") and "light" (also called "thin"). In general, the dark sauces are less salty than the light ones. Mushroom soy sauce, a "dark" variation flavored with Chinese straw mushrooms, is also widely available. In Chinese cuisine, dark sauces are used as tabletop condiments and in cooking with meats and with heartier, strongly flavored foods. Thin sauces are used where a light-color sauce is more visually appropriate (seafood and shellfish dishes), in marinades, and as seasoning for vegetables and poultry.

It's important to note that Japanese and Chinese soy sauces cannot be used interchangeably in recipes. While the somewhat sweeter, less salty Japanese shoyu can be used with success in Chinese recipes, the thick, dark, more powerfully flavored Chinese sauces cannot be successfully substituted for less aggressively flavored Japanese shoyu.

The third category is chemical synthetic nonbrewed soy sauces. Thick and extremely dark (almost black), these concoctions have a strong, rather yeasty aroma and a somewhat metallic taste. The most inexpensive of all soy sauces, they are made from hydrolyzed vegetable protein and hydrochloric acid, with caramel and corn syrup added for coloring and flavor, plus, in most instances, preservatives. Because these sauces are not brewed, they can be manufactured in just a few days. These sauces, including supermarket brands such as Chun King and La Choy, along with those ubiquitous little packets of sauce that accompany Chinese takeout, are what most Americans grew up thinking of as soy sauce.

Low-Sodium Alternative

For consumers concerned about cutting back on sodium, the interesting news is that soy sauce and tamari can be useful alternatives to salt in cooking. A single teaspoon of soy sauce or tamari containing 320 mg of sodium is the seasoning equivalent of a full tablespoon of salt, which contains 6,900 mg of sodium. Then there are reduced sodium soy sauces, a relatively new category introduced to the market about 15 years ago in response to American consumers' interest in low-sodium products as part of overall health consciousness and for special dietary needs. These contain an average of between 35–40 percent less sodium than regular sauces and they taste mellower than higher sodium versions (interestingly, an Eden Foods low-sodium shoyu was among our tasters' top picks). Kikkoman produces a Lite Soy Sauce containing 40 percent less sodium than their regular version (8.6 percent sodium vs. 13.5 percent) as well as a Less Salt Soy Sauce with a sodium content of 7.9 percent. In both, sodium is reduced by applying a dialysis process to the brewed sauce.

How Soy Sauce is Made

Like wines, natural soy sauce and tamari are the result of fermentation, and the brewing process for both sauces is quite similar, bearing in mind that the formula for tamari does not include wheat. For soy sauce, equal amounts of soy beans and wheat are blended, a seed mold called aspergillus is introduced, and the mixture is allowed to incubate, or mature, for several days. The resulting culture, known as *koji*, is then mixed with a salt brine to produce a mash called *moromi*, which brews in leisurely fashion in fermentation tanks for six months to two or more years, depending on the manufacturer.

It is this slow fermentation and aging process that creates the more than 285 flavor components, including nearly 20 amino acids, present in soy sauce. The presence of the amino acids account for soy sauce's ability to boost food flavors without masking them. Once aged, the now mellow moromi, which is a thick paste, is filtered; the unrefined soy sauce is pressed from the mature moromi mash, and then refined and pasteurized. Because it is a product of fermentation, soy sauce emerges with many of the same aromatic compounds found in roasted coffee and in whiskey; other compounds produce the scents of fruits and even of flowers like roses and hyacinths.

The issue of the material used for the tanks in which moromi ages (and whether this affects flavor) is a matter hotly debated among streamlined mass producers who use stainless steel or fiber-reinforced plastic, and smaller, artisanal manufacturers who still use traditional wooden vats. It's worth pointing out that among the 14 sauces explored by our tasting panel, those rated numbers one and six had been aged in cedar, which suggests that the difference can be detected. Whether the difference would remain evident when the sauces are used in cooking was not explored.

While most natural Chinese soy sauces are manufactured in the People's Republic of China and exported to the United States, and most Japanese natural shoyu and tamari sold in America is brewed in Japan (where there are more than 2,500 breweries), several Japanese firms are brewing sauces in this country. Kikkoman Foods, Inc., the world's largest soy sauce producer, whose roots date back to the seventeenth century, established a brewing facility in Wisconsin in 1972, while San-Jirushi, the world's largest producer of naturally brewed tamari, which was founded in 1804, produces tamari and shoyu at its Virginia brewery, which has been in operation since 1987. ■

Joni Miller, a New York–based writer, is the author of *True Grits* (Workman, 1990).

Storing Soy Sauce

All soy sauces are long-lasting and, with proper storage, will remain usable for a year or more after opening. The subtle bean aroma of light-colored versions is more likely to fade slightly several months after opening, so purchase these in smaller bottles. Once opened, tightly cap bottles and store in the refrigerator or in a cool, dark place.

Cutting Up Poultry, Step-by-Step

Buying whole birds is not only cheaper than buying parts, it also lets you customize your cuts. With this guide, you can learn how to cut up chicken and other birds in a number of different ways for a variety of uses, and how to "stuff" chicken skin without cutting at all.

Cutting Up a Whole Bird for Frying, Sautéing, or Broiling

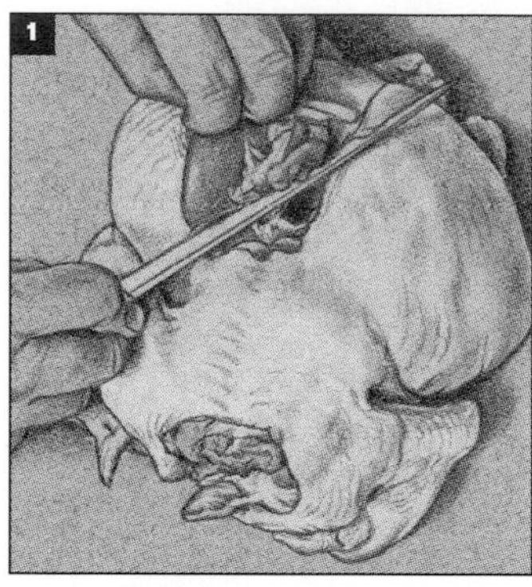

1. Turn the bird breast down and using a well-sharpened boning knife, cut under the "oyster," the nugget of meat running from the backbone into the leg. Do not sever it from the leg. Repeat on other side.

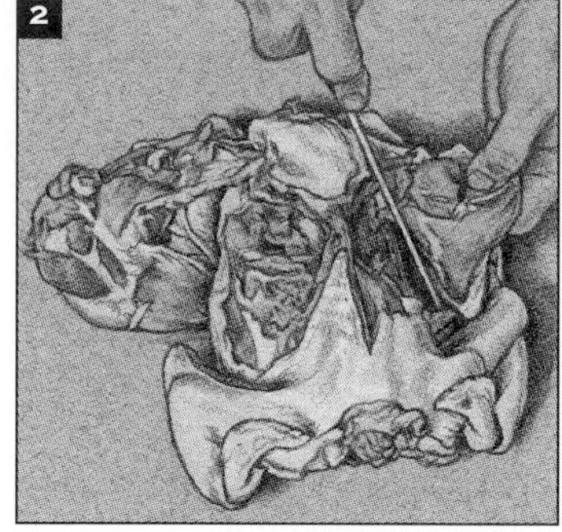

2. Cut through the skin and between the leg meat and the carcass of the chicken, following the shape of the bird with the boning knife. Pull the leg away from the body as you cut. Repeat on other side.

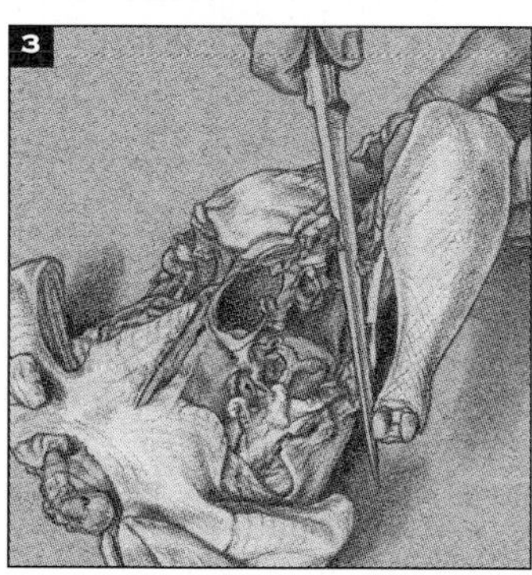

3. Pop the leg out of its socket. Cut through the remaining skin, holding the leg to the body. Repeat on other side.

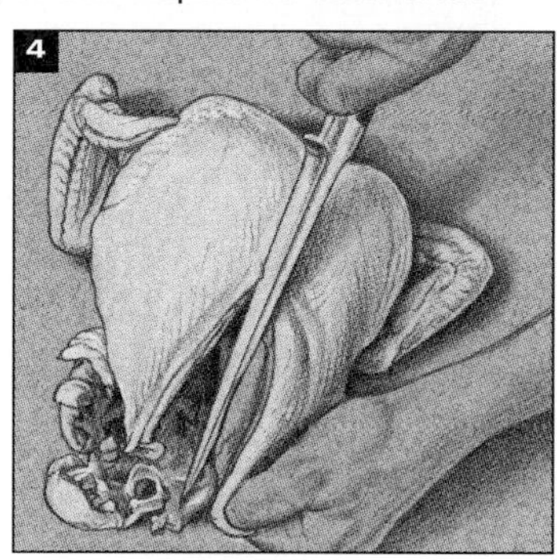

4. Turn the bird over and change to a large knife, such as a 10-inch chef's knife. Starting at the tail end, cut straight down through the breastbone on either side of the large white "keel" bone. Keep cutting until you hit the wishbone (at the neck end of the bird), then follow the wishbone down.

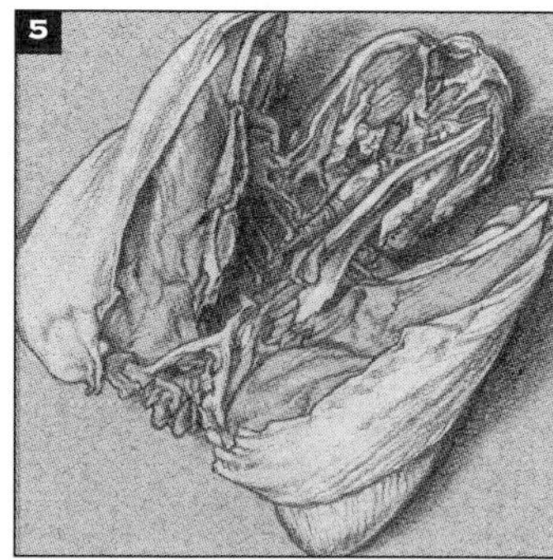

5. When you have completed step 4, both halves of the breast will be cut from the center bone, with wishbone exposed.

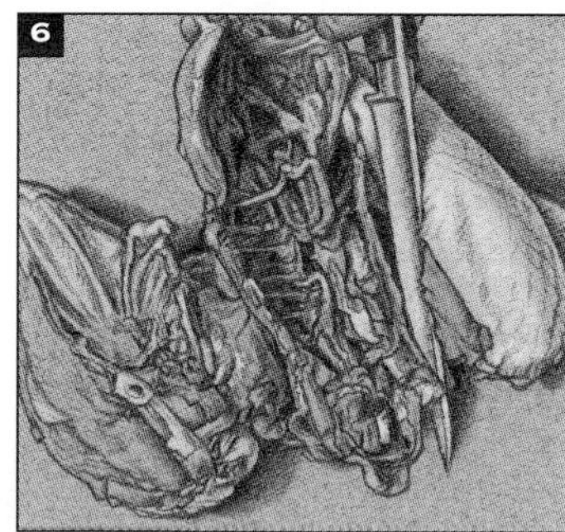

6. Cut through the "shoulder" joint between the wishbone and the breast; this will free the breast entirely.

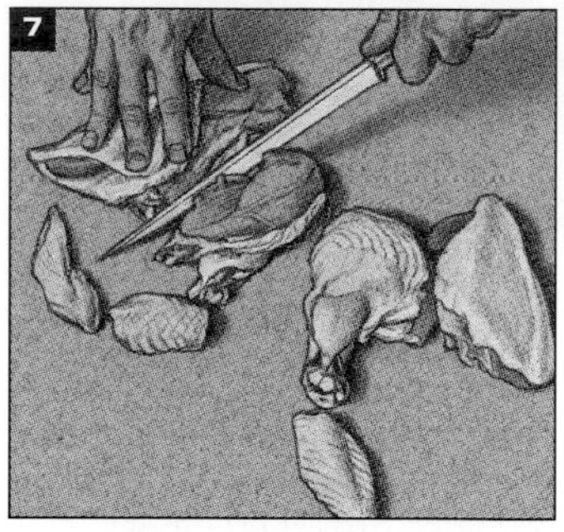

7. Sever the two outer wing joints, then cut the wing from the breast. (You may also cut the breast halves themselves in two.)

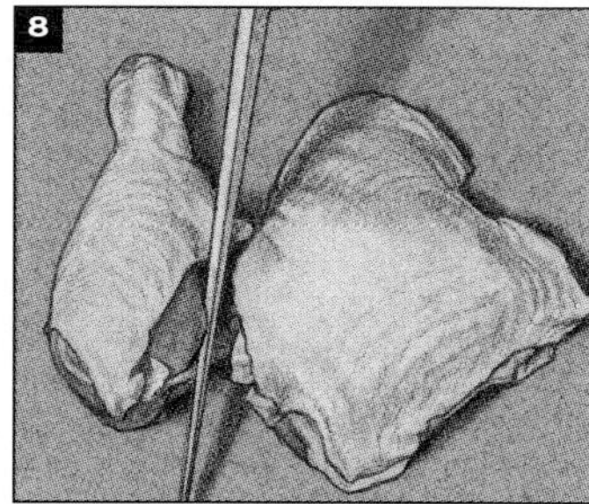

8. Cut the leg in two; you can feel the joint with the tip of your knife.

To Make "Lollipops" for Hors d'Oeuvres

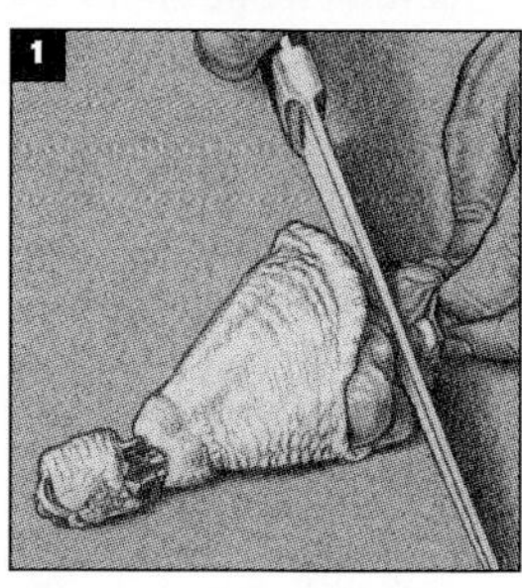

1. Using a 12-inch chef's knife or cleaver, hack off both ends of the drumstick. With a smaller knife, push up meat and skin one-half to one inch from the thin end of the leg.

2. The finished lollipop. The same technique can be used to make smaller lollipops out of the largest section of the wing.

Illustrations by Alan Witschonke

Removing Boneless Breast Meat

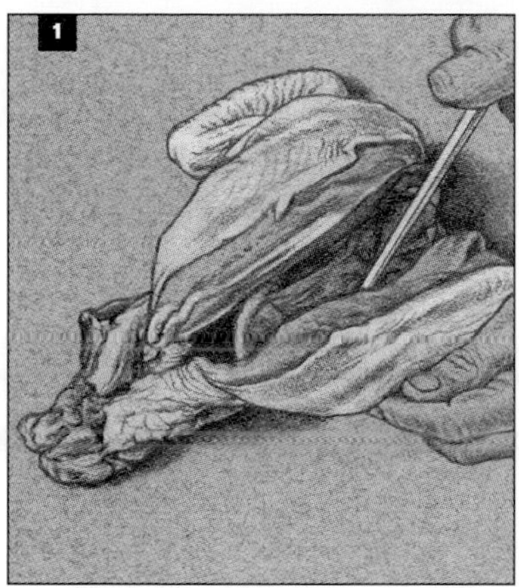

1. This technique differs only slightly from that used to remove the breast with the bone. Using a thin-bladed boning knife, cut on either side of the keel bone, following the rib cage down and separating the meat from the bone structure. (This is somewhat easier if the legs are removed first.)

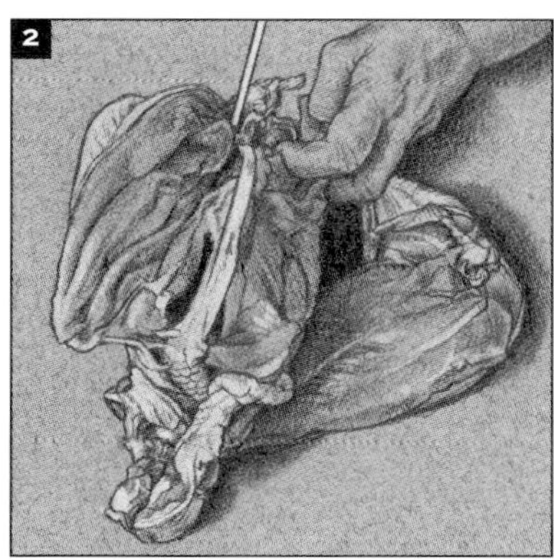

2. The entire half-breast, with the wing, can be removed in one cut, leaving all other bones behind.

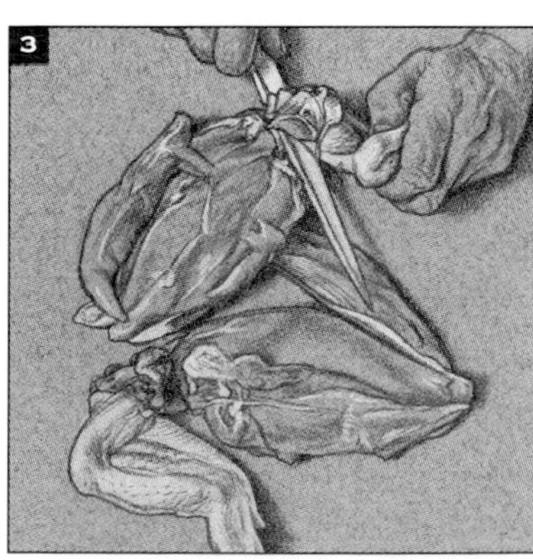

3. Cut the wing from the breast. If you like, you can also separate the thin strip of "tenderloin" from the main section of the breast meat.

Boning the Thigh

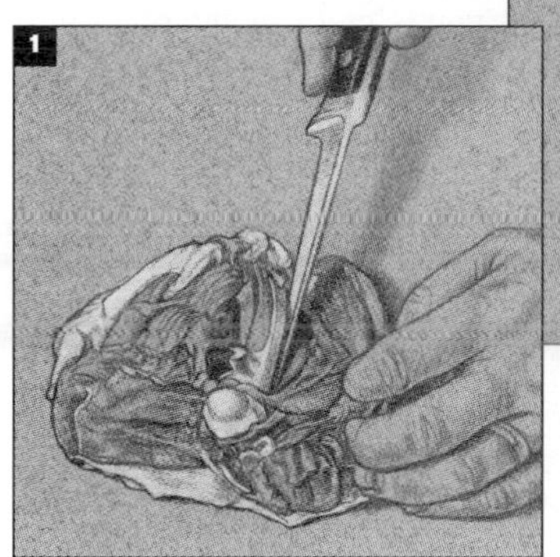

1. Using a boning knife, cut along one side of the thigh bone, angling the knife so that it cuts slightly under the bone.

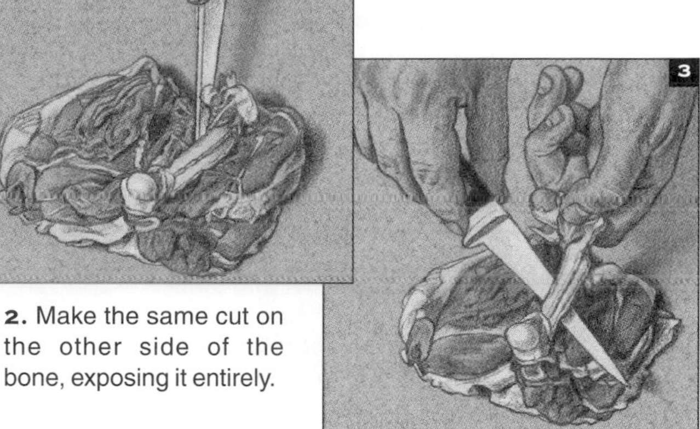

2. Make the same cut on the other side of the bone, exposing it entirely.

3. Slide the knife under the bone and sever it completely. The thigh meat is best grilled or used in stir-fries.

Butterflying for Grilling or Broiling

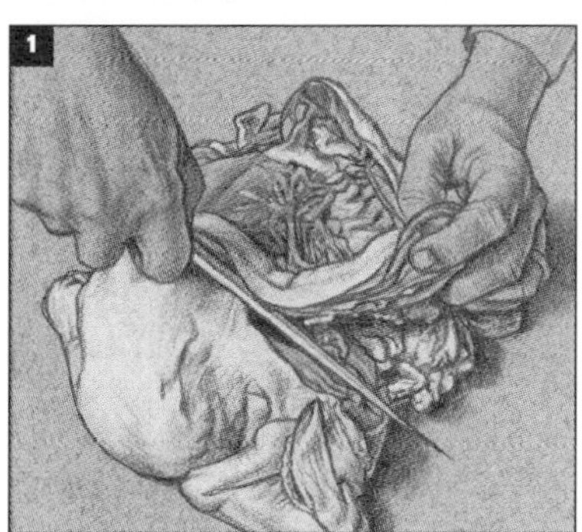

1. Place the bird breast side down. Using a sharp, heavy knife, such as a 10- or 12-inch chef's knife, cut on either side of the backbone, the entire length of the bird. Remove the backbone.

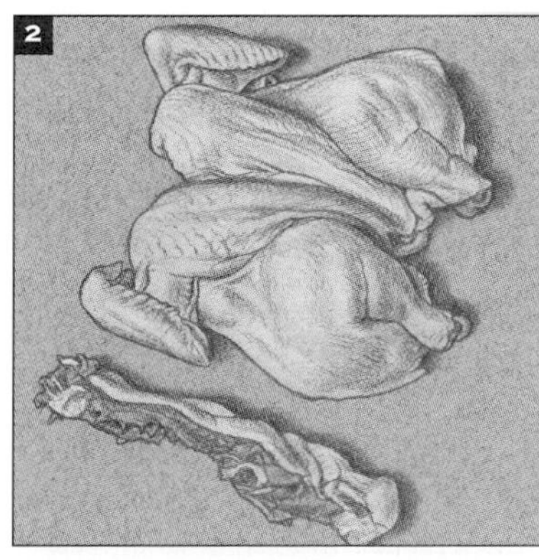

2. Turn the bird over and flatten it with the palm of your hand. Reserve the backbone for stock.

To "Stuff" the Skin before Roasting

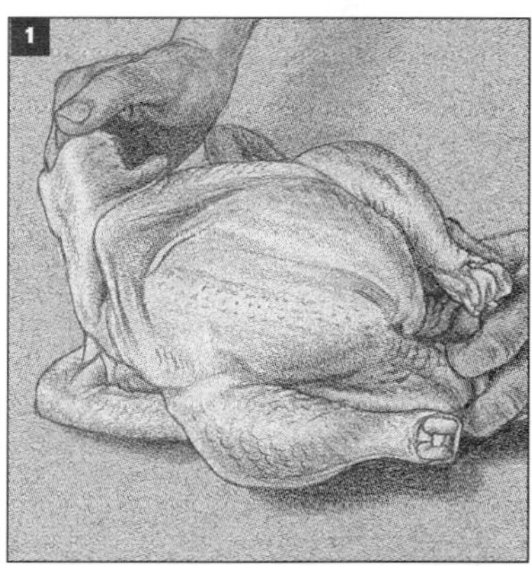

1. You need no knife for this technique. Gently separate the skin from the breast meat, starting at the neck.

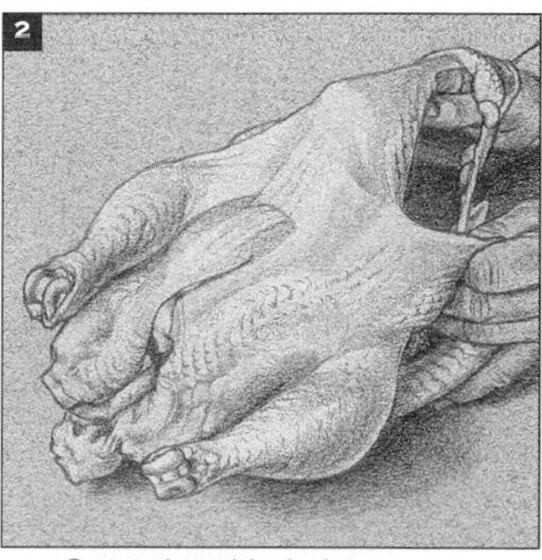

2. Once the skin is loose, you can use your hand to loosen the skin from the entire bird, even along the leg.

Stir-Frying Comes Home

Now you can stir-fry at home without the benefit of a high-heat restaurant wok.

BY PAM ANDERSON

The stir-fry is everything we like and need in an everyday dish — it's attractive, healthy, economical, quick, and complete. So why do we eat it in restaurants instead of cooking it at home? Maybe it's because many cooks don't know how to do it right; I didn't, until recently.

I was Chinese-cookbook dependent, and intimidated by long ingredient lists. Many times I'd close the book and decide once again to sauté those chicken breasts. When I was able to get past the ingredient list, I was often disenchanted with the final dish. My meat stewed or stuck instead of stir-fried, my ginger and garlic burned, my sauce was too gloppy or too thin.

But the potential of stir-fry remained great; it's too important a dish *not* to know how to make. I wanted to go to the refrigerator, find chicken, broccoli, and carrots, and feel just as comfortable stir-frying them as I did sautéing the chicken and steaming the vegetables. I wanted to understand the technique, to get out from under the recipes.

I had questions about every aspect of the process: How much protein and vegetables would I need for each person? Must I marinate the meat or would the other ingredients add enough flavor? If marinating was necessary, what was the simplest way to do it? How much of the essential trio of ginger, scallions, and garlic did I need? Could I determine a standard amount of these aromatics that would work for all meat and vegetable combinations? When was it best to add them? What cooking order made sense: vegetables or meat first? What vegetables needed cooking before stir-frying? Once I developed a basic master stir-fry recipe, how would I vary the flavor? Would simply changing the meats and vegetables, or stirring in some sesame oil or chili paste, offer enough variety to put the dish on the menu at least once a week?

For an expert opinion, I sought out Barbara Tropp, chef/owner of China Moon Cafe in San Francisco. She put me at ease initially, saying, "There is no right way to stir-fry." Then came the bad news: "It's impossible for people in this country to stir-fry." The reason she gave for this latter opinion is that, at about 20,000 Btu (British thermal units), the average gas burner doesn't come close to the 150,000 Btu in the well of a commercial wok. At best, home cooks would have to be content with a sort of sauté/stir-fry.

One key to stir-frying is knowing the proper ratio of vegetables and seasonings to meat or seafood. With that in mind, you can make stir-fries with whatever ingredients you have on hand, using Chinese Flavoring Sauces (page 19) to add even more variety.

Since Americans include more protein and less rice in their diet than Asians do, Tropp also suggested that American stir-fries should contain a significant amount of meat or seafood. Finally, since we tend to make an entire meal from a stir-fry, Tropp added that American stir-fries should be more highly seasoned than the Asian versions, which typically complement other dishes at the same meal.

Keeping all this in mind, I started testing with a ratio of three-quarters of a pound of meat or seafood to one and one-half pounds of vegetables, plus two tablespoons scallions, one tablespoon garlic, and two teaspoons ginger. (If you don't have a scale, you can approximate this proportion by using about two to three times as many vegetables as meat by volume.)

Do Marinades Matter?

Since most recipes begin with marinating, I made five tests to determine whether it was necessary and, if it was, which marinade was simplest and best. For each test, I used chicken breast, celery, and blanched carrots. In the first test, I simply salted the chicken, stir-fried the three ingredients, then thickened and flavored them with a mixture of chicken stock, soy sauce, sherry, and cornstarch. In test two, I marinated the chicken in soy sauce and rice wine prior to cooking, then added sherry and the unabsorbed soy sauce to a cornstarch/chicken stock mixture stirred in at the end of cooking. On the theory that a cornstarch/soy sauce coating seals in the juices, the chicken in test three was tossed with equal parts of soy sauce and

PHOTOGRAPH BY RICHARD FELBER

cornstarch, and finished with chicken stock, rice wine, and more soy sauce and cornstarch. Batch four was the same, except I added some oil to the soy/cornstarch marinade.

The differences were remarkable. Although the sauce in the salt-only stir-fry was flavorful, the chicken itself was hopelessly bland, and the meat stuck to the pan during cooking. The soy sauce and rice wine penetrated the meat and gave it a good flavor in the second stir-fry, and I had fewer problems with sticking. The cornstarch in the third batch compounded the sticking problems; the meat actually tore this time. Since I added less cornstarch at the end of cooking, this one also lacked the appealing glaze of its predecessor. Furthermore, the extra cornstarch on the meat absorbed a lot of stir-fry liquid, leaving less sauce. The addition of oil to the marinade in test four didn't improve the sticking problem enough to justify it.

In my fifth batch, I tried "velveting," the process of marinating the meat in egg white, soy sauce, and rice wine, then pre-cooking in hot oil or water before stir-frying to produce a smooth, velvety coating. The results were hardly worth the effort for a weekday get-it-on-the-table-in-under-30-minutes dish. My conclusion: the simple soy/wine marinade showed that less — but not nothing — is more.

Dealing with Vegetables

During the course of these tests, I also discovered that Tropp was right — my domestic stove couldn't handle large batches of uncooked anything. I had to blanch all the harder vegetables and to cook the meat in two batches. (While some recipes instruct you to steam hard vegetables in the middle of the stir-fry process by covering the wok, I preferred to blanch the vegetables earlier, so that I didn't have to change gears once I started to stir-fry.) When I added too many raw vegetables, my wok started chugging like the locomotive in *The Little Engine that Could.* But it couldn't. Eventually, I took to blanching even snow peas and asparagus.

I also found it impossible to add the ginger, scallion, and garlic when I first started cooking. In theory, adding them at the beginning flavors the entire dish, but they always turned to burnt bits by the end. I had better results by adding them just seconds before tossing in the first batch of vegetables.

Still, although the ginger and garlic made their presence known, I wasn't tasting the scallion at all. I moved the scallions from the aromatics category over to the vegetables. If I wanted scallion flavor in a given stir-fry, I'd cut them into lengths or shred them, then add them with the vegetables so they could really stand out in the dish.

"When making stir-fry sauces," cautions cookbook author Hugh Carpenter, "stir in only enough thickener so the sauce lightly glazes the food."

Quick-Change Artistry

I next approached the Big Question. I had developed a basic stir-fry recipe using soy sauce, dry sherry, ginger, and garlic, but I was already getting tired of it. How to vary the dish, simply and quickly?

Hugh Carpenter, co-author of *Chopsticks* (Stewart, Tabori, & Chang, 1989), furnished the answer. "I've got what you need," he said, and within five minutes the recipes for eight Chinese flavoring sauces (*see* below) were rolling out of my fax machine. Not only did these sauces provide the variety I was looking for — lemon, oyster, Szechwan, sweet and sour, black bean — but Carpenter's recipes worked exactly with the proportions I had developed. Call it good karma, a miracle, or a reward for hard work: I had found my way to stir-fry.

MASTER RECIPE FOR STIR-FRY

Serves 4

This recipe is easily halved (in fact it's even better, because you avoid the batch-cooking that you encounter with the full recipe). The typical wok holds up to 3 quarts water, which will com-

CHINESE FLAVORING SAUCES

Knowing the amount and ratio of meat to vegetables gives you the freedom to create a stir-fry with almost any ingredients. That knowledge, combined with Hugh Carpenter's sauces, make for an almost infinite number of stir-fry combinations. All the ingredients are readily available at a supermarket. For each sauce, mix the ingredients together and add them to the stir-fry as indicated in the Master Recipe.

Tomato Fireworks Sauce
2 tablespoons dry sherry, 3 tablespoons tomato sauce, 1 tablespoon oyster sauce, 1 tablespoon light soy sauce, ½ teaspoon sugar, and 1 teaspoon sesame oil.

Lemon Sauce
¼ cup lemon juice, 1 tablespoon sugar, 2 tablespoons chicken stock, 1 tablespoon light soy sauce, ¼ teaspoon salt, and 2 teaspoons lemon zest.

Sweet and Sour Sauce
¼ cup red wine vinegar, ¼ cup sugar, 2 tablespoons tomato sauce, 2 tablespoons pineapple juice, and ¼ teaspoon salt.

Black Bean Sauce
1 tablespoon salted black beans, rinsed, chopped, and added to ginger and garlic, 3 tablespoons dry sherry, 2 tablespoons chicken stock, 1 tablespoon light soy sauce, ½ teaspoon sugar, 1 tablespoon sesame oil, and ¼ teaspoon ground black pepper.

Oyster Flavored Sauce
2 tablespoons oyster sauce, 3 tablespoons dry sherry, 1 tablespoon sesame oil, ½ teaspoon sugar, and ¼ teaspoon ground black pepper.

Coconut Curry Sauce
2 tablespoons chicken stock, 2 tablespoons dry sherry, 1 tablespoon light soy sauce, 1 tablespoon curry powder, ½ teaspoon sugar, ½ teaspoon salt, and ½ cup coconut milk (not cream).

Spicy Tangerine Sauce
1 tablespoon each of minced, fresh hot chiles, and tangerine zest added to ginger and garlic, 1 tablespoon light soy sauce, 1 teaspoon heavy soy sauce, 3 tablespoons dry sherry, 1 teaspoon red wine vinegar, ½ teaspoon roasted and ground Szechwan peppercorns, 1 tablespoon sesame oil, ¼ teaspoon sugar, and ¼ teaspoon salt.

Szechwan Chili Sauce
1 tablespoon light soy sauce, 1 tablespoon sesame oil, 3 tablespoons dry sherry, 1 tablespoon chili paste, 2 teaspoons heavy soy sauce, ¼ teaspoon roasted and ground Szechwan peppercorns, ¼ teaspoon sugar, and ¼ teaspoon salt.

To Produce Uniform Pieces of Chicken Breast

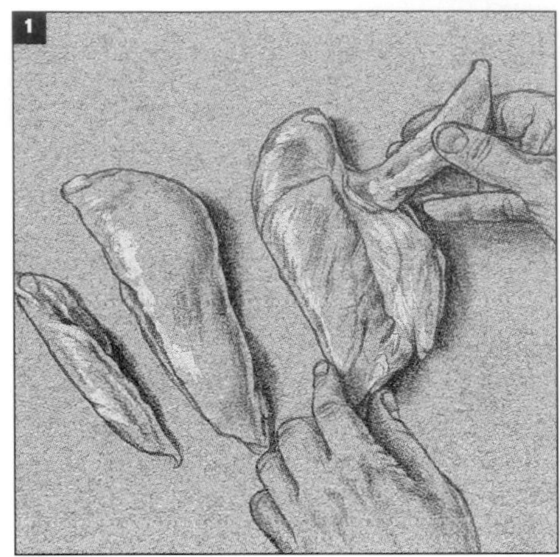

1. Separate tenderloin from partially frozen chicken breast.

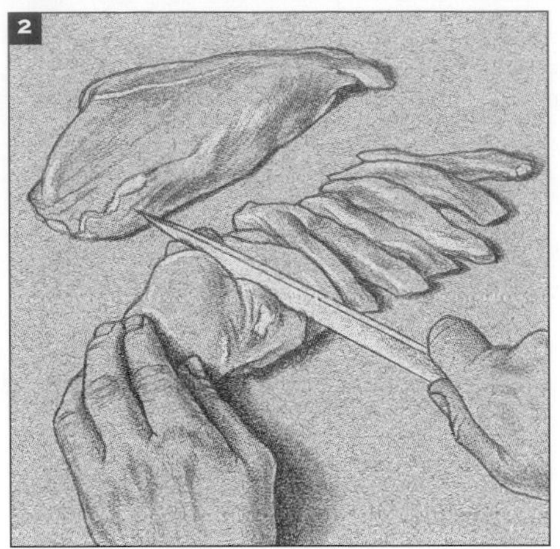

2. Slice breast, across the grain, into slices about ¼-inch wide and 1½ to 2 inches in length. Center pieces will need to be cut in half so they are of approximately the same length as end pieces.

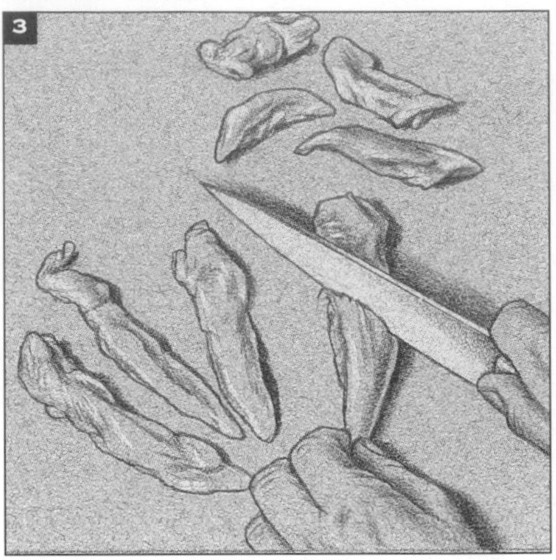

3. Cut tenderloins on the diagonal to produce pieces of the same size as breast pieces.

To Vary Slices of Long Vegetables

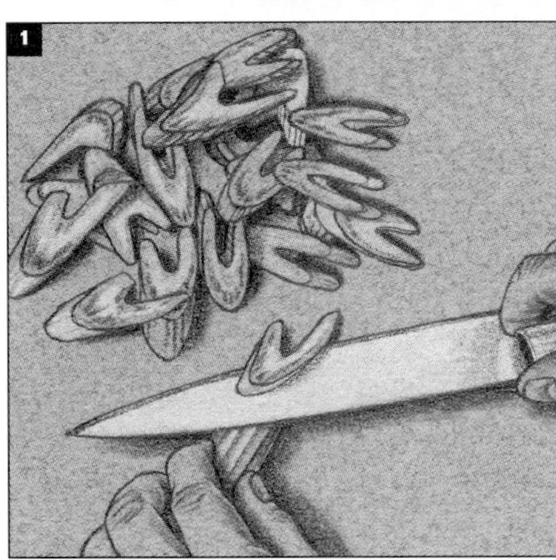

1. Slice vegetable with knife at a fairly steep (about 60-degree) angle to the cutting surface.

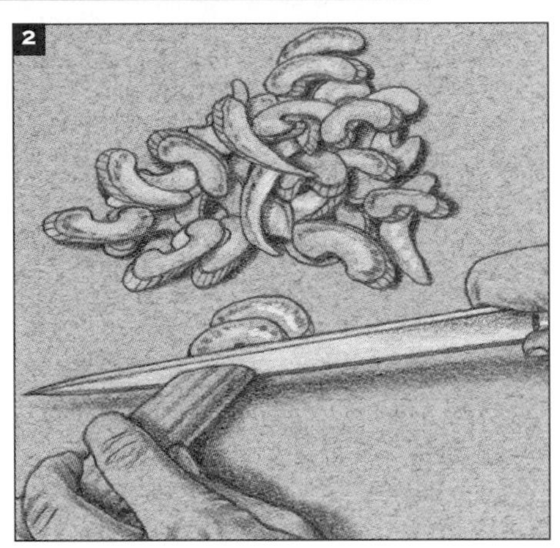

2. Slice vegetable with knife at a 45-degree angle to the length of the vegetable.

To Roll-Cut Vegetables

Holding knife at approximately 30-degree angle to the vegetable, make a diagonal cut near stem end, and discard the stem. Roll vegetable ¼ to ⅓ turn away from you, then cut again at the same angle, about 1½ inches further down the vegetable. Continue until entire vegetable is cut up.

To Quick-Shred Long, Round Vegetables

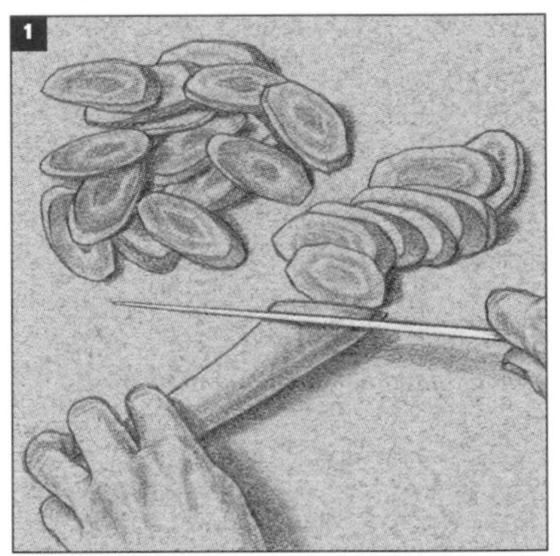

1. Slice vegetables into rounds on the diagonal.

2. Fan vegetable rounds and thin-shred or julienne them lengthwise.

Illustrations by Alan Witschonke

To Mince Ginger

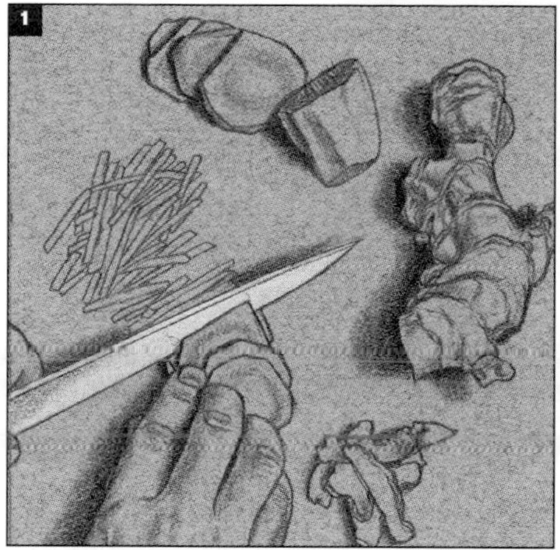

1. Peel and trim ginger and slice into thin rounds. Fan rounds and cut into matchsticks.

2. Chop matchsticks crosswise.

fortably cook 1 pound of vegetables. If you are blanching all the vegetables, you may want to use a large pot.

- ¾ pound of meat or seafood, cubed, diced, sliced thin, or julienned
- 1 tablespoon soy sauce
- 1 tablespoon dry sherry
- Salt
- 1½ pounds vegetables, cut in approximate size of the selected meat or seafood
- 1 recipe flavoring sauce (*see* "Chinese Flavoring Sauces," page 19)
- 3 tablespoons peanut or vegetable oil
- 1 tablespoon minced garlic
- 2 teaspoons minced ginger
- 2 tablespoons chopped scallions
- 1 tablespoon cornstarch mixed with
- 2 tablespoons water or chicken broth

1. Toss first ingredient with soy sauce and sherry in a medium bowl; set aside.

2. Meanwhile, heat enough water in the wok to blanch harder vegetables. Add ¾ teaspoon salt per quart of water, then add hard vegetables. Simmer until vegetables brighten in color and soften slightly. Time will vary based on type and cut of vegetables. Drain vegetables under cold, running water; set aside.

3. Prepare sauce.

4. Heat wok over high heat until it begins to smoke; drizzle 1 tablespoon oil around lower circumference of pan to lightly coat sides. Scatter ½ of meat or seafood around bottom and up sides of wok and stir-fry until meat is seared and just cooked through. Shovel or spoon cooked meat or seafood into serving dish; add another tablespoon oil, and repeat cooking process with remaining meat; transfer second batch of meat or seafood to serving dish.

5. Drizzle in remaining tablespoon oil; add garlic and ginger and almost immediately add raw vegetables and scallions. Stir-fry until vegetables are just tender-crisp. Add cooked vegetables and stir-fry until all vegetables are sizzling hot.

6. Return cooked meat or seafood to wok, stir in sauce, and stir-fry to coat all ingredients. Stir cornstarch mixture and add; stir-fry until wok juices become saucy and glossy. If wok juices look too thick, stir in a tablespoon or so more water or chicken stock. Serve immediately with steamed rice.

Tips for Novices

Harder vegetables — carrots, snow peas, asparagus, green beans, broccoli, and cauliflower — need blanching. Vegetables with a high water content — onions, scallions, bell peppers, and mushrooms —don't. However, if you julienne or shred the hard vegetables, you can eliminate blanching.

Frozen vegetables such as green peas must be thawed; canned vegetables such as water chestnuts and bamboo shoots must be drained. After that they may be treated as if they were blanched.

If you are using more than one kind of raw vegetable, add the one with the longer cooking time first — zucchini, for example, before onion. Even if the vegetables seem to have similar cooking times, give one a head start; unless you have a powerful stove, the wok is burdened by the addition of more than three-quarters of a pound of raw vegetables at once.

For both practical and aesthetic reasons, cut meats and vegetables uniformly. Cooking will be more even, and the finished dish more appealing.

Pineapple or other fruits can be substituted for some of the vegetables in stir-fries flavored with the Sweet and Sour Sauce (*see* "Chinese Flavoring Sauces," page 19). I use one pound pineapple along with eight ounces of red pepper and scallions. Add the fruit as you would blanched vegetables.

You can flavor stir-fries with a few ounces of cashews or other nuts. Add them to the wok after removing the second batch of meat, just before adding the aromatics. Leave them in the wok while you finish cooking.

To firm up steak or chicken breasts and make them easier to cut, freeze the meat for an hour or two. If it's frozen to begin with, transfer it from the freezer to the refrigerator in the morning. By evening, the steak or chicken should be a not-quite-thawed texture that's perfect for slicing, cubing, dicing, or julienning. ■

A Variety of Chinese Cookbooks

Nahum Waxman, owner of Kitchen Arts and Letters, a bookstore in New York City dedicated exclusively to food and wine, developed this short list of Chinese cookbooks for those who are ready to trade their chef's knife for a cleaver. Reading the first two will give you a comprehensive approach akin to that of *Mastering the Art of French Cooking.*

The Key to Chinese Cooking
By Irene Kuo
Alfred A. Knopf, 1977; $27.50
Recipe-oriented, quite complete.

The Modern Art of Chinese Cooking
By Barbara Tropp
William Morrow, 1982; $30.00
Comprehensive but distinctly American approach.

Chinese Cooking Techniques
California Culinary Academy
Chevron Chemical Company, 1987; $9.95
User-friendly, with lots of useful color photographs.

Ken Hom's Quick and Easy Chinese Cooking
By Ken Hom
Chronicle Books, 1990; $14.95
Practical, with shopping lists and preparation and cooking times. Ken Hom's recipes always work.

Florence Lin's Complete Book of Chinese Noodles, Dumplings and Breads
By Florence Lin
William Morrow, 1986; $19.95
Once you've mastered stir-frying, this respected teacher can show you how to make Chinese noodles and doughs.

Leg of Lamb with Red Chile Crust and Jalapeño Preserves

Use classic French techniques to create a dish that's utterly southwestern.

Mesa Grill doesn't look like a restaurant with serious food; in fact, it has all the earmarks of a super-trendy New York spot. A former factory in the Flatiron district, it has 25-foot ceilings (maybe higher — no one seems to have measured recently), and is decorated in primary colors with a mildly amusing cowboy motif. It's noisy, and the crowd is young. The restaurant even has a logo.

When you look at Mesa Grill's thoroughly southwestern menu, though, you begin to realize that someone here is quite serious. Dishes like Crisp Whole Red Snapper with Tangerine-Ancho Chile Sauce; Grilled Pork Chops Adobo with Spicy Apple Chutney; Sweet Potato Soup with Smoked Chiles; and Shrimp and Roasted Garlic Corn Tamale are immediately and enormously appealing.

The serious person behind these creations is Bobby Flay, the 28-year-old chef who moved here just over two years ago after making a splash at the Miracle Grill, a smaller restaurant farther downtown. Flay grew up in the restaurant business, started cooking professionally when he was 17, attended the French Culinary Institute, and worked in three of Jonathan Waxman's restaurants before taking an interest in southwestern cooking. "When you think about it," he says now, "southwestern food is the truest regional American food."

Whether or not you agree with that sweeping statement, you will find Flay's food is straightforward, direct, and supremely flavorful. These qualities put his creations in that rare camp of dishes that are not only great restaurant food, but are also nearly perfect for home cooking. Once you have collected a few special ingredients (mostly an assortment of chiles, readily available by mail — *see* Sources and Resources, page 32), the rest is easy. To make his perennially popular Roast Leg of Lamb with Red Chile Crust, for example, Flay bones a whole leg of lamb, stuffs the meat with cilantro pesto, rolls and ties it, rubs it with a paste containing freshly made chili powders, and roasts it. Marinating before roasting is optional, and gives you the flexibility to do everything except roast the lamb a day — or even two — in advance. Flay serves the roast with a thin,

At Mesa Grill in New York City, chef Bobby Flay makes high-intensity southwestern food that you can recreate at home.

hot-and-sweet jam made from red bell and jalapeño peppers, a play on the mint jelly theme.

There are no tricks involved in making this dish. For the most part, it follows traditional French techniques for dealing with lamb; a beginning cook would have little trouble with it. The boning can be done by a butcher (even most supermarkets sell boned leg of lamb), the cilantro pesto is as straightforward as "regular" basil pesto, and the jalapeño preserves are similar to strawberry preserves. Tying, a useful technique that is mastered by few home cooks, is as easy as tying your shoes, if you follow the illustrations (at right). And the most challenging aspect of the homemade chili powders is obtaining dried ancho and pasilla chiles.

You might be tempted to substitute store-bought chili powder for these, and certainly such a switch would be no crime. But Flay discourages this. "Store-bought chili powder is bitter and without much character," he says. "You cannot compare it to powder made from dried ancho and pasilla chiles."

There's really very little reason to make the substitution. Making chili powder at home takes less than 10 minutes, and the flavor makes a wonderful contribution to this impressive dish.

ROAST LEG OF LAMB WITH RED CHILE CRUST AND JALAPEÑO PRESERVES

Serves 12–16

To toast the cumin seeds for the marinade, heat a small skillet, add the cumin seeds, and toast over medium-high heat, shaking the pan constantly, until seeds are fragrant, about 15 seconds. Grind in a coffee grinder or with a mortar and pestle. Do not more than triple the Jalapeño Preserve recipe.

1 leg of lamb (about 7 pounds), boned and butterflied
Salt and ground black pepper

Red Chile Marinade

2 ancho chiles, stemmed, seeded, and halved
1 pasilla chile, stemmed, seeded, and halved
1 small chile chipotle pureed with a bit of adobo to yield 1 tablespoon
1 tablespoon toasted cumin seed, ground
2 tablespoons olive oil

Cilantro Pesto

2 cups packed cilantro, leaves only
2 large garlic cloves
2 tablespoons pumpkin seeds
2 tablespoons lime juice from 1 large lime
Salt and ground black pepper
5 tablespoons olive oil

PHOTOGRAPH BY RICHARD FELBER

Jalapeño Preserves

1 medium red bell pepper, seeded and cut into ½-inch dice
2 jalapeño peppers, seeded and minced
1⅓ cups sugar
6½ tablespoons red wine vinegar
¼ cup fruit pectin

1. *For the marinade,* heat oven to 350°. Set ancho and pasilla chile pieces in a small pan; place pan in oven until chile pieces develop a sheen, no more than 30 seconds. Cut chiles into pieces small enough to grind in a mini-chopper or coffee grinder. Grind chiles to a powder. Mix with next 3 ingredients to form a smooth paste. Set aside.

2. *For the pesto,* place first 4 ingredients, plus 2 teaspoons salt and 1 teaspoon pepper, in the workbowl of a food processor fitted with a steel blade; process until cilantro is minced. With machine on, slowly add the olive oil so that pesto emulsifies. Transfer to a small container; cover and refrigerate.

3. *For the preserves,* bring first 4 ingredients to boil in a medium nonreactive saucepan. Adjust heat to medium-low and simmer, stirring every 5 minutes, for a total of 20 minutes. Remove from heat, stir in pectin. Return saucepan to heat and bring mixture to boil. Let preserves cool to room temperature; they will be on the thin side. Transfer to a non reactive container and refrigerate. (Refrigerated preserves will last at least 3 months; if canned, preserves can be stored indefinitely.)

4. Lay the butterflied leg of lamb, cut side up, so that its short end faces you; trim off excess meat, particularly the shank piece, so that leg forms a rough rectangle. (Meat scraps can be placed on thinner sections of the butterflied leg for more uniform height.) Pound particularly thick leg muscles to facilitate rolling. Spread about ⅔ of the Cilantro Pesto in a thin layer over leg, leaving at least a 1-inch border around the perimeter. (If spread too close to the edge, pesto will ooze out when leg is tied.) Reserve remaining pesto for serving. Starting with the short side closest to you, roll leg into a tight cylinder. Following the illustrations below, tie roast to secure. Place lamb leg on a roasting pan; rub roast on all sides with the chile marinade. (Can cover and refrigerate up to 48 hours.)

5. Bring lamb roast to room temperature. Adjust rack to low position and heat oven to 450°; roast lamb for 15 minutes. Reduce oven temperature to 350°; roast until a meat thermometer inserted into the thickest part registers no more than 120° to 125°, about 1½ hours. Let roast rest at room temperature for 15 minutes. Cut lamb into slices ½-inch thick . Drizzle with remaining pesto and serve with Jalapeño Preserves passed separately. ■

Sorting Out Chiles

The jalapeño (at left) and the chipotle (at right) are the same pepper. To make chipotles, jalapeños are smoked. You can find them dried (and reconstitute them yourself), but it's easier to buy them canned, in *adobo*—a tomato, vinegar, and herb paste. For this recipe you'll need the canned version.

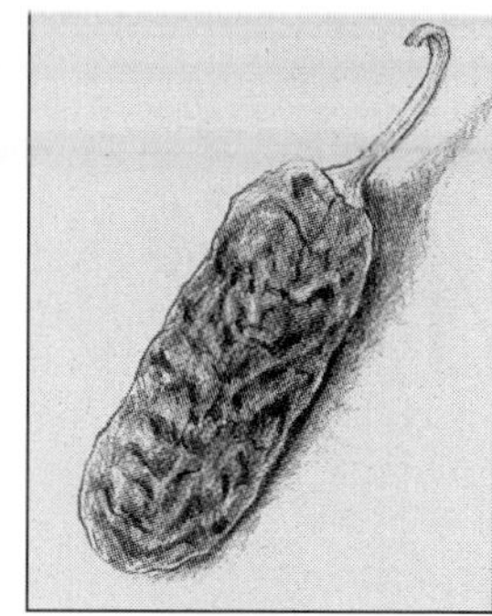

The triangular ancho (left) and longer pasilla (right) have a similar wrinkled, reddish-brown skin, but their aroma and taste are quite different. Ancho has a fruity rather than hot flavor — it's a little like a spicy raisin — while pasilla is everything you want from a fiery pepper: dark, earthy, and rich.

Tying the Leg of Lamb

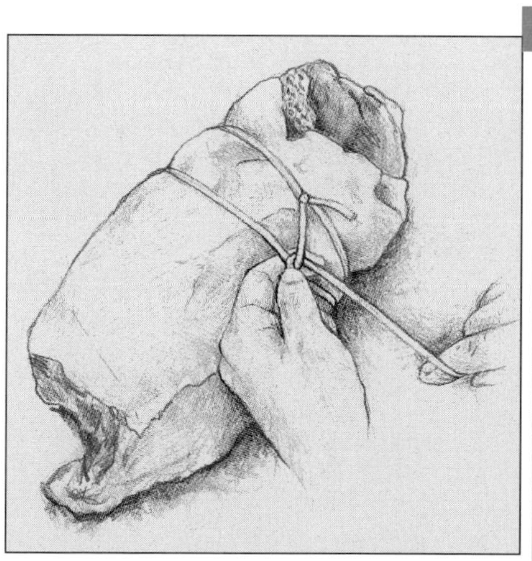

1. Start with a piece of string 4 or 5 feet long. Hold one end on top of the rolled lamb, then wrap the other end around the meat. Tie in a knot. Move the long end about an inch down the roast, loop it around your finger, then wrap it under and around the roast. Run it through the loop you've made and pull tight.

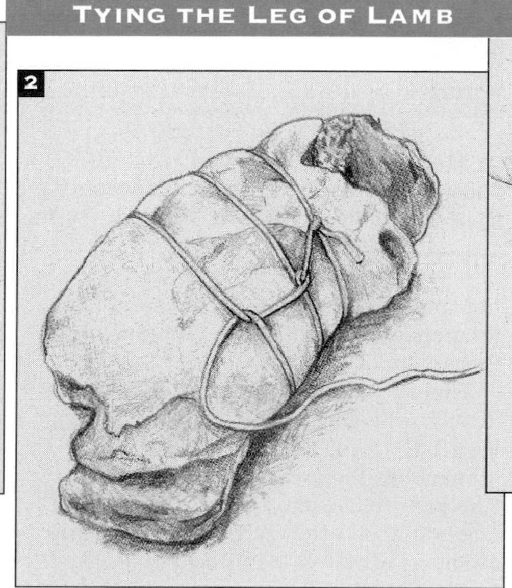

2. Repeat step 1 as necessary, moving down the lamb.

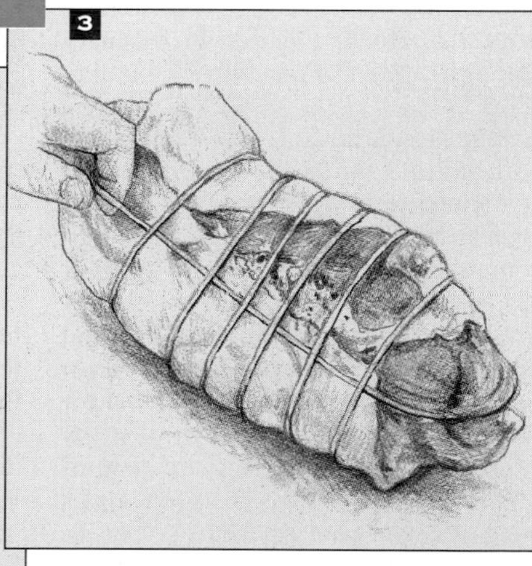

3. When you reach the other end of the rolled lamb, run the string along the bottom of the roast, passing it through each of the loops. Bring it up to the original knot, pull tight, tie, and cut excess string.

ILLUSTRATIONS BY KATHY BRAY

How to Poach Fruit

With two basic techniques and syrups of varying densities and flavors, you can make an infinite variety of simple poached fruit desserts.

BY NICK MALGIERI

To maintain pears' subtle color, peel them and then plunge them immediately into an acidulated water bath made by combining two quarts of water with the strained juice of two lemons and one quart of ice cubes.

Poaching is a particularly apt way to cook fruit. Unlike other cooking methods, poaching allows the shape, texture, and basic flavor of fruit to remain intact, while improving its tenderness and enhancing rather than masking its flavor. Perfectly ripe fruit poaches quickly and easily. But I have found that poaching is also a perfect remedy for underripe or bland fruit, rendering it immediately edible. Several different strengths of sugar syrups and flavorings for fruit are recommended in the chart on page 26 — once you get the hang of it, you can vary them as you like.

Preparing the Fruit

Readying fruit for poaching is rarely more than a matter of peeling and coring, pitting, or hulling. Stainless-steel knives or peelers are best for these tasks; carbon steel reacts with the acid in fruit and imparts a metallic flavor to all but the first few pieces cut.

The cut surfaces of some fruit, especially pears, apples, peaches, cherries, and apricots, discolor when exposed to air. This oxidation, caused by an enzyme called polyphenoloxidase, can be retarded by refrigeration, surface application of acids such as lemon juice, or salting — hardly practical for fruit. The easiest way to prevent browning is to poach the fruit immediately after prepping. The exception is pears, which discolor so quickly that they must be plunged directly into acidulated water to prevent browning.

Poaching Techniques

Poaching performs two distinct functions: it softens fruit's cellulose, or fiber, and concentrates its natural sugars, allowing the fruit to retain its shape and most of its texture.

Poaching does present one unique problem, however: if the fruit is poached in plain water, osmotic pressure — the process by which the cell walls of fruit seek to equalize the concentration of molecules on both sides of the wall — will expel the fruit's sugars from its cells, making it less sweet. That's the reason to poach in sugar syrup — not only to allow the fruit to absorb some of the sugar from the syrup, but also to prevent it from losing its own sugars. Assuming the quantity is not excessive, sugar also intensifies the existing flavors of many fruits.

Poaching technique does differ slightly depending on the ripeness of the fruit you are using. When poaching firm and underripe fruit, you need only combine the fruit with the elements of the syrup and bring it to a simmer before allowing it to cool in the liquid. This slow cooking and cooling permits the fruit fiber to soften gently and absorb maximum flavor from the syrup. For soft, delicate fruit, it is preferable to make the syrup first then, while it is hot, pour it over the fruit. The water trapped in the cell walls of the fruit cools slowly enough to actually cook the fruit even though the fruit itself spends no time on the fire.

Poaching Syrups

To prepare cold poaching liquid, combine water (or other liquid, *see* "Seasonings for Poaching Syrup") and sugar in a large nonreactive saucepan; add fruit and selected seasonings. Follow the cooking instructions for specific fruit (*see* chart page 26).

To prepare hot poaching liquid, combine the cooking liquid and sugar in a nonreactive pan. Bring to a boil over low heat, stirring occasionally to dissolve sugar crystals. Use immediately or reheat, returning syrup to a full boil (or simmer, depending on the fruit) before

POACHING SYRUPS

Each recipe makes enough syrup for poaching up to two pounds of fruit at one time.

Light syrup	Medium syrup	Heavy syrup
2 cups water	2 cups water	2 cups water
½ cup sugar	1 cup sugar	1½ cups sugar

ILLUSTRATION BY MELINDA MAY SULLIVAN

adding fruit and selected seasoning.

STRAWBERRY AND RHUBARB COMPOTES WITH SUGARED PECANS

Serves 6–8

One of the mainstays of the lunch menu at Windows on the World restaurant, this continues to be one of my favorite simple, make-ahead desserts.

Strawberry Compote

- 1 quart strawberries, prepared according to chart
- 1 recipe medium syrup
- 1 tablespoon lemon juice
- 1 tablespoon Kirsch

Rhubarb Compote

- 1½ pounds fresh rhubarb, prepared according to chart
- 1 recipe heavy syrup, replacing 1 cup of the water with 1 cup orange juice

Sugared Pecans

- 2 cups pecan halves
- 1 egg white
- 1 cup sugar

1. For the Strawberry Compote, follow cooking instructions on chart, page 26; flavor cooled berries with lemon juice and Kirsch. Cover and refrigerate.

2. For the Rhubarb Compote, follow cooking instructions on chart, page 26; cover and refrigerate.

3. For the Sugared Pecans, adjust rack to middle position and heat oven to 325°. Toss pecan halves with egg white in a 9-by-13-inch baking pan until nuts are completely coated; stir in sugar. Bake, stirring the mixture every 5 minutes, until pecan coating turns a nutty brown, 25 to 30 minutes. Immediately transfer nuts to a clean pan in a single layer to cool. Cool, then cover and store at room temperature.

4. Spoon a portion of each fruit, with a bit of its poaching liquid, into each dessert bowl. Top with Sugared Pecans and serve immediately.

POACHED PEARS WITH STAR ANISE

Serves 6

Chris Kump, joint chef/owner with his wife, Margaret Fox, of Cafe Beaujolais in Mendocino, California, frequently serves these pears with vanilla ice cream or uses them as a base for pear soufflé.

- 3 ripe Bartlett or other pears, prepared according to chart on page 26
- 1 recipe medium syrup
- 1 vanilla bean
- 1 star anise
- 1 tablespoon pear eau-de-vie
- 1 pint vanilla ice cream

1. Follow cooking instructions on chart, adding vanilla bean and star anise with the

To Core a Pear

1. Use a melon baller to cut around the central core with a circular motion.

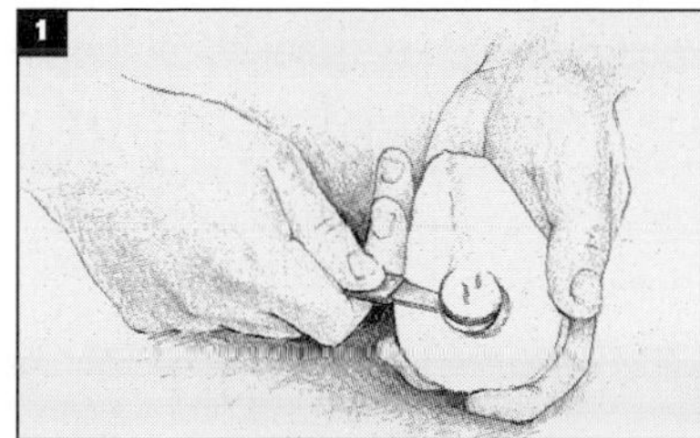

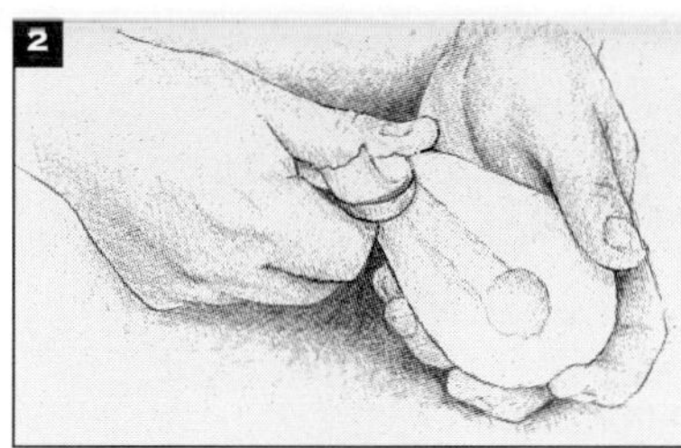

2. Draw the melon baller from the central core to the top of the pear, removing the interior stem as you go.

Slicing Pineapple

1. Slice the top and bottom from the pineapple, then cut off the rind without cutting too far into the fruit.

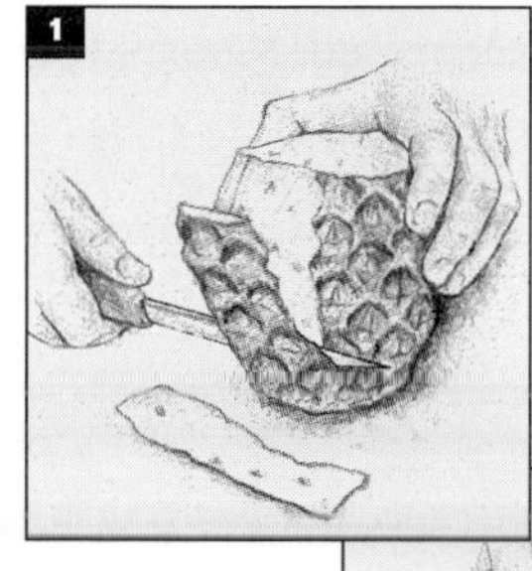

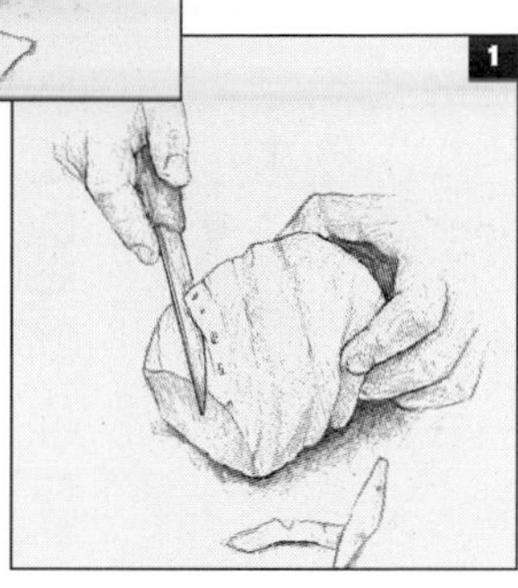

2. Remove the "eyes" from the pineapple by cutting a spiraling ridge from bottom to top.

Seasonings for Poaching Syrup

Sugar syrups may be seasoned with a wide variety of flavors; these are the most widely used.

Liquors and liqueurs: A small amount of the eau-de-vie of the same fruit — such as Calvados with apples — enhances most poached fruits. Add it after the fruit has cooled to room temperature. Use sparingly — start with no more than a tablespoon — or the bitterness of the alcohol will overwhelm the fruit. In addition, try any of these combinations:

Armagnac: *plums or prunes*
Bourbon: *apples, pears*
Cognac: *apples, pears*
Framboise: *figs, plums, raspberries, strawberries*
Herb liqueurs *(Benedictine, Chartreuse, Strega): pears in vanilla syrup with no other seasonings*
Kirsch: *all fruit*
Orange liqueur: *all fruit*
Rum: *white with delicate and/or acidic fruit; dark with apples, pears.*

Caramel: Caramelize half the sugar for the syrup, then add water and the remaining sugar. Adds an elusive flavor and magnificent color to apples and pears.

Citrus zest: Strip the zest from one lemon or orange with a vegetable peeler — press lightly so as not to remove the white pith beneath the zest — and add to poaching liquid. Remove zest after several hours or it will impart a bitter flavor.

Fruit juices: Replace half the water in sugar syrup with raspberry or orange juice. Great for figs, pears, and peaches.

Herbs: Thyme and/or bay leaves with figs; lemon verbena or lemon balm with pears or apricots; mint with pears. Use a sprig or branch, or one teaspoon, dried, wrapped in cheesecloth.

Spices: One cinnamon stick, with apples or pears; two to three cloves, with apples or pears; six black peppercorns, with pears poached in red wine; two pieces star anise, for pears.

Vanilla bean: Add a whole vanilla bean to any preparation of poached fruit. Don't split the bean or the fruit will be covered with tiny black specks. Leave the vanilla bean in the syrup until the fruit has cooled, then remove, dry, and reuse it.

Wines: Replace all or part of the water. Red wine is good with apricots, cherries, peaches, pears, plums, and strawberries. White wine is best with apples, oranges, pears, and pineapple. Avoid sweet fortified wines — Port, Madeira, and Marsala — with all fruits except pears; they are too strong for all others.

ILLUSTRATION BY KATHY BRAY

Poaching Fresh Fruit

This chart describes methods for poaching a variety of fresh fruit. If the fruit is extremely tart, substitute heavy syrup where medium is suggested. Pineapple (unless perfectly ripe) and rhubarb always need heavy syrup. Once poached, keep the fruit loosely covered so it does not cool too rapidly. After the fruit has cooled, refrigerate it in its syrup; it will keep for five days.

Fruit	Preparation	Syrup	Cooking Method
Apple	Use a paring knife to peel, quarter or halve; core with a melon baller or spoon; add syrup immediately to prevent discoloration.	Medium	Combine all syrup ingredients; add apples and bring to a slight simmer; cool in syrup.
Apricot	Do not peel; cut in half and remove pit.	Medium	Bring syrup to a boil, add apricot halves and seasonings and allow to cool.
Sour Cherry	Stem and pit, using chopstick or paring knife to force out pit, cutting from stem end.	Heavy	Bring syrup to a boil and pour over cherries; allow to cool.
Sweet Cherry	Stem and pit, using a chopstick or paring knife to force out the pit, cutting from stem end.	Light	Bring syrup to a boil and pour over cherries; allow to cool.
Fig	Stem, peel, and cut in half.	Light	Bring syrup to a boil and pour over figs.
Orange	Peel, using a serrated knife, and section.	Heavy	Bring syrup to a boil, add oranges and return to a slight simmer. Remove oranges and allow to cool; allow syrup to cool, then pour over oranges.
Peach	Blanch in boiling water; remove skin and pits; cut in half.	Medium	Bring syrup to a boil and add peach halves; allow to cool.
Pear	Peel with a knife, quarter or halve, and core with a melon baller or spoon; plunge into acidulated water to prevent discoloration.	Medium	Combine all syrup ingredients; add pears and bring to a full simmer; cool in syrup.
Pineapple	Peel with a knife; remove eyes (*see* illustration page 25), quarter, and core.	Heavy	Combine all syrup ingredients; add pineapple and bring to a slight simmer; cool in syrup.
Plum	Do not peel; cut in half and remove pit.	Medium	Bring syrup to a boil, add plums and seasonings, and allow to cool.
Rhubarb	String (*see* illustration, page 4) and cut into 2-inch lengths.	Heavy	Bring syrup to a boil and pour over rhubarb; allow to cool.
Strawberry	Hull with paring knife; leave whole.	Medium	Bring syrup to a boil and pour over berries in a shallow nonreactive pan.

pears. Remove vanilla bean and star anise; cover pears and cool to room temperature, then refrigerate.

2. Spoon a half pear into each serving bowl and sprinkle with a few drops of eau-de-vie. Place a scoop of ice cream alongside each pear and serve immediately.

PEACHES AND CHERRIES POACHED IN SPICED RED WINE

Serves 6

The accompanying chart is simply a guide. Here's an example of a variation, particularly useful when you want to poach mixed fruits. Since the peaches are sliced rather than halved, they'll be cooked, cherry-style, with the hot syrup poured over them. Serve this compote as is, with a bit of the poaching syrup, or as a shortcake topping.

- 1 pound peaches, peeled, pitted, and sliced
- 1 pound sweet cherries, prepared according to chart above
- ½ cinnamon stick
- 2 cloves
- 1 recipe medium syrup, replacing the 2 cups of water with 2 cups of red wine

1. Place the fruit in a large bowl, along with cinnamon stick and cloves. Pour boiling syrup over fruit; cover and cool to room temperature. Remove spices and refrigerate until ready to serve. ■

Nick Malgieri is the author of *Great Italian Desserts* (Little, Brown, 1990) and is currently at work on a complete baking guide to be published by HarperCollins.

Using and Rating Immersion Blenders

It can fill in for the whisk, it can substitute for the blender, and it can do some things better than either.

BY MICHELE ANNA JORDAN

The immersion blender, a hand-held wand with a rotating blade on one end and a motor and electric cord on the other, arrived on the culinary scene nearly a decade ago. There are at least eight immersion blenders available (*see* page 29 for *Cook's* evaluation of these), and — although you wouldn't guess it from late-night television commercials — they can be helpful kitchen tools.

I have always thought of the immersion blender as a miniature version of the soup gun, which is an oversized professional tool used to blend huge pots of soup and to emulsify vast quantities of salad dressings. The home kitchen models perform these same functions well, too, in smaller quantities. But professional chefs are also using immersion blenders to make quick and easy emulsified sauces, replacing not only their soup guns, but also the hand-held whisk.

Less Fat, More Speed

Chef Jean-Louis Gerin of Restaurant Jean-Louis in Greenwich, Connecticut, for example, calls immersion blenders "revolutionary." "Where I once used a whisk," he says, "I now use the immersion blender. I have two, one at the seafood station, one at the meat station." Gerin uses the tool for making fine emulsified sauces. In these, he often includes Dijon mustard, which is a natural emulsifier, and purees of roasted shallots or garlic, which he refers to as "the glue," and which allow him to reduce the amount of butter he uses. With the addition of vegetable broth, truffle juice, or stock, he can make a light, emulsified sauce in seconds. "The immersion blender incorporates more air into the mixture than I can by hand," says Gerin. Because of this, the blenders allow users to combine virtually any liquid and fat to produce a fine sauce.

Charles Saunders, chef/owner of the Eastside Oyster Bar and Grill in Sonoma, California, uses the immersion blender to make a more-or-less standard *beurre blanc,* but says the immersion blender works much more quickly than almost anyone can use a whisk, thus simplifying the difficult and often tricky incorporation of the butter.

These are not the only tasks for which immersion blenders are suited. I use mine for all kinds of emulsions, including mayonnaise and vinaigrette. But my favorite use for the blender is in soup making. It is perfect for pureeing mixtures of vegetables and broth, tomatoes or beets, any type of beans, or any combination of liquid and vegetables that would normally have been pureed in the blender or food processor. Besides, the immersion blender is easy to use and clean up.

The immersion blender can not do everything, though. Manufacturers' recommendations notwithstanding, these blenders make dreadful mashed potatoes and, with one exception (*see* page 29), they are also useless for chopping.

Containers

The container you use is almost as important as the blender itself. In some instances, you can work in the container in which you are cooking: simply submerge the blender in your beans and whir away — nothing could be easier. But

THE TOP THREE IMMERSION BLENDERS

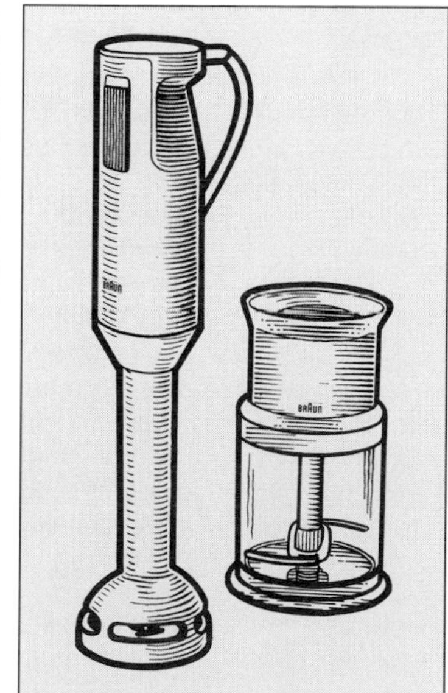

1. Braun MR380*:* $38.00. The Minichopper attachment included with the Braun model allows it to mince herbs and chop nuts.

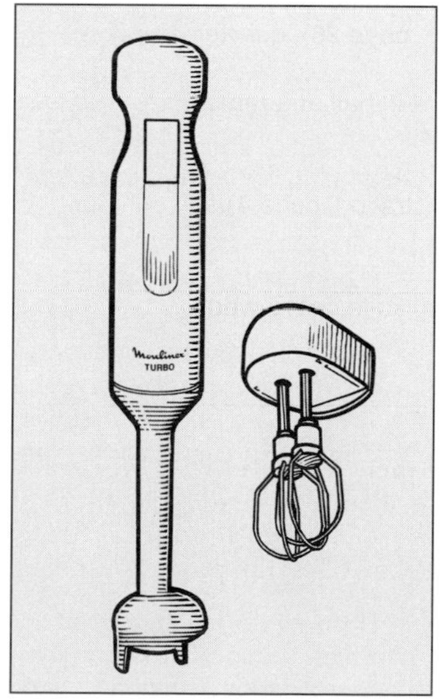

2. Moulinex Turbo 071*:* $30.00. The Moulinex blender comes with a rotary beater attachment for whipping cream and mixing batters.

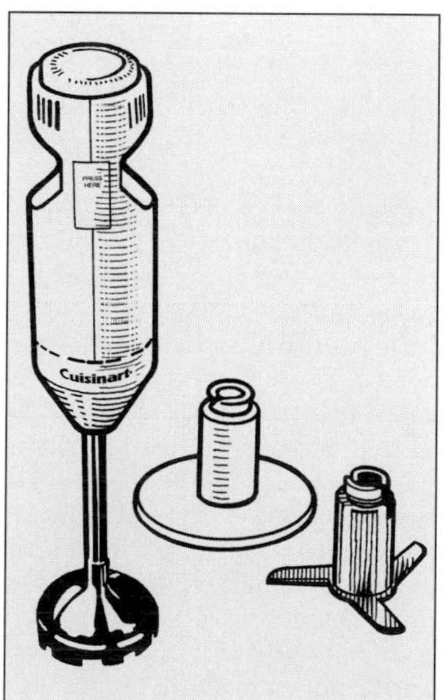

3. Cuisinart CSB-1C*:* $50.00. The Cuisinart model includes separate blades for whipping and puréeing and blending.

ILLUSTRATIONS BY DAN KROVATIN

when making sauces with immersion blenders, the shape of the container becomes more important. The tapered slope of the container that comes with the Cuisinart immersion blender is particularly useful, especially for sauces such as beurre blanc. Since you begin with a small quantity of liquid, the narrow bottom makes the initial submersion of the tool much easier; its outward flare allows you to hold the blender at a slight angle, and to see the sauce as it comes together; and it provides ample clearance for adding butter.

The depth of the container is also worth considering. You should be able to move the blender up and down through the liquid in order to incorporate all ingredients smoothly or to obtain a full emulsion. Use caution as the blender nears the top — should the rotary blade break the surface, you will be splashed, an inconvenience at best, and a possible danger.

ROAST CHICKEN WITH DIJON MUSTARD-THYME SAUCE

Serves 4

Jean-Louis Gerin of Restaurant Jean-Louis in Greenwich, Connecticut, serves this sauce with butterflied baby chicken *(poussin)*. The immersion blender transforms all the wonderful tasting (but not-so-wonderful looking) browned mustard bits and pieces into flecks, giving the sauce a smooth, more refined look.

½ cup Dijon mustard
1 tablespoon fresh thyme, stems removed
4 chicken breast halves or 4 whole chicken legs
2 tablespoons butter
1½ cups chicken stock
¼ cup heavy cream

1. Mix Dijon mustard and thyme; coat chicken pieces with this marinade. Cover and refrigerate for 24 hours.

2. Bring chicken to room temperature and heat oven to 350°. Melt 1 tablespoon butter in a skillet. Add 2 breasts and cook, skin side down, over medium-high heat, until well browned, about 6 minutes. Transfer breasts to a roasting pan. Repeat cooking process with remaining chicken, adding another tablespoon butter, if necessary. Transfer chicken to the oven; roast until juices run clear when pierced with a fork, 20 to 25 minutes.

3. Meanwhile, add chicken stock to skillet; bring to boil, scraping up any brown bits that have stuck to the pan; simmer until stock reduces to ¾ cup, about 10 minutes. Add cream; return to simmer for 1 minute. Pour sauce into an appropriate container. Submerge an immersion blender and blend until sauce is smooth and frothy. Place a piece of chicken on each of 4 dinner plates. Spoon a portion of sauce over each piece of chicken and serve immediately.

GINGER BEURRE BLANC

Makes approximately 1 cup

Chef Charles Saunders uses his immersion blender to make this velvety, ginger-flavored classic, excellent on most light-fleshed fish.

½ cup Chardonnay
2 tablespoons white wine or rice wine vinegar
1 tablespoon minced ginger
1 tablespoon minced garlic
1 tablespoon minced shallots
¼ cup heavy cream
12 tablespoons room-temperature unsalted butter, cut into ½-inch pieces
Salt and cayenne pepper

1. Bring first 5 ingredients to boil; adjust heat to medium-high and reduce mixture by half, about 5 minutes. Add cream; reduce by half again, 2 to 3 minutes.

2. Strain mixture through a fine sieve into a warm container (*see* "Immersion Blender Tips," this page). Add 2 pieces of butter, submerge immersion blender; blend until mixture is smooth. Continue adding butter, 1 piece at a time, until it has all been incorporated.

3. Add about ½ teaspoon salt and a pinch of cayenne pepper; blend well. Taste and adjust the seasonings and serve. (Can store in a thermos bottle or over a pan of warm water up to 1 hour.) ■

IMMERSION BLENDER TIPS

Immersion blenders are top-heavy. Don't leave yours upright in a container and walk away (I learned this the hard way). Set it on a cutting board or other work surface.

To facilitate clean-up, have a container of clean water nearby. As soon as you've completed your soup, sauce, or dressing, run the blender briefly in the clean water. Then unplug it and rinse it under warm water before putting it away.

If you are pureeing hot soup or beans, move the pot off the stove before blending. A cord resting on a hot burner or passing over a forgotten flame could be dangerous.

Once a sauce is made, you can hold it by transferring it to a heat-retaining container. A good thermos, properly used, can allow you to make a delicate beurre blanc or hollandaise an hour or more in advance. In recent tests, I found a glass thermos most efficient.

Michele Anna Jordan, the author of *The Good Cook's Book of Oil & Vinegar* (Addison-Wesley, 1992)and *A Cook's Tour of Sonoma* (Addison-Wesley, 1990), lives in northern California.

FIVE USEFUL IMMERSION BLENDER RECIPES

"Margarine"
Blend together equal amounts of room-temperature butter and virgin olive oil. Chill and use as you would butter, except in baking or fine saucemaking.

Raspberry Mayonnaise
Place 1 whole egg, 1 egg yolk, 1 teaspoon dry mustard, 1 teaspoon sugar, ½ teaspoon salt, ¼ cup low-acid raspberry vinegar, and ¼ cup extra virgin olive oil in an appropriate container. Submerge the blender, blend ingredients together, then slowly add ½ cup olive oil and ½ cup vegetable oil until emulsified. Taste and correct the seasoning.

Honey-Pepper Vinaigrette
Place ¼ cup warm honey, ¼ cup balsamic vinegar, 1 minced shallot, 2 minced garlic cloves, 1 teaspoon salt, and 2 teaspoons freshly ground black pepper in an appropriate container. Submerge the blender, blend ingredients together, then slowly add ¾ cup extra virgin olive oil. Taste and correct seasonings. Excellent as a dressing for pasta, tomatoes, grilled lamb, or seafood salads.

Gazpacho
Puree with blender 2 cups (about 1 pound) fresh tomatoes, peeled, seeded, and coarsely chopped, with 2 cups chicken stock. Stir in 1 avocado, peeled and diced; 1 small cucumber, peeled and diced; 1 medium red pepper, diced; ¼ small red onion, chopped fine; 2 garlic cloves, minced; 1 jalapeño, minced; 2 tablespoons minced parsley or cilantro; 2 tablespoons extra virgin olive oil, 2 tablespoons red wine vinegar, and salt and pepper to taste. Serve chilled.

Dessert Sauces
Puree with blender 1 pint of raspberries or hulled and quartered strawberries, ¼ cup sugar, and ¼ cup liqueur — Framboise, Cointreau, or Grand Marnier. (If making raspberry sauce, strain out seeds.) Use as a sauce for soufflés, ice cream, crepes, or other desserts.

Rating Immersion Blenders

Price and Variety of Attachments Are Key to Buying the Right Immersion Blender.

By Jack Bishop

Spurred by the market for diet shakes (one blender even comes with a packet of Ultra Slim-Fast in the box), sales of immersion — or hand-held — blenders are increasing at a rate of 20 per cent annually; one out of every three blenders sold is an immersion blender.

As noted in the accompanying story (see page 27), hand-held blenders can make milk-shakes and puree soups with the added convenience of putting the whirring blades directly into simmering pots and frosty glasses. Some manufacturers also claim that their machines can handle tougher tasks. To test these claims, I attempted to whip cream, mince parsley, grind almonds, semi-puree black beans, puree a vegetable soup (containing carrots, leeks, turnips, herbs, and potatoes), and make the Ginger Beurre Blanc on page 28. While doing these tests, I also rated the design and versatility of each blender.

When it comes to their most important uses — pureeing and emulsifying — all eight of the machines did an adequate job. For pureeing, the Hamilton Beach and the Moulinex are slightly better than the crowd; the Salton is noticeably worse. For emulsifying, all the machines were about equal.

Generally, I would limit an immersion blender to those uses, although the gadgets and accessories offered with some do allow them to perform additional tasks. With an attachment that includes two rotary beaters, the Moulinex blender is easily the best at whipping cream and can be used much like a hand mixer. The Braun model, which comes with a chopping attachment, is the only one I would recommend for mincing herbs or chopping nuts. The Cuisinart has the advantage of coming with three separate blades and has the best container.

Overall, it's safe to say that cheaper machines perform fewer tasks than models with attachments. Since the difference in cost is not great, I have rated the most versatile blenders highest. Finally, a note about prices: hand blenders usually sell for less than the manufacturer's suggested retail price; I have included the "actual" retail price when possible.

Blenders In Order Of Preference

Manufacturer	Speeds	Power	Price	Accessories	Performance in Tests	General Comments
Braun MR380	One	120 watts	$38 (actual)	Chopping attachment with lid, whipping disk, clear graduated beaker, wall mount.	Whips cream adequately; chops parsley and almonds perfectly. Purees well. Beaker comes in handy when emulsifying sauces.	Best overall design. Easiest machine to handle and very quick to wash.
Moulinex Turbo 071	One	150 watts	$30 (actual)	Attachment with two small rotary beaters for whipping cream or mixing batters; pureeing/ mashing blade for fruits and vegetables; clear graduated beaker with fine sieve;wall mount.	Best machine for whipping cream; not designed for chopping herbs or nuts. Produces extra-smooth purees. Sieve insert is excellent for straining and emulsifying in one container.	The biggest blender with the most clunky design; whips and purees extremely well.
Cuisinart CSB-1C	Variable	150 watts	$50 (actual)	Separate blades for whipping, blending and chopping; clear graduated plastic beaker and metal beaker; wall mount.	Special blade yields excellent whipped cream; chopping blade does poor job overall. Purees well but food gets caught in blade. Wide stainless-steel beaker is top choice.	Best user's manual, with intriguing recipes and extensive tips. Clean-up is cumbersome.
Singer 795	Two	100 watts	$25 (actual)	Separate blades for whipping, mincing, and mixing; clear beaker without measuring lines; wall mount.	Special disk whips cream well (but disk is impossible to remove unless fingers are very small); sauce emulsifies nicely in wide beaker.	Light, compact, and versatile with a low price considering the number of extras.
Rival 951W	Two	100 watts	$31 (suggested)	Opaque beaker without measuring lines.	Whips cream adequately; not designed for mincing herbs. Purees, emulsifies sauce nicely on low.	Light and easy to use. Shallow well for blade makes cleaning easy.
Waring HHB75-1	Two	NA	$35.95 (suggested)	Opaque beaker without measuring lines .	Whips cream adequately; not designed to chop herbs or nuts. Purees beans and soup well; emulsify sauce on low to prevent excess foam.	Compact design and very easy to clean.
Hamilton Beach 57900	One	80 watts	$25 (suggested)	None.	Whips cream adequately; not designed for mincing herbs. Chops nuts unevenly and makes a mess. Excellent for soup; emulsifies sauce well.	Power button is hard to engage since it must be snapped into place. User's manual provides little information. Curved three-sided shaft is hard to grip.
Salton MX 1	One	150 watts	$15 (actual)	None.	Worst at whipping cream; does not chop or mince despite claims. Emulsifies sauce without problems.	Light design but only moderate success in tests.

For information about finding individual blenders, see Sources and Resources, page 32.

Cooking Under Wraps
By Nicole Routhier
William Morrow, $27.00

In this book, Nicole Routhier shows she is more than an expert on Vietnamese cooking; she's also at home on international culinary turf. Building on the magic she worked with rice paper in her first book (*The Foods of Vietnam*, Morrow, 1989), she turns to other wrapping mediums: phyllo, vegetables, yeast breads, flatbread, crepes, even chocolate.

Many of the recipes in this book are challenging, long, even tedious, but Routhier is a gifted recipe writer and never abandons the reader. She knows the minefield of a tough recipe and draws good maps, complete with detailed, step-by-step instructions; "Cook's Notes," giving a variety of information about substitutions, shortcuts, and unfamiliar products; and "Planning Ahead" notes, telling the cook exactly how far in advance each portion of the recipe can be made.

Although this is not a cookbook for weeknights, two of the five recipes we tested will join our permanent repertoire for casual summer entertaining. Souvlaki Gyros, marinated, grilled leg of lamb cubes nestled inside homemade pita breads, are topped with a sauce of cucumbers and yogurt, thin slices of tomato, and red pepper mayonnaise. Molded Provencale Salad is another winner — individual rice salads filled with vegetables, tossed with mustard vinaigrette, and wrapped in Swiss chard. Neither of these dishes lacked anything; both were well balanced and perfectly seasoned. The same held true with the more difficult Scoubidou, a filled pizza rolled up struedel-style, and Grilled Lime Chicken in Rice Crepes, served with peanut sauce.

Only Chocolate Sushi Truffle, a sushi-looking white and dark chocolate candy, was a disappointment. The white chocolate mixture was melted with so much liquid that it never hardened sufficiently to be rolled as directed.

We have always had trouble with technique-based cookbooks — do you say to yourself, "I think I'll make something wrapped tonight?" — but *Cooking Under Wraps* is a good one. If the concept is a bit odd, the execution is complete, and there's a lot for most of us to learn, from new ideas for filling frozen puff pastry to tackling homemade phyllo.

A Treasury of Southern Baking
By Prudence Hilburn
HarperCollins, $15.00 paper

Southern baking runs the gamut from super-fresh peach cobbler, made by hands so experienced they need no recipe, to strawberry shortcake constructed from store-bought pound cake, frozen sweetened strawberries, and Cool Whip. Both styles are served in mansions and shanties alike. Fortunately, Prudence Hilburn concentrates on the former, and it turns out to be a very worthwhile topic.

After raising a family in Alabama, Hilburn made the New York scene, studying with James Beard and Simca Beck and teaching at Peter Kump's Cooking School. But while her cosmopolitan cooking experience broadened her style, it didn't much alter it. This is the work of an experienced southern baker who may have moved North, but whose heart stayed home.

All five of the recipes we tested were winners. Southern Yeast Biscuits, triple-leavened with baking soda, baking powder, and yeast, combine the soft fluffy texture and quick cooking time of southern biscuits with the fragrance and flavor of yeast. The dough can be made and refrigerated for up to one week, "so that no one," Hilburn writes, "should be without biscuits for breakfast." Leftover biscuits can be used to make Biscuit Pudding with Caramel Apple Sauce, a superior version of bread pudding, topped with a sauce made not by caramelizing sugar syrup, but by tossing brown sugar, butter, an egg yolk, and a bit of water together in a saucepan and simmering until slightly thickened — a foolproof and carefree way to make caramel sauce.

Ambrosia Pound Cake, flavored with coconut and orange, had a delicate, crispy crust around a buttery, tender crumb. And Hilburn's Deep-Dish Fresh Peach Cobbler — definitely not a recipe for ascetics — is a wonderful taste of southern baking.

Emeril's New New Orleans Cooking
By Emeril Lagasse and Jessie Tirsch
William Morrow, $23.00

We've been waiting for years for the definitive cookbook about the great food of New Orleans. This isn't it. Rather, it's a showcase for the personal style of Emeril Lagasse, one of the most consistently creative and intelligent chefs in the United States. Originally from the multicultural town of Fall River, Massachusetts, Lagasse has not only adopted New Orleans cuisine, he has broadened it.

But, like so many chefs before him, Lagasse fails to make the leap from restaurant to home kitchen. Typically, chefs' cookbooks are filled with ingredients we can't find, techniques we can't master, equipment we don't have, quantities we dare not use, and steps that require not only a sous-chef but a dishwasher. Few cookbook authors could run a kitchen, and few chefs can put together first-rate books. Lagasse, unfortunately, is not one of them. More often than not, testing his recipes was disappointing. Quantities are off, cooking instructions are not descriptive enough even for experienced home cooks, and the recipes are far from universally appealing.

Lagasse's signature Banana Cream Pie with Banana Crust and Caramel Drizzles, for example, contains six cups of heavy cream. It overflowed the nine-inch pie pan called for, and was even too much for a deep dish nine-incher. When cooked, the filling was gummy and runny. Still, we sliced it, drizzled it, whipped-creamed it, garnished it with chocolate, and served it. But the pie was too rich for more than a couple of bites; our guests sampled it politely, then pushed their plates away.

Even though Emeril's New New Orleans Paellaya calls for a "large stockpot," I don't think most home cooks have a pot large enough to fit everything he puts into this jumble—1 whole chicken, andouille sausage, 3 cups *uncooked* rice, 3 small lobsters, 36 littleneck clams, 36 mussels, and 18 shrimp. Even with a large wok, by the end we were bailing out cooked seafood to make room for the uncooked stuff. And the game wasn't worth the candle.

Some of Lagasse's dishes were true to form, the kind of things that make so many people drive straight from the airport to his restaurant when they hit New Orleans. Tuesday's Red Bean Soup, for example, was superb, as was Artichoke Seafood Salad (illustrated on the back cover of this issue). But the book as a whole is far from a success. Lagasse and other chefs should hire professional recipe developers to assist on cookbook projects, especially if they think they're only going to do it once — or if they ever want a chance to do it again. ■

French Rosés Still the Best—Barely

In a blind tasting of dry pink wines, there were two winners: a classic Tavel won first prize while a $4 Spanish rosé raced to an upset victory in third place.

BY MARK BITTMAN

"Blush," "pink," or "white zinfandel" are among the most popular wines in America. Most are uncomplicated drinks, with a fair amount of residual sugar that may make them fun to drink, but hardly make them interesting or useful companions at mealtime. Unfortunately, this style of wine has lent its negative cachet to the original rosé wines, which are bone-dry or nearly so, and even somewhat complex. Blush wine drinkers avoid dry rosés because they're too dry, and fans of dry wines avoid rosés for fear of seeming unsophisticated.

There is one benefit to the negative aura surrounding dry rosés: they remain relatively inexpensive. The average retail price of the 13 wines in our tasting was under $10, and our top three wines sell for $11, $9, and $4, respectively. Most of the wines were enjoyable, fruity, and extremely versatile; they complement a wide range of foods. None of this would come as any surprise to the people of southern France, who often choose rosé wines for backyard meals, picnics, sipping in cafes, or meals by the sea.

Rosé wines — the modifier is French for pink — are not a blend of white and red wines, but are made from dark grapes, especially those indigenous to the Côtes-du-Rhône, such as grenache, syrah, or zinfandel, a glut of which was responsible for the creation of the blush wines of California around 10 years ago. Once the grapes are pressed, the liquid is allowed to mingle with the skins long enough to absorb some color, but not so long that the juice becomes red. From that point on, the wines are treated as if they were white, spending most of their time in stainless steel and glass. They are almost always drunk young and cool.

Because of their versatility, dry rosés are increasing in popularity not only among open-minded wine drinkers, but also among California winemakers, who are beginning to take traditional Côtes-du-Rhône grapes and vinify them, French-style. The results are impressive: three out of the top six wines in our tasting were from California, and the best of them finished in a virtual dead heat for first place.

The tasting was held in New York City's Rainbow Room, by a panel of ten. As in the first *Cook's Illustrated* wine tasting, the panel was made up of professionals and amateurs — in this case five wine professionals (a salesman, a sommelier, a consultant, a writer, and a retailer), and five people whose work has nothing to do with wine but who enjoy it with meals several times a week. The wines were tasted blind; their identities were revealed only after the poll of preferences was made.

When it came to judging the wines, opinions varied little between professionals and amateurs. The top wine took four first-place votes, two from each group, and was named in the top five wines by nine of ten tasters. The second- and third-place wines showed similarly wide appeal. This makes sense: dry rosés are straightforward, uncomplicated wines, with few of the hidden aesthetics that make other tastings controversial. What was found here was a group of delightful, affordable wines for a wide variety of summer occasions. ■

Mark Bittman writes about wine for the *Hartford Courant.*

BLIND TASTING RESULTS

Wines are listed in order of preference. Seven points were awarded for each first-place vote; six for second; five for third; four for fourth; three for fifth; two for sixth; one for seventh. Prices are average retail in the New York metropolitan area.

1. 1991 Chateau de Trinquevedel Tavel (France, 39 points), $11: *With four first-place votes, this fragrant, fresh wine had great appeal. "This is just the wine for a picnic by the sea," said one taster.*
2. 1990 Joseph Phelps Vin du Mistral Grenache Rosé (California, 38 points), $9: *Two first-place votes; voted in the top five by nine of ten tasters. Rich and plummy, with good body. "Outspoken — the best by far," said one of its admirers.*
3. René Barbier Mediterranean Rosé (Spain, 30 points), $4. *Its first-place vote was from a sommelier, who said, "Full and berryish — I want to drink this." A surprise and a terrific bargain.*
4. 1990 Côtes de Provence (St. Tropez), Les Maitres Vienerons (France, 21 points), $9. *One first-place vote. Placed in top five wines by five tasters. "Has character and complexity."*
5. 1991 Bonny Doon Vin Gris de Cigare Pink Wine (California, 17 points), $9. *Some found this wine "sprightly," or "lively", others found it "metallic."*
6. 1992 Cline Cellars Angel Rosé (California, 14 points), $9: *Ranked in the top five by two tasters; some found it "soapy," "sweetish," or "light-bodied."*
7. 1991 Domaine Tempier Bandol (France, 10 points), $19: *Ranked first by one experienced taster, who found it subtle and well-balanced. Majority found it "generic" or "lacking in fruit." From a winery of no small reputation; note price, by far the highest.*
8. 1990 Chateau St. Jean Cuvée Natacha, Coteaux D'Aix en Provence (France, 9 points), $6: *One taster found this "creamy;" many others thought it to be "old," with "off-flavors."*
9. 1990 Sancerre Les Baronnes (France, 9 points), $15: *Favorable comments such as, "A beautiful, long, fruity finish," did not translate into high ranking.*
10. 1990 Chateau Court-les-Muts Bergerac (France, 7 points), $8. *Comments ranged from "full and pleasant tasting" to "lacks character" and "astringent."*
11. 1991 Chateau d'Aqueria Tavel (France, 7 points), $12: *Many tasters picked up a variety of off-scents and off-flavors. Another surprise, since this wine has a good reputation.*
12. 1991 Chateau de la Mascarone Les Pierres Rosés, Côtes de Provence (France, 5 points), $12: *One taster found this "nondescript but likable," most thought it "dull."*
13. 1991 Duboeuf Syrah Vin de Pays D'Oc (France, 4 points), $6: *Most frequently mentioned descriptor: "Flat."*

SOURCES

AND RESOURCES

DRIED CHILES Los Chileros de Nuevo Mexico sells a wide selection of dried chiles by mail, including anchos, chipotles, mulatos, japones, pasillas, cascabels, de arbols, piquins, and New Mexico greens and reds. In addition to whole chiles, the company also offers powdered anchos, chipotles, de arbols, and red and green jalapeños, as well as a dozen blue and yellow corn products. For a catalog, contact Los Chileros de Nuevo Mexico (P.O. Box 6215, Santa Fe, NM 87502; telephone 505-471-6967). Their products are also sold in better supermarkets and specialty stores.

SPATZLE MACHINE Most well-stocked kitchen stores should carry a spatzle machine. However, if you have trouble locating one or would like to purchase the model pictured on page 2, contact Bridge Kitchenware (214 E. 52nd Street, New York, NY 10022; telephone 800-274-3435). The cost for this machine is $7.95 plus shipping. Also ask for a copy of their extensive catalog — it contains more than 1,800 items for the home and professional kitchen. The catalog costs $3, with the price deducted from your first purchase.

IMMERSION BLENDERS Most stores stock only one or two immersion blenders, which can make it a challenge to locate the model with the features you want. (If you want to dial just one number and have a blender delivered to your doorstep, call Williams-Sonoma at 800-541-2233. They sell the Cuisinart blender for $50 plus shipping.) Here are the telephone numbers for blender manufacturers: Braun, 617-596-7300; Moulinex, 201-784-0073; Cuisinart, 800-726-0190; Singer, 800-877-1329; Rival, 816-943-4100; Waring, 203-379-0731; Hamilton Beach, 800-851-8900; Salton, 800-233-9054.

PEA SHOOTS Fresh pea shoots are sold by many Asian greengrocers in New York, San Francisco, Los Angeles, and other cities with large Chinatowns. Pea shoots are also available by mail from Aux Delices des Bois (4 Leonard Street, New York, NY 10013; telephone 212-334-1230). The cost is $8 per pound plus shipping.

SOY SAUCES Some of the soy sauces tested on page 14 are available in health food stores; the most difficult to find is Ohsawa Nama Shoyu, which is sold primarily in natural foods stores with an emphasis on macrobiotic products. This brand is also available by mail from Gold Mine Natural Food Company (1947 30th Street, San Diego, CA 92102; telephone 800-475-3663). A 10-ounce bottle costs $3.99 plus shipping. Mitoku Macrobiotic Johsen Organic Shoyu is available by mail from Granum (2901 Northeast Blakeley Street, Seattle, WA 98105; telephone 206-525-0051). A 10-ounce bottle costs $4.14 plus shipping.

COLD-PRESSED PEANUT OIL Whether made from olives or walnuts, the flavor and aroma of cold-pressed oils are superior to those of refined oils, and peanut oil is no exception. A brand of particular note is Loriva Supreme Peanut Oil. When heated for stir-frying, this robust oil fills the kitchen with the scent of freshly roasted peanuts. Even cold, the aroma is intoxicating. A 12.7-ounce bottle retails for about $3 in most major supermarket chains around the country.

COOKING SCHOOLS The comprehensive *Guide to Cooking Schools* has been updated for 1993 and gives detailed descriptions of 350 programs — from culinary vacations to professional schools — in 39 states and 22 countries. Published by Shaw Guides, the book costs $16.95 and is available at Williams-Sonoma stores across the country. To order directly from the publisher, call 305-446-8888. There is a $3 shipping charge. ■

The 201-acre Whipporwill Farm has been in the same family for 100 years and is dedicated to organic farming.

ORGANIC MEATS Organic meats of uncommon quality are available from Whippoorwill Farm in the hills of northwestern Connecticut. Owner Malcolm MacLaren has sold beef, veal, lamb, and pork products at New York's farmers' market in Union Square for the past several years. He is now expanding his business and offering his top-quality meats by mail. Available cuts (prices are per pound) include lamb chops ($13), leg of lamb ($7), veal loin chops ($14), lean ground beef ($7), sirloin steaks ($9), fresh ham ($5), smoked ham ($6), and sage breakfast sausage ($5). For more information and a complete list of cuts and prices, contact Whippoorwill Farm (P.O. Box 717, Lakeville, CT 06039; telephone 203-435-9657).

COOKBOOK CARD SERIES

CULINARY NOTECARDS Galison Books has just published a series of culinary notecards. On the front of each folded card is a photograph or illustration from a favorite cookbook. On the back is the recipe and inside there is plenty of room to write a quick note or a thank-you for a wonderful meal. Recipes come from *The New Basics* by Julee Rosso and Sheila Lukins, *The International Cookie Cookbook* by Nancy Baggett, *Chopstix* by Hugh Carpenter, *Spirit of the Harvest* by Beverly Cox, *The Little Bean Cookbook* by Patricia Stapley, and *Seeds* from the Sierra Club. The cards are packaged in boxes of 20 that retail for $12.50. To locate a gourmet shop or department store that carries Cookbook Cards, call Galison Books at 212-354-8840. The cards may also be ordered over the phone from the publisher. Add $3.95 for shipping up to two boxes.

RECIPE INDEX

MAIN COURSES

Artichoke Cups with Seafood Salad and Herb Vinaigrette....back cover
Leg of Lamb with Red Chile Crust and Jalapeño Preserves....22
Master Recipe for Stir-Fry....19
Roast Chicken with Dijon Mustard-Thyme Sauce....28
Seared Snapper with Pea Shoots and Coconut Curry Sauce....2

SIDE DISHES

Buttered Spatzle....2
Gazpacho....28
Grilled Asparagus....7
Jumbo Asparagus Salad with Parma Ham, Parmesan, and Lemon Vinaigrette....7
Master Recipe for Steamed Asparagus....7
Thai-Style Asparagus with Chiles, Garlic, and Basil....7

BREADS AND PIZZAS

Cheddar Biscuits....12
Flaky Biscuits....12
Fluffy Biscuits....12
Grilled Shrimp Pizza Topping with Roasted Tomatoes and Farmer's Cheese....9
Herb Biscuits....12
Master Recipe for Garlic-Herb Pizza Crust....8
Roasted Tomato Pizza Topping with Fennel and Asiago....9
Simple Pizza Topppings....9

SAUCES

Blender Dessert Sauce....28
Blender "Margarine"....28
Chinese Flavoring Sauces for Stir-Fries....19
Black Bean Sauce, Coconut Curry Sauce, Lemon Sauce, Oyster Sauce, Spicy Tangerine Sauce, Sweet and Sour Sauce, Szechwan Chili Sauce, Tomato Fireworks Sauce
Ginger Beurre Blanc....28
Honey-Pepper Vinaigrette....28
Raspberry Mayonnaise....28

DESSERTS

Peaches and Cherries Poached in Spiced Red Wine....26
Poached Pears with Star Anise....25
Strawberry and Rhubarb Compotes with Sugared Pecans....25
Strawberry Shortcake....12

MASTER RECIPE FOR STIR-FRY page 19

POACHED PEARS page 25 **WITH RASPBERRY SAUCE** page 29

STRAWBERRY SHORTCAKE page 12

ASPARAGUS SALAD WITH PARMA HAM AND LEMON VINAIGRETTE page 29

LEG OF LAMB WITH RED CHILE CRUST AND JALAPEÑO PRESERVES page 22

GRILLED SHRIMP PIZZA AND ROASTED TOMATO PIZZA WITH FENNEL AND ASIAGO page 24

Artichoke Cups with Seafood Salad and Herb Vinaigrette

Heat 1 inch of water to boiling in a large soup kettle. Arrange 4 trimmed and stemmed artichokes (*see* step 1, page 5), stem side up, in a collapsible steamer basket. Place basket in kettle, cover, and steam over medium-high heat until artichoke base is easily pierced with the tip of a knife, 30 to 40 minutes. Cool slightly, then hollow each artichoke, following steps 2, 3, and 4 on page 5. Cover and refrigerate. Whisk 1 tablespoon lemon juice with 3 tablespoons white or sherry vinegar, 1 tablespoon Dijon-style mustard, and 1 minced small garlic clove. Add 2 tablespoons minced parsley, 2 tablespoons shredded basil leaves, and salt and pepper to taste. Whisk in ⅔ cup virgin olive oil; set aside. Toss ½ pound cooked and peeled medium shrimp with ½ pound crabmeat, 1 minced scallion, and ¼ cup of the dressing. Drizzle an additional 2 tablespoons of vinaigrette onto each artichoke so that each leaf is lightly coated. Toss remaining vinaigrette with 1½ cups each of shredded radicchio and bibb lettuce. Arrange a portion of shredded lettuce on each of 4 salad plates; fill each artichoke cup with a portion of seafood salad. Place a filled artichoke on top of each bed of lettuce and serve. Serves 4 for lunch or as a substantial first course.

NUMBER THREE ◆ JULY/AUGUST 1993

FOUR DOLLARS

COOK'S ILLUSTRATED

Taste-Testing Sparkling Waters

Perrier Wins in Blind Tasting

The Best Vanilla Ice Cream

Less Cream and Sugar Makes the Perfect Ice Cream

Grill Roasting

How to Slow Cook over Indirect Heat for Spectacular Results

Do Marinades Really Work?

They Add Flavor but Do They Tenderize?

CORN OFF THE COB

HOW TO COOK EGGPLANT

RATING ICE CREAM MAKERS

LOBSTER, STEP-BY-STEP

BEST DRY WHITE WINES

JULY/AUGUST 1993

TABLE OF CONTENTS

VOLUME ONE • NUMBER THREE

~2~

Notes from Readers:

Deep-Fried Devils, a letter from Julia, skinning hazelnuts, Mississippi Mud Cake, marinade injectors, and superfine sugar.

~4~

Quick Tips

How to get the fruit from a mango, seed cucumbers, clean leeks, extract juice from ginger, separate eggs, and peel and core a roasted pepper.

~6~

How to Cook Eggplant

To get the best results, there is no substitute for salting and pressing eggplant to remove excess liquid before cooking.
By Stephen Schmidt

~8~

Corn off the Cob

Three different techniques for removing corn from the cob are used in recipes from salsa to chowders to puddings.
By Rebecca Wood

~10~

Do Marinades Work?

Tests show that marinades are ineffective tenderizers, but add deep flavor if used for the right amount of time. We offer master marinade recipes for fish, poultry, and beef. *By Jack Bishop*

~13~

Common Fresh Herbs

Illustrations of ten herbs frequently used in cooking.

~14~

Raw Tomato Sauces

Uncooked sauces marry the flavors of ripe tomatoes with just a hint of other ingredients. *By Michele Scicolone*

~16~

How to Prepare Lobster

Everything you need to know, in 16 step-by-step illustrations.

Peaches are one of summer's great pleasures, as are eggplants (story, page 6), corn (page 8), tomatoes (page 4), and fresh herbs (page 13).

ILLUSTRATION BY BRENT WATKINSON.

Fresh Raspberry Summer Bread Pudding can be served a few hours after it is assembled or refrigerated and eaten the following day.

ILLUSTRATION BY FRANCIS LIVINGSTON.

~18~

Grill Roasting

Indirect grilling, over gas or charcoal, saves effort and gives spectacular results — golden chicken, smoky ribs, perfect fish.
By Pam Anderson

~21~

Taste-Testing Sparkling Waters

Despite many new competitors, Perrier comes in first, with an American water tied for second place. *By Joni Miller*

~23~

Master Class: Roasted Salmon with Kasha and Leek Stuffing

Michael Roberts's boned and butterflied whole salmon makes a spectacular bed for either a kasha or rice stuffing.

~26~

The Best Homemade Vanilla Ice Cream

The best recipe uses egg yolks but, for optimum flavor, cuts back on cream and sugar. ***Also*** Rating Ice Cream Makers: the most expensive model comes out on top, but the inexpensive second-place model offers both electric and hand cranks.
By Jack Bishop.

~30~

Non-Chablis Wines Dominate "Chablis" Tasting

A $40 Grand Cru Chablis won our tasting but an $11 Connecticut wine placed second. *By Mark Bittman*

~31~

Book Reviews

A top contender fails to win the race for the all-purpose healthful cookbook, but a celebration of American feasts offers rustic food and loving photos.

~32~

Sources and Resources

Products from this issue, plus a corn-kernel cutter, spicy foods catalog, mail-order sausages, and a spectacular poster.

Publisher and Editor
CHRISTOPHER KIMBALL

Executive Editor
MARK BITTMAN

Managing Editor
JOHN WILLOUGHBY

Food Editor
PAM ANDERSON

Senior Writer
JACK BISHOP

Copy Editor
DAVID TRAVERS

Art Director
MEG BIRNBAUM

Food Stylist
MARIE PARINO

Circulation Director
ADRIENNE KIMBALL

Circulation Manager
MARY TAINTOR

Circulation Assistant
JENNIFER L. KEENE

Production Director
JAMES MCCORMACK

Treasurer
JANET CARLSON

Cook's Illustrated is published bimonthly by Natural Health Limited Partners, 17 Station Street, Box 1200, Brookline, MA 02147. Copyright 1993 Natural Health Limited Partners. Application to mail at second class postage rates is pending at Boston, MA and additional mailing offices. Editorial office: 17 Station Street, Box 5690, Brookline, MA 02147 (617) 232-1000, FAX (617) 232-1572. Editorial contributions should be sent to: Editor, *Cook's Illustrated*, 17 Station Street, Brookline, MA 02147. We cannot assume responsibility for manuscripts submitted to us. Submissions will be returned only if accompanied by a large self-addressed stamped envelope. Subscription rates: $24.95 for one year; $45 for two years; $65 for three years. (Canada: add $3 per year; all other foreign add $12 per year.) Postmaster: Send all new orders, subscription inquiries, and change of address notices to *Cook's Illustrated*, P.O. Box 59046, Boulder, CO 80322-9046, or telephone (800) 477-3059. Single copies: $4 in U.S., $4.95 in Canada and foreign. PRINTED IN THE U.S.A.

EDITORIAL

THE SCIENCE OF BUTTERMILK

Sundays are pancake day in our household. I make them with thick, tangy buttermilk and I separate the eggs, beating the whites for a fluffy, sky-high rise. Our two young daughters help out, adding the salt, stirring the batter; the older, who's four, takes her turn flipping them. Hundreds of flapjacks later, I've come to learn a few things about both kids and pancakes.

CHRISTOPHER KIMBALL

I've always made pancakes and waffles with buttermilk, following the conventional wisdom that buttermilk makes better, fluffier baked goods than those made with sweet milk. By nature, however, I am not inclined to trust traditional kitchen lore. If I'm told to scald milk, I don't bother. If a recipe calls for egg whites at room temperature, I leave them in the refrigerator until the last minute to see what happens (in fact, cold egg whites whip as well as warm ones). So I thought that, in the *Cook's* tradition, it was about time to put buttermilk to the test.

I like a thick pancake, so one Sunday I used one cup of flour, one-half teaspoon salt, one-half teaspoon baking soda, one cup of buttermilk, two tablespoons of melted butter, and one separated egg. I whisked the dry ingredients together in a bowl, beat the egg yolk lightly with the buttermilk and melted butter, and poured the liquid ingredients slowly into the flour mixture, stirring gently with a rubber spatula. Then I beat the egg white and folded it in. For the sweet-milk version I used one teaspoon of baking powder in place of the soda.

The resulting batters were remarkably different. The buttermilk batter started to rise immediately, looking a bit like a sponge for bread. The sweet-milk batter was thinner and denser, although it did thicken as it sat in the bowl for about 10 minutes before cooking. The buttermilk pancakes rose at least 50 percent higher, and had a fluffier texture. The sweet-milk pancakes were good, but more compact and somewhat tougher. There was no discernable difference in taste, which surprised me, since most baked goods made with buttermilk have a distinctive flavor.

I guessed that the acidity of the buttermilk reacts in a more pronounced manner with the baking soda than the sweet milk does with the baking powder. For a more detailed description, I turned to our technical consultant, Harold McGee.

According to McGee, double-acting baking powder is designed to create gas (carbon dioxide) at both room and baking temperatures (single-acting baking powder only creates gas at room temperature). If too much of the rise occurs at room temperature, gas begins to escape before the high heat has the chance to "set" the cake by trapping the carbon dioxide. When baking pancakes, however, the batter is not subjected to heat for very long, so less gas is developed during cooking, and the rise is smaller. You can make your own single-acting baking powder by adding a bit of cream of tartar to baking soda (for detailed instructions, *see Biscuits*, May/June, 1993 issue). This should give you a faster rise, more appropriate to pancakes.

Buttermilk, on the other hand, is full of lactic acid, which reacts at room temperature with the baking soda. As I observed in my test, the buttermilk batter started to rise immediately (this is why some buttermilk biscuit recipes recommend that biscuits sit 10 minutes before baking — they begin rising at room temperature) and the final pancake was lighter and fluffier than the sweet-milk version. For quick cooking, buttermilk has a clear advantage.

When serving up breakfast that morning, I followed all of the rules drilled into me by our kids — use lots of butter (if it melts, it doesn't count), make sure that some of the syrup spills onto the plate (so they can scoop it up with a spoon), and don't cut the pancakes ahead of time (they have to ask). Everything was served up perfectly and the kids were called to the table. They sat down, took one look at their two fluffy buttermilk pancakes and said, "Dad, we wanted *waffles* this morning." I guess pancakes are easier to figure out than children. ■

PHOTO BY JIM THOMAS

Chinese Fried Bread

On a recent trip to China, I sampled a light, crisp fried bread that I have been trying to duplicate at home ever since. The loaf is about 12 inches long and 1 inch in diameter; sometimes it is actually two loaves attached like the wings on a butterfly. Could you supply a recipe?

Linda Vodangson
San Diego, CA

The following bread recipe, adapted from Florence Lin's *Complete Book of Chinese Noodles, Dumplings, and Breads* (Morrow, 1986), matches your description perfectly. Two unusual ingredients, alum and ammonium carbonate powder, give this bread its unique character. "The alum makes the dough harder and therefore very crisp when fried," says Florence Lin, "and the ammonium carbonate makes it puff up." Both ingredients are sold in most pharmacies or may be ordered by mail from The Spice Corner (904 S. Ninth Street, Philadelphia, PA 19147; telephone 215-925-1660).

DEEP-FRIED DEVILS
Makes about 20 fried breads

- 2 teaspoons coarse salt
- 1 teaspoon alum
- 1 teaspoon ammonium carbonate powder
- 1 teaspoon baking soda
- 1 teaspoon baking powder
- 1¼ cups tepid water
- 3½ cups unbleached flour
- 1½ quarts oil for frying

1. Mix together first 5 ingredients in a medium bowl. Stir in water until powders and salt dissolve. Using your hands, mix in 3 cups flour with a pressing/pushing motion to form a soft dough. Work in remaining flour, if necessary, so that dough is not sticky.

2. Transfer dough to a floured work surface and knead until smooth, 2 to 3 minutes. Halve dough, then shape into 2 oblong loaves. Coat with oil, wrap tightly in plastic wrap, and allow to stand at room temperature for at least 4 hours. (Can be held at room temperature for up to 8 hours.)

3. Flour a large cutting board or work surface. Stretch each loaf by hand to measure 14 by 3 inches. Flour tops of loaves, then roll each into a 16-by-4-inch rectangle, about ¼-inch thick. Cover with a damp cloth and let rest for 10 minutes.

4. Meanwhile, heat oil in a wok or large, deep pan. Line a cookie sheet with paper towels. When oil reaches about 350 degrees, cut 4 crosswise strips of dough, each about ⅔-inch wide, from one of the rectangles (illustration 1). Brush 2 of the dough strips with water, then lay the other two strips on top (illustration 2). Press a chopstick lengthwise on top of each pair of strips to seal them together (illustration 3). Holding one end in each hand, pick up one dough strip and stretch to about 10 inches, then lower into the hot oil. Repeat with second dough strip. Fry, turning gently, until breads are golden brown, about 2 minutes (illustration 4). Drain on paper towels. Repeat cutting and frying process with remaining dough. Serve.

Preparing Deep-Fried Devils

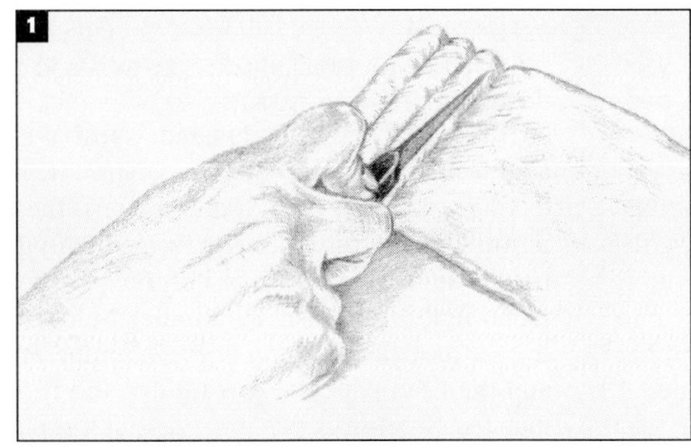

1. Cut dough into strips two-thirds inch wide.
2. Brush two strips with water, then lay strips on top of each other to form double width.

3. With a chopstick, press double strips to seal them together.
4. Dough will quadruple in size when fried.

Illustrations by Dorothy Gulick

Kudos from Julia

Congratulations on a wonderful issue. Everyone is delighted to know that you are back in print, and the magazine looks great. Here's wishing you the best of success.

JULIA CHILD
Cambridge, MA

Skinning Hazelnuts

Recently I made a cookie recipe that called for skinned hazelnuts, but I had trouble getting rid of the skins. What's the best way to remove them?

PEGGY ROSEN
New York, NY

Baking expert Rose Levy Beranbaum passed along this quick, effective technique for removing hazelnut skins, which she learned from food-processor inventor Carl Sontheimer.

To skin one cup of hazelnuts, bring three cups of water to boil in a deep pan. Add nuts and one-quarter cup baking soda and boil for 4 minutes. The water will fizz and blacken. Drain the nuts, rinse them under cold water, and a quick rub should slip the skins right off. The skinned nuts are soggy at this point, so we recommend putting them on a baking sheet and toasting in a 350-degree oven until dry and golden, about 10 minutes.

Mississippi Mud Cake

I have been unsuccessful to date in my attempts to recreate the scrumptious texture of a Mississippi mud cake that I bought at the Greenmarket in New York City some time ago. It was wonderfully fudgy, while at the same time delicate and moist. The cake contains coffee, chocolate, and liquor. Most importantly, the texture was light. Can you offer some suggestions or a recipe?

CATHERINE MALINOWSKI
Avon, NJ

This finely textured cake is based on a recipe developed by Chris Schlesinger and John Willoughby (also managing editor of *Cook's Illustrated*) for their book *The Thrill of the Grill* (Morrow, 1990). We have added nuts, marshmallows, and a bourbon-chocolate glaze to keep the delicate cake moist and fudgy.

MISSISSIPPI MUD CAKE
Serves 10–12

- 2 cups flour
- 2 teaspoons baking soda
- 1 teaspoon salt
- 6 ounces unsweetened chocolate
- ½ cup strong-brewed coffee
- ½ cup bourbon
- ½ pound butter
- 1½ cups sugar
- 4 large eggs
- 2 teaspoons vanilla extract
- 1½ cups miniature marshmallows
- 1 cup chopped pecans

Chocolate-Bourbon Glaze

- 3 ounces bittersweet chocolate
- 3 tablespoons butter, softened
- 2 tablespoons hot water
- 1 teaspoon corn syrup
- 1 teaspoon bourbon

1. *For the cake,* heat oven to 350 degrees; grease the bottom of a 13-by-9-inch baking pan. Line pan bottom with foil, extending the foil over pan ends by 2 inches to facilitate cake removal; grease and flour pan bottom and sides and set aside. Sift together flour, baking soda, and salt; set aside.

2. Heat next 4 ingredients in a double boiler until chocolate and butter melt. Off heat, stir in sugar until dissolved. Whisk eggs and vanilla together in a medium bowl until well combined. Slowly whisk ¼ of chocolate mixture into beaten eggs, then whisk egg mixture back into chocolate mixture.

3. Stir dry ingredients into chocolate mixture in small batches, until fully incorporated.

4. Pour batter into prepared pan and bake until a cake tester, inserted in the cake's center, comes out clean, 25 to 30 minutes. Remove cake from oven and sprinkle marshmallows and pecans over cake top. Return to oven and bake until marshmallows and nuts toast, about 5 minutes. Transfer cake in pan to a wire rack and cool for 15 minutes. Use foil handles to remove cake from pan; cool cake completely. Remove the foil liner.

5. *For the glaze,* melt chocolate in a double boiler or microwave. Stir in butter, one tablespoon at a time. Stir in water, then corn syrup and bourbon.

6. Drizzle glaze over cake top; let stand until glaze sets, about 15 minutes, and serve.

What Is It?

I found these surgical-looking instruments in a local kitchen supply shop. Can you tell me what they are and how they operate?

KURT KRUGER
Camden, ME

You have stumbled upon two excellent devices for injecting marinades into meats. The instant marinating needle (at right) is quite thin and is therefore best for injecting liquids like juice, wine, or oil directly into meat. The needle holds about one-quarter cup of liquid and is also useful for injecting liquor (such as vodka) into large fruits (such as watermelon).

The stainless-steel baster (bottom) has a larger capacity (about one-half cup) and a wider tube that allows pureed solids such as garlic or herbs to be injected into foods. Marinades (*see* recipes, on pages 11 and 12) should be pureed until smooth and then sucked into the bulb baster. The injection tube screws into the baster and can be stuck deep into ham, leg of lamb, large cuts of beef, or whole roasting chickens.

For information on where to buy these tools, *see* Sources and Resources, page 32.

Superfine Sugar

I recently ran across a recipe that called for superfine sugar. What is this, and can I substitute confectioners' sugar?

BETH BLOOMBERG
Arlington, VA

Sorry, but the two are quite different. Confectioners' is sugar that has been ground into a powder and mixed with 3 percent cornstarch to prevent clumping; superfine is simply regular granulated sugar that has been further processed so the crystals are smaller.

Professional bakers often prefer superfine sugar, particularly for cakes, pastries, or meringues, because the smaller crystals are easier to incorporate into batters and result in a finer crumb and a lighter texture. If you cannot find superfine sugar in your supermarket, you can make a very close approximation by grinding regular granulated sugar in a food processor for a minute or two. ■

Quick Tips

Cutting Mangoes

When buying mangoes, look for fruit that gives slightly when pressed but is not mushy. Firm mangoes will ripen at room temperature. Also, smell the stem end when purchasing mangoes; the aroma should be faintly sweet and floral.

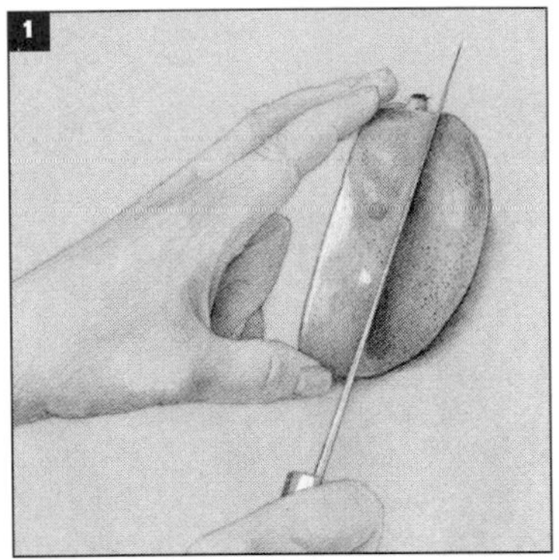

1. Cut through the mango on either side of the flat pit in the center, slicing the mango into three pieces.

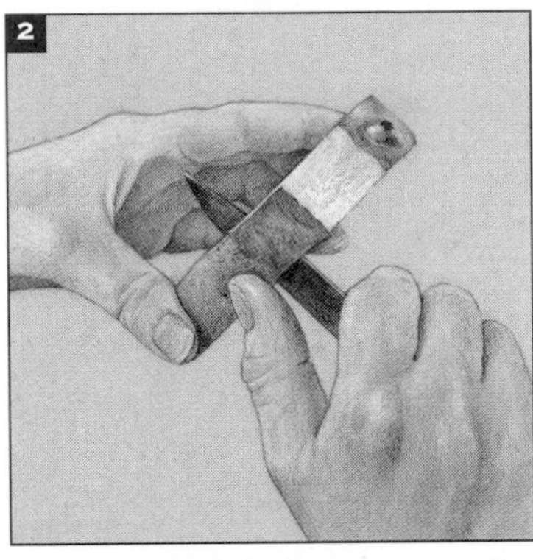

2. Use a sharp knife to remove the peel from the section that contains the pit.

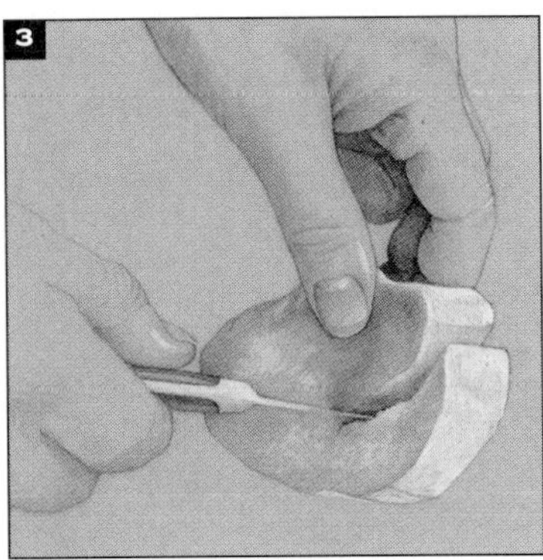

3. Slide the knife around both sides of the pit to remove the attached fruit.

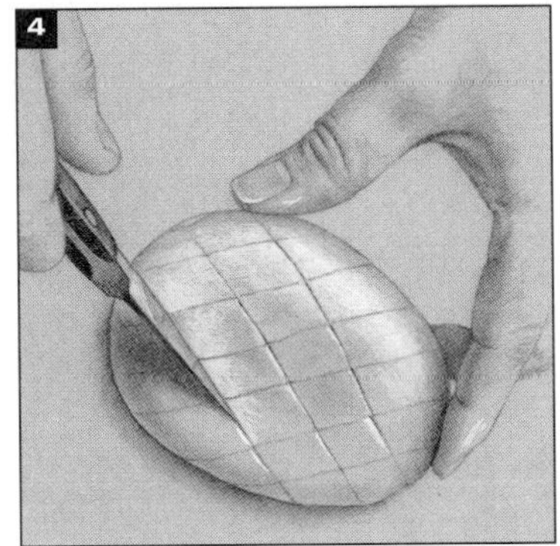

4. Make diagonal cross-hatches on each of the two remaining mango pieces, slicing down to (but not through) the peel.

5. Place your hand under each of the mango sections and push upward to invert the fruit; the cubes will rise and separate.

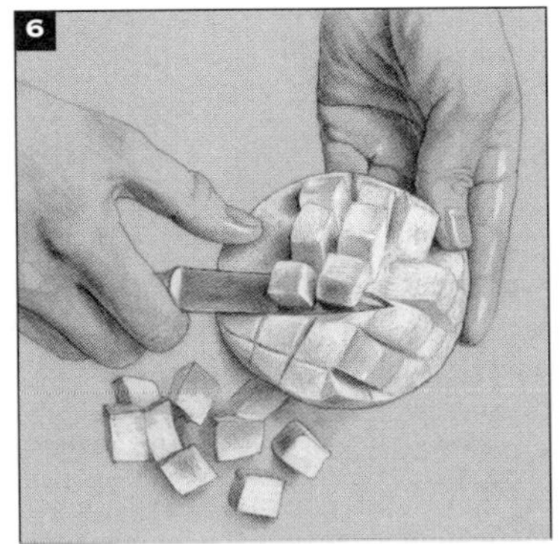

6. Slide the knife along the base of the cubes to separate them from the peel.

Seeding Cucumbers

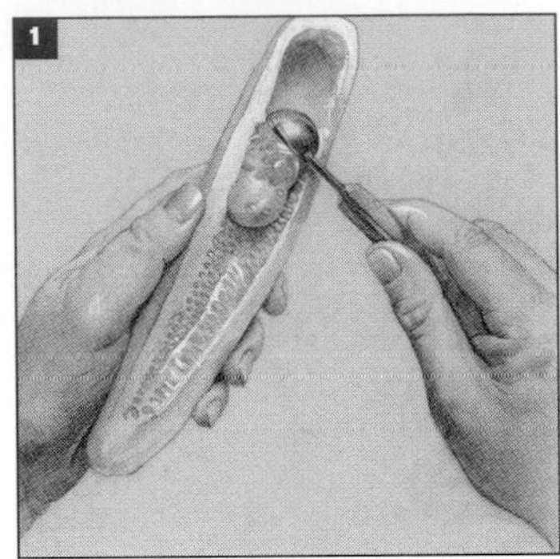

1. Peel the entire cucumber and slice it in half lengthwise. Use a melon baller or small spoon to scoop out the seeds and surrounding gelatinous material from each half. Stuff cucumber boats or proceed to step 2.

2. To create firm cucumber slices for use in grain salads, salsas, or dressings, place the seeded cucumber halves on a cutting board, open side down, and slice into thin half-moon-shaped rings.

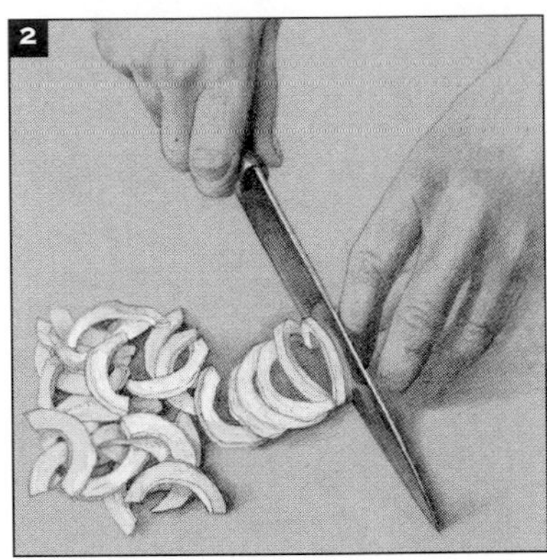

Cleaning Leeks

Leek leaves are somewhat delicate, but they also have many crannies where dirt particles can hide. This procedure allows you to thoroughly clean the leaves while still keeping them whole.

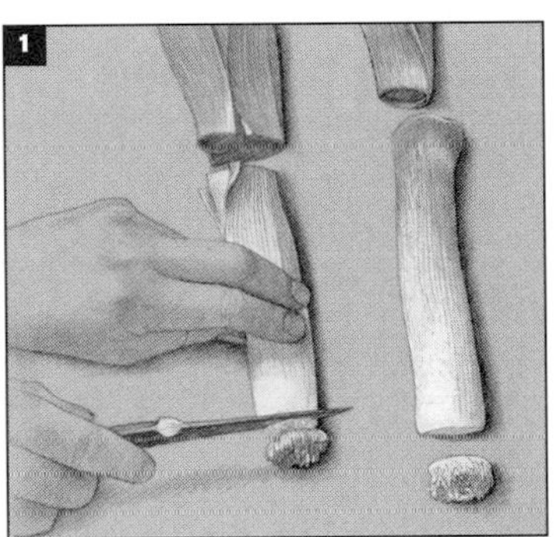

1. Cut off the dark green top and trim off the root end of each leek.

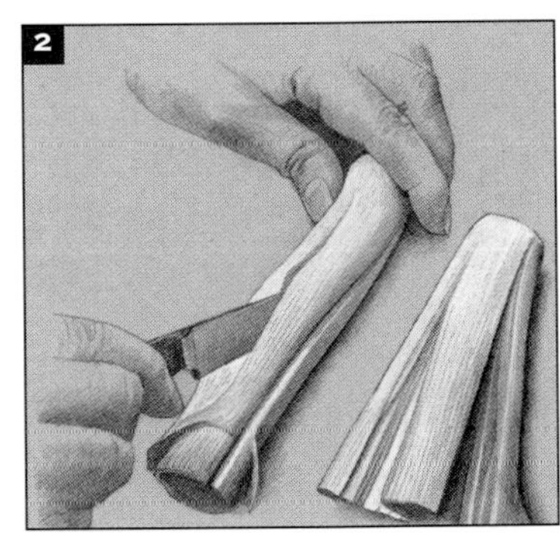

2. Beginning about one-half inch up from the root end, slice the remaining length in half.

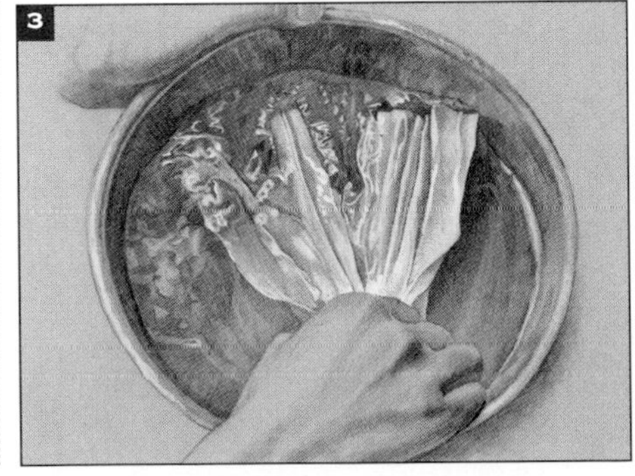

3. Fan out the leek leaves in a bowl of cold water and swish them gently to loosen dirt. If necessary, repeat with a fresh bowl of water until the leek is completely cleaned.

ILLUSTRATIONS BY ANATOLY

Extracting Ginger Juice

Clear ginger juice can be used in dishes where the taste but not the texture of ginger is needed. It is especially useful in smooth dressings, sauces, broths, and puddings (*see* Shaker-Style Creamy Corn Pudding, page 9).

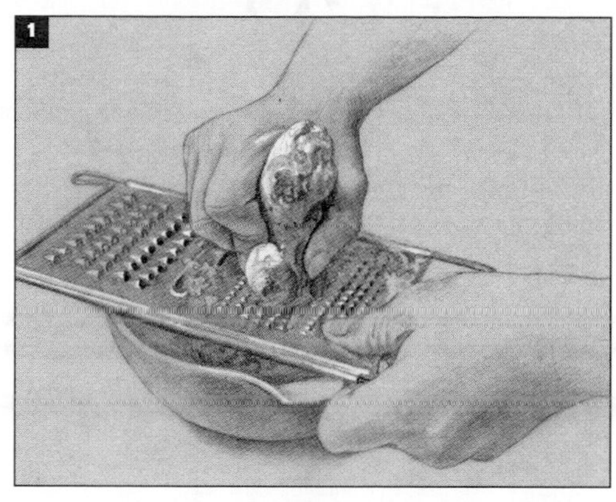

1. Finely grate unpeeled ginger into a small bowl.

2. Wrap the grated ginger in a single layer of cheesecloth. Twist and press cloth to extract the juice

Separating Eggs

The traditional method of separating an egg by tossing the yolk back and forth from one shell to the other often results in a pierced yolk. Hands have no sharp edges that can break the yolk apart. Make sure to wash hands thoroughly after separating eggs.

1. Crack the egg over the bowl that will hold the whites. Place a second bowl nearby for the yolks. Use the thumb of one hand to pull the halves of the shell apart, being careful to keep the yolk fully contained in one of the halves.

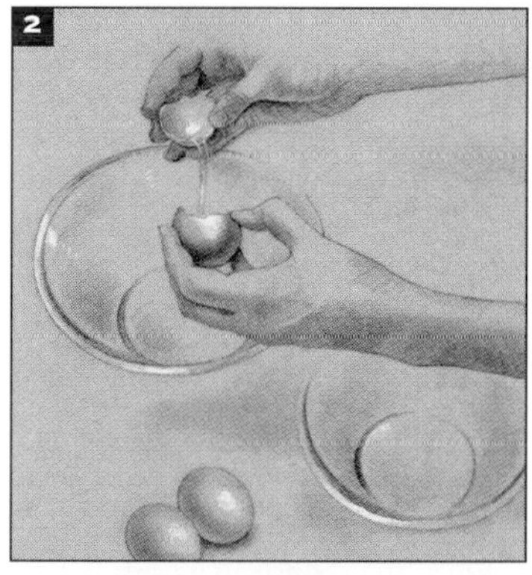

2. Separate the shells and allow as much white as possible to drop into the bowl below. Do not pass the yolk from one shell to the other.

3. Pour the yolk and remaining white into the palm of one hand. Open fingers slightly, allowing the white to drop into the bowl below. Place the whole yolk into the other bowl.

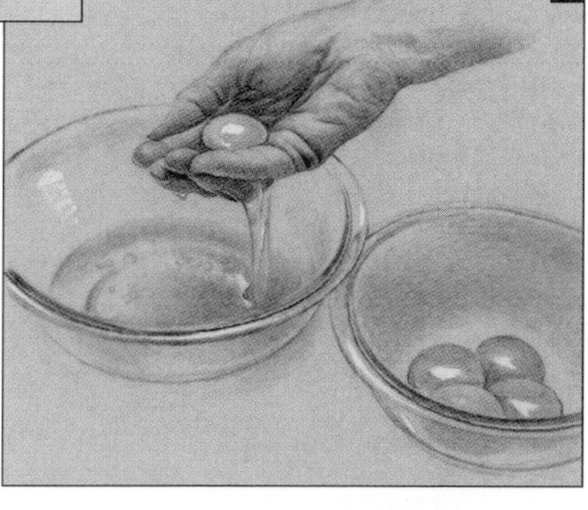

Peeling and Seeding Roasted Peppers

Peppers become so soft during roasting that the stem, core, and seeds can be removed by hand. Cleaned whole peppers can be stuffed or stored in oil for later use. Begin by roasting peppers under a broiler or directly over a gas flame until the skin blackens. Place the charred peppers in a paper bag for 10 minutes to sweat off the skins.

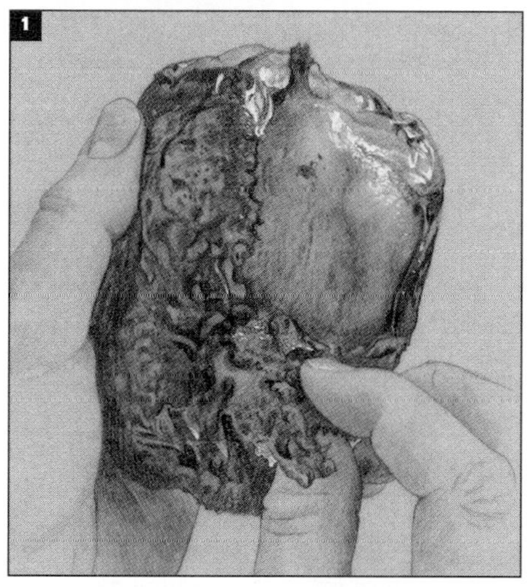

1. Remove peppers from bag and peel off the blistered skin with your fingers.

2. Place your thumb and index finger on either side of the stem and lift up to remove stem, core, and seeds in one piece. Rinse the inside of the pepper with water to remove any remaining seeds. ■

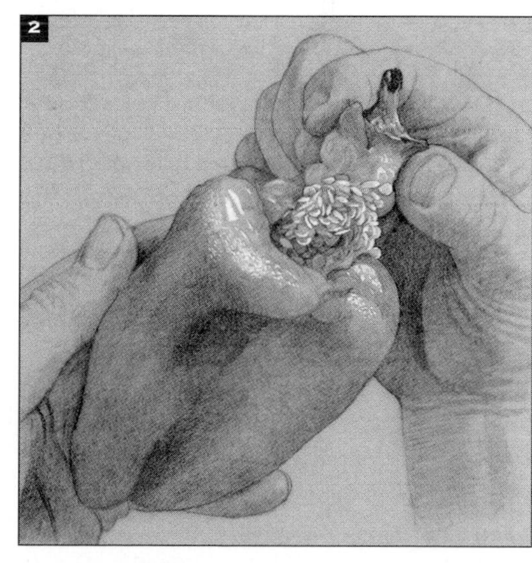

ATTENTION READERS: FREE SUBSCRIPTION FOR PUBLISHED TIPS. Do you have a unique tip you would like to share with other readers? We will provide a one-year complimentary subscription for each quick tip that we print. Send a description of your special technique to *Cook's Illustrated,* P.O. Box 1200, Brookline Village, MA 02147. Please write "Attention: Quick Tips" on the envelope and include your name, address, and daytime phone number. Unfortunately, we can only acknowledge receipt of tips that will be printed in the magazine.

How to Cook Eggplant

To get the best results with eggplant, there is no substitute for salting and pressing to remove excess liquid before cooking.

BY STEPHEN SCHMIDT

Many people complain that their eggplant dishes are either tough, pithy, and astringently bitter, or oil-soaked, slimy, and tasteless. This is not inevitable. Eggplant can (and should) be firm and meaty, with a rich, sweet, nutlike flavor. As many cookbooks tell you, this effect can only be achieved if the eggplant is macerated in salt, rinsed, and then pressed nearly dry before cooking. Now that I have experimented with eggplant in a formal and systematic way, I better understand why this procedure works and how best to do it.

To remove excess liquid, eggplant must macerate in salt for at least 1½ hours, preferably for 2 to 3, prior to pressing and cooking. It will not be harmed by macerating for as long as 24 hours.

Dealing with Excessive Liquid

I always thought that the reason you had to rid eggplant of much of its liquid before cooking is because the liquid is bitter. It turns out, however, that this is not the case. The real problem is that eggplant is packed with water. When I dried inch-thick slices in the oven, for example, they lost two-thirds of their weight long before they were dry.

Eggplant is extremely porous. When not first salted and pressed, it drinks up oil like a sponge, presenting cooks with two equally bad options: To keep the eggplant from sticking and burning, he or she can simply quit frying it long before it is cooked through. Unfortunately, this leaves the eggplant tough and bitter. Alternatively, the cook can continue to pour more oil into the pan and keep cooking the eggplant until tender. But, with all that juice turning to steam inside it, the eggplant dissolves into a soupy, oil-soaked mush by the time it is cooked.

The solution is salting. Salt draws water out of cells by creating such a high concentration of dissolved ions outside the cell walls that water inside is drawn out. Salting alone, however, is not sufficient. The flesh of the eggplant must also be firmly pressed between sheets of paper towels; pressing extrudes the juice and compacts the flesh.

To confirm this, I generously salted three-quarter-inch eggplant slices and let them sit for a full five hours. I then divided the slices into two equal portions. The first portion I just rinsed and patted lightly with paper towels; the second portion I pressed until the flesh had shrunk in weight and volume by roughly half and had become a translucent brownish-green. I then sautéed each batch separately in a nine-inch nonstick skillet over medium-low heat, using one and one-half tablespoons of olive oil each time.

The slices that had been only patted dry drank up every drop of oil almost at once, and ended up tasting greasy and bland. Furthermore, they become so mushy that they all but fell apart on the spatula when I removed them from the pan. The pressed slices, by contrast, absorbed just a teaspoon of the olive oil, and they turned out delicious — firm, sweet, and covered on both sides with a lovely crisp, chewy, caramelized glaze.

Finally, to make sure that salting actually was a prerequisite to pressing, I attempted to press some unsalted eggplant slices. As I had expected, they were too punky to bear the pressure and simply crumbled when pressed; sautéed, they turned to mush.

For the salt to do its job, eggplant must macerate for at least one and one-half hours, preferably for two to three. But I found that steaming is an acceptable last-minute alternative. If short on time, steam the eggplant over rapidly boiling water for three to five minutes, or just until a firm pinch will dent it rather than causing it to break apart. Turn the eggplant out onto a triple thickness of paper towels and let it cool until it's comfortable to handle. Next, cover it with additional towels and press to release the moisture, exerting rather gentle pressure lest you mash it to a pulp. Steaming makes for a softer and less flavorful final result than salting, but it is far better than no preliminary attention at all.

Particulars of the Process

One bit of advice that I had sometimes ignored and sometimes heeded was to salt eggplant in a colander. My experiments indicate that this is indeed a good idea. Even after a thorough rins-

PHOTOGRAPH BY ERIC ROTH

ing, eggplant that was macerated in a bowl was markedly saltier than that which had been drained in a colander, perhaps because it had been actually sitting in a salt water solution. Conscientious rinsing is also important: it not only floods away excess salt but softens the eggplant, facilitating pressing.

Then there is the matter of the skin. I have almost always peeled eggplant, believing that the skin would not soften sufficiently during cooking. But, when salted and pressed, whether broiled, baked, or fried, eggplant was delicious with the skin left on. When I simmered the sautéed eggplant in crushed tomatoes or in some other liquid, as many of the recipes given below suggest, the peel was even further softened. Since the skin is not only pretty but also helps the pieces to hold their shape, it usually should be left on. Finally, no matter what the cooking method, eggplant always comes out firmer, browner, and sweeter when cooked slowly rather than quickly.

MASTER RECIPE FOR SAUTÉED EGGPLANT

Serves 4–6

- 2 pounds eggplant (about 2 medium eggplants)
- 1 tablespoon salt
- 3 tablespoons extra virgin olive oil
- Ground black pepper
- 1 tablespoon minced garlic
- 2–4 tablespoons minced parsley or finely shredded fresh basil

1. Cut off and discard stem and bottom end of each eggplant. Cut eggplants crosswise into ¾-inch slices, then cut slices into ¾-inch strips. Place strips in a colander, sprinkle with salt, and toss. Set colander over a bowl or in the sink and let eggplant stand for at least 1½ hours, preferably for 2 to 3, stirring it a couple of times.

2. Rinse eggplant under cold, running water, rubbing the strips lightly in your hands. Shake colander to drain. Lay strips about 1 inch apart on a triple thickness of paper towels; cover with another triple layer of towels. Using your palms, press each eggplant strip very firmly until it looks green and translucent and feels firm and leathery when pressed between fingertips. Repeat pressing process on fresh toweling if eggplant has not yet reached this stage. Repeat with remaining eggplant strips. (Can refrigerate up to 3 hours before cooking.)

3. In a heavy-bottomed 12-inch skillet, heat oil until it shimmers and becomes fragrant. Add eggplant strips; sauté until they begin to brown, about 3 minutes. Reduce heat to medium-low and cook, stirring occasionally, until eggplant is fully tender and lightly browned, 15 to 20 minutes. Stir in pepper and garlic; cook to blend flavors, about 2 minutes. Off heat, stir in herbs, adjust seasonings, and serve.

SAUTÉED EGGPLANT WITH CRISPED BREAD CRUMBS

Serves 4–6

Add ½ cup fine-textured fresh bread crumbs with the garlic in the Master Recipe; toss lightly to coat strips. Turn heat to high; cook until crumbs begin to brown, about 1 minute. Toss and cook until crumbs brown, about 1 minute longer. Off heat, stir in basil.

SAUTÉED EGGPLANT IN SPICY GARLIC SAUCE

Serves 4–6

Substitute 2 tablespoons dark sesame oil and 1 tablespoon peanut or vegetable oil for the olive oil in the Master Recipe. Increase garlic to 2 tablespoons, and add 2 teaspoons minced fresh ginger and ¼ teaspoon crushed red pepper flakes with the garlic. Cook to blend flavors, about 1 minute. To this, add a mixture of 2 tablespoons dry sherry, 2 tablespoons dark soy sauce, 2 tablespoons vinegar (any kind), and 1 teaspoon sugar; simmer until liquid absorbs into eggplant, about 1 minute. Substitute 2 tablespoons minced cilantro and 2 tablespoons thin-sliced scallions for parsley or basil.

SAUTÉED EGGPLANT IN TOMATO SAUCE WITH BASIL

Serves 4–6

Stir in 1¼ cups crushed tomatoes after the garlic has cooked for a minute in the Master Recipe. Simmer until tomatoes thicken slightly, 2 to 3 minutes. Stir in ¼ cup finely shredded fresh basil.

MASTER RECIPE FOR BROILED EGGPLANT SLICES

Serves 2 as a main course, 4–6 as a side dish

As an alternative to broiling, you can bake the eggplant in the upper third of a 375-degree oven for 20 to 25 minutes, turning it once. The effect is virtually the same.

- 2 pounds eggplant (about 2 medium eggplants)
- 1 tablespoon salt
- 2 tablespoons extra virgin olive oil
- 4 teaspoons balsamic vinegar
- 2 teaspoons minced garlic
- 2–3 tablespoons minced parsley or finely shredded fresh basil
- Ground black pepper

1. Cut off and discard stem and bottom end of each eggplant. Do not peel. Cut eggplants crosswise into ¾-inch slices. Lay slices out on a work surface, sprinkle tops with half the salt, and rub it in with your fingers. Turn eggplant slices over and repeat procedure with remaining salt. Place eggplant in a colander, set colander over bowl or in sink, and let eggplant stand for at least 1½ hours, preferably 2 to 3.

2. Rinse eggplant under cold, running water, rubbing slices lightly in your hands. Shake colander to drain. Lay slices about an inch apart on triple thickness of paper towels; cover with another triple layer of towels. Using your palms, press each eggplant slice very firmly until it looks green and translucent and feels firm and leathery when pressed between fingertips. Repeat pressing process on fresh toweling if eggplant has not yet reached this stage. Repeat with remaining eggplant slices. (Can refrigerate up to 3 hours before cooking.)

3. Heat broiler. Mix oil, vinegar, and garlic in small cup. Arrange eggplant slices fairly close together on a baking sheet; brush tops with half of oil mixture. Turn slices over and brush with remaining oil mixture. Broil eggplant slices about 8 inches from heat source until tops turn mahogany brown, 6 to 8 minutes. Turn slices over; broil until other sides brown, an additional 6 to 8 minutes. Sprinkle eggplant with herbs and pepper, adjust seasonings, and serve.

BROILED EGGPLANT SLICES WITH TWO CHEESES

Serves 2 as a main course, 4–6 as a side dish

Follow Master Recipe for Broiled Eggplant Slices, then sprinkle cooked eggplant with a mixture of ¾ cup (3 ounces) shredded fresh mozzarella cheese and 6 tablespoons (1½ ounces) grated Parmesan cheese. Return eggplant to broiler until cheese melts and becomes a little crusty. Sprinkle with parsley or basil and serve, accompanied by marinara-style tomato sauce if desired. ■

Stephen Schmidt, a caterer and cooking teacher, is the author of *Master Recipes* (Ballantine, 1987) and the forthcoming *Dessert America* (Morrow).

PRESSED VS. UNPRESSED EGGPLANT

Eggplant that has been salted and pressed (at right in drawing) has a drier, more compact structure for easier cooking.

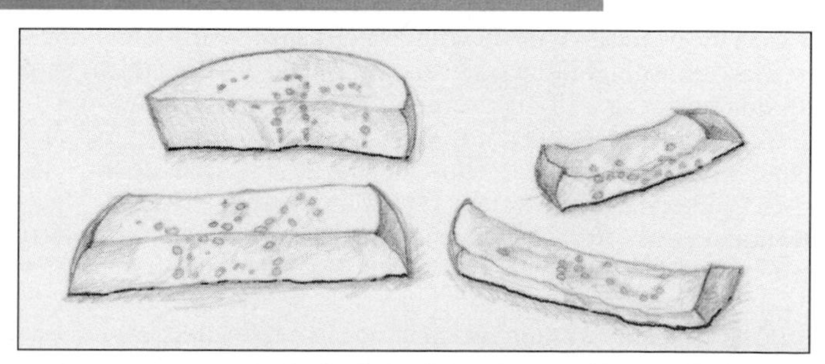

ILLUSTRATION BY KATHY BRAY

Corn off the Cob

Three different techniques for removing corn from the cob are used in recipes from salsa to chowders to puddings.

BY REBECCA WOOD

Corn should be eaten as soon after picking as possible. Unless it is one of the new "super-sweet" varieties, over half of the sugar in an ear of corn is converted to starch within 24 hours, and the corn also begins to dehydrate and become hard.

In our family, we eat a great deal of corn when it's in season, and over the years, we have learned the joys of eating corn *off* the cob. The trick is to use the technique for removing kernels that is best suited to the recipe. I have found that slicing off whole kernels works well for some recipes, such as relishes, but not so well for chowders or baked goods: The ideal chowder or pudding is made with grated corn. Biscuits and rolls, on the other hand, are best with double-cut or half-size kernels, enjoyably chewy but not so large that they overpower the recipe.

I recommend three different kernel-removal techniques, and offer four recipes that demonstrate how to use them.

Slicing Whole Kernels

Slice as-close-to-whole-as-possible kernels from the cob for use in relishes, salsas, chowchows, pickles, or any other dishes where you want a whole grain texture. Some corn pulp will remain on the cob; scrape this for another use or use the cob for a delicious corny-tasting stock. Many turn-of-the-century cookbooks advise plunging an ear of corn into boiling water and then into cold water in order to facilitate removing the kernels and to minimize the corn juices spurting when cut. I tested that practice and found that there was no difference between uncooked and quick-cooked corn on either count.

Grating and Scraping

Grated corn enhances soufflés, soups, chowders, fritters, puddings, corn oysters, and other delicate dishes. Grate the corn into a bowl using the large holes in a standard vegetable grater. Next, with the back of a knife, firmly scrape the cob to extract remaining pulp. Be careful not to scrape too hard, or hulls will also be pulled from the cob. This technique yields lush, smooth-textured, hull-free corn puree.

A second traditional method of making corn puree is to slice through each row of kernels and then to scrape the pulp from the cob. However, cutting and scraping takes twice as long as grating, is more cumbersome, and gives the same result, so I don't recommend it.

Double-Cutting

This technique yields halved corn kernels, which retain just enough texture to complement vegetable mixtures such as Corn and Zucchini Sauté with Chiles, as well as breads, biscuits, and rolls. With a sharp knife, slice down one side of an ear of corn, slicing halfway through the kernels. Rotate the cob and continue until all the kernels are sliced in half. Then repeat the slicing a second time to remove the bottom halves of the kernels.

ROASTED CORN SALSA

Serves 8

The serrano chile fires up this dish; omit it for a mild to medium salsa. If neither poblanos nor serranos are available, substitute 2 small red bell peppers and 1 jalapeño, both roasted and seeded (*see* Quick Tips). Cut the red pepper into a small dice and mince the jalapeño.

- 5 ears corn in the husk
- 2 poblano chiles, roasted, peeled, seeded, and cut into small dice
- 1 serrano chile, roasted, peeled, seeded, and minced
- ½ cup oil-packed sun-dried tomatoes, drained and cut into small dice
- 3 tablespoons oil from sun-dried tomatoes
- 2 tablespoons minced cilantro
- 2 teaspoons minced fresh oregano
- ½ small red onion, minced
- 2 garlic cloves, minced
- 3 tablespoons juice from 1 large lime
- ½ teaspoon celery seed
- Salt and ground black pepper to taste

1. Heat grill or oven to 400 degrees. Soak

PHOTOGRAPH BY ERIC ROTH

corn in water for 30 minutes.

2. Place ears of corn on hot grill rack; cover and grill, turning often, until outer husks brown and corn is cooked, about 20 minutes. Alternatively, place corn on oven rack and roast until outer husks brown, about 20 minutes. Cool corn slightly, then husk. Slice whole corn kernels from the cobs.

3. Mix corn kernels with remaining ingredients in a medium bowl. (Can cover and refrigerate overnight.) Let stand at room temperature for 1 hour before serving.

CORN AND CLAM CHOWDER WITH ROASTED PARSNIPS

Serves 6

Steaming moistens the parsnips a bit so that they don't wither on the grill or in the oven. However, be careful not to overcook the parsnips, either at the steaming or roasting stage, or they will turn to mush.

- 5 ears corn in the husk
- 2 large parsnips
- 2 pounds littleneck clams, shells well scrubbed under cold running water
- 2 tablespoons butter
- 1 large onion, chopped
- Salt and pepper to taste
- ¼ cup minced cilantro

1. Heat grill or oven to 400 degrees. Soak corn in water for 30 minutes. Steam whole parsnips to soften slightly, about 5 minutes.

2. Place ears of corn and steamed parsnips on hot grill rack; cover and roast, turning often, until parsnip skins and outer corn husks brown, 8 to 10 minutes for parsnips and about 20 minutes for corn. Alternatively, place corn and parsnips in a roasting pan and roast until parsnip skins and outer corn husks brown, about 10 minutes for parsnips and about 20 minutes for corn. Cool corn and parsnips slightly. Dice parsnips and set aside; shuck corn.

3. Use the double-cutting method (*see* illustrations below) to remove kernels from each cob of corn.

4. Bring clams and 1 cup water to simmer over medium-high heat in a large saucepan. Cover and cook until clams just open (discard any that don't), about 8 minutes. Off heat, drain clams and reserve cooking liquid. Remove clams from shells and discard shells; chop clams coarsely, cover, and set aside. Strain the clam cooking liquid through a coffee filter or double thickness of cheesecloth; set aside.

5. Heat butter in a large saucepan; add onions and sauté until softened, about 5 minutes. Add the corn, parsnips, clam liquor, 3 cups water, and salt and pepper to taste. Bring to a boil; simmer to blend flavors, about 5 minutes. Add the chopped clams and simmer 5 minutes longer; adjust seasonings. Stir in cilantro and serve.

SHAKER-STYLE CREAMY CORN PUDDING

Serves 8 as a side dish

To make a sweet version of this pudding add (in place of the chives) 6 tablespoons sugar, 1 teaspoon minced orange zest, and 2 teaspoons ginger juice (*see* Quick Tips) to the grated corn. To make individual puddings, you can divide the mixture among 8, 6-ounce custard cups and bake until set, about 25 minutes.

- ¼ cup bread crumbs
- 10–12 ears corn, husks and silk removed
- 2 eggs, beaten
- ½ teaspoon salt
- 3 tablespoons chives, chopped
- 2 tablespoons butter, melted
- 1 cup milk

1. Heat oven to 350 degrees. Grease a 1½ quart casserole dish, add bread crumbs, and roll them around the dish to evenly coat bottom and sides.

2. Grate each ear of corn on a coarse grater to extract 3 cups of corn pulp (*see* illustrations below). Mix grated corn with next 5 ingredients.

3. Pour corn mixture into prepared dish. Bake until the center is barely set, 45 to 50 minutes. Serve hot or warm.

CORN AND ZUCCHINI SAUTÉ WITH CHILES

Serves 4 as a side dish

Don't let looks deceive you. This utterly unassuming dish, known as *calabacitas,* is the most popular summertime vegetable dish in New Mexico — and probably has been for a long time. If garden-fresh zucchini are not available, draw out the bitter flavor that develops with age by tossing the zucchini rounds in a colander with 1 teaspoon salt; let stand over a plate or in the sink for ½ hour. Rinse the zucchini, then dry on paper towels.

- 3–4 ears corn in the husk
- 2 tablespoons butter
- 1 onion, sliced
- 2 garlic cloves, minced
- 4 medium-small zucchini, sliced into thin rounds
- 2 New Mexico or other fresh red chiles, roasted, peeled, seeded, and diced
- Salt and pepper
- ½ cup grated cheddar cheese

1. Use the double-cutting method (*see* illustrations below) to remove kernels from each cob, to yield about 1½ cups.

2. Heat butter in a large skillet over medium-high heat. Add onions and garlic; sauté until almost softened, about 2 minutes. Add zucchini; sauté until almost softened, about 2 minutes. Add corn and chiles; sauté until corn is cooked, about 2 minutes longer. Season to taste with salt and pepper. Stir in cheese and serve. ■

Rebecca Wood is the author of *The Whole Foods Encyclopedia.*

GRATING AND SCRAPING CORN

1. Grate the corn using the large holes in a standard vegetable grater.

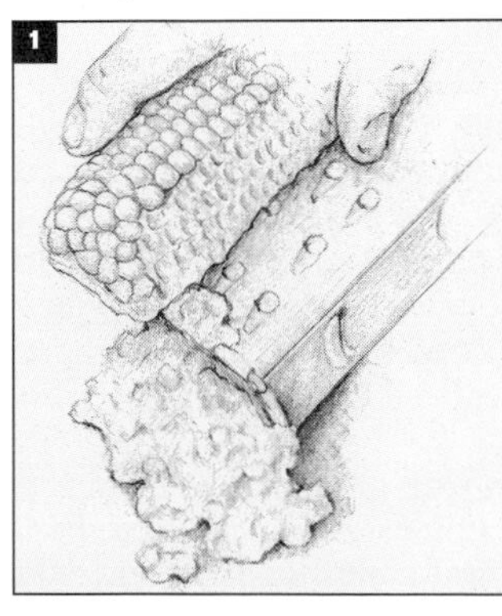

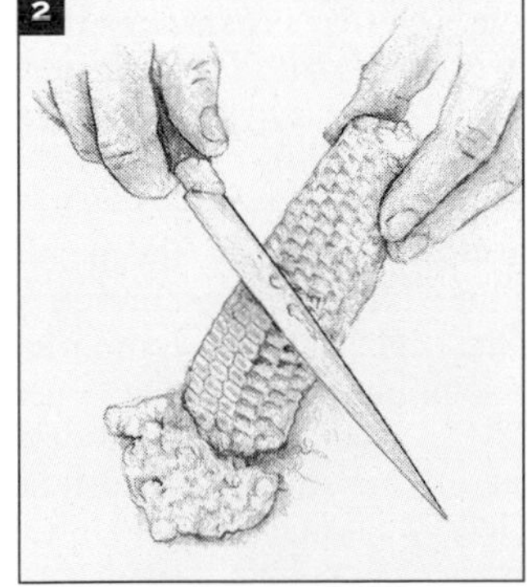

2. Using the back of a knife, firmly scrape the remaining pulp from the cob.

DOUBLE-CUTTING CORN

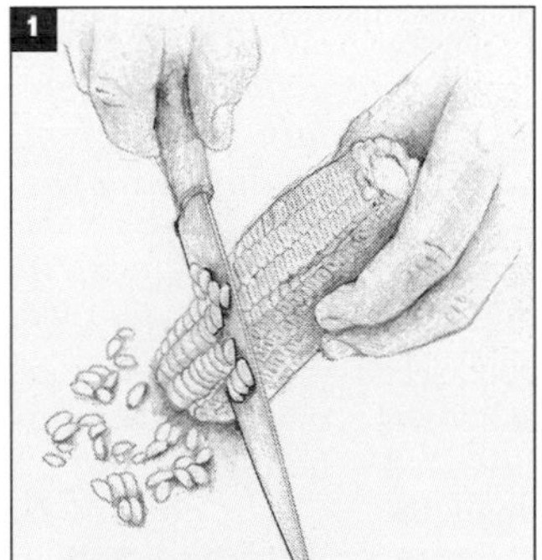

1. Holding ear of corn in an upright position, slice corn kernels from each cob, shaving off only half of each kernel.

2. Repeat, shaving off the remaining half of the kernels.

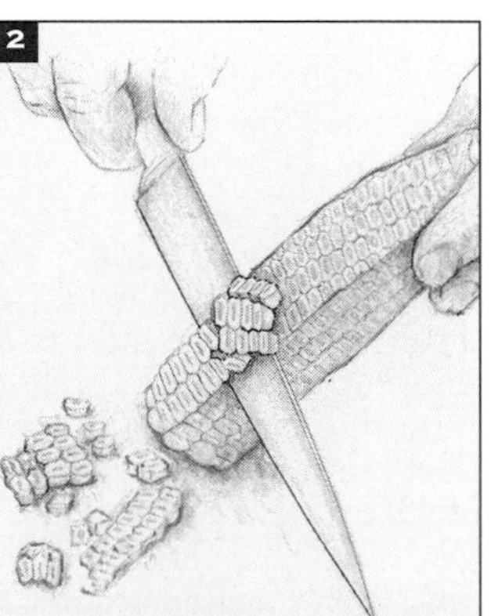

ILLUSTRATIONS BY KATHY BRAY

Do Marinades Work?

Marinades are ineffective as tenderizers, but add deep flavor if used for the correct amount of time.

BY JACK BISHOP

Can tough cuts of beef, lamb, and pork yield tender results? Many cookbook authors and chefs suggest tenderizing tough meat in acidic marinades. A look at current scientific journals shows that the laboratory community also regards marinades as tenderizers. But these studies fail to ask basic questions: How does marinated meat taste? What exactly happens to the texture? And, most importantly, is it worth the bother?

To answer these questions, I conducted several dozen tests in my kitchen to gauge the effects of marinades on beef, chicken, fish, and vegetables. In all cases, I assessed the effects in terms of both tenderizing and flavor.

According to common wisdom, the two substances most effective in tenderizing meat are acid and enzymes called proteases. Marinades designed to tenderize therefore usually contain lime or lemon juice for acid, and may derive proteases from a number of fruits, including papayas, pineapples, kiwis, and figs.

Finding the Optimum Mixture

Before I began the experiments, I called Dr. Barbara Klein, Professor of Food and Nutrition at the University of Illinois at Urbana, to find out what happens at the molecular level when a piece of meat sits in a marinade.

According to Klein, the "tenderizing" process actually has three steps. "When you put a piece of meat into an acidic or alkaline solution the water is drawn out," she explains. "The acid or base then moves into the meat, taking the place of the water and breaking apart the protein strands. Finally, the acid moves out of the meat and the water returns." Klein says this process takes a minimum of 24 hours, which is why short marinades have little effect on texture.

Since alkaline marinades are not practical — "Drano is one of the few alkaline substances strong enough to break down meat proteins, but you can't pour it on foods," notes Klein wryly — we are left with acids. Lemon juice, lime juice, and vinegar are the strongest culinary acids; other fruit juices and wines are less acidic.

In addition, certain fruits contain proteases, enzymes that speed up the natural breakdown of muscle. Papain, the most commonly used protease, comes from papaya. It is the main ingredient in commercial meat tenderizers, like Adolph's, that our mothers might have sprinkled on steaks. Pineapples, kiwis, and figs also contain powerful proteases.

With this information in mind, I went into the kitchen to develop the maximum-strength marinade. To do so, I took London Broil from the round (a particularly lean and therefore tough piece of meat), cut it into two-inch cubes, then marinated the cubes in various solutions for 24 hours.

The control sample without any marinade was tough and dry when broiled. Meat marinated in one-quarter cup lemon juice per pound of beef (along with one-quarter cup olive oil) was slightly more tender, especially on the outside. Lower amounts of lemon juice, however, had no effect, while more lemon juice "cooked" the meat, making it gray and dry. This was a recurring problem throughout my tests with lemon juice: To get any tenderizing effect, I had to use such large quantities that it made the meat dry and chewy. Even after 48 hours the third step described by Dr. Klein — where the acid left the meat and water returned — did not seem to occur.

As for fruits with proteases, I chose papaya since it has the mildest flavor. I pureed the flesh and added several tablespoons of oil to thin it out. I also added one cup lemon juice to one

PHOTOGRAPH BY ERIC ROTH

batch. Papaya alone did soften the meat, but the amount required was about one cup papaya per pound of meat. When the cup of lemon juice was added to the papaya, the tenderizing effect was the greatest; the color of the meat was bright and rosy when cooked and the meat was very soft.

I also experimented to find the ideal length of time for marinating. Meat that was marinated for 3 hours, 6 hours, and 12 hours, respectively, in the papaya-lemon juice mixture showed little improvement over the unmarinated control. Meat marinated 24 hours was noticeably softer, but was already starting to become mushy on the outside. At 48 hours, the meat was soft and unappealing.

But How Does it Taste?

At this point in my experimentation, however, I ran up against a rather subjective but critical criterion — taste. To be honest, in many cases "tenderized meat" translated as "mushy meat" and, in order for the papaya-lemon juice mixture to be effective, it had to be used in such quantity that its taste was overwhelming and unpleasant. This may not make much difference in the laboratory, but in the kitchen it is all-important.

In an attempt to remedy this problem, I threw several batches on the grill, since grilled foods usually taste better than foods broiled in home ovens. Although charring the outside does mask some of the marinade flavor (and some marinade actually burns off), grilling does not noticeably affect the texture. Once meat is softened by a highly acidic papaya marinade, cooking can do little to firm it up.

I also repeated the tests with thicker pieces of meat and found the effects were negligible and definitely not worth the effort. I therefore concluded that cuts with a relatively large surface area as compared to total volume are the best candidates for tenderizing, while roasts and other thick cuts are the worst. For instance, a butterflied leg of lamb will absorb more marinade than a bone-in leg, as the former has much more surface area.

What I found, then, is that if you want tender meat, marinating is not the answer. In fact, when it comes to tenderizing red meat, it seems that history has mistermed the process; acidic marinades do soften tough cuts, but they are unable to give a lean or sinewy piece of beef a more tender texture. If you want tender meat, you should either buy naturally tender cuts (those with some marbling of fat or from parts of the animal that are barely exercised, like the tenderloin) or, if you buy tough cuts, braise or stew them, since prolonged exposure to moist heat softens connective tissue and makes tough cuts fall apart.

Marinating for Flavor

The news is not all bad when it comes to marinades, though. While their ability to tenderize meat is marginal at best, there is no question that they add flavor — if you soak food in them long enough.

Without the high acid content designed to tenderize, marinades seep slowly into foods through osmosis. The length of time you leave the food in the marinade is critical. To understand the effect of time, I marinated beef cubes, various chicken parts, a mild flaky fish (flounder), a strong steakfish (tuna), and vegetables (an absorbent type, zucchini, and one with a thick skin, bell peppers) for various periods. In all cases, I kept the acid content to a minimum to prevent softening. (Acid can be eliminated entirely, but I prefer some lemon or vinegar to balance flavors.)

I first experimented with beef, and found that marinating in olive oil, balsamic vinegar, garlic, and herbs for anywhere from 3 to 12 hours makes only a slight difference in internal flavor. After 24 hours, though, the flavors of the marinade had penetrated into the center of two-inch cubes for shish kabob. After that, more time did not translate into more flavor.

The effect of the marinade on chicken varied quite dramatically according to whether I left the skin on. With skin on, in 3 hours the flavors on the skin were quite intense and there was even a mild lemony undertone in the meat. At 6 and 12 hours, there was little change. After 24 hours in the marinade, though, there was a noticeable difference; the meat was now redolent with lemon, garlic, and rosemary. After 48 hours, the meat had turned opaque and was actually starting to fall off the bone before cooking. Despite this dramatic change little flavor was added by the extra day. For optimum flavor and texture, 24 hours is by far the best, unless you like chicken seviche.

Skinless, boneless chicken breasts yielded very different results. After 1 hour, the chicken picked up little flavor, but pieces marinated for 3 hours were pleasantly lemony and juicy. Because there is no skin to protect the flesh, boneless breasts should not be marinated in acidic solutions for more than 3 hours; long marinating "cooks" exposed meat and dries it out.

Similarly, because acids begin to "cook" fish in a matter of minutes, I recommend very low-acid marinades for seafood, so that flavor absorption, not fear of making seviche, determines the length of time the fish is marinated. A quick bath in a marinade with less than one tablespoon of acid per pound of fish is fine. Generally, you should marinate delicate white fish like flounder for 15 minutes; stronger fish like tuna can withstand 30 minutes but not much more.

Absorbent vegetables such as zucchini, eggplant, and mushrooms act like sponges and soak up flavor over the course of 1 or 2 hours. Vegetables with a more pronounced flavor, such as bell peppers, begin to lose their characteristic taste after just 15 minutes; the marinade seemed to sit on the skin, making the peppers bitter and harsh. In general, be careful not to mask the natural sweetness in vegetables when choosing a marinade.

The master marinade recipes contain enough acid to provide good flavor (I find all-oil marinades heavy and dull) but not enough to cause tenderizing. Zipper-lock plastic bags are great for holding liquids and solids; shake several times during marinating to redistribute the contents. One final precaution: make sure to boil

Guide to Marinating for Flavor

This chart provides a general guide to amounts of marinade and marination time when using the low-acid Master Marinades, designed to provide flavor rather than to tenderize.

Product	Amount of Marinade	Optimum Marinating Time
Beef	¼ cup per pound of beef	24 hours
Chicken, skin on	¼ cup per pound of chicken	24 hours
Chicken, skinless	¼ cup per pound of chicken	3 hours
Delicate white fish (e.g., flounder)	2 tablespoons per pound of fish	15 minutes
Strong-textured fish (e.g., tuna)	2 tablespoons per pound of fish	30 minutes
Absorbent vegetables (e.g., zucchini)	3 tablespoons per pound of vegetables	1 hour
Thick-skinned vegetables (e.g., bell pepper)	2 tablespoons per pound of vegetables	15 minutes

the marinade before using it in sauces or to baste foods as they cook; this kills any bacteria that may have migrated from the flesh into the liquid.

MASTER RECIPE FOR ASIAN MARINADE

Makes ½ cup

¼ cup soy sauce or tamari
2 tablespoons dark sesame oil
2 tablespoons rice vinegar
1 tablespoon minced garlic
1 tablespoon minced ginger
1 scallion, sliced thin (about 2 tablespoons)
Ground black pepper to taste

Whisk ingredients (with additions, below, if desired) together in a small bowl. Place meat, poultry, fish, or vegetables in zipper-lock bag or in shallow, nonreactive pan. Pour marinade over contents and seal or cover. Marinate as directed in accompanying chart, turning zipper-lock bag or stirring contents of pan occasionally to evenly distribute marinade.

Additions: To vary or enhance flavor, add any one of the following to the Asian Marinade: 1 teaspoon wasabi or to taste; 1 tablespoon minced citrus zest; 1 teaspoon toasted and ground Szechwan peppercorns; 1 teaspoon dry mustard; 1 teaspoon five-spice powder.

Spicy Black Bean Variation: Substitute 1 tablespoon chili oil for 1 tablespoon of the sesame oil, and add 1 tablespoon chopped Chinese fermented black beans.

Lemon Fish Sauce Variation: Substitute 2 tablespoons fermented fish sauce such as *nuoc mam* for 2 tablespoons of the soy sauce or tamari, and add 1 tablespoon finely minced lemon zest or 2 tablespoons minced lemon grass.

MASTER RECIPE FOR MEDITERRANEAN MARINADE

Makes ½ cup

Balsamic and red wine vinegar will color poultry and fish. In place of the lemon juice or vinegar, you may substitute an equal amount of orange juice or white or red wine.

5 tablespoons olive oil
3 tablespoons lemon juice or balsamic, red, or white wine vinegar
1 tablespoon minced garlic
2 tablespoons minced fresh basil, parsley, tarragon, oregano, mint, or snipped chives or 1 tablespoon minced fresh thyme or rosemary
Ground black pepper to taste

Whisk ingredients (with additions, below, if desired) together in a small bowl. Place meat, poultry, fish, or vegetables in a zipper-lock bag or in a shallow, nonreactive pan. Pour marinade over contents and seal or cover. Marinate as directed in accompanying chart, turning zipper-lock bag or stirring contents of pan occasionally to evenly distribute the marinade.

Additions: To vary or enhance flavor, add any one of the following to the Mediterranean Marinade: 1 tablespoon olive paste; 1 tablespoon minced sun-dried tomatoes packed in oil; 1 tablespoon tomato paste.

Southwestern Variation: Substitute lime juice for lemon juice or vinegar; use 2 tablespoons minced cilantro for the herb; and add 1 teaspoon each of ground cumin, chili powder, and turmeric, along with 1 jalapeño chile, seeded and minced.

Indian Variation: Decrease olive oil to 3 tablespoons and lemon juice to 1 tablespoon; use 2 tablespoons minced cilantro or mint for the herb; and add 1/4 cup plain yogurt and 1 teaspoon curry powder.

SPICY SOUTHWESTERN FLANK STEAK

Serves 4

Flank steak is a relatively inexpensive cut that can be tough if not properly prepared. To make sure that the meat is tender, do not overcook (rare or medium-rare is best). Because flank steak is a very thin cut, the marinade may flavor the meat in less than 24 hours. Cut steak into thin slices across the grain.

1 Master Recipe for Mediterranean Marinade, Southwestern Variation
1 flank steak (about 2 pounds), trimmed of excess fat
Salt

1. Prepare marinade and marinate flank steak (*see* Master Recipe for Mediterranean Marinade). Refrigerate at least 3 hours, 24 hours if possible.

2. Heat grill or broiler. Remove steak from bag or pan and sprinkle with salt. Place on a roasting pan or hot grill rack. Cook steak on grill or under broiler, turning once, until medium-rare, 8 to 10 minutes. Transfer steak to a platter and cover with aluminum foil to let juices settle, about 5 minutes. Holding knife at a slight angle, cut thin slices across the grain. Serve immediately.

GRILLED CHICKEN WITH OLIVES, ROSEMARY, AND GARLIC

Serves 4–6

Chicken dripping marinade into hot coals can potentially catch fire. If you don't want to watch over the chicken as it cooks, you can build an indirect fire (*see* illustrations, pages 19 and 20) and roast the chicken on the grill.

1 Master Recipe for Mediterranean Marinade, doubled (use rosemary for the fresh herb)
2 tablespoons olive paste
1 whole chicken (about 4 pounds), cut into 8 pieces
Salt

1. Prepare marinade and marinate chicken pieces (*see* Master Recipe for Mediterranean Marinade). Refrigerate at least 3 hours, 24 hours if possible.

2. Heat grill. Remove chicken pieces from bag or pan and sprinkle with salt. Bring remaining marinade to a boil and set aside. Place chicken pieces, skin side down, on the hot grill rack. Cover and cook chicken over a medium-hot fire, turning once and brushing frequently with remaining marinade, until juices run clear when skin is pierced, about 30 minutes.

GRILLED TUNA WITH GINGER AND GARLIC

Serves 4

Since the tuna steaks spend so little time in the marinade, place them in a nonreactive pan rather than in a zipper-lock bag.

4 tuna steaks (about 8 ounces each)
½ Master Recipe for Asian Marinade
Salt

1. Prepare marinade (*see* Master Recipe for Asian Marinade). Place tuna steaks in a nonreactive dish and brush both sides with marinade. Cover and refrigerate for 30 minutes, turning once after 15 minutes.

2. Heat grill. Sprinkle tuna steaks with salt and place them on the hot grill rack. Cook over a medium-hot fire, turning once, until medium-rare, about 8 minutes. Serve immediately.

GRILLED SKEWERED LAMB WITH YOGURT, CURRY, AND MINT

Serves 6

Skewer vegetables like zucchini, bell peppers, and onions along with the lamb and serve them over a bed of basmati rice. You can also serve the lamb with pita bread, shredded lettuce, chopped tomato, and cucumber-yogurt sauce.

1 Master Recipe Mediterranean Marinade, Indian Variation
2 pounds boneless lamb, cut into 1½-inch cubes
Salt

1. Prepare marinade and marinate lamb cubes (*see* Master Recipe for Mediterranean Marinade). Refrigerate at least 3 hours, 24 hours if possible.

2. Heat grill. Remove lamb cubes from bag or pan and sprinkle with salt. Thread ⅙ of lamb cubes onto each of 6 skewers. Place skewers on the hot grill rack. Cover and cook over a medium-hot fire, turning once, until medium-rare, about 7 to 8 minutes. ■

ILLUSTRATION BY ALAN WITSCHONKE

Raw Tomato Sauces

Uncooked tomato sauces marry the aromatic flavors of ripe tomatoes with just a hint of other ingredients.

BY MICHELE SCICOLONE

Canned tomatoes are fine for cooked sauces; but to take advantage of the fleeting flavor of homegrown, vine-ripened tomatoes, it's best to make uncooked sauces.

Few foods are more appealing than sweet, fresh tomatoes. During their all-too-brief season, it seems a shame to sully their direct appeal with complicated preparations and unnecessary blandishments. Still, there are times when I crave something a bit more complex than sliced fresh tomatoes, tomatoes layered with basil, or tomatoes sprinkled with olive oil and balsamic vinegar.

On those occasions, I turn to uncooked tomato sauces. While I enjoy the cooked tomato sauces that can be made all year long using canned tomatoes, raw sauces are an August specialty — one I have looked forward to every year since learning how to make them a few summers ago in Rome.

When there, my husband and I headed for our favorite trattoria every day, where we'd lunch on pasta dressed with chopped ripe tomatoes, basil, olive oil, and diced fresh mozzarella. At home, I recreate the same sauce — without the cheese — to spoon on toasted bread for bruschetta, or to top grilled fish, chicken breasts, or chops. It also makes a fine light dressing for vegetables and salads.

There is some question as to whether it's best to peel and seed tomatoes for this basic uncooked sauce and its variations. I usually don't bother to remove the seeds or skins; I want both their fiber and their nutrients, and diced or cubed pieces hold their shape and look better if the skin is left intact. In addition, seeded tomatoes lose much of their juice and, for an uncooked sauce — especially one for pasta — I like to use all of the juices. This helps moisten the pasta without having to add too much oil. You might, however, want to remove the skins when serving the sauce over pasta (*see* illustrations, page 15).

In those cases where I want a thick sauce — as in the Tomato-Yogurt variation on the Master Recipe, for example — I squeeze the tomatoes to extract both juice and seeds. To use this method, simply cut the peeled or unpeeled tomato in half crosswise (*not* through the stem), then hold each half over a bowl or sink and squeeze gently while shaking somewhat vigorously. Remove any remaining seeds with a spoon or dull knife, remove the stem end, and chop as needed. Plum-shaped tomatoes, sometimes called Romas, contain fewer seeds than round tomatoes, and can be substituted in recipes where seeds are not wanted.

Some people salt tomatoes to remove their juice and intensify their flavor. I found that salted tomatoes do tend to lose some of their juice, but that their flavor was not more intense, just saltier. Futhermore, rinsing and drying the tomatoes did nothing to remove the saltiness. I have found, however, that if tomatoes are less than perfect — due to the time of year, the crop, or whatever the reason may be — a pinch of sugar sprinkled on them after dicing boosts their flavor considerably.

MASTER RECIPE FOR FRESH TOMATO-HERB SAUCE

Makes 2 cups

Serve this sauce or the variations that follow over pasta, toasted bread, grilled fish or chicken, or salad greens.

- 2 medium tomatoes, cut into a medium dice (peeling and seeding optional)
- 3 tablespoon minced fresh herbs such as basil, parsley, cilantro, mint, oregano, or tarragon
- 1 teaspoon minced garlic
- ¼ cup virgin olive oil
- Salt and ground black pepper

Mix all ingredients, including salt and pepper to taste, in a medium bowl. The mixture can be set aside at room temperature for a couple of hours, but should not be refrigerated or it will lose flavor.

Additions: To vary or enhance flavor, add any one of the following to the Master Recipe: 2 tablespoons finely chopped onions or scallions; ¼ cup chopped cured black olives; ¼ cup grated Parmigiano Reggiano or Pecorino Romano cheese; 1 tablespoon balsamic vinegar.

MEXICAN-STYLE SALSA CRUDA

Makes about 2 cups

Serve with scrambled eggs, grilled meat or fish, or Mexican dishes. You can also add ¼ cup red bell pepper to this salsa.

Follow the Master Recipe, omitting the olive oil and using 3 tablespoons cilantro. Add 2 tablespoons finely chopped red onion and half of a seeded and minced jalapeño pepper.

TOMATO YOGURT SAUCE

Makes about 2 cups

Serve with grilled fish, boiled potatoes, or as a filling for pita bread. You can also add 2 tablespoons chopped scallion or ¼ cup diced cucumber to this sauce.

Follow the Master Recipe, omitting the olive oil, substituting 1 cup plain yogurt for 1 cup of the tomatoes, using mint as the herb, and adding ½ teaspoon cumin. ■

Michele Scicolone is the author of *La Dolce Vita* (Morrow, 1993) and *The Antipasto Table* (Morrow, 1992).

ILLUSTRATION BY JACQUI MORGAN

Two Ways to Peel Tomatoes

Both of these methods are effective; I use the boiling water method when I have many tomatoes to peel — it's quicker. Note that, while some cookbooks say tomato skins can be removed by using a microwave, I had no luck with this method, and one of my tomatoes burst open while I was trying. I don't recommend this technique.

Stovetop Method:

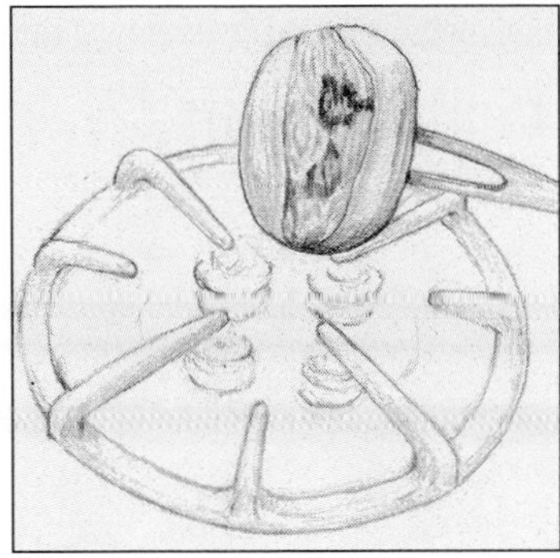

Use a pair of tongs to hold a ripe tomato over a gas or electric burner with the heat on high. Turn the tomato often until the skin is blistered and lightly blackened in spots if using a gas burner (left), or until the skin starts to blister and separate from the tomato if using an electric burner (right), about 30 seconds in either case. Let the tomato cool, then pull off the skin with your fingers.

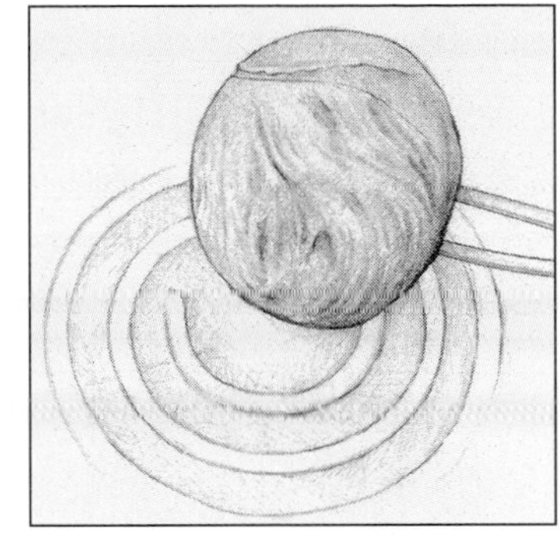

Boiling Water Method:

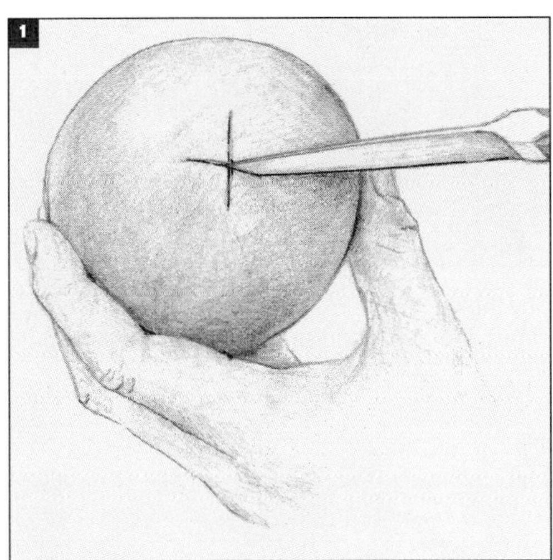

1. Bring a pot of water to boil. Cut a small cross in the base of a ripe tomato; put it in the water for 30 seconds.

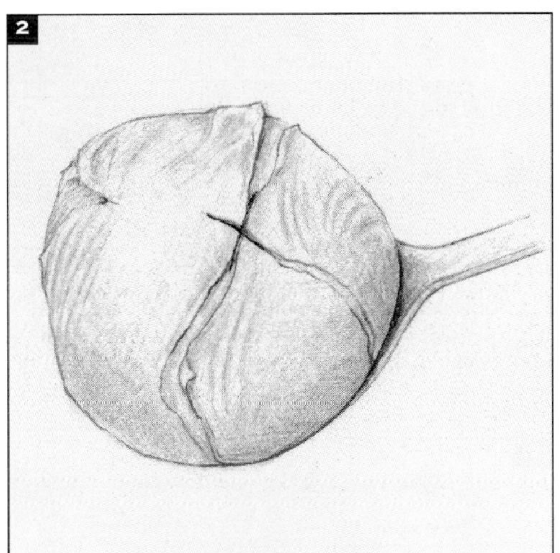

2. Remove the tomato with a slotted spoon and put it in a bowl of ice water for 30 seconds.

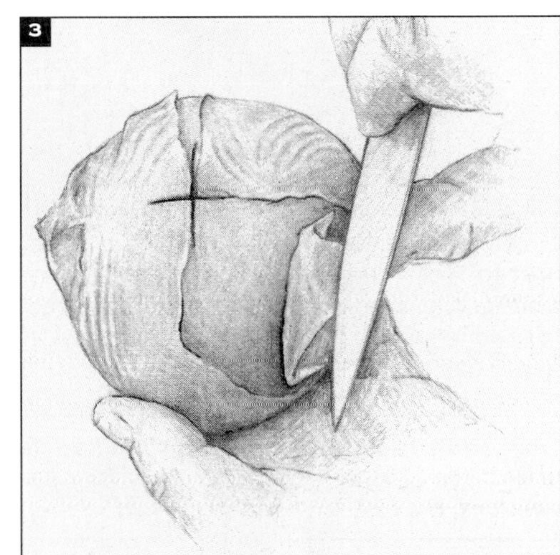

3. Remove from the water and peel off the skin, using your fingers and a knife as shown.

Dicing Tomatoes

Choose a firm, ripe tomato. Peel it if you like, using one of the methods above. Use a serrated knife to cut slices off both stem and bottom ends.

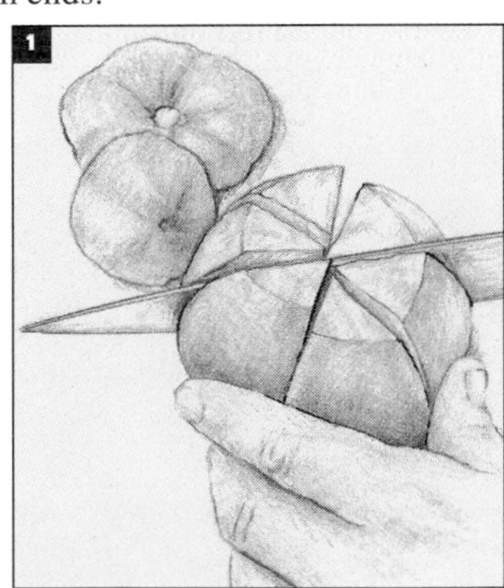

1. Stand the tomato on one flattened end and cut it into 6 or 8 wedges, depending on the size of the tomato.

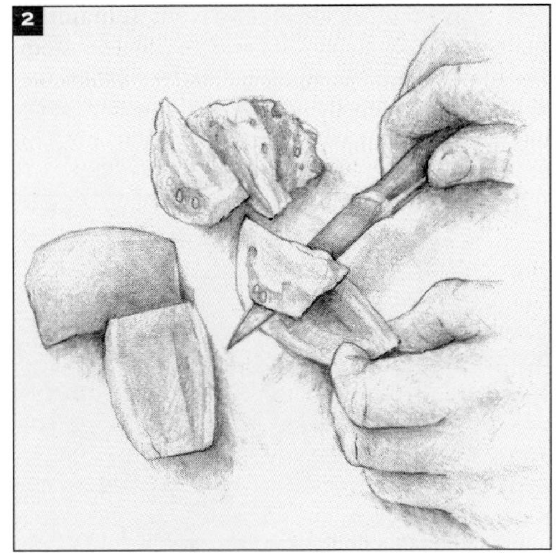

2. With a sharp paring knife, cut the outer tomato flesh where it joins the soft inside, as if you were peeling an orange wedge. Scrape away any seeds from the flesh.

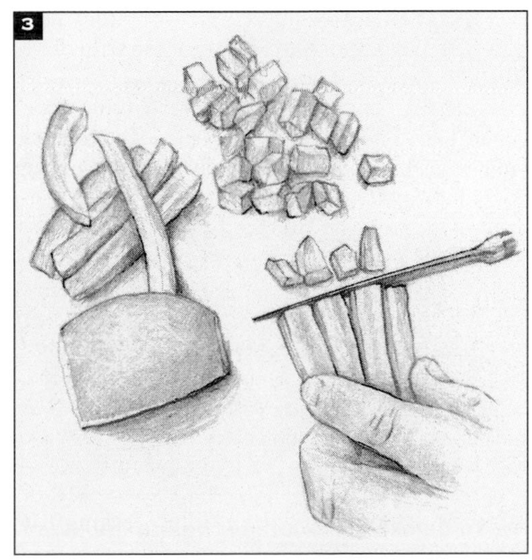

3. Cut into narrow strips, then into dice.

ILLUSTRATIONS BY KATHY BRAY

How to Prepare Lobster

Everything you need to know to select, prepare, and eat lobster.

Telling Male from Female

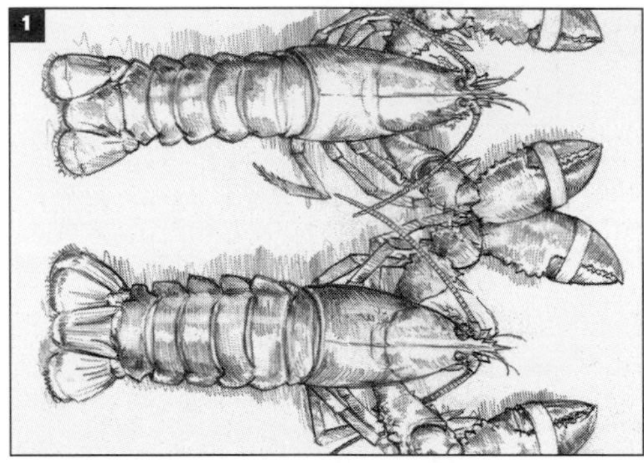

1. Female lobsters (bottom) have a greater meat-to-shell ratio than males (top), and may contain coral, or roe, which is delicious and can be used in sauces. From the back, the female usually has a broader tail.

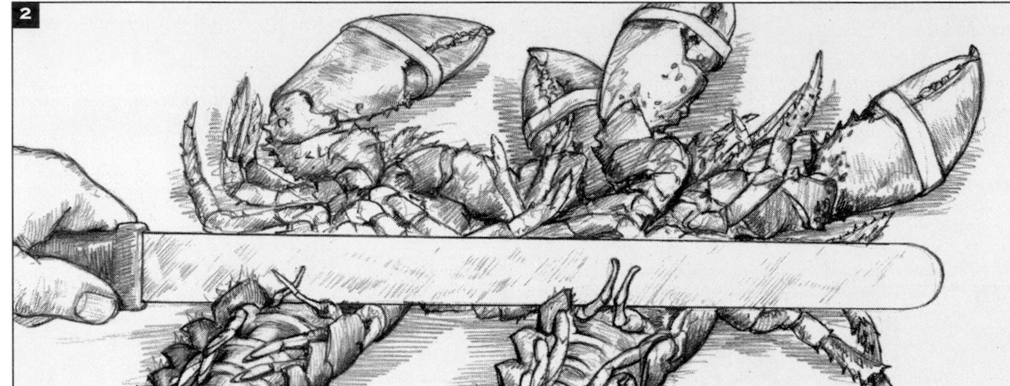

2. Lobsters can be sexed more reliably from the front, by looking at their "swimmerets," the little claw-like appendages at the top of the tail. The males' (right) are hard, and may even resemble small claws; the females' are softer and often smaller.

To Prepare for Grilling or Broiling

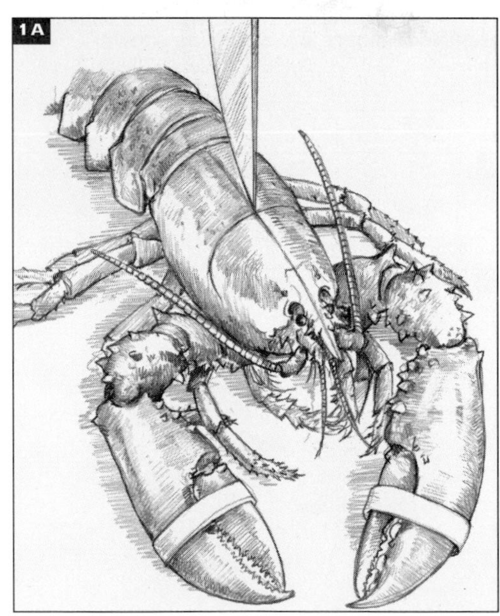

1A. To quickly kill a lobster before grilling or broiling, use a sharp 10- or 12-inch chef's knife. Place the point of the knife right at the cross-hatch in the middle of the top of the lobster's body.

2A. Insert the knife straight into the lobster, cut an inch or so towards the tail, then turn the knife and cut straight up through the head.

3A. Cut all the way through the head, then cut all the way back through the tail.

4A. This is what a lobster looks like cut in half. Remove and discard the watery head sac (top left) and the long, thin intestine (top right) with a knife; each must be removed from both halves.

5A. The pale green tomalley (liver) can be removed with a spoon, and should be reserved for sauces. Note the long strip of coral above the tail meat. This can also be used in sauces, or left in the lobster; it turns coral-colored when cooked.

To Prepare for Sautéing or Stir-Frying

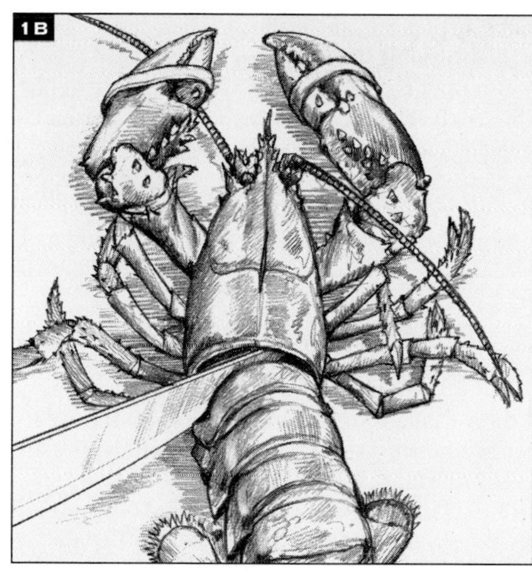

1B. For stir-frying or sautéing, you will want to remove the claws and crack them, and to remove the tail and section it. To remove the tail, insert the point of a chef's knife into the gap between tail and body, and pry and cut simultaneously. It will come off easily.

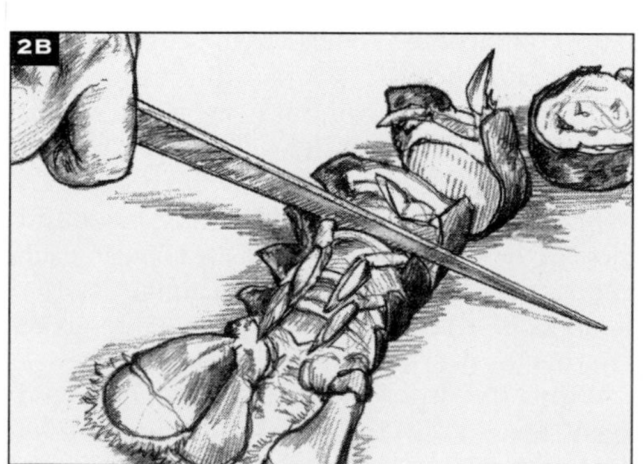

2B. Cut the tail into 3/4- to 1-inch sections, cutting from the underside.

3B. Remove the claws from raw or cooked lobster by twisting them where they join the body. Crack them as you would after cooking.

To Eat Boiled Lobster

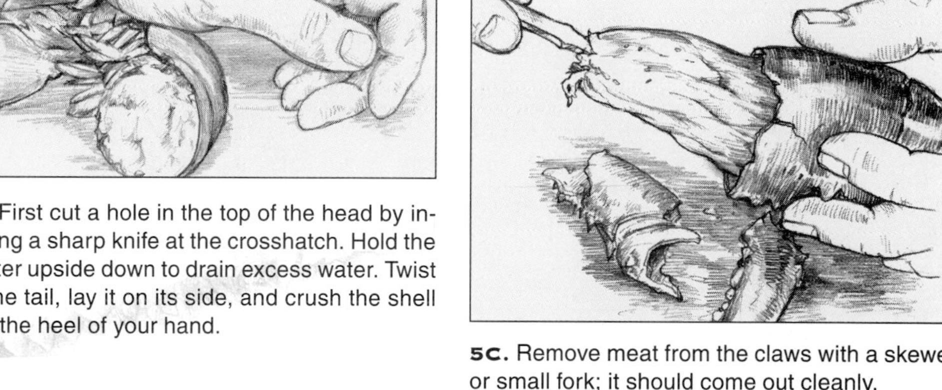

1C. First cut a hole in the top of the head by inserting a sharp knife at the crosshatch. Hold the lobster upside down to drain excess water. Twist off the tail, lay it on its side, and crush the shell with the heel of your hand.

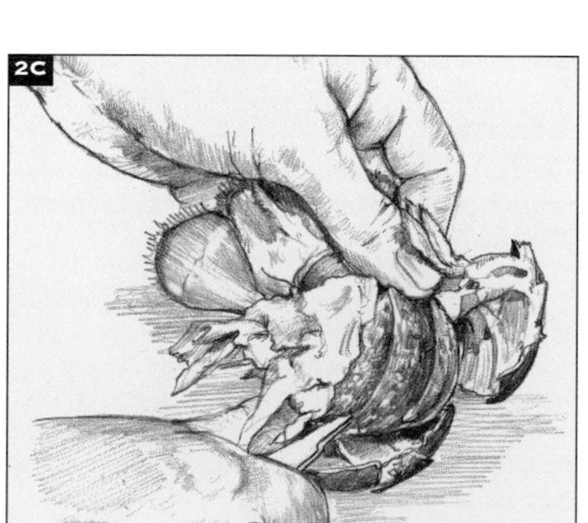

2C. Twist and break the shell to free the tail meat; it will come out cleanly.

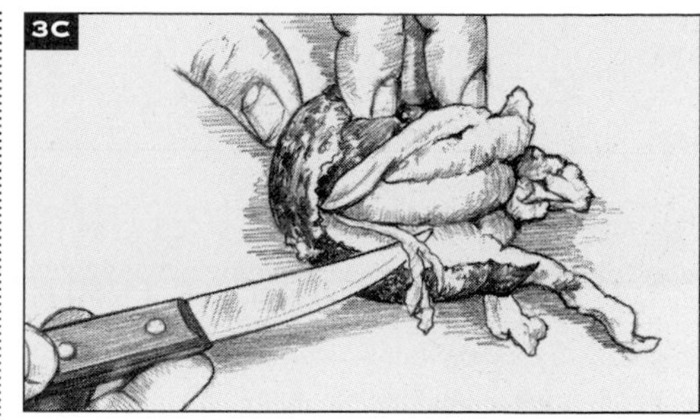

3C. Cut a small lengthwise slit in the center of the back of the tail and remove the pinkish intestine.

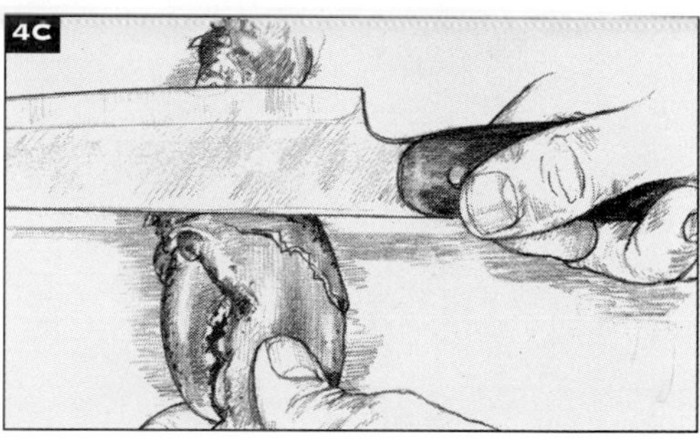

4C. Remove the claws (*see* illustration 3B). Crack the claws with a couple of sharp blows with the back of a heavy knife. Break them in half.

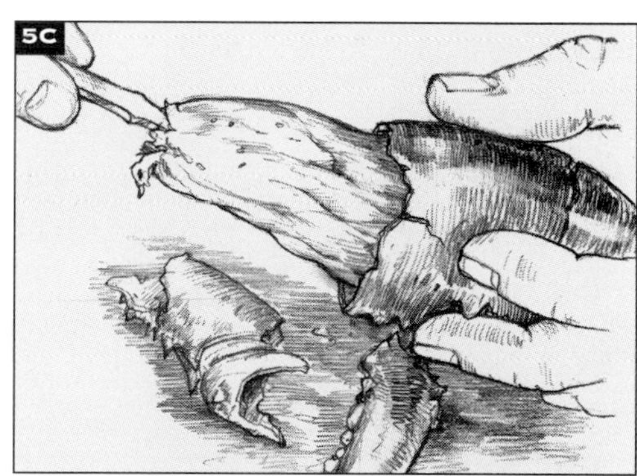

5C. Remove meat from the claws with a skewer or small fork; it should come out cleanly.

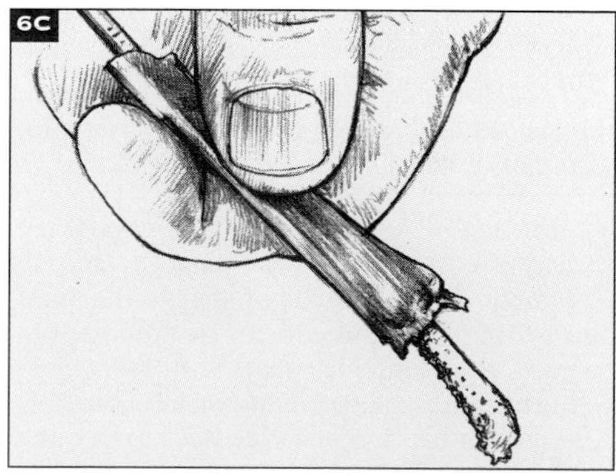

6C. On larger lobsters, there is plenty of meat in the small legs attached to the body. Twist them off, break them in half, and push the meat out with a skewer or small metal pick. ■

ILLUSTRATIONS BY ELAINE SEARS

Grill Roasting

Indirect grilling, over gas or charcoal, saves effort and gives spectacular results — golden chicken, smoky ribs, perfect fish.

BY PAM ANDERSON

Grill roasting can be used for whole vegetables as well as for meat and fowl. Vegetables such as potatoes and onions may need to roast for the entire cooking time; faster-cooking items, such as tomatoes and corn, can be added during the last few minutes of roasting.

I grew up in Florida, where outdoor cooking was possible almost year-round. Everyone I knew — especially my father — did all of their grilling over direct heat. He stood out in the yard, following his rituals with great care, lovingly tending his pieces of chicken, his steaks, even his burgers. Needless to say, the results were memorable.

But my father's outdoor cooking, like that of so many of the men of his generation (and remember that most of the outdoor cooking was done by men in those days), was limited to small pieces of meat, especially burgers, steaks, chops, and chicken.

That's probably why it seemed like such a revelation when, several summers back, a good friend showed me how to make her summertime specialty, hickory-roasted chicken. She built a fire on one side of her kettle grill, threw wet hickory chips on top of the coals after they were white, stuck a whole, untrussed bird on the other side of the grill, and walked away, to busy herself with the other affairs of dinner. She glanced at the grill, but didn't really pay much attention to it. I was a little worried, but decided my friend must know what she was doing. Sure enough, when she returned to it, 45 minutes later, she revealed a fully cooked, beautifully tanned chicken, the likes of which I had never seen outside of a restaurant.

I readily added this simple recipe to my admittedly limited grilling repertoire, but it took me years to see the real possibilities of grill-roasting. It was almost as if I learned how to make bread dough without realizing I could make pizza.

But playing with the gas grill I was given last Christmas triggered my memory, and started to make me think about expanding my grill-roasting skills. Why not fire up one side and cook on the other, replicating the technique my friend used on her charcoal grill? And — as long as I was at it — why not begin to use my kettle grill to its full potential, trying the indirect grilling method on foods other than chicken?

Cooking with Charcoal

It didn't take long for me to figure out how to get my kettle grill to act pretty much like an oven, maintaining a fairly constant temperature of 350 to 400 degrees. All I did was load up my chimney starter with about 60 coals — full to the top — light it, and wait about half an hour, until the top of the heap was coated with a thin layer of white ash. After that, by judiciously adjusting the grill's top and bottom vents, I could maintain a steady, moderate heat without much fuss.

My kettle grill has two half-moon-shaped metal baskets, which I can put on opposite sides of the bottom of the kettle, leaving a space down the center of the grill rack (*see* illustration page 19). The food goes over this center strip, where it's away from direct heat. This two-basket method produces wonderfully even heat. Of course, you don't need grill baskets; just build a fire in the grill and push half the coals to each side, or pour hot coals from the chimney starter on opposite sides, using long-handled tongs or a fireplace poker to move stray coals.

With a bit of practice, I learned that I could roast almost anything — not just whole chicken, but large pieces of meat, pork, or lamb, and even whole fish — without paying too much attention. And the results were terrific —

PHOTOGRAPH BY ERIC ROTH

lovely and golden in appearance, slightly smoky in flavor. Only racks of ribs, which require a great deal of surface area on the grill, needed to be rearranged during cooking, and that only once. (And only with ribs did I find it best to put all the coals in one basket, to maximize the cooking area.) Still, I had smoky, moist ribs ready in about an hour and with a minimum of effort.

While mastering my technique, I found that by topping the coals with either wood chips or larger chunks of hardwood — soaked in water for as little as 20 minutes or as long as overnight — I could gain the intensely flavored, richly colored meats I was after. I prefer the chunks, because wood chips are spent after just a few minutes on the coals; when I used them, I usually threw on a second batch about halfway through the cooking time to increase the smokiness. (If you prefer a more subtle smoky flavor, however, one batch of chips will suffice.)

The only other accessory that I found helpful is a homemade drip pan. (I can't stand foil drip pans that aren't cheap enough to throw out and yet are impossible to clean.) A big rectangle of heavy-duty aluminum foil—with its edges turned up to form a lip—will catch the drippings of anything you cook; and when the fat cools off and solidifies, you can just wrap up the foil and toss it out. (Many people who recommend foil pans also suggest that you put water in the pan to keep the fat from spattering. I never had a problem with grease fires while using the foil, and I suspect a little fat spattering onto the coals now and again actually helps the flavor.)

Several weeks after I first began experimenting — and after charcoal roasting at least 50 pounds of chicken, plus ribs, salmon, and beef — I'm starting to feel as enthusiastic as Cort Sinnes, author of the excellent book *The Grilling Encyclopedia* (Atlantic Monthly Press, 1992), who states, "When I pull a leg of lamb, turkey, or prime-rib off the covered kettle grill, it does my sense of history good to know that it was prepared in the time-honored method — charcoal roasted. I say leave the oven for what it does best — namely, baking pies, breads, cakes, and cookies."

Cooking with Gas

Although the construction of gas grills vary from one to the next, most have in common two adjustable burners and a half-size "warming" rack on top. The burners make it possible to adjust the temperature, but — for reasons inherent in the design of gas grills — most people complain that even the lowest flame on their grill is often too high for roasting without causing frequent flare-ups and, conversely, that even the highest flame is not high enough for direct grilling.

I soon realized that using the gas grill to mimic the indirect method of charcoal grilling was going to take some creativity. For starters, cooking on the off side would not work for everything. With only one burner going (heating just one side of the grill), the ambient heat in the closed chamber — which isn't nearly as tight as the chamber of a kettle grill — hovers in the neighborhood of 300 degrees. Therefore, unless you're using wood chips, the meat doesn't brown.

I also quickly discovered that, unlike chickens and roasts, 18-inch long specimens such as whole fish or beef tenderloin were not going to fit on one side of the gas grill. Nevertheless, I was determined to roast one of my salmons over gas (I'd already had success in the kettle grill). Staring at the gas grill's open mouth, I realized that long, narrow foods would fit perfectly on the elevated warming rack; that way, I could use both burners but keep the flames at bay.

This technique worked beautifully with the salmon — I got fish that was moist and tender inside, with a slight hint of smoke — but was not as successful with chicken and ribs. Both meats cooked nicely for the first 75 percent of their cooking time, but during the last 10 to 15 minutes—the point when the juices started flowing—the fire inevitably flared up. Grease fires are not so much of a problem if you're standing by your grill, but the whole idea of indirect grilling was to let me grill, make a salad, set the table, and open the wine at the same time. I was discouraged; what good was top-rack roasting if I had to hover over whatever I cooked?

Then I tried my improvised drip pan and was quickly back in business. I cooked ribs, chicken parts, and a tenderloin. When the juices hit the hot foil they spattered and made smoke, but no fire. And there was an added benefit: the foil shielded the food from any direct heat. This was indirect grilling with the least effort yet.

One unresolved problem remained, however. Although soaked chips, when thrown directly on the lava rocks, give gas-grilled foods a mild smoky flavor, I couldn't make the larger chunks of hardwood work. They always caught fire no matter how long I soaked them, no matter what I tried.

No one can question the ease and handiness of a gas grill, but I invariably preferred food that was roasted over charcoal in the kettle grill. The gas-grilled food was fine; it just wasn't quite as good as charcoal-grilled. Of course, if lack of time, the need for convenience, or cold weather keep you from building a real fire, the gas grill is a good second choice. After all, that's why we all have them.

To Set Up a Charcoal-Roasting Grill

Use a chimney starter (*see* Sources and Resources, page 32) to heat 60 charcoal briquets so that even those coals at the top are covered with a thin layer of white ash. Remove the grill rack. Place heavy-duty aluminum foil, with sides turned up to form a shallow lip, down the center of the grill. Pour half the hot coals into each grill basket or into two piles on opposite sides of the grill.

If you heat the coals in the grill (rather than in the chimney starter), use long-handled tongs to separate the coals into two piles, on opposite sides of the grill, once they have heated. Next, carefully place the shaped foil in the grill between the coals. (When grill-roasting ribs, place all the coals on one side of the grill, thus providing more surface area for the meat.)

If you are using soaked wood chunks, add them at this point. Replace the grill rack and lid. You may also want to place an oven thermometer on the grill rack (over the foil, not on the coals) to keep track of the temperature. Open the bottom and lid vents halfway and heat grill to about 350 degrees. This should take about five minutes.

Remove the grill lid. If you're adding wood chips, use tongs to pull the rack halfway off the grill. Toss a small handful of soaked chips into each pile of coals. Return the rack and place food on the rack over the foil. Cover and roast until the food is done; add a second batch of wood chips about halfway through the cooking process if you desire a stronger smoked flavor.

Remember that removing the grill lid is like opening an oven door; each time you do it, you lose heat (and, by adding oxygen, cause the charcoal to burn faster). Without adding coals to the fire, you should have enough heat to last about 90 minutes. If you are cooking food that takes longer, start another batch of coals about 45 minutes after the meat starts cooking, so that you're adding hot coals to the fire.

ILLUSTRATION BY ELAINE SEARS

To Set Up a Gas-Roasting Grill

The first technique, which I prefer, will work for anything that will fit on the top rack — ribs, whole fish, butterflied poultry or poultry pieces, pork and beef tenderloins. Tall roasts and whole birds won't fit on the top rack and must be cooked using the second method.

For the double-burner, top-rack method, turn both burners on high, place an oven thermometer on the top rack, and heat the grill to about 400 degrees. Cut a piece of heavy-duty foil slightly larger than the length and width of the top rack. Turn up the sides and ends to form a shallow lip. If you're adding wood chips, use tongs to remove the grill racks, then toss the soaked chips onto the lava rocks; return the bottom grill racks. Put the foil on the bottom rack, then place prepared meat, poultry, or fish on the top rack and close the lid. (When grill roasting a whole fish like salmon, it's better to cook the fish directly on a piece of heavy-duty foil rather than over it. The foil helps when it comes time to move the delicate cooked fish to a serving platter.) Roast until the food is done; add a second batch of wood chips about halfway through the cooking process if you desire a stronger smoked flavor. If the grill temperature exceeds 400 degrees, lower the heat.

For the one-burner method, cut a piece of heavy-duty foil slightly larger than the roast and turn up the sides to form a shallow lip. Put it under the grill rack, on the side that will eventually be turned off. Turn both burners on high and heat the grill to about 400 degrees. Turn off the heat on the foil side, and put the roast on the rack, over the foil. If you are using wood chips, use tongs to remove the other rack, and toss a large handful of soaked chips over the hot lava rocks. Close the lid and roast until the meat is done; add a second handful of soaked chips, halfway through the cooking process if you desire a stronger smoked flavor. You may start off with a 400-degree temperature, but with only one burner going, the temperature will eventually fall to about 300 degrees.

GRILL-ROASTED SALMON WITH ALDERWOOD
Serves 6–8

Perfectly cooked salmon is like well-cooked red meat — it's done when the meat thermometer, inserted at the thickest point, registers 130 degrees. You can use chunks or chips on the charcoal grill, but stick to chips when roasting on the gas grill. Whole fish need to be roasted on foil — they're too fragile to move from grill to platter with just a spatula.

1 whole salmon (about 5 pounds)
2 tablespoons olive oil
Salt and ground white pepper
3 cups chips or about 6 chunks of alderwood or other aromatic hardwood

1. Set up charcoal grill (*see* illustration, page 19) or set up gas grill using the double-burner, top-rack method (*see* illustration above).

2. Brush salmon, including cavity, with olive oil and sprinkle with salt and pepper. Place salmon on a sheet of heavy-duty aluminum foil, place on grill rack, and grill roast according to directions under selected method. Roast salmon until meat thermometer inserted into the thickest point registers 130 degrees, 30 to 40 minutes. Transfer salmon to a platter and remove bottom foil; cover and let rest 10 minutes. Serve.

GRILL-ROASTED SPARERIBS WITH BARBECUE SAUCE
Serves 4

Since only one rack of spareribs fits comfortably down the center aisle of most standard charcoal grills, I prefer to build the fire on one side of the grill and to cook on the other. This provides the extra space to roast another ½ rack of ribs.

1½ racks spareribs (5 to 5½ pounds)
Salt and ground black pepper
1 cup barbecue sauce

1. Set up charcoal grill with all coals on one side, or set up gas grill using the double-burner, top-rack method.

2. Sprinkle ribs with salt and pepper. Place ribs on grill rack, meaty side up, and grill roast until ribs brown and render most of their fat, 45 to 60 minutes.

3. Brush one side of each rack with barbecue sauce, cover, and roast for 5 minutes. Turn the ribs, brush other side with sauce, cover, and roast until sauce adheres to ribs, about 5 minutes longer. Serve.

GRILL-ROASTED HICKORY CHICKEN
Serves 4

I might perform a more elaborate truss for company, but for everyday chicken, I just tuck the third wing joint under the chicken and tie the legs together.

1 chicken (3½ pounds)
1 tablespoon olive oil
Salt and ground black pepper
3 cups hickory chips or 6 hickory chunks

1. Set up charcoal grill or set up gas grill using the one-burner method.

2. Brush chicken, including cavity, with oil and sprinkle with salt and pepper. Truss chicken (*see Cook's Illustrated,* May/June, 1993). Grill roast chicken, adding chips or chunks at specified times, until a meat thermometer inserted into the thigh registers between 160 and 165 degrees, about 1 hour, depending on the grill temperature. Remove from grill, let rest for 10 minutes, and serve.

GRILL-ROASTED BEEF TENDERLOIN
Serves 12

1 beef tenderloin, trimmed and tail end tied up to make a more uniform roast (6 to 6½ pounds, net weight)
1 tablespoon olive oil
2 tablespoons minced garlic
1 tablespoon *herbes de Provence*
Salt and ground black pepper

1. Set up charcoal grill or set up gas grill using double-burner, top-rack method.

2. Brush tenderloin with oil, press garlic onto meat, and sprinkle with herbs, salt, and pepper. Grill roast beef until meat thermometer inserted into the thickest point registers 125 degrees for medium-rare, about 1 hour and 15 minutes, depending on the grill temperature. Remove from grill, let rest for 10 minutes, and serve. ■

ILLUSTRATION BY ELAINE SEARS

Taste-Testing Sparkling Waters

Despite many new competitors, the venerable Perrier comes in first, with a trendy Italian and an American tied for second place.

BY JONI MILLER

With more than 75 brands of domestic and imported sparkling waters to choose from, it's no wonder thirsty American consumers feel as though they're swimming in the stuff. The spectrum of taste-styles can be daunting to the uninitiated, and each month a new contender seems to bubble to the surface. The double-digit growth rates have calmed down a bit since the former *Cook's* explored bottled sparkling waters in 1989, during the boom years of sky-rocketing sales and of Perrier's preeminence. Even so, Americans bought 172.3 million gallons of sparkling water last year, up 9.4 percent from 1991's figures.

We drink sparkling water primarily as a sugar-free, caffeine-free, low- (or no) sodium, healthful alternative to soft drinks and alcohol. Most, though not all, sparklers are mineral waters, and their characteristic bubbly effervescence comes from carbonation which may occur naturally or be added as part of the bottling process.

A Closely Regulated Drink

With increased health concerns over local and municipal water supplies (a scare last April in Milwaukee was front-page news), it's worth pointing out that domestic sparkling water is considered a "food" by the United States government. As such, it must meet regulations established by the Food and Drug Administration (FDA), the Environmental Protection Agency's "Safe Drinking Water Act," plus laws set by state and local governments. Additional new FDA regulations may recommend even stricter maximum levels of certain substances, among them lead.

Two states, California and New York, where bottled water consumption is among the nation's highest, have their own stringent regulations. Additionally, the International Bottled Water Association, whose membership includes around one thousand bottlers and distributors, has its own regulatory program which requires its members to allow mandatory, unannounced annual facilites inspections. Imported mineral waters are not specifically regulated by the FDA (they're not considered a food), but are subject to strict regulation by European governments and must meet all federal "Good Manufacturing Practices," health and safety standards, and FDA labeling requirements.

Cook's Illustrated gathered a panel of five tasters — a professional chef, two food and beverage writers, a representative from the Northeast's major bottled-water distributor, and an interested consumer — to taste 13 domestic and imported sparkling waters at the Sign of the Dove restaurant in New York City. To avoid any chance that the waters' carbonation would dissipate from standing too long, tasters sipped each chilled water from a wine glass within seconds of pouring. This was a blind tasting in which all bottles had been carefully camouflaged to obscure their labels, color, and shape.

The gates of the Source Perrier grounds open to the site of the famous Perrier spring in the south of France.

Americans Opt for Lack of Flavor

Tasters' overall opinions lent substance to the conventional wisdom that in choosing a sparkling water, Americans are not looking for flavor per se. Indeed, our panelists were quick to identify the overt presence of tastes they disliked, and the "gold standard" in sparkling bottled water emerged as a neutral-tasting, clear, crisp water with small bubbles producing moderate to high carbonation that felt refreshing. Only the subtlest hint of mineral flavor was seen as positive. (European water drinkers might judge waters differently, seeking a distinctive mineral taste.)

To everyone's surprise, the winner in our tasting was the perennial best-selling sparkling water in America, Perrier, a highly carbonated, low-mineralized water from France that captured consumers' imaginations in the 1980s and made it chic to drink bottled water.

Tied for second place were San Pellegrino, a lightly carbonated water from the San Pellegrino springs in the Italian Alps, and Saratoga, which comes from an underground spring in the Adirondack foothills.

Among the waters tasted were two relative newcomers to the American market, both of which court attention with unusual bottle designs. Loka from Sweden, rated fourth in our tasting, is a sparkler with low-mineral content that comes from the Loka Brunn Spa in the forested central part of Sweden, site of a famous health spa that dates back to 1720. It was first introduced in America around 1988 and is sold in a distinctive, clear glass, Champagne-style bottle.

One of the newest sparkling waters on the market fared less well in the tasting. Ty Nant Original Natural Spring Water, whose Welsh name translates as "small cottage by a stream," made its debut here two years ago, attracting frenzied attention with its unique cobalt-blue bowling-pin-shaped bottle (now *the* stylish impromptu bud vase of the 1990s). This is a lightly mineralized water from a network of springs, discovered in 1976 by a water diviner, which lie beneath the Cambrian mountains in a remote part of Wales.

Canada Dry Seltzer, Schweppes Club Soda, and Vintage Seltzer (a widely available East Coast supermarket brand) were also included in the tasting. The bottled water industry considers these "soft drinks," and they are usually filtered municipal water that has been carbonated. While seltzer is generally salt-free, club sodas are often fortified with mineral salts for flavor, which increases their sodium levels. Canada Dry Seltzer, rated sixth in the tasting, was considered "refreshing."

With regard to the overall outcome of the

tasting, it's worth noting that there was tremendous disparity between tasters' positive reactions to the four top-ranked waters, which scored between 22 and 16 points, and their less-than-enthralled impressions of the other nine waters, which ranged from 12 to 2 points. Each of the top three waters provided positive sensations and a level of refreshment that the others simply did not come close to offering. It's good to know that two of the top three waters — Perrier and San Pellegrino — are readily available nationwide, and that Saratoga, once sold primarily in the Northeast, is beginning to spring up on shelves in other parts of the country. ■

Sparkling Water Blind Tasting

Waters are listed in order of overall preference. The first three were universally favored by the panelists. The next two were generally liked; the remainder were considered unappealing for a variety of reasons. Ratings were based on a 10-point maximum for individual panelists' scores for each water. There was a potential 50-point maximum score per water based on the combined points given by all panelists. Note that there were three overall ties. Prices are not included, since they vary more than 50 percent from store to store.

Sparkling Waters Listed in Order of Preference

1 **Perrier Sparkling Mineral Water** (*France*). Best-liked of all the waters tasted, Perrier's "tiny" bubbles were admired by all the tasters, although everyone perceived the water's effervescence as slightly "too aggressive"; several found it "painful on the tongue." Nonetheless, there was a definitive consensus that Perrier's taste was the most "appealing" of all the waters. Interestingly, that taste, described by one imbiber as more like "a presence on the tongue than a taste," did not remind tasters of any specific flavor or attribute, a reminder that American water drinkers prefer an absence of overt taste in their bottled waters.

2 **San Pellegrino Sparkling Natural Mineral Water** (*Italy*). San Pellegrino and Saratoga Water tied for second place, receiving identical scores. Described as tasting "very, very good" in an overall sense, the panel liked the small size and balanced quality of Pellegrino's bubbles, which rose up in "small streams" in the glass. Tasters zeroed in on Pellegrino's "faint mineral" flavor and "clean, natural" taste, for which they expressed real enthusiasm. While three tasters commented on mildly pronounced "saltiness," they viewed this as an asset.

3 ✶ **Saratoga Naturally Sparkling Water** (*New York*). The second most well-liked, along with Pellegrino, Saratoga's "tiny" bubbles also appealed to panelists. As with San Pellegrino, tasters were drawn to the water's "pleasant, slightly salty" taste with a hint of mineral flavor; most described the taste as balanced and "very pleasant" overall; one found it a bit "too minerally." The consensus: "Well-balanced taste with some flavor."

4 **Loka Sparkling Mineral Water of Sweden** (*Sweden*). In a dead heat for fourth-place ranking with Lurisia, Loka's "Champagne-like trail" of "very active" tiny bubbles attracted some tasters. But on the taste front, panelists mused over an "unidentifiable flavor" variously described as "slightly fishy, almost sour" and "aggressive," and remarked on an "aluminum-like" aftertaste.

5 ✶ **Lurisia Carbonated Spring Water** (*Italy*). "Too effervescent" for some, who found that it tasted "neutral, "neither good nor bad," and a "little salty." Lurisia's relatively high ranking reflects the positive views of two tasters, one of whom found it "perky"; the other liked the "slightly mineral" taste.

6 **Canada Dry Seltzer** (*U.S.A.*) "Looks like seltzer," noted one taster. "Bubbly to the point of being painful" and "biting," it hit some palates "like a ton of bricks." Opinion was divided on taste, which some liked because it was "fresh," "wonderfully clean and refreshing," but others found "too salty," with a "metallic taste and medicinal smell."

7 **Schweppes Club Soda** (*U.S.A.*) "Heavy effervescence" due to "too many big bubbles" put Schweppes midway in the rankings. Slightly salty, it was described as rather "blah," with "no character."

8 **Ty Nant Original Carbonated Natural Spring Water** (*Wales*). Opinion was divided about whether the "lowish level of effervescence" was a plus; "light" and "springy" to those who liked it, others attributed a "nondescript," "plain water" taste to "large, inactive bubbles." A "faint, citrus-like" taste was detected by one taster, who found it "pleasant." A readily detectable aftertaste, variously described as "tinny" and "seltzer-like," was perceived as a drawback. A "strong mineral flavor" was cited by two tasters, with one commenting that "the minerals were fighting each other."

9 **Artesia Sparkling Natural Artesian Water** (*Texas*). Panelists liked the "soft, soothing effervescence" from "nice, fine bubbles" that were "fuzzy on the tongue," but were less positive about the overall taste, summed up by one as a "nondescript, aggressive bicarbonate flavor." Several cited an unpleasant but indefinable aftertaste. Two found unexpected flavor present, which one identified as "a slight citrus taste" and another likened to "flavored water." One taster summarized: "Not tasteless but with a bit more carbonation than I like."

10 **Vintage Seltzer** (*Pennsylvania*). "Numbing," "strong, almost overwhelming" effervescence, combined with a pronounced "powerfully salty" or "sodium" taste with "metallic" overtones, caused tasters to reject this water on the basis that it was "rough" tasting.

11 **Crystal Geyser Sparkling Mineral Water** (*California*). In a tie with Poland Spring for second-least-appealing water, Crystal Geyser's "strong, heavy" effervescence was a drawback, though one taster who liked it called it "perky." Panelists seemed slightly baffled by an unpleasant, "unidentifiable flavor," pinpointed variously as "slightly sour" and "chlorinated," and the water was judged "too salty." A taster who liked the "clean, grassy" taste objected to a "soapy smell."

12 ✶ **Poland Spring Natural Spring Water** (*Maine*) "Painfully bub bly" effervescence, attributed to "too many bubbles" that made the water "biting on the tongue," was cited as a negative by all but one taster, who liked it. While some appreciated a "pleasant saltiness," others did not, finding it "seltzer-tasting." "Not very refreshing" was the general consensus.

13 **Henniez Sparkling Mineral Water** (*Switzerland*). Lowest-rated Henniez had "too many bubbles" for several panelists and was rejected as "tasteless" and "flat, very neutral in taste." Also on the negative side, one taster identified it as having a "sea-like" taste, another described it as "slightly musty." "Less salty than some of the others we've tasted," summed up one panelist, "but dries your mouth instead of quenching your thirst."

✶ Indicates that the water was tied with the water listed directly above.

MASTER CLASS

Roasted Salmon with Kasha and Leek Stuffing

Michael Roberts's boned and butterflied whole salmon makes a spectacular bed for either a kasha or rice stuffing.

Chef Michael Roberts knows that preparing fish for a large group can be overwhelming, but a boned whole salmon makes an elegant presentation that requires almost no last-minute cooking. Consider this your fish dish for a crowd.

Los Angeles chef and cookbook author Michael Roberts finds himself increasingly drawn to rustic French home cooking. In fact, having recently closed his groundbreaking West Hollywood restaurant, Trumps, Roberts is now spending several months in Paris researching a new cookbook. "I am talking with butchers, fishmongers, greengrocers, and average home cooks to understand what's going on night after night in Parisian kitchens," he says.

Roberts's whole, boned stuffed salmon, with its hearty kasha and leek stuffing and simple roasted vegetable garnish, takes its cue from traditional Gallic cuisines. Boning the fish is a bit complicated, but everything else is simple and straightforward.

Of course, the one essential element for success with this dish is an impeccably fresh fish. When buying whole salmon, look for bright red or pinkish gills; gray gills indicate a fish past its prime. The fish's eyes should be clear and ballooned, the skin slightly slimy and moist, and the flesh clean-smelling. Depending on the species and time of year, whole salmon range in size from 5 to 20 pounds. We used a 9-pound fish here. Note that specimens much larger than 10 pounds may be difficult to work with or to cook in home ovens.

Central to Roberts's recipe is his technique for removing the spine and rib bones (*see* illustrations, page 24). Two knifes, both with blades about six or seven inches long, are required for the job. Use a sliding motion with the flexible blade to separate the flesh from the bones. The stiff blade is best for piercing the skin and cutting with a sawing motion. Don't worry if you slash or mash some of the flesh. "Salmon is a very forgiving fish," says Roberts. "Accidental cuts will heal in the oven."

Once boned, the two sides rest next to each other and form a bed for any number of stuffings or sauces. In addition to kasha and leeks, Roberts offers an alternative stuffing with eggplant, summer squash, and rice. Either way, the whole salmon with a bed of stuffing cooks remarkably fast, in about 30 minutes.

This recipe itself may seem dauntingly long, but many parts can be prepared well in advance of serving. The stuffing may be refrigerated in a sealed container for one day. The salmon can be boned several hours in advance and refrigerated. The roasted and braised vegetables can be prepared early in the day and reheated at serving time. Likewise, the sauce (all except stirring in the butter) can be made ahead of time. In fact, the roasted salmon can be roasted ahead and served at room temperature (with warm sauce) if you like.

ROASTED SALMON WITH KASHA AND LEEK STUFFING
Serves 10–12

Kasha and Leek Stuffing
- 5 tablespoons olive oil or butter
- 2 medium leeks, white and light green parts sliced thin (about 3 cups), ½ cup dark green tops reserved for broth
- 1½ cups buckwheat groats (kasha)
- Salt and ground black pepper

Roasted Salmon
- 1 whole salmon (8 to 9 pounds), boned (*see* page 24), bones reserved for sauce
- 3 tablespoons butter, melted
- Salt and ground black pepper
- ¾ cup dry white wine
- Parsley sprigs for garnish

1. *For the stuffing,* heat oil in a large saucepan; add leeks and sauté, stirring occasionally, until softened, about 10 minutes. Stir in kasha and coat with oil. Add 3¾ cups water, pepper and salt to taste; simmer, covered, until kasha softens and puffs, about 10 minutes. Set aside.

2. *For the salmon,* heat oven to 350 degrees. Lay salmon in a large baking pan lined with a double thickness of foil. (A 17-by-11-inch jelly

PHOTOGRAPH BY GEOFFREY MONTAGU, STYLING BY NORMAN STEWART

Boning the Whole Salmon

1. Lay salmon on its side. Place one hand on top of the fish to steady it; hold the fish in a dishcloth to protect your hand. Pierce the skin at the back of the head with the inflexible knife. With tip of blade feel for the backbone and begin making a shallow incision just above the bone. Continue cutting, using a saw-like motion, so that a half-inch deep incision runs from just behind the head down past the top of the dorsal fin to the beginning of the tail.

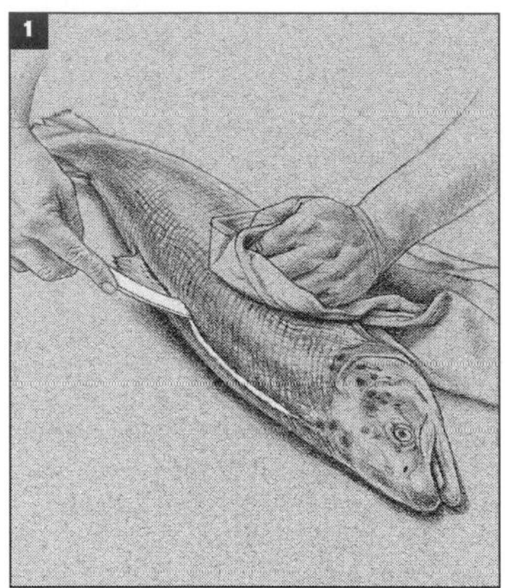

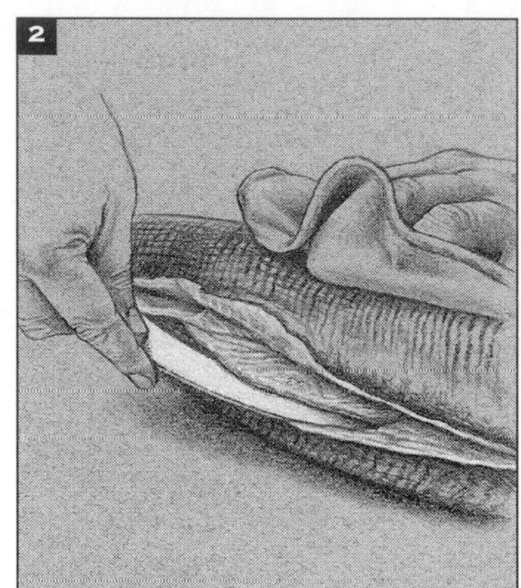

2. Place blade of flexible knife in the slit just behind the head. With blade parallel to work surface, press down and slowly slide knife along flesh to increase the depth of the slit. The blade will bend as the fish opens little by little. Once knife reaches the tail end of the slit, return blade to the top and repeat to widen the slit even further.

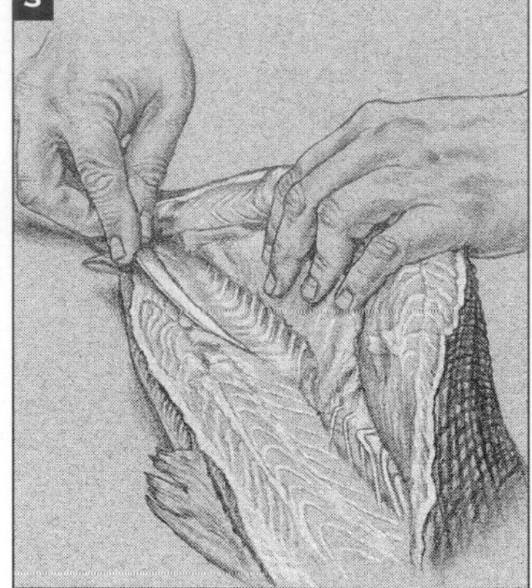

3. Lift top fillet to expose small rib bones that are attached to backbone. Glide knife along the top of the backbone to further separate the fillets.

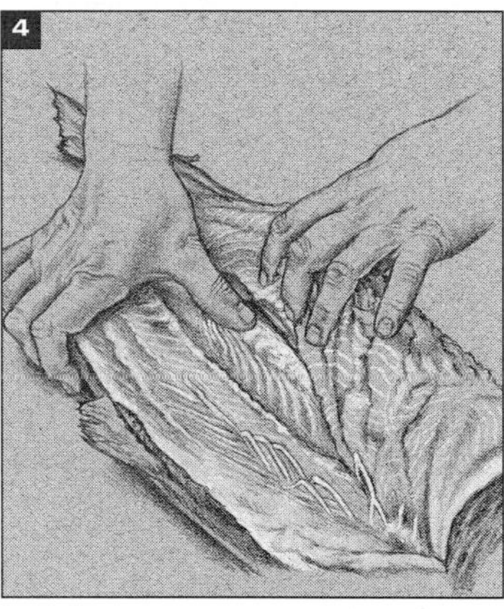

4. To accomplish the complete separation of the fillets, use fingers to press against bottom fillet and find the stomach slit made when the fish was eviscerated.

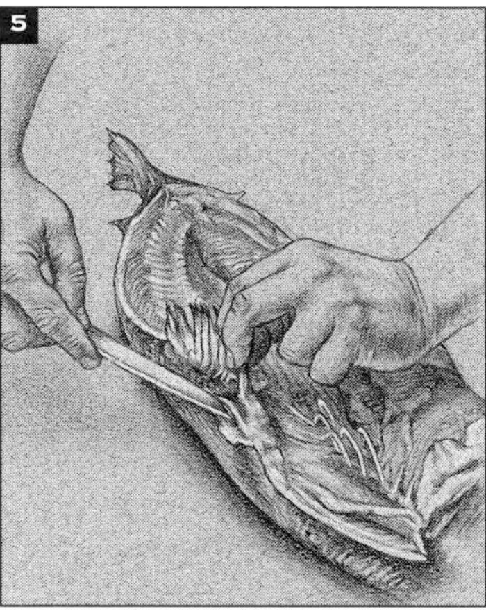

5. Use inflexible knife to cut around dorsal fin.

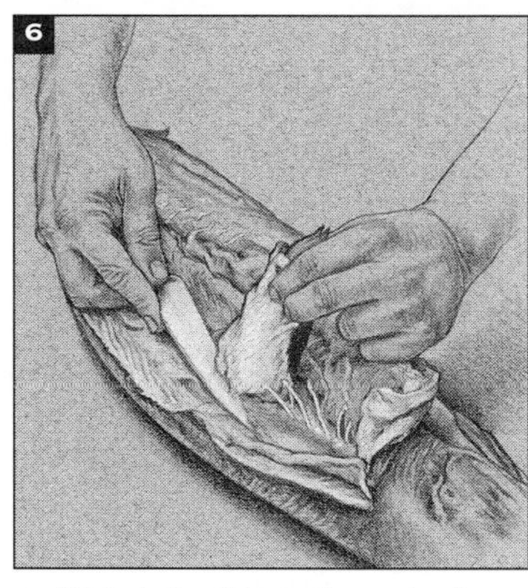

6. Slide inflexible knife under loosened dorsal fin to cut away the white flesh and root bones adjacent to the fin. Stop when you reach the pink meat. Discard dorsal fin and root bones.

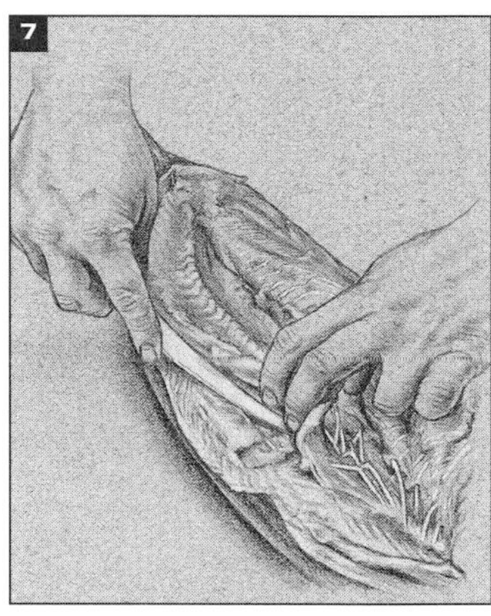

7. Once dorsal fin has been removed, insert the flexible knife into the natural separation that extends under the backbone.

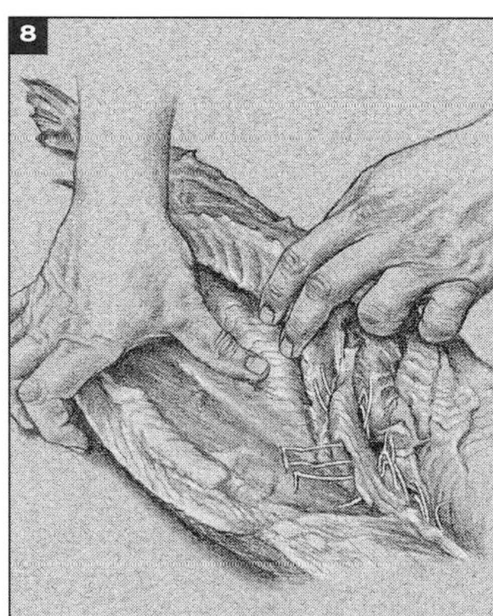

8. Use hands to lift backbone, ribs, and attached flesh away from the bottom fillet.

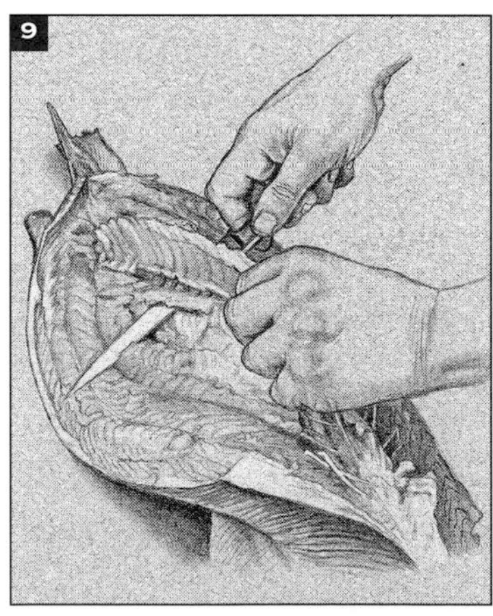

9. Holding backbone mass away from fillet use knife to free spine from the bottom fillet.

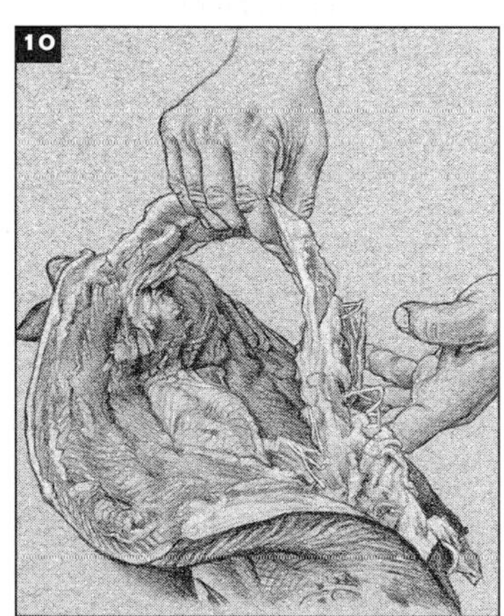

10. Backbone matter is now free from fish except at head and tail ends.

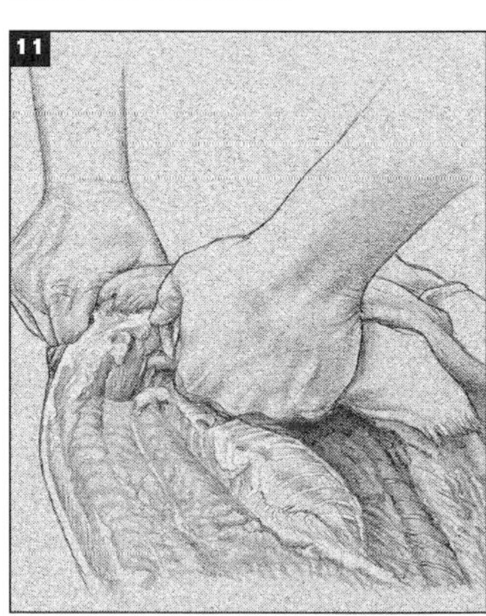

11. Wrap dishcloth around tail end of backbone and twist to pull out the spine. Repeat procedure at head end of fish.

ILLUSTRATIONS BY ALAN WITSCHONKE

roll pan works well.) Brush flesh with butter and sprinkle with salt and pepper.

3. Mound stuffing down the center of the salmon, where the two fillets meet. Pour wine onto foil to keep fish from sticking. Bake fish until a meat thermometer inserted into thickest point of fish registers 130 degrees, 25 to 30 minutes. Remove pan from oven and carefully transfer fish atop foil to a large platter. Gently slide and tear foil out from under fish and discard. Garnish with parsley sprigs and serve warm sauce passed separately.

ROASTED CARROTS AND PARSLEY ROOTS

Serves 12

If parsley roots cannot be found, other root vegetables, brussels sprouts, and/or cauliflower may be substituted. Roasting the vegetables concentrates their flavor and brings out their sweetness.

- 12 small carrots, peeled and all but 1 inch of green top removed (reserve ½ cup peel for broth)
- 12 small parsley roots, peeled and all but 1 inch of green tops removed
- 1 tablespoon butter
- Salt to taste

1. Heat oven to 375 degrees. Place carrots and parsley roots in a roasting pan along with butter and ½ cup water. Sprinkle with salt to taste. Roast vegetables until tender, about 20 minutes. (Can loosely cover and set aside at room temperature up to 6 hours.)

2. (Heat roasted vegetables in the oven or microwave.) Arrange atop fish and stuffing; serve.

BRAISED CELERY

Serves 12

When preparing the celery, make sure not to trim off the root end—you'll need it to hold the stalks together.

- 2 tablespoons butter
- 1 tablespoon olive oil
- 2 large heads celery, tough outer stalks removed; each head cut, lengthwise, into 6 pieces (reserve ½ cup leafy tops for sauce)
- ½ teaspoon salt

1. Heat oven to 375 degrees. Heat butter and oil in a large ovenproof skillet. Add celery pieces and sauté, turning once, until golden on both sides, about 10 minutes. Sprinkle celery with salt, add ½ cup water, and transfer skillet to oven.

2. Braise celery for 10 minutes, then turn. Continue braising celery until tender but not falling apart, another 10 or 15 minutes. Return skillet to stove; simmer celery over medium heat until any remaining liquid thickens to form a nice glaze. (Can loosely cover and set aside at room temperature up to 6 hours.)

3. (Heat braised celery in the oven or microwave.) Arrange atop fish and stuffing; serve.

WARM BALSAMIC VINEGAR SAUCE WITH BACON

Makes about 2 cups

This sauce may seem overpowering when tasted straight from the pan, but the lush, rich salmon tones down it acidic intensity. When straining the broth, don't press too hard on the solids; you'll release the oil from the fish bones which, in the end, overpowers the sauce.

Quick Salmon Broth

- 1 tablespoon butter
- Reserved salmon bones, broken into several pieces
- ½ cup reserved leek trimmings (dark green part), chopped
- ½ cup reserved carrot peelings
- ½ cup reserved leafy celery tops, chopped
- 1 cup dry white wine
- 2 bay leaves
- ½ teaspoon minced fresh thyme or 1/4 teaspoon dried
- 6 black peppercorns
- ½ pound bacon, diced
- 1 cup balsamic vinegar
- 3 tablespoons lemon juice
- 3 tablespoons butter

1. Heat butter in a 2-quart saucepan. Add fish bones and vegetable trimmings; sauté and stir until vegetables soften, about 5 minutes.

2. Add wine, 2 cups water, herbs, peppercorns, and bring to a boil; cover and simmer to blend flavors, about 10 minutes. Strain and discard solids; set broth aside.

3. Heat bacon in a 2-quart saucepan, stirring occasionally, until bacon starts to crisp, about 5 minutes. Add broth, vinegar, and lemon juice. Simmer over medium heat until liquid is reduced by half, 20 to 30 minutes. (Can be covered and refrigerated overnight; return sauce to a simmer.)

4. Remove sauce from heat; whisk in remaining 3 tablespoons butter. Serve warm sauce with fish.

SUMMER VEGETABLE AND RICE STUFFING

Serves 10–12

This stuffing relies on eggplant, summer squash, leeks, and cooked rice and makes an equally attractive summer partner with roasted salmon. When using this stuffing, Michael Roberts serves the salmon at room temperature with an herb mayonnaise instead of the warm balsamic vinegar sauce. There is also no need to prepare the roasted vegetable garnish.

- 1 large eggplant (about 1¼ pounds), peeled, and cut into small dice
- 3 medium carrots (about ⅓ pound), peeled, and cut into small dice
- 3 medium onions, peeled, and cut into small dice
- 2 medium leeks (about 1½ pounds), white part only, cut into small dice
- 2 small yellow squash, cut into small dice
- 2 small zucchini squash, cut into small dice
- 1 large green cabbage, shredded fine
- 1½ tablespoons minced garlic
- ¾ cup cooked rice
- 3 tablespoons rice or malt vinegar
- ¼ cup soy sauce
- 1½ teaspoons tomato paste
- ¾ teaspoon thyme
- 1½ teaspoons sage
- 1½ cups fresh or canned chicken broth
- Salt and ground white pepper to taste
- 1¼ cups sour cream

Place all ingredients except sour cream in a large soup kettle. Cover and cook over medium heat for 10 minutes. Remove cover and cook, stirring occasionally, until liquid almost evaporates, 20 to 30 minutes longer. Transfer stuffing to a bowl and stir in sour cream. Cool stuffing slightly, then proceed with step 3 of Roasted Salmon with Kasha and Leek Stuffing. ■

THE FINAL STEPS

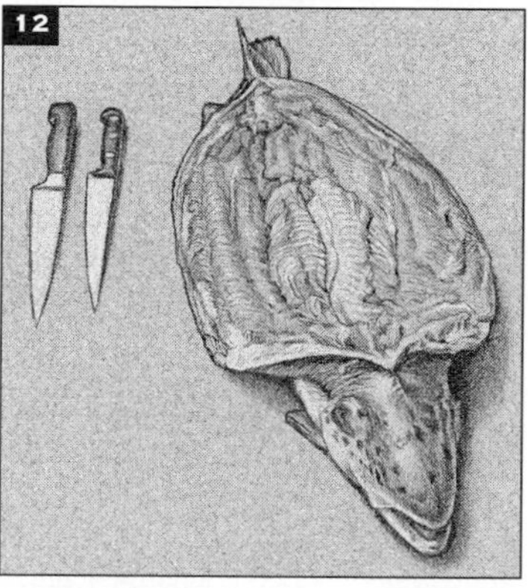

12. Two sides of fish now lay flat on the work surface. Also pictured are the two knives used in the process: The thinner blade (on the right) is the flexible knife that does most of the boning. The thicker blade (which is inflexible) is best for piercing the skin and cutting away the dorsal fin.

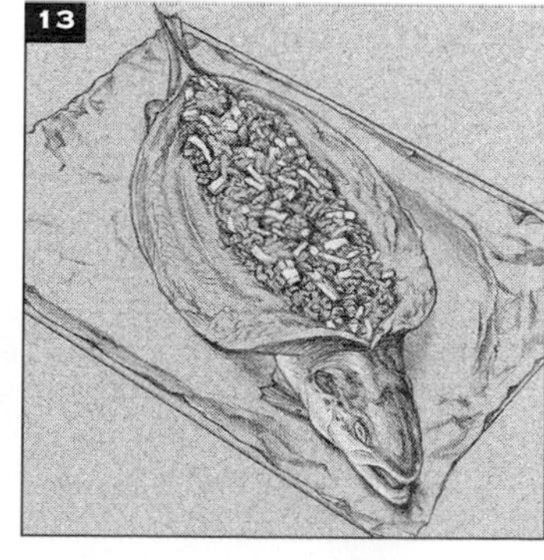

13. Transfer boned fish to foil-lined baking tray and cover belly cavity with stuffing.

The Best Homemade Vanilla Ice Cream

The very best ice cream is made with egg yolks but, for optimum flavor, cut back on the cream and sugar.

BY JACK BISHOP

Making ice cream used to involve lengthy hand cranking, with rock salt and ice acting as the freezing agent. Today the cream-egg-sugar mixture is still much the same, but supercoolants and electric motors have replaced the old hand crank.

The ingredients for making vanilla ice cream could not be simpler — cream, milk, sugar, vanilla, and sometimes eggs. The results, however, vary greatly, depending on the quantities of each ingredient and the techniques used. To find out how to make the very best vanilla ice cream at home, I made dozens of batches, varying each individual ingredient.

Egg Yolks Give Essential Richness

Early in the testing process it became apparent that "French vanilla," made with a custard base relying on egg yolks, far surpasses "Philadelphia-style" vanilla, made without eggs. In texture as well as flavor, the French version simply had far more of the richness and creaminess that we look for in ice cream.

Why is ice cream made with egg yolks richer and creamier than ice cream without eggs? Partially because yolks are about 10 percent lecithin, an emulsifier which helps maintain the even dispersal of fat droplets throughout the mixture and keeps ice crystals small, which helps trap air in the mixture. The overall effect is one of smoothness and richness.

My Master Recipe calls for six yolks, which at first glance may seem like a lot. Commercial ice creams (even premium brands) are much paler, and presumably use fewer yolks than my recipe. However, more yolks guarantees better texture. As few as three yolks makes an excellent ice cream, but with three more the texture is considerably silkier. I tried eight yolks, but found that at that level, an eggy taste dominated the ice cream, so six yolks seems to be the optimum number.

Yolks need to be beaten very well with some of the sugar before being combined with the other ingredients. If the yolks are only lightly beaten, the color of the finished ice cream is shockingly yellow. Prolonged beating — two minutes with an electric mixer or four minutes with a wire whisk, at which point the mixture will fall in ribbons — insures a lighter color, helps dissolve the sugar, and, perhaps most importantly, evenly disperses the emulsifying agent in the yolks. This maximizes the emulsifying power of the eggs once they are added to the custard.

Cream and Sugar: More Is Not Necessarily Better

Ice cream buffs may wonder why my "decadent" Master Recipe has only one part cream to two parts milk. I tried a number of different combinations — everything from two parts cream and one part half and half, all the way down to all milk — and found that more cream is not necessarily better. In fact, with high quantities of fat, the ice cream takes on an undesirable "buttery" quality. From a scientific point of view, this results from the fact there is so much fat that the globules stick together and are more noticeable on the tongue. The trick to perfect ice cream is in balancing ingredients, not in excess.

Sugar plays a dual role in ice cream. Besides adding sweetness, it gives a smoother, softer, more "scoopable" end product. This is because sugar both reduces the number and size of ice crystals and lowers the freezing temperature of the mixture. The latter allows you to beat the mixture longer before it freezes, incorporating more air into the ice cream.

The texture of a quart of ice cream made with

PHOTOGRAPH FROM CULVER PICTURES

one cup sugar is wonderful, but the sweetness, at least to my taste, overpowered the vanilla. Three-quarters cup is enough sugar to make the ice cream soft without killing the other flavors. In fact, as little as one-half cup can be used, but ice cream made with so little sugar will freeze much harder and be more difficult to scoop straight from the freezer.

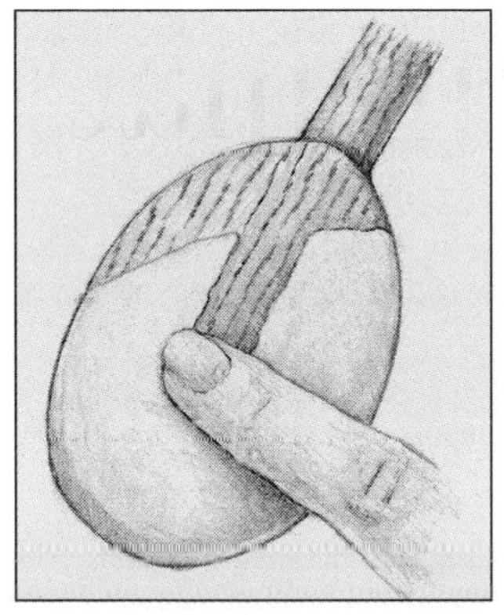

Custard is thick enough when a line drawn through it on the back of a spoon holds for several seconds.

In Search of "Diet" Ice Cream

My original goal in testing recipes was to also offer a master recipe for lower-fat ice cream akin to regular commercial products. The mechanics of making ice cream at home, however, made this challenge impossible.

I wanted to emulate the snowy-white Philadelphia-style ice creams that do not contain eggs. The problem was that without eggs I needed an emulsifier to improve the texture. At first I resisted, but eventually I gave in and tried making ice cream with gelatin, which seemed to me the best home substitute for the gums and starches used to provide texture to cheap commercial ice creams. Although gelatin gave the ice cream a slightly gummy texture, it was an improvement over eggless ice cream made with just dairy and sugar.

My real problem, however, came with the dairy ingredients. My Master Recipe for Vanilla Ice Cream is already fairly lean (about 15 percent milkfat), with two parts milk to one part cream. Cutting back on the cream made the eggless ice cream extremely icy. After ten tries it became apparent that I needed something all around me but unusable — air.

Commercial ice cream may contain as much as 50 percent air, which keeps ice crystals apart and gives a lower-fat product a better mouthfeel. The industry terms this process "overrun," and it partially explains why some ice cream appears to be so cheap. Ice cream in gallon containers often has 100 percent overrun (the volume doubled during churning) while premium brands (usually in small pint containers) have only 20 or 30 percent overrun. When there is more air, you pay less.

While some home ice cream makers add more air than others, none come close to doubling the volume of the ice cream during churning. Without an industrial pump that can shoot air into ice cream in seconds, I was unable to make an acceptable ice cream with appreciably fewer calories or fat than in my custard-based recipe.

Keeping Ice Cream

Ice cream made in any of the machines I tested was excellent after three days in the freezer. In fact, with all the machines except for the Simac, the ice cream is very soft after churning and should be frozen for several hours before serving. Leftover ice cream can be stored in plastic containers with very tight lids. Manufacturers claim that ice cream can be stored in the freezing vessels, and all suggest covering with plastic wrap rather than aluminum foil. However you store your ice cream, be sure it is tightly sealed; the flavor and texture of ice cream is so delicate that any contact with air causes quick deterioration.

Finally, a note about freezers. If your freezer is above zero degrees, you may have problems with ice cream machines that use coolant, since the coolant will not get cold enough. My freezer fluctuates between -4 and 2 degrees, depending on how many times I have opened the freezer door. At these temperatures, ice cream emerges from the freezer at around 7 degrees. Since the ideal temperature for eating ice cream is 10 degrees, I let it soften for several minutes before serving. Note that most ice cream makers only bring the temperature down to 25 degrees, which is slightly warmer than commercially available soft ice creams.

MASTER RECIPE FOR VANILLA ICE CREAM

Makes 1 quart

If necessary, two teaspoons of vanilla extract may be substituted for the vanilla bean. To maximize the extract's potency, stir it into the chilled custard just before churning.

2 cups whole milk

For Vanilla, You Can't Beat Beans

When it comes to ice cream, vanilla is America's flavor of choice, outselling its nearest competitor (chocolate) three to one. But, sadly, most of the vanilla ice cream sold in supermarkets is made with artificial vanillin. Even a premium brand such as Haagen-Dazs (which is made with real extract) paled when tested against the real vanilla flavor of homemade ice cream. The tiny, unctuous seeds release a powerful flavor that simply is not available in store brands.

When shopping for vanilla, look for glossy, black beans; dull, brownish pods have less flavor. A whole vanilla bean (which usually measures about 8 to 10 inches long) is too strong for one quart of ice cream. A 4-inch piece delivers the right flavor.

Cut beans in half lengthwise with a small, sharp knife. Place the side of a knife at one end and press down to flatten the bean as you move the knife away from you (*see* illustration below). The seeds should accumulate on the edge of the knife. Drop seeds into a saucepan and repeat with the other half of the bean. The pods have plenty of flavor (and may contain some seeds) so add them to the ice cream base during cooking. Remove pods just before the custard is frozen.

Vanilla extract, which is made by macerating the pods in alcohol and then combining the infusion with sugar syrup, may be used in a pinch. However, don't add liquid vanilla to hot custard, since much of the aroma will dissipate in the steam. Instead, add extract just as the base is going into the ice cream machine.

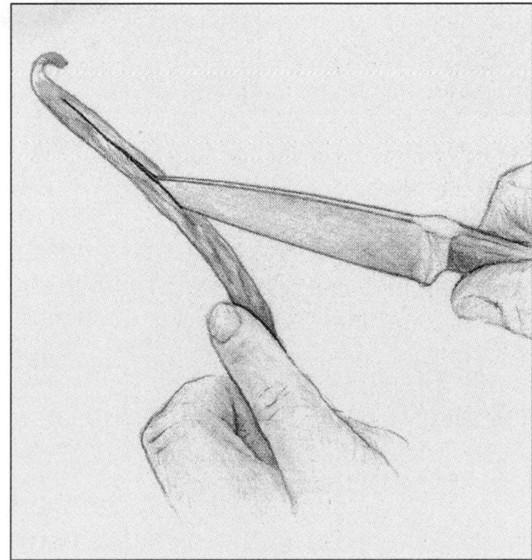

Cut beans in half lengthwise with a small, sharp knife.

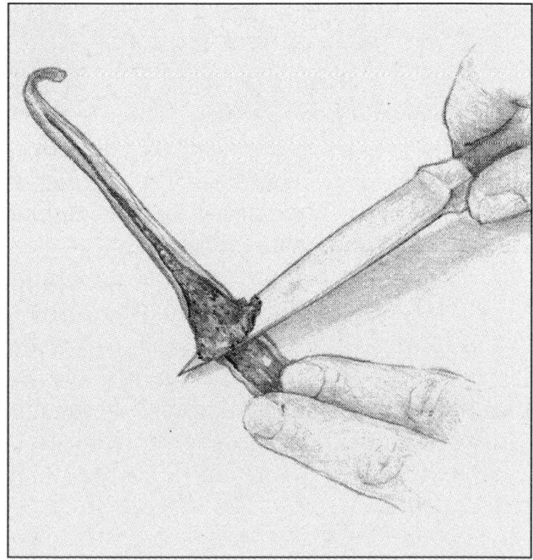

Place the side of a knife at one end and press down to flatten the bean as you move the knife away from you.

ILLUSTRATIONS BY KATHY BRAY

¾ cup sugar
4-inch piece of vanilla bean, slit lengthwise and seeds removed (*see* illustration), pod reserved
6 large egg yolks
1 cup heavy cream

1. Bring milk, ¼ cup sugar, and vanilla seeds and pod to 175 degrees in a heavy saucepan over medium heat, stirring occasionally to dissolve sugar and break up vanilla seeds.

2. Meanwhile, beat remaining sugar with yolks until mixture turns pale yellow and thickens so that it falls in ribbons, about 2 minutes with an electric mixer or 4 minutes with a whisk.

3. Remove ½ cup hot milk from pan and slowly whisk it into beaten yolks. Then gradually whisk yolk mixture into saucepan and, stirring constantly, heat this mixture over medium-low heat to 180 degrees, 8 to 10 minutes. Remove saucepan from heat; strain custard into a plastic or nonreactive metal bowl and stir in cream. Retrieve vanilla pods from strainer and add them to the mixture. Place bowl in a larger bowl of ice water to bring custard to room temperature.

4. Seal container and refrigerate until custard is no more than 40 degrees, 4 to 8 hours. (This is unnecessary with self-contained electric model). Remove vanilla pods (or add extract) and pour custard into an ice cream machine. Churn until frozen.

COFFEE ICE CREAM

Makes 1 quart

Instant espresso powder adds a strong jolt of coffee flavor without adding liquid, which would cause iciness.

Follow the Master Recipe, adding 3 tablespoons instant espresso powder (in place of vanilla bean) to hot milk mixture in step 1; stir until dissolved. Add 1 teaspoon vanilla extract as directed in step 4.

CHOCOLATE ICE CREAM

Makes 1 quart

Cocoa adds a rich flavor without too much fat. For a truffle-like ice cream, add two ounces of chopped bittersweet or semisweet chocolate to the finished, but still hot, cocoa custard and stir constantly until chocolate melts.

Follow the Master Recipe, omitting vanilla bean and adding 2 tablespoons sugar to the original ¼ cup in step 1. When the egg mixture has reached the ribbon stage in step 2, beat in ⅓ cup unsweetened cocoa powder until mixture is smooth. Add 1 teaspoon vanilla extract as directed in step 4.

STRAWBERRY ICE CREAM

Makes 1 quart

Other soft fruits can also be turned into ice cream using this technique. Good candidates include peaches, nectarines, and plums (all peeled and sliced), and raspberries and blackberries (seeds may be strained from both after the fruit has macerated).

Follow the Master Recipe omitting vanilla bean in step 1. While custard is chilling, sprinkle 1 pint stemmed and halved strawberries with 2 tablespoons sugar and 1 teaspoon vanilla extract; crush lightly with a potato masher and let macerate for 1 hour. Stir berries into cold custard and refrigerate mixture again (if necessary) until temperature falls to 40 degrees. ■

CHOOSING AN ICE CREAM MAKER

There are three basic types of ice cream makers now on the market. Traditional models (many in wooden buckets) require rock salt and ice and often are quite messy to use. These old-fashioned makers are also less reliable, and therefore are not considered here.

Of the remaining two types, the frozen-canister technology used by the popular Donvier has spawned several imitators. The idea behind this clever gadget is simple. An aluminum canister filled with a patented super-coolant is placed in the freezer overnight; a chilled custard is then poured into the very cold canister, and a hand crank is attached for churning. In about 25 minutes, the ice cream is ready.

Its French-sounding pedigree notwithstanding, the name Donvier actually comes from the Japanese for "very cold." This ingenious invention was created by accident about ten years ago. Apparently a Japanese engineer thought of the idea after one of his children spilled milk on an aluminum cooling tray for sushi. He redesigned the tray, which used the same powerful coolant, into a canister shape more appropriate for ice cream making.

An alternative to this relatively inexpensive technology are the self-contained electric freezers, from Italy, that are based on commercial models. These units are twice the size of a large food processor and weigh at least 30 pounds. The Simac is currently the only brand sold in this country.

Without a doubt, this Rolls Royce of ice cream makers produces the best frozen desserts I have ever tasted. The texture is silky and smooth, without a hint of ice or graininess. There is no downtime between batches (in Donvier-type machines, the canister must be refrozen overnight before making a second batch). The only drawback is cost. Although $500 may seem steep, the passionate (and frequent) ice cream maker will find this advanced technology worth every penny.

There are cheaper models of self-contained electric freezers, all under $100; the main difference is found in the churning mechanisms. Either an electric motor or hand crank drives a plastic paddle. Machines with an electric motor beat much more air into the ice cream and produce a fluffier texture.

Machines with hand cranks yield denser frozen desserts, resembling Italian gelati. The Waring provides the option of using either a crank or motor and can produce dense or fluffy ice cream; I have ranked it first among the cheaper machines and second overall.

I much prefer denser ice creams and I have ranked the Donvier third, just ahead of the smaller Simac with the attachable motor. The Salton (with hand crank) is less powerful than either, and yielded grainy ice cream. It is the only machine I do not recommend.

THE WINNERS

1. Simac II Gelataio Magnum $499.00. This expensive, self-contained electric model made the smoothest ice cream.

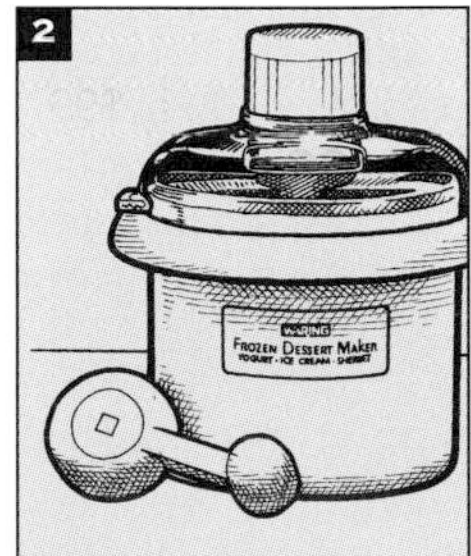

2. Waring Frozen Dessert Maker FDM-810: $68.00. With both hand and electric cranks, the Waring makes either dense or fluffy ice cream.

3. Donvier Premier: $60.00. The original frozen-canister model is still good enough for the top tier.

ILLUSTRATIONS BY DAN KROVATIN

Rating Ice Cream Makers

Models are listed in order of preference. Performance was based on making the Master Recipe for Vanilla Ice cream (page 27), with the following assumptions: the smoother and creamier the texture of the finished product, the better; the colder the ice cream when churning is complete, the better; the higher the yield from the same amount of custard, the better.

Name	Cost	Design and Use	Texture	Freezing Time	Temperature	Yield	General Comments
Simac II Gelataio Magnum	$499	Self-contained electric freezing unit that weighs 33 pounds. Must be kept upright to function properly. This mini-freezer is a bit bulky, but easy to use.	Dense, creamy, and silky smooth; best ice cream you'll ever taste.	40 minutes	18 degrees	4 cups	Unlike other machines, this one can be used to make several batches every day. Also, ice cream is cold enough to eat right from machine. Note cost, however.
Waring Frozen Dessert Maker FDM-810	$68	Canister design that comes with both an electric motor attachment and hand crank. Very easy to assemble and operate. Hole in lid allows air to be beaten into ice cream as it churns.	Creamy, airy, and smooth; no trace of ice.	24 minutes	24 degrees	5 cups with motor; 4¼ cups with hand crank	Flexibility, low cost, and simple design make this machine a winner.
Donvier Premier	$60	Canister design with hand crank. Solid paddle causes ice cream to build up on one side of canister during churning. Must remove lid and redistribute contents at least once during freezing. Otherwise, very easy to use.	Creamy and dense; excellent.	24 minutes	24 degrees	3¾ cups	Superb gelato-style ice cream.
Simac II Gelataio SC	$99	Canister design with electric motor attachment that can be a bit tricky to assemble.	Very light and fluffy; almost marsh-mallow-like.	50 minutes	27 degrees	5¼ cups	Slower and not as "cold" as other machines. Also, by the time the machine is assembled the mixture can freeze the blade in place.
Salton Big Chill ICM-1	$40	Canister design with hand crank. Very easy to assemble and use.	Too dense and a bit grainy.	40 minutes	26 degrees	3½ cups	Machine gives low yield and does not beat in enough air; not recommended.

For information about locating individual ice cream makers, see Sources and Resources, page 32.

Non-Chablis Wines Dominate "Chablis" Tasting

BEST WINE

A $40 Chablis won our tasting, but an $11 Connecticut wine placed second.

BY MARK BITTMAN

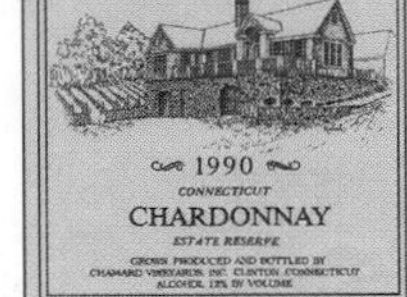

The classic wine to drink with raw oysters, Chablis is the driest and most subtle of the white Burgundies, known for its "flinty" flavor, which is attributed to the soil of Northern Burgundy and to the fact that the wines are not fermented in wood.

Most wine drinkers admire Chablis, but do not consider it to be in the same class as some other great wines made from the Chardonnay grape, especially its heavily oaked cousins such as Montrachet. The Californian growers, who clearly prefer the flavors wood lends to wine, mimic these, but not always successfully; if there has been a consistent criticism of the best California Chardonnays, it is that they emphasize wood over grape. (As one French winemaker said to me recently, "They sometimes forget that wood is like garlic; it must be used judiciously.")

Consequently, when it came to finding wines to compete with true Chablis in our blind tasting of Chablis-style whites, we found few entrants from California. In fact, we wound up with just three: an inexpensive wine from the producer Callaway (their other wines are wood-aged); a reasonably well-established wine from Napa's Mt. Veeder; and an unheard of $6 entry from Nominée, in Paso Robles. These were among the least expensive wines at the tasting, but none did especially well, although the Nominée might be considered the second most surprising wine at the tasting.

Tops in the "surprise" category, though, was the 1990 Chamard Estate Reserve Chardonnay, a Connecticut wine that is considered to be the best made in that state (which, until now, was not saying much). At $11, this most resembled the top-ranked Grand Cru.

Otherwise, it might be said that the French swept the tasting — but, unexpectedly, the wines from Chablis did not. The third-place wine was a Pinot Blanc from Alsace, made from a grape related to Chardonnay. Its combination of spicy crispness and flowery fruit appealed to the tasters, none of whom were overly impressed by any of the wines except for the first-place finisher. And an inexpensive wine from Macon — Southern Burgundy — finished fourth.

As in the previous *Cook's Illustrated* wine tastings, the panel was made up of professionals and amateurs — in this case, five wine professionals (two wholesalers, a retailer, an importer, and a winemaker), and five nonprofessionals who routinely enjoy wine with meals. The wines were tasted blind; their identities were revealed only after the poll of preferences was made.

When it came to judging the wines, opinions varied widely. The top wine garnered only two first-place votes, although seven of the tasters placed it in their top seven. What the top two wines had in common — and they finished well ahead of the pack — was a concentration of fruitiness balanced by high levels of acid. The question is, Why did other wines from Chablis not do better? It may be that even the French are not making Chablis as well as they once did. ■

BLIND TASTING RESULTS

Wines are listed in order of preference. Seven points were awarded for each first-place vote; six for second; five for third; four for fourth; three for fifth; two for sixth; one for seventh. Prices are average retail in the Northeast.

1. 1990 Fevre Grand Cru "Les Clos" (Chablis, 38 points), $40. Not exactly a dark horse; there are only seven Grand Cru vineyards in Chablis, and Fevre is a fine producer. Those who liked it, loved it ("rich with good concentration and depth"); those who didn't found it "out of balance" and "a little punky."
2. 1990 Chamard Estate Reserve Chardonnay (Connecticut, 36 points), $11. From a fledgling vineyard by the Long Island Sound, this wine demonstrates that the East Coast holds great promise for the future of Chardonnay in the United States. Most tasters found it a bit austere but extremely well made.
3. 1991 Leon Beyer Pinot Blanc (Alsace, 28 points), $8. Spicy, crisp, and rich; two tasters pegged it as a non-Chardonnay, but one called it "the second-best Chablis of the tasting."
4. 1990 Domaine des Vielles Pierres (Macon Vergisson, 26 points), $11. From the southernmost region of Burgundy, this wine was rated first by one of the professionals. Round, ripe fruit, with no wood.
5. 1992 Nominée Paso Robles Chardonnay (Central Coast, 25 points), $6. A good example of what can be done by taking decent grapes and treating them simply. "Good, rich fruit, if a bit disjointed." Note price.
6. 1990 Callaway Calla-Lees Chardonnay (California, 23 points), $9. Probably the most controversial wine of the tasting. Some found it "delicate, flowery, and crisp"; others thought it smelled and tasted like chemicals.
7. 1988 Montée de Tonerre Premier Cru (Chablis, 23 points), $50. Even the professionals found little right with this prestigious wine, which they described as "vinegary" and "lacking in fruit."
8. 1990 Mt. Veeder Chardonnay (Napa, 22 points), $12. The taster who ranked this first found it "rich and remarkably complex," but the majority detected a variety of off-flavors and aromas.
9. 1988 Jeanne Paule Filippi (Chablis, 17 points), $12. An inexpensive, inoffensive Chablis that excited no one and struck at least two tasters as "boring."
10. 1990 Alain Corcia Premier Cru Montman (Chablis, 15 points), $15. Those who liked this wine said it "typified inexpensive Chablis" and was the "perfect seafood wine," but still ranked it fourth or fifth. Others found it "harsh" and even "bad."
11. 1991 Jermann Chardonnay del Friuli (Italy, 12 points), $22. Generally considered one of the best Chardonnays from Italy, this weak wine was outclassed by the others tested.

Great Good Food
Julee Rosso
Crown, $19.00 paper

The race is on — and it has been for some time — to be the first cookbook author to appeal to the tens of millions of Americans who presumably want to lower their fat intake but just can't figure out how to do it. The odds-on favorite, at press time, is Julee Rosso, co-author of the two *Silver Palate* books and *The New Basics,* and author of *Great Good Food* — not so much because we like the book, but because of the prodigious marketing effort behind it (more than 300,000 copies came rolling off the presses during the first printing), combined with Rosso's deserved reputation as a roper of current trends.

We believe that her lasso has missed its mark this time around. No one knows for certain, of course, but it's our guess that people who actually *cook* at home (as distinguished from those who reheat at home) are not really searching for low-fat substitutes for cream or for hollandaise with reduced calories (both of which you can find here), but for easy-to-cook, highly flavorful dishes that are not super-high in fat. Rosso goes through convolutions to meet the latter qualification, but seems to have overshot the goal that has made Mediterranean food in general, and that of Tuscany in particular, the biggest thing to hit home kitchens since *Mastering the Art of French Cooking.*

If you look at Martha Rose Schulman's classic, *Mediterranean Light,* you find a collection of basic recipes that have been modified, with a nod to available ingredients and current fashion, in order to make them more accessible as well as more acceptable to the hordes of home-cooking, health-conscious Americans. If you look at *Great Good Food,* you find a hodgepodge of somewhat contrived recipes arranged seasonally in a cookbook so overdesigned that even if it were the second coming of James Beard's *Delights and Prejudices* you wouldn't know it.

You might argue that none of this would matter if Rosso's new recipes struck our collective nerve — or palate — as did those of Rosso and former partner Sheila Lukins when they ushered in the 1980s with their high-impact, high-flavor first book. And we agree — contrived or not, if Rosso gave us flavorful, low-fat recipes of a new order, we'd be impressed. In fact, we'd be overwhelmed.

Unfortunately, that didn't happen. On the contrary, *none* of the recipes we tested did much to alter our initial impression of this book as one we could easily live without. Nonnie's Cinnamon Rolls were dry and hard, and what they needed was obvious — more fat. Similarly, creme brulée made with skim milk, 4 egg yolks, 12 egg whites, and potato starch provides a sugar fix and little else. It's not as if we make a staple of creme brulée; when we do eat it, it might as well bring tears of joy to our eyes (as does Joel Robuchon's version, to which Rosso alludes).

Big Beef Burgers — a mixture of ground sirloin, ground turkey, and nonfat yogurt — are undoubtedly a nutritional improvement on the real thing. But they still derive 38 percent of their calories from fat, a full 8 percent more than the most liberal health-conscious dietary guidelines recommend. And, as you would expect, the taste and texture were far from that of a good homemade burger. Vegetable Lasagna with Wild Mushroom Sauce took two hours to make (not the half hour that Rosso allows) and, although it was reasonably flavorful, it was Spartan in character.

Of the *Great Good Food* recipes we tested, our favorite was guacamole. But it doesn't stray far from the standard, although it is made with extra tomato and Rosso's "Low-Fat Blend" (a mixture of cottage cheese and yogurt). The result, though high in fat (as anything containing avocado must be), contains a mere 14 calories per serving, so you don't feel guilty when you tear open that bag of chips. That is, until you realize that a serving is a teaspoon. No fair.

A Book of Feasts
Kay Goldstein and Liza Nelson
Photography by Al Clayton
Longstreet Press, $29.95

This is a quintessential American book, 10 short stories about different families and groups celebrating their holidays. The writing, though a tad sentimental, is far from sloppy, and the book is filled with color photographs — warm, candid, loving ones of people, and minimally propped, appetizing ones of food. It's a book that welcomes you, at least initially.

As for the recipes, although they don't go very far, most of them are simple and appealing, the kind found in the spiral-bound community cookbooks that sometimes contain undiscovered gems. The problem is that they're not nearly as varied as they could be; too many are for standard American holiday fare, such as Roast Turkey with Giblet Gravy, Bourbon-Glazed Baked Ham, Cheese Straws, and Fried Chicken. You wouldn't have to look far to find these elsewhere.

Thankfully, others are much funkier, comforting and familiar if your grandmother made them, exotic and even exciting if she didn't. Macaroni with Milanese Gravy, for example — an Italian-American name for a pasta dish if ever there was one — contains a tomato sauce made chunky with celery, peppers, onions, fennel, artichokes, olives, pine nuts, and raisins. After this "gravy" is tossed over pasta, it's topped with browned bread crumbs.

A Book of Feasts makes no claims to be comprehensive, so it can't be downgraded for its lack of range; no attempt has been made to be all-inclusive, and this is not "American Immigrant Cooking." Nor can it be faulted for its failure to add much to the lexicon of American dishes; we've seen almost all of these before, and while the selection is limited it is, at least, tasteful.

But the authors and editors can be taken to task for providing recipes that lack detail. Potatoes and Goat Cheese in Pastry, for example, a smart-looking free-form potato pie, would not have been so dry had not much of the cream leaked from the pastry during baking — a mishap that could have been avoided with some dough-handling tips.

We also object to the authors' consistently heavy editing of recipes. We're told about Anne Madorsky's carrot *tsimmes,* which includes sweet potatoes, beef bones, orange marmalade, and apricots, and which is given "long baking in her oven — a very traditional approach." Yet the recipe we're offered is for an almost meager dish of carrots, orange juice, prunes, stock, honey, and spices, cooked on top of the stove. No Jewish grandmother would call this *tsimmes.*

Thanks to the authors' obvious love of food and their respect for people, and to Al Clayton's talent with the camera, *A Book of Feasts* is lovely and . . . well . . . pleasant. But we still wish that Goldstein and Nelson had taken their subject a little more seriously, and given us a little more to enjoy. ■

SOURCES
AND RESOURCES

CHERRY PITTER Removing pits from cherries for pies or quick preserves and jams can be an annoying chore without a cherry pitter. Once common in American kitchens, this little item has become something of a rarity. Well-stocked kitchen stores should carry a cherry pitter, but not all do. If you cannot find one in your local store, contact Williams-Sonoma; their catalog offers a sturdy aluminum pitter ($8 plus shipping) that punches out stones from cherries as well as olives. For more information on this model, call 800-541-2233.

ICE CREAM MAKERS If you are having trouble finding a particular brand that we tested this month, call the following for help in locating a source in your area: For either Simac machines, contact the U.S. distributor, Lello Appliances (355 Murray Hill Parkway, East Rutherford, NJ 07073; telephone 201-939-2555); they suggest looking for the top-rated Simac Magnum at Williams-Sonoma stores nationwide. The North American distributor for Donvier is Browne & Co. (100 Esna Park, Markham, Ontario, Canada L3R 1E3; telephone 416-475-6104). For Waring and Salton machines, contact the manufacturer directly for details on availability. Waring can be reached at 203-379-0731, and Salton at 800-233-9054.

UNIQUE SAUSAGES Sausage connoisseurs looking for something more adventurous than breakfast patties should link up with Jody Maroni's Sausage Kingdom in Los Angeles. His Yucatan chicken and duck sausages with cilantro and beer, or Moroccan lamb and pork links flavored with tangerines, wine, and currants can spice up any summer barbecue. Other delicious varieties — all made without nitrates or preservatives — include pork sausages with sun-dried tomatoes, prosciutto, and pine nuts; Bombay lamb and pork links with curry and raisins; and Chinese chicken and duck "haute dogs" with cashews, oranges, scallions, and sesame seeds. A five-pound sampler (with up to five different varieties) costs $65, including overnight shipping. For more information, contact Jody Maroni's Sausage Kingdom (2011 Ocean Front Walk, Venice, CA 90291; telephone 310-390-9252).

CORN POSTER Ten Speed Press has issued another in its series of acclaimed food posters. "Indian Corn of the Americas" is the brainchild of chef and cookbook author Mark Miller. Heirloom varieties like red stardust (grown by the Hopi and Zuni tribes in Arizona) are featured side-by-side with modern strains like extra-sweet silver queen. The 24-by-36-inch poster comes with two backgrounds (one black, the other sand-colored) and retails for $15; $25 for both. Look for the posters in bookstores or order directly from Ten Speed by calling 800-841-2665. While you're at it, you might want to ask them about Miller's chile posters, as well as Alice Waters' tomato poster.

SPICY FOODS CATALOG If you are addicted to spicy foods, then you need to know about Mo Hotta-Mo Betta, a catalog devoted to foods that will clear your sinuses and make your eyes water. Tim and Wendy Eidson have searched the globe from Southeast Asia to South America looking for salsas, hot sauces, spicy oils and vinegars, potent pickles, barbecue sauces, curries, chutneys, spice rubs, chili mixes, jerk sauces, and spicy snack foods. Ask about the Six-Pack from Hell with sauces like Jamaica Hellfire, Hellfire and Damnation, and Satan's Revenge. It costs $41, plus $4 if you want it gift-wrapped. To receive a catalog call 800-462-3220.

CORN-KERNEL CUTTER An ingenious device from Williams-Sonoma strips whole kernels of corn from the cob in just one stroke. Simply place the circular cutting blade over one end of a husked ear, then squeeze the flexible plastic handles as you push the blade down the length of the corn. There is no better way to remove kernels for chowders, breads, salsas, or salads. The kernel cutter costs $7.50 plus shipping and can be ordered by calling Williams-Sonoma at 800-541-2233.

CHIMNEY STARTER This no-fuss device starts a fire without lighter fluid and is completely portable. The best models have an aluminum or steel cylinder (it looks like an extra-large coffee can) and a heat-resistant wooden handle. Also look for a separate chamber on the bottom in which to place pieces of crumpled newspaper. Most hardware stores carry some sort of chimney. We are particularly impressed with the Fire Cone Charcoal Starter made by Williams-Sonoma, which costs just $16 plus shipping. For more information, call 800-541-2233.

MARINATING NEEDLES If your local kitchen supply store does not carry the marinating baster mentioned in Notes from Readers (page 3), a stainless steel version with injection needle attachment is available from Bridge Kitchenware (214 East 52nd Street, New York, NY 10022; telephone 212-688-4220). The 10-inch baster, which also comes with a cleaning brush, costs $9.95, plus shipping. A thin marinating needle (called Zap!) is available at Lechter's Housewares stores nationwide. The cost is $6. ■

RECIPE INDEX

BROILED EGGPLANT SLICES WITH TWO CHEESES page 7

GRILL-ROASTED HICKORY CHICKEN page 20

SOUPS AND BREADS
Corn and Clam Chowder with Roasted Parsnips 9
Deep-Fried Devils 2

FISH AND SHELLFISH
Grill-Roasted Salmon with Alderwood 20
Grilled Tuna with Ginger and Garlic 12
Roasted Salmon with Leek and Kasha Stuffing 23
Roasted Salmon with Summer Vegetable and Rice Stuffing 25

MEAT AND FOWL
Grilled Chicken with Olives, Rosemary, and Garlic 12
Grilled Lamb with Yogurt, Curry, and Mint 12
Grill-Roasted Beef Tenderloin 20
Grill-Roasted Hickory Chicken 20
Grill-Roasted Spareribs 20
Spicy Southwestern Flank Steak 12

VEGETABLE SIDE DISHES AND MAIN COURSES
Braised Celery 25
Broiled Eggplant Slices with Two Cheeses 7
Corn and Zucchini Sauté with Chiles 9
Master Recipe for Broiled Eggplant 7
Master Recipe for Sautéed Eggplant 7
Roasted Carrots and Parsley Roots 25
Roasted Corn Salsa 8
Sautéed Eggplant in Spicy Garlic Sauce 7
Sautéed Eggplant in Tomato Sauce with Basil 7
Sautéed Eggplant with Crisped Bread Crumbs 7
Shaker-Style Creamy Corn Pudding 9

MARINADES AND SAUCES
Master Recipe for Asian Marinade 12
Master Recipe for Fresh Tomato-Herb Sauce 14
Master Recipe for Mediterranean Marinade 12
Mexican-Style Salsa Cruda 14
Tomato-Yogurt Sauce 14

DESSERTS
Chocolate Ice Cream 28
Coffee Ice Cream 28
Fresh Raspberry Summer Pudding ..... back cover
Mississippi Mud Cake 3
Strawberry Ice Cream 28
Master Recipe for Vanilla Ice Cream 27

CORN AND CLAM CHOWDER WITH ROASTED PARSNIPS page 9

STRAWBERRY ICE CREAM page 28

SPICY SOUTHWESTERN FLANK STEAK page 12

ROASTED SALMON WITH LEEK AND KASHA STUFFING page 23

ALL PHOTOGRAPHS BY ERIC ROTH

THIS PHOTO: GEOFFREY MONTAGU, STYLING: NORMAN STEWART

Fresh Raspberry Summer Bread Pudding

Mix 3 cups fresh raspberries with 3 tablespoons sugar. Set aside until berries and sugar form a syrup, at least 30 minutes. Remove the crusts from 6 slices of high-quality white sandwich bread and cut into 1-inch squares. Whip 1½ cups heavy cream with 3 tablespoons sugar into stiff peaks; fold in 2 tablespoons Grand Marnier. Spoon about ¼ cup berries, with their juices, into each of 4 large dessert goblets and top each with about ¼ cup whipped cream. Top each portion of whipped cream with a layer of bread squares. Repeat the process: berries, whipped cream, bread squares, berries, and finally whipped cream. Refrigerate at least 4 hours. (Can be covered and refrigerated overnight.) Garnish the top of each dessert with fresh berries and serve. *Serves 4.*

NUMBER FOUR ◆ SEPTEMBER/OCTOBER 1993

$4.00 U.S./$4.95 CANADA

COOK'S ILLUSTRATED

How to Make Professional Muffins at Home

The Secrets of Dramatic, High-Capped Muffins

Juicy, Tender Sautéed Chicken

A Foolproof Recipe

Filled Pastas

16 Steps to Tortelli, Ravioli, and Tortellini

Sweet Roasted Garlic

How to Poach, then Roast

CRISPS AND BETTIES

MAKING VINEGAR AT HOME

TESTING ESPRESSO MACHINES

RATING PINOT NOIRS

30-MINUTE PEKING DUCK

SEPTEMBER/OCTOBER 1993

TABLE OF CONTENTS

VOLUME ONE • NUMBER FOUR

2

Notes from Readers:

Stir-frying in a skillet; cutting board controversy; making a bouquet garni; an antique apple peeler; a stuffed veal breast recipe; and French and American rolling pins.

4

Quick Tips

How to prepare monkfish for cooking; quickly seed and chop dried chiles; make scallion brushes; remove avocado pits; pit olives; chop fennel bulbs; and separate cauliflower.

6

How to Make Professional Muffins at Home

Learn the secrets of making dramatic, high-capped muffins that stay tender. *By Marcy Goldman*

9

How to Sauté Chicken

High heat, perfect timing, and the right amount of oil and butter yield juicy and tender boneless breasts. *By Stephen Schmidt*

12

Master Class: 30-Minute Peking Duck

California chef David SooHoo simplifies this Chinese-restaurant dish for preparation at home.

14

Fresh Mushrooms for Cooking

15

Three Filled Pastas

In one hour, you can make ravioli, tortelli, or tortellini by following these 16 step-by-step illustrations. *By Jack Bishop*

19

Roasting Garlic

For the sweetest, creamiest garlic, poach it in milk before roasting. *By Elizabeth Hilts*

"The Fruits of Fall" Pears are delicious in both crisps and betties. See page 26.

ILLUSTRATION BY BRENT WATKINSON

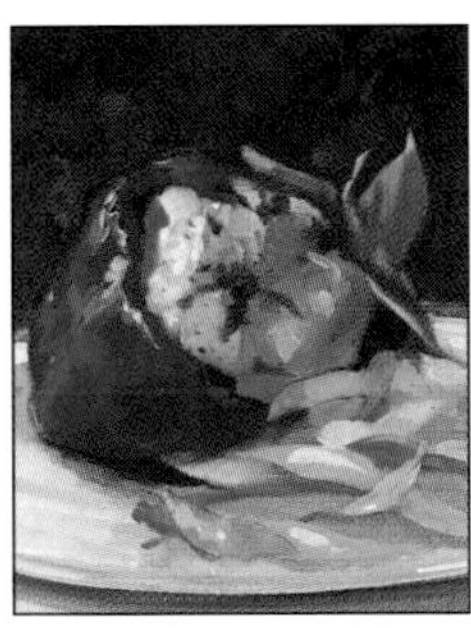

Chicken Roasted in Red Pepper from *Michel Richard's Home Cooking with a French Accent* reviewed on page 31.

ILLUSTRATION BY FRANCIS LIVINGSTON

21

Omelets Revisited

Use a no-stick pan for a no-hassle omelet. *By Stephanie Lyness*

23

Making Your Own Vinegar

You need little more than time to turn leftover wine into inexpensive and full-bodied vinegar. *By Lynn Alley*

24

Rating Red Wine Vinegars

An inexpensive American vinegar tops the field. *By Joni Miller*

26

Crisps and Betties

Make dozens of quick fruit desserts with these simple toppings. *By John Phillip Carroll*

27

Secrets of Homemade Espresso

Is a $200 espresso machine worth the investment? We test five brands to find out. Plus: Techniques for perfect cappuccino. *By Jack Bishop*

30

American Pinot Noirs Eclipse French Burgundies

A $6 Napa Pinot Noir showed better than pricey, well-known Burgundies in our blind tasting. *By Mark Bittman*

31

Book Reviews

Chef Michel Richard creates great recipes for the home kitchen; German food is lighter than expected; a new collection of James Beard essays proves irresistible.

32

Sources and Resources

Products from this issue, plus espresso aides, mushrooms by mail, exotic tropical jams, glass vinegar flasks, and replacement parts for kitchen appliances.

Cook's Illustrated (ISSN 1068-2821) is published bimonthly by Natural Health Limited Partners, 17 Station Street, Box 569, Brookline, MA 02147. Copyright 1993 Natural Health Limited Partners. Application to mail at second class postage rates is pending at Boston, MA and additional mailing offices. Editorial office: 17 Station Street, Box 569, Brookline, MA 02147 (617) 232-1000, FAX (617) 232-1572. Editorial contributions should be sent to: Editor, *Cook's Illustrated,* 17 Station Street, Brookline, MA 02147. We cannot assume responsibility for manuscripts submitted to us. Submissions will be returned only if accompanied by a large self-addressed stamped envelope. Subscription rates: $24.95 for one year; $45 for two years; $65 for three years. (Canada: add $3 per year; all other foreign add $12 per year.) Postmaster: Send all new orders, subscription inquiries, and change of address notices to *Cook's Illustrated,* P.O. Box 59046, Boulder, CO 80322-9046, or telephone (800) 477-3059. Single copies: $4 in U.S., $4.95 in Canada and foreign. PRINTED IN THE U.S.A.

EDITORIAL

THE JOY OF COOKING

CHRISTOPHER KIMBALL

My family and I live in Boston's South End, a melting-pot neighborhood with its share of typical inner-city problems. When I tell people where we live, they usually play back the newspaper's page-one version of city living — drive-by shootings, rapes, crack dealers, racial tensions, and crumbling infrastructure. What never makes it into the news are the sounds of the choir from the nearby Baptist church, the pleasures of a walk home past the Victorian brownstones, the gathering of neighbors to prune the rose bushes in our park on a crisp October morning, or the delicious steamed dumplings in yellow curry sauce at the local Korean grill.

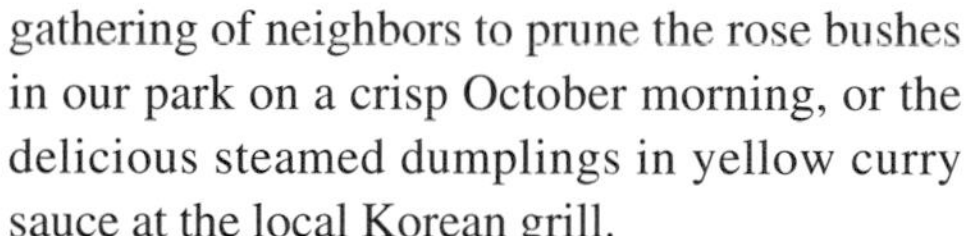

Like city living, food should be a day-to-day affair, not just page-one stories of bioengineering, pesticides, and irradiation. Food should be a fresh-baked buttermilk biscuit with homemade blackberry jam. A quick stir-fry for unexpected neighbors. Pears poached in white wine, liqueur, and white peppercorns. A loaf of rye bread, still warm from the oven, and a shaker of salt given to the new family across the street. The first crisp bite of native corn in August.

Perhaps cooking has become too everyday in an age in which everything "worthwhile" must have global impact. Can we enjoy a splash of cream from time to time without thinking about the cost of long-term health care? Can we make the time to prepare food at home when we should be thinking about the rain forest, Bosnia, or the national debt? Daily life is intrinsically repetitive, mundane, and predictable — but it is also more compelling, satisfying, and fascinating than the global world of page one. On many days, there is more sense to be found in a good recipe for roast chicken than in all the news on the front page of the *New York Times.*

At the height of the food mania of the 1980s, a restaurant owner took me aside and whispered, "You know — it's only food." That's right. Food is to be eaten, not worshipped. And therein lies the romance of it all. James Beard captured it best, in *Delights and Prejudices,* when he extolled "the exquisite pleasure of a simple piece of broiled meat." Beard was a truly honest home cook, a man who preferred dining home alone to "endless luncheons in smart restaurants, endless tasting, endless talk about food."

Cooking is rarely glamorous. More often, it takes hard work, training, patience, thought, practice, and repetition. It is, after all, a craft rather than an art. But, for all of us here at *Cook's Illustrated,* it is not only the page-one story but our passion. And we're glad so many of you (75,000 new readers in the last six months) have taken the time to stop by and share our table and our enthusiasm. We appreciate your support, your letters (we've received a stockpot full of them), and your comments. One of my favorite letters expressed concern about our decision not to take advertising. "Do you have a benevolent friend or relative willing to indulge your purist approach?" it asked. The answer is, no, we do not. What we do have is thousands of commonsense readers who love to cook.

Not too long ago, the page-one news was that home cooking was dead. It was the age of the microwave (the use of microwaves for home cooking has steadily declined since 1990), a time when dining out had replaced eating at home (since 1985, annual per capita restaurant visits have dropped by more than 10 percent). So much for trends. All of you know what so many others have forgotten — good home cooking matters. As Julia Child says, "The pleasures of the table depict food . . . as a delightful part of civilized life." In an age when the major headlines are anything but civilized, perhaps we can rediscover a sense of purpose and enlightenment in the kitchen. ■

PHOTO BY JIM THOMAS

NOTES
FROM READERS

Stir-Fry in a Skillet

I have been stir-frying at home for decades and found your advice ("Stir-Frying Comes Home," May/June, 1993) sound and admirable. A suggestion, if I may be so bold, from my own experience.

I believe we have to abandon the wok for stir-frying in the American home. As you pointed out, the wok is built for a degree of heat and a kind of flame that is impossible on a normal home gas or electric range. What does work on the American stove is the kind of pan the stove was built for — the old-fashioned cast-iron skillet. Particularly on electric stoves, where the pan makes direct contact with the red-hot burner, cast-iron skillets can reach a temperature that approaches restaurant cooking in a wok.

A few adjustments must be made when stir-frying in a skillet. Doing things in batches is a given. The wok is designed so that cooked food can be pushed up on the sides while searing still continues in the center of the pan. With a skillet, items must be removed when cooked and then recombined at the end. However, the results are the same once one gets used to new cooking times. For instance, foods continue to cook after they have been removed from the pan and while other batches are in the skillet.

With practice, cast-iron skillets can yield restaurant-quality results. So put away those woks and adapt the cooking principles to the equipment at hand.

JOHN MATHIESEN
Portland, OR

Cutting-Board Controversy

Several years ago I put away my wooden cutting boards and bought plastic ones after reading a story about the dangers of salmonella poisoning. Now a friend tells me that potentially harmful bacteria can grow on plastic boards as well. Is plastic still safer than wood? Are there any precautions I should be taking to prevent bacterial contamination from my cutting board?

MARGOT LEVIN
Yardley, PA

An unpublished study conducted by microbiologists at the University of Wisconsin has many food scientists shaking their heads. In the study, several kinds of wood and plastic surfaces were purposely contaminated with various bacteria. After about three minutes, most of the bacteria were no longer present on the wooden boards. In contrast, the bacteria actually multiplied on plastic surfaces.

These results have not been duplicated in other laboratories, though, so don't throw out your plastic boards yet. With either type of material it is important to keep the surface clean, especially after raw meats have been in contact with the cutting board. Wash boards (as well as your hands and knives) with hot soapy water or run the boards and knives through the dishwasher. It is also a good idea to soak boards occasionally in a light chlorine bleach solution for several minutes; two teaspoons of bleach per quart of water is adequate. Remember to wash the board well with clean water after soaking in the bleach solution.

Bouquet Garni

What's the role of bouquet garni in soups and stocks? Can you use dried herbs instead of fresh? What about variations? Is it necessary to wrap the herbs in cheesecloth?

SUSAN DAY
Ithaca, NY

Bouquet garni is a bunch of aromatic herbs used to flavor stocks, soups, casseroles, and other liquid-based dishes. There is no such thing as a universal recipe, although most variations begin with fresh parsley stems, sprigs of thyme, and a dried bay leaf, all wrapped together with kitchen twine (*see* illustrations). Possible additions include rosemary, celery (leaves and/or ribs), the green part of the leek, tarragon, savory, or fennel. In some parts of France the mixture may contain spices (especially whole peppercorns or cloves) as well as a slice of bacon to serve as a wrapper.

The untied end of the string is often left long enough to wrap around the handle of the pot; when cooking is finished the herb bundle is then easily retrieved and discarded. If dried herbs are used, the mixture is traditionally enclosed in a small piece of cheesecloth and tightly tied to prevent leakage. The main reason for this is aesthetic — herb flecks can mar an otherwise clear broth. However, we often omit the cheesecloth, since many clear broths are poured through a fine-mesh strainer anyway.

Back Issues Available

I just learned of (and subscribed to) your great magazine. Can I get the early issues I missed?

JANE STOVER
Spruce Pine, NC

We're glad you like the magazine. Back issues (Charter, May/June 1993, and July/August 1993 issues) are now available for $5.00 per issue. To order, send check, money order, or MasterCard/Visa/American Express information (no cash) to *Cook's Illustrated* Back Issues, P.O. Box 569, Brookline Village, MA 02147. Please allow three to four weeks for delivery. (Availability of issues is subject to change without notice.)

What Is It?

I found this device at a tag sale while vacationing in Pennsylvania Dutch country. I think it has some sort of culinary purpose. Can you tell me how this utensil was once used?

JENNIFER GONZALEZ
Santa Cruz, CA

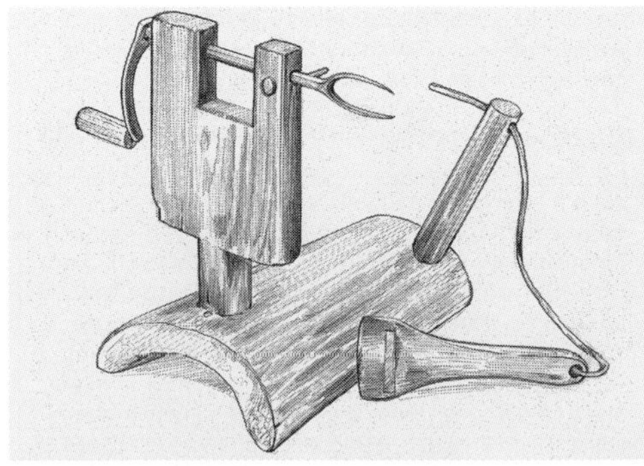

You have indeed stumbled across a piece of culinary equipment that was quite popular during the nineteenth century. This "mobile"

ILLUSTRATIONS BY ELAYNE SEARS

apple parer could be tied around the user's thigh and taken into the field or to harvest festivals called "apple bees." An apple was skewered on the two prongs and then rotated by turning the handle on the left. A sharp knife blade was held against the apple as it turned, removing the peel in one long piece.

Stuffed Veal Breast

When I was a child, my grandmother used to prepare stuffed veal breast for family dinners every Sunday. I remember enjoying this dish and was wondering if you could give me some tips on preparing and cooking veal breast. Also, can you recommend an Italian-style stuffing recipe?

ROY PIZZARELLO
Phoenix, AZ

Veal breast is one of the most underrated cuts of meats. Extremely moist and tender, it is also very inexpensive (we paid only $1.39 per pound at the butcher), especially when compared to other veal cuts. A whole breast can feed 10 or 12 adults, making it an excellent choice for parties or holiday meals. Because of the bones, plan on about one pound of veal per adult.

Generally, only the first seven ribs contain enough meat to make a pocket suitable for stuffing. If your butcher has not already done so, trim the meat and bones after the seventh rib (illustration 1). The excess meat may be ground and used in the stuffing and the bones can be used to make veal stock, as in the recipe below. Next, open a cavity in the breast by cutting along the top of the ribs (illustration 2). Gently fill the cavity but do not overstuff it.

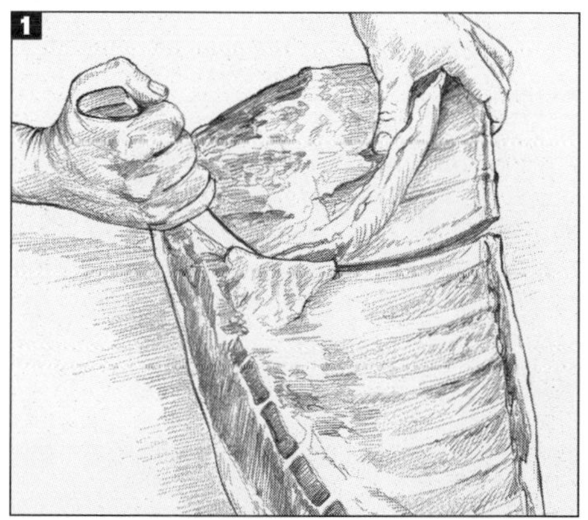

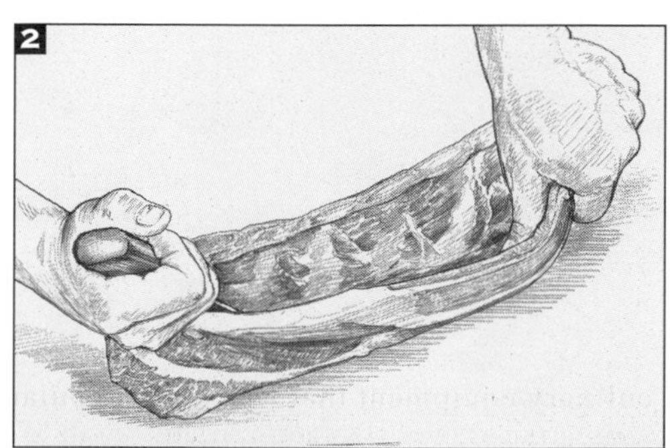

To close the pocket, tie three or four pieces of kitchen string parallel to the ribs and around the entire breast. After the veal is removed from the oven, it should be allowed to rest so that the stuffing and meat stay together when sliced. Veal breast is excellent when served at room temperature or even chilled.

BRAISED VEAL BREAST WITH SAUSAGE, OLIVE, AND SWISS CHARD STUFFING

Serves 10–12

Simple Veal Stock

- 2 pounds veal bones
- 1 tablespoon vegetable oil
- 1 small onion, peeled
- 1 small carrot, peeled
- ½ small celery stalk

Sausage, Olive, and Swiss Chard Stuffing

- 2 tablespoons olive oil
- 1 large yellow onion, chopped
- 4 medium garlic cloves, minced
- 1 pound Swiss chard, stemmed, washed, and chopped coarse
- 1 teaspoon fennel seeds
- ¼ teaspoon hot red pepper flakes
- Salt
- 1 pound mild Italian sausage, removed from casing
- ½ pound ground veal from veal breast trimmings
- ½ cup grated Parmesan cheese
- ½ cup black olives, pitted and chopped coarse
- 1 cup fresh bread crumbs

- 1 veal breast (first 7 ribs), trimmed and prepared for stuffing (*see* above)
- 2 tablespoons olive oil
- Salt and ground black pepper
- ½ cup dry white wine

1. *For the stock,* heat oven to 400 degrees. Toss bones with oil in a baking pan. Roast bones, turning occasionally, until brown, about 40 minutes. Transfer bones to a large saucepan along with vegetables. Spoon excess grease from roasting pan, then add 1 cup water, scraping pan bottom with a wooden spoon to loosen browned bits. Pour this liquid into saucepan with enough water to cover bones and vegetables by 1 inch; bring to a simmer over low heat, skimming foam as it floats to the surface. Simmer until bones and vegetables have completely given up their flavor to liquid, 3 to 4 hours. Skim fat, strain, and refrigerate until ready to use. You should have 3 to 4 cups stock. (Can be refrigerated up to 5 days or frozen.)

2. *For the stuffing,* heat oil in a large skillet or dutch oven. Add onions; sauté until they start to soften, about 2 minutes. Add garlic, sauté until both soften, about 2 minutes longer. Add Swiss chard, fennel, red pepper flakes, and 1 teaspoon salt. Sauté until chard wilts, liquid evaporates, and flavors blend, 3 to 4 minutes. Transfer mixture to a medium bowl and cool slightly. Stir in remaining ingredients.

3. Spoon stuffing into veal breast pocket; do not overstuff. Secure pocket by tying veal breast with kitchen twine at 2-inch intervals running parallel to rib bones. Brush veal breast with oil and sprinkle lightly with salt (too much and pan juices will be salty) and pepper.

4. Heat oven to 325 degrees. Heat large roasting pan (at least 15-by-11-by-3 inches) over medium-high heat. Brown veal breast on all sides, about 15 minutes total. Add wine and stock and bring to a simmer. Cover pan with foil and put in oven. Braise until meat is tender and a meat thermometer inserted into thickest section of roast registers between 160 and 170 degrees, about 3 hours. Remove veal breast from oven and transfer to a cutting board and let rest for at least 20 minutes. Meanwhile pour braising liquid into a saucepan and reduce over high heat to about 2 cups.

5. Remove twine and carve veal breast, leaving rib bones on platter. Serve with pan juices passed separately.

Rolling Pins

I know there are several kinds of rolling pins but I'm confused about which ones are best. Are there special uses for tapered pins? What about pins with handles and ball bearings?

ANGIE CHOW
San Francisco, CA

There are three main types of rolling pins. American-style pins have a metal dowel running through the center, handles on either end, and are usually 10 to 15 inches long, not including handles. They are best for heavy bread or Danish doughs, since the ball bearings and handles allow extra pressure to be exerted during rolling.

French pins are usually 18 or 20 inches long and have no handles or ball bearings, but are simply round lengths of wood (no more than dowels, really) which can be used to roll out any dough. French pins are generally felt to convey a better feel for dough, since hands are placed directly on the barrel and not on handles.

Some French pins are tapered, with the ends narrower than the middle. This makes them lighter and more delicate, and therefore more precise. Additionally, by "anchoring" one end of the pin with one hand, the pin can be pivoted in a circle, facilitating the making of round pastries such as pie crusts. ■

Quick Tips

Preparing Monkfish

Sweet and meaty, monkfish is an increasingly popular fish in the U.S. It is often available ready to cook. However, if you find it skin-on, you can easily prepare it yourself for cooking. First, slide a knife between the skin and the flesh along the head side of the fish.

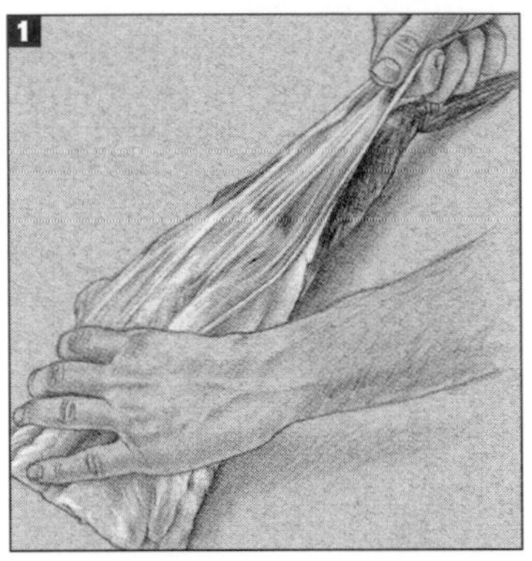

1. Grasp the skin firmly between thumb and forefinger and hold the fish with the opposite hand; peel the skin away from the flesh, cut off, and discard.

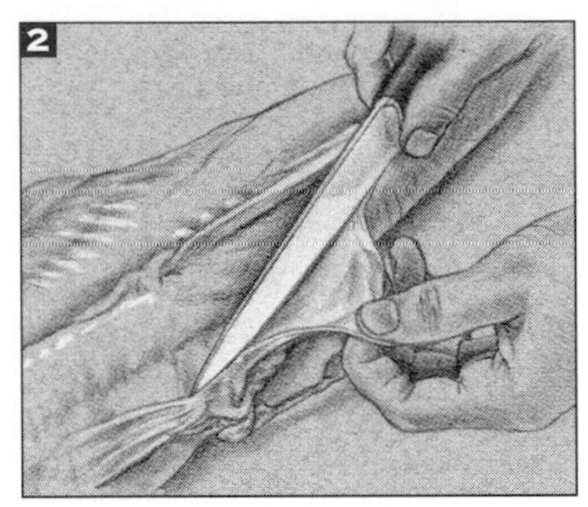

2. Monkfish is covered with a thin membrane under the skin, which also must be removed. Peel the membrane away with a filleting knife; cut close to the flesh and pull the membrane away with your fingers. Discard the membrane.

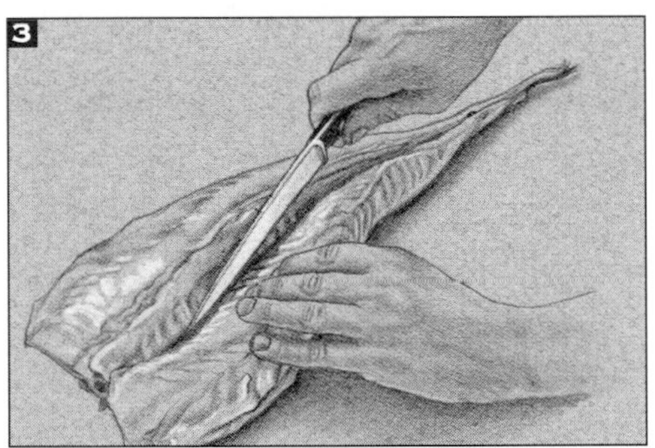

3. Slice along one side of the fish's backbone to remove one fillet; repeat on the opposite side. Discard the backbone, and rinse and dry fillets before cooking.

Making Scallion Brushes

Decorative scallion brushes can be used to spread hoisin sauce over Asian pancakes or as a plate garnish for dishes such as Peking Duck (page 12). Begin by trimming the roots and dark green tops.

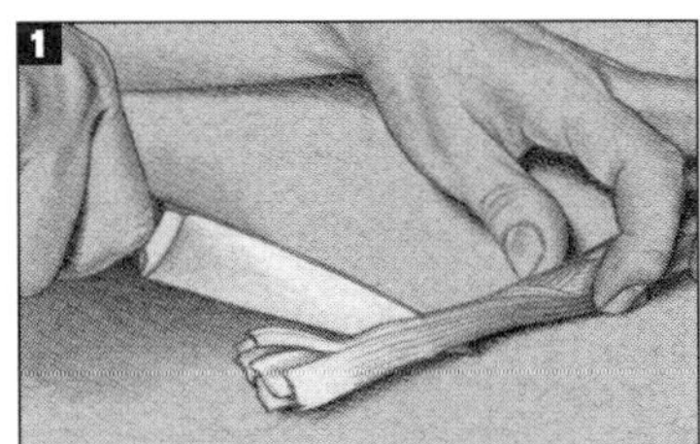

1. Use a small, sharp knife to make a cut that extends about one inch up from the root end. Roll scallion one-quarter turn and make a second similar cut.

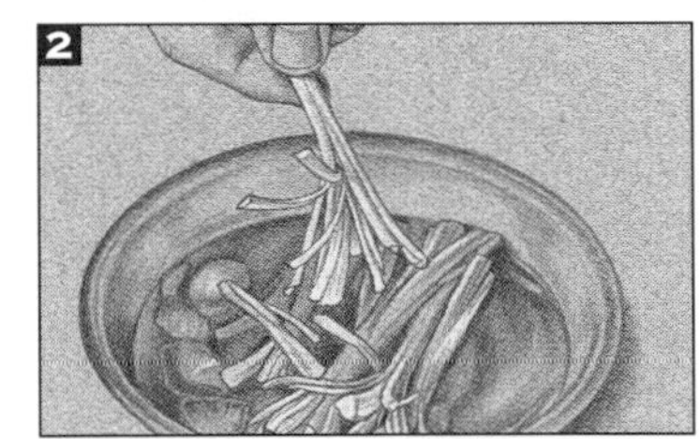

2. Chill cut scallions in a bowl of ice water for at least five minutes. When ready to use, shake to remove excess water and separate ends.

Cutting and Seeding Dried Chiles

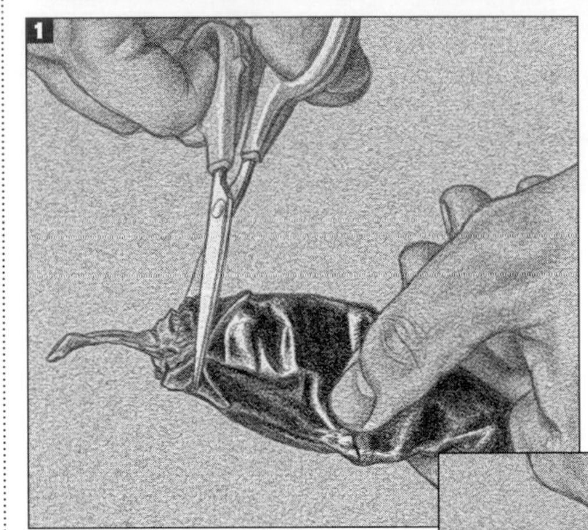

1. Dried chiles are often leathery and can be difficult to cut with a knife. A pair of scissors does the job with ease. To begin, snip off and discard the stem.

2. Beginning at the stem end, cut chile lengthwise in half.

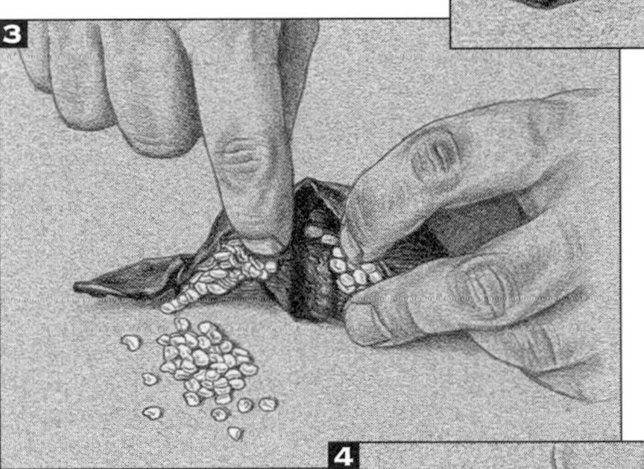

3. Use your fingers to brush out seeds from inside the chile halves.

4. Cut seeded halves into thin strips that can be toasted, stir-fried, or added to sauces and salsas.

Illustrations by Alan Witschonke

Pitting an Avocado

Removing pits without mashing the flesh is important when making avocado vinaigrette or when using avocado halves to hold salad. Avocados with pebbly skins (as opposed to the larger variety with smooth skins) are creamier and better in salads.

1. Slice around the pit by cutting through both ends.

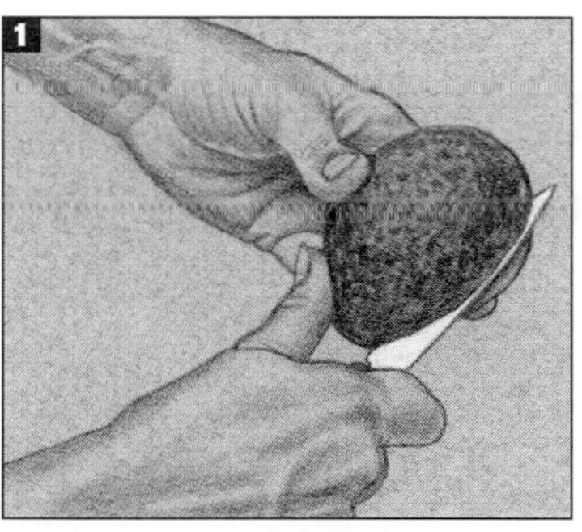

2. Twist to separate halves and stick the blade of a large knife sharply into the pit.

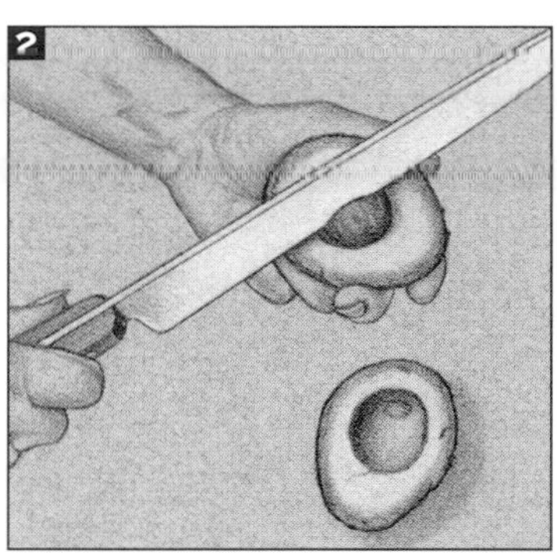

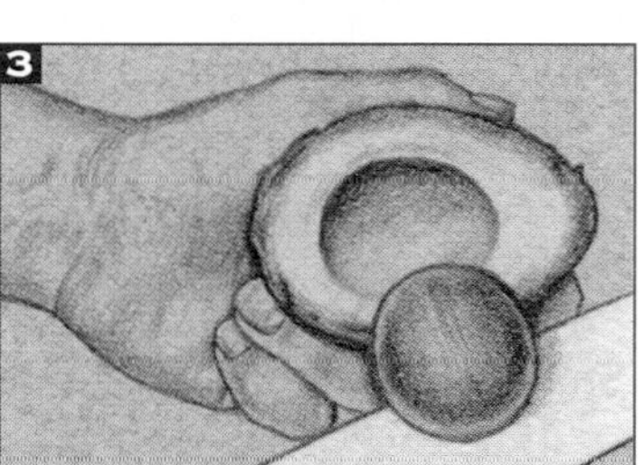

3. Lift blade, twisting if necessary to loosen and remove the pit. Avocado halves may be filled with vinaigrette or peeled with a paring knife and cut into strips.

Trimming and Slicing Fennel

Raw fennel has an anise-like flavor that is excellant in salads or crudités. When sautéed or braised, fennel loses some of its pungency, but the slices soften nicely.

1. Chop off the feathery fronds and tough stems. Save fronds for salads or garnishes and use stems in stocks in place of celery.

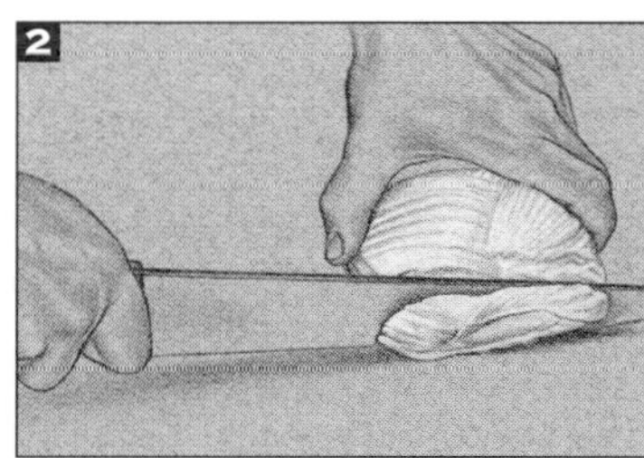

2. Cut fennel bulb in half through the bottom and stem ends. Trim and discard bottom end.

3. Place fennel cut side down on a cutting board and slice into thin half-circles.

Pitting Olives

This technique can be used with any olives in brine. Oil-cured olives, on the other hand, can be seeded by simply squeezing the olive to pop out the pit.

1. Place olive on a work surface and hold flat edge of a large chef's knife over olive. Hit blade with fist to smash olive.

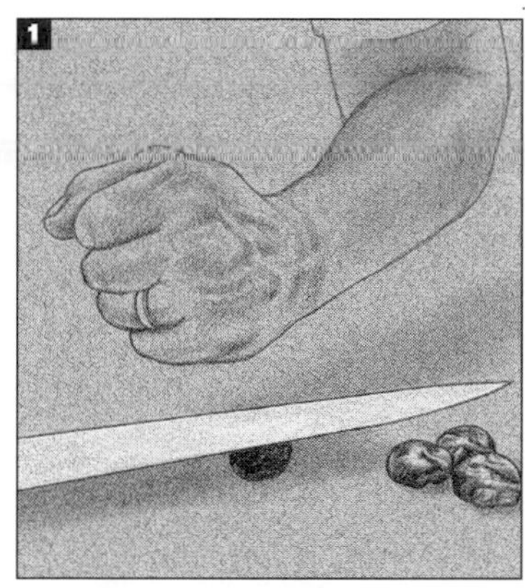

2. Separate pit from olive meat with fingers.

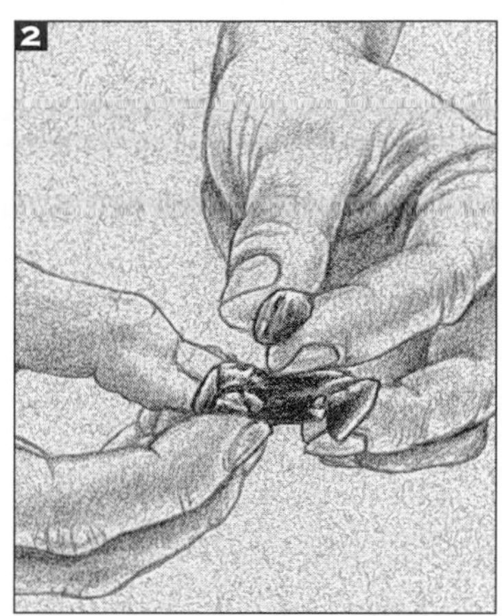

Breaking Cauliflower into Florets

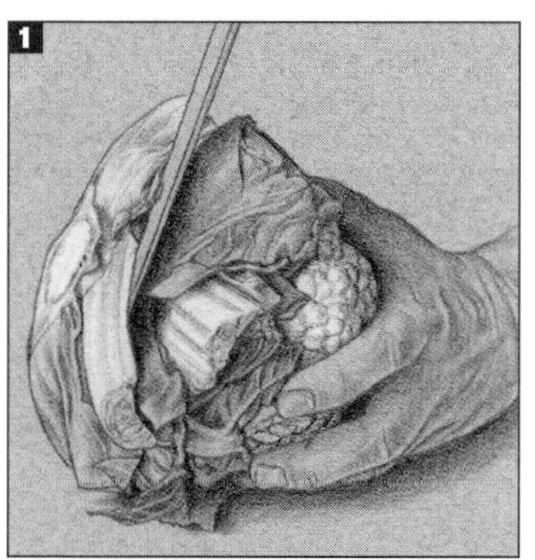

1. Slice through the stem end with a sharp knife to remove the outside leaves.

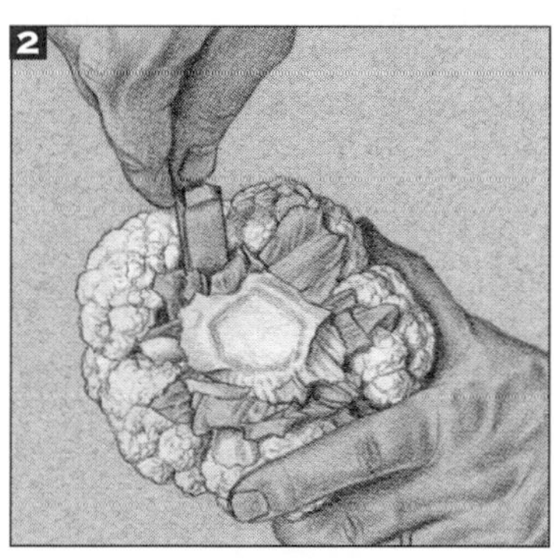

2. Cut around the core as close as possible to the florets in order to remove core and tough stems in one piece.

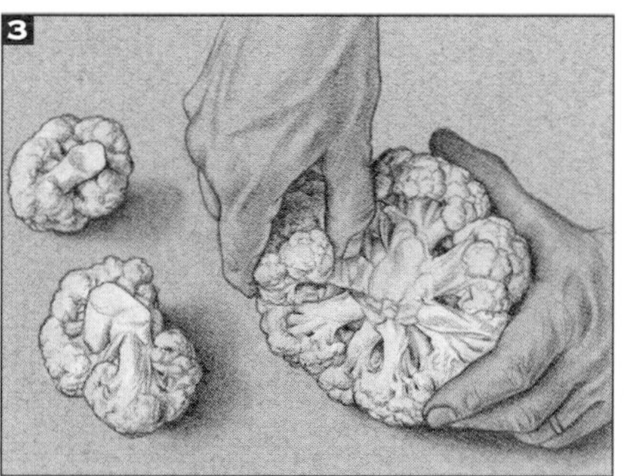

3. Separate florets by hand into small chunks.

ATTENTION READERS, FREE SUBSCRIPTION FOR PUBLISHED TIPS. Do you have a unique tip you would like to share with other readers? We will provide a one-year complimentary subscription for each quick tip that we print. Send a description of your special technique to *Cook's Illustrated,* P.O. Box 569, Brookline Village, MA 02147. Please write "Attention: Quick Tips" on the envelope and include your name, address, and daytime phone number. Unfortunately, we can only acknowledge receipt of tips that will be printed in the magazine.

How to Make Professional Muffins at Home

Learn the secrets of making dramatic, high-capped muffins that stay tender.

BY MARCY GOLDMAN

Muffins — one of the first baked goods people tackle — run the gamut from terrific to mediocre. Even great-tasting homemade muffins, however, may lack the star quality of the fabulous, high-domed muffins sold in stores. In fact there is no reason that home bakers can't make a high-rising, tender, eye-catching muffin that rivals those made by the pros.

Ingredients: Simple but Crucial

Although many pastry chefs ordinarily scoff at using all-purpose flour, most concede that it is the flour of choice for muffins. This is because it has sufficient body to hold things together and to support extras such as nuts and raisins, yet it is not so high in protein that the final product is coarse or tough.

DIP AND SCOOP

1. To accurately measure flour, pour the flour into a large bowl, stir it with the measuring cup to aerate it, then dip the measuring cup completely into the flour.

2. Using a spatula, scrape all excess flour back into the bowl, leaving a precisely filled measuring cup.

Muffins can be made with almost any liquid at all. Juices add flavor and a pleasant touch of acidity (orange muffins made with fresh-squeezed orange juice are sensational), and the sugar and fat content of milk and other dairy products assist with browning, moistness, and a pleasant-textured crumb.

I am particularly partial to buttermilk, as many bakers are. There are several reasons for this: I like the punch and accent it lends to the flavor of the batter, and there is no question that it gives better rise, thanks primarily to the reaction between its acidity and the baking soda. The acid in buttermilk also inhibits gluten development, and buttermilk is less calorie-laden than sour cream, which also works well. Finally, buttermilk is more romantic-sounding — and better-tasting — than plain old soured (not spoiled!) milk (*see* "Soured Milk Substitute?," page 7). Yogurt, another good option, varies so widely in texture that it is difficult to give directions for using it in recipes; it's best to experiment with the brand you usually buy, or with the yogurt you make at home.

I have found that muffins made with sweet milk are adequate, but they lack tang, don't rise as high, and are often more dense than those made with more acidic dairy products. There are sweet-milk–based recipes that compensate by using extra baking powder; although they are nice and high, the taste is somewhat compromised. When you have a choice, use (in order of preference) buttermilk, yogurt, or soured milk.

You also have a choice when it comes to fat. Liquid oils have several advantages: they are easier to blend with other ingredients, contain little dietary cholesterol (although, of course, they have no fewer calories or grams of fat than butter), are relatively inexpensive, and produce muffins that keep exceptionally well. Solid fats produce lighter muffins because they are creamed before being mixed with other ingredients, which incorporates air. Butter adds its unrivaled flavor, and assists a muffin in browning becomingly. Shortening offers a higher burning point than both, a neutral flavor, and the ability to produce a distinctively light crumb; however its use is declining as research indicates it may have many of the health-shortcomings of butter with none of the flavor.

I tested all of the recipes below with oil, shortening, butter, and a combination of shortening and butter. Oil works quite effectively in bran muffins, but I prefer creamed solid fats for corn muffins; the flavor and texture are better. All the results were good; as I said, you have a choice when it comes to fat.

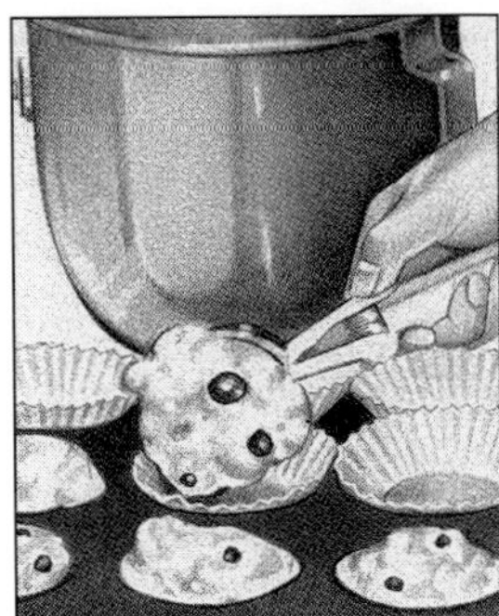

For clean dispensing and uniform size, use an ice-cream scoop to fill muffin tins.

Use a Whisk Lightly

Regardless of your choice of liquids and fat, there is no real choice when it comes to blending the ingredients — the utensil to use is a wire whisk.

Whisk the dry ingredients together, aerating and combining them at the same time. Then use a solid, heavy-duty whisk for the liquid and fat, too, thoroughly creaming the sugar, eggs, oil, and/or solid fat. (Sometimes when you do this, the mixture may look curdled. If this happens, add in a bit of the recipe's flour as a binder. This will also help incorporate the remainder of the dry ingredients more readily.) After you've creamed the moist ingredients, add some of the flour mixture with the whisk; as the batter becomes thick and sticky, switch to a large rubber spatula or a wide wooden spoon. When the dry ingredients have been partially blended, fold in any extras such as fruit and nuts, and finish off the job with a few more thorough but gentle stirs. Hand-mixing with a spoon, spatula, or whisk guarantees that the batter will not be overbeaten, and makes for a nice, smooth batter.

Speaking of smooth batter, muffin recipes are well known for warning home bakers not to overmix batters. If you do, say these recipes, the gluten will become elastic, resulting in inedible,

ILLUSTRATIONS BY MICHELE AMATRULA

tough muffins. This is absurd. The following recipes are rich enough to protect themselves from becoming tough or too chewy. The extra fat, sugar, and, if you use it, buttermilk, inhibit gluten development and act as tenderizing agents. Consider, too, that most muffins are mixed by hand (it just isn't worth hauling out the electric mixer to whip up a batch), and never really beaten, which might provoke unwanted gluten development. As long as you don't bludgeon your muffin batter, it makes little sense to work with a batter that is filled with lumps of unblended flour and leavener.

DOUBLE-CORN MUFFINS

Makes 1 dozen

The "double" refers to the cornmeal softened in the buttermilk, as well as the bit of dry cornmeal thrown into the batter at the end. The result is a moist, but resoundingly cornmeal-tasting muffin. It is not necessary to use paper baking liners if the muffin tin is commercial, glazed, or nonstick. You can add one cup semifrozen berries — blueberries, cranberries, or raspberries — to the finished batter. You may also garnish each cup with a sprinkling of cornmeal or with very thin slices of quartered lemon.

- 1 cup buttermilk, warmed
- ½ cup plus 1 tablespoon cornmeal (white or yellow), preferably stoneground
- 2¼ cups unbleached all-purpose flour
- 1 teaspoon baking soda
- 2 teaspoons baking powder
- Pinch of salt
- ¼ cup unsalted butter, softened
- ¼ cup shortening, softened
- 1 cup sugar
- 1 tablespoon minced zest from 1 lemon
- 2 eggs, lightly beaten
- ¾ teaspoon vanilla extract

1. Adjust oven rack to middle position and heat oven to 400 degrees. Lightly grease the top of a 12-cup muffin pan; use liners, if necessary (*see* note, above). Mix buttermilk with ½ cup cornmeal; set aside.

2. Whisk together remaining cornmeal with next 4 ingredients; set aside.

3. Cream butter and shortening with a whisk or by using the paddle attachment of an electric mixer on slow speed. Whisk or blend in sugar, then zest, eggs, and vanilla. Whisk soaked cornmeal mixture into batter; then whisk in dry ingredients to partially blend. Continue mixing batter with a rubber spatula, making sure that ingredients at the bottom are incorporated into batter. (If adding fruit, carefully fold in at this point.)

4. Using an ice-cream scoop, place a portion of batter into each muffin cup, filling to the brim. Bake until muffins are golden brown, 18 to 20 minutes. (If muffins are not done after 20 minutes, reduce temperature to 350 degrees and bake until muffins test done.) Let muffins cool in pan for 5 minutes then transfer them to a wire rack. Serve warm or at room temperature.

REFINING THE TECHNIQUE

I have gone to great lengths to try to duplicate the high cap of commercial muffins. At first, I tried increasing the amount of baking soda or powder. But the muffins began to taste soapy, and, even worse, they sometimes collapsed or literally blew their cap off. I tried a stiffer batter by adding more flour: this produced gloriously mammoth muffins. Unfortunately, they were abysmally dry.

Finally, I concluded that a muffin's cap is a matter of balance. The best combination of flavor, texture, and appearance results from preheating the oven to a higher than usual temperature, lowering it during baking, and baking in the upper third of the oven (*see* recipes). These tactics — combined with the following directions — had a wonderful affect on the muffins' visual appeal without compromising the most important criteria: taste and texture.

To make lovely, high-capped muffins, work with room-temperature eggs and fats whenever possible. When you use cold eggs and chilly butter, ingredients simply do not incorporate as well. In addition, a cold batter entering a hot oven has to work harder to boost itself up. When a room-temperature batter enters a hot oven, things start happening much faster.

When you fill muffin tins, scoop the batter generously, filling the individual cups almost to the top. (The traditional counsel about filling them two-thirds full usually results in short muffins.) Allow baked muffins to rest five minutes before removing them from the pan, since just-baked muffins can be fragile and have been known to collapse or have their tops sheer off. When you do remove the muffins, put them on a wire rack to cool; muffins that are allowed to cool in a hot pan will "sweat" and leftovers will become stale prematurely.

BIG BRAN MUFFINS WITH RAISINS AND DATES

Makes about 20 muffins

This recipe turns nutritious ingredients into great-tasting, moist muffins. It can easily be doubled and freezes well. Garnish batter in muffin cups with wheat germ or oat bran, or sesame or sunflower seeds. You can substitute one cup oat bran for the wheat germ for a wholesome, but slightly more dense, muffin.

- 2½ cups plus 2 tablespoons unbleached all-purpose flour
- 4½ teaspoons baking soda
- 1 tablespoon baking powder
- 2 teaspoons ground cinnamon
- ⅛ teaspoon salt
- ¾ cup vegetable oil
- 2 tablespoons honey
- ¼ cup molasses
- 1 cup plus 2 tablespoons light brown sugar, packed firm
- 1 teaspoon vanilla extract
- ¾ teaspoon maple extract
- 1½ teaspoons butter extract or flavoring
- 3 large eggs, lightly beaten
- 2 cups buttermilk
- 1 cup wheat germ
- 1 cup natural bran (not the cereal)
- ½ cup dates, plumped with scalding water, drained, and coarsely chopped
- 1 cup dark raisins, plumped with scalding water and drained

1. Whisk first 5 ingredients together in a medium bowl; set aside.

SOURED-MILK SUBSTITUTE?

To determine if soured or "clabbered" milk is an acceptable substitute for buttermilk in muffins, we compared corn muffins made with the two types of milk.

Tasters easily identified the batter made with soured milk; it not only lacked the distinctive buttermilk "tang," but also had a texture more like cake batter. In cooked form, the soured-milk muffin still reminded tasters of cake. Compared to the buttermilk one, it was flat and dull, with a sweet finish and a smooth texture. The buttermilk muffin sparkled; each bite triggered bursts of tart and sweet, as the buttermilk seemed to heighten the lemon and sugar flavors.

With this overwhelming endorsement of buttermilk, should you ever consider soured milk? Certainly. If it's Sunday morning and using buttermilk means getting dressed and going to the store, consider soured milk. But if both are available, definitely opt for the buttermilk.

To make soured milk, bring the milk to room temperature. (If the milk is too hot, it will form one large curd rather than lightly curdling when added to vinegar or lemon juice.) Measure one tablespoon distilled white vinegar or lemon juice into a one cup measure, add the milk to make one cup, and let the mixture stand until it curdles. (If the milk is at the right temperature, it will curdle almost instantly.) Allow to stand for five minutes after curdling, then proceed with the recipe.

—Pam Anderson

Using Whole Grains in Muffins

Granular, nonglutenous flours — such as wheat or oat bran, corn- or oatmeal, or wheat germ — add unusual flavor and texture to muffins (along with their purported health benefits, of course). I think of them as healthy "sand"; if you don't treat them with additional solicitude, you will be rewarded with a gravelly, dry, coarse muffin. Roughage is fine in a muffin, but you want moistness and a delicate crumb as well.

I have experimented with whole grains in muffins for years, and have come to this conclusion: they all profit from some sort of pretreatment. (Think of these grains as edible "sponges," just waiting to soak up flavor and moisture.) When making bran muffins, for example, I

found that soaking the bran for a while in the recipe's liquid allowed it to swell, tenderize, and combine more easily with the remaining dry ingredients.

Even better — and particularly convenient if you want to eat your muffins fresh and hot for breakfast — is to allow the batter to rest overnight in the refrigerator, which accomplishes the same goal. When I first tried this, I was concerned that the leaveners might lose some of their punch. But the chilly temperature and the use of double-acting baking powder (which responds partly to hydration, partly to heat) retarded much of this action, saving it for the oven. The reward is an easily handled batter and higher, lighter bran muffins.

I also tested both presoaking and precooking cornmeal. Precooking the grain in the recipe's liquid gave inconsistent (although sometimes quite wonderful) results. Ultimately, I decided this was an added bother, and not worth doing regularly.

Presoaking the cornmeal in buttermilk worked well, but I did want to retain some of the sandy texture, since it is characteristic of cornmeal. So I usually presoak most of the cornmeal and incorporate a little more directly into the batter. The result is a moist corn muffin with full corn flavor, and an appreciable and characteristic — though not overstated — graininess.

2. In a large bowl, whisk next 7 ingredients together. Whisk in eggs, then buttermilk, wheat germ, and bran. Let batter rest 10 minutes.

3. Whisk dry ingredients into wet mixture to partially blend. Continue mixing batter with a rubber spatula, making sure that ingredients at the bottom are incorporated into batter. Fold in dates and raisins.

4. Cover batter with plastic wrap and refrigerate at least 1 hour, preferably overnight.

5. Adjust oven rack to middle position and heat oven to 400 degrees. Lightly grease the top surface of 2, 12-cup muffin pans; use liners, if necessary (*see* note in Double-Corn Muffins). Using an ice-cream scoop, place a portion of batter into each muffin cup, filling to the brim. Fill empty muffin cups with water to ensure even baking. Bake until muffin tops brown, about 20 minutes. (If muffins are not done after 20 minutes, reduce temperature to 350 degrees and bake until muffins test done.) Let muffins cool in pan for 5 minutes then transfer them to a wire rack. Serve warm or at room temperature.

ANY-FRUIT-WILL-DO MUFFINS WITH STREUSAL TOPPING

A Master Recipe

Makes 1 dozen

To simplify muffin making, quadruple the streusal topping recipe and freeze. Orange, lemon, or lime zests can be used to flavor the muffins, if you like. Lemon works well with blueberry; orange zest with cranberry or rhubarb; lime zest with banana chunks. Almost any fruit works in this recipe. Good choices include: fresh or frozen rhubarb, diced; cranberries, coarsely chopped; blueberries; apples, cut into small dice; bananas, cut into firm, small chunks; raspberries; strawberries, quartered or cut into small dice; dried sour cherries or cranberries. To prevent delicate, highly colored fruits like raspberries, cranberries, and blueberries from getting mashed and discoloring the batter, use semi-frozen fruit.

Streusal Topping

- 1/3 cup brown or white sugar
- 1/2 teaspoon ground cinnamon
- 1 tablespoon unsalted butter
- 1/2 cup finely chopped walnuts

Any-Fruit-Will-Do Muffins

- 2 1/2–2 3/4 cups unbleached all-purpose flour
- 1 teaspoon baking soda
- 2 teaspoons baking powder
- 1/2 teaspoon ground cinnamon
- Pinch of salt
- 1 1/3 cups light brown sugar, packed firm
- 2/3 cup vegetable oil
- 1 tablespoon minced citrus zest (*see* note, above) from 1 lime, lemon, or orange
- 1 egg
- 1 cup buttermilk
- 2 teaspoons vanilla extract
- 1 3/4 cups fruit (*see* note, above), lightly packed

1. *For the topping,* mix sugar and cinnamon in a small bowl or workbowl of a food processor; add butter. If mixing by hand, use fingertips, a pastry blender, or 2 forks to blend the fat into dry ingredients until mixture looks like coarse irregular crumbs, with no visible lumps of fat. If mixing in a food processor, pulse about 10 times, then process 5 to 10 seconds, until there are no visible lumps of fat; stir in nuts and set aside.

2. *For the muffins,* adjust oven rack to middle position and heat oven to 400 degrees. Lightly grease the top surface of a 12-cup muffin pan; use liners, if necessary (*see* note in Double-Corn Muffins). Whisk 2 1/2 cups flour with next 4 ingredients in a medium bowl; set aside.

3. Whisk together next 4 ingredients in a large bowl; whisk in buttermilk and vanilla. Gently whisk dry ingredients into wet ingredients to partially blend. Continue mixing batter with a rubber spatula, making sure that ingredients at the bottom are incorporated into batter; fold in fruit. (Frozen fruit will help "firm" up batter. If batter seems too wet add a few more tablespoons of flour — up to 1/4 cup — to stiffen batter.)

4. Using an ice-cream scoop, place a portion of batter into each muffin cup, filling to the brim. Sprinkle a portion of streusal topping over batter in each muffin cup.

5. Bake 15 minutes; reduce heat to 350 degrees and bake until muffins are golden brown and spring back when lightly pressed with fingertips, 10 to 12 minutes. Let muffins cool in pan for 5 minutes then transfer them to a wire rack. Serve warm or at room temperature. ■

Marcy Goldman is a Montreal-based professional pastry chef, baker, and food journalist.

When baking less than a full tin, fill empty compartments with water to ensure that heat is evenly conducted.

ILLUSTRATION BY MICHELE AMATRULA

How to Sauté Chicken

High heat, perfect timing, and the right amount of oil and butter yield juicy and tender boneless breasts.

BY STEPHEN SCHMIDT

To avoid being splashed with hot fat when putting chicken cutlets into the pan, lay them in thick side first, hanging on to the tapered end until the whole cutlet is in the pan.

Although there are several keys to correctly sautéing boneless chicken breasts, one is paramount: there must be enough heat. Home cooks often shy away from the smoke and spatters that can accompany strong heat. But a thin, delicate food like boneless chicken must be cooked through quickly. Cooking over low or even moderate heat pushes the meat's moisture to the surface before any browning occurs, and once the juices hit the exterior of the meat, it will not brown at all, unless it is cooked for a long, long time. Furthermore — and this is especially true in a lean piece of meat such as a chicken breast — these same juices provide the lion's share of moisture; expel them, and the result is a tough, leathery piece of meat rather than a tender, moist one.

There are other points to bear in mind, as well. After you have trimmed excess fat from the cutlets and removed the tendon, if desired (*see* illustrations, page 10), rinse them quickly under cool water if they seem sticky or have even the slightest off-scent. (The surface of foods is usually the first part to go bad, and rinsing can do wonders to salvage the flavor.) Then dry the meat thoroughly with paper or cloth towels; again, if it is wet, it will not brown. For best flavor, salt and pepper both sides; I use a full teaspoon of salt for four pieces of chicken. Although flouring cutlets is not absolutely essential, it does promote juiciness and add color, so I recommend it (*see* "Is Flouring Necessary?," page 11).

The Right Way to Sauté

Your skillet must measure at least nine inches across the bottom in order to comfortably hold four six-ounce chicken cutlets (crowded meat will not brown well), and the bottom should be reasonably heavy, or else the chicken will scorch. I tested nonstick and enamel-coated pans and found them perfectly acceptable, but I prefer bare metal — stainless steel or an alloy — as it seems to yield more intense color. I do not recommend cast iron because it may react with any acidic ingredient you use in a deglazing sauce, such as tomato or lemon juice, leaving a metallic taste.

The best cooking medium for chicken cutlets is a mixture of butter and oil. Butter contains milk solids, which brown during cooking, providing a beautiful rich color; it also contributes mightily to flavor. Adding oil reduces the proportion of burnt milk solids and helps keep the fat from blackening.

I discovered something else about fat in the course of my experiments. In a concession to the reigning wisdom about health, I tried sautéing a batch of cutlets in just the sheerest film of fat, much less than I usually use. The results were disastrous. The fat burned, the outside of the chicken became dry and stringy, and the crust was very disappointing, nearly blackened in some spots and a strange yellowish color in others. For sautéed food to become crisp and uniformly brown, the entire surface must stay in contact with the fat; meat has an irregular surface, and any part which is not in contact with the cooking medium — in this case, the oil — is steamed by the moisture generated by the cooking meat, and therefore will not brown. You will need about one-eighth inch of fat in the pan at the start. Assuming that your skillet measures nine inches across the bottom, one and one-half tablespoons each of butter and oil is about right. If your skillet is wider, you may need closer to two tablespoons of each.

Place the butter and oil in the skillet and set it over high heat — everyone's stove is different, of course, but most home burners are quite weak, so when I say "high," I mean "high." Hold the skillet by the handle and swirl it a few times until the butter melts. Now you must pay close attention. At first, the butter will foam, and possibly sputter, as the moisture boils out. As the foam subsides, the butter will become fragrant and begin to darken. At just the moment when the butter turns the pale brown color of roasted peanuts, quickly lay in the chicken cutlets, with the tenderloin side down, holding onto the tapered end as you lay the cutlet down flat.

Maintain the heat at the point where the fat remains at a fast sizzle but does not quite smoke. If you see more than just a wisp or two

WHEN IS IT DONE?

I sautéed some two dozen six-ounce cutlets following the procedure described in this article. In all cases, they were perfect when cooked four minutes on the first side and three to four minutes on the second. It takes a bit of practice to determine if that eighth minute is required, but there are some indications: The thickest part of the breast should feel firm rather than squashy when pressed with a finger. Also look for the emergence of clotted juices in the crack between the tenderloin and the top meat.

Until you learn to judge doneness by appearance, you may cut into one breast to check, but you will be sacrificing both good looks and a bit of juice. You can also use an instant-read thermometer, inserted horizontally or diagonally into the thick part of the breast; the meat is done at 150 degrees, and overdone at 160 degrees. You have about a minute before the temperature goes from the minimum to the maximum.

PHOTOGRAPH BY ERIC ROTH

of smoke, immediately slide the pan off the burner, turn down the heat, and wait a few seconds before returning the pan to the flame. Be advised that there will be some spattering.

Serve with a Sauce

After cooking (*see* "When Is It Done?," page 9), your plump, moist, beautifully brown chicken cutlets may be served just as they are. But it seems a pity to waste the browned bits left in the skillet, when these can so easily be "deglazed" to make a simple, lovely sauce. To make the most basic sauce, pour one-half cup water into the skillet, turn the heat way up, and boil the water until it's reduced by half; use a wooden spoon to scrape up the browned bits. For a more refined and flavorful sauce, replace the water either with wine (virtually any kind), brandy, vinegar, chicken broth, heavy cream, or fruit juice. After reducing the liquid, take the pan off the heat and swirl in one or more tablespoons of soft butter to give the sauce added richness and deeper flavor. Once you try the quick and easy deglazing sauces below, you'll have no trouble thinking up 50 more.

If you wish to use butter to thicken a deglazing sauce — in addition to enriching its flavor — you must observe these rules: The sauce must be slightly syrupy, and be well reduced; it takes about three tablespoons of butter to thicken one-third cup of sauce. Add the butter off the heat, and do not return the pan to the heat once the butter is incorporated, or the sauce will separate and thin out. Finally, swirl the pan by the handle or stir very gently until the butter is incorporated and the sauce thickened. Note also that acidic deglazing sauces — those made with a high proportion of lemon juice or vinegar — are more stable and thicker than others.

GETTING READY TO SAUTÉ

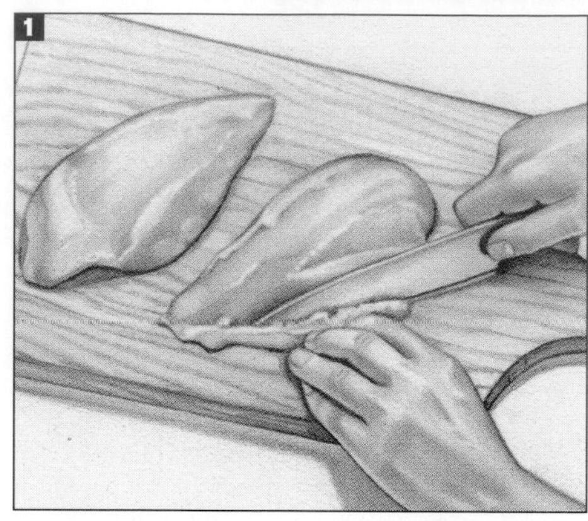

1. To prepare a chicken cutlet, lay it tenderloin side down and smooth the top with your fingers. Any fat will slide to the periphery, where it is easy to see; trim it with a knife.

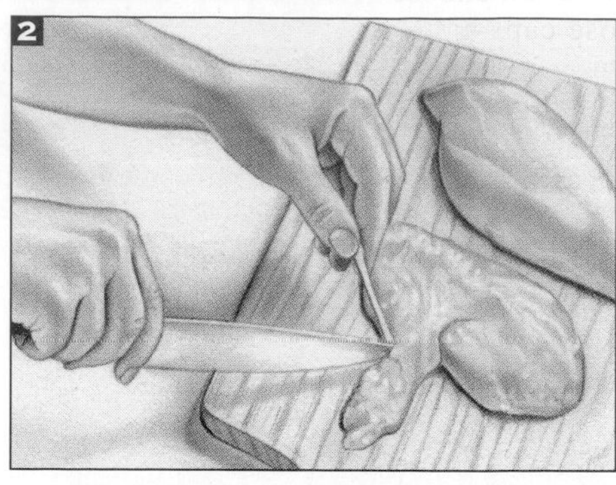

2. To remove the tendon, turn the cutlet tenderloin side up and peel back the thick half of the tenderloin so it lies top down on the work surface. Use the point of a paring knife to cut around the tip of the tendon to expose it, then scrape the tendon free with the knife.

MASTER RECIPE FOR SAUTÉED CHICKEN BREAST CUTLETS

Serves 4

- 4 chicken breast cutlets (1½ pounds), trimmed, tendons removed, rinsed and thoroughly dried
- Salt and ground black pepper
- ¼ cup all-purpose flour
- 1½ tablespoons unsalted butter
- 1½ tablespoons neutral vegetable oil or olive oil

1. Sprinkle 1 teaspoon salt and ¼ to ½ teaspoon pepper on both sides of the cutlets. Measure flour onto a plate or pie tin. Working with one cutlet at a time, press both sides into flour. Make sure tenderloin is tucked beneath and fused to main portion of breast. Pick up cutlet from tapered end; shake gently to remove excess flour.

2. Heat butter and oil in a heavy-bottomed skillet measuring at least 9 inches across bottom. Swirl skillet over high heat until butter has melted. Continue to heat skillet until butter stops foaming and has just begun to color. Lay cutlets in skillet, tenderloin side down.

3. Maintain medium-high heat, so fat sizzles but does not smoke, and sauté cutlets until browned on one side, about 4 minutes. Turn cutlets with tongs (a fork will pierce meat); cook on other side until meat feels firm when pressed and clotted juices begin to emerge around tenderloin, 3 to 4 minutes. Serve immediately, or, if making one of the sauces, transfer cutlets to a plate, keep warm in oven set at lowest temperature possible, and continue with recipe.

OAXACAN-STYLE SAUCE WITH CLOVES AND CINNAMON

Serves 4

- 1 small onion, minced (about ½ cup)
- 2 large or 3 small jalapeño peppers, seeded and minced
- 2 garlic cloves, minced (about 1 tablespoon)
- ½ teaspoon ground cinnamon
- ¼ teaspoon (scant) ground cloves
- ½ cup chicken stock or low-salt canned broth
- 1 tablespoon cider vinegar
- ½ cup unsweetened crushed pineapple, undrained
- ⅓ cup pimiento-stuffed green olives, sliced thin
- ¼ cup currants or chopped raisins
- ¼ cup crushed tomatoes
- 1½ tablespoons minced fresh cilantro
- 3 tablespoons pine nuts, toasted (optional)

1. Follow Master Recipe for Sautéed Chicken Breast Cutlets. Without discarding fat, set skillet over medium heat. Add onions and jalapeños and sauté until softened, about 1 minute. Stir in garlic, cinnamon, and cloves and cook until garlic softens, about 30 seconds longer. Add stock and vinegar and bring mixture to a boil, scraping bottom of skillet with a wooden spoon to incorporate browned bits. Add pineapple, olives, currants, and tomatoes, increase heat to high, and boil sauce, stirring, until thick, about 3 minutes.

2. Return cutlets to pan, spoon sauce over cutlets. Cover and let cutlets stand over very low heat to blend flavors, about 5 minutes. Adjust seasonings; transfer cutlets to a plate, spoon sauce over cutlets, and sprinkle with cilantro and optional pine nuts; serve immediately.

LEMON-CAPER SAUCE

Serves 4

- 1 shallot or scallion, minced (about 2 tablespoons)
- 1 cup chicken stock or low-salt canned broth
- ¼ cup juice from 1 large lemon
- 2 tablespoons small capers, drained
- 3 tablespoons unsalted butter, softened

Follow Master Recipe for Sautéed Chicken Breast Cutlets. Without discarding fat, set skillet over medium heat. Add shallots; sauté until softened, about 1 minute. Increase heat to high, add stock, and scrape skillet bottom with wooden spatula or spoon to loosen browned bits. Add lemon juice and capers; boil until liquid reduces to about ⅓ cup, 3 to 4 minutes. Add any accumulated chicken juices; reduce sauce again to ⅓ cup. Off heat, swirl in softened butter until it melts and thickens sauce. Spoon sauce over cutlets; serve immediately.

SHERRY-CREAM SAUCE WITH MUSHROOMS

Serves 4

White wine, champagne, port, or Madeira can be substituted for the sherry in this classic

ILLUSTRATIONS BY MICHELE AMATRULA

chicken sauté; in that case, the mace should be omitted or replaced by a speck of nutmeg. For best flavor, choose "ripe" button mushrooms whose caps have darkened and lifted away from the stems, or use "wild" mushrooms of any kind.

- 2 shallots or scallions, minced (about ¼ cup)
- 8 ounces mushrooms, sliced thin (about 2½ cups)
- ⅓ cup sherry, preferably cream or Amontillado
- ½ cup chicken stock or low-salt canned broth
- 1 cup heavy cream
- 2 tablespoons minced parsley leaves
- Pinch of ground mace
- Salt and ground black or white pepper
- 1 small piece of lemon

Follow Master Recipe for Sautéed Chicken Breast Cutlets. Without discarding fat, set skillet over medium heat. Add shallots; sauté until softened, about 1 minute. Increase heat to high, add mushrooms, sauté until limp and brown, 2 to 3 minutes. Add sherry; boil until sherry completely evaporates, about 1 minute. Add stock and cream; boil, stirring frequently, until sauce reduces to about ⅔ cup and is thick enough to lightly coat a spoon, about 5 to 6 minutes. Add any accumulated chicken juices; reduce sauce to previous consistency. Stir in parsley and mace and season to taste with salt, pepper, and drops of lemon juice. Spoon sauce over cutlets and serve immediately.

TOMATO-BASIL SAUCE WITH CAPERS

Serves 4

- 2–3 shallots or scallions, minced (about ⅓ cup)
- 3–4 garlic cloves, minced (about 2 tablespoons)
- 2 medium-large tomatoes (about 1 pound), seeded and chopped (about 2 cups)
- ¼ cup dry white wine or 3 tablespoons dry Vermouth
- 2 tablespoons small capers, drained
- 2 tablespoons shredded basil leaves or minced parsley leaves
- Salt and ground black pepper

Follow Master Recipe for Sautéed Chicken Breast Cutlets. Without discarding fat, set skillet over medium heat. Add shallots and sauté until softened, about 1 minute. Stir in garlic, then tomatoes. Increase heat to high and cook, stirring frequently, until tomatoes have given up most of their juice, forming a lumpy puree, about 2 minutes. Add wine, capers, and any accumulated chicken juices; boil sauce until thick enough to mound slightly in a spoon, about 2 minutes. Stir in herbs and season with salt and pepper. Spoon sauce over chicken and serve immediately.

ASIAN-STYLE SWEET AND SOUR PAN SAUCE

Serves 4

- 2–3 cloves garlic (1½ tablespoons), minced
- 2 teaspoons minced fresh ginger
- ¼ teaspoon crushed red pepper flakes
- ¼ cup dark brown sugar, packed firm
- ¼ cup distilled white vinegar
- 2 tablespoons soy sauce
- ½ teaspoon anchovy paste or Thai or Vietnamese fish sauce
- 4 medium scallions, including the tender green parts, sliced thin

Place first 3 ingredients on a cutting board; mince further to pulverize the pepper. Follow Master Recipe for Sautéed Chicken Breast Cutlets. Without draining fat, return skillet to medium heat; add garlic mixture and sauté until softened, about 1 minute. Increase heat to high; add next 4 ingredients and accumulated pan juices; boil, stirring to loosen browned bits from pan bottom, until mixture thickens to a light syrup, less than a minute. Pour sauce over chicken cutlets, scatter scallions on top, and serve immediately.

PEACH SALSA

Serves 4

- 2 small peaches or nectarines, peeled and cut into small dice (about 1 cup)
- ½ large cucumber (5 to 6 ounces), seeded, and cut into small dice (about ⅔ cup)
- 1 plum tomato, seeded and cut into small dice (about ¼ cup)
- 2 tablespoons chopped red onion
- 1 serrano or jalapeño chile pepper, seeded and minced
- 4 teaspoons juice from 1 lime
- Salt
- 1 cup chicken stock or low-salt canned broth
- 2 teaspoons juice from 1 small lemon (or additional lime juice)

1. Mix first 6 ingredients in a medium bowl. (Can cover and refrigerate up to 24 hours.) Shortly before serving, season the salsa with ¼ teaspoon salt or to taste; set aside at room temperature and follow Master Recipe for Sautéed Chicken Breast Cutlets.

2. Pour off any remaining chicken fat, set skillet over high heat; add stock and boil until it reduces to ⅓ cup, scraping up browned bits from pan bottom. Add any accumulated chicken juices and reduce sauce to previous consistency; stir in citrus juice. Moisten chicken with pan reduction. Spoon salsa alongside chicken and serve immediately. ■

Stephen Schmidt, a caterer and cooking teacher, is the author of *Master Recipes* (Ballantine, 1987).

FANNING CHICKEN BREASTS

It isn't difficult to make an eye-pleasing presentation with a simply sautéed chicken cutlet. Using a 10-inch chef's knife, cut the breast on the bias as shown below, cutting all the way through the breast. Then arrange the segments in a fan shape, spreading them out on the plate around a central axis.

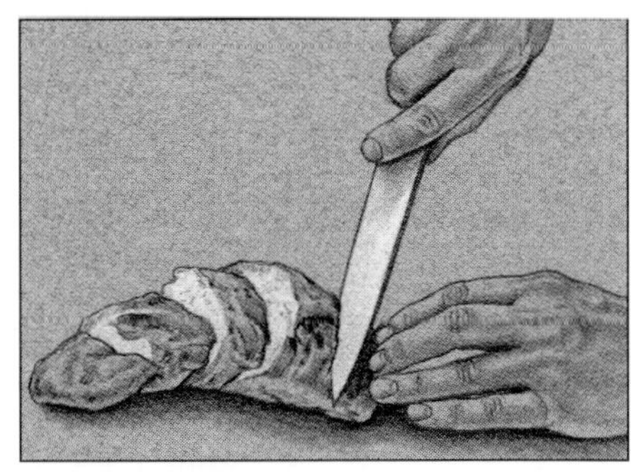

IS FLOURING NECESSARY?

Following the procedure in the Master Recipe, we sautéed both floured and unfloured chicken cutlets to determine any differences in taste, texture, and juiciness.

We immediately noticed a more dramatic sizzle when the unfloured cutlet hit the pan, and while both cutlets sizzled during cooking, the unfloured cutlet "spit" a bit more. The flour seems to offer a barrier between the fat in the pan and the moisture in the cutlet. The floured cutlet also moved about more freely; while neither version stuck to the skillet, the floured cutlet skated easily when we swirled it about.

When cooked, the floured cutlet displayed a consistently brown crust, almost resembling a skin. The uncoated breast was a spotty brown. Both breasts were equally moist, but the floured cutlet offered better mouth feel with its contrasting crispy exterior and juicy, tender meat. The floured cutlet, reminiscent of fried chicken, was also more flavorful than its uncoated counterpart.

Our advice: flour those cutlets.

—Pam Anderson

ILLUSTRATION BY ALAN WITSCHONKE

MASTER CLASS

30-Minute Peking Duck

California chef David SooHoo simplifies this classic Chinese-restaurant dish for home preparation.

There is a good reason why some dishes remain popular for centuries. In the case of Peking Duck, which dates back at least four hundred years, it is the alluring combination of crackling pieces of crisp skin and juicy (but not fatty) slices of meat. Most Americans know this dish as a Chinese-restaurant classic. However, with a few simple modifications, an excellent Peking Duck can be prepared at home with minimal fuss.

This technique was developed by California chef David SooHoo and calls for equipment rarely seen in the kitchen — an electric fan and a metal hanger from the dry cleaners. SooHoo uses these modern tools to cut drying time from three days to several hours. Best of all, his streamlined preparation (which takes less than 30 minutes of hands-on time) guarantees that the duck will have crisp, dark skin and moist, flavorful meat.

Even in SooHoo's modernized version of Peking Duck, there are two steps, in addition to the drying process, that will be unfamiliar to most American cooks. The first is a part of the traditional recipe, and involves pumping air into the bird to separate the skin from the meat. "The idea is to lift the skin from the meat so it will crisp when cooked, not to make a balloon," cautions SooHoo, who uses a basketball pump or even a straw for the task, and says not to worry if the air escapes once it has done the job.

The second unfamiliar step is SooHoo's trademark wok bath. For this, the chef fills a large wok or stockpot with boiling water and vinegar, then ladles the hot liquid over the duck's skin to open the pores — look for goose bumps as you do this. "The vinegar literally pulls the fat right out of the bird," says SooHoo.

When the bird is done, SooHoo likes to carve separate slices of skin and meat from the roasted bird and then reassemble them on the carcass in the traditional manner. Of course, for quicker service, simply place separate slices of skin and meat directly on a platter. Either way, it is a delicious feast.

The son of a prominent Sacramento restaurant family, chef David SooHoo grew up on traditional American food prepared with a Chinese twist. "My family celebrated Thanksgiving with a turkey — but we air-dried the bird and seasoned it with soy sauce," he recalls.

PEKING DUCK

Serves 4

Traditional recipes call for a duck with both the head and feet still attached. Whole birds are available at Asian butcher shops in most major cities. This recipe can also be prepared using a supermarket duck. To make two ducks, double the amount of marinade, cilantro, and scallions but keep ingredients for the wok bath the same.

Garlic-Ginger Marinade

- 4 cloves garlic, peeled
- 2 ½-inch slices ginger root, peeled
- 1 tablespoon salt
- 2 tablespoons sugar
- ½ teaspoon five-spice powder or 1 whole star anise
- 1 tablespoon ground bean paste
- 2 tablespoons rice wine or white wine

Peking Duck

- 1 four- to five-pound duck (with or without head and legs)
- 1 small bunch cilantro, leaves and stems (about 1 cup)
- 2 whole scallions, roots trimmed
- ½ cup distilled white vinegar
- ½ cup cornstarch
- 1 tablespoon Kitchen Bouquet
- ½ cup sugar or honey

1. Puree marinade ingredients in a blender or food processor until smooth; set aside.

2. Wet a 6-inch piece of string and tie it tightly around the neck to stop the flow of air. If you have bought a duck without a head, gather excess fat around the neck and tie it tightly together as close as possible to the body.

3. Pull out fat that lines the sides of the back cavity and discard. Pour marinade into open cavity and stuff bird with cilantro and scallions.

4. Pierce the two flaps on either side of the back cavity with a 6-inch long wooden or metal skewer. Thread the skewer through the two flaps of skin several times to close the cavity (*see* illustration 1, page 13). Tighten seal by tying an 18-inch piece of wet string under the skewer several times (illustration 2).

5. Insert the needle of a basketball pump (or a thin straw) between the two flaps of skin and into the back cavity. Pump several times to lift the skin from the meat (illustration 3). Do not overinflate. As long as skin has visibly detached from meat it does not matter if the air slowly escapes from the duck.

6. Fold up both ends of a metal hanger from the dry cleaners. Slide ends of hanger under the wings of the bird (illustration 4). Secure hanger by tying an 18-inch piece of wet string through the ends of the hanger and around the bird (illustration 5).

7. Bring 1 gallon water and ½ cup vinegar to boil in a large wok or stockpot. Use hanger to hold duck above wok and ladle hot liquid over the surface of the duck until goose bumps are visible on the skin, 1 to 2 minutes (illustration 6). Do not let duck rest for long periods in the water or it will begin to cook. Set duck aside and discard all but 2 quarts of liquid from wok. Dissolve cornstarch in 1 cup cold water and whisk mixture into liquid in the wok. Whisk in Kitchen Bouquet and sugar and stir until mixture is smooth. Use hanger to hold duck above wok and ladle hot paste over skin. Make sure that all parts of the duck are coated with the thick brown liquid.

8. Hang duck away from the sunlight in a cool, dry place (either over a work sink or a cov-

PHOTOGRAPH BY KENT LACIN MEDIA SERVICES

ering of newspaper.) Place an electric fan set to high about 1 foot from the duck. Blow-dry, turning duck once, until skin between the leg and belly is translucent, 4 to 8 hours depending on the heat and humidity. (Duck can be dried overnight and then refrigerated during the day until cooking time.)

9. Preheat oven to 350 degrees. Untie string that secures the hanger, discard string and hanger. Wrap head (if present), legs, and wings with aluminum foil to prevent them from burning.

10. Roast duck for 1 hour. Remove foil and continue cooking until meat juices from leg run clear, 15 to 30 minutes more depending on size of duck.

11. Remove and discard all strings and skewers. Remove head (if present) and use as a garnish for the meat platter, if desired. Detach legs and wings and carve meat from both. Slice skin and meat from the body and place all carvings on a large platter. ■

How to Prepare Duck for Air-Drying

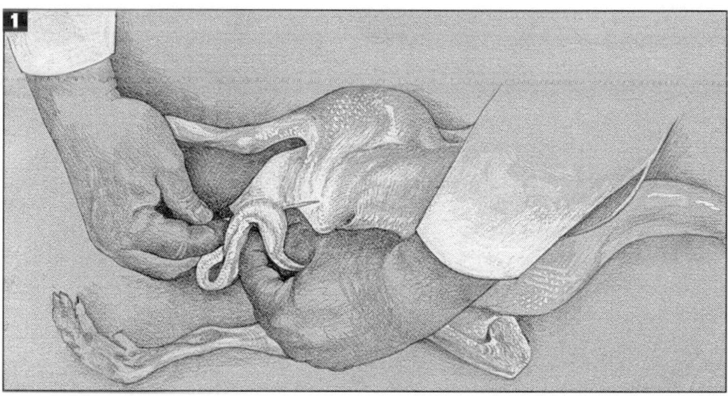

1. Thread a 6-inch skewer through the two flaps of skin on either side of the back cavity several times to close the cavity.

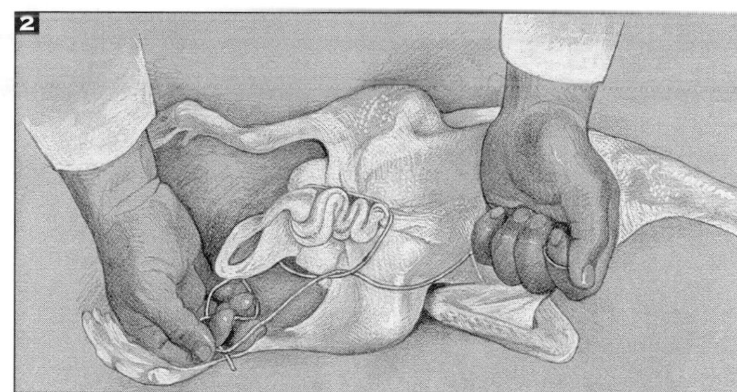

2. Tie an 18-inch piece of wet string under the skewer several times.

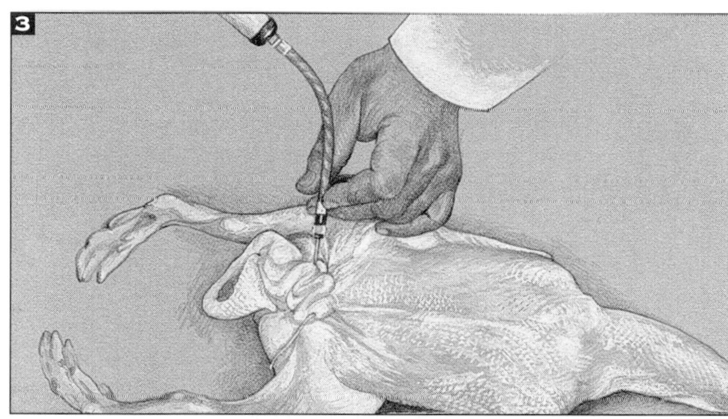

3. Insert the needle of a basketball pump or a thin straw between the two flaps of skin and into the back cavity. Pump several times to lift the skin from the meat.

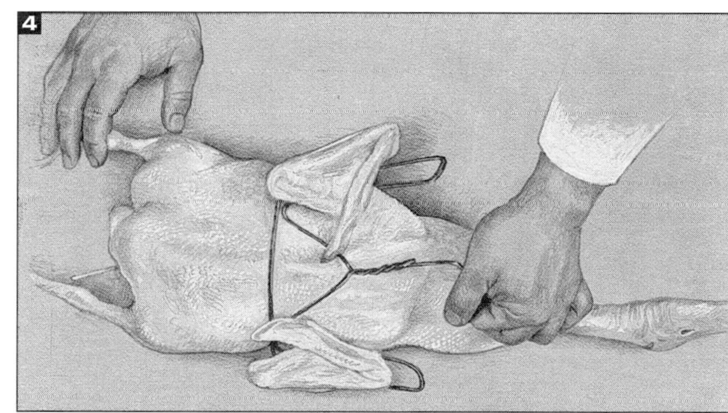

4. Fold both ends of a metal clothes hanger and slide them under the wings of the bird.

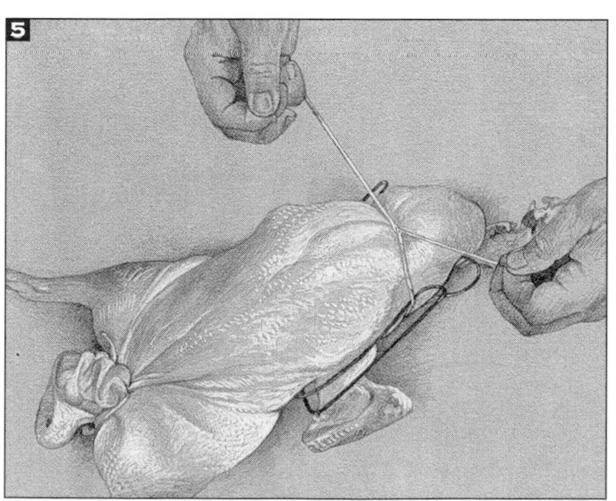

5. Tie an 18-inch piece of wet string through the ends of the hanger and around the bird.

6. Hold the duck above the wok bath and ladle hot liquid over the surface of the duck until goose bumps are visible on the skin.

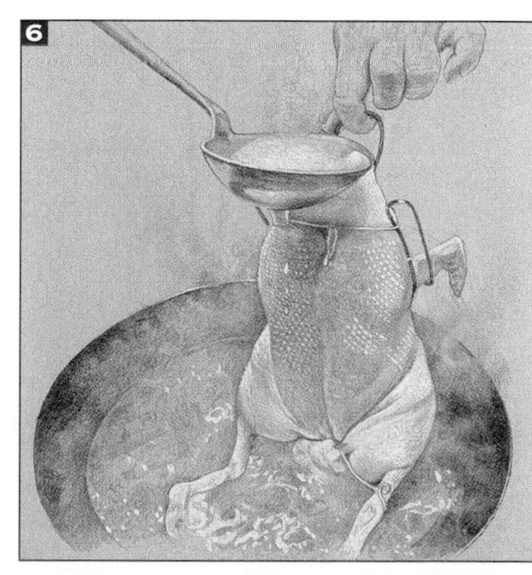

ILLUSTRATIONS BY ANATOLY

COOK'S FIELD GUIDE

Fresh Mushrooms for Cooking

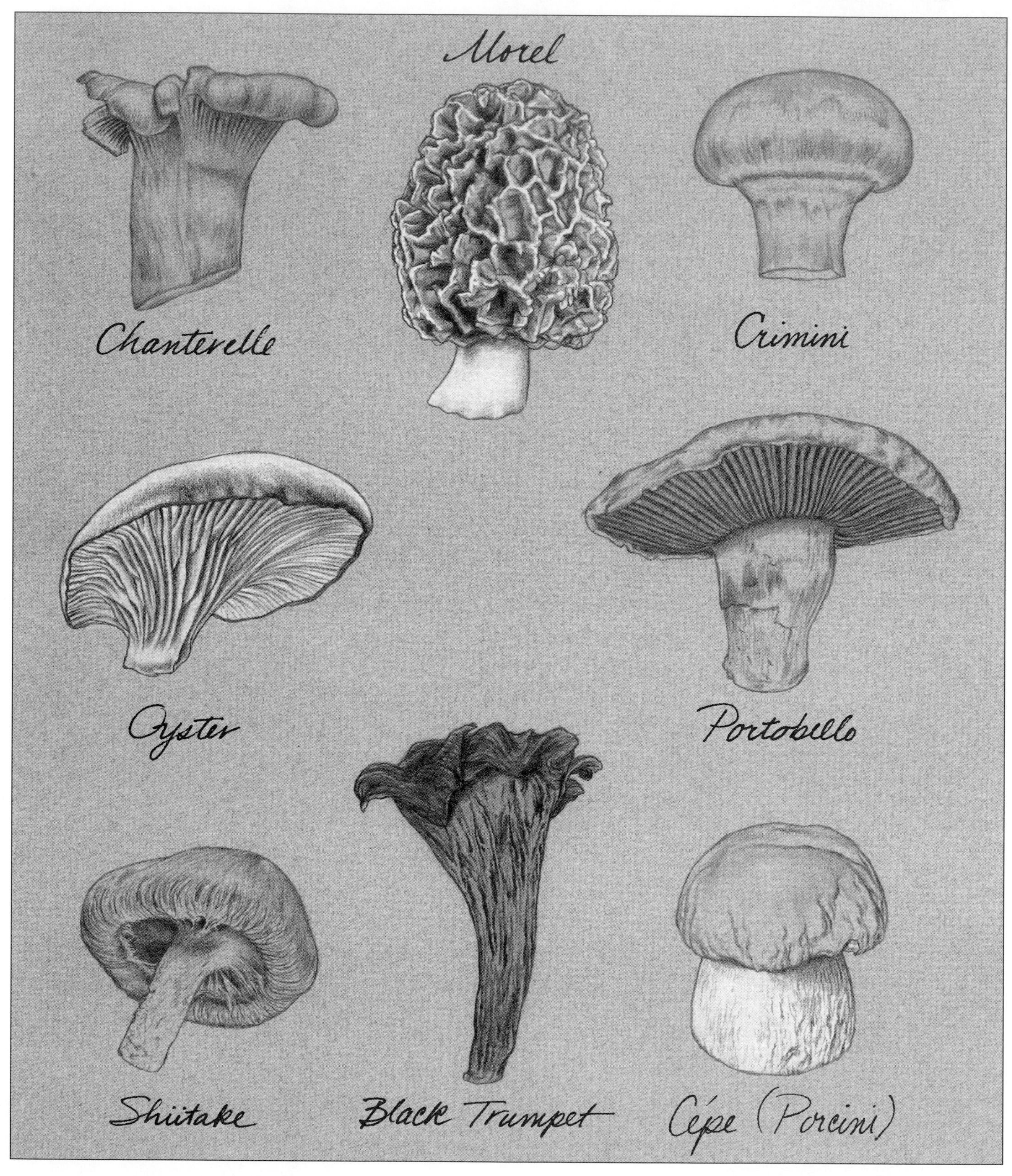

ILLUSTRATION BY ALAN WITSCHONKE

Three Filled Pastas

In one hour, you can make ravioli, tortelli, or tortellini by following these 16 step-by-step illustrations.

BY JACK BISHOP

Making pasta dough from scratch and then rolling, shaping, and stuffing it to produce ravioli, tortellini, and other varieties will never be quick. But stuffing pasta at home is simple, and the entire process — from making the pasta and filling to combining the two — can often be completed in about an hour. Best of all, the results put the frozen (and so-called "fresh") filled pastas sold in supermarkets — with their lack of flavor and rubbery texture — to shame. Truly fresh pasta is incomparably better, with more tender texture and richer flavor.

There are only two essential ingredients for pasta dough: flour and eggs. I recommend all-purpose flour and a ratio of two-thirds cup flour to one large egg. This yields a dough that is elastic and strong enough to roll and manipulate, is not sticky, and is wonderfully tender after cooking. Slight variations in egg size or in heat and humidity can affect results, but after making pasta once or twice you'll know whether it is too wet or dry.

Pasta making is greatly speeded up by using modern cooking tools. I use a food processor to combine ingredients and to knead the dough, and a manual pasta machine — the Atlas brand is by far the most common — to roll it out.

Once the pasta is made, you can fill it with almost any combination of ground meats, vegetables, cheeses, herbs, and/or spices, and you should feel free to invent your own stuffings. Just make sure that the mixture is thick, not runny; that you use egg yolk as a binder; and that you season it generously so that it contrasts with the bland pasta.

When filling pasta, resist the temptation to overload it with filling. Bulging ravioli are difficult to seal and may break when cooked. A fluted pastry wheel is best for cutting ravioli and twisted tortelli; use a pizza wheel for cutting out squares for tortellini, and seal it with your fingers. A handy device called the KrimpKut Sealer (*see* Sources and Resources, page 32) does an excellent job of sealing and scalloping the edges of ravioli in one motion.

For illustrated instructions on making several filled pasta shapes, see pages 16 and 17. One word of advice — don't worry if your filled pastas are slightly irregular; it will only add to their homemade appeal.

MASTER RECIPE FOR PASTA DOUGH

Makes about 1 pound fresh pasta

Individual recipes give yields in terms of pieces of stuffed pasta, but all three variations produce enough pasta to feed six as a main course and eight or even ten as a first course. To freeze the stuffed pastas, place them on a lightly floured cookie sheet and freeze. Transfer frozen pastas to zipper-lock bags and return to freezer. Make sure to add at least three minutes to the cooking time when cooking frozen pastas.

2 cups all-purpose flour
3 large eggs, beaten

1. Pulse flour in workbowl of a food processor fitted with the metal blade to evenly distribute. Add eggs; process until dough forms a rough ball, about 30 seconds. (If dough resembles small pebbles, add water, ½ teaspoon at a time; if dough sticks to side of workbowl, add flour, 1 tablespoon at a time, and process until dough forms a rough ball.)

2. Turn dough ball and small bits out onto a dry work surface; knead until dough is smooth, 1 to 2 minutes. Cover with plastic wrap and set aside (*see* steps 1 through 3, below).

3. Cut about ¼ of dough from ball and flatten into a disk; rewrap remaining dough. Run dough through widest setting of a manual pasta machine. Bring ends of dough towards the middle and press down to seal. Run dough, open end first, through the widest setting again. Fold, seal, and roll again. Without folding, run pasta through widest setting about two more

KNEADING DOUGH IN A FOOD PROCESSOR

1. If after 30 seconds the dough resembles small pebbles, it is too dry. With motor running, add one-half teaspoon of water. Repeat one more time if necessary.

2. If dough sticks to the sides of the workbowl, it is too wet. Add one tablespoon flour at a time until dough is no longer tacky.

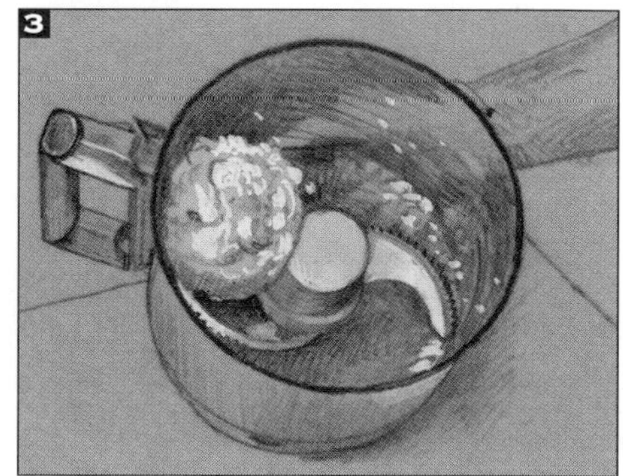

3. Dough that is of proper moistness will come together in one large mass. If there are some small bits that remain unincorporated, turn contents of workbowl onto a board and knead together.

ILLUSTRATIONS BY ANATOLY

times, until dough is smooth. If at any point dough is sticky, lightly dust with flour. Continue to run dough through machine; narrow the setting each time, until you use last setting on machine, and outline of your hand is visible through dough sheet (see steps 1A through 1E, right).

4. Follow instructions below for cutting and shaping each pasta. After one sheet of pasta has been cut, stuffed, and set aside, roll out another quarter of the dough ball, along with trimmings from previous sheet.

TWISTED TORTELLI

Makes about 36

Many Americans are not familiar with this pasta from northern Italy. The shape is extremely easy to prepare and takes little time to execute; it's twisted form resembles candy wrappers.

- 1 pound fresh pasta sheets
- 1 filling recipe
- 1 tablespoon salt
- 1 sauce recipe

1. Follow steps 4A through 4C, page 17, to form tortelli.

2. Bring 4 quarts water to boil in a large stockpot. Add salt and half the pasta. Cook until twisted ends are *al dente,* about 6 minutes. With a slotted spoon, transfer tortelli to warmed bowls or plates; add sauce. Meanwhile, put remaining tortelli in boiling water and repeat cooking process. (Or bring two pots of water to boil and cook both batches simultaneously.) Serve immediately.

RAVIOLI

Makes about 60

This recipe produces two-inch square ravioli with three fluted edges and one folded edge. The folded edge may be trimmed with a fluted pastry wheel if you like.

- 1 pound fresh pasta sheets
- 1 filling recipe
- 1 tablespoon salt
- 1 sauce recipe

1. Follow steps 2A through 2D, page 17, to form ravioli.

2. Bring 4 quarts water to boil in a large stockpot. Add salt and half the pasta. Cook until doubled edges are *al dente,* 4 to 5 minutes. With a slotted spoon, transfer ravioli to warmed bowls or plates; add sauce. Meanwhile, put remaining ravioli in boiling water and repeat cooking process. (Or bring two pots of water to boil and cook both batches simultaneously.) Serve immediately.

TORTELLINI

Makes about 90

Tortellini's rounded shape is more labor intensive than either ravioli or tortelli, making it a good choice when there are several people

Shaping Filled Pastas

Rolling Out Pasta with a Manual Machine

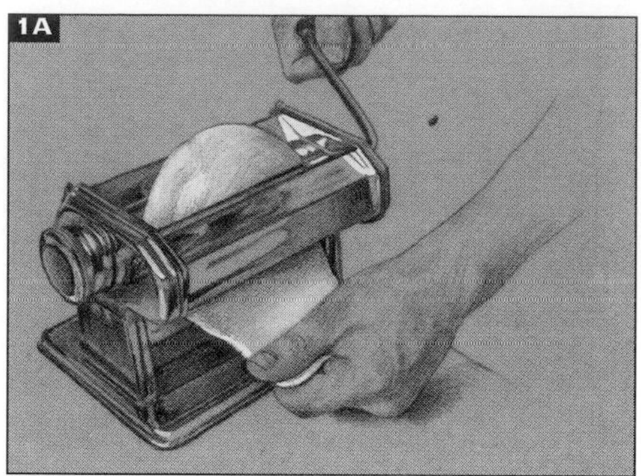

1A. Cut about one-quarter of dough from ball and flatten into a disk. Run disk through rollers set to widest position (setting one on the Atlas machine).

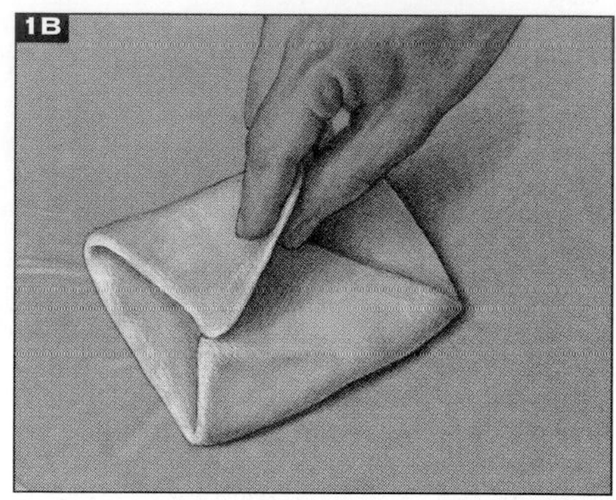

1B. Bring ends of the dough towards the middle and press down to seal.

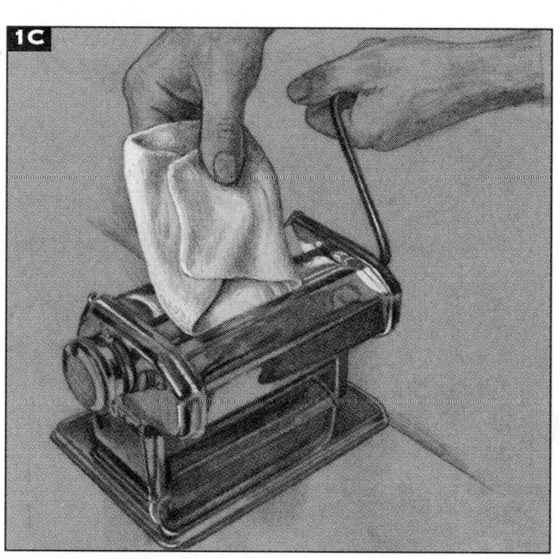

1C. Feed open end of pasta through the rollers. Repeat steps 1B and 1C.

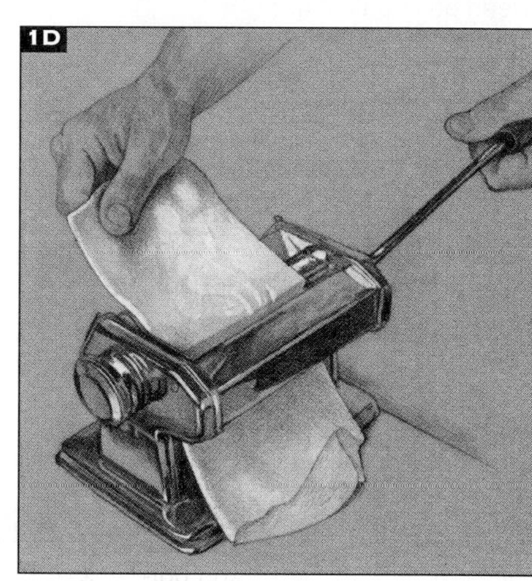

1D. Without folding again, run pasta through widest setting twice or until dough is smooth. If dough is at all sticky, lightly dust it with flour.

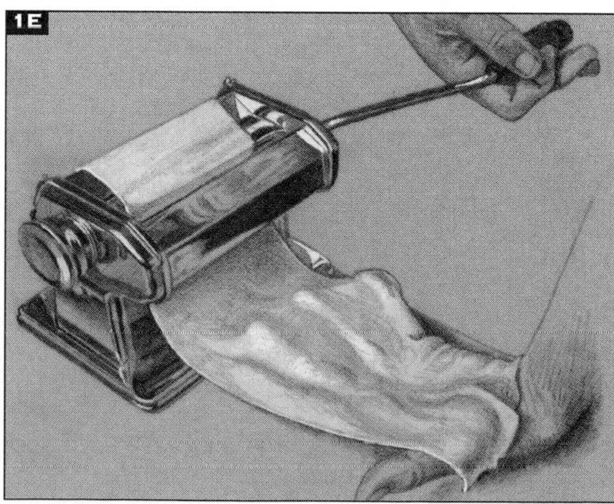

1E. Begin to roll pasta thinner by putting it through the machine repeatedly, narrowing the setting each time. Roll until dough is thin and satiny (setting seven on the Atlas machine), dusting with flour if sticky. You should be able to see the outline of your hand through the pasta.

Making Ravioli

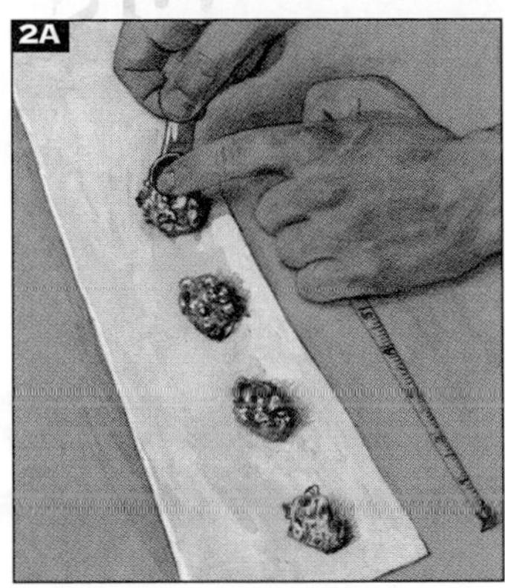

2A. Use a pizza wheel or sharp knife to cut sheets into long rectangles measuring four inches across. Place small balls of filling (about one rounded teaspoon each) in a line one inch from the bottom of the pasta sheet. Leave one and one-quarter inches between each ball of filling.

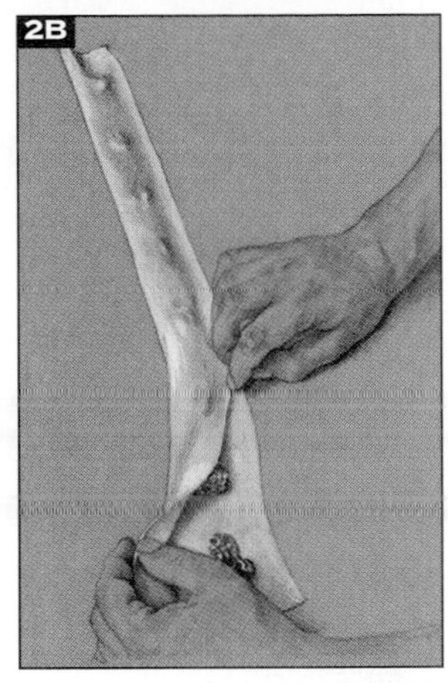

2B. Fold over the top of the pasta and line it up with the bottom edge. Seal bottom and the two open sides with your finger.

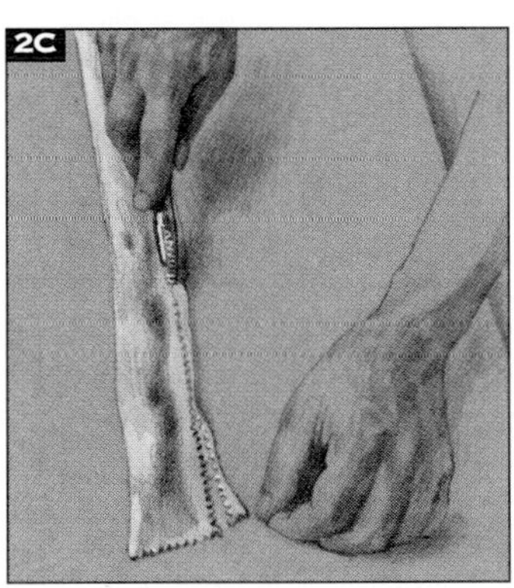

2C. Use fluted pastry wheel to cut along the two sides and bottom of the sealed pasta sheet.

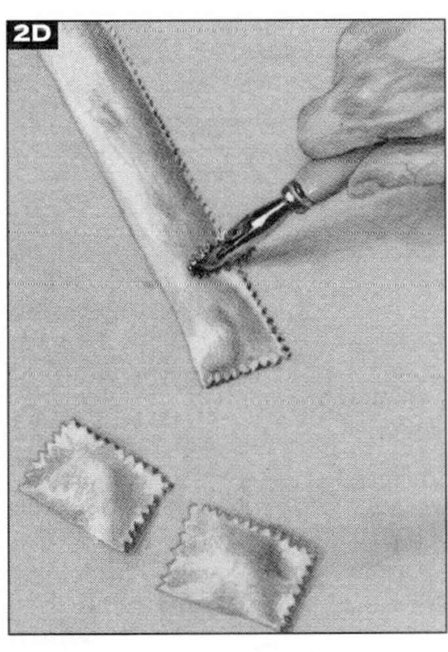

2D. Run pastry wheel between balls of filling to cut out the ravioli.

Making Tortellini

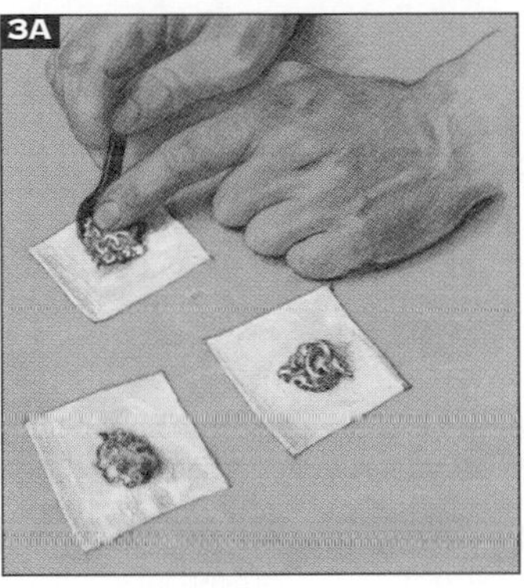

3A. Use a pizza wheel or sharp knife to cut pasta sheet into two and one-half inch squares. Lift one square from work surface (otherwise it may stick when stuffed) and place it on another clean part of the counter. Place one-half teaspoon filling in the center of square.

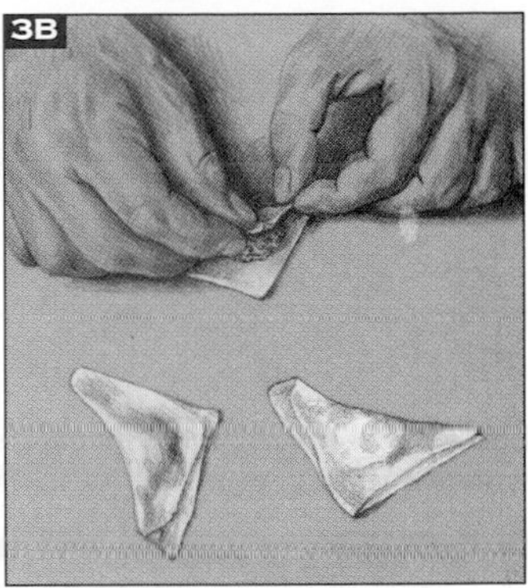

3B. Fold square diagonally in half to make two triangles. Make sure that the top piece of dough covers the filling but leaves a thin border of the bottom triangle exposed. Seal edges with finger.

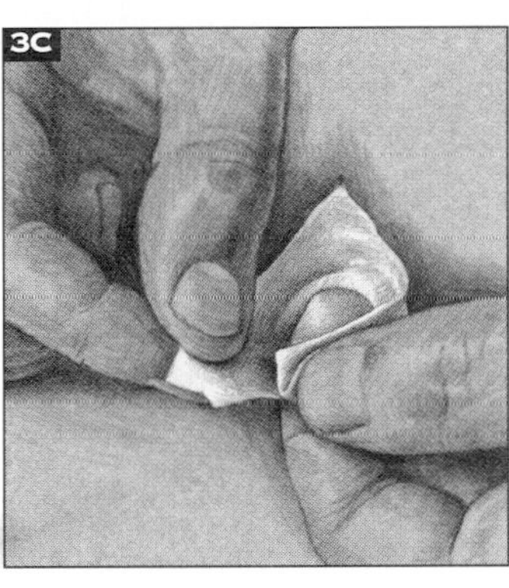

3C. Lift filled triangle from counter and wrap the back of the triangle around the top of your index finger. Squeeze the two bottom corners of the triangle together.

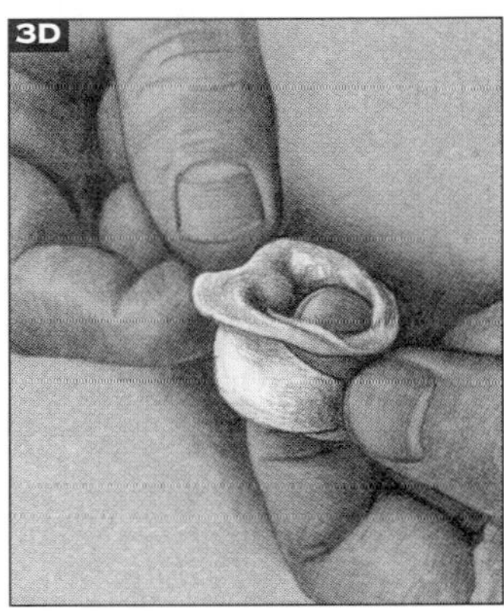

3D. As you pull back the top peak of the triangle, gently fold over the top ring of pasta so that the stuffing is completely enclosed. Slide the filled pasta off your finger.

Making Twisted Tortelli

4A. Use a fluted pastry wheel to cut pasta sheet into rectangles measuring four-by-five inches. Lift one rectangle from work surface (otherwise it may stick when stuffed) and place it on another clean part of the counter. Place a rounded tablespoon of filling in the center of rectangle.

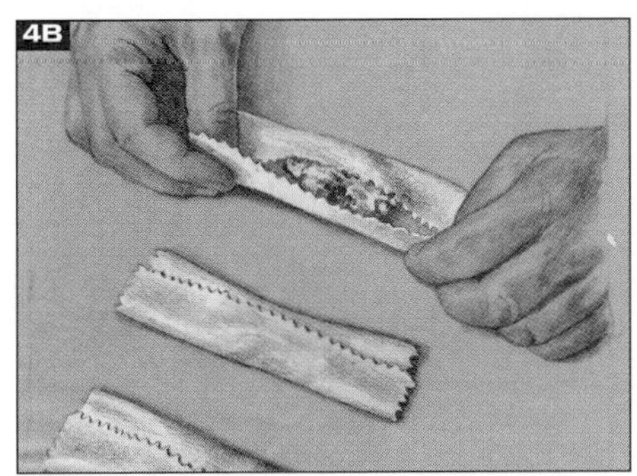

4B. With a long side facing you, fold the bottom third of the rectangle over the filling. Next, fold the top third over the filling so that it just barely overlaps with the folded piece from the bottom.

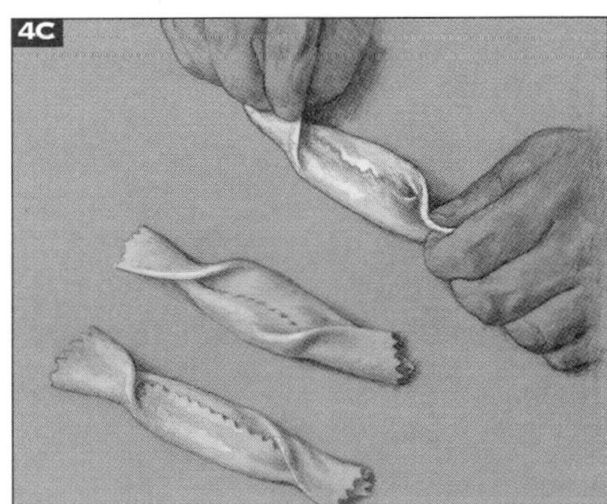

4C. Place hands at either end of the pasta and twist in opposite directions to form candy-wrapper shape.

Illustrations by Anatoly

working in the kitchen. This recipe produces relatively large tortellini; to make tortellini for soup, cut pasta into one and one-half- or two-inch squares.

- 1 pound fresh pasta sheets
- ½ filling recipe
- 1 tablespoon salt
- 1 sauce recipe

1. Follow steps 3A through 3D, page 17, to form tortellini.

2. Bring 4 quarts water to boil in a large stockpot. Add salt and half the pasta. Cook until tortellini are *al dente,* about 4 minutes. With a slotted spoon, transfer tortellini directly to warm bowls or plates; add sauce. Meanwhile, put remaining tortellini in boiling water and repeat cooking process. (Or bring two pots of water to boil and cook both batches simultaneously.) Serve immediately.

SPINACH AND RICOTTA FILLING FOR PASTA

Makes about 2½ cups

This filling works well with either the tomato or brown butter sauce (*see* recipes, below). Other leafy vegetables such as kale and Swiss chard may be substituted for the spinach. Three-quarter cups frozen chopped spinach may be used if desired; defrost spinach and squeeze out excess liquid before cooking it with the onions.

- ¾ pound fresh spinach leaves, stemmed and washed
- 2 tablespoons butter
- ½ small onion, minced (about ¼ cup)
- Salt
- 1 cup ricotta
- ¾ cup grated Parmesan cheese
- 1 egg yolk

1. Place cleaned spinach leaves and any water that clings to them in a nonreactive soup kettle. Cover and cook over medium heat until spinach wilts, about 5 minutes. Cool spinach slightly, squeeze out the excess liquid, and chop fine; set aside.

2. Heat butter in a small skillet. Add onions and sauté until translucent, about 5 minutes. Stir in chopped spinach and salt to taste; cook for 1 minute.

3. Transfer spinach mixture to a medium bowl. Stir in remaining ingredients; adjust seasonings, and set aside. (Can be covered and refrigerated overnight.)

SQUASH, PROSCIUTTO, AND PARMESAN FILLING FOR PASTA

Makes about 2½ cups

Fresh sage perfumes this autumnal stuffing that is best paired with the brown butter sauce (*see* below). Other hard squash or pumpkin also work well in this filling. You can also substitute frozen pureed squash for the fresh squash. Two 12-ounce packages of frozen squash cooked over medium heat for 10 minutes (to thicken the squash puree) yields about two cups, more than the one and one-half cups you'll need in this recipe.

- 2 small acorn squash (about 1½ pounds), halved and seeded
- ¼ pound prosciutto, minced fine
- 1 egg yolk
- 1 cup grated Parmesan cheese
- 1 tablespoon minced fresh sage leaves
- ⅛ teaspoon grated nutmeg
- Salt to taste

1. Heat oven to 400 degrees. Place squash, cut sides down, on a small baking sheet; bake until tender, about 35 minutes. Cool squash, then scoop out the flesh (about 1½ cups).

2. Mix squash with remaining ingredients; set aside. (Can be covered and refrigerated overnight.)

MEAT AND RICOTTA FILLING WITH BASIL FOR PASTA

Makes about 2½ cups

This filling is especially delicious with beef, veal, or pork. Use any combination of these meats and pair this hearty filling with tomato sauce (*see* below).

- 1 tablespoon olive oil
- 2 garlic cloves, minced
- ½ pound ground meat
- 1 cup ricotta
- ¼ cup grated Parmesan cheese
- 1 egg yolk
- ¼ cup minced fresh basil leaves
- Salt and ground black pepper

Heat oil in a medium skillet. Add garlic and sauté until lightly colored, about 1 minute. Add meat; cook over medium-high heat, stirring to break up larger pieces, until liquid evaporates and meat browns, 3 to 4 minutes. Drain off fat; transfer meat mixture to a medium bowl. Stir in remaining ingredients and set filling aside. (Can be covered and refrigerated overnight.)

WILD MUSHROOM FILLING FOR PASTA

Makes about 2½ cups

This earthy filling can be served with either sauce. Reserve the porcini soaking liquid for soups or rice dishes.

- 1 ounce dried porcini mushrooms
- 2 tablespoons olive oil
- 2 garlic cloves, minced
- 10 ounces fresh wild or domestic mushrooms, cleaned and minced
- ¼ cup minced fresh parsley leaves
- Salt and ground black pepper
- 1 cup ricotta
- ⅓ cup grated Parmesan cheese
- 1 egg yolk

1. Cover porcini with boiling water and soak 30 minutes. Drain and reserve liquid for another use. Mince porcini and set aside.

2. Heat oil in a medium skillet. Add garlic and sauté over medium heat until golden, about 2 minutes. Add fresh mushrooms and cook until wilted, about 4 minutes. Stir in porcini, parsley, and salt and pepper to taste. Cook until liquid evaporates, about 2 minutes.

3. Off heat, stir in remaining ingredients and adjust seasonings; set aside. (Filling can be covered and refrigerated overnight.)

GARDEN TOMATO SAUCE

Makes about 2½ cups

Carrots and onions give this sauce a sweetness that contrasts nicely with either the spinach or meat fillings.

- 3 tablespoons butter
- 1 small onion, minced
- 1 medium carrot, peeled and minced
- 1 can (28 ounces) crushed tomatoes
- Salt

Melt butter in a medium saucepan. Add onion and carrots; cook over medium heat until vegetables soften, but do not brown, about 5 minutes. Add tomatoes and ½ teaspoon salt; bring to boil; simmer until sauce thickens, about 1 hour. Adjust seasonings.

For a chunky, more rustic sauce, stir in 2 tablespoons minced fresh parsley or basil leaves. Toss with pasta and serve with grated Parmesan cheese.

For a smooth, more refined sauce, puree mixture in a food processor or blender. Return pureed sauce to pan and stir in ½ cup heavy cream. Cook, stirring constantly, until sauce starts to bubble and thicken, 1 to 2 minutes. Toss with pasta and serve with grated Parmesan cheese.

BROWN BUTTER AND PINE NUT SAUCE

Makes about 1 cup

This simple, elegant sauce is the perfect match for the squash filling; it also works quite nicely with spinach-filled pasta.

- ½ cup pine nuts
- ¼ pound butter
- Salt
- ¼ cup minced fresh parsley leaves

1. Heat oven to 325 degrees. Toast nuts on a small baking sheet until golden, about 5 minutes; set aside.

2. Melt butter in a medium skillet; cook over medium heat, swirling pan, until butter turns golden brown, about 5 minutes. Stir in reserved nuts, ½ teaspoon salt, and parsley. Toss with pasta and serve with grated Parmesan cheese. ■

Roasting Garlic

For the sweetest, creamiest garlic, poach it in milk before roasting.

BY ELIZABETH HILTS

When choosing garlic, look for well-formed heads with cloves that have grown tightly together. Avoid sprouted garlic or heads that have dark "bruises" or soft spots; these must be removed or they will affect the taste of the entire head.

Few foods are as flavorful, nutty, and downright sweet as roasted garlic, which has a wonderful, soft consistency that makes it perfect to spread on crusty bread, to bind or accentuate sauces, or to add marvelous flavor to roasts.

Many cookbooks recommend drizzling garlic with olive oil, wrapping it in aluminum foil, and tossing it in the oven; I've never been completely satisfied with that method. For one thing, it's unreliable: Some bulbs cook faster and burn before others become tender. Also, garlic roasted in this fashion sometimes has a bitter taste. Since I love roasted garlic, I set out to find a way to eliminate these problems.

Because garlic is relatively dry, I wanted to add some moisture to the heads as they roast. But when I roasted garlic with chicken broth, it not only changed the flavor of the garlic but made it mushy — it had, in effect, been braised. Vegetable broth affected the flavor less, but the consistency still suffered.

A friend suggested I try poaching the heads of garlic before roasting. Once again, chicken and vegetable broths masked the flavor of the bulb. Poaching in wine worked nicely, but I felt that the distinct flavor this produced would limit the uses of the roasted garlic. As it turns out, milk is the best medium for poaching. With a quick rinse between poaching and roasting (*see* Master Recipe), the final product is beautifully golden in color and perfectly tender. Use this method and you'll never be disappointed with your roasted garlic.

By the time you've removed the garlic from its skin (*see* "Before and After Roasting Garlic", page 20), it's already pretty well pureed, but you can mash it further with a fork or with the back of a wooden spoon. Each head will yield approximately one-quarter cup of garlic puree. You can spread the cloves on bread, either plain or grilled (*see* recipe below) or use the puree in salad dressings, tomato-based sauce for pasta, fresh mayonnaise, or in any recipe where you might prefer the mellower taste of roasted garlic. In addition, the garlic puree may be used in place of butter in reduction sauces; it acts as an emulsifying agent when added in the final minutes of cooking.

MASTER RECIPE FOR ROASTED GARLIC PUREE

Makes 1 cup

Use this roasted garlic paste as you would use minced raw garlic — in salad dressings, pasta sauces, and salsas. You can grill the garlic as well — just cook the packets, covered, over a medium-hot fire about one hour, or two hours over slow coals.

- 4 heads of garlic
- 1 cup milk
- 2 teaspoons olive oil or melted butter

1. Loosen papery outside skin by rolling each head of garlic back and forth across a cutting surface; rub away loose skin. Cut off about ½ inch from tip end of each garlic head with a sharp knife, so that most clove interiors are exposed and garlic heads sit straight (*see* illustration 1, page 20).

2. Place garlic heads, cut side down, in a medium saucepan. Add milk and bring to simmer. Poach garlic over low heat, until softened slightly, about 10 minutes. Drain garlic (reserve milk if making Linguine with Garlic Cream Sauce, page 20) and rinse under cold running water to remove milk residue.

3. Heat oven to 350 degrees. Place 1 head of garlic in the center of an 8-inch square of aluminum foil. Drizzle ½ teaspoon oil over the garlic. Gather the corners of the foil over garlic; twist to seal. Repeat with remaining heads of garlic and oil.

4. Roast garlic packets in a small baking dish until garlic is very soft, about 1 hour. Let packets cool. Remove from foil. Squeeze out softened garlic by hand or with the flat edge of a chef's knife, starting from the root end of the head and working down (*see* illustrations 2 and 3, page 20). Transfer garlic puree to a small bowl. Mash garlic with a fork or with the back of a wooden spoon to fully puree, if desired. Continue with one of the following recipes, or store puree in a small jar; top with olive oil. (The puree can be stored at room temperature for 1 week or refrigerated up to 1 month.)

GRILLED BREAD WITH ROASTED GARLIC AND FRESH TOMATO SAUCE

Makes 1 dozen

- 2 medium tomatoes, seeded and chopped
- 2 tablespoons minced fresh basil
- Salt and ground black pepper
- 1 loaf French bread (½ pound), cut on the diagonal into 12, ¼-inch slices
- ¼ cup Roasted Garlic Puree
- 2 tablespoons olive oil

1. Heat grill or broiler. Mix tomatoes, basil, and salt and pepper to taste in a small bowl; set aside.

2. Grill bread over a medium-hot fire or broil, turning once, until bread is toasted on both sides, 3 to 4 minutes. Spread a portion of garlic paste over each slice of toast; drizzle with olive oil. Top each toast with a portion of tomato sauce and serve immediately.

Basil Pesto Variation: To make the pesto, process ½ cup Roasted Garlic Puree with 2 cups fresh basil leaves and ¼ cup walnuts in a food

PHOTOGRAPH BY ERIC ROTH AND DAVID HENDERSON

processor fitted with a steel blade. Transfer mixture to a small bowl; stir in ¼ cup fresh-grated Parmesan cheese and ½ cup olive oil. Top pesto-spread toast with slices of fresh tomato and sprinkle with salt and pepper.

GARLIC AND BASIL ROAST CHICKEN WITH LEMON PAN SAUCE

Serves 6

If you're using canned chicken broth in the sauce, use the low-salt variety; regular chicken broth is salty enough straight out of the can and when reduced by half, as for the sauce in this recipe, it's practically inedible. Serve the chicken with mashed potatoes and broccoli rabe or some other assertive fall green.

- 6 tablespoons fresh basil leaves, rinsed and stems removed
- 3 tablespoons Roasted Garlic Puree
- 3 tablespoons olive oil
- Salt and ground black pepper
- 1 chicken (about 4 pounds), rinsed and giblets removed
- ½ cup dry white wine
- ¼ cup juice from 1 large lemon
- 1 cup chicken stock or low-salt chicken broth

1. Heat oven to 450 degrees. Mince basil leaves in a food processor fitted with a steel blade; pulse in 2 tablespoons garlic puree. With processor on, add 2 tablespoons oil in a slow, steady stream; mixture will emulsify slightly. Season to taste with salt and pepper.

2. Use fingers to gently separate chicken skin from meat all the way down breastbone, being careful not to pierce skin. Loosen skin around leg and thigh. Spread ¼ cup garlic mixture under skin, starting on leg and working across breast. Press skin to evenly distribute mixture. Spread 1 tablespoon of garlic mixture in cavity. Truss chicken (*see* May/June, 1993 issue, page 3) or simply tie its legs together and tuck third joint of each wing under back. Brush chicken with remaining 1 tablespoon oil and sprinkle with salt and pepper.

3. Place chicken in a nonreactive roasting pan; add wine and lemon juice. Lower oven temperature to 350 degrees; roast chicken, basting often until juices run clear, about 1½ hours. Transfer chicken to a platter. Degrease pan juices, add chicken broth, and stir to loosen browned bits. Pour pan juices into a medium saucepan and boil until reduced by half; whisk in remaining 1 tablespoon garlic puree. Carve chicken; serve sauce separately.

LINGUINE WITH GARLIC CREAM SAUCE

Serves 4–6

Although this pasta dish is not totally cream-free, the garlic puree and poaching milk make appealing and tasty substitutes for the amounts of cream and butter usually found in standard Alfredo-style sauces.

- 1 cup milk (reserved from garlic poaching)
- ½ cup heavy cream
- ¼ teaspoon hot red pepper flakes, or to taste
- 1½ teaspoons fresh oregano leaves, minced, or ½ teaspoon dried oregano
- ¼ cup Roasted Garlic Puree
- ½ cup grated Parmesan cheese
- Salt and ground black pepper
- 1 pound linguine

1. Bring 4 quarts of water to boil in a large soup kettle.

2. Bring milk, cream, red pepper, and oregano to boil in a medium saucepan; simmer, whisking constantly, until milk mixture reduces by half. Lower heat; whisk in garlic puree until sauce emulsifies slightly, 2 to 3 minutes. Whisk in Parmesan cheese and salt and pepper to taste; cover and keep warm.

3. Meanwhile add 1 tablespoon salt and the linguine to the boiling water; boil until linguine is just tender, 7 to 9 minutes. Drain pasta, reserving some of the cooking water. Toss linguine with sauce. If the sauce is too thick to coat pasta evenly, add the cooking water 1 tablespoon at a time. Serve with additional finely grated Parmesan and ground black pepper. ■

Elizabeth Hilts, a Connecticut-based freelance writer, is presently working on a humor book.

To prepare garlic for roasting, remove the papery outside skin by rolling the whole heads of garlic across a cutting board, then rubbing it with your hands. When it becomes difficult to remove the skin, you have removed enough of it. (The cloves will begin to loosen from the root end if you remove too much skin, which will make it more cumbersome to cook and will spoil the presentation of garlic served whole.) Next, slice off the tips of the cloves with a sharp knife (*see* below).

After roasting, squeeze the garlic out of their skins with your fingers. Start at the root end of the head and work down to the sliced end (*see* below). If you prefer, you may use the flat edge of a knife for this task: grasp the cooled head of garlic in one hand, place it on its side on a dish or cutting board, and, starting at the root end of the head and working toward the top of the cloves, press the garlic out of its skin with the knife edge, rotating the head as you work to evenly remove the garlic (*see* below). Store roasted garlic in a jar, covered lightly with olive oil; it will keep for up to a month in the refrigerator. Do not freeze.

TIPS AND TECHNIQUES FOR ROASTED GARLIC

1. Before poaching the garlic, slice off about one-half inch from the top of the head, making sure that the tips of almost all the cloves are exposed.

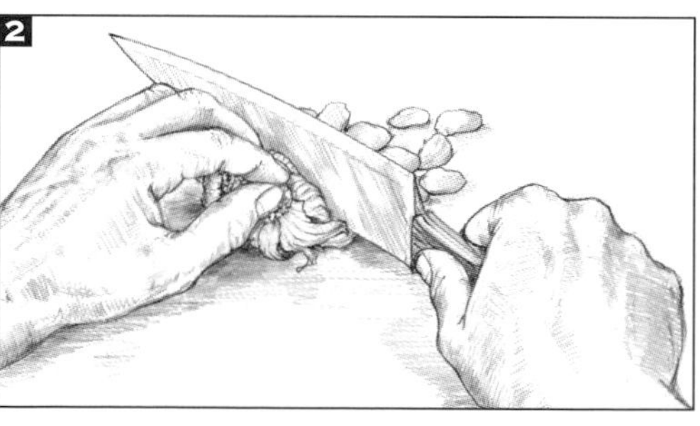

2. After poaching and roasting, you can easily press the softened cloves out of their skins with the back of a knife.

3. It is equally easy, if slightly messier, to remove the cloves from their skins by pushing up from the root end of the garlic head with your fingers.

ILLUSTRATIONS BY ELAYNE SEARS

Omelets Revisited

Use a no-stick pan for a no-hassle omelet.

BY STEPHANIE LYNESS

FOUR STEPS TO A PERFECT OMELET

1. When the bottom layer of eggs has cooked, pull a portion of the cooked eggs from the side of the pan toward the center; then tilt the pan so the uncooked eggs run to the bottom of the pan.

2. Jerk the pan toward you to slide the omelet partway up the opposite side, then tip the pan and use a fork or spatula to fold the far edge over onto itself.

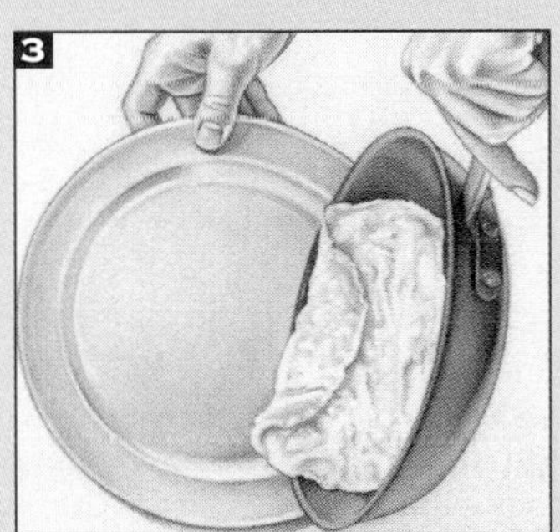

3. To remove the omelet, grasp the pan as far down the handle as possible, then rest the far edge of the pan on the serving plate.

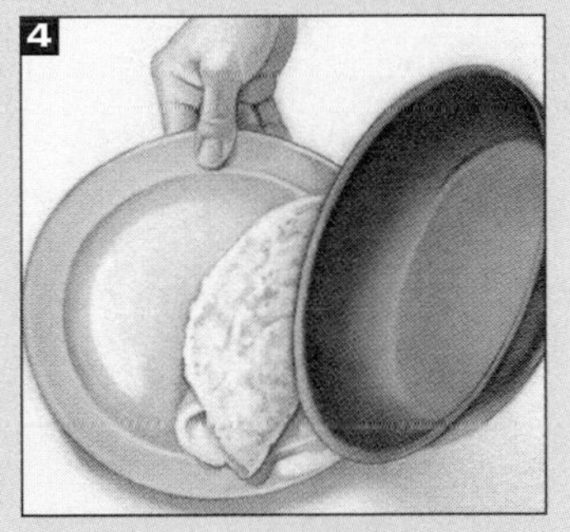

4. Gently roll the omelet onto the serving plate to give the final fold.

Many people have been led to believe that you must be a trained chef, or at least a *very* serious cook, to turn out a decent omelet. The truth is, while this may once have been the case, nonstick pans now make omelets a cinch. And, with the ever-present demand for tasty, instant meals, omelets fit the bill handily: they are quick, satisfying, and can be made with almost anything you have on hand, providing a terrific way to use leftovers or to savor some fresh herbs. Besides, you almost always have eggs in your refrigerator.

A big part of the omelet mystique centers around the pan in which they are cooked. Traditional omelet pans are made of heavy iron with an absolutely flat bottom and sloping sides to help ease the omelet out of the pan. These pans are carefully seasoned before use to prevent the omelet from sticking; in order to prevent rusting, they are never washed thereafter — just wiped out with a towel.

It is still true that the proper pan is essential to good omelet making. Today, however, that pan is a simple, nonstick skillet; it is already "seasoned," and requires no special care. It just needs to be the right size for the job.

The traditional technique for cooking omelets involves a number of fairly tricky arm motions that take practice — stirring with the flat of a fork in a circular motion until the mixture has thickened, tapping the handle to dislodge the set egg, and sliding the omelet up one side of the pan. However, the no-stick pan makes most of this unnecessary.

Testing the Classic Technique

Using two eggs and one-half tablespoon butter (olive oil is also delicious and works just fine) for each omelet, I tested the classic technique to determine the simplest way to cook an omelet without compromising the taste. The vehicle was a nine-inch nonstick pan with sloping sides; the flat bottom of the pan measures about five inches. My first series of tests determined how best to beat the eggs and which utensil to use — most classic recipes merely dictate that the eggs be "completely incorporated," although some say "beat until frothy" and others "beat until barely combined."

I tried three methods of mixing the eggs: beating them lightly with a fork to barely combine the yolk and white; beating more vigorously with a fork to completely mix them; and using a whisk to beat them until they turned frothy. The easiest and best method is to mix the eggs with a fork until they're well mixed; this gives the omelet a more uniform texture than if the eggs are beaten less. Beating with a whisk simply doesn't improve the texture.

The next step was to find the best heat for cooking. Since most egg preparations call for gentle heat, I wondered if low heat would make a more tender omelet. It doesn't. All it does is slow down the cooking (the basic goal here is to coagulate proteins; the rate at which you do it has little effect on the ultimate result, as long as you don't overcook it). Medium-high to high heat cooks the eggs quickly, helping you to achieve the true omelet, what Escoffier called "scrambled eggs enclosed in a coating of coagulated egg," with a lovely brown exterior.

I also tried adding liquid to the eggs; I used a bit less than a tablespoon each of water, milk, and cream in three separate egg mixtures. The addition of any liquid at all helps the omelet remain moist in the event of overcooking, but it also makes the omelet's taste and texture meager. I could discern no difference in taste or texture between the addition of milk and water; while I could taste the cream, I felt that it overshadowed the purity of the egg flavor. My conclusion is that, if you're careful not to overcook your omelet, there's no reason to add liquid.

I then investigated the necessity of stirring the eggs as they cooked. The classic technique is to stir them until they thicken, then pull in the edges to finish. I also tested pulling in the edges until the omelet was set without any stirring. The results were clear. Stirring breaks up and integrates the cooked egg with the soft por-

ILLUSTRATIONS BY MICHELE AMATRULA

tions, giving the finished omelet a very consistent texture and a smooth appearance. If the eggs are not stirred during cooking, the omelet has a less homogeneous texture and a more uneven exterior. Stirring also shortens the cooking time. I prefer the texture of the stirred omelet, but not by much. Stirring, then, classifies as a nonessential refinement, but one that is worth the small amount of extra work it takes.

I tried various methods of getting the omelet out of the pan, both with and without utensils. The technique of tapping the handle to slide the omelet up in the pan is one of the trickiest in cooking. But with a nonstick pan you can use a simple jerk of the handle to accomplish the same thing. Folding is easiest with a spatula; you can make the final fold before you turn the omelet out of the pan.

It is also quite possible to make an omelet without using any utensils. The result is a cross between an omelet that has been stirred and one that has not. Begin the omelet as in the Master Recipe, add the eggs to the hot pan and let them set slightly, then jerk the pan several times so that the cooked egg bunches up and folds back on itself, leaving room for the uncooked egg to run into the unoccupied space in the pan to cook. Fold and turn out the omelet as in the Master Recipe.

FILLING THE OMELET

Omelets are enormously versatile. They are delicious plain or, like a sandwich, they can be stuffed with almost anything. The important thing to remember about filling omelets is that it is the egg, not the filling, that should take center stage. Do not add so much filling or so many ingredients that the filling overpowers the simple pleasure of the egg. In the course of my kitchen tests I tried leftover cooked spinach, chopped and sautéed in a little butter or olive oil; leftover steamed vegetables, already marinated in olive oil; a boiled potato, sliced and sautéed in butter; and an onion, thinly sliced and cooked in butter until it became soft and sweet.

If you are flavoring the omelet with herbs, grated dry cheese, or a small dice of onion or sweet pepper, just whisk the ingredient into the egg mixture. Add chunkier, more substantial fillings just after the omelet has set, before you fold it. For a filling that must be cooked first (like the potato filling below), you can simply pour the egg mixture over the cooked filling, then cook and fold the two together.

MASTER RECIPE FOR BASIC OMELET

Serves 1

- 2 large eggs
- Salt and freshly ground black pepper
- ½ tablespoon butter

1. In a small bowl, lightly beat eggs and a pinch of salt and pepper with a fork until mixed.

2. Heat butter in an 8- to 9-inch nonstick pan over medium-high heat. When butter stops foaming and just begins to color, pour in eggs. Wait a few seconds until edges of omelet begin to set. With the flat of a fork, stir in a circular motion until slightly thickened. Use a wooden spoon or spatula to pull in cooked egg at side of pan toward center; tilt pan to one side so that uncooked eggs run to edge of pan (*see* illustration 1, page 21). Repeat until omelet is just set but still moist on top. Cook a few more seconds to brown bottom.

3. To fold omelet, jerk pan sharply toward you a few times to slide omelet up far side of pan. Jerk pan again so that far edge just folds over onto itself or use fork or spatula to fold edge over (illustration 2, page 21). Grasp pan as far down handle as possible with your palm facing up; rest far edge of pan on serving plate (illustration 3, page 21) and gently roll omelet onto plate so that it gets its final fold (illustration 4, page 21). Use a fork or spatula to tuck in any edges. Serve immediately.

Smoked Salmon Omelet: Make omelet according to Master Recipe. Just before folding, sprinkle in 1 teaspoon minced fresh dill, chives, or scallion greens, then place 2 tablespoons thin-sliced smoked salmon strips over center third of omelet. Fold and turn out as in Master Recipe.

Fines Herbes *Omelet:* Make *fines herbes* by mincing equal parts fresh parsley, chives (or scallion greens), tarragon, and chervil, if available, to yield 1 tablespoon. Beat eggs with *fines herbes*. Make omelet according to Master Recipe.

Cheese Omelet: Make omelet according to Master Recipe. If using a hard cheese like Parmesan, beat 1 tablespoon grated cheese into eggs before cooking. If using softer cheeses, such as Monterey Jack, cheddar, or soft goat cheese, sprinkle over center third of omelet just before folding. Fold and turn out as in Master Recipe.

Asparagus Omelet: Steam 4 to 8 asparagus tips (depending on size) over boiling water until bright green, about 2 minutes. Halve tips lengthwise, if large. Heat ½ tablespoon butter in omelet pan over medium heat. Add asparagus, sprinkle with salt, and roll in melted butter; transfer to plate and set aside. Add 1 teaspoon butter to pan and make omelet according to Master Recipe. Just before folding, arrange asparagus tips over center third of omelet. Fold and turn out as in Master Recipe.

POTATO, HAM, AND PARSLEY OMELET

Serves 2

Note that this omelet requires a larger pan than the single-serving recipes. You can add another egg without changing any of the other proportions.

- ½ tablespoon plus 1 teaspoon butter
- 1 small waxy potato (about 3 ounces), peeled, quartered, and sliced thin
- Salt
- ¼ cup julienned ham
- 1 teaspoon minced parsley leaves
- Freshly ground pepper
- 3 large eggs, beaten

Heat butter in 9- or 10-inch nonstick pan over medium-high heat. Add potato and a pinch of salt and sauté until tender and golden brown, 4 to 5 minutes. Off heat, stir in ham and parsley; season to taste with salt and pepper. Return pan to heat, add remaining butter and beaten eggs. Finish omelet according to Master Recipe. ■

Stephanie Lyness, a freelance food writer and cooking teacher living in New York City, is at work on a translation of a French book about steamed food, to be published by William Morrow.

LOW-CHOLESTEROL OMELETS

Many chefs have experimented with either egg-white or reduced-yolk omelets at the request of their clientele. Bradley Ogden, the chef at Lark Creek Inn and One Market Restaurant in the Bay Area, makes an egg-white omelet with a vegetable filling. He starts by beating the whites briefly in a mixer, then cooks them over low heat, without browning — high heat makes whites tough. Ogden finishes it just like a standard, folded omelet.

Ercolino Crugnale, the chef at San Francisco's Stanford Court, uses a similar technique for his egg-white omelet, but he folds about one-quarter cup blanched, pureed spinach into the whites before cooking.

I tested egg-white omelets as well as reduced-yolk omelets, and found whites-only omelets to be anemic — they did not even begin to satisfy my desire for an omelet. But one whole egg plus one or two whites makes a fine individual omelet; if your filling is especially rich, you may even find this slightly leaner mixture preferable to a whole-egg omelet.

Making Your Own Vinegar

You need little more than time to turn leftover wine into inexpensive and full-bodied vinegar.

BY LYNN ALLEY

Why bother making vinegar at home? The main benefit is vinegar that is stronger and more flavorful than most vinegar you can buy. It's also a great use for leftover wine and it is very easy to do.

The Materials

All you need to make vinegar are a container, some wine (or beer), and a starter. The container can be a plain glass jug, a ceramic crock, or a small oak barrel (*see* below). Barrels lend a softer, more interesting flavor to vinegar, but they are also far more expensive ($70 or more) than an empty gallon jar.

Wine itself is easy enough to come by — just add your leftovers to the barrel or jug. Red wine, which usually has fewer sulfites than white, is more easily cultured; if you'd like to use white wine, start with a mixture of wine and water, in a ratio of about two to one.

Until fairly recently, if you left wine to stand, the ubiquitous airborne bacteria called *acetobacter* turned it to vinegar. Today, winemakers commonly use sulfites or other preservatives to inhibit bacterial growth. As a result, an active bacterial culture must be added to wine in order to make vinegar.

This is the trickiest part — finding a good starter. If you have a friend who's already making vinegar, just get a piece of his or her "mother," the large, slimy substance that forms on top of developing vinegar. Otherwise, buy an 8- or 12-ounce bottle of unpasteurized vinegar (also sold as "starter" from suppliers, *see* page 32). This is enough to start a batch of vinegar, and you'll never have to buy it again.

The Process

First, fill your container about half full of wine. Let it stand uncovered overnight to aerate; the bacteria need plenty of oxygen. The following day, add the starter and cover the holes in the jug or barrel with cheesecloth or with a piece of coarsely woven cotton cloth that will let in oxygen but keep out insects and debris. Finally, set the container in a dark location with a fairly constant temperature. You may add leftover wine from time to time, but never fill the container more than two-thirds full.

After a while — as little as two weeks in hot weather, and as long as two months at normal to cool room temperatures — a moldlike film will form on the surface of the liquid. This is the beginning of the mother. Within a few more weeks it will thicken, and you may remove it and use it to start your next batch of vinegar. You may choose not to remove it, but you should still take out a good portion from time to time, or it will continue to grow and take over your whole container.

Whether you remove the mother or not, the bacteria will remain active, and eventually the liquid will begin to smell more like vinegar than like wine. At this point — usually within two weeks after the mother develops — you can bottle the vinegar. Fill the bottles as full as possible, since you now want to exclude oxygen, and tightly cork them. Don't use metal caps, as vinegar will erode them. Lay down the bottles to age for a few months; this will mellow the sharpness and allow the flavors to become more complex.

You don't have to bottle all the vinegar at once. Simply draw off enough for a bottle every now and then, and continue to replenish the vinegar in the barrel, keeping the container about two-thirds full. In fact, you don't have to bottle and age the vinegar at all — it can be used straight from the bottle, as long as you don't mind a fairly rustic brew. ■

Lynn Alley, a San Diego–based cooking teacher and food writer, is the author of *Herban Kitchen*.

PREPARING VINEGAR BARRELS

You can purchase a one- or two-gallon oak barrel from any good winemaking supply shop (*see* Sources and Resources, page 32). However, these barrels are ordinarily intended for making wine, and need to be altered accordingly.

When making wine, the object is to exclude oxygen from the process; therefore the barrel has a small bunghole with a cork in it. When making vinegar, you want the bacteria which convert wine into vinegar to have plenty of oxygen. Therefore ask the supplier to enlarge the bunghole to a diameter of two and one-half to three inches. You should also ask the supplier to install a spigot near the top of the barrel for extracting the vinegar.

Since all barrels leak to some degree, fill your barrel with water and let it sit outside or in the bathtub for two or three days to allow the wood to swell and seal any leaks before you proceed.

TROUBLESHOOTING VINEGAR

If, after following the general directions above, you have one or more of the following problems, try the following solutions.

❧ Nothing happened: The wine you used may have been heavily treated with sulfites, which act as stablizing and preserving agents; try diluting it with about one-third water. Alternatively, you might try a different wine, preferably red, from one of the several organic wineries of France or California; these wines contain no sulfites.

❧ Nothing happened (again): Your unpasteurized vinegar may not have contained viable bacteria. Try buying starter from one of the sources listed on page 32.

❧ The vinegar doesn't smell good: Your bacteria may not have had enough oxygen. Try pouring the vinegar back and forth from one container to another several times, then wait a couple of days. Also, make sure you cover containers only with cheesecloth or cotton, and that the openings are fairly large.

❧ Your once-potent vinegar has weakened: After a while, bacteria convert acetic acid to carbon dioxide and water; you must draw off vinegar from time to time and add new wine, so the vinegar has alcohol on which to work.

Rating Red Wine Vinegars

An inexpensive American vinegar tops the field.

BY JONI MILLER

Oil and vinegar have long been culinary partners, a sort of gastronomic Fred Astaire and Ginger Rogers, with oil providing unctuous fluidity while vinegar zips along in tandem supplying acidic razzle-dazzle and a flagrant kick of flavor.

Recently, much attention has been focused on olive oils *(see Cook's Illustrated*, Charter Issue, for example), and the result has been a vast new and useful literature for consumers. Certainly balsamic vinegar (*aceto balsamico*) has been explored with equivalent thoroughness over the past several years. In the quest for new taste thrills, however, some serviceable and seemingly more mundane occupants of the cook's pantry have been shunted aside and taken for granted. The time has come to rediscover red wine vinegar.

The word vinegar comes from the French *vin aigre,* or "sour wine." Its history stretches back more than ten thousand years, and one can reasonably assume its initial appearance on the scene was accidental. A quantity of open wine was simply left uncovered and unattended long enough to ferment and the result was the first crude version of vinegar.

From the beginning, vinegar has been used for a wide range of medicinal as well as culinary purposes. Possibly one of the first antibiotics, it was used by Hippocrates to treat patients; during the Civil War it was on active duty to prevent scurvy; and even today it figures extensively in folk remedies. In the prerefrigeration era, vinegar was a convenient food preservative and, of course, it is still used in canning and preserving.

How Commercial Wine Vinegar Is Made

All vinegar is made by a double fermentation process. During the initial fermentation, sugar in the wine or other liquid is converted into alcohol; during the second phase, bacteria called acetobacters convert the alcohol into acetic acid.

Commercial vinegar producers use three distinct fermentation methods to produce their vinegars. Experts agree that the Orleans method, named for the French port city on the Loire River where it originated, produces the most complex, flavorful vinegars. Three of the four top-ranked vinegars in our tasting (L'Estornell, Paul Corcellet, and Maison Martin Pouret) are produced using this method.

In this lengthy and costly procedure, wine is slowly and naturally fermented in oak barrels for one to three months without heat, until a sticky-skinned mass of bacteria known as the "mother" forms on the surface. The fermentation process is then allowed to continue until all alcohol has been converted to acetic acid.

The second method — called the "quick process" method — is faster and therefore less expensive. Wine trickles slowly into a heated tank that is loosely filled with wood shavings or chips, charcoal, or corncobs. As the bacteria in these materials begins to act on the wine, a circulating generator blows air up from the bottom of the tank, exposing the liquid to the maximum amount of oxygen. After about one week of this treatment, the mother will have completely digested the alcohol in the wine, a signal that fermentation is complete.

Since the temperature in the fermentation tank is artificially maintained at about 100 degrees during the quick process, some of the wine's delicate flavors may dissipate. To compensate for this, vinegars made in this fashion are usually aged in wood for several weeks at the end of their production cycle.

The most rapid and least costly method is the continuous or "submerged fermentation" process. Most vinegar manufactured in the United States by high-volume producers is made in this way, including the Heinz vinegar that placed first in our testing. In this method, wine and acetobacter microorganisms are processed in large-capacity stainless-steel tanks in which a giant spindle or propellor agitates the liquid, aerating it for a speedy fermentation period of around 24 hours, at up to 100 degrees. The resulting vinegar is aged for several months in wood tanks, but the aging tanks hold several thousand gallons as opposed to the 50-gallon or less tanks or barrels used in the other two processes.

To complete any of the three processes, most vinegars are filtered or pasteurized prior to sale. This is done to remove any remaining vestiges of the mother, to curtail further bacterial activity, and to preserve the vinegar's strength and quality of flavor. Some inexpensive brands may also use sulfites for the same purpose.

Acetic Fermentation Process

Wine vinegars are produced from the acetic fermentation of wine. Although any wine (champagne, varietals, fortified wines such as sherry) may be used to make vinegar it is important to bear in mind that the finer the wine used, the more flavorful the vinegar. A good red wine vinegar should at least give a strong hint of the wine from which it was made and also reflect an appropriate mellowness.

During fermentation, acetic acid develops as a result of the bacteria in the "mother" attacking the alcohol in the wine and oxidizing it into oblivion (*see* "How Commercial Wine Vinegar Is Made," left). Most vinegar labels indicate the "strength," or amount of acetic acid present, in much the same way that alcohol levels are noted on wine labels. This is shown either by percentage or by "grain"; the higher the number, the stronger the vinegar. The minimum acidity level for commercial vinegars is 4 percent but most fall into the 5–7 percent range. A milder 5 percent — or five-grain — red wine vinegar (such as most domestic supermarket brands) contains less acid than a 7 percent or seven-grain variety (including many imported brands).

As a general rule of thumb, the higher quality, more costly vinegars have a higher acidity level; less expensive and/or presumably less flavorful ones are apt to have a lower one. Strength and a pleasantly developed full flavor are not necessarily synonymous, however. In our tasting, the top-ranked vinegar was the five-grain Heinz; L'Estornell Garnacha Tinto, also five-grain, tied for second place with the seven-grain Paul Corcellet. ■

Joni Miller, a New York–based writer, is the author of *True Grits* (Workman, 1990).

Red Wine Vinegar Blind Tasting

The *Cook's Illustrated* panel for our tasting of red wine vinegars included Dean & DeLuca specialty-foods buyer Geri Ackert; chef Ed Brown from Tropica; restaurant consultant and cookbook author Rozanne Gold; food writer and New York *Daily News* restaurant reviewer Arthur Schwartz; *Cook's Illustrated* executive editor Mark Bittman; author Joni Miller; and a home cook. The tasting was held at Tropica in New York City, where an array of 10 domestic and imported red wine vinegars were evaluated on the basis of color, clarity, aroma, and taste. This was a blind tasting in which the vinegars were poured from numbered bottles into clear wine glasses. Tasters dipped an oblong, slow-dissolving sugar cube into each sample, drawing the liquid into their mouths. Prices listed are per bottle; note that there was some variation in bottle size. All vinegars were purchased in the New York metropolitan area; prices vary nationally.

Vinegars are listed in order of preference (an asterisk next to a vinegar indicates that it tied with that immediately below it). In the judging, seven points were awarded for each first-place vote; six for second; five for third; four for fourth; three for fifth; two for sixth; one for seventh. Two of the three top-ranked vinegars were on the lower end of the acidity scale (5 percent) and each was admiringly described as berrylike in both aroma and taste.

Red Wine Vinegars Listed in Order of Preference

1 **Heinz Gourmet Fine Wine Vinegar** (United States), 12 ounces, $1.69; 5 percent acidity; 21 points. Surprisingly, the top-ranked vinegar turned out to be an unsophisticated American supermarket staple that tasted "familiar." Clarity of color and flavor were singled out as positives. A clear, rich pink vinegar with a mild, faintly fruity aroma tinged with a hint of strawberry. Pleasant, well-balanced, clean taste. Responsiveness to low acidity may have been a factor in high scores. A dissenting taster found the flavor "thin." Made from "grape wine" diluted with water to 5 percent acidity. Sulphur dioxide added "to protect color." Quite inexpensive and definitely worth trying. *Widely available.*

2 * **L'Estornell Garnacha Tinto Fine Wine Vinegar** (Spain), 12.7 ounces, $7.95; 5 percent acidity; 17 points. A low-acidity vinegar tied for second-place honors. It's worth noting that tasters' comments verged on the euphoric in some instances, with one scribbling "I think I'm in love!" This vinegar is the color of a burgundy or a tawny port with drifts of very visible sediment. A pronounced medicinal alcohol aroma was not judged unpleasant but the contrast between the aroma and taste universally surprised tasters. A delicious, smooth, almost portlike taste that "smacked" of berries and/or dried fruits also hinted at wood. This vinegar, introduced in the States two years ago, is made in Catalonia by the Orleans method from 100 percent garnacha tinto grapes, aged for nine months, and bottled in Sarroca de Lerida near Barcelona on the 200-year-old estate of the Vea family, which also produces organic and extra virgin olive oils. *Selected specialty food stores.*

3 **Paul Corcellet Red Wine Vinegar** (France), 8.5 ounces, $4.25; 7 percent acidity; 17 points. Tied for second place, this vinegar is cloudy and brownish with a pronounced sweet berry aroma; praised for a mellow and complex fruity flavor that suggested to several tasters it had been aged longer than the others. *Widely available in specialty food stores.*

4 **Maison Martin Pouret Bordeaux Wine Vinegar** (France), 6.9 ounces, $6.39; 7.5 percent acidity; 13 points. Cloudy garnet color with a full, fruity aroma; berrylike bouquet with hints of raspberry. Sweet, rather lively taste with overt fruit flavor tinged with a mellow hint of age. Manufactured in Orleans using the city's namesake method, made from wine "usually from the Loire Valley," and aged in oak for six months. *Maitre vinaigrier* Jean Francois Martin's family founded the firm in 1797; today it makes 14 kinds of vinegar. *Specialty food stores.*

5 **Regina Red Wine Vinegar** (United States), 12 ounces, $1.69; diluted with water to 5 percent acidity; 12 points. Very clear, light ruby-red color with an unpleasantly sharp, almost sour, stinging aroma with hints of fruit. Weak, flat, and thin taste with an unpleasant sharp edge. Tasters who disliked this vinegar loathed it but several others found the taste clean. Made from "100 percent California wine" by a division of Nabisco Brands, Inc.; sulfur dioxide added "to protect color." *Widely available.*

6 **Badia a Coltibuono Aceto di Vino** (Italy), 16.9 ounces, $20; 7 percent acidity; 9 points. Clear, tawny, pinkish copper color with an offbeat, musty, slightly unpleasant aroma also described as astringently sharp; a hint of fruit. Although its raspberry overtones were viewed as positive, overall tasters found the flavor flat; one found it lip-puckering. Produced in the heart of Tuscany's Chianti Classico region. Aged for three years in oak barrels. *Selected specialty food stores.*

7 * **Marcel Recorbet Red Wine Vinegar** (France), 8.5 ounces, $2.99; 7 percent acidity; 8 points. Opinions quite divided. Cloudy, heavily sedimented, and golden brown in color with an interesting sherry or molasseslike nose. Favorable responses focused on a mild, rich, complex taste described as honest by one taster; those who disliked the vinegar found it overly acidic. *Selected specialty food stores.*

8 **Spice Islands Premium Red Gourmet Red Wine Vinegar** (United States), 12.7 ounces, $2.89; 5 percent acidity; 8 points. Mixed response. Slightly cloudy, brown color with glints of red. An off-putting, faintly sour aroma variously described as musky, brackish, and woody. Disliked by those who felt it tasted the way it smelled, with discomfitingly acidic high notes; those who liked it found it smooth and unambiguously mellow. Sulfites added; water listed as second ingredient. *Widely available.*

9 **Dessaux Pure Wine Vinegar** (France), 25.25 ounces, $4.10; 7 percent acidity; 6 points. A cloudy, murky-looking pale brown vinegar with a very unpleasant, musty, rotten aroma likened to a barnyard smell. Unbalanced, acidic taste matched aroma; taste closer to that of a cider vinegar. Made in Dijon. *Widely available in specialty food stores and some supermarkets.*

10 **Colavita Aged Red Wine Vinegar** (Italy), 16.9 ounces, $1.98; 6 percent acidity; 4 points. Clear, vivid Kool-Aid pink with a hint of brown and an overtly alcoholic, chemical aroma. Astringent and sour tasting, but a bit fruity and with a touch of flavorful depth suggestive of a California Rosé. Contains sulfites. *Widely available.*

** Indicates that the vinegar was tied with the one listed directly below.*

Crisps and Betties

Make dozens of quick fruit desserts with these simple toppings.

BY JOHN PHILLIP CARROLL

Crisps and betties are ideal easy desserts: slice the fruit, mix the topping, and bake. While these two desserts are similar, they differ in one important respect — the toppings. Crisps are covered with a streusel of brown sugar, flour, oatmeal, and butter, while betties are blanketed with buttered bread crumbs.

For betties, I made toppings with a variety of bread crumbs, from whole wheat to rye to cornbread, but the classic approach is best: fruit, sweetened with granulated sugar, then layered and topped with buttered white bread crumbs.

Crisps allow more latitude for experimentation, since there are more ingredients in the topping. I tested several varieties of each of the topping's main components. I found that all-purpose flour works as well as any other kind and that, while white sugar is acceptable, brown sugar gives a richer, caramel-like flavor and a better color. As for fat, I recommend a combination of two parts butter to one part vegetable shortening, to obtain both the tastiness of butter and the crunch that shortening adds.

A crisp's topping can be made by hand or in a food processor, and the Master Recipe gives instructions for each. The processor takes just a few seconds; use chilled fat to help prevent over-blending. On the other hand, mixing by hand using room-temperature butter and shortening demands only a couple of minutes and minimal effort. I also feel it gives you more control and a better feel for the ingredients, especially if you use your fingertips.

When it comes to baking, crisps do best in a shallow pan about two inches deep. Betties work best in a deep pan, such as a round soufflé dish three to four inches deep and about eight inches in diameter. In a shallower pan, the betty crumbs become sodden.

MASTER RECIPE FOR FRUIT CRISP

Serves 6

If you make the crisp topping in large quantities and freeze it, this dessert can be as simple as slicing up some fruit. Just store the topping in a large container or zipper-lock bag. When you need a quick dessert, scoop out the required amount (about two cups for the quantity of fruit in this recipe), sprinkle it over the prepared fruit, and bake.

- 7 cups prepared fruit
- 1 teaspoon grated zest and
- 1 tablespoon juice from 1 lemon
- ⅔ cup brown sugar, packed firm
- ½ cup all-purpose flour
- ½ cup quick-cooking oatmeal
- ½ teaspoon ground cinnamon or nutmeg
- ¼ teaspoon salt
- 4 tablespoons butter, cut into small bits (chilled, if using food processor)
- 2 tablespoons vegetable shortening, cut in small bits (chilled, if using food processor)

1. Heat oven to 425 degrees. Toss fruit with lemon zest and juice in a large bowl. Spread evenly in 8-inch square baking pan, pressing down lightly.
2. Mix next 5 ingredients in a medium bowl or in workbowl of a food processor; add butter and shortening. If mixing by hand, use fingertips, a pastry blender, or 2 forks to blend fat into dry ingredients until mixture looks like coarse irregular crumbs, with no visible lumps of fat. If mixing in a food processor, pulse about 10 times, then process 5 to 10 seconds, until there are no visible lumps of fat.
3. Spread topping over prepared fruit; bake for 15 minutes. Reduce heat to 350 degrees; bake until topping browns and fruit is tender when pierced, 30 to 40 minutes. Serve warm or at room temperature.

MASTER RECIPE FOR BASIC BETTY

Serves 6

- 9–10 slices (about 8 ounces) firm white sandwich bread, processed to yield 3 lightly packed cups bread crumbs
- ¼ pound (1 stick) butter, melted
- 7 cups prepared fruit
- 1 teaspoon grated zest and
- 1 tablespoon juice from lemon
- ⅔ cup sugar
- ½ teaspoon ground cinnamon or nutmeg
- ¼ teaspoon salt

1. Heat oven to 400 degrees. Toss bread crumbs with melted butter in a medium bowl; set aside.
2. Mix remaining ingredients in a large bowl.
3. Spread ½ cup bread crumbs over the bottom of a deep 2-quart baking pan, such as a soufflé dish. Top with half the fruit, sprinkle another ½ cup crumbs over fruit. Top crumbs with remaining fruit with their juices; press down gently. Top with remaining crumbs. Lightly butter a sheet of foil large enough to cover the dish; place foil, buttered side down, over dish and seal closed.
4. Bake for 25 minutes and remove foil. Bake uncovered until crumbs brown, juices bubble, and fruit is tender when pierced, 30 to 40 minutes. Serve warm or at room temperature. ■

PREPARING FRUITS FOR CRISPS AND BETTIES

FRUIT	AMOUNT	PREPARATION
Apples	2½ pounds (*about 6 apples*)	Peel, core, and thinly slice.
Apricots	3 pounds (*15 to 20 apricots*)	Pit and quarter.
Berries	2 pounds	Rinse and pat dry; if tart, add 1 tablespoon or more of sugar to taste.
Nectarines, peaches	2½ to 3 pounds (*8 to 10 pieces of fruit*)	Peel, pit, and cut into sixths.
Pears	2½ to 3 pounds (*6 to 7 pears*)	Peel, core, and thinly slice
Plums	3 pounds (*15 to 20 plums*)	Pit and quarter.

John Phillip Carroll, is the co-author of *California, the Beautiful Cookbook.*

Secrets of Homemade Espresso

Is a $200 espresso machine worth the investment? We test five brands to find out.

BY JACK BISHOP

Because one doesn't always want to go out for coffee — especially with cafés and restaurants charging as much as four dollars for cappuccino — more Americans are trying to make high-quality espresso at home.

Espresso professionals compare their brew to wine. In many respects they are right: espresso is an extremely complex beverage with more than six hundred individual flavor components, and there are tremendous differences between beans grown in different areas. But there is one clear difference in the nature of espresso and wine. Wine is ready to drink when you buy it; making good espresso requires a good machine and proper technique. The type of beans, roasting method, and grinding process all make a difference, and even the best coffee can be easily ruined by bad form at home.

A New Coffee Creation

Most coffee is brewed by letting water drip or percolate slowly through the ground beans. Espresso, on the other hand, is a relatively new creation, dependent upon high-tech devices that generate enough pressure to force hot water through finely ground coffee, quickly extracting the flavor. The first modern espresso machine, which used a manually operated piston, was invented at the end of World War II; electric pump machines date to the 1950s.

Only these two types of machines can create a true cup of espresso. The best of them heat the water to 192–198 degrees (hotter water scalds the coffee and imparts bitterness; cooler water does not extract as much flavor). The typical "pull" — the term used to describe forcing heated water through compacted grounds — lasts about 20 seconds. When done properly, the result is a thick, rich brew that captures the essence of the coffee bean. Good espresso never tastes burnt, harsh, or bitter, but is somewhat buttery, with a pleasing level of acidity and a bittersweet flavor that is rich with subtle undertones.

A properly made espresso also features the characteristic light brown topping called *crema*. This foamy extraction adds a smoothness and creaminess not found in other coffee drinks. The presence of a well-defined crema (there should be enough crema to briefly trap sugar crystals sprinkled over the espresso) is a sign that the right coffee has been paired with the right extraction technique.

Begin with the Beans

High-quality espressos start with quality arabica beans. "I always recommend buying a good espresso blend rather than 'varietals'," states Nick Jurich, coffee guru and author of *Espresso* (Missing Link Press, 1991). "Knowledgeable roasters create blends that accentuate the positive attributes of each bean." Most coffee professionals agree that few varietals are suited for the quick extraction process of espresso. Even top varietals such as Kenya AA or Costa Rican Tres Rios are usually more one-dimensional than a well-crafted blend.

While there is some agreement among experts about blends, there is little consensus about roasting. On the West Coast (and particularly in Seattle), beans are generally roasted until very dark. East Coast roasters — as well as many Italians — think their Western counterparts go too far and actually scorch the beans. Of course, since most espresso in Seattle is consumed with plenty of milk, the bitter taste is less noticeable than it would be in a straight cup.

The key to buying beans for espresso at home is to find a store with good beans and then experiment to find a roast that suits your palate. Look for dark brown but not black beans that have an oily sheen; dry, cracked beans are well past their prime.

"At least 70 percent of coffee's quality is freshness," says David Baron, director of marketing at Torrefazione Italia, one of Seattle's leading roasters. "So make sure to buy from a store with very high turnover or buy by mail.

WHICH MILK IS BEST?

Most people wonder which milk is best for frothing; some have had luck with low-fat milk, others insist only full-fat does the job. But my tests showed that temperature and age are much more important than fat content. Skim, low-fat, and whole milk can all be steamed successfully, although skim milk produces drier foam and whole milk yields creamier foam. Because I prefer creamier froth, I use either 2 percent or whole milk. Half-and-half and light cream contain too much fat to froth.

Regardless of the type of milk, I found that milk below 40 degrees froths much better than that which is warmer. Avoid pouring cold milk into a warm frothing container; you might even chill the container in the freezer for several minutes before frothing.

Milk foam is created when the proteins trap the air emitted by the steaming wand. Garth Rand, professor of food science at the University of Rhode Island, says these proteins are more stable, and thus better able to trap air, at colder temperatures.

Still more noticeable is the effect time has on milk's ability to froth. Milk that has been opened and left in the refrigerator for a week — even if it is still technically "fresh" — may be impossible to froth. Milk sugars (lactose) are constantly breaking down into lactic acid (which causes the sour taste in old milk), so milk begins to "spoil" from the moment it is produced, long before we can taste it. This increased acidity compromises the ability of the proteins to trap air.

In sum, the freshest, coldest milk will produce the most foam when steamed.

PHOTOGRAPH BY BRUCE MILLETTO

When properly stored, the beans are at their peak of flavor for only two weeks after roasting." The best strategy, then, is to ask the retailer when the beans were roasted; if he or she doesn't know (or if it has been more than a few days), shop elsewhere.

Ideally, you should buy a small quantity of fresh whole beans and grind them yourself as needed. But most experts dismiss inexpensive blade grinders: "They chop the beans and create friction that causes heat and the evaporation of oils," warns Baron. "They also tend to produce an uneven grind not suitable for espresso."

Jurich is slightly more optimistic. He suggests grinding only small quantities (fill the grinder halfway) and wiping the container clean after each use to prevent a buildup of oils. He also suggests holding the grinder securely together and shaking it as you grind, much as you might shake a martini. I was pleased with this method, which seems to give good, consistent results; beans ground for espresso should be gritty — like coarse salt — rather than powdery.

But Jurich is quick to point out that electric burr grinders — which use plates to crush the beans without heating them — are far superior. The problem is that good burr grinders cost $125 or more. If you're not pleased with a blade grinder and can't afford a plate grinder, you might consider buying small quantities of ground coffee from the store.

Ground or not, coffee should be stored in an airtight container, away from sunlight. Trained palates may pick up a decrease in flavor after just a day or two, but in my tests I found that this method preserved flavor for a week, even with ground coffee. Freezing causes the natural oils to congeal and, in my tests, produced coffee with less crema. But if you plan to keep coffee for more than a week or two, it's best to store it in the freezer to protect flavor, even at the risk of reducing crema slightly.

A final note about grinding and storing: Coffee inspires a fair amount of zealotry. Many devotees go through the same rituals day in and day out. (One told me he packs beans, a small blade grinder, and a drip coffee maker when he goes on the road.) Your passion for coffee, coupled with your ability to distinguish differently handled beans, should determine how much fuss you are willing to endure.

Ground Coffee Becomes Espresso

Properly blending, roasting, and grinding coffee is half the battle; technique is equally important. Since lukewarm espresso is unappealing and will not hold crema, begin by preheating the filter holder, basket, and coffee cup — just run the machine without coffee, letting the water drip into the cup.

Then fill the filter basket (the correct amount, technically, is seven grams of coffee for each cup) and lightly tamp the grounds. Some machines come with a special tool, and others have a built-in tamper; you can also use the back of a small measuring cup. Tamping is important because, if the grounds are loose, the water will run through them too quickly and the espresso will be watery. However, avoid overtamping, which can completely prevent the water from seeping through the grounds. The correct amount of tamping depends to some extent on the grind. Coffee that is slightly coarse should be firmly packed; coffee that is a tad too fine should be lightly tamped.

Wipe the excess coffee from the rim of the basket to ensure a firm seal between the holder and the brew head, and slide the filter holder tightly into place. You are now ready to brew.

Turn on the pump and allow espresso to slowly flow out of the machine for about 20 seconds, or until the coffee stream has turned light brown. Shut off the pump, and allow the stream to finish dripping for several seconds. If the brew head continues to leak, remove the filter holder. (In any case, do not leave the filter holder in the machine when it's not in use, as this may weaken the brew head seal.)

Frothing the Milk

If anything, frothing milk is even more challenging than brewing espresso. With most of the machines tested, I was able to make an excellent cup of espresso on the first try, but my initial attempts at frothing milk were erratic. Although each machine has its own peculiarities, there are a number of general guidelines.

First, place fresh, cold milk in a narrow container — the most common vessel is stainless steel, but you can use a ceramic mug. Make sure the container is not more than one-third full. When the steam light goes on, open the steam valve into an empty cup to let out any accumulated water. Place the steam valve into the milk, just below the surface, open the valve, and gently move the container in a circular fashion to steam and froth the milk. After about 20 seconds (a little longer with the Krups machine), there should be a nice head of froth on top of the steamed milk.

When you're done, open the steam valve into an empty container to remove clogged milk, then wipe the wand to remove any milk particles before they harden. ■

Espresso Drinks

Although Americans tend to think more is better, a single portion of espresso contains just 1½ ounces of liquid, and should be served in a warmed, 2- to 3-ounce demitasse. Espresso can be sipped slowly or quaffed, Italian style, in one or two gulps. If you want more coffee, make a lungo or doppio (*see* below).

Espresso Ristretto: A short or "restricted" espresso of about 1 ounce. To make this, simply cut short the flow of water when brewing this intense espresso.

Espresso Lungo: The opposite of a ristretto, this is made by adding an ounce or two of hot water (not from the brew head) to make a milder or "long" cup. When diluted with more hot water (at least 3 or 4 ounces), this drink is sometimes called an Americano.

Espresso Doppio: A double: 3 ounces of espresso made by filling the two-cup basket and letting contents drip into one 4- to 5-ounce cup.

Espresso Macchiato: Single

espresso "marked" by a tablespoon of frothed milk.

Espresso con Panna: Single shot of espresso with a small dollop of whipped cream.

Espresso Romano: Espresso served with lemon peel. Italians turn up their noses at this American invention for good reason — the acidity in the lemon peel does not enhance the flavor of the espresso.

Espresso Corretto: A single espresso that has been "corrected" with a splash of brandy or other spirits.

Cappuccino: Single espresso topped with equal amounts of steamed milk and frothed milk and served in a 5- to 6-ounce cup. Europeans usually add plain or vanilla-scented sugar, but many Americans dust the top of the foam with cocoa powder, cinnamon, or nutmeg as well.

Caffè Latte: "Coffee with milk" (known as café au lait in French or cafè con leche in Spanish), made with a double shot of espresso, 5 or 6 ounces of steamed milk, and very little or no froth. Add more espresso or milk to strengthen or weaken and serve in large, bowl-shaped cups (about 9 or 10 ounces) or tall, wide-mouthed glasses.

Latte Macchiato: Tall glass of steamed milk (sometimes with froth) into which a single espresso is slowly poured to "mark" the milk with coffee.

Caffè Mocha: Single espresso flavored with ½ ounce of chocolate syrup and then topped with 4 or 5 ounces of steamed milk and whipped cream. Dust with cocoa or shaved chocolate if desired.

Mocha Latte: Latte with chocolate syrup added to espresso but no whipped cream or grated chocolate. Other syrups, especially almond, hazelnut, and orange, can be used in the same way to create exotic lattes.

Rating Espresso Machines

Buying an espresso machine is an expensive proposition. In earlier tests, I found that those models costing less than $100 are a waste of money. Since they are not equipped with a pump, such machines use steam to force water through the coffee grounds; but without the pressure created by a pump, they fail to extract all the flavor from the coffee. The result is espresso with little or no crema, and anemic frothing. We chose, therefore, to test only those machines with electric pumps. (Piston machines with a manually operated lever also yield excellent results, but start at about $400 and are more difficult to master.)

There may be as many as 50 electric pump machines sold in this country for home use, ranging in price from $175 to $1,200. We have considered only the least expensive models. Spending more money will get you a sturdier machine with more bells and whistles, somewhat better frothing, a heavier filter holder, a solid metal housing, a larger reservoir, and other features you may or may not need. Although higher priced machines may be superior, most first time buyers are probably just as well off with one of these relatively inexpensive machines, unless price is no object.

Among the machines tested, the Krups, Saeco, and Braun are clearly superior to the DeLonghi and Gaggia models. Although all five machines consistently turn out good-to-excellent cups of espresso, the top three are much better at frothing milk. In addition, the DeLonghi and especially the Gaggia are plagued by a number of design flaws.

Krups receives the top ranking not only for performance but for design — it's the only machine with an all-metal exterior, it takes up the least amount of counter space, and it's good looking. In addition, it produced the hottest water, and never leaked water after the pump was turned off — a sure sign that the brew head seal is tight. The Saeco ran a very close second because of its reliable and powerful frothing. The Braun is also an excellent machine with great frothing ability but ranks third because of its slightly higher price and significantly larger size.

Espresso machines, which are far more complicated than drip coffee makers, do need occasional repairs. (In fact, two of the five machines I ordered came with malfunctioning pumps. While experts tell me this is rare, obviously it's not rare enough.) Therefore, I recommend buying espresso machines from specialty kitchen and coffee stores, which generally offer more knowledgeable salespeople who can help with any necessary repairs. (Some stores will ship machines by mail; *see* Sources and Resources, page 32.)

Espresso Machines in Order of Preference

FIRST PLACE
Krups Espresso Novo 964

SECOND PLACE
Saeco Gran Crema Super Idea

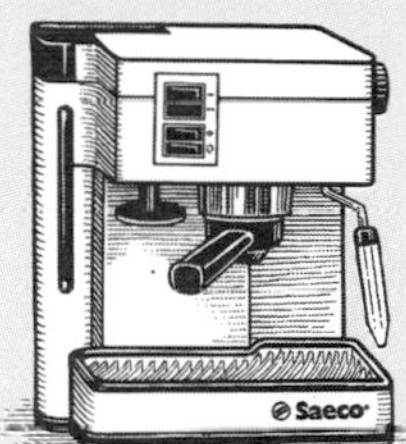

THIRD PLACE
Braun Espresso Master Professional E400T

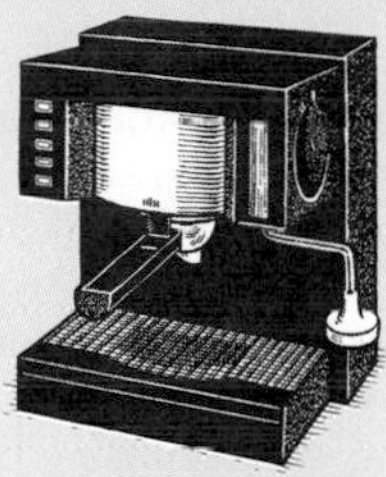

KRUPS ESPRESSO NOVO 964
Price: $200
Power: 1,000 watts
Tank Capacity: 30 ounces
Warm-Up Time: 1½ minutes
Design: Sleek and sturdy stainless-steel exterior; best looking of models tested. Buttons are easy to read, although water gauge is in the back and hidden from view.
Performance: Excellent espresso with rich crema. Frothing is slow but steady with generally good results.
General Comments: Dependable, easy-to-use machine. Unlike plastic machines, this one makes an attractive addition to kitchen counter. It's also considerably smaller and won't take up so much space. Only machine that never leaked when pump was turned off.

SAECO GRAN CREMA SUPER IDEA
Price: $199 (discounted to $180)
Power: 960 watts
Tank Capacity: 45 ounces
Warm-Up Time: 1½ minutes
Design: Handy built-in tamper. Two-cup filter basket is welded into holder. (For one cup, simply fill basket halfway with one coffee scoop.) Cheap-looking plastic housing; well-constructed engine.
Performance: Thick crema on espresso with excellent frothing. Except for occasional dripping after espresso was made, no complaints.
General Comments: A nice machine that is especially good at frothing milk. Comes with an excellent instruction video and a well-written manual.

BRAUN ESPRESSO MASTER PROFESSIONAL E400T
Price: $249 (discounted to $225)
Power: 1,000 watts
Tank Capacity: 28 ounces
Warm-Up Time: 1½ minutes
Design: Metal exterior with some plastic. Frothing attachment is easy to clean but a bit awkward to maneuver, especially with tall pitchers. Two-cup filter basket holds only 1½ scoops of coffee.
Performance: Thick crema on espresso with dense frothed milk. Easy to use but machine dripped frequently.
General Comments: Impressive machine (although too large for cramped countertops) that gets the job done with ease.

DELONGHI CAFFE ITALIA BAR 16
Price: $179
Power: 1,100 watts
Tank Capacity: 36 ounces
Warm-Up Time: 1½ minutes
Design: Filter holder is a bit difficult to pull into place. Frothing wand is easy to clean. Built-in tamper is convenient.
Performance: Espresso with thick crema. Frothing wand lacks the power to greatly increase the volume of milk — milk would not even double while some machines were able to triple its volume.
General Comments: In addition to erratic frothing, I have my doubts about the factory workmanship. One machine was dead on arrival (the pump didn't work) and the second came with a misshapen filter holder that just wouldn't pull into place — I had to use the holder from the dead machine.

GRAN GAGGIA
Price: $210
Power: 680 watts
Tank Capacity: 42 ounces
Warm-Up Time: 6 minutes
Design: Filter holder is extremely difficult to slide into place. Power button cycles on and off so it's not clear when water is hot enough to make espresso.
Performance: Fine espresso but frothing is erratic. Even when filter holder is removed the machine frequently leaked after espresso was made.
General Comments: A messy leaking problem (by far the worst among the machines tested) may indicate that the brew head seal is weak. Very slow warm-up (due to wimpy power rating) and confusing lights and buttons.

ILLUSTRATIONS BY DAN KROVATIN

American Pinot Noirs Eclipse French Burgundies

BEST WINE

A $6 Napa Pinot Noir showed better than pricey, well-known Burgundies in our blind tasting.

BEST BUY

BY MARK BITTMAN

Pinot noir, the red wine grape of Burgundy, creates what is arguably the greatest alcoholic drink known to humankind. At its best, the wine — usually called Burgundy (*Bourgogne*) in France, and Pinot Noir elsewhere — is delightful, soft, sweet, and at the same time meaty and complex. Even the merely good wines made from pinot noir are fruity, soft, and alluring; bad ones, and there are plenty, are thin and acidic.

Until recently, few wine aficionados would argue that any Pinot Noirs made outside of Burgundy were worthy of serious consideration. Then some quite decent wines from Oregon cropped up, and, not surprisingly, California made its mark soon thereafter.

We set out to taste what we hoped would be Pinot Noirs for good-to-great current drinking and included six West Coast wines in our tasting, along with eight Burgundies. (No other region produces world-class Pinot Noir.) We did not put a ceiling on price, but made certain of their availability; consequently, all of the wines are from 1988 or later vintages.

This choice may have worked against the best French wines, which tend to be vinified in a more traditional style requiring longer aging than their West Coast cousins. Such wines might make great drinking five or ten years from now, or they might not — cellaring wine is a gamble.

Something worked against the French wines, because a $30 Oregon newcomer finished first, a $6 California wine came in second, and another Oregonian finished third. In addition, our most experienced tasters agreed that the first and third finishers were not only delicious now but also have great aging potential, further enhancing their value. You must look in fourth place to find the familiar name of Vosne-Romanée, the most expensive bottle of the tasting, at nearly $50.

This tasting shows that good-quality Pinot Noir can be made and sold for less than $10. This is, in itself, an important revelation. In this context, and because of their reputation and scarcity, top red Burgundies are relatively overpriced.

One cannot conclude, however, that American wines have become "better" than their French counterparts; another tasting, with different Burgundies, could yield entirely different results.

As in our previous tastings, our panel was made up of both wine professionals and amateur wine-lovers; the wines were tasted blind. When scanning these results, note the precipitous drop-off in points from the first wine to the second, and from the group of wines from second through fifth place to those below. ■

BLIND TASTING RESULTS

Wines are listed in order of preference (an asterisk next to a wine indicates that it tied with that immediately below it). In the judging, seven points were awarded for each first-place vote; six for second; five for third; four for fourth; three for fifth; two for sixth; one for seventh. Prices are average retail in the Northeast; consumers on the West Coast can expect to pay somewhat less for wines from California and Oregon, and somewhat more for those from France.

1. 1990 Domaine Drouhin Pinot Noir (Oregon, 45 points), $30. Full-bodied wine with rich, intense flavor and a long finish. Should improve with age. Four first-place votes (out of a possible nine), with comments like "brilliant" and "spectacular."
2. 1991 Napa Ridge North Coast Pinot Noir (California, 30 points), $6. "Big, rich fruit" with "good balance of oak." "Somewhat simple" but incredible at this price.
3. 1989 Arterberry Pinot Noir (Willamette Valley, Oregon, 29 points), $19. "Rich and complex" wine with "wonderful finish."
4. 1988 Vosne-Romanée Les Chaumes, Jean Tardy (Burgundy, 26 points), $48. Featured "some of the complexity one expects from good Burgundy," but "short finish" cost it points.
5. 1990 Mondavi Reserve Pinot Noir (Napa, 24 points), $29. "Rich," "spicy and pleasant." Not especially complex, but "no real flaws," either. One first-place vote, from taster who found it "sweet and beautifully perfumed."
6. 1990 Gevrey Chambertin, Philippe Rossignol (Burgundy, 18 points), $27. "No fruit," wrote one taster, and most others agreed, calling it "dry" and "too tannic" and "very lean." Two tasters, however, found it "sweet and rich" and "yummy."
7. 1988 Morey St. Denis, Domaine Dujac (Burgundy, 16 points), $38. "Soft, pleasant wine." One experienced taster placed it first, calling it "by far the wine of the tasting."
8. * 1991 Cosentino Pinot Noir (Napa, 11 points), $18. "Acidic," with "little fruit."
9. 1989 Chambolle Musigny, Drouhin (Burgundy, 11 points), $30. "Round," but with "little intensity or complexity."
10. * 1990 Pommard, Domaine Pothier-Rieusset, Alain Corcia (Burgundy, 10 points), $21. A wine whose value could vastly improve with age: "closed and tannic," but "big in the mouth" with "great potential."
11. 1990 Saintsbury Pinot Noir (Carneros, 10 points), $17. Confusing wine, with comments ranging from "tannic and very dry" to "smooth, rich" and "nicely balanced."
12. 1990 Monthelie, Latour (Burgundy, 9 points), $13. "Light and thin."
13. 1990 Mercurey Domaine de Croix Jacquelet, Faiveley (Burgundy, 7 points), $15. Some tasters found "decent fruit," others thought it "thin and not very exciting."
14. 1990 Bourgogne Pinot Noir, Domaine Virely Arcelain (Burgundy, 5 points), $8. "Lean," with "little fruit" and "no finish."

BOOK REVIEWS

Michel Richard's Home Cooking with a French Accent
Michel Richard with Judy Zeidler and Jan Weimer
William Morrow, $25.00

A more descriptive title for this enjoyable cookbook might be *Cooking at Home with a Zany, Americanized French Chef.* Richard is delightfully iconoclastic, and he has considerable experience and creativity — he runs Citrus, the cutting-edge Los Angeles restaurant, and several others, including a deli. From Roast Chicken with Garlic, Shallots, and Potatoes (as basic a recipe as you could ask for), to Rabbit with Endive and Sage (spectacular, delicious, and eminently doable), there is something here for everyone.

Here is a chef's book that makes sense, and that isn't surprising: these are home recipes, not restaurant recipes and Richard — or his editor — was wise enough to hire two veteran food writers, author Judy Zeidler and former *Bon Appétit* executive food editor Jan Weimer. We tested 10 of the book's recipes; we found no significant errors, and we loved the results. Richard's work will be instantly appealing to a broad spectrum of home cooks.

There are recipes for french fries, stuffed cabbage with pork and tomato sauce, and onion and olive tarts (made, you should know, with frozen puff pastry). Then there are recipes that look common at first, but show sparks of creativity in technique or flavoring: potato pancakes are stir-fried, then baked, for precooked convenience and superb crispness; duck salad with citrus is seasoned with cinnamon, which lends a surprising sweetness; couscous with orange and pistachios is a dessert rather than a side dish.

The real fun begins, though, with the dishes few of us could imagine, some of which are so bizarre as to be off-putting, but many of which are, on second look, worth a shot. We tried scallop asparagus lollipops, in which the vegetable spears are used as an edible skewer; baked brie filo bars with mesclun, a knockoff on the bistro salad with poached egg, which combines runny brie, crisp filo, and crunchy greens in a great hazelnut-curry dressing; salmon with couscous crust; tunaburgers, which are both logical and delicious; and the somewhat ironically named turkey corn dogs, a fun combination of ground turkey, toasted pecans, and corn, wrapped in plastic (why not? that's what most sausage casing is) and poached and served on hot dog buns or, if you insist, on real bread.

Richard's book is brilliantly organized, with solid technique tips accompanying every recipe, variations when appropriate, and information for planning ahead and storing. Although the techniques are essentially French, there are influences from all over the world here, and few recipes beyond the reach of even beginning cooks. Nearly everyone will find some value in this chef's book — we only wish there were more like it.

— Mark Bittman

The New German Cookbook
Jean Anderson and Hedy Würz
HarperCollins, $27.50

From the recipe titles alone, you know that this is not a spatzle-sauerkraut-schnitzel book. See-it-on-the-plate, taste-it-in-your-mouth names like Braised Red Cabbage with Onions and Apples in Red Wine Sauce, or Potato Salad in a Light Chervil Dressing, give the recipes a contemporary, international feel.

But — as you would expect from any book involving the talented and experienced cookbook author Anderson (no relation) — *The New German Cookbook* delivers more than alluring recipe titles. What ultimately matters is how easy it is to follow the recipes, and, of course, how good the food tastes. It's rare to find recipes as clear, concise, and informative as these. Neither the ingredient lists nor the recipe instructions leave the cook guessing, and well-researched, pertinent information appears alongside each recipe.

"Modern German cooks," say Anderson and Würz, "are every bit as frugal as their mothers and grandmothers." Therefore, you can save your asparagus stems and peelings to make the Asparagus-Rice Soup, in which tarragon and a squeeze of lemon support the bold, clean flavor of asparagus while rice lends body. (One of our testers thought, however, that cooking and rinsing the rice before adding it to the soup was an unnecessary step. So we tried it again, our way — the soup was cloudy, and we learned something.)

The slightly bizarre-sounding Cod with Sauerkraut and Tarragon Sauce proved a happy combination. Anderson and Würz have successfully lightened Roulades of Beef for today's more health-conscious cooks; the process, from start to finish, was perfectly clear, and the results memorable. Despite the updating, we loved the toothpick-speared beef rolls resting in a pool of rich beef gravy — it reminded us of Mom's cooking.

The New German Cookbook will still be very much with us next December, as we pull the best of 1993's fruits from the Rum Pot, begun in May with strawberries. Equal weights of fruit and sugar, covered with dark rum and stored in a crock, are left to macerate in a dark corner from late spring to the end of the year. This is old-world cooking at it's best — a welcome addition in today's kitchens.

— Pam Anderson

James Beard's Simple Foods
James Beard
Macmillan, $22.00

In 1974, James Beard began writing a monthly column for the in-flight magazine *American Way*. Over the next several years, he produced about 70 such columns, on topics ranging from shopping in San Francisco to how to properly use your hands while cooking. This book, a collection of 40 of these essays, is probably the last original work of James Beard we'll see published and, like so many of its predecessors, it reminds us of why he deserved his reputation as America's leading good eater, great cook, and beloved teacher.

The man who hated the term "gourmet" ("What gourmet cooking is I will never know") was expert at identifying, cooking, and eating the best food. He preferred eating at home to eating in restaurants — probably because the food was better.

In person and in print, Beard was opinionated, talented, warm, and accessible. Like much of Jim Beard's work, this is a prose book, with few formal recipes. Fifteen years old and more, most of these essays remain relevant and insightful. His breezy writing is, as always, a joy to read, and — for us at least — an inspiration. There's nothing like a little Beard to send you off into the kitchen, dying to get your hands into a lump of dough, a pile of potatoes, a nice piece of fish. Novice and experienced cooks alike will find *Simple Foods* simply delightful. ■

— Mark Bittman

SOURCES AND RESOURCES

COMMERCIAL MUFFIN TINS

There is no need to use paper liners when baking with heavy-duty commercial muffin tins, since these specially glazed pans prevent sticking and are easy to clean. La Cuisine Kitchenware (323 Cameron Street, Alexandria, VA 22314; telephone 800-521-1176) carries a full line of pans from Lockwood Manufacturing. James Beard was a big fan of Lockwood tins, and we are especially impressed by their dark glaze and deep cups. Ekco-Glaco also makes a full line of superior commercial muffins tins; they are carried by the King Arthur Flour Baker's Catalogue (P.O. Box 876, Norwich, VT 05055; telephone 800-827-6836).

PROFESSIONAL ICE-CREAM SCOOPS

Professional ice-cream scoops insure uniform size and clean dispensing when placing muffin dough into tins. Excellent stainless-steel scoops with heavy-duty springs are made by Zyliss Switzerland and sold by the King Arthur Flour Baker's Catalogue (*see* above). The scoops come in sizes for both mini and standard muffins and cost $23.95 each plus shipping.

ESPRESSO MACHINES

We have located low-priced sources for the three top-rated espresso machines in our testing (*see* page 29). The Krups Espresso Novo 964 is available at Williams-Sonoma stores nationwide for $200 plus shipping; to order from their catalog, call 800-541-2233. The Saeco Gran Crema Super Idea is sold for $180 in Peet's Coffee and Tea stores in the San Francisco area, and may be ordered by calling 800-999-2132. The Braun Espresso Master Professional E400T is available at Coffee Connection stores in the Boston area or by mail from their catalog for $225 plus shipping; to order, call 800-284-5282. For information about the DeLonghi machine, contact the distributor at 800-322-3848. Gaggia operates a consumer assistance office at 800-527-4336.

ESPRESSO AIDES

If you are interested in learning more about espresso there are a number of good books and even a video on the subject. *Espresso,* by Nick Jurich (Missing Link Press, 1991), is a 200-page primer packed with information about machines, grinders, and mail-order coffee sources. It is available at major coffee chains, including Starbucks and Coffee Connection; or order directly from Missing Link Press (3213 W. Wheeler Street, Suite 179, Seattle, WA 98199; telephone 206-285-9016) for $11.95 plus $3 shipping. Another excellent resource is *Crema,* a 44-page booklet on making espresso. Published by Trendex International (1540 Merchandise Mart, Chicago, IL 60654; telephone 312-644-7754), the pamphlet is available in coffee stores for $4.95 or by mail for $6 including shipping. Trendex also sells a 30-minute videotape on espresso, priced at $15 including shipping.

PASTA MACHINE

The steel exterior and nickel-plated rollers of the Atlas pasta machine are durable and should last a lifetime. The machine, which clamps onto the side of most work surfaces and comes with an attachment that cuts pasta sheets into either wide fettuccine or thin spaghetti, is available at Williams-Sonoma stores nationwide. To order from their catalog, call 800-541-2233. The price is $45 plus shipping.

RAVIOLI CUTTERS

The KrimpKut Sealer can be used to seal and scallop ravioli edges in one motion. It is sold at kitchen supply shops and Williams-Sonoma stores across the country for about $9. Ravioli can also be punched from sealed dough using special cutters. Available in both round and square versions (either two inches or two and one-half inches in diameter), these cutters have sturdy wooden handles and sharp metal edges for slicing through dough. They range in price from $2.95 to $4.50 (depending on the shape and size) and are available by mail from Bridge Kitchenware (214 E. 52nd Street, New York, NY 10022; telephone 800-274-3435).

MUSHROOMS BY MAIL

Aux Delices des Bois offers more than 20 kinds of mushrooms by mail. Unusual cultivated mushrooms like shiitake, cremimi, portobello, oyster, and white trumpet are sold almost year-round, along with seasonal varieties. This fall's seasonal choices include hen of the woods, wine cap, lactaire, and matsutake. Prices (without shipping) range from $6 a pound for cremini to $13 for white trumpets. For information about gift packs or to receive their catalog, contact Aux Delices des Bois (4 Leonard Street, New York, NY 10013; telephone 212-334-1230).

EXOTIC TROPICAL JAMS

Lost Acres Rain Forest Preserves come in three exotic combinations — Pineapple, Papaya, Acerola, and Lilikoi; Pineapple, Guava, and Cupuassu; and Mango, Apricot, Guanabana, and Lilikoi. While pineapples and papayas are common, few Americans have ever heard of (let alone tasted) some of these fruits from the Amazon basin. Acerola, for example — also known as a Barbados cherry — is a bright red cousin to our native cherry but has three pits and an acidic, raspberry-like flavor. The jams made from these exotic fruits come in 10-ounce jars and are sold in gourmet and specialty stores for $3.50 each. They are also available by mail from Country Cupboard (126 Jefferson Street, Ripon, WI 54971; telephone 800-JEL-LIES); call for prices. A portion of sales is donated to Cultural Survival, an organization dedicated to supporting the rain forest and its inhabitants.

VINEGAR EQUIPMENT

There are a number of companies around the country that sell equipment for making vinegar and wine at home. Barrel Builders (P.O. Box 268, St. Helena, CA 94574; telephone 800-365-8231) offers small, high-quality barrels as well as cradles and oak chips; write or phone for their catalog. Cantinetta Tra Vigne (1050 Charter Oak Avenue, St. Helena, CA 94574; telephone 707-963-8888) is a mail-order business run by chef Michael Chiarello of the famed Tra Vigne restaurant. Among the products he sells are an unpasteurized Zinfandel vinegar and an attractive ceramic crock for storing vinegar; write or call for a newsletter. Beer and Wine Crafts (450 Fletcher Parkway, Suite 112, El Cajon, CA 92020; telephone 619-447-9191) supplies bottles, corks, reliable unpasteurized vinegar, and barrels. On the East Coast, Milan Home Brew Shop (57 Spring Street, New York, NY 10012; telephone 800-BEER-KEG for orders) carries an extensive line of vinegar-making equipment.

GLASS VINEGAR FLASKS

Homemade vinegars can be displayed or bottled for special gifts in handsome, clear glass flasks. Sur La Table (84 Pine Street, Seattle, WA 98101; telephone 800-243-0852), a leading kitchen shop in the Pacific Northwest, sells two sizes (8 ounces and 17 ounces) with wire-hinged plastic stoppers to seal in freshness. The smaller flasks cost $2.95 each; larger flasks are $3.95, and both are available by mail order.

REPLACEMENT PARTS FOR APPLIANCES

A California company has hit on a sensible idea by stocking replacement parts and accessories for household appliances made by 20 leading manufacturers. Culinary Parts Unlimited (80 Berry Drive, Pacheco, CA 94553; telephone 800-543-7549, or 800-722-7239 within California) stocks more than 40 Cuisinart accessories and attachments. The company also carries parts for appliances made by KitchenAid, Krups, Braun, Oster, Salton, Farberware, Hamilton Beach, Proctor Silex, and more than a dozen other companies. ■

RECIPE INDEX

POTATO, HAM, AND PARSLEY OMELET
page 22

BREADS AND MUFFINS

Any-Fruit-Will-Do Muffins with Streusal Topping....8
Big Bran Muffins with Raisins and Dates....7
Double-Corn Muffins....7
Grilled Bread with Roasted Garlic and Fresh Tomato Sauce....19

OMELETS

Asparagus Omelet....22
Cheese Omelet....22
Fines Herbes Omelet....22
Master Recipe for Basic Omelet....22
Potato, Ham, and Parsley Omelet....22
Smoked Salmon Omelet....22

SAUCES AND SALSAS

Asian-Style Sweet and Sour Pan Sauce....11
Brown Butter and Pine Nut Sauce....18
Garden Tomato Sauce....18
Lemon-Caper Sauce....10
Master Recipe for Roasted Garlic Puree....19
Oaxacan-Style Sauce with Cloves and Cinnamon....10
Peach Salsa....11
Sherry-Cream Sauce with Mushrooms....10
Tomato-Basil Sauce with Capers....11

PASTA AND FILLINGS

Linguine with Garlic Cream Sauce....20
Master Recipe for Pasta Dough....15
Meat and Ricotta Filling with Basil for Pasta....18
Ravioli....16
Spinach and Ricotta Filling for Pasta....18
Squash, Prosciutto, and Parmesan Filling for Pasta....18
Tortellini....16
Twisted Tortelli....16
Wild Mushroom Filling for Pasta....18

MEAT AND FOWL

Braised Veal Breast with Sausage, Olive, and Swiss Chard Stuffing....3
Chicken Roasted in Red Peppers....Back Cover
Garlic and Basil Roast Chicken with Lemon Pan Sauce....20
Master Recipe for Sautéed Chicken Cutlets....10
Peking Duck....12

DESSERTS

Master Recipe for Basic Betty....26
Master Recipe for Fruit Crisp....26

PLUM BETTY
page 26

GRILLED BREAD WITH ROASTED GARLIC AND FRESH TOMATO SAUCE
page 19

THIS PHOTO: KENT LACHIN MEDIA SERVICES

PEKING DUCK
page 12

ALL PHOTOGRAPHS BY ERIC ROTH

ANY-FRUIT-WILL-DO MUFFINS WITH STREUSAL TOPPING page 8

TWISTED TORTELLI page 16
WITH GARDEN TOMATO SAUCE page 18

Chicken Roasted in Red Peppers

Marinate 8 boneless, skinless chicken thighs for at least 4 hours in a mixture of ¼ cup olive oil; 2 large garlic cloves, minced; ¼ cup minced basil leaves or other fresh herb; and ground black pepper to taste. Slice tops off four large, flat-bottomed red bell peppers and remove seeds and veins. Brush the inside of each pepper with olive oil and sprinkle with salt and pepper. Stand peppers on end in an 8-inch square baking pan. Sprinkle chicken with salt, roll each thigh jelly-roll fashion, and put two thighs inside each pepper. Bake in a 350-degree oven until chicken juices run clear when pierced with a fork, 45 to 50 minutes. Accompany with sautéed vegetables, if desired. *Serves 4.*

NUMBER FIVE ◆ NOVEMBER/DECEMBER 1993

$4.00 U.S./$4.95 CANADA

COOK'S ILLUSTRATED

Holiday Turkey Perfected

The Secret of Moist Breast Meat and Fully Cooked Legs

One Dough, Many Cookies

One Master Recipe Yields 12 Variations

Pumpkin Pie

Crisp Crust Plus Smooth Filling

Solving the Waffle Mystery

The Science of Perfect Waffles

PRICEY CHAMPAGNES FIZZLE

•

DINNER ROLLS ILLUSTRATED

•

ULTIMATE MASHED POTATOES

•

HOW TO BUY CAVIAR

NOVEMBER/DECEMBER 1993

TABLE OF CONTENTS

VOLUME ONE • NUMBER FIVE

~2~

Notes from Readers

Oyster varieties; keeping broccoli green; slow-rise breads; eggplant gender confusion; homemade vanilla extract; grated parmesan; whole-egg mayonnaise; converted rice; an English cake whisk; and bell-pepper tricks.

~4~

Quick Tips

How to stem and cut winter greens; extract pomegranate seeds; prepare lemongrass; make a disposable piping cone; flavor roasts with garlic; and carve slices of rib roast.

~6~

One Dough, Many Cookies

One master recipe for holiday cookies yields a dozen perfectly moist and tender variations. The secret ingredient? Cornstarch. *By Marcy Goldman*

~10~

Making Perfect Mashed Potatoes

For a fluffy, light, flavorful version of this classic, use high-starch potatoes and the right tool . . . and don't overcook. *By Eric Wolff*

~12~

Master Class: Country Ham Stuffed with Greens

Stuffing a country ham with greens and grits adds moisture and contrasting flavors and textures to a holiday favorite. *By Jack Bishop*

~14~

Autumn and Winter Squashes

~15~

Shaping and Baking Dinner Rolls

Make eight types of dinner rolls from a single dough by following these 26 step-by-step illustrations. *By Nick Malgieri*

"A Holiday Table"
A simple centerpiece will complement a holiday table laden with perfect roast turkey (page 18), mashed potatoes (page 10), dinner rolls (page 15), pumpkin pie (page 22), and holiday cookies (page 6).

ILLUSTRATION BY BRENT WATKINSON

Chocolate Trinity Parfait, adapted from *Death by Chocolate* (Rizzoli, 1992) by Marcel DeSaulnier.

ILLUSTRATION BY FRANCIS LIVINGSTON

~18~

The Holiday Turkey Perfected

After roasting 30 birds, we discover an unusual technique for producing exceptionally moist breast meat and fully cooked legs. *By Pam Anderson with Karen Tack*

~22~

The Only Pumpkin Pie Recipe You'll Ever Need

For the best of both worlds — pumpkin pie with smooth, delicious filling and a crisp crust — precook both before baking. *By Stephen Schmidt*

~24~

Caviar Tasting Finds Quality Disappointing

Spending $30 an ounce doesn't guarantee an exciting culinary experience. *By Joni Miller*

~27~

The Mystery of the Ideal Waffle

The best waffles are crisp on the outside and creamy on the inside, like a soufflé with crunch; the secret is buttermilk. *By Christopher Kimball*

~30~

Pricey Champagnes Fizzle in Tasting

California sparklers have made great strides, but our tasting found that the best Champagnes are still made in France — and they don't cost a fortune. *By Mark Bittman*

~31~

Book Reviews

Two new Provencal cookbooks and a Greek entry are notable improvements in their respective fields.

~32~

Sources and Resources

Products from this issue, plus adjustable roasting racks, the best potato peeler, country hams, citrus oils, cookie cutters, and exotic produce by mail.

Cook's Illustrated (ISSN 1068-2821) is published bimonthly by Natural Health Limited Partners, 17 Station Street, Box 569, Brookline, MA 02147. Copyright 1993 Natural Health Limited Partners. Application to mail at second class postage rates is pending at Boston, MA and additional mailing offices. Editorial office: 17 Station Street, Box 569, Brookline, MA 02147 (617) 232-1000, FAX (617) 232-1572. Editorial contributions should be sent to: Editor, *Cook's Illustrated,* 17 Station Street, Box 569, Brookline, MA 02147. We cannot assume responsibility for manuscripts submitted to us. Submissions will be returned only if accompanied by a large self-addressed stamped envelope. Subscription rates: $24.95 for one year; $45 for two years; $65 for three years. (Canada: add $3 per year; all other foreign add $12 per year.) Postmaster: Send all new orders, subscription inquiries, and change of address notices to *Cook's Illustrated,* P.O. Box 59046, Boulder, CO 80322-9046, or telephone (800) 477-3059. Single copies: $4 in U.S., $4.95 in Canada and foreign. Back issues available for $5 each. PRINTED IN THE U.S.A.

PHOTO BY JIM THOMAS

EDITORIAL

ALCHEMY OR CALCULUS?

CHRISTOPHER KIMBALL

I have often been asked why I started a cooking magazine. The answer is that I had to, in order to find satisfying answers to basic cooking questions. How many times have you leafed through cookbooks looking for a definitive recipe for pie pastry, for example, only to find that each author had a different technique, different proportions, even different ingredients? Although it's true that cooking is closer to alchemy than to calculus — that's part of its charm — it's also true that cooking is not a discipline devoid of fundamental truths.

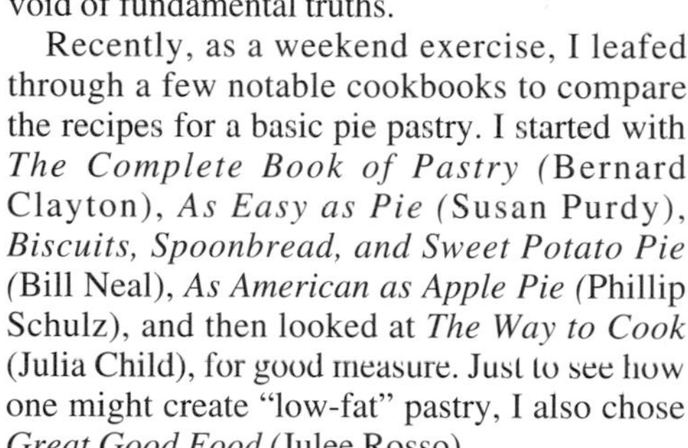

Recently, as a weekend exercise, I leafed through a few notable cookbooks to compare the recipes for a basic pie pastry. I started with *The Complete Book of Pastry* (Bernard Clayton), *As Easy as Pie* (Susan Purdy), *Biscuits, Spoonbread, and Sweet Potato Pie* (Bill Neal), *As American as Apple Pie* (Phillip Schulz), and then looked at *The Way to Cook* (Julia Child), for good measure. Just to see how one might create "low-fat" pastry, I also chose *Great Good Food* (Julee Rosso).

I started with the basic ingredients and their ratios. The average proportion of fat to flour was one to two, although one recipe offered a ratio of only one part shortening to three parts flour. Salt varied from one-tenth teaspoon per cup of flour to one-half teaspoon per cup. Authors recommended as little as three tablespoons of chilled water per cup of flour, and as many as five tablespoons, a large variation. The recommended fat went from all lard, to a lard/butter combination, to all butter, to canola oil. Sugar and egg were often optional.

The directions for making the dough were eye-opening. Some authors recommended cutting the shortening into the flour until it reached the size of "small peas." Another suggested melting the shortening in boiling water, cooling it, then adding it to the dry ingredients. For cutting in the shortening, some claimed hands were best, while others went to bat for a variety of implements including a food processor, a pastry blender, knives, and even a mixer.

All of this leads to endless questions. What is the right amount of water? Is there no consensus about salting pastry dough? If cold shortening is so important how can authors suggest that you melt fat with boiling water or add room-temperature vegetable oil? Why do you let pastry dough rest? Do all of these recipes even work?

As a first step to answering this question, I decided to compare a basic recipe for Pâte Brisée Fine to the one found in a popular low-caloric cookbook. The low-cal version calls for no butter or shortening, just a half-cup of canola oil cut (with two knives) into two and two-thirds cups all-purpose flour. To this, the recipe adds one-quarter teaspoon salt, four tablespoons sugar, six tablespoons ice water, and, in a purely symbolic nod to the cholesterol police, one tablespoon of *skim* milk. Despite culinary warning bells, I made the recipe and used it to prebake a pie crust. The result was a tough, inedible dough that even my kids wouldn't touch. Suspecting that the oil and flour should be mixed with a fork instead of two knives (as called for in the recipe), I tried the recipe a second time with better results but the pastry was still brittle and undersalted; more like a cookie than a pie crust.

After this, the classic Pâte Brisée Fine, was like arriving home after a long and unpleasant business trip. It calls for one part cake flour to three parts all-purpose flour, a combination that results in a more tender crumb. There is plenty of butter and vegetable shortening (three parts butter to one part shortening) and, to my great relief, sufficient salt to give the pastry some bite. I prebaked a nine-inch tart shell and went on to make a quick fruit tart. The result was more than satisfactory — the crust was tender, rich in flavor, properly salted, and delicate.

It seems that there is, in fact, a right way and a wrong way to make pie pastry. Certainly there are variations on a theme, from a flaky American pie pastry to a "shorter" Pâte Brisée, but underneath it all, there is a discipline, a carefully acquired body of knowledge that gives cooking a firm grounding in fact.

Like music, cooking is a tempestuous marriage of art and discipline. You need to be well-grounded to take flight, you need to practice to get off the ground. Through hours of kitchen testing and first-hand observation, the staff of *Cook's Illustrated* aims to provide the right balance between basic training and flights of fancy. We hope that you enjoy both. ■

Editor's note: A thorough investigation of pie pastry will appear in an upcoming issue.

NOTES FROM READERS

Oyster Varieties

I have been living in California for several years and have never been able to find local oysters that taste like the ones I had while growing up in New York. What makes Pacific oysters so different from those I enjoyed as a kid on Long Island?

DEIRDRE PAONE
San Diego, CA

There are four distinct species of oysters found in the waters off North America. On the West Coast, meaty Pacific oysters (left) dominate. The native Olympia oyster, a much smaller and less hearty species with a round shape (right), can also be found in some parts of Washington and British Columbia, but it is not nearly as common as Pacific oysters. Unlike Pacific oysters, the tiny Olympia oysters are rarely cooked and almost always served on the half shell.

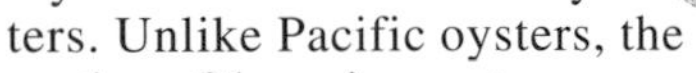

On the East Coast, Atlantic oysters (left; also known as Eastern oysters) can be found from Canada to the Gulf of Mexico. Like Pacific oysters, Atlantic oysters are generally good-sized and may be eaten raw or cooked.

The fourth species, European flat oysters (right; also called Belons or Wescotts), are farmed on both coasts. Named for a region in Brittany, these prized French oysters are often on the small side but are wonderful raw. Unlike Atlantic and Pacific oysters, European oysters usually have round shells and are fairly flat.

Keeping Broccoli Green

I usually blanch broccoli and then sauté it in olive oil, garlic, and lemon juice. Sometimes, however, the broccoli turns an unattractive gray color. What causes a vegetable to change from bright green to dull gray, and how can I prevent this?

PAT REBUCCI
Mountain Lakes, NJ

Your problem might be the lemon juice. Chlorophyll, the pigment in green vegetables, is highly susceptible to heat and acids. Although most green vegetables will brighten when thrown into boiling water, they become dull with prolonged cooking. If boiled in an acidic solution, they quickly become gray. Even without the addition of lemon juice or vinegar, heat causes the release of acids naturally present in green vegetables that can lead to color loss.

For centuries, a common solution to this problem has been to make the cooking water alkaline by adding baking soda. However, this is not recommended, because alkaline solutions damage cell structure and lead to mushy vegetables. Another once-common solution that is no longer recommended is cooking in unlined copper pots. Metal ions keep vegetables bright green, but they also pose a health hazard. It is therefore necessary to resort to other means.

First and foremost, avoid adding lemon juice or other acidic ingredients to green vegetables until after they have cooled slightly. (Chlorophyll will not degrade at lower temperatures.) Also, cook vegetables uncovered in abundant quantities of water to dilute the natural acids from the vegetables and allow them to escape in the steam.

Unfortunately, boiling in abundant water also promotes some loss of nutrients. Because vegetables come into contact with less water when steamed, this method preserves more water-soluble nutrients such as vitamin C and B vitamins. But, since the natural acids remain in the vegetables it can promote color loss if vegetables are steamed for more than a couple of minutes. For these reasons, you may want to consider the microwave for cooking green vegetables. Its fast heat does not destroy as much color or nutrients. Otherwise, boil or steam briefly.

Slow-Rise Breads

The article on breadmaking in the Charter Issue was useful and interesting, but I suggest that you were too casual in dismissing the "myth" that slow-rising breads taste better. If one were to set aside a sponge dough (admittedly, not a "basic bread") for 12 hours, one would certainly taste a distinct difference.

MIKE WARSHAUER
Hearthstone Bakery
Mountain View, AR

We agree that slow rising will make a tremendous difference for sourdough breads. However, with standard bread recipes that rise for just a few hours, we found no difference in flavor when using rapid-rise, regular dry active, or cake yeast. In fact, even the rising times were fairly close. (This may account for the similar flavor and texture of breads prepared with each type of yeast.) Look for more about starter-type breads such as sourdough in future issues.

Gender Confusion

*I am writing to correct an error in the May/June, 1993 issue of your magazine. There is no such thing as a male or female eggplant (*see Quick Tips, page 5*). While it is true that some plants have separate male and female individuals, or that the same plant can have male and female flowers, eggplant is not among these plants. It would be a shame to perpetuate this misinformation in your magazine.*

JULIE WOLIN
Assistant Professor of Biological Sciences
Western Michigan University
Kalamazoo, MI

After hearing from numerous sources that there *was* a gender difference in eggplant, we tested the theory by purchasing several eggplants that matched the supposed male and female external characteristics. Perhaps just by chance, it turned out that the "males" had fewer seeds. Several biologists wrote to advise us that there is no gender difference, so we stand corrected.

We also heard from Paula Wolfert, a respected cookbook author and leading expert on Mediterranean cuisines. She says the only way to choose eggplant with fewer seeds is to judge the weight of same-sized samples. A lighter eggplant generally has fewer seeds.

Homemade Vanilla Extract

Is it possible to make vanilla extract at home using vanilla beans? If so, how should I go about doing this?

JENNIFER GOREN
Brookline, MA

Commercially sold vanilla extract is made by steeping chopped vanilla beans in vats of warm alcohol and water. When the flavor of the tiny black seeds has been extracted, the beans are

ILLUSTRATIONS BY ELAYNE SEARS

strained and discarded. A touch of sugar or corn syrup may be added for sweetness before the potent liquid is bottled.

It is possible to duplicate the commercial process at home with excellent results. Pour one-half cup vodka — it's a good choice since it has little aroma or flavor, but brandy or rum may also be used — into a small container or jar with a tight-fitting lid. Split a six-inch vanilla bean lengthwise and add it to the alcohol. Cover the container tightly and shake once a day for at least a week to loosen the seeds from the pods. (The beans can steep indefinitely, but need a week to yield most of their flavor.) When stored in a cool, dark place, homemade vanilla extract should last indefinitely.

In a side-by-side test, butter cookies made with homemade extract were deemed superior to cookies made with bottled pure extract; they had a much stronger vanilla aroma as well as a truer vanilla flavor.

Grated Parmesan

All my cookbooks say to grate Parmesan cheese only "as needed." Will the flavor of grated cheese really deteriorate if stored in the refrigerator?

MARCIA KAPLAN
New York, NY

Since most experts warn against using pregrated Parmesan cheese, we decided to put this notion to the test. We purchased a hunk of Parmigiano-Reggiano that had been freshly cut from a large wheel. At home, we grated some and divided it between two airtight containers. One batch went into the refrigerator, the other into the freezer. The remaining hunk of cheese was wrapped in a fresh piece of plastic and sealed in a zipper-lock plastic bag.

One week later we compared freshly grated cheese against the pregrated. When sampled alone, freshly grated was a slight favorite if only because it was warmer and therefore had a fuller taste. However, the slight differences in taste among the three samples disappeared when tossed with buttered hot pasta. We did the same test again after two and three weeks, and neither time could we detect significant differences between freshly grated and pregrated Parmesan. It was only after four weeks that there was a slight but noticeable decline in the quality of the refrigerated and frozen samples; both had become fairly dry and slightly bitter.

While we would never recommend bottled Parmesan (it's usually made from lower-quality cheese), it is clearly acceptable to grate top-notch Parmigiano-Reggiano yourself and then store it in either the refrigerator or freezer for several weeks until needed.

Whole-Egg Mayonnaise

Can mayonnaise be made with whole eggs to reduce cholesterol? What are the differences between whole-egg mayonnaise and the traditional version?

ELEANOR PROUTY
Cordelia, CA

Although traditional mayonnaise contains yolks only, a successful version can be made using both yolks and whites — it will be lighter in color and have a somewhat less eggy taste.

The basic recipe for yolks-only mayonnaise calls for two large egg yolks, one tablespoon red wine vinegar or lemon juice, one-half teaspoon Dijon mustard, salt to taste, and oil. Once the yolks, acid, mustard, and salt are combined, the oil is slowly incorporated with a whisk; two egg yolks require about one and one-half cups of oil to form a thick mayonnaise.

One whole egg may be used instead of two yolks, if desired. However, two cups of oil must be whisked in to create a sauce with the characteristic thickness. A better alternative is to use a food processor instead of a whisk to incorporate the oil. The powerful motion of the metal blade creates a thick, luscious mayonnaise with just one and one-quarter cups oil. The color (which is white) and texture are akin to commercial products, but the taste is superior. (Traditional mayonnaise with just yolks may also be made in a food processor, using about one-half cup oil per yolk.)

Although whole-egg mayonnaise has half the cholesterol of the original, the number of calories and fat grams are basically the same — very high. In its favor, whole-egg mayonnaise has a mellower flavor, and the recipe comes in handy when there are few eggs on hand. Just don't think of it as "lite" mayo.

Converted Rice

The rice I like to buy says "converted" on the label. What does this mean? Does this kind of rice have fewer nutrients than regular rice?

JEFF LOUIE
San Francisco, CA

"Converted" rice (also known as "parboiled" rice) has been treated with steam pressure to ensure that the rice grains cook up fluffy and separate. In this process, the whole grain (including the strawlike hull) is soaked, steamed, and dried; the outer hull is then removed during milling. This treatment gelatinizes the starch in the center of the grain and removes some of the starch from the rice exterior, which makes the rice less likely to become starchy or sticky when cooked.

This process toughens the rice kernel and therefore adds at least five minutes to the cooking time when compared to regular long-grain rice. Converted rice also requires about two and one-half cups of cooking water per cup of rice, as compared to two cups of water for every cup of regular long-grain rice. In terms of nutrition, parboiled rice actually has more nutrients than unenriched regular rice. However, since almost all American rices (whether or not they have been converted) are enriched after milling, the differences are slight among white rices. Of course brown rice, which has the whole bran layer intact, is more nutritious than either converted or regular white rice.

You can usually identify raw parboiled rice by its color — it is a very light brown, as opposed to regular white rice. (The color bleeds from the straw-colored hull during soaking.) Many restaurants use parboiled rice because it is harder to overcook and will hold for longer periods of time without becoming sticky. At home, converted rice is a good choice for pilafs or other fluffy rice dishes.

What Is It?

I collect odd kitchen equipment and sometimes buy things I don't know how to use. I picked up this item at a tag sale and was told it is a cake maker. Is this right? If so, how do you use it?

ELLEN YOHAI
Oakland, CA

This item is usually called an English cake mixer or cake whisk, and has been made in Great Britain for more than one hundred years. The open wire blade allows more air to be incorporated into batters than a closed wooden or metal spoon. Therefore, this tool is especially useful when beating air by hand into cake batter or meringue. Of course, an electric mixer (not available to nineteenth-century cooks) will add air even more quickly. For information about ordering an English cake maker (yes, it's still made for people who like to mix batter by hand), *see* Sources and Resources on page 32.

Bell-Pepper Tricks

I'm glad I found Cook's. *It's great to read a real magazine with no fall-out cards or advertisements. The quick tip for trimming bell peppers (May/June, 1993) tickled my curiosity. I have never been troubled by the inner flesh of the pepper. But the outer skin has always seemed to be a tough, waxy, and nonflavorful barrier to half of the pepper. (Try chewing a mouthful of pepper peels to see if they have any merit.) So when I want full pepper smoothness and taste, I always use a vegetable peeler to remove the peel. This is much easier to do after the pepper has been cut into three or four sections along its natural creases.* ■

WILLIAM VAN DRUTEN
Duluth, MN

Quick Tips

Stemming and Cutting Winter Greens

Winter greens such as kale and Swiss chard as well as spinach can be stemmed and then roll-cut into thin julienne.

1. For tender greens, simply break off tough stems.

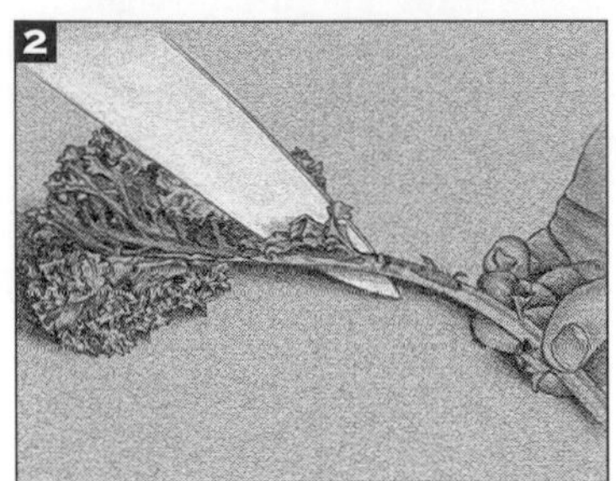

2. For tougher greens, cut the center rib from between the leaf, and cut it off along with the stem.

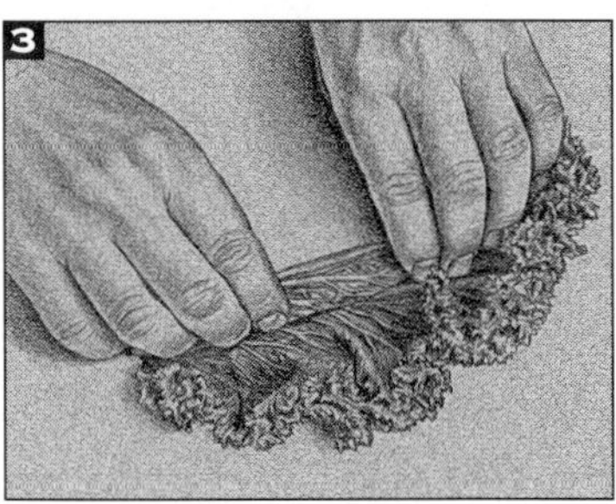

3. Lay several leaves on top of each other and tightly roll them into a long cigar shape.

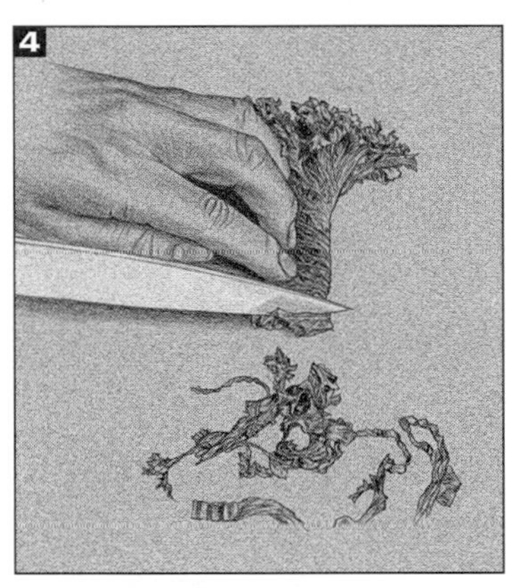

4. Slice rolled leaves into thin strips and separate.

Extracting Pomegranate Seeds

One pomegranate holds hundreds of small, tart seeds. The ruby seeds can stain, so work carefully as you open the fruit.

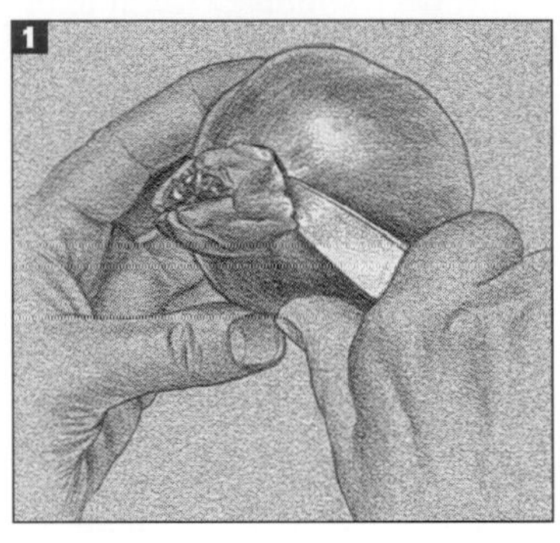

1. Use a sharp knife to cut through the stem end of the pomegranate; discard the stub.

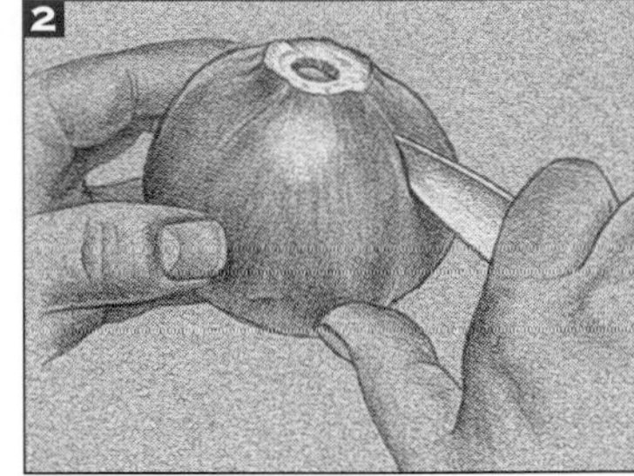

2. Starting at the exposed stem end, cut through the thin skin (but not the flesh), separating the pomegranate into quarters.

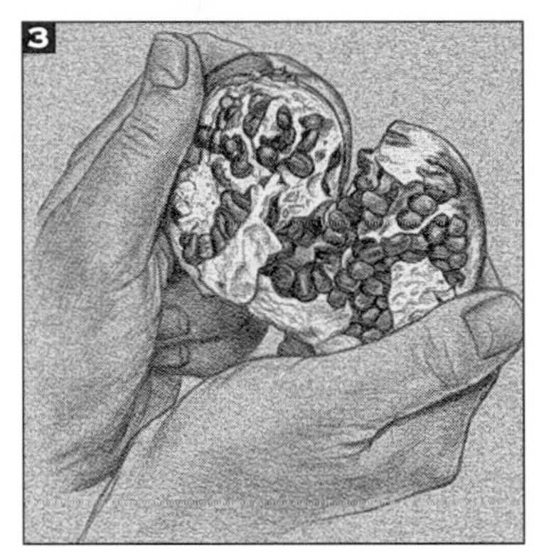

3. Use your hands to break apart the scored fruit into quarters.

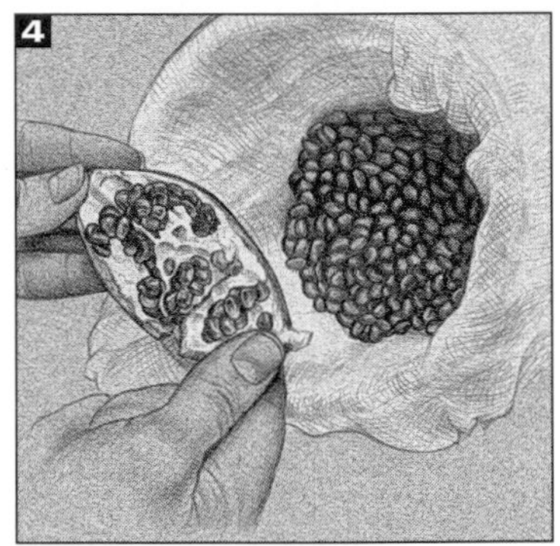

4. Turn the quarters inside out and shake the seeds into a bowl. Use your fingers to loosen the remaining seeds.

Preparing Lemongrass

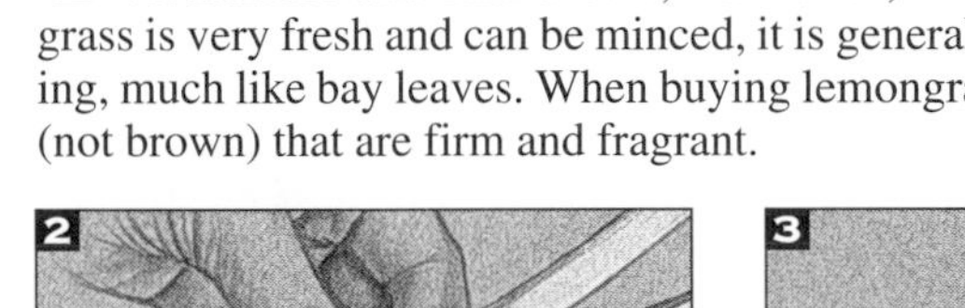

The tender heart of the long lemongrass stalk is used to flavor many Vietnamese and Thai broths, marinades, and sauces. Unless lemongrass is very fresh and can be minced, it is generally removed before serving, much like bay leaves. When buying lemongrass, look for green stalks (not brown) that are firm and fragrant.

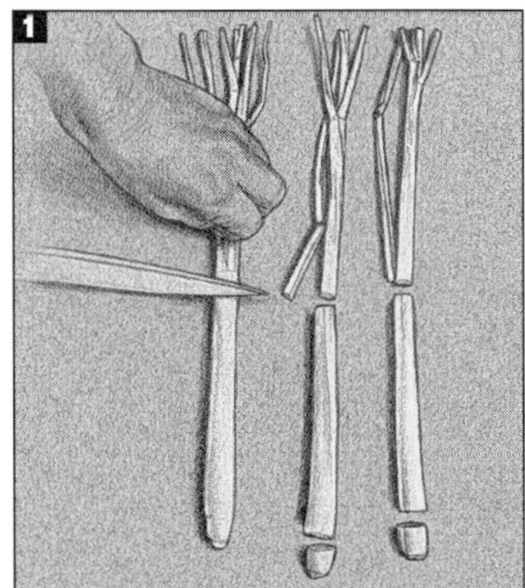

1. Trim the dry leafy top (this part is usually green) and the tough bottom of each stalk.

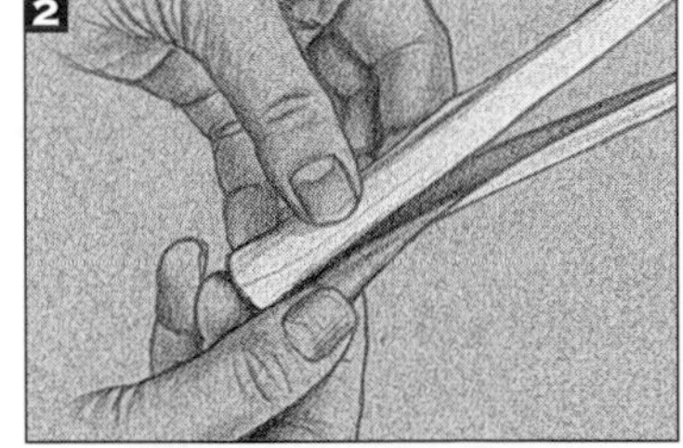

2. Peel and discard dry outer layers until the moist, tender center is exposed.

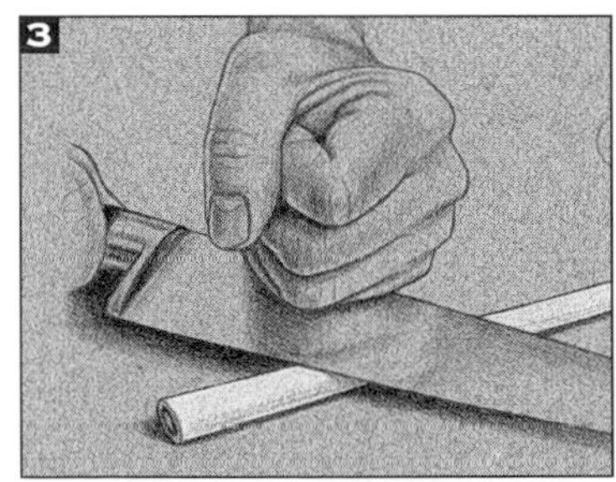

3. Smash the peeled stalk with the side of a heavy knife.

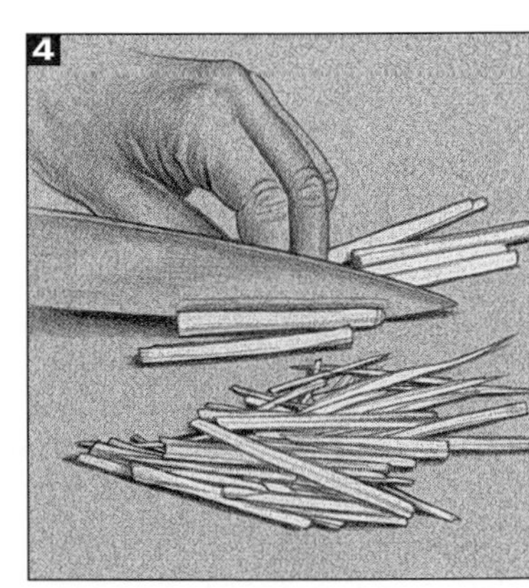

4. Cut the smashed stalk into long strips that can be removed when the dish is finished cooking. Freeze extra strips for later use.

Illustrations by Alan Witschonke

Making a Disposable Piping Cone

These disposable cones are useful for making desserts such as the Chocolate Trinity Parfaits shown on the back cover.

1. Fold an 8-x-14-inch sheet of parchment paper in half on the diagonal and cut along the fold.

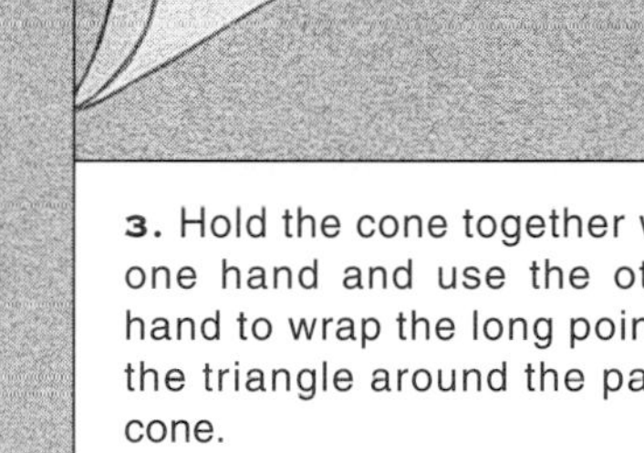

2. Fold the short side of one of the triangles over to the right-angled corner, thus forming a cone.

3. Hold the cone together with one hand and use the other hand to wrap the long point of the triangle around the paper cone.

4. Tuck the exposed point of the paper inside the cone, positioning it between the inner and outer layers of the cone to secure it.

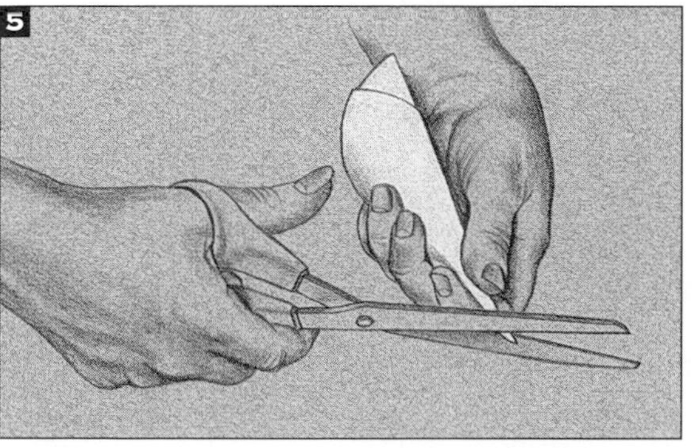

5. Use a scissors to snip a hole in the point of the cone; make a very small hole for decorative piping, a larger one for less delicate tasks.

Flavoring Roasts with Garlic

Fresh herbs and slivers of garlic can be inserted into any roast, including lamb, beef, or pork, so that the flavor permeates the entire piece of meat as it cooks. You can insert up to two dozen slivers or sprigs of herbs, depending on the size of the roast and your individual preference.

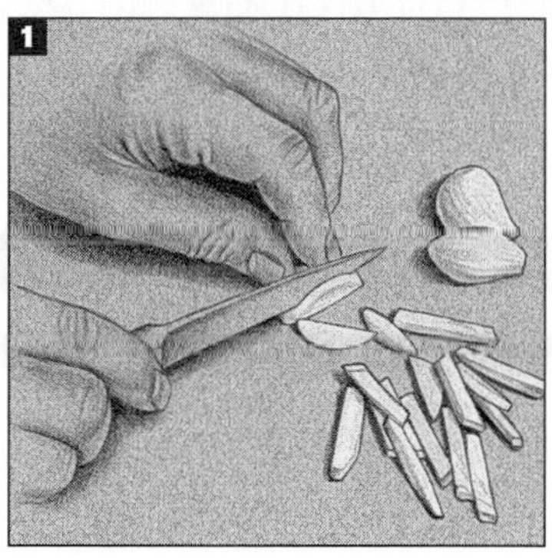

1. Separate garlic into cloves, peel the cloves, and cut each one lengthwise into several small slivers.

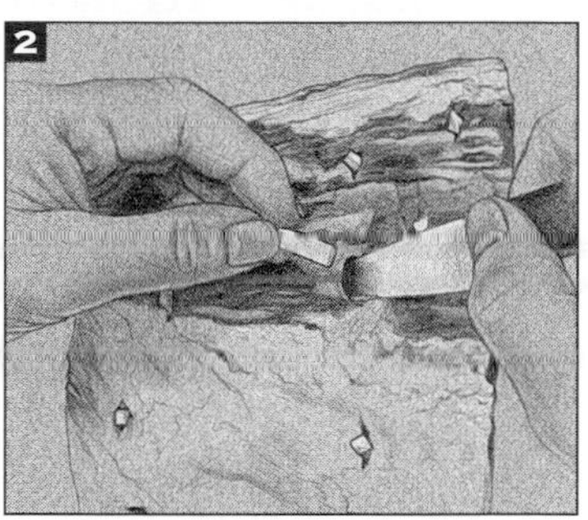

2. Push the tip of your knife about one inch into the meat, force the meat to one side of the opening, slide the garlic sliver to the bottom of the opening, and remove the knife.

Carving a Rib Roast

There are two ways to carve a rib roast — either with the rib attached for prime rib or without the rib for slices of any thickness.

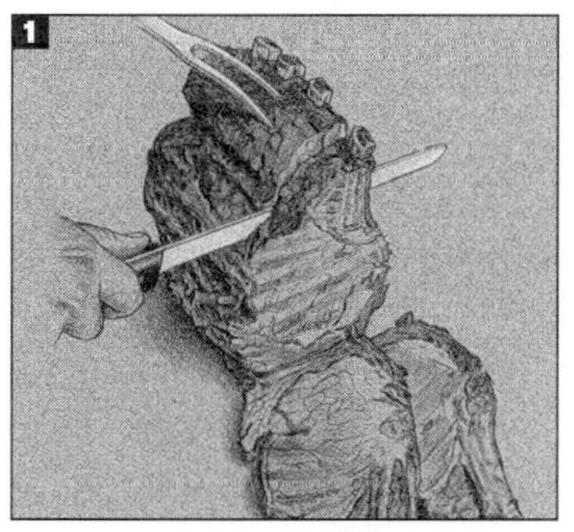

1. For thick prime rib slices, stand roast on end with ribs facing up and slice between each rib.

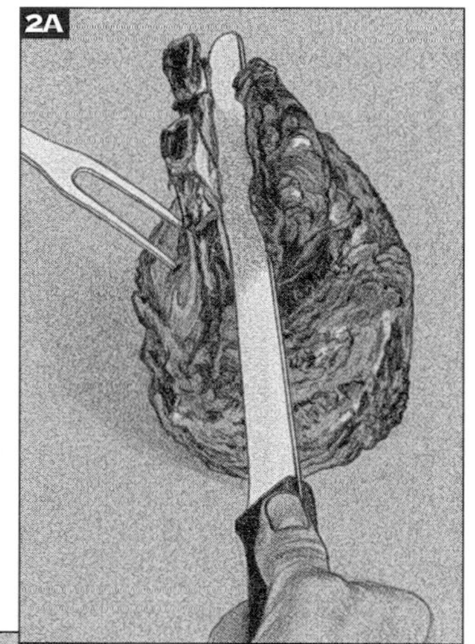

2A. For slices without bone, detach the roast from the bones by cutting along the inside of the ribs.

2B. Turn the roast onto a counter and slice into pieces of desired thickness.

ATTENTION READERS, FREE SUBSCRIPTION FOR PUBLISHED TIPS. Do you have a unique tip you would like to share with other readers? We will provide a one-year complimentary subscription for each quick tip that we print. Send a description of your special technique to *Cook's Illustrated,* P.O. Box 569, Brookline Village, MA 02147. Please write "Attention: Quick Tips" on the envelope and include your name, address, and daytime phone number. Unfortunately, we can only acknowledge receipt of tips that will be printed in the magazine.

One Dough, Many Cookies

One master recipe for holiday cookies yields a dozen perfectly moist and tender variations. The secret ingredient? Cornstarch.

BY MARCY GOLDMAN

The quintessential holiday cookie can be easily rolled, molded, cut, and handled without breaking, yet retains a buttery quality when eaten. Good holiday cookies should almost melt in your mouth, with a sensation close to that of shortbread.

This is a tall order, to be sure, because the dough for tender, buttery cookies is notoriously hard to work. But there is such a cookie, and it has the added benefit of being easily varied. In the cookie dough I have developed, two strategies work in your favor: the use of extra tenderizing agents in the batter, and the use of the refrigerator to firm up the rich, otherwise temperamental dough.

Making a Tender Cookie

My emphasis on tenderness is not just about taste; shaped or decorated cookies, always popular at this time of year, are necessarily subjected to more handling than the drop variety. There is rolling and cutting, even rerolling of scraps, all of which would provoke a less tender dough into toughness. A purposefully rich and short dough, however, braces itself against the negatives of constant working by calling on every ingredient that offers tenderness — egg yolks, fat, sugar, and cream — and avoiding those that don't, such as hard or too much flour, egg whites, and extra liquid (*see* "'Short' Dough Makes Tender Cookies," page 7).

The classic butter cookie, much like good bread, should win raves on its own, long before the chocolate chips, garnish of sprinkles, or colorful frosting are added. Therefore the foundation ingredients — sweet butter, cane sugar, pure vanilla, and other extracts — must be of premium quality.

The primary fat must be sweet butter; there is no mistaking its distinct aroma and flavor. Do not be tempted to substitute margarine for the butter; it performs differently and the result is far inferior. The judicious addition of vegetable shortening, on the other hand, does little to detract from the full butter flavor, and its higher burning temperature and lower moisture content allows for additional shortness of crumb.

Egg yolks and cream follow in the tenderness scheme. While most cookie recipes use whole eggs, I omit them here. Egg whites are a terrific help when you need a dough with more body, but can compromise this cookie's flaky appeal. (Don't chuck the whites however; keep them covered in the fridge for use as an egg wash or cookie "glue," to make sprinkles and other surface decorations adhere.) The small amount of cream in the recipe binds the batter together, and the extra fat content added by the cream helps with browning as well.

Perfect holiday cookie dough combines workability with tenderness. If children are helping shape cookies, add two to three tablespoons extra flour to the recipe to create a firmer dough.

A Secret Ingredient: Cornstarch

When I first began to examine the vast number of heirloom holiday cookie recipes, I was immediately struck by the fact that many of them call for confectioners' sugar, which is no more than cornstarch and sugar pulverized together. The cornstarch serves as a "carrier" for the sugar, preventing it from caking, which is why this type of sugar works so well for icings and decorative dusting.

Confectioners' sugar does a good job inside a cookie dough, too, because it softens the flour, but it is more difficult to regulate its sweetening effect, since it carries starch and sugar as a fused partnership. I prefer to separate the cornstarch from the sugar, which allows me to adjust the sweetness of the dough by altering the sugar alone, without disturbing the dry ingredients' balance.

Furthermore, cornstarch diminishes the hardness of all-purpose flour, providing the baker with a softer flour without the necessity of any special trips to the supermarket for cake flour. (Cornstarch can dramatically improve or alter the texture in other cookie recipes, as well; *see* "The Cornstarch Connection," page 9.)

Baking powder is the leavener of choice to provide the required lightness of crumb in these cookies; baking soda cannot be used here because it requires the presence of an acid to work. Pure vanilla and the merest touch of salt help round out the flavors.

Mixing, Handling, and Baking

As with most butter-based cookies, you begin by creaming the butter and shortening with the sugar. It is important to blend the two fats well, and doing this task along with the sugar allows the sharp crystals of the sugar to break up the fat and drag in more air, which makes for lightness. Egg yolks, extracts, and cream are blended in next, quickly followed by the preblended dry ingredients.

Having ingredients just a bit cooler than room temperature assists proper blending and results in a dough that is ready to roll. If a dough does begin to get too soft to be workable, simply pop it in the fridge for about ten minutes and you're back in business. Chilling the dough prevents you from adding extra flour, which would firm up the dough but can make the final product tough.

Any pastry chef will readily admit that, after quality ingredients, the refrigerator is his or her primary asset. It is a tool available to everyone, but home chefs tend to underestimate the fridge's ability to salvage warm, slightly greasy doughs that otherwise can be nearly impossible to work with.

Once, under duress, I tried to rush a warm dough along into a hasty quartet of jaunty gingerbread men. The dough instantly laminated itself to my rolling pin — a partnership forged in warm fat. As I scraped the whole mess off and gathered the floppy strips together, I wryly recalled my own council as a professional baker: Don't rush. And, when in doubt, chill out.

Even if you do manage to make a cleanly cut shape out of such a dough, the oven heat, hitting the warm dough, will cause the butter to melt and the cookies to splay outwards before they set up. The result: flat, amorphous shapes.

PHOTOGRAPHS BY ERIC ROTH

I recommend that you make a few batches of the doughs you need, then freeze them in flattened disks (each recipe makes two rounds of just over three-quarters of a pound each) or refrigerate them for up to three days. This way, you can defrost cookie dough as needed; it softens in just about an hour on the counter. Having ready-made packets of dough allows you to simply bake and decorate cookies in small batches as you need them, ensuring fresh, buttery cookies throughout the holidays.

When baking your cookies, I recommend that you cover the cookies sheets with baking parchment or silicone paper (*see* Sources and Resources, page 32). This professional baker's item eliminates the need for both pregreasing and washing several cookie sheets, and makes for uniform cookies with consistent, rounded edges. You will eliminate scorched bottoms and the cookies will slide right off.

Finally a note on baking time. Lightly baked, golden cookies are visually very pretty, but darker browned cookies, baked an additional two to four minutes, bring out the butter flavor. This is what I recommend. Cool your cookies on a wire rack and store them in a covered container — if you leave them out, they become soft in a few hours.

All of the variations on the Master Recipe can be made into a variety of shapes, using a spritz gun, a pastry bag, your hand (as in the crescents), or standard cookie cutters. Some doughs are best used for a particular presentation, and we have included some suggestions.

MASTER RECIPE FOR HOLIDAY BUTTER COOKIE DOUGH

Yields approximately 6 dozen single-layer cookies or 3 dozen sandwich cookies

- 2½ cups all-purpose flour
- ¼ cup cornstarch
- 2 teaspoons baking powder
- Tiny pinch salt
- 2 egg yolks
- 3 tablespoons light cream
- 1½ teaspoons vanilla extract
- 1 cup white sugar
- 12 tablespoons unsalted butter, softened
- 4 tablespoons vegetable shortening

1. Heat oven to 350 degrees. Line 2 baking sheets with parchment or silicone paper.
2. Mix flour, cornstarch, baking powder, and salt in a medium bowl. Mix yolks, cream, and vanilla together in a measuring cup.
3. Cream sugar with butter and shortening until lightened and pasty. Beat yolk mixture into creamed butter until just combined.
4. Add dry ingredients and beat until mixture begins to clump together (about 18 to 20 seconds on lowest speed of electric mixer).
5. Turn dough out onto a lightly floured board and knead gently to shape into a soft dough. (Can be wrapped in plastic wrap and refrigerated up to 3 days or frozen up to 6 months.) Proceed with rolling, shaping, and baking instructions under selected cookie.

Suggested shapes: Classic cut-outs; spirals made with another colored dough; turnovers; mock thumbprints; petticoat tails.

CHOCOLATE BUTTER COOKIE DOUGH

Follow the Master Recipe, adding 1 ounce each melted unsweetened and semisweet chocolates after sugar has been creamed with butter and shortening.

Suggested shapes: Pinwheels with butter cookie dough; classic cut-outs garnished with icing or melted white chocolate; Linzer cookies filled with apricot or raspberry preserves; crescents coated with confectioners' sugar.

NUT BUTTER COOKIE DOUGH

Follow the Master Recipe, adding 1 cup toasted and cooled walnuts, pecans, hazelnuts, or almonds after the dry ingredients are almost incorporated. If using walnuts, pecans, or hazelnuts, add ½ teaspoon cinnamon and ¼ teaspoon nutmeg to the dry ingredients. If using almonds, reduce vanilla to ¾ teaspoon and add ¾ teaspoon almond extract.

Suggested shapes: Linzer cookies or Viennese crescents; simple cut-outs; mock thumbprints.

CITRUS BUTTER COOKIE DOUGH

Citrus oils are available at candy-making supply stores or through specialty mail order (*see* Sources and Resources, page 32).

Follow Master Recipe; reduce vanilla to ¼ teaspoon and add ¼ teaspoon each orange oil, lemon oil, and citric acid to the egg yolk mixture. After the sugar has been creamed with the butter and shortening, add 1 tablespoon each orange, lemon, and lime zest, minced fine.

Suggested Shapes: Classic cut-outs; citrus pinwheels.

SPICE BUTTER COOKIE DOUGH

Follow Master Recipe; reduce baking powder

"SHORT" DOUGH MAKES TENDER COOKIES

Perfect cookies are a balance between fats and proteins, softness and structure. Too much fat and the cookies will literally run off the baking sheet in the oven; too much protein and they will be tough and chewy. The Master Recipe calls for a number of unusual ingredient tricks to achieve the right balance.

Solid fats are also called shortening because of the effect they have on proteins in flour. About 80 percent of the protein in flour is gluten. When exposed to water, the gluten proteins bond together, as they do in bread dough, forming a strong network that gives texture and shape to baked goods. In cookies and other pastries, however, gluten formation is not desired. Previous generations believed that cutting solid fat into flour "shortened" the gluten strands. Although we now know the term is not completely accurate, fat does inhibit gluten formation.

According to Carl Hoseney, a professor at Kansas State University, particles of flour that are coated with fat absorb water more slowly than uncoated particles. "If the flour doesn't take up water the glutens can't interact with one another and won't form a continuous network," says Hoseney. Excessive mixing or rerolling, however, will increase the rate of water absorption by flour molecules, even when fat is present. "Shortening keeps gluten strands smaller by slowing down the natural interaction of flour and water," continues Hoseney.

The high sugar content of cookie doughs (particularly the Master Recipe here) also slows down gluten formation, since the sugar molecules are in intense competition with the flour molecules for the small amount of liquid that the dough contains.

With this explanation, it becomes clear why the Master Recipe is so successful. Butter is roughly 80 percent fat and 18 percent water, plus milk solids. Vegetable shortening is 100 percent fat. In terms of "shortening" ability, butter is the second choice because of its water content; it's the first choice for flavor, however. The compromise struck in the Master Recipe of three parts butter to one part shortening keeps the rich, buttery flavor while reducing the amount of water, and therefore the formation of gluten, in the cookies.

Likewise, the decision to omit egg whites is based on the fact that they contain 90 percent water and 10 percent albumen proteins, which coagulate and toughen — think of a fried egg — when heated. In addition to supplying fat, the yolks contain lecithin, a powerful emulsifier that surrounds the fat molecules and helps prevent the absorption of water by the flour. As for the use of cream, some liquid is needed to bind ingredients in the batter. The choice of high-fat, low-water cream — instead of thinner milk — again helps reduce gluten formation.

—Jack Bishop

to 1½ teaspoons and add ½ teaspoon baking soda. To the dry ingredients add: ¾ teaspoon cinnamon, ¼ teaspoon cloves, ¼ teaspoon allspice, ¼ teaspoon ginger, ⅛ teaspoon mace, and a tiny pinch nutmeg. Substitute 1 cup brown sugar for the white sugar and add 2 tablespoons molasses when creaming the sugar with the butter and shortening. Reduce light cream from 3 tablespoons to 2 tablespoons.

Suggested shapes: Gingerbread men; classic cut-outs; Linzer cookies filled with lemon curd.

MINCEMEAT OR JAM TURNOVERS

Makes about 4 dozen

Follow recipe for one of the butter cookie doughs. Working with ¼ of the dough at a time, roll to about ⅛-inch thick. Using a 3-inch round cookie cutter, cut dough rounds. Transfer rounds to prepared cookie sheet. Fill the center of each with a scant ½ teaspoon of prepared mincemeat, jam, or apricot or prune butter. Fold in half (*see* illustration 1); crimp edges with a fork. Turn corners up and around so that they come within ½-inch of meeting (illustration 2). Arrange shaped cookies about 1½ inches apart. Bake at 375 degrees until golden brown, 15 to 17 minutes. Dust with confectioners' sugar if desired.

MOCK THUMBPRINTS

Makes about 4 dozen

Follow recipe for one of the butter cookie doughs. Divide dough into eighths. Roll a portion into a 12-inch log and place on prepared cookie sheet. Use the handle of a wooden spoon to make a deep indentation down the center of each log (*see* illustration 3). Repeat with remaining dough, placing each log about 1½ inches apart. Bake, remaking the indentation once during baking if necessary, until cookies are golden, 15 to 17 minutes. Transfer to a cookie sheet to cool. Pipe or spoon about 2 tablespoons jam per cookie down the center of each warm cookie (illustration 4). Let stand until jam sets. Cut each cookie diagonally into 1½- to 2-inch bars.

CLASSIC CUT-OUTS

Makes about 6 dozen 2-inch cookies

Follow recipe for one of the butter cookie doughs. Working with ¼ of the dough at a time, roll to about ⅛-inch thick on a well-floured work surface. Use cookie cutter of your choice to cut out shapes. Using a spatula, transfer cut-outs to prepared baking sheet, placing them about 1 inch apart. Bake at 350 degrees until golden, 10 to 12 minutes. Repeat with remaining dough. Transfer to a wire rack and cool to room temperature.

PINWHEELS

Makes about 6 dozen

Make ½ recipe each of 2 of the butter cookie doughs of different colors (e.g. chocolate and butter). Halve each half-batch of dough; roll a portion of each dough on parchment to a 9-by-7-inch rectangle about ¼-inch thick; brush one dough rectangle with egg wash. Carefully invert other dough rectangle on top of the egg-washed dough. Remove parchment paper from the inverted dough. With the long side of the rectangle facing you, use the bottom sheet of parchment paper as a guide to gently roll the two doughs up, jellyroll-style, pulling paper off as you roll (*see* illustration 5). Wrap dough log in plastic wrap and chill for at least 15 minutes. Repeat process with remaining dough. Cut each chilled log into ¼-inch slices. Place dough pinwheels about 1 inch apart on prepared cookie sheet (illustration 6); bake at 350 degrees until golden, 12 to 15 minutes.

For citrus spirals, use a colored dough (yellow or orange) along with the plain or vanilla dough and precede as for regular pinwheels.

SHAPING THE COOKIES

TURNOVERS

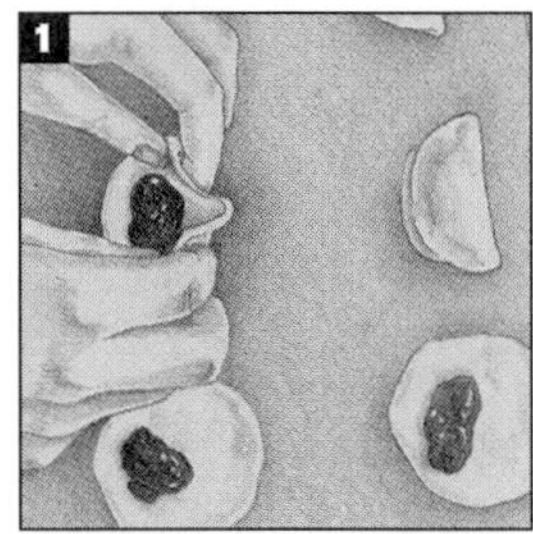

1. After filling centers of rounds, fold them in half.

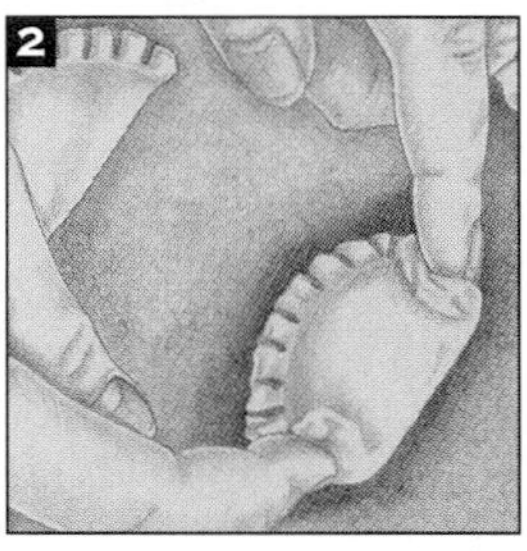

2. Crimp ends of turnovers with a fork, then turn corners up and fold them over.

MOCK THUMBPRINTS

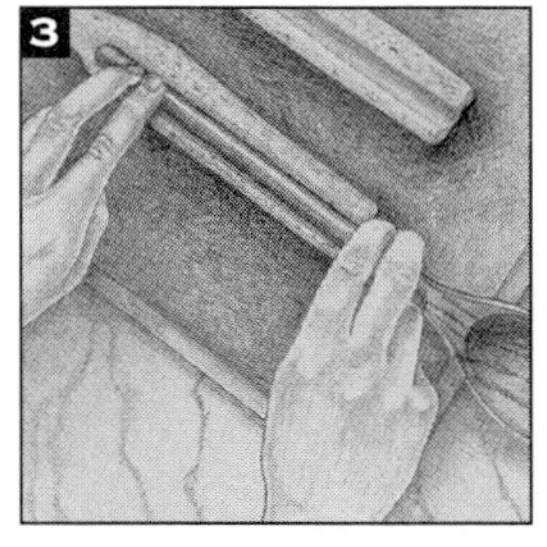

3. Make a deep indentation down the center of each log with a wooden-spoon handle.

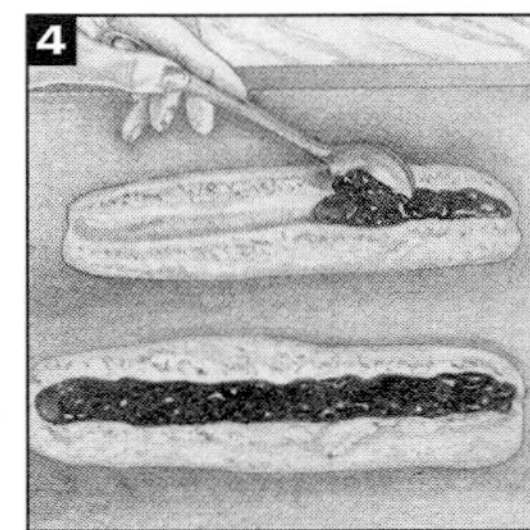

4. Pipe or spoon jam down the center of each baked log and cut into pieces.

PINWHEELS

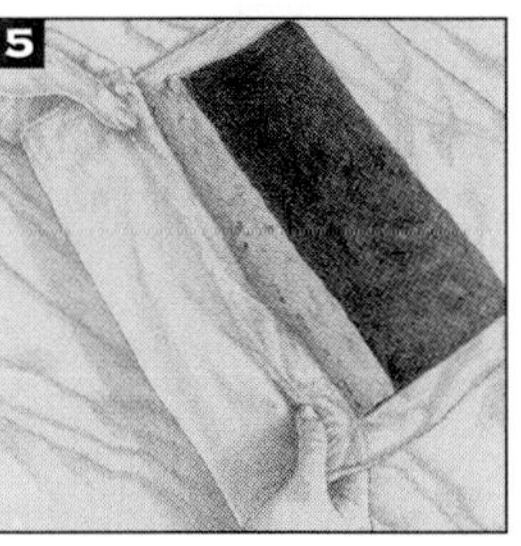

5. Use parchment paper to roll the superimposed rectangles of different-colored doughs into a log.

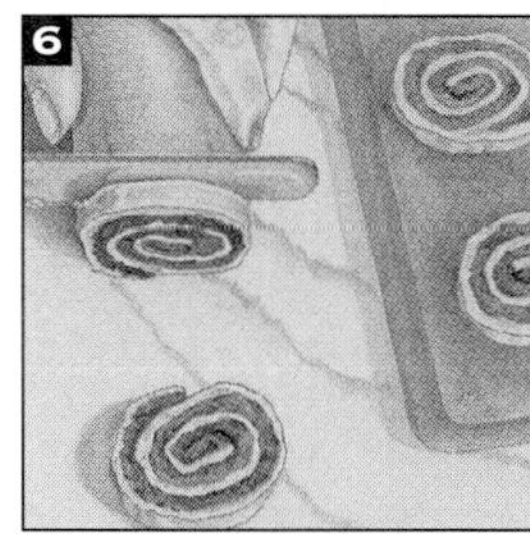

6. Slice logs and place about one inch apart on a prepared cookie sheet.

LINZER COOKIES

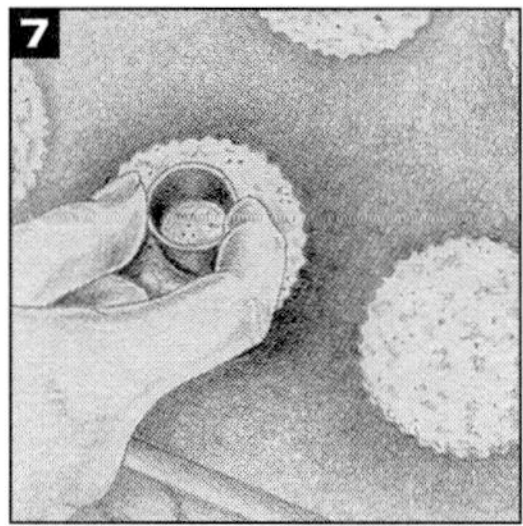

7. Use a one-half inch cutter to cut holes in half the unbaked dough rounds.

8. Place jam in center of uncut rounds, then place holed rounds on top

PETTICOAT TAILS

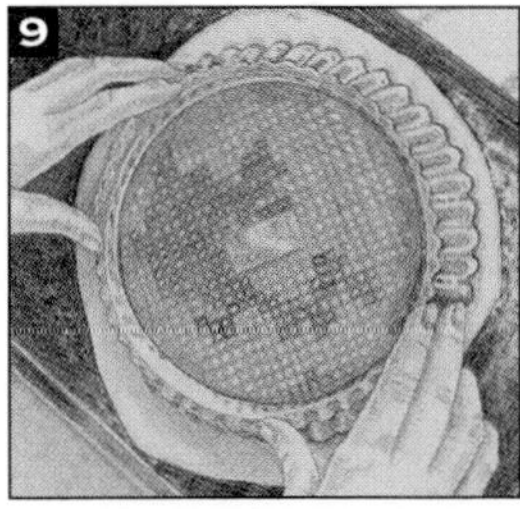

9. Use an eight-inch-diameter fluted tart pan to cut a fluted circle.

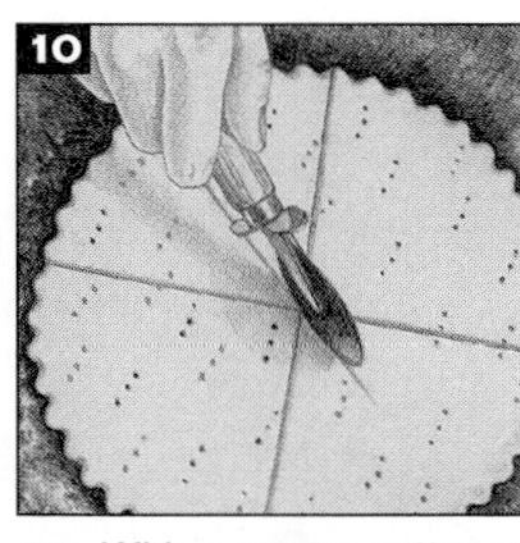

10. With a pastry cutter or sharp knife, cut the circle into eight wedges.

VIENNESE CRESCENTS

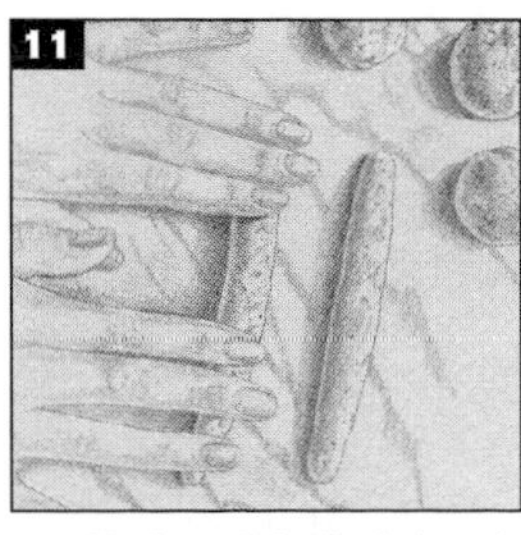

11. Roll each ball of dough into three-inch log with tapered ends.

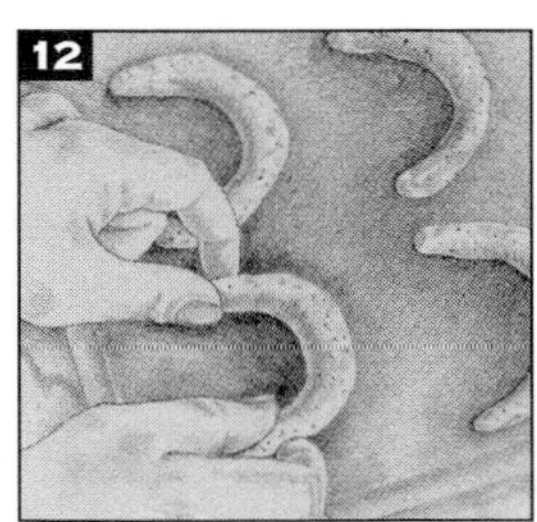

12. Turn ends of each log down so that a crescent shape is formed.

ILLUSTRATIONS BY DOROTHY GULICK

Brush slices with egg wash, and dust with sanding sugar or plain table sugar.

For jam pinwheels, roll out 1 rectangle of dough as described above. With long end of rectangle facing you spread a thin layer of thick preserves (3 to 4 tablespoons) over dough leaving a 1-inch border along the side opposite you. Roll up, jelly-roll style. Follow above instructions for chilling, cutting, and baking.

LINZER COOKIES
Makes 3 dozen sandwich cookies

1. Follow recipe for one of the butter cookie doughs. Working with about ¼ of the dough at a time, roll dough to about ⅛ inch thick. Using a 2-inch serrated cookie cutter, cut dough rounds. Place about 1 inch apart on prepared cookie sheets. Using a ½-inch cutter (the bottom of a pastry tip works well), cut a hole in the center of half the dough rounds to make cookie tops (*see* illustration 7). Bake until golden, 10 to 12 minutes. Transfer to a wire rack and cool completely.
2. Smear a heaping ½ teaspoon complementary jam (or chocolate frosting or lemon curd) on each cookie bottom, mounding center a bit more generously. Gently place top cookie over filling (illustration 8). Dust with confectioners' sugar.

For chocolate Linzer cookies, dust with a mixture made up of equal parts cocoa and confectioners' sugar.

For spice Linzer cookies, fill layers with store-bought lemon curd. Finish with confectioners' sugar.

PETTICOAT TAILS
Makes about 4 dozen

Follow recipe for one of the butter cookie doughs. Divide dough into sixths. Working with one portion at a time, roll dough to an 8½-inch circle on parchment paper. Invert an 8-inch fluted tart pan onto dough to form fluted circle (*see* illustration 9). (Or use an 8-inch pie pan to cut dough circle, then crimp perimeter with a fork.) Using a pastry cutter or a sharp knife, cut the dough circle into 8 wedges (illustration 10). Prick dough all over with fork. Bake the round at 350 degrees until golden, 15 to 17 minutes. While cookie is still warm, use pastry wheel or sharp knife to reestablish original cut marks. Transfer wedges to wire rack and cool to room temperature. Dip in melted chocolate, if you like.

VIENNESE CRESCENTS
Makes about 4 dozen

Follow recipe for one of the butter cookie doughs. Working with about 1 tablespoon dough at a time, roll each portion of dough into a ball. Roll ball into a 3-inch length with tapered ends (*see* illustration 11); turn ends down to form a crescent shape (illustration 12). Repeat with remaining dough. Place dough crescents about 1½ inches apart on prepared cookie sheet. Bake at 350 degrees until golden, 15 to 17 minutes. While cookies are still warm, dip them in sifted confectioners' sugar, then place on a wire rack to cool to room temperature. Dip cooled cookies again in confectioners' sugar.

DECORATIVE ICING
Coats about 2 dozen 2-inch cookies

1–2 tablespoons milk
1 cup confectioners' sugar
Food coloring (optional)
2–3 drops flavored extracts (vanilla, peppermint, cherry, banana, almond, etc.), to taste (optional)

1. Stir minimum amount of milk into confectioners' sugar with a small wire whisk or a fork to make a soft smooth icing. (Stir in optional food coloring and flavor extracts.) If mixture is too stiff, add milk in very tiny increments until correct consistency is reached.
2. Pipe icing from a pastry bag to outline cookies or make simple motifs, or simply drizzle on designs. If coating the cookie, use a small metal spatula to spread icing over entire top surface or dip cookie into icing, using the metal spatula to trim away excess. (If mixture hardens, remix with a bit of water, whisking well to make icing smooth.) Allow cookies to dry to a dull shine before storing. ■

Marcy Goldman is a Montreal-based professional pastry chef, baker, and food journalist.

THE CORNSTARCH CONNECTION

Perhaps the most unusual ingredient in the Master Recipe is cornstarch. Diluting all-purpose flour with inert starch creates a type of flour that is best for cookies, one which is not otherwise available to all home cooks.

Flour contains between 7 and 14 percent protein. Bread flours, which are designed to promote strong gluten formation, generally have more protein; pastry flours generally have less.

Given what we know about gluten formation and toughness (*see* "'Short' Dough Makes Tender Cookies" page 7), why not choose flours with a low-protein content for cookies? P. J. Hamel, senior editor at King Arthur Flour, says unbleached pastry flour, which has a protein content between 7.5 and 8 percent, can make wonderful cookies. However, Hamel adds that it can be difficult to work with because it's so delicate. "It's the choice of many professional bakers but is less practical for people at home," says Hamel.

Cake flour, with a slightly higher protein content of 8 to 9 percent, might seem like a better choice; it is available in most supermarkets and is easier to handle. But cake flour is bleached with chlorine, which increases the ability of gluten proteins to bond with sugar and helps cakes rise and hold their shape. These traits, though welcome in cake making, increase toughness in cookies. Carl Hoseney, a professor in the Cereal Science and Industry Department at Kansas State University, says unbleached cake flour is ideal for cookies. Unfortunately, this product, which is sometimes called cookie flour, is available only to food manufacturers.

Adding cornstarch to unbleached all-purpose flour is an easy way to make this commercial product at home. Substituting one-quarter cup cornstarch for the same amount of flour (as directed in the Master Recipe) lowers the protein content by about 1 percent. If you start with a low-protein, all-purpose flour (look on the label for a brand with 11 grams of protein per four ounces), you can create your own unbleached cake flour. (Note: To calculate the exact protein percentage in any flour, divide protein grams per four ounces — the number listed on the label — by 1.13.)

This trick of diluting all-purpose flour with cornstarch can be used in almost any cookie. To gauge the effects on a classic recipe, I prepared chocolate chip cookies with two and one-quarter cups unbleached all-purpose flour. (My regular flour contains 11 percent protein.) In a second batch, I replaced one-quarter cup flour with an equal amount of cornstarch. For a third batch, I replaced one-half cup flour with cornstarch.

The batch with one-quarter cup cornstarch was very similar to the original recipe. The cookies were cakey, chewy, and even crunchy as they cooled. However the third batch, with one-half cup cornstarch, was markedly different. The cookies were tender, light, and airy. As opposed to the cakey originals, this batch was almost wispy.

Using about 1 part cornstarch to 4 parts high-protein, unbleached all-purpose flour (12 to 13 grams of protein per four ounces) can benefit many cookie recipes. With low-protein, unbleached all-purpose flour (no more than 11 grams of protein per four ounces), just 1 part cornstarch per 10 parts flour (the ratio used in the Master Recipe) will work.

Of course, if you like cakey chocolate chip cookies, replacing some of the flour with cornstarch is not for you. However, with rolled holiday cookies, tenderness is always an asset and cornstarch a ready ally.

—Jack Bishop

Making Perfect Mashed Potatoes

For a fluffy, light, flavorful version of this classic, use high-starch potatoes and the right tool . . . and don't overcook.

BY ERIC WOLFF

Nearly every home cook mashes potatoes from time to time, but few know how to make this quintessential American dish truly flavorful, with the full and fluffy texture that makes it so satisfying.

Yet there are few secrets. I've found that the major factors are the potatoes and the equipment you use; timing is important as well. During the course of my research, I also explored whether peeling really does cause great nutritive loss and whether the added milk should be hot or cold. Finally, I looked for a good low-fat version, and for easy, flavor-boosting additions.

The Potato: High Starch is Best

Although you can mash any type of potato, the variety you choose *does* make a significant difference in the ultimate quality of the dish. Potatoes are composed mostly of starch and water. The starch is in the form of granules, which in turn are contained in starch cells. The higher the starch content of the potato, the fuller the cells. In high-starch potatoes, the cells are completely full — they look like plump little beach balls. In medium- or low-starch potatoes, the cells are more like underinflated beach balls. The space between these less-full cells is mostly taken up by water.

The full starch cells of high-starch potatoes are most likely to maintain their integrity and stay separate when mashed, giving the potatoes a delightfully fluffy, full texture. In addition, the low water content of these potatoes allows them to absorb milk, cream, and/or butter without becoming wet or gummy. Starch cells in lower-starch potatoes, on the other hand, tend to clump up when cooked and break more easily, allowing the starch to dissolve into whatever liquid is present. The broken cells and dissolved starch tend to make sticky, gummy mashed potatoes.

I recommend Russet or Yukon Gold potatoes, both of which have a high starch content as well as rich flavor. I like the buttery color of the Yukon Golds for certain variations, and prefer the stark white of Russets for basic mashed potatoes. Russets, which are often marketed as Idaho Baking Potatoes, can be found virtually anywhere. Yukon Golds are less common but are sold in many supermarkets and produce stores. In a pinch, you can use Eastern potatoes, which have a lumpy appearance, with a thick brown skin. They have a medium-high starch content, and will give you decent texture and pleasing whiteness, although not quite as good a texture or flavor as Russets. Do not use low-starch waxy, red bliss, or California White; when I made mashed potatoes with these, the result was a thin dish similar to the kind made with instant potato buds. Regardless of the potato variety you use, old ones are always better than new for mashing: during storage, water evaporates.

The Best Tool

My favorite device for mashing potatoes (and I've tried them all) is an Italian tool resembling a giant garlic press. Although it is sold under the name of *schiacciapatate,* or potato masher, it is actually not a masher per se, but the best-made ricer I've ever seen (*see* Sources and Resources, page 32). Made of stainless steel and with a capacity of about two-cups, it rices beautifully and is very easy to clean. It is sold with two removable disks, one with large holes and one with small holes. If you like some lumps in your mashed potatoes use the large holes; if not, use the small. At $37.50 it is not inexpensive, but it is so convenient and so well made that your great-grandchildren will still be using it to make their mashed potatoes while praising their ancestor's consumer wisdom.

Some people, including potato notables such as Lydie Marshall, author of *A Passion for Potatoes* (HarperCollins, 1992), like to force potatoes through a kitchen strainer to mash. This works well if the strainer's holes are big enough — use a wooden spoon to force the potatoes through the strainer — but it is both time consuming and messy.

Whether you choose the ricer or the strainer, both offer the advantage of mashing the potato before adding other ingredients. That way, you can blend in butter and milk with a wooden spoon or a stiff whisk, which is gentler on those starch cells and therefore helps ensure consistently fluffy mashed potatoes.

Some people, including the late James Beard, recommend using an electric mixer to mash. I found this acceptable, as long as I kept the mixing time as short as possible. Mixing too long caused the potatoes to lose their fluffiness. If you have a KitchenAid, use the paddle, as it is relatively gentle and will not immediately overwork the potatoes. Never use a food processor for mashing, since it will transform your potatoes into lifeless soup.

The more traditional mashers are usually of two types: a disk with large holes in it or a curvy wire loop. I found the disk to be more efficient for reducing both mashing time and the number of lumps in the finished product. (Besides, the one I use was my grandmother's, and sentiment is an important ingredient in cooking.) If you choose one of these mashers, don't use a spoon to blend in the other ingredients, as recommended with the ricer and strainer, but blend and mash at the same time to minimize stickiness. I recommend mashing a little, then stirring a bit, then mashing, and so on, finishing with a brisk stirring.

I also discovered a mashing gizmo consisting of a spring-loaded, double-decker wire loop. When you mash down, the top row of loops moves down to meet the bottom row and then springs back up as you raise the masher. This device did mash quickly, but is difficult to clean. I found it works better as a conversation piece than as a mashing device.

The last and least favorite of the mashing tools is the fork. Some people say it's the only way, but I found it all too easy to burn my knuckles on the side of the bowl, and equally

Mashing tools include (left to right) a spring-loaded double-wire loop; disk; single-wire loop; and the Italian ricer called schiacciapatate, *the clear favorite.*

ILLUSTRATION BY DAN KROVATIN

easy to overwork the potatoes and increase gumminess.

On Peeling and Cooking

Many experts recommend leaving the skin on potatoes because of its high nutritive value; common wisdom also holds that there is a layer of rich nutrients just below the skin. In fact, the only nutritive substance in potato peels that isn't contained in the flesh is dietary fiber. And nutrients are not concentrated under the skin; rather, they are distributed throughout the potato. Therefore, unless you like skins in your mashed potatoes (and many people do), you might as well peel them before cooking.

There is also another reason to peel. Potatoes exposed to light develop a toxin called solanine, which may contribute a green tinge to the skin itself and frequently turns the flesh directly under the skin a bright green. Botanists theorize that solanine, an alkaloid, is present to discourage insects from eating the potato, especially the growth buds (eyes). Fatal poisoning is only theoretically possible, but solanine is indigestible, and enough of it may cause stomach discomfort. So, whether you choose to peel or not, I recommend cutting out the eyes and any green patches; if you use potatoes that have been stored in light conditions, be sure to peel them.

If you do peel, you should know that there really is a better peeler; on this model, the blade is mounted horizontally on a U-shaped handle. It peels just about anything more quickly, more easily, and with less waste than the more common vertical-style peeler (*see* Sources and Resources, page 32).

Be careful not to overcook potatoes you plan to mash, because the starch cells will break down and create a sticky mash. Cook them just until a thin-bladed knife meets a bit of resistance. It is also important to drain the potatoes well after cooking; again, excess water combining with starch produces gumminess.

Many recipes call for heating milk before adding it, and justify this by saying that cold milk makes mashed potatoes sticky. But my repeated experiments have demonstrated that this is not true. Cold milk does cool the potatoes, which you really don't want to do, but the stories about the milk forming strange, gummy substances are poppycock. (Adding boiling milk, however, does tend to make mashed potatoes sticky, because the additional heat breaks up the starch cells.) My choice is to use warm milk, but only because it keeps the potatoes up to temperature. Similarly, when adding butter to mashed potatoes, be sure that it is presoftened so that it melts quickly.

VARIATIONS, YES; SUBSTITUTIONS, NO

Mashed potatoes can be combined with a great many other vegetables and flavorings. A good rule of thumb for proportion is to use equal parts of potato and the added vegetable. You can also add grated cheese; I sometimes add about a cup to the Master Recipe, although you can certainly use more if you like. When using softer, more strongly flavored cheeses like Gorgonzola, half that amount should do.

Unfortunately, I didn't find any satisfying recipe for low-fat mashed potatoes. I tried several combinations, the most promising of which required boiling garlic along with the potatoes, reducing the potato/garlic water, and using that to thin the potatoes, which I then finished with a tablespoon or two of olive oil. But I found the result uninteresting and unpleasantly starchy. I also tried using yogurt instead of butter, but this did not taste anything like the real thing. If you have an interest in low-fat mashed potatoes, use skim milk and less butter rather than substituting.

MASTER RECIPE FOR MASHED POTATOES

Makes about 4 cups (6–8 servings)

If you're serving mashed potatoes with sauce or gravy, this is the recipe you want. It delivers spectacularly smooth, fluffy potatoes, not too rich and not too assertively flavored. Consider one of the variations when the mashed potatoes will stand alone.

- 2 pounds Russet or Yukon Gold potatoes, peeled, eyes and blemishes removed; cut into 2-inch chunks
- ¾ teaspoon salt, total
- 6 tablespoons butter, softened
- 1 cup whole milk or half-and-half, warm
- Ground black pepper to taste

1. Put potatoes in a large saucepan; add cold water to cover and ½ teaspoon salt. Bring to boil and continue to cook over medium heat until potatoes are tender when pierced with a knife, 15 to 20 minutes.
2. Drain potatoes well and return pan to low heat. Rice or strain potatoes into pan if using these methods. With whisk or a wooden spoon blend in butter, then warm milk. Or, return potatoes to saucepan; mash over low heat with a potato masher, adding butter as you mash. Stir in warm milk. Season with ¼ teaspoon salt and a pinch of black pepper, or to taste. Serve immediately.

Mashed Potatoes with Poached Garlic and Olive Oil: Follow Master Recipe, adding 2 large peeled garlic cloves and 2 bay leaves along with water in step 1. Remove bay leaves as potatoes are drained, and mash garlic with potatoes. Decrease butter to 2 tablespoons and stir in ¼ cup virgin olive oil with butter. Stir in warm milk as in Master Recipe.

Mashed Potatoes with Parmesan Cheese and Lemon: Follow Master Recipe, stirring in 2 tablespoons lemon zest and 1 cup grated Parmesan cheese to finished potatoes.

Variations: You can cook any number of other vegetables with potatoes. Try celery root, carrots, turnips, or parsnips. Follow Master Recipe, substituting 1 pound of your chosen vegetable for 1 pound of potatoes; cut other vegetable into pieces that will cook in the same amount of time as potatoes (cut softer vegetables into larger pieces than potatoes and cut harder vegetables into smaller ones).

MASHED POTATOES AND APPLES WITH BACON AND BROWNED ONIONS

Makes about 4 cups (6–8 servings)

This is a traditional German dish my grandmother taught me called *Himmel und Erde,* or Heaven and Earth.

- 1 pound Russet potatoes, peeled, eyes and blemishes removed; cut into 1-inch cubes
- 1 pound tart apples such as Granny Smith, peeled, cored, and quartered
- ½ teaspoon salt plus more to taste
- 4 tablespoons plus 1 teaspoon butter
- 1 small onion, sliced very thin
- 1 teaspoon cider vinegar
- Pinch sugar
- 2 slices bacon, fried and crumbled

1. Put potatoes and apples in a large saucepan; add cold water to cover and ½ teaspoon salt. Bring to a boil and continue to cook over medium heat until both are tender when pierced with a fork, about 15 minutes.
2. Meanwhile, heat 1 teaspoon butter in a small skillet; sauté onions over medium-high heat until browned, 4 to 5 minutes.
3. Drain potatoes and apples well and return to pan to low heat. Rice or strain them into pan if using these methods. Then with a whisk or a wooden spoon, blend in remaining butter and the vinegar. Or, return potatoes and apples to saucepan; mash potatoes and apples over low heat with a potato masher, adding remaining butter then vinegar as you mash. Season to taste with additional salt and a pinch of sugar. Transfer to serving dish; top with onions and bacon and serve immediately. ■

Eric Wolff has been pursuing the art of cooking since he was seven and now cooks and writes in Manhattan.

MASTER CLASS

Country Ham Stuffed with Greens

Stuffing a country ham with greens and grits adds moisture and contrasting flavors and textures to a holiday favorite.

BY JACK BISHOP

Chef Susan McCreight Lindeborg respects Southern traditions, but also believes that "something new always adds to the festivities."

Although unfamiliar to many Northerners, country ham is a staple on Southern holiday buffet tables. Susan McCreight Lindeborg, chef at the Morrison-Clark Inn in Washington, D.C., adds a modern twist to this Southern classic by stuffing the meat with a mixture of greens, grits (which act as a binder), vegetables, and aromatic spices. The stuffing provides a visual and gustatory contrast to the rich ham.

Unlike other hams, country ham is dry-cured with a mixture of salt, sugar, black pepper, and other spices, in much the same manner as Italian prosciutto. After curing, the hams are usually smoked over a wood fire, and then hung in cool sheds for at least six months to age. The most famous of the American country hams are Smithfield hams, made exclusively in the town of Smithfield, Virginia.

Lindeborg says many Northerners are afraid that country hams will be too salty or too strong; she always soaks the ham for about 12 hours and changes the water twice to reduce the saltiness and soften the meat. She also suggests buying a ham that has been cured for six to nine months. "Old" hams, cured for a year or longer, generally do have a stronger flavor and can be quite salty. Lindeborg uses hams from S. Wallace Edwards & Sons (*see* Sources and Resources, page 32) in the restaurant and recommends them highly.

When stuffing the ham, it is important to make cuts all the way down to the bone, and to stagger the cuts so that every slice will have some stuffing (*see* illustration 5). Also, be sure to pry the cuts open with your fingers and put in as much stuffing as possible.

Busy holiday cooks can break the preparation for this dish into three segments — soaking, simmering and stuffing, and glazing — that can be done on different days. While steps one and two should be done on consecutive days, the final glazing and baking can be done up to a week later.

Lindeborg serves her stuffed ham with freshly cooked greens, fluffy biscuits, and spiced peaches, another Southern favorite at holiday time. The flavors are bold but complementary — sweet, salty, spicy, and acidic all have a place on this overflowing plate. This is right in line with the chef's idea of Southern cooking which, she says, is "all about generosity and hospitality, with lots of vegetables and little tastes."

COUNTRY HAM STUFFED WITH SPICY SOUTHERN GREENS

Serves 18

Because the ham is so rich and salty, it is usually served with poultry (a roasted turkey is perfect) and an assortment of vegetables. Greens, simmered in a bit of broth from the ham, are a must. This stuffing can also be prepared with kale, collards, or any available winter greens.

1 country ham (12–16 pounds)

Spicy Greens Stuffing

- 1 cup water
- 1/4 teaspoon salt
- 3 tablespoons quick grits (not instant)
- 1/4 cup reserved ham broth
- 3/4 pound mustard greens, stemmed, washed thoroughly, and chopped coarsely
- 3/4 pound spinach, stemmed and washed thoroughly
- 1 tablespoon reserved ham fat or olive oil
- 1 small onion, chopped
- 2 garlic cloves, minced
- 2 celery ribs, cut into small dice
- 1 small red bell pepper, cut into small dice
- 3 scallions, sliced very thin
- 1 1/2 teaspoons celery seeds
- 1 1/2 teaspoons mustard seeds
- 1/8 teaspoon cayenne pepper
- Ground black pepper to taste

Brown Sugar and Honey Mustard Glaze

- 1/2 cup light brown sugar
- 1/4 cup honey mustard
- 1 tablespoon water

1. Remove cheesecloth casing and scrub mold and excess black pepper from ham's surface. Place ham in a large stockpot, cover with water, and soak for 12 hours, changing water at least once, twice if possible.

2. Drain ham and cover with fresh water. Bring water to boil over medium-high heat; simmer, adding hot water as necessary to keep ham covered, until it softens, about 2 hours. Remove ham from pot and cool to room temperature, reserving ham broth.

3. Clean outside of cooled ham, wiping off excess black pepper that has been loosened during simmering. Use a sharp knife to remove excess fat from around outside of ham (*see* illustrations 1 through 4), reserving 1 tablespoon of fat.

4. Meanwhile, *for the stuffing,* bring water to boil in a small saucepan. Add salt, then gradually stir in grits. Simmer, stirring frequently, until grits start to thicken, 5 to 7 minutes; transfer to a large bowl and set aside.

5. Heat 1/4 cup of reserved ham broth in a large nonreactive soup kettle. Add greens and spinach, cover and cook over high heat until just wilted, about 5 minutes. Transfer to a colander; drain for 15 minutes. Squeeze excess moisture from greens and chop fine. Add greens to bowl with grits.

6. Heat reserved fat in a large skillet; sauté onions until softened slightly, 3 to 4 minutes. Stir in garlic, celery, red pepper, and scallions; sauté until softened slightly, 3 to 4 minutes longer. Add sautéed vegetables to bowl with greens and grits. Stir in next 4 ingredients.

7. Cover top of ham with a series of parallel cuts down to the bone. Cuts (about 12 in all) should be about 3 inches long and about 1 inch

PHOTOGRAPH BY RENÉE COMET

apart; to ensure that each slice of ham contains some stuffing, stagger cuts so they are not in even rows. Use fingers to open slits and fill generously with stuffing (*see* illustration 5).

8. Place 2 doubled pieces of cheesecloth, each measuring 2 feet across and 3 feet long, on top of each other. Place ham near top of cheesecloth and tightly roll cheesecloth around ham. Twist ends of cheesecloth and tie tightly with butcher's twine or thick string in a double knot to prevent cheesecloth from unwrapping.

9. Return wrapped ham to pot containing reserved ham broth. Bring ham to a boil; simmer until ham is tender, 2 to 3 hours. (Total simmering time before and after stuffing is about 20 minutes per pound.) Turn off heat and allow ham to rest in broth for 1 hour. Remove ham from broth, unwrap, and refrigerate overnight or up to 1 week. Reserve defatted ham broth for future use.

10. *For the glaze,* heat oven to 375 degrees. Mix brown sugar, honey mustard, and water in a small saucepan; simmer gently, stirring frequently, until sugar melts, about 5 minutes. Brush chilled ham with glaze and bake until lightly browned, about 20 minutes. Cool ham to room temperature and then refrigerate for at least 2 hours (or overnight) before serving.

11. When ready to serve, begin at hock end and make thin slices perpendicular to bone. Serve ham with biscuits, freshly cooked greens, and spiced peaches.

SPICED PEACHES

Makes about 2 pounds

If fresh peaches are available (or if you want to plan ahead next summer for the holiday season), follow Fresh Peach Variation below.

- 1 cup sugar
- 1 cinnamon stick (about 3 inches long)
- 1 teaspoon whole allspice
- 1 teaspoon whole cloves
- 1 ounce ginger, peeled and sliced thin
- 1 cup water
- 2 cups rice wine vinegar (you may substitute distilled white vinegar)
- 2 cans (1 pound 13 ounces each) peach halves (about 18 halves), drained and rinsed

Combine first 7 ingredients in a large nonreactive soup kettle; simmer until sugar dissolves and spices begin to flavor pickling syrup, about 20 minutes. Add peaches and turn off heat; cool peaches to room temperature in pickling syrup. Refrigerate spiced peaches for at least 2 days to allow flavors to develop. Serve peaches in pickling syrup next to ham.

Fresh Peach Variation: Simmer 2 pounds ripe but firm peaches in abundant boiling water until skins loosen, about 30 seconds. Drain peaches, run them under cold, running water, then remove skins with fingers. Add peaches to simmering pickling syrup. Bring peaches to simmer, then remove from heat. Cool peaches to room temperature in pickling syrup. Refrigerate peaches for at least 5 days, preferably a couple of weeks. Just before serving, halve and pit peaches.

CREAM BISCUITS WITH HERBS

Makes about 40, 1½-inch biscuits

Beaten biscuits are traditionally served with country ham; these small biscuits are just as delicious and much less work.

- ¼ teaspoon dried thyme
- ¼ teaspoon dried basil
- ¼ teaspoon dried oregano
- ¼ teaspoon dried sage
- 3 cups all-purpose flour
- ¾ teaspoon salt
- 1½ tablespoons baking powder
- 1½ tablespoons sugar
- 6 tablespoons chilled butter
- 1½ cups heavy cream

1. Heat oven to 425 degrees. Place first 8 ingredients in a large bowl. Cut butter into dry ingredients until mixture resembles coarse meal. Stir in cream until mixture forms into a soft, sticky ball.

2. Roll dough on floured surface to ½-inch thickness. Use a 1½-inch round cutter to punch out dough rounds. (Scraps can be rolled again but do not overwork.) Arrange on ungreased cookie sheet, about 1 inch apart.

3. Bake until biscuits are golden brown, 15 to 20 minutes. Serve warm with ham. ■

TRIMMING AND STUFFING COUNTRY HAM

The hock (the narrow end) of most country hams is covered with fat and skin. Follow steps 1 through 3 to remove this protective covering in one long piece. Remove fat from the wide end of the ham (step 4) to complete trimming. When stuffing the ham, fill the holes generously.

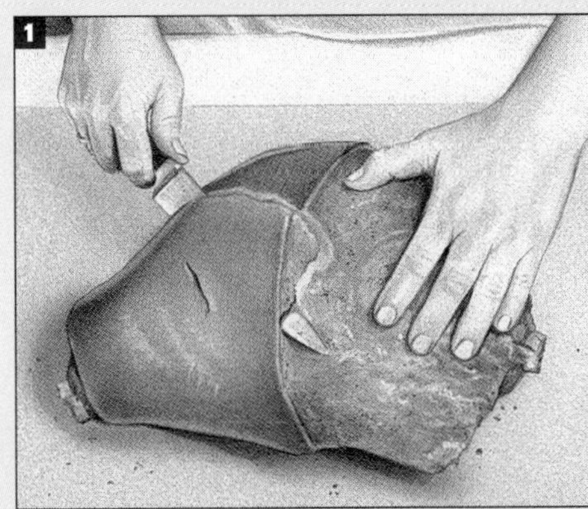

1. Slide knife under skin and fat that cover the top (rounded) side of the ham.

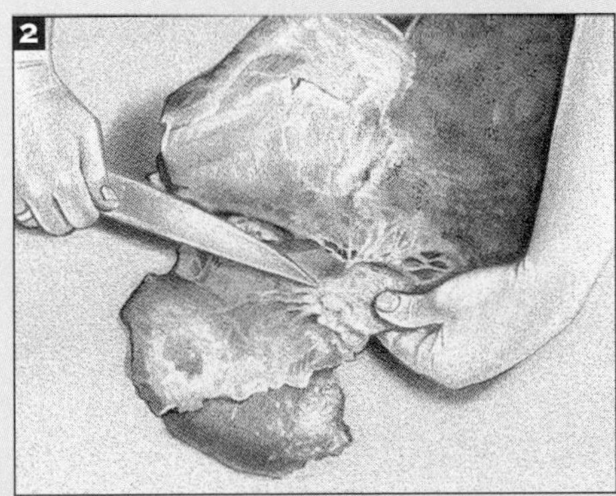

2. Continue cutting off fat and skin with knife. Use other hand to pull fat back in one long piece.

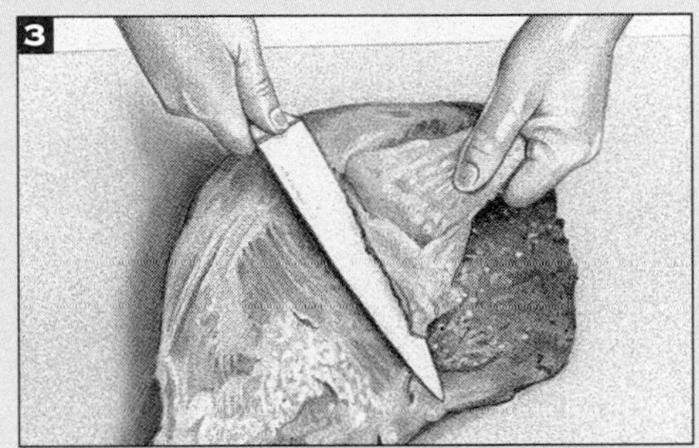

3. Flip ham over and trim fat from underside (the flat side). Use other hand to separate fat from the meat.

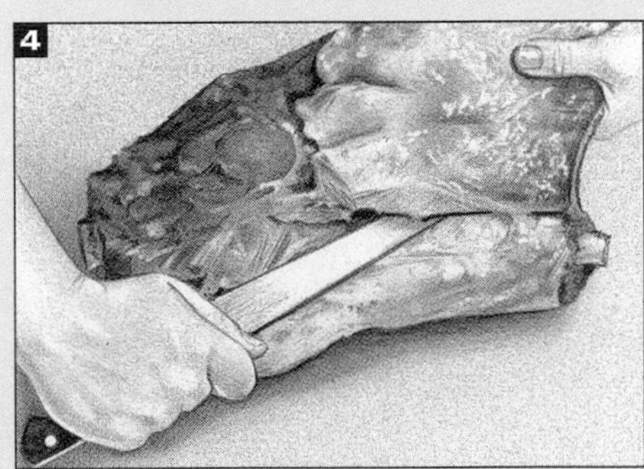

4. Slide knife under remaining fat and cut toward the wide end of the ham to remove. Trim until pink meat is exposed. Some fat may be left on the ham to provide moistness during cooking.

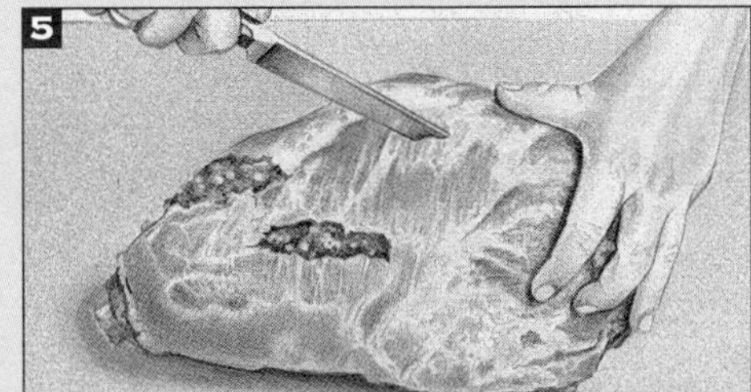

5. To stuff the ham, use a sharp knife to make parallel cuts down to the bone. Stagger cuts so that no slice of meat will be without stuffing.

ILLUSTRATIONS BY MICHELE AMATRULA

Cook's Field Guide

Autumn and Winter Squashes

Illustration by Alan Witschonke

Shaping and Baking Dinner Rolls

How to make eight types of dinner rolls from a single dough.

~ BY NICK MALGIERI ~

Individual dinner rolls have been popular since the middle of the nineteenth century, when the brioche conquered Paris. In fact, for the roll variation here, I originally tried a dough that was closer to brioche, with a high butter, sugar, and egg content. But rolls made with this dough, although delicious, were too rich to eat with a meal.

Nick Malgieri believes that dinner rolls are popular because they are delicate in appearance, as well as easy to serve and eat.

The recipe I settled upon falls right in between good-quality white bread and brioche. Since these rolls are meant to accompany a meal, the sugar is kept to a minimum, just enough to impart a pleasantly sweet flavor that supports and enhances the flavor of the wheat. In addition, the dough is made with water rather than milk for ease of handling (the fat solids in milk can cause doughs to be stickier) and to prevent unnecessary richness. Eggs and either oil or butter are added for tenderness as well as color and flavor.

Once the dough has been made, you are ready to begin shaping it into various forms. First divide the dough in half. For all shapes except crescent, butterfly, and Parker House rolls, form the dough into small individual pieces. When doing so, be sure to stretch a smooth, even skin around the outside of the sphere in the final step (*see* illustration 3, right); the skin will become the crust of the roll, and blemishes will mar its final appearance.

After rounding the pieces of dough, allow them to rest for a few minutes under a towel. This resting period makes the elastic gluten strands in the dough relax so the dough is easy to handle and does not spring back when shaped; keeping the dough covered as it rests prevents it from forming a thick, uneven crust.

To make rolls of various shapes, follow the illustrated steps on pages 16 and 17.

When baking the rolls, I use a short, high-temperature bake. This encourages tenderness in the finished product because the interior retains moisture that migrates back to the surface, thus softening it; long, slow baking at a low temperature, conversely, would provide a thick, hard crust.

MASTER RECIPE FOR DINNER ROLLS

Makes 16

- 4½ cups unbleached, all-purpose flour
- 1 tablespoon sugar
- 1 tablespoon salt
- 2 teaspoons active dry yeast
- 1 cup warm water, about 110 degrees
- 2 large eggs
- 4 tablespoons melted butter or mild olive oil

Egg Wash

- 1 egg, well beaten with a pinch of salt

1. Measure flour, sugar, and salt into workbowl of a food processor fitted with a steel blade, or a mixer bowl fitted with dough hook, or a large mixing bowl. Dissolve yeast in water; stir in eggs, then butter or oil. Pour yeast mixture over dry ingredients; if using food processor, pulse 6 or 8 times to form a dough ball; then process until dough is smooth and elastic, about 30 seconds. If using mixer, mix on low speed for 1 minute. Stop and scrape bowl to incorporate all ingredients, then continue mixing on low speed until dough is smooth and elastic, about 5 minutes. If mixing by hand, stir liquid with rubber spatula until dry ingredients are evenly moistened and dough is ropy and uneven in appearance. Cover bowl tightly with plastic wrap and allow dough to rest 5 minutes. Then beat dough vigorously with rubber spatula or heavy wooden spoon until smooth and elastic, 8 to 10 minutes.

2. Put dough in a large lightly greased bowl; cover with a damp cloth and let rise until dough doubles in bulk, 1 to 1½ hours.

3. Turn dough onto a lightly floured work surface; press with palms of hands to deflate. If making crescents or butterflies, follow specific rolling and shaping instructions, (*see* page 17). For remaining shapes, halve the dough and roll each half to a thick cylinder (*see* illustration 1); cut each cylinder into 8 pieces (illustration 2); round each piece by rotating your hand over it while gently pressing to form the dough into a sphere (illustration 3); allow rounded pieces to rest under a towel for 5 minutes; then form individual shapes as shown in illustrations on pages 16 and 17.

4. Arrange shaped dough on 2 cookie sheets covered with lightly greased parchment paper. Cover with a damp towel or oiled plastic; let rise until almost doubled, 30 to 45 minutes.

5. Preheat oven to 400 degrees. Set one rack to upper third position, the other to lowest position. Brush risen rolls with egg wash.

6. Bake until golden brown and an instant-read thermometer, when plunged into the roll's center, registers 200 degrees, 15 to 20 minutes. Remove from oven and serve at once or allow to cool to room temperature. Rolls can be loosely covered at room temperature up to 24 hours or placed in a plastic bag and frozen. ■

Nick Malgieri is the author of *Perfect Pastry* (Macmillan, 1989) and *Great Italian Desserts* (Little, Brown, 1990).

PREPARING THE DOUGH

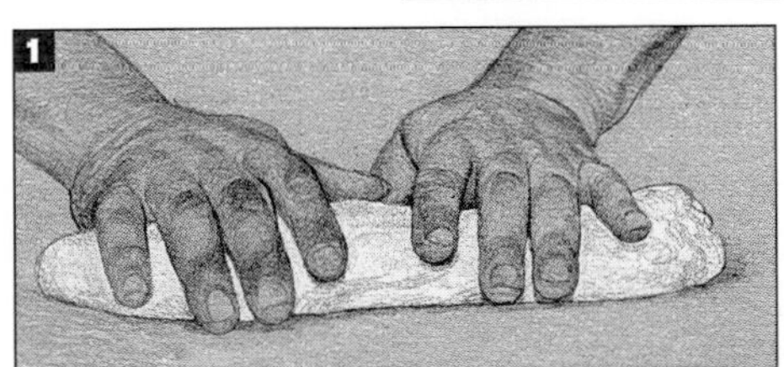

1. After dividing dough in half, roll each half into a thick cylinder.

2. Cut each cylinder into eight equal pieces.

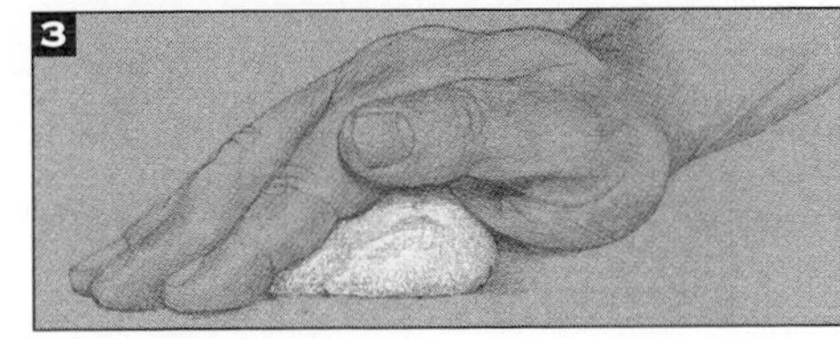

3. Round each piece by rotating your hand over it while gently pressing to form a sphere.

PHOTOGRAPH BY RICHARD FELBER, ILLUSTRATIONS BY ANATOLY

Shaping Individual Dinner Rolls

You can form an entire batch of dough into rolls of the same shape, or create several shapes from a single batch. For all shapes except crescent, butterfly, and Parker House rolls, first follow steps 1 through 3 on page 15 to divide the dough and round the individual pieces.

Eyeglasses

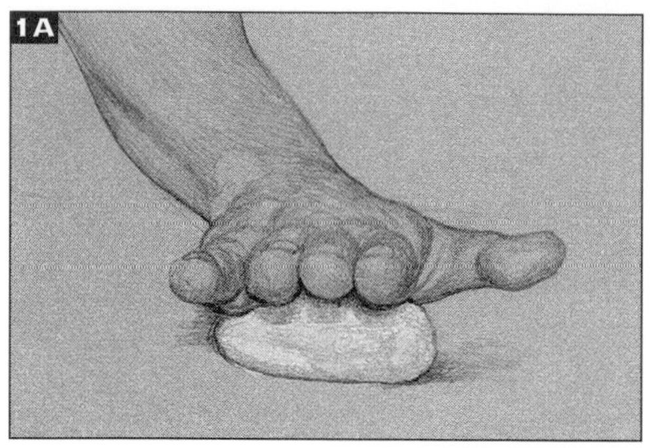

1A. Gently roll rounded dough piece to elongate it into a 12-inch strand; be sure to position dough seam side down.

1B. Form a loop at each end of the strand, leaving a small gap in the center.

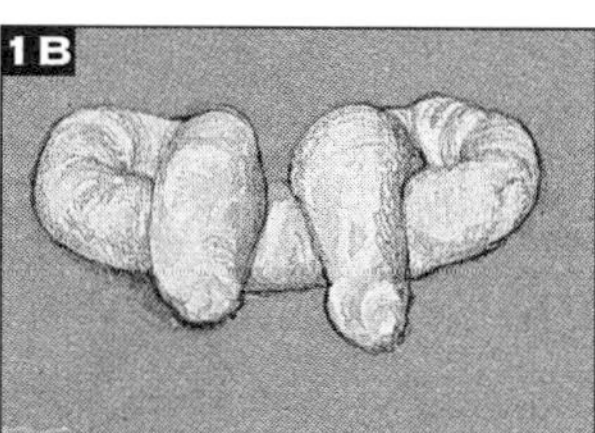

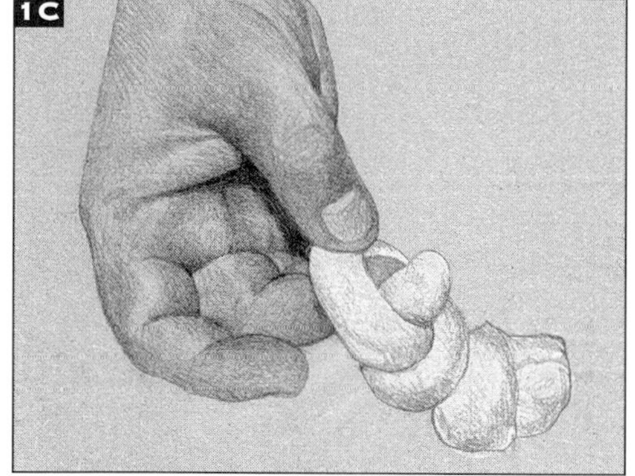

1C. Pull each end under and then up through the corresponding loop.

1D. Finished eyeglasses.

Small Braid

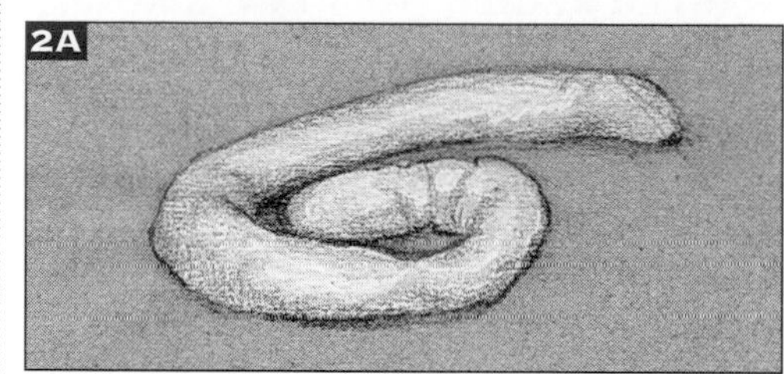

2A. Gently roll rounded dough piece into a 16-inch strand. Form the strand into the shape of a "6."

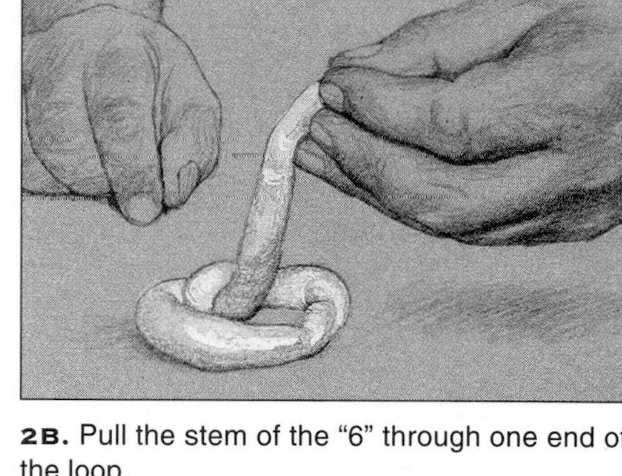

2B. Pull the stem of the "6" through one end of the loop.

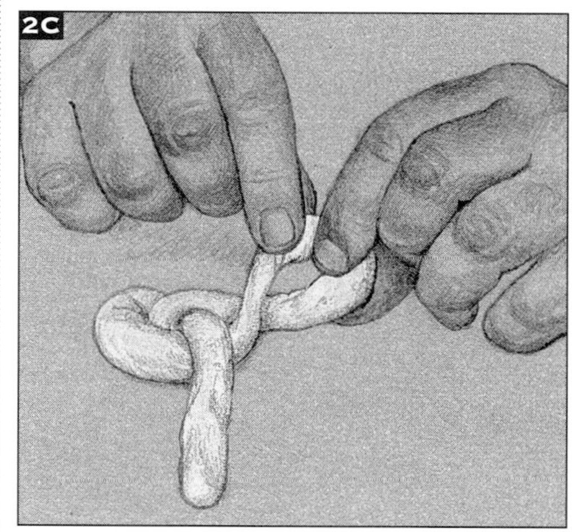

2C. Twist the other end of the loop toward you, flipping it over completely.

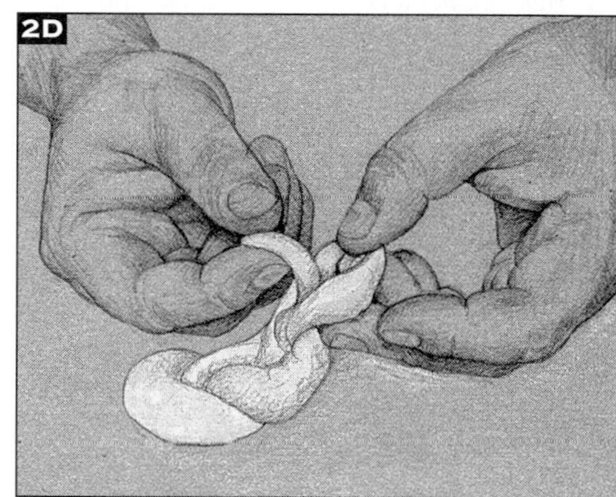

2D. Thread the end of the stem under and through the twisted loop.

Single Knot

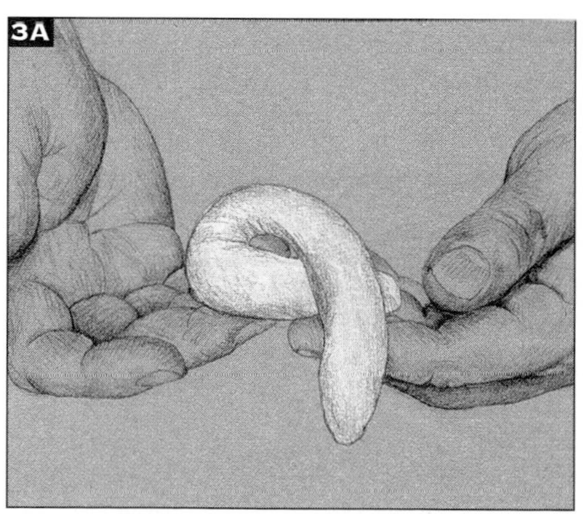

3A. Gently roll rounded dough piece into a 9-inch strand. Form strand into the shape of a "9."

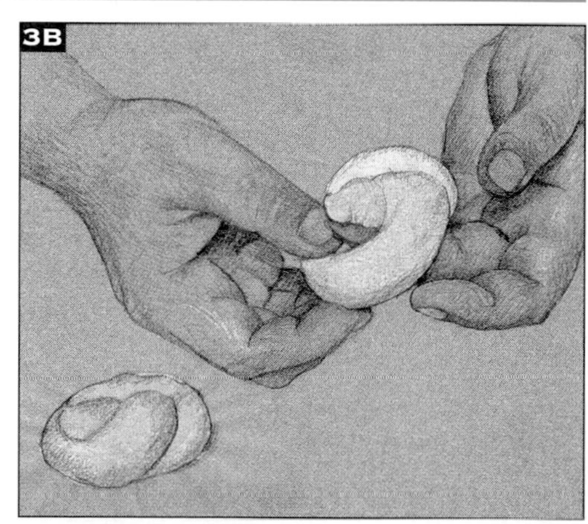

3B. Thread the long end of the "9" under and through the loop to form a knot.

Butterfly

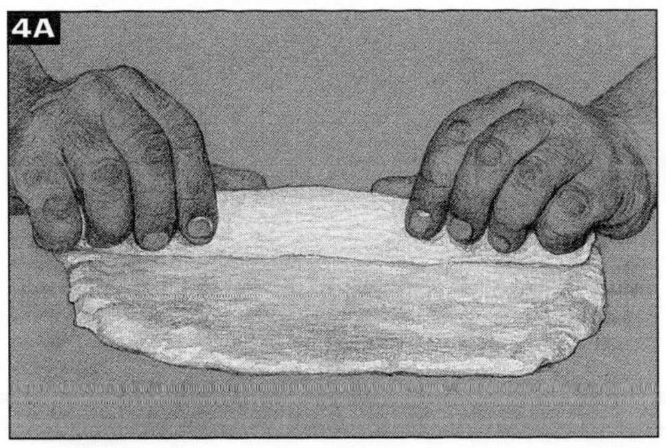

4A. Roll half of the dough into a 10-inch square, brush the square with two teaspoons melted butter or oil, roll up, and place seam-side down.

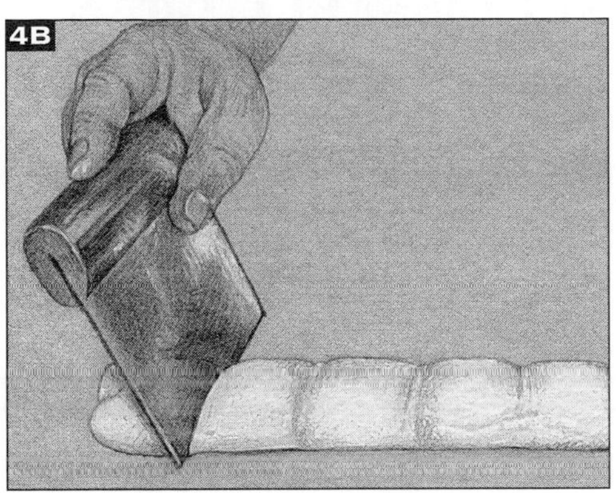

4B. Mark and cut into eight separate pieces.

4C. Press each piece of dough firmly with the handle of a wooden spoon to form butterflies.

Stick or Twist

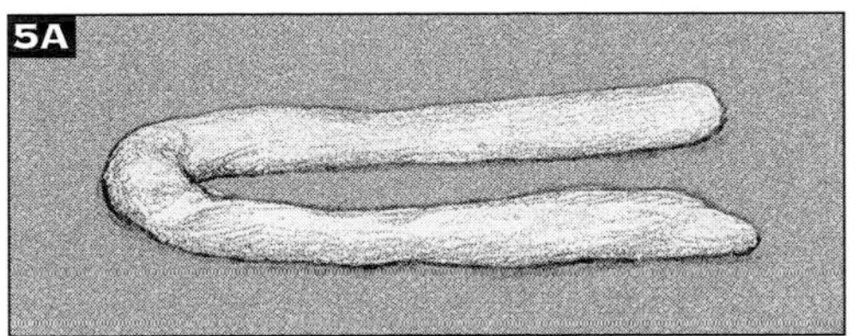

5A. Roll dough piece into a 12-inch strand. Form the strand into an elongated "U."

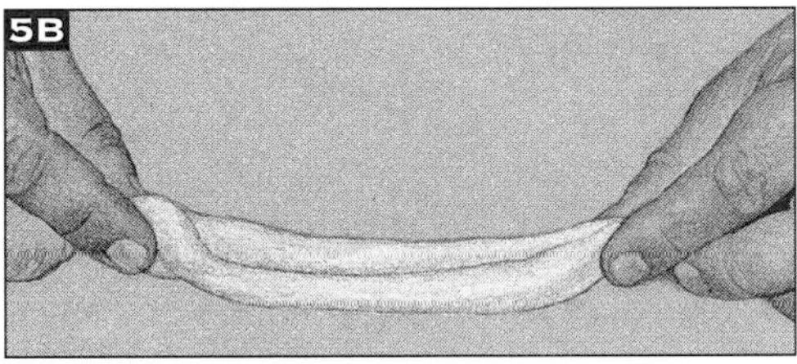

5B. Pinch the ends of the "U" firmly together.

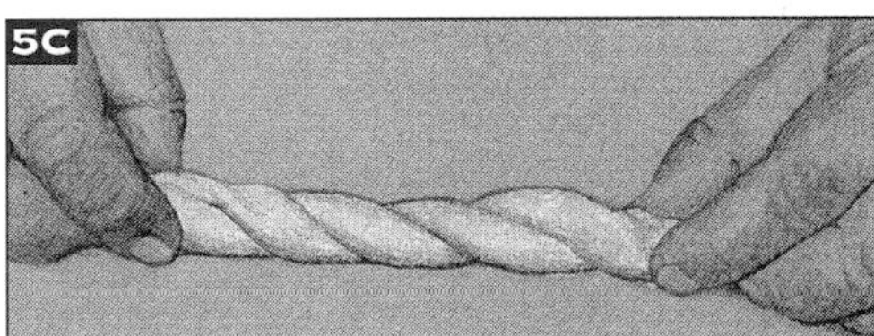

5C. Grasp one end with each hand and twist several times in opposite directions.

Double Knot

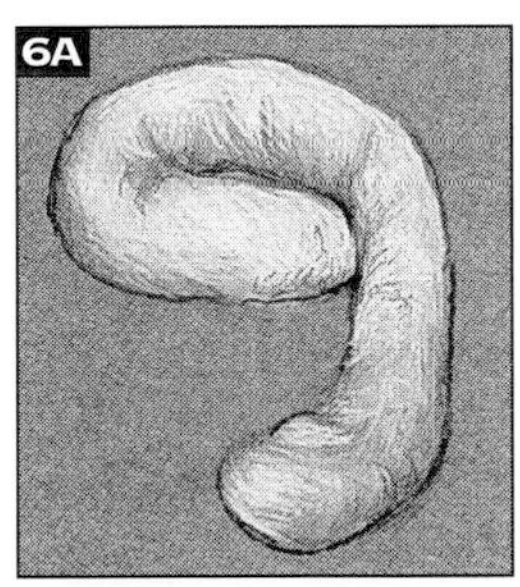

6A. Roll rounded dough piece into a 12-inch strand. Form the strand into a loop in the shape of a "9," as in single knot, but with longer end and wider opening.

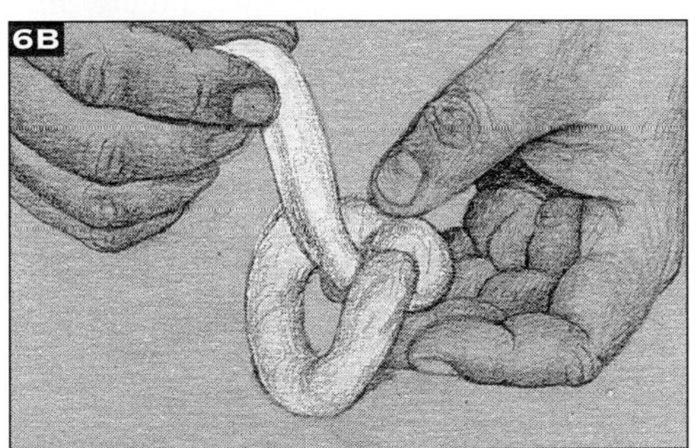

6B. Thread the stem of the "9" under and through the loop. Repeat, threading the stem through the remaining open section of the loop.

6C. Finished double knots.

Crescent

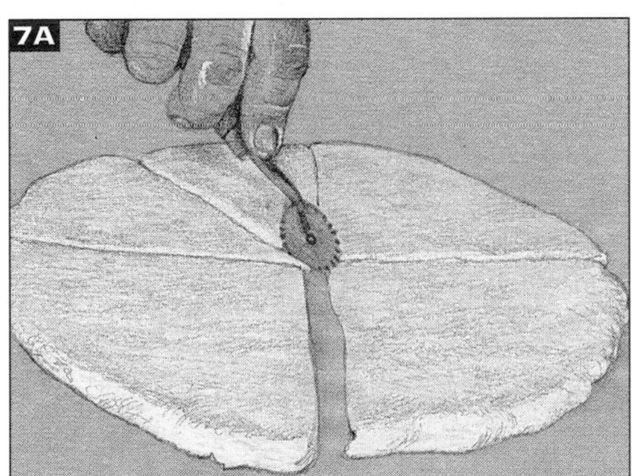

7A. Roll half of the dough into a 12-inch disk and cut it into eight wedges.

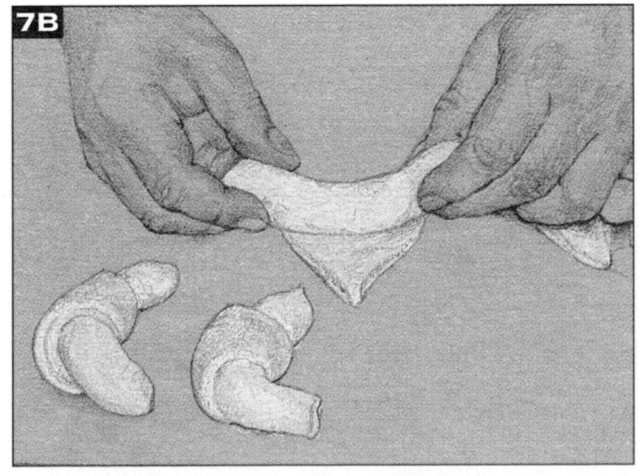

7B. Brush the disk lightly with melted butter or oil, roll up each section from the base of the wedge, and curve into crescents.

Parker House

8A. Wrap a small heavy pan in a towel (not terry cloth) and flour the towel. Place the ball of dough on a floured surface and slam the pan against the dough to flatten it. Form dough into a 3-inch disk about ½-inch thick. Mark the diameter, pressing with wooden spoon handle.

8B. Brush lightly with melted butter and fold over so top half covers bottom half.

ILLUSTRATIONS BY ANATOLY

The Holiday Turkey Perfected

After roasting 30 birds, we discover an unusual technique for producing exceptionally moist breast meat and fully cooked legs.

~ BY PAM ANDERSON WITH KAREN TACK ~

Although turkey has become commonplace, most cooks roast whole birds only at holiday time. We all know why this is, too: the bird may look lovely on the platter, but more often than not it's bland and dry, salvaged only by good gravy and wonderful side dishes.

Is it possible to roast a turkey perfectly? Usually juicy breast meat comes with a price — shocking pink legs and thighs. You have some leeway with the dark meat, which is almost impossible to dry out during normal roasting times. The trick is that the breast, which is exposed to direct heat and finishes cooking at a lower temperature, becomes parched while the legs and thighs take their time creeping to doneness. Nearly every roasting method in existence tries to compensate for this; few succeed.

There are literally hundreds of different methods of roasting turkey; we tested a dozen or so fairly different ones, from traditional to idiosyncratic. Our goals were to end up with an attractive bird, to determine the ideal internal temperature, and find a method that would finish both legs and thighs simultaneously.

There were other issues as well: We like stuffing, but wondered whether, by necessitating longer cooking times, it leads to drier meat. Is basting a ritual done more for the sake of the cook, or is it time well spent? Is stuffing the cavity with herbs and vegetables a waste of good thyme, not to mention celery, carrots, and onions? Perhaps roasting these same vegetables alongside the turkey makes for more flavorful pan juices and therefore better gravy? These were our original questions for research. Once we started roasting, we realized there were others we didn't even know to ask.

How Not to Roast a Turkey

Our first roasting experiments used the method most frequently promoted by the National Turkey Federation, the United States Department of Agriculture, and legions of cookbook authors and recipe writers. This, of course, features a moderate (325-degree) oven, a breast-up bird, and an open pan. We tried this method twice, basting one turkey and leaving the other alone. The basted turkey acquired a beautifully tanned skin, while the unbasted bird remained quite pale. Both were cooked to 170 degrees in the leg/thigh. Despite the fact that this was 10 degrees lower than recommend by the USDA and most producers, the breasts still registered a throat-catchingly dry 180 degrees.

We quickly determined that almost all turkeys roasted in the traditional, breast-up manner produced breast meat that was consistently 10 degrees ahead of the leg/thigh meat (tenting the breast with heavy-duty foil was the exception; read on). Because white meat is ideal at 160 degrees, and dark thigh meat just loses its last shades of pink at about 162, you might conclude, as we did, that roasting turkeys with their breasts up is a losing proposition.

Still, we pressed on, next trying a 2-hour turkey — essentially braising the bird at 425 degrees in air-tight heavy-duty foil for the first hour, then removing the foil and roasting at a slightly lower temperature for the second. Like all of the other breast-up methods, this produced white meat that was 10 degrees hotter than dark meat, but at least this turkey seemed a bit juicier than those cooked with purely dry heat. However, the turkey's spotty brown skin, which looked sticky, thin, and translucent, was a definite drawback. And because the pan juices sweated along with the bird for the first hour of cooking, the liquid added to the pan finished thin and brothy — great for turkey soup, but not intense enough to make a good pan gravy. A related technique, turkey roasted in a chemical-free brown bag atop carrots, celery, and onions, received a high score for its beautiful brown skin. Its taste and texture, however, were only average; the bird was typically dry and bland.

One recipe instructed us to make a paste of flour and butter, then rub it onto the turkey skin before roasting. The ensuing crust would theoretically seal in the juices and roast the turkey to perfection. The results were disappointing; the turkey's skin was swelled and soggy and the breast meat was dry and chalky, leaving only a flavorless pasty feeling in the mouth.

A number of recipes call for placing butter-soaked cheesecloth over the breast for most of the roasting time, augmented by occasional basting. The cheesecloth is removed during the last minutes of cooking to allow the skin to brown. This technique produces magazine-cover turkey, but does nothing to lower the temperature of the breast meat or to improve the flavor. It joined most of the others in the reject pile.

Injecting butter into the turkey was another logical-sounding attempt to keep it juicy and make it flavorful. But while the skin ballooned during roasting, it deflated once out of the oven, and much of the injected butter wound up in the bird's cavity; the rest of it formed pockets at injection sites rather than infusing the whole bird as we had hoped. Even though the meat surrounding the pockets was nicely seasoned, the overall results were inconsistent, and the technique felt contrived.

We also discovered that stuffing a bird virtually guarantees overcooked meat. Because it slows interior cooking (our tests showed a nearly 30-degree difference in internal temperature after an hour in the oven), stuffing means longer oven times, which translates to bone-dry surface meat. Unless stuffing is your passion, cook your dressing separately.

On the Right Track

Of all the breast-up methods, tenting the bird's breast and upper legs with foil, as suggested by

AN EASY TRUSSING METHOD

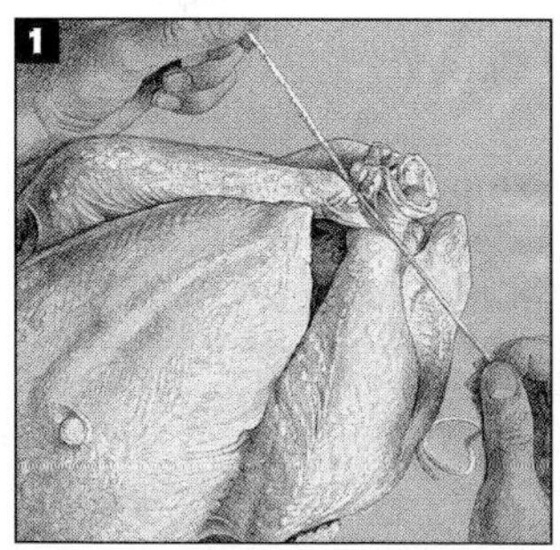

1. Using the center of a five-foot length of cooking twine, tie the legs together at the ankles.

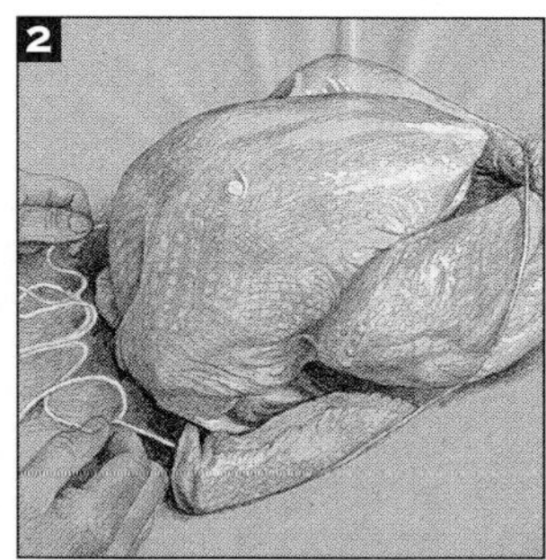

2. Run the twine around the thighs and under the wings on both sides of the bird, pulling tightly.

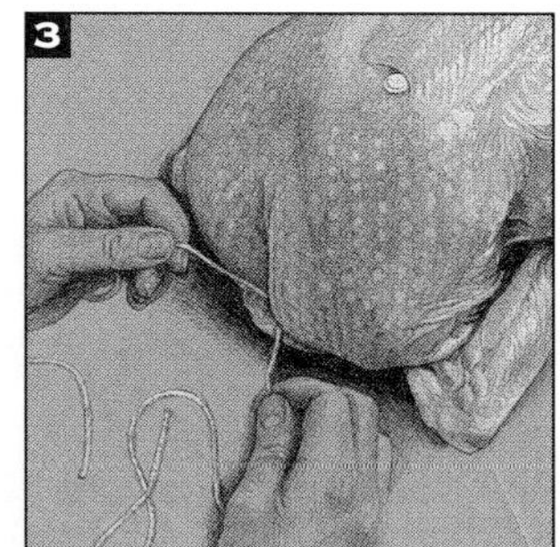

3. Keeping the twine pulled snug, tie a firm knot around the excess flesh at the neck of the bird. Snip off excess twine.

ILLUSTRATIONS BY ANATOLY

numerous authors, including Rick Rodgers, worked the best. The foil deflects some of the oven's heat, reducing the ultimate temperature differential between white and dark meat from 10 to 6 degrees. The bird is roasted at a consistent 325-degree temperature, and during the last 45 minutes of roasting the foil is removed, allowing enough time for lovely browning. If you're partial to open-pan roasting and don't care to follow the technique we developed, try the foil shield; it certainly ran a close second.

Many people resort to butchery in an attempt to compensate for the fact that white meat roasts more quickly than dark. A friend roasts his turkey whole, removes the breast, and returns the legs to the oven while he carves white meat at the table. Guests enjoy white meat the first time around and dark meat for seconds. This is fine for those who like both parts of the bird, but an informal poll revealed that dark-meat-only lovers do not receive this method well.

Then there were the really unusual methods, such as Julia Child's clever technique of roasting breast and legs/thighs separately. You might think dismantling a turkey is difficult, but cutting out the backbone and separating the whole legs from the breast takes less than 10 minutes. We liked how quickly the turkey parts roasted: the legs cooked more quickly than the breast, and were done in 45 minutes, and the breast followed with a temperature of 160 to 165 about 10 minutes later. In an attempt to make the bird appear whole, we secured the legs to the breast with skewers, put it on a serving platter, and garnished it with garlands of herbs. Although not quite what we wanted, this method does have two advantages: it is quick, and you can easily roast each portion perfectly.

A related but somewhat less drastic technique is to remove the backbone of the bird before cooking, on the theory that the portions of meat nearest the cavity take the longest to cook. Although this technique reduced the temperature variation between breast and leg and produced juicy meat, the bird looked fat, stubby, and unnatural at the table. After dissecting a number of birds in various ways, we decided that, although these techniques are perfectly acceptable at other times during the year, the holiday turkey should be spared the knife until it reaches the table.

The Science of Brining

Our tasters found that brining the turkey for four hours gives roasted birds firm, meaty texture and well-seasoned flavor. They also reported that brined turkeys are moister and juicier. To explain these sensory perceptions, we attempted to gather some empirical data. We started by weighing several 11-pound birds after they had been brined for four hours, and found an average weight gain of almost three-quarters of a pound. Even more impressive, we found that brined birds weighed six to eight ounces more after roasting than a same-sized bird that had not been brined. Our taste buds were right: brined birds are juicier.

Jane Bowers, head of the Department of Foods and Nutrition at Kansas State University, says salt is used in meat processing to extract proteins from muscle cells and make these proteins more viscous: "Brining turkey causes a change in the structure of the proteins in the muscle. They become sticky, which allows them to hold more water." Citing a similar example, she says frankfurters without sodium are limp. "It is the salt that gives hot dogs their plumpness," she says.

Tina Seelig, scientist and author of *The Epicurean Laboratory* (W. H. Freeman, 1991), says salt causes protein strands to become denatured, or unwound. This is the same process that occurs when proteins are exposed to heat, acid, or alcohol. "When protein strands unwind, they get tangled in one another and trap water in the matrix that forms," says Seelig.

And Dr. Bill Schwartz, director of technical services at the Butterball Turkey Company, adds that when these unravelled proteins are exposed to heat they gel — much like a fried egg white — and form a barrier that prevents water from leaking out of the bird as it cooks. The capillary action that draws blood out of the meat and gives it a milky-white color also helps the brining solution penetrate deep into the meat, according to Schwartz. This accounts for the pleasant salty flavor even of the inner breast meat.

—*Jack Bishop*

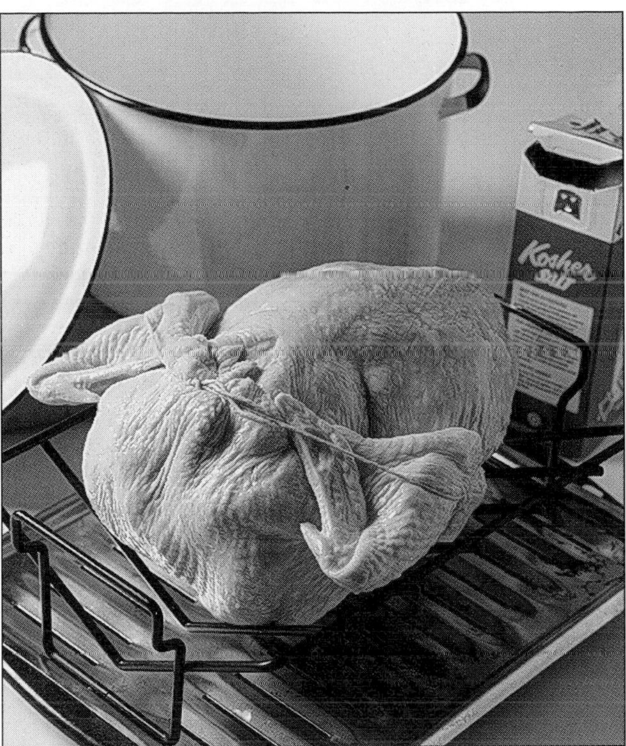

Brining (soaking in salt water) is a time-honored culinary technique. In our tests, it resulted in a juicier, more well-seasoned turkey. Roast the bird as soon as possible after brining, or some of the brining solution will leech out of the meat.

The Successes

Amidst all these failures and near-successes, some real winners did emerge. Early on, we became fans of Maria Da Mota's method, described in Jean Anderson's *Foods of Portugal* (William Morrow, 1986); most other turkeys were bland and boring compared to this one. The secret: the turkey soaks in water seasoned with two pounds of salt for up to 24 hours. When we first removed the brined turkey from the refrigerator, we found a beautiful, milky-white bird. Following recipe instructions, we roasted it breast-side up in a 400-degree oven. Except for some parched marks along the breast bone and leg tops, this nicely browned turkey showed well.

More important, the texture of the breast was different from that of the other birds we had cooked; they were firm and juicy at the same time. And the turkey tasted fully seasoned; others had required a bite of skin with the meat to achieve the same effect. The drawbacks: this bird might be a bit too salty for some, although we thought it perfect, and its pan drippings were inedibly salty by any standards. We experimented with the brining time, and found that 4 to 6 hours in a cool spot (a winter basement would be fine in cool climates, a refrigerator elsewhere) produces pleasantly seasoned turkeys and not overly salty pan juices.

Brining was our first real breakthrough; we now believe it to be essential in achieving perfect taste and texture. But we had yet to discover the way to roast.

Our most successful attempt at achieving equal temperatures in leg and breast came when we followed James Beard's technique of turning the turkey as it roasts. In this method, the bird begins breast side down on a V-rack, then spends equal time on each of its sides before being turned breast side up. The V-rack is important not just to hold the turkey in place, but

PHOTOGRAPH BY ERIC ROTH

Grilling The Holiday Bird

In *The Grilling Encyclopedia* (Atlantic Monthly Press, 1992), Corte Sinnes published a fascinating recipe for Pandora's Turkey, so-called because under no circumstances can you peek during roasting. Following his instructions, but using a smaller turkey, we arranged five pounds of hot coals on opposite sides of a grill, set the turkey in a roasting pan on the grill rack, and closed the lid. Using the grill's built-in thermometer, we tracked the temperature, which never fell below 450 degrees during the first hour and a half. Seeing this, we decided to risk the curse and check our bird. This was one of the few times during our testing that we actually saw a pop-up timer standing tall; this bird was way overcooked.

Still, the technique had much to commend it. Using the grill frees the oven for all the side dishes. The skin color was a smashing mahogany, and the smoke lent the meat a subtle flavor. We decided to refine the technique.

Because frequent turning was not a good option, we began by tenting the breast with foil, but the grill heat was so intense that this was ineffective. So we tried one turn during roasting, and produced turkeys with bronzed backs, lily-white breasts, and a long cooking time. Sinnes was right: removing the lid kills the heat, making it impossible to both turn the bird and brown it nicely. Finally, we tried adding a burst of hot coals at the midpoint turn. The result: Juicy breast. Well-seasoned meat. Good color. Mission accomplished.

to elevate the turkey, affording some protection from the heat of the roasting pan. This combination of rack and technique produced turkey with breast temperature as low as, and sometimes lower than, that of the legs.

Perfecting Oven Technique

Because we were using smaller turkeys than Beard had used, we had to fine-tune his method. Large turkeys spend enough time in the oven to brown at 350 degrees; our turkeys were in the 10-pound range and were cooking in as little as 1½ hours, yielding quite pale skin. Clearly, we needed higher heat.

Reviewing our notes, we noticed that the basted birds were usually the evenly browned, beautiful ones. So we turned up the heat to 400 degrees, basted faithfully, and got what we wanted. In an effort to streamline, we tried to skip the leg-up turns, roasting only breast side down, then breast side up. But in order for the turkey to brown all over, these two extra turns were necessary. Brining, turning, and basting are work, yes, but the combination produces the best turkey we've ever had.

The Subtleties

During our first few tests, we discovered that filling the cavity with aromatic herbs and vegetables made for a subtle but perceptible difference in flavor. This was especially noticeable in the inner meat of the leg and thigh; turkeys with hollow cavities, by contrast, tasted bland.

Roasted alongside the turkey, the same combination of carrot, celery, onion, and thyme also did wonders for the pan juices. But these vegetables dry up fairly quickly, burning rather than caramelizing over the 2-hour-plus roasting period. Roasting the turkey on a broiler pan with a perforated cover kept the juices from evaporating too quickly; we also added just enough stock to keep the vegetables moist until the turkey juices started to flow.

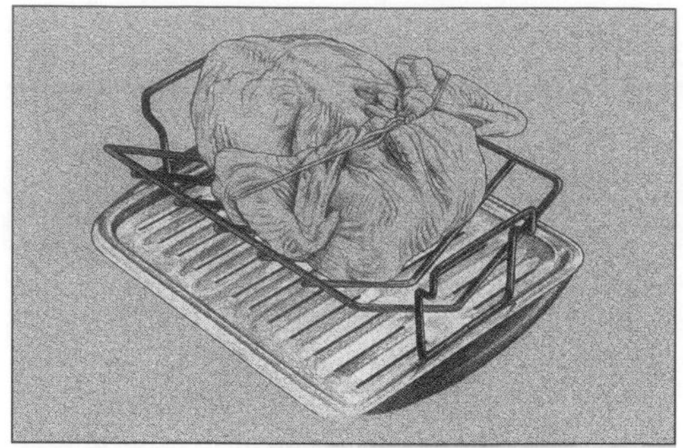

Because it elevates the bird, a V-rack promotes even roasting and prevents overcooked breast meat.

The Best Oven-Roasted Turkey with Giblet Pan Sauce

Serves 10–12

The ideal roasting equipment for the turkey is a shallow broiler pan with a perforated cover. It's important that the pan be shallow (about one-inch high); if the covered pan is too deep, the turkey may not fit in your oven when the bird roasts on its side. The perforated cover allows the turkey drippings to flow down to the vegetables, while keeping the pan juices from evaporating too quickly.

- 1 turkey (12 to 14 pounds gross weight), rinsed thoroughly, giblets and tail removed
- 2 pounds salt
- 3 medium onions, chopped coarse
- 1½ medium carrots, chopped coarse
- 1½ celery stalks, chopped coarse
- 6 thyme sprigs
- 1 bay leaf
- 1 tablespoon butter, melted, plus extra for basting
- 3 tablespoons cornstarch

1. Place turkey in a pot large enough to hold it easily. Pour salt into neck and body cavities; pour salt all over turkey and rub into skin. Add cold water to cover, rubbing bird and stirring water until salt dissolves. Set turkey in a refrigerator or other cool location for 4 to 6 hours. Remove turkey from salt water and rinse both cavities and skin under cool running water for several minutes until all traces of salt are gone.

2. Meanwhile, reserve liver and put giblets, neck and tail piece, ⅓ of the onions, celery, carrots, thyme sprigs, and the bay leaf in a large saucepan. Add 6 cups water and bring to a boil, skimming foam from surface as necessary. Simmer, uncovered, adding liver during last 5 minutes of cooking, for a total of about 1 hour. Strain broth (you should have about 4½ cups); set neck, tail, and giblets aside. Cool to room temperature, and refrigerate until ready to use. Remove meat from neck and tail, cut giblets into a medium dice, and refrigerate meat and giblets until ready to use.

3. Heat oven to 400 degrees. Toss another ⅓ of onions, carrots, celery, and thyme with 1 tablespoon butter and place in body cavity. Bring turkey legs together and perform simple truss (*see* illustrations, page 18).

4. Scatter remaining vegetables and thyme over a shallow roasting pan; pour 1 cup reserved broth over vegetables. Put perforated cover on roasting pan; set a V-rack (preferably nonstick) adjusted to widest setting on top of the cover. Brush entire breast side of turkey with butter, then place turkey, breast side down, on V-rack. Brush entire back side of turkey with butter.

5. Roast for 45 minutes. Remove pan from oven (close oven door); baste turkey with butter. With a wad of paper toweling in each hand, turn turkey, leg/thigh side up. If broth has totally evaporated, add an additional ½ cup stock to pan. Return turkey to oven and roast 15 min-

How Much Does a 12-Pound Turkey Weigh?

The real weight of turkeys readied for cooking is quite different from the package weight. After removing the packaging and giblets (which sometimes included the tail piece), and allowing the birds to drain, we found variations of up to 1½ pounds from sticker weights. One 11¾-pound turkey, for example, wound up with a true net weight of 10¼ pounds. This affects both serving size and scheduling: If you calculate cooking times for a 12-pound turkey that is actually closer to 10, and use the inaccurate but common rule of 20 to 25 minutes per pound, your turkey could be done 40 to 50 minutes early. If you've already figured in a 30-minute rest, you'll be serving cold turkey. Not only that, there will be considerably less of it than you originally thought.

utes. Remove turkey from oven again, baste, and again use paper toweling to turn the other leg/thigh side up; roast for another 15 minutes. Remove turkey from oven for final time, baste, and turn it breast side up; roast until meat thermometer stuck in leg pit registers 165 degrees, about 30 to 45 minutes. Breast should register 160 to 165 as well. Transfer turkey to platter; let rest for 20 to 30 minutes.

6. Meanwhile, strain pan drippings into a large saucepan (discard solids) and skim fat. Return broiler pan to stove and place over 2 burners set to medium heat. Add 3 cups reserved broth to the broiler pan and, using a wooden spoon, stir to loosen brown bits. When pan juices start to simmer, strain into saucepan along with giblets; bring to a boil. Mix cornstarch with ½ cup water and gradually stir into saucepan. Bring to boil; simmer until sauce thickens slightly. Carve turkey; serve with gravy.

THE BEST GRILL-ROASTED TURKEY

Serves 10–12

This is an adaptation of a recipe from Corte Sinnes, author of *The Grilling Encyclopedia* (Atlantic Monthly Press, 1992). My chimney starter holds about four of the five pounds of charcoal needed to roast this turkey. I place the other pound of charcoal in two piles on opposite sides of the grill and simply pour the hot coals over them; within minutes all the coals are red hot. Make sure your grill lid is tall enough to accommodate a turkey.

1. Follow steps 1, 2, and 3 (except heating oven) in recipe above.

2. Heat 5 pounds of charcoal (*see* note, above). If using a chimney starter, pour half the coals into 2 piles on opposite sides of grill; otherwise use long-handled tongs to separate coals into 2 piles, on opposite sides of grill; put grill rack in position.

3. Scatter remaining vegetables and thyme over a 15-by-10-inch roasting pan; pour 1 cup reserved broth over vegetables. Set a V-rack adjusted to its widest setting in pan. Cover pan, excluding rack area, with foil to keep pan juices from evaporating. Brush breast with butter, then position turkey, breast side down, on V-rack, and brush back with butter as in step 4 above.

4. Grill-roast turkey, positioning pan between 2 piles of coals, for 1 hour. About 40 minutes into roasting, heat an additional 1½ pounds of charcoal. Remove turkey from grill, remove grill rack, stir up coals, and add half new hot coals to each pile; replace lid. Baste back side of turkey with butter, then with a wad of paper toweling in each hand, turn turkey breast side up and baste. Check pan drippings and add an additional ½ cup broth if vegetables are starting to burn. Return pan to the grill; quickly replace lid, roast until meat thermometer stuck in leg pit registers 165 degrees, about 1 hour to 1 hour and 15 minutes longer. Transfer turkey to a platter; let rest for 20 to 30 minutes.

5. Follow step 6 above for pan sauce. ■

HOW DO POP-UP TIMERS WORK?

More than a decade ago, some poultry suppliers began inserting automatic pop-up timers in their birds. The technology behind this device is quite simple. A compound with a known melting temperature is liquefied in the bottom of the timer device. A spring is compressed into the molten material as it cools and hardens. The timer is then inserted in the thickest part of the breast. When the material at the bottom of the timer melts again during cooking, the spring is free to expand and the plastic stem rises.

While frequent basting can sometimes clog the spring mechanism or cause it to pop up too quickly (the very hot liquid may melt the base material too early), there is a more basic problem with pop-up timers. Volk Enterprises in California, the only American producer of the devices, calibrates theirs to "pop" at 178 degrees, a temperature chosen to guarantee that the legs will be well done — but that also ensures that the breast meat will be way overcooked. (The company's timers for turkey breasts sold separately are calibrated at 163 degrees, a temperature that is much more friendly to delicate white meat.) Our advice: ignore the timer that comes with your holiday turkey and rely on your own thermometer.

—Jack Bishop

INTERNAL TEMPERATURE — HOW MUCH IS ENOUGH?

Industry standards developed by the United States Department of Agriculture and the National Turkey Federation call for whole birds to be cooked to an internal thigh temperature of 180 to 185 degrees. The breast temperature, according to these standards, should be 170 degrees. Our kitchen tests showed, however, that breast temperature rarely drops below that of the thigh, no matter how you cook the bird. And no meat is at its best at a temperature of 180 or 185 degrees.

While the USDA might have us believe that the only safe turkey is a dry turkey, this just isn't true. The two main bacterial problems in turkey are salmonella and campylobacter. According to USDA standards, salmonella in meat is killed at 160 degrees. Turkey is no different. So why the higher safety standard of 180 degrees?

Susan Connolly, director of the USDA Meat and Poultry Hotline, believes that "Most people think that turkey, especially dark meat, tastes better when cooked to 180 degrees." Perhaps more convincing is her claim that stuffing must reach an internal temperature of 165 degrees to be considered safe. (Carbohydrates such as bread provide a better medium for bacterial growth than do proteins such as meat; hence the extra safety margin of 5 degrees). In order to raise stuffing temperature to safe levels, thigh meat must usually top 180 degrees.

Since we recommend roasting a turkey without bread-based stuffing, a finished temperature of 160 to 165 degrees is more than adequate to kill possible pathogens, even according to USDA standards. A number of food scientists all confirmed the safety of this recommendation.

E. M. Foster, a professor of food microbiology at the University of Wisconsin at Madison, says that killing salmonella depends on a complex relation between temperature and time. To rid foods of bacteria, the industry uses two common methods, "fast" and "slow." In the slow method, food is held at 143 degrees for 30 minutes, eliminating the salmonella. Salmonella will also be killed when the food maintains a temperature of 160 degrees for 15 seconds; this is the "fast" method.

Because home conditions are imprecise, Foster doesn't recommend the slow method. But as long as meat temperature is properly measured in the deepest part of the thigh and away from the bone, he is confident that a reading of 160 degrees will certainly last for 15 seconds and indicate that any possible salmonella bacteria has been killed. And campylobacter, the other important bacterial contaminant, is even more sensitive to heat than salmonella.

The final word on poultry safety is this: As long as your thermometer reaches 160 degrees, all unstuffed meat (including turkey) should be bacteria-free. Since home thermometers may vary by a couple of degrees, you may want to wait until the thermometer registers 165 degrees, just to be safe (we found that dark meat also tastes better at this temperature). But bacteria in meat cooked to 180 or 185 degrees is long gone — as is moistness and flavor.

—Jack Bishop

The Only Pumpkin Pie Recipe You'll Ever Need

For the best of both worlds — pumpkin pie with smooth, delicious filling and a crisp crust — precook both before baking.

BY STEPHEN SCHMIDT

The colonial forerunners of pumpkin pie were usually called "puddings," essentially rich custards in pastry, with a bit of pumpkin and spice added. Even today, many pumpkin pies are no more than variations on custard pie, and present the baker with identical challenges — making the crust crisp while developing a custard that is firm but still tender. After baking countless pumpkin pies, I have found the solution.

Crisping the Crust

Creating crisp pastry shells is a problem for many bakers. For years, I used partially baked shells, which always turned out soggy. I remedied this with a threefold approach. First, I began baking my crusts almost completely before filling them; that way I knew they started out crisp. Next, I made sure that both shell and filling were hot when I assembled the pie, so the custard could begin to firm up almost immediately, rather than soaking into the pastry. Finally, I baked the pie quickly, in the bottom of the oven, where the bottom of the crust is exposed to the most intense heat. (Baking in the top of the oven exposes the rim of the crust to the most intense heat, while baking in the middle fails to expose the crust to intense heat from any source.)

This technique produced a wonderfully crisp pastry, but a couple of refinements were needed. With a total baking time of about 50 minutes, the shell began to blacken around the rim; I avoided this by covering the shell and the vulnerable rim with foil during the first 15 minutes of baking. I also began using glass pie pans, those wonderful American inventions, which hold heat better and therefore are superior to metal when it comes to crisping and browning the crust.

Avoiding Curdled Custard

Because it sets the filling quickly, high oven heat works to the advantage of all custard pies; the quicker the pie gets out of the oven, the less likely that the filling will soak into the crust and make it soggy. But baking at high heat also has its perils — when overbaked, custard will curdle, becoming grainy and watery. Regardless, however, of the heat level, curdling can be averted if the pie is taken out of the oven *immediately* once the center thickens to the point where it no longer sloshes but wiggles like gelatin when the pan is gently shaken. Residual heat will finish the cooking outside the oven. Because the presence of the pumpkin dilutes the egg proteins and therefore interferes with curdling, you have a window of about five minutes between "set" and "curdled," considerably longer than with most other custards.

The best pumpkin pie combines modern techniques for crisp crust, plus the custard-type filling of the colonial era.

Two other features of my recipe provide additional anticurdling insurance. First, because the filling is hot when it is put into the shell, the center cooks quickly, thus making it less likely that the edges, which receive the most direct heat, will become overcooked. Second, as with colonial recipes, this recipe calls for heavy cream, in addition to milk, and a goodly quantity of sugar. These ingredients not only improve the flavor but also protect the texture, since both fat and sugar serve to block the curdling reaction. (In this context please note that I would relegate to the trash all those "healthy" custard recipes concocted out of skim milk, egg whites, and artificial sweeteners. Even if they tasted good, which they do not, their fatless, sugarless composition virtually assures that they will turn into curdled, wheyish messes.)

Colonial bakers, of course, started with fresh pumpkin, which they stewed, strained, and pressed dry between heavy cloth napkins. I have on occasion done the same myself (*see* "Using Fresh Pumpkin," page 23). However, canned pumpkin is surprisingly good, and, given a little special treatment, it can be as tasty as fresh; in a recent informal taste test I organized, a roomful of food professionals could not tell the difference between a pie made with canned pumpkin and one made with fresh.

One problem with canned pumpkin is its fibrous nature, easily corrected by pureeing it in a food processor. A blender also works well, with the minor adjustments described in the introduction to the recipe. As I learned from cookbook author Marcia Adams, you can freshen the taste of canned pumpkin by cooking it with the sugar and spices before combining it with the custard ingredients. As the pumpkin simmers, you can actually smell the unwelcome canned odor give way to the sweet scent of fresh squash. This is a small but delightful culinary miracle.

THE BEST PUMPKIN PIE

Serves 8

If you do not have a food processor, the pumpkin may be put through a food mill or forced through a fine sieve with the back of a wooden spoon. Alternatively, you can cook the pumpkin, sugar, and spices together *before pureeing,* then whir the mixture in a blender, adding enough of the cream called for in the recipe to permit the pumpkin to flow easily over the blades. In either case, heat the pumpkin with the (remaining) cream and milk, as indicated, then slowly whisk the mixture into the beaten eggs.

Flaky pastry can be successfully produced using any all-purpose flour, but a low-protein

PHOTOGRAPH BY ERIC ROTH

brand (such as Gold Medal) produces a more tender crust. Doughs made with low-protein flours are also easier to handle, and, perhaps most important, they are less likely to buckle and shrink out of shape during baking. If you wish to blend the fat and flour with your fingertips or with a pastry tool instead of using a machine, decrease the butter to six tablespoons and add two tablespoons of chilled vegetable shortening. The pie may be served slightly warm, chilled, or — my preference — at room temperature.

Flaky Pastry Shell

- 1¼ cups all-purpose flour, measured by dip and sweep (*see* September/October, 1993, issue page 6)
- ½ teaspoon salt
- ½ teaspoon sugar
- 10 tablespoons (1¼ sticks) unsalted butter, chilled and cut into ¼-inch pats
- 3–3½ tablespoons ice water

Spicy Pumpkin Filling

- 2 cups (16 ounces) plain pumpkin puree, canned or fresh
- 1 cup packed dark brown sugar
- 2 teaspoons ground ginger
- 2 teaspoons ground cinnamon
- 1 teaspoon fresh grated nutmeg
- ¼ teaspoon ground cloves
- ½ teaspoon salt
- ⅔ cup heavy cream
- ⅔ cup milk
- 4 large eggs

Brandied Whipped Cream

- 1⅓ cups heavy cream, cold
- 3 tablespoons confectioners' sugar
- 1 tablespoon brandy

1. *For pastry shell,* mix flour, salt, and sugar in a food processor fitted with steel blade. Scatter butter over dry ingredients; process until mixture resembles cornmeal, 7 to 12 seconds. Turn mixture into a medium-sized bowl.

2. Drizzle 3 tablespoons of water over flour mixture. With blade side of a rubber spatula, cut mixture into little balls. Then press down on mixture with broad side of spatula so balls stick together in large clumps. If dough resists gathering, sprinkle remaining water over dry, crumbly patches and press a few more times. Form dough into a ball with your hands; wrap in plastic, then flatten into a 4-inch disk. Refrigerate for at least 30 minutes. (Can be refrigerated for 2 days or, if sealed airtight in a plastic bag, frozen for up to 6 months.)

3. Generously sprinkle a 2-foot square work area with flour. Remove dough from wrapping and place disk in center; dust top with flour. (If it has been chilled for more than 1 hour, let dough stand until it gives slightly when pressed, 5 to 10 minutes.) Roll dough in all directions, from center to edges, rotating a quarter turn and strewing flour underneath as necessary after each stroke. Flip disk over when it is 9 inches in diameter and continue to roll (but don't rotate) in all directions, until it is 13 to 14 inches in diameter and just under ⅛-inch thick.

4. Fold dough in quarters and place the corner in the center of a Pyrex pie pan measuring 9 to 9½ inches across top. Carefully unfold dough to cover pan completely, with excess dough draped over pan lip. With one hand, pick up edges of dough; use index finger of other hand to press dough around pan bottom. Use your fingertips to press dough against pan walls. Trim dough overhanging the pan to an even ½ inch all around.

5. Tuck overhanging dough back under itself so folded edge is flush with edge of pan lip. Press double layer of dough with your fingers to seal, then bend up at a 90-degree angle and flute by pressing thumb and index finger about ½ inch apart against outside edge of dough, then using index finger (or knuckle) of other hand to poke a dent through the space. Repeat procedure all the way around.

6. Refrigerate for 20 minutes (or freeze for 5 minutes) to firm dough shell. Using a table fork, prick bottom and sides — including where they meet — at ½-inch intervals. Flatten a 12-inch square of aluminum foil inside shell, pressing it flush against corners, sides, and over rim. Prick foil bottom in about a dozen places with a fork. Chill shell for at least 30 minutes (preferably an hour or more), to allow dough to relax.

7. Adjust an oven rack to lowest position, and heat oven to 400 degrees. (Start preparing filling when you put shell into oven.) Bake 15 minutes, pressing down on foil with mitt-protected hands to flatten any puffs. Remove foil and bake shell for 8 to 10 minutes longer, or until interior just begins to color.

8. *For filling,* process first 7 ingredients in a food processor fitted with steel blade for 1 minute. Transfer pumpkin mixture to a 3-quart heavy-bottomed saucepan; bring it to a sputtering simmer over medium-high heat. Cook pumpkin, stirring constantly, until thick and shiny, about 5 minutes. As soon as pie shell comes out of oven, whisk heavy cream and milk into pumpkin and bring to a bare simmer. Process eggs in food processor until whites and yolks are mixed, about 5 seconds. With motor running, slowly pour about half of hot pumpkin mixture through feed tube. Stop machine and scrape in remaining pumpkin. Process 30 seconds longer.

9. Immediately pour warm filling into hot pie shell. (Ladle any excess filling into pie after it has baked for 5 minutes or so — by this time filling will have settled.) Bake until filling is puffed, dry-looking, and lightly cracked around edges, and center wiggles like gelatin when pie is gently shaken, about 25 minutes. Cool on a wire rack for at least 1 hour.

10. *For whipped cream,* beat cream at medium speed to soft peaks; gradually add confectioners' sugar then brandy. Beat to stiff peaks. Accompany each wedge of pie with a dollop of whipped cream. ■

Stephen Schmidt, a caterer and cooking teacher, is the author of *Master Recipes* (Ballantine, 1987).

Using Fresh Pumpkin

Properly handled, canned pumpkin works quite well in pies (*see* text), but you may be curious to start with fresh. Having tried virtually every conceivable method of preparing fresh pumpkin, I have concluded that the following one works best: First, choose one of the smaller pumpkins, sometimes called sugar pumpkins, which are firmer, meatier, and sweeter than those grown for jack-o'-lanterns. Split the pumpkin in half (or in quarters, if it is very large), carve out the stem, and scrape out the seeds and stringy bits. Next, arrange the pumpkin with the rind side down on a lightly oiled roasting pan, cover it tightly with foil, and bake at 325 degrees for 75 minutes. Remove the foil and bake for 30 to 45 minutes longer, or until the flesh is extremely soft and yields hardly any moisture when pressed firmly with the back of a spoon. Remove from the oven and allow to cool.

When the pumpkin is cool enough to handle, scrape the flesh free of the rind and mash it to a pulp. An ordinary whisk will serve here; you will be pureeing the pulp when you make the pie, so it isn't necessary to use a food processor at this point. Line a colander with a triple thickness of cheesecloth that has been rinsed in very hot water and thoroughly wrung out. Turn the pumpkin into the colander, wrap the protruding ends of the cheesecloth over the top, and cover with a cake pan topped with a five-pound weight. Put the colander in the sink and let the pumpkin drain for one hour.

You will need at least four pounds of fresh pumpkin — and I'd recommend five or even six pounds, just to be safe — to make one pound of stewed, mashed, and drained puree.

Caviar Tasting Finds Quality Disappointing

Spending $30 an ounce doesn't guarantee an exciting culinary experience.

BY JONI MILLER

Caviar's ineffable mystique is best summed up in the words of one of the world's preeminent caviar purveyors, Armen Petrossian, who once observed, "I don't sell caviar, I sell dreams." Our tasting of a dozen caviars found that many of these dreams are little more than overpriced nightmares.

As has been the case in *Cook's Illustrated* tastings of other foods, there was near-consensus in choosing the highest and lowest ranked caviars, with a rather dramatic schism marking the cutoff between the two. What was markedly different here, however, was that at least half of the 12 caviars tasted displayed below-par texture, appearance, and flavor, and even the best did not live up to expectations.

Although it is salted, caviar is a relatively delicate product with a finite shelf life, one which must be well handled. Given that our tasting was held in midsummer, we expected to be sampling caviar from the spring catch; given that we purchased our caviar from reputable dealers, we expected to have been sold what we thought we were buying. But our panelists, many of whom were veteran caviar tasters, guessed that many of the caviars were older than they should have been ("probably not spring 1993 catch"), that some had been improperly stored, and that we may have tasted some "mixed batches," a no-no in the world of fine caviar.

The tasting certainly raised some questions about buying caviar, with so many reputable brands displaying unsatisfactory texture, appearance, and flavor. After the tasting, I interviewed several industry sources and found that it was unlikely that any of the caviars we tasted could have come from the spring 1993 catch. Due to political and economic turmoil in Russia and the as-yet incomplete establishment of firm, new controls in the country's caviar industry, shipments of the spring catch to the United States had been delayed past their customary July arrival dates.

Last April's Caspian Sea symposium of hundreds of caviar producers and importers theoretically worked on solving problems such as this and on reinstating some order in the industry (it is probably not chauvinistic to observe that an industry dominated by Russian and Iranian bureaucracies is

BUYING AND SERVING FRESH CAVIAR

To avoid confusion at the caviar counter, be aware that fresh, hand-packed *malossol* caviar — the kind we tasted — is usually sold to consumers in round tins with an air-tight seal provided by a wide, thick rubber band securing the seam where the two halves of the tin meet.

Each plump grain of top-quality, fresh caviar should be smooth-skinned and glistening with a light sheen of oil. If there is any aroma, it should be a faint, clean, fresh sea-air smell. The eggs should be whole and separate, not bruised or broken (as were many in our tasting). In the mouth, when the grains are gently pressed against the palate, they should hold firm for an instant, then burst or "pop", releasing a frisson of subtle, unsalty, unfishy flavor containing a suggestion of the eggs' natural oils. Dull, broken eggs that are mushy or gummy may reflect improper storage or handling, or signify eggs past their prime. A combination of firm, separate grains and broken ones may indicate rough handling or that eggs from several batches have been mixed together.

Because they are only lightly salted, fresh malossol caviars are quite perishable. Good caviar purveyors store their products at between 28 degrees and 32 degrees, and so should you. When you purchase caviar in a retail store it should be packed in an insulated bag with a frozen gel pack to keep it cool; mail-ordered caviar, shipped overnight, is similarly protected. At home, an unopened tin should be kept in the coldest part of the refrigerator (usually the bottom shelf, although this may not be true for many new refrigerators). Set it on top of a frozen gel pack or in a bowl of crushed ice, and use it within two to four weeks, replacing the ice as needed. Caviar should never be frozen.

The best way to serve fine caviar is alone, without distracting embellishments. Garnishes such as chopped onion or hard-boiled egg, sour cream, or lemon are completely unnecessary. Caviar should be eaten chilled; remove the tin from the refrigerator no more than 30 minutes before serving, leaving the lid on until the last minute. Once a tin is opened, the caviar should be consumed that day; it deteriorates rapidly.

For real elegance, you might set the tin, or a chilled glass bowl into which the eggs have been carefully transferred, into a large bowl set on a bed of crushed ice. Spoon caviar directly from the tin or bowl to your mouth, using a small bone, horn, or wooden spoon (plastic, although less suave, works just fine). Never use metal, as it oxidizes instantly upon contact with the roe and ruins the flavor; gold is an exception.

Well-chilled or frozen vodka, of course, is caviar's classic accompaniment, though Champagne is also delicious. An advantage of vodka is that it cuts through the slight oiliness of the eggs, cleansing the palate in preparation for the next unctuous spoonful.

LESSER TYPES OF CAVIAR

Pasteurized *malossol* caviar is sold in glass jars. The eggs have been vacuum-sealed in the jars and "cooked" at 149 degrees. They have a different taste, consistency, and texture than unpasteurized eggs and are considerably less expensive. Pressed caviar (*payusnaya*) is the least expensive. Sold in tins, it is usually made from a combination of all three types of eggs (beluga, ossetra, and sevruga) broken during whole-grain caviar processing and those deemed overripe for preserving whole, along with more mature eggs "harvested" toward the end of the season. With a saltier and more intense flavor than that of either fresh or pasteurized whole-grain caviars, pressed caviar is best eaten on bread or with blinis and sour cream, or as a baked potato topping.

not likely to run smoothly any time in the near future). In late August, fishery officials from Russia, Iran, Azerbaijan, Kazakhstan, and Turkmenistan announced the formation of a cartel to control the supply of caviar and to coordinate its marketing. Consumers can realistically expect that caviar prices, which have declined somewhat over the past two years, will rise as a result.

In the meantime, as our tasting showed, finding fine caviars worth indulging in may require some extra diligence on your part. The finest caviar sources encourage consumers to taste their offerings before buying. Customers who ignore this custom risk disappointment, but those who have confidence in their tastebuds and in their supplier can still find delight in the pearls of the Caspian.

The Caviar Troika

Caviars take their names from the species of sturgeon that is their source. The rarest and priciest are beluga, ossetra, and sevruga, all of which come from sturgeon in the Black and Caspian seas and the Sea of Azov. Each has distinctive size, color, and flavor characteristics.

Beluga, the most expensive, is held in high esteem for its large eggs, which are taken from the largest sturgeon. Although an average beluga may weigh around 800 or 900 pounds and reach a length of approximately 15 feet, some mammoth specimens have been logged in at up to 2,500 pounds and around 20 feet long. The female beluga takes 20 years to reach maturity, another factor contributing to expense. Belugas yield the largest eggs, soft, tender *petits pois*-size grains two and one-half to three millimeters in diameter and pale to dark gray or silver. The eggs' flavor should be barely salty, subtle, somewhat ethereal, and almost buttery.

The smaller ossetra sturgeon, around 6 feet long and weighing anywhere from 250 to 600 pounds, reach maturity at 12 to 15 years of age and produce medium-size eggs which, because they are firmer and "crisper" than beluga, are less likely to be crushed during processing and shipping. Their color varies from a golden yellow to shades of brown and occasionally darkish gray, and the pronounced flavor, nutlike or even fruity, is preferred by many aficionados.

Sevruga, the smallest and most abundantly spawned eggs, are from considerably smaller sturgeon (around 5 feet long and weighing 50 pounds) that are also the fastest maturing (7 years). Despite their small size, these eggs are the strongest and most assertively flavored of the three caviar types. They range in color from light to dark gray. Their relative abundance is a function of sevruga sturgeon's short maturation period and this is reflected in the price, for sevruga is the least expensive caviar.

All caviars are expensive, but price alone is no indication of quality or desirability. Consumers' subjective opinions based on the flavor and textural attributes of each type of roe are what count. The greatest enjoyment of caviar comes after exploring each and zeroing in on the one that sparks the pleasure principle on your palate. As Susan R. Friedland, author of *Caviar* (Scribners, 1986) points out, "There is no 'best' sturgeon caviar; what you like best is best."

We decided to concentrate on ossetra and sevruga caviar. These generally sell for considerably less than beluga, which, at the going rate of at least $25 to $30 per ounce, is out of range for most people. Our quest was for fine, relatively inexpensive caviar, and we found at least one, our second-place finisher.

For our tasting, then, we chose 10 fresh Russian ossetra and sevruga caviars and, for a bit of contrast, one fresh Russian beluga and one less familiar Chinese beluga (from sturgeon in the Aurora River near Beijing). All caviars tested were *malossol,* a term which means "little salt" in Russian, indicating that 3 to 6 percent salt in relation to the amount of roe was used in processing. ■

Joni Miller, a New York–based writer, is the author of *True Grits* (Workman, 1990).

Transforming Fish Eggs into Caviar

The Food and Drug Administration defines caviar exclusively as processed sturgeon roe, and strictly enforced federal controls are exercised to ensure this is the case. All other eggs (including those from salmon, carp, lumpfish, paddlefish, steelhead trout, and whitefish) must be clearly labeled with the fish of origin (as in "salmon caviar").

The finest caviar, of course, comes from sturgeon species in the Caspian Sea. Most caviar sold in the United States has been harvested and processed in Russia; due to trade embargoes, Iranian caviar, still available in Europe, may not legally be sold here.

In Russia, the season for sturgeon fishing is limited to spring and fall "catches." Enormous care and expertise are required in the processing of the sturgeon roe, a task considered to be an art; each rapidly performed, hand-labor-intensive step contributes to caviar's high cost.

It begins when live female sturgeon, captured in nets set up across the rivers leading to the Caspian, are transported with great haste to one of two Russian processing centers. Within minutes of arrival, the roe sacs, which look like clusters of tiny grapes, are removed from the fish and taken into cold processing rooms. Here, the eggs are separated from the membrane that holds them together by gently passing the sacs over huge sieves with openings that are slightly larger than the eggs. After being gently rinsed by hand in icy cold water, the eggs are drained on fine screens, before proceeding to the ministrations of highly skilled *nastavnic,* or master tasters, for sorting, grading, and salting; all of this takes place, quite literally, within minutes.

To ensure unbroken eggs, everything from sorting to salting to packing the tiny eggs in tins is done by hand.

These specialists, whose craft ranks alongside those of winemakers and perfumers, grade the eggs based on a combination of factors that include size, color, flavor, and firmness, as well as the uniformity and consistency of each grain. Master tasters base the crucial decision as to how much purified salt to fold into the roe on the roe's size and condition and the weather. (The caviar's destination is also a factor. Borax, another preserving agent, is combined with salt for caviar shipped everywhere but the United States, where FDA regulations forbid its use. The borax/salt combination uses less salt, which results in a sweeter, moister caviar preferred by many aficionados.) The salt acts as a preservative and also ripens the roe into caviar; *malossol* ("little salt") caviar, treated with a less than 6 percent salt-to-roe ratio, is the most prized.

After salting, the roe is once again placed on fine sieves, which are shaken for a precisely gauged number of minutes until the caviar is dry. In another rapid-fire step, the roe is mounded into two-kilo (4.4-pound) tins, which are marked by the master with the fish's identification number and the roe's grade. The tins are covered with varnished, concave lids to force out the excess brine, heavy weights are applied, and the caviar "cures" for seven or eight hours before each tin is sealed air-tight with a large rubber band around its circumference. Maintaining a temperature of between 26 degrees and 30 degrees during storage and shipping is crucial (the eggs may spoil above 35 degrees), and tins must be turned every two to four weeks so the oils are evenly distributed. Caviar, in its original two-kilo tins, has a shelf life of five to six months.

PHOTOGRAPH COURTESY OF PETROSSIAN INC.

Caviar Blind Tasting

Our blind tasting, held at The Russian Tea Room in New York City, had as its panel *Cook's Illustrated* executive editor Mark Bittman; Salvatore J. Conti, a senior buyer for the Cunard Line, one of the world's major purchasers of caviar; newspaper and magazine food writer and columnist Florence Fabricant; chef Paul Ingenito of The Russian Tea Room; food writer and New York *Daily News* restaurant critic Arthur Schwartz; restaurant consultant Clark Wolf; author Joni Miller; and two home cooks.

The caviars were purchased anonymously from well-known caviar purveyors in New York City, each of whom will ship orders. In each instance, the buyer requested spring 1993 catch. Prices quoted are for one-ounce jars or tins (enough to serve one or two people as an appetizer), and will vary.

Caviars are listed in order of preference (an asterisk next to a caviar indicates that it tied with that immediately below it). In the judging, seven points were awarded for each first-place vote; six for second; five for third; four for fourth; three for fifth; two for sixth; one for seventh.

Caviars Listed in Order of Preference

1 **Caspian Sturgeon Caviar Ossetra Malossol** (Caviarteria), $18.50; 44 points. The hands-down favorite, and not a bad price. A "nicely textured" dark charcoal-gray ossetra with firm "but not too hard" eggs that showed good separation and "popped" in the mouth. Despite a slightly "fishy" smell, the flavor was pleasantly nutty, well-balanced, and "mellow," if a bit "one-dimensional."

2 **Caviar Aristoff Sevruga Malossol** (Caviar & Fine Foods), $9.50; 33 points. The "small but mighty tasting" slightly greenish, pearl-gray berries showed well on the taste front but did not meet all the criteria for a good caviar in appearance and texture, as some grains were broken. "Softish," mushy texture with inconsistent pop. "Clean, "subtle, "scent of the sea." "Complex" flavor, a shade on the salty side; "quite delicious" and "pleasant overall" with several levels of taste. Two tasters detected "a slightly bitter finish," but this caviar must be considered a bargain.

3 **Caviar Aristoff Beluga Malossol** (Caviar & Fine Foods), $31.25; 20 points. One of two belugas in the tasting; a "pleasant," "acceptable" caviar. Experienced tasters on the panel identified it as a beluga based on the large-size charcoal-gray eggs which were firm with good separation. Grains were "velvety on the tongue." Faint aroma and subtle taste were "gently sea-like" and "clean." Several panelists suggested it was "a bit oilier" than it should have been.

4 ***Caviar Aristoff Ossetra Malossol** (Caviar & Fine Foods), $13.50; 18 points. Firm, "glistening, well-separated, picture-perfect blackish-bronze" eggs with "great pop" and a clean "slightly saline" aroma reminiscent of the sea. A "fresh sea-taste" with qualities typically associated with ossetra; "nutty" flavor, likened to that of "walnuts" or "hazelnuts." On the downside, one taster detected an unpleasant "cheesy" flavor.

5 **Petrossian Paris Sevruga Malossol** (Petrossian Paris), $21; 18 points. The taste of this sevruga was more appealing than its "mushy" appearance suggested. Smallish charcoal-gray grains described as "loose," "watery," or "almost like a paste." Positive comments on the "clean," "complex" taste. One taster noted it was "oily" and "coated the teeth." "Good flavor, good quality" was the consensus.

6 **Petrossian Paris Ossetra Malossol** (Petrossian Paris), $29; 17 points. Intensity of flavor and aroma were hallmarks of this ossetra, which had firm, "crisp," dark-gray berries with good separation and pop. A taster who found the eggs "a bit dehydrated" doubted this was spring catch because "it doesn't seem fresh enough." But panelists were positive about a much more "pungent," "stronger," "richer," and "more briney" aroma than detected in the other caviars. (A dissenting view identified a "fake, chemical" aroma.)

7 **Zabar's Sevruga Malossol** (Zabar's), $9; 14 points. Very unappealing in appearance and in the mouth. Small, light-gray "soft and broken" grains were "mushy" and "gooey," and noted as "decomposed" with "minimal separation." A "clean," "mild" aroma was a positive, however, with one taster noting it was "a tad sweet and grassy." At best, the taste was "decent;" "awful" was the general consensus.

8 **Zabar Ossetra Malossol** (Zabar's), $10.50; 10 points. A middle-of-the-road caviar with poor appearance and texture. Reactions ranged from faintly positive ("a caviar to eat in a pinch") to vigorously negative ("yuck!"). Very small, almost black, "soft," "oily" grains were mushy and "gluey" with minimal pop. Likened by one taster to "pressed caviar without as much concentrated flavor."

9 **Iron Gate Malossol Sevruga** (Macy's), $11; 8 points. "Pinpoint" grains of "texturally unsubstantial," "uneven-size" eggs. "Unappealing" pale-gray, slightly "greenish" color. "Oddly chewy," noted several tasters, but "not sticky," with a clean, mild aroma. Detectable flavor described as "vegetal" or "seaweedlike." Lack of distinctive flavor and "Jurassic" appearance prompted several panelists to question whether these were "actually" sturgeon eggs. "Another species?" one wondered.

10 **Aristoff Imperial Chinese Beluga** (Caviar & Fine Foods), $13.75; 6 points. Too "salty" for most tasters. Big "gluey dark grayish-brown eggs" were a mixture of broken and whole berries. "Strong," "fishy" aroma and taste. Several detected a slight "bitterness" and an after-taste. "Grabs me in the throat," noted one taster.

11 **Caspian Sevruga Malossol** (Caviarteria), $20; 4 points. This sevruga's "intense" distinctive flavor was described positively as "gutsy" and "rustic"; negatively as "salty and fishy", "sour and synthetic," or "metallic." The small, "buckshot-colored" grains were "oddly sticky." A combination of firm-textured whole eggs with soft, "mushy," damaged ones; "grainy in the mouth." A pronounced, "sharp and unpleasant," "almost sour" aroma. "Could be fresher," several panelists commented, while one quipped that it tasted like it "had been purchased in a Russian hotel hallway."

12 **Iron Gate Malossol Ossetra** (Macy's), $13; 0 points. No points were given this caviar, which elicited harsh evaluations. Interestingly, its appearance, about which there was no criticism (firm, largish, gray-brown eggs showed good separation), did not serve as an indicator of its unacceptable taste. Once in the mouth, "hard, dried out" grains "smacked of badly stored caviar" to one taster, while another wondered if the "tough" skin signaled a "pasteurized" product. There was consensus about its strong, "nasty," "harsh" taste.

The Mystery of the Ideal Waffle

The best waffles are crisp on the outside and creamy on the inside, like a soufflé with crunch; the secret is buttermilk.

BY CHRISTOPHER KIMBALL

You might ask, "What could be more straightforward than finding the best recipe for waffle batter?" But starting this quest is akin to the innocuous beginning of a Sherlock Holmes mystery, in which the theft of a pair of boots evolves into a search for the Hound of the Baskervilles.

What is the perfect waffle? My ideal is a crisp, well-browned exterior — browning develops flavor — with a moist, fluffy interior. It should be like a rich, just-cooked soufflé encased in a flavorful crust. After testing more than 15 variations on a basic recipe and speaking with a trio of food scientists, I found that the basic waffle described in most cookbooks sheds little light on the inner workings of a recipe that requires a delicate balance of imperfectly understood chemical reactions. Two things became clear during my work: My ideal requires a thick batter, so the outside can become crisp while the inside remains custardy. And it takes quick cooking, because slow cooking overcooks the center.

The Ingredients

I started with the batter. The proportion found in most recipes is one cup of milk to one cup of flour. This makes a rather thin batter, which results in a gummy waffle with a dry, unappealing interior. I found that seven-eighths cup of buttermilk, or three-quarters cup of sweet milk, to one cup of flour is a far better proportion.

Most recipes omit buttermilk entirely, or at best list it as an option. Yet I found that buttermilk is absolutely crucial. Why? Because buttermilk and baking soda create a much thicker batter than the alternative, which is sweet milk and baking powder (*see* "Double-Acting Baking Powder and Waffles Don't Mix," page 28), and, again, a thick batter is key. If you do not have buttermilk on hand, follow my sweet-milk recipe; it not only has a reduced proportion of milk to flour, but contains a simple homemade baking powder which creates a much thicker batter than can be made with sweet milk and store-bought baking powder.

Although you need not add baking powder when using the buttermilk/baking soda combination (the cream of tartar is an acidic ingredient in baking powder and is made superfluous by the acidity of buttermilk), many recipes call for it. But when I eliminated the baking powder and increased the amount of baking soda, the batter improved and my waffle cooked up crisper. Out of curiosity, I also tried to make a waffle with buttermilk and baking powder, eliminating the baking soda. This was inedible by any standard, since there was too much acid and not enough baking soda.

Because crispness is so important in waffles, I tried substituting cornmeal for a bit of the flour, and found that one tablespoon per cup of flour adds extra crackle to the waffle. I also experimented with cake flour, whose lower gluten, or protein, content produces a finer crumb and a more tender product. I started by replacing one-third of the all-purpose flour with cake flour, and was disappointed. The waffle was indeed tender, but it lacked sufficient contrast between crisp exterior and creamy interior. When I reduced the amount to two tablespoons, the results were better, but still not worth the trade-off; I want as much crispness as I can get.

Buttermilk batter, gentle but thorough mixing, and a machine capable of maintaining high heat throughout the cooking time combine to produce the best waffle.

Although I am not a fan of low-fat recipes, I felt obliged to attempt to create a lower fat waffle by removing the melted butter from the recipe. This created a bland, tasteless waffle, with a limp exterior. Why? Well, when butter or oil is added, the outside of the waffle will cook at a higher temperature. Oil is a better conductor of heat than the water, egg, flour, and other ingredients in the waffle batter. The oil also improves the heat transfer from the waffle iron to the batter itself. Inside the waffle, however, the batter is being steamed (even with the addition of butter) and the interior will reach no more than 212 degrees as long as it is still moist (an instant-read thermometer inserted into the middle of a just-cooked waffle will read about 200 degrees). That is why the exterior of a waffle is crisper than the interior — two different cooking processes are at work. Vegetable oil will produce the same outside crispness as butter, although with a loss of flavor. (I recommend this substitution only if you are desperate to reduce the saturated fat in your diet; the caloric content is the same.)

The Technique

Separating the egg and beating the white before folding it into the mixed batter is another important step, making the batter glossier and the waffle fluffier. If you cut through a cooked waffle made with beaten egg whites, you can actually see pockets of air trapped inside. Cutting through a waffle made with whole egg reveals a flatter, more consistent texture.

Look at a number of waffle recipes and you'll see a wide range of recommendations as to how to combine ingredients. One author carefully mixes with a whisk until the liquid and dry ingredients are *just* combined; another throws everything into the bowl of an electric mixer and cranks up the horsepower. But most have this in common: they add all of the liquid at once. This practice necessitates overmixing, and usually results in clumps of unmoistened flour. When I used a whisk to combine the ingredients until they were smooth, the batter was thin and the waffle tough.

The objective in all of this is to moisten the flour thoroughly, not to create a smooth batter, and for this there is no question that a gentle hand is crucial. This is the technique I have found works best: Whisk together the dry ingredients, whisk together the liquid ingredients, and then pour the liquid ingredients into the dry ingredients very slowly, mixing gently with a rubber spatula. Use a thin steady stream, as you would when you add oil to vinegar to form an emulsion for salad dressing, and be careful not to let the addition of the liquid get ahead of mixing. When most of the liquid has been added, the batter becomes thicker; switch to a folding motion, similar to the folding of egg whites, to finally combine and moisten the batter. Then fold in the egg white.

There is also debate about resting the batter before baking. I let two different batters rest in the refrigerator for about an hour: a whole egg recipe and one in which the egg white was separated and beaten. In both cases, the results were disappointing. The theory of resting waffle or pancake batter is based on the notion that the gluten (protein) in all-purpose flour has a chance to relax, producing a more tender product. But the quick development of carbon dioxide in a buttermilk-based batter, which makes the batter thick and puffy, mandates a quick move to a hot waffle iron. Letting the batter sit only allows the gas to escape, deflating the batter and the final waffle. In a pinch, the batter can sit for up to 15 minutes at room temperature without ill effect.

The Baking

When you bake waffles, remember that darker waffles are better than lighter ones. In scientific terms, this is due to the Maillard reaction, which refers to the reaction and subsequent transformation of carbohydrates at temperatures of more than three-hundred degrees. This is why meat is browned before stewing, why dark beers have more flavor than regular brews, and why nuts are roasted before use in pesto or desserts. This chemical reaction, which is evidenced by browning (and *not* by "tanning"), creates a lot of flavor. Waffles should therefore be cooked to a medium-brown, not a light brown. Empirically, I also found that light brown waffles become soggy more quickly than darker counterparts. It's as if the waffle has to "set" properly, much like a cake or soufflé. Just don't overdo it — the perfect waffle is still moist and creamy inside.

Usually, you must check each waffle visually; the conventional wisdom about a waffle being properly cooked when the iron stops steaming is useless (the waffle will be overcooked if you wait this long). The top waffle iron (the Vitantonio) has a green light that really works — it goes on when the iron is back up to temperature which coincides with the exact moment when the waffle is perfectly cooked. For most models, however, you must check the waffle after three minutes of cooking time. Again, the exterior should be a toasty brown; manila-colored waffles turn soggy in seconds.

It's surprising how quickly even properly cooked waffles begin to deteriorate; a minute after you remove them from the iron, the crispy exterior starts to absorb the moisture from the softer interior; all too soon, the result is a limp, soggy square. This problem is compounded if the waffle is left on a plate; the bottom of the waffle quickly turns soggy as the moisture from the interior of the waffle cannot escape into the air — it condenses and turns the bottom of the waffle mushy. To combat this problem, make sure that you thoroughly cook the waffle as described above; a crisp exterior holds its texture better. You can also hold waffles on a cake rack in a two-hundred degree oven for up to five minutes. This helps the exterior remain crisp. Unfortunately, it causes the interior to start to become dry, dense, and tough; that fluffy, moist texture does not hold for long. My advice is to eat each waffle immediately. Like a soufflé or a morsel of fried food, the ultimate waffle is a passing delicacy.

THE BEST BUTTERMILK WAFFLES

Makes 3–4

The secret to great waffles is a thick batter, so don't expect to pour this one. Make toaster waffles out of leftover batter — undercook the waffles a bit, cool them on a wire rack, wrap them in plastic wrap and freeze. Pop them in the toaster for a quick breakfast.

- 1 cup all-purpose flour
- 1 tablespoon cornmeal (optional)
- ½ teaspoon salt
- 1 teaspoon baking soda
- 1 egg, separated
- ⅞ cup buttermilk
- 2 tablespoons unsalted butter, melted

1. Heat waffle iron. Whisk dry ingredients together in a medium bowl. Whisk yolk with buttermilk and butter.
2. Beat egg white until it just holds a 2-inch peak.
3. Add liquid ingredients to dry ingredients in a thin steady stream while gently mixing with a rubber spatula; be careful not to add liquid faster than you can incorporate it. Toward end of mixing, use a folding motion to incorporate ingredients; gently fold egg whites into batter.
4. Spread appropriate amount of batter onto waffle iron. Following manufacturer's instructions, cook waffle until golden brown, 2 to 5 minutes. Serve immediately. (You can can keep waffles warm on a wire rack in a 200-degree oven for up to 5 minutes.)

ALMOST-AS-GOOD-AS-BUTTERMILK WAFFLES

Makes 3–4

If you're out of buttermilk, try this sweet-milk variation. By making your own baking powder using baking soda and cream of tartar and by cutting back on the quantity of milk, you can make a thick, quite respectable batter. The result is a waffle with a crisp crust and moist interior.

Follow Steps 1 through 4 in The Best Buttermilk Waffles, adding 2 teaspoons cream of tartar to the dry ingredients and substituting a scant ¾ cup milk for the buttermilk. ■

DOUBLE-ACTING BAKING POWDER AND WAFFLES DON'T MIX

Baking powder is made from an acid, such as cream of tartar, and baking soda. When baking soda comes in contact with a moist, acidic environment, it forms carbon dioxide gas, creating "rise." This chemical reaction is quite pronounced in a buttermilk batter, because the large amount of lactic acid in buttermilk reacts with the soda, generating a thick, spongy batter in seconds. The air bubbles (carbon dioxide gas) are trapped by the structure of the batter much like whipped cream thickens when aerated through beating.

Baking powder is useful in doughs or batters that don't contain other acidic ingredients; that is, those in which sweet milk is used rather than buttermilk or yogurt. But the combination of sweet milk and powder is not as powerful as that of buttermilk and soda; the batter remains thin. This is partially because most baking powder is "double-acting" — it contains two different acid ingredients (different baking powders use different acids including a few — how about sodium acid pyrophosphate? — that sound distinctly unappetizing), one of which creates carbon dioxide at room temperature, the other at temperatures of 120 degrees or higher.

Double-acting baking powder is designed to create gas slowly and over a longer period of time, so that a cake, for example, has time to bake and set before all of the bubbles dissipate. I have found that the rise from baking powder occurs mostly at oven temperatures. But with waffles (and pancakes), which cook quickly, you want the rise to take place at room temperature. Store-bought baking powder doesn't do this.

It's best then, when using sweet milk, to make your own baking powder right in the bowl, adding cream of tartar to the baking soda (*see* "Almost-As-Good-As-Buttermilk Waffles"). And if you have a favorite waffle recipe containing both buttermilk and baking powder, try substituting the same amount of baking soda; you'll probably see an improvement.

Rating Waffle Irons

THE COSTLIEST MODEL TESTED IS AMONG THE WORST; THE LEAST EXPENSIVE MACHINE TAKES SECOND PLACE.

Waffle irons are definitely *not* all the same; they vary widely in quality, even within the same price range. As a result, choosing your iron is an important part of making waffles: even the best batter can make terrible waffles when poured into the wrong machine. Using our buttermilk batter (*see* The Best Buttermilk Waffles, page 28), I found that the top-rated Vitantonio yielded perfect waffles in just 2 minutes, while the bottom-rated Toastmaster Family Size could take as long as 10 minutes to crank out rubbery disks better suited to sporting events than to breakfast.

Among the eight waffle irons tested, the Vitantonio Premier Classic is in a league of its own in both design and performance. This is largely because the machine achieves a temperature of 470 degrees (versus the 400 to 450 degrees of other machines), which allows quick cooking. If you don't want to spend $50 on a waffle iron, however, the Dazey Short Order Chef makes four crisp waffles at once and is a best buy at just $30.

In the second tier, the Black & Decker, Toastmaster Cool-Touch, and Oster models all have a similar modern design that is quite easy to use. However, the Black & Decker and Toastmaster irons have an edge — they make crisper waffles and signal when they are done, although not always accurately. (The B & D also has a chirping ready tone, which my dog liked but you may not.) The Palmer machine turns out fine waffles but has no ready light and is relatively expensive.

Steer clear of the Broil King Hurry Hot (the name is appropriate, given the scorching handles) and Toastmaster Family Size.

For information about locating individual waffle irons, *see* Sources and Resources, page 32.

Waffle Irons in Order of Preference

FIRST PLACE
Vitantonio Premier Classic Waffler 1800

SECOND PLACE
Dazey Short Order Chef DWG-300

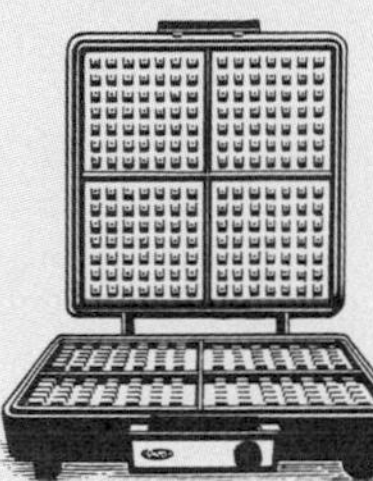

THIRD PLACE
Black & Decker Sweet Hearts Wafflebaker G12

VITANTONIO PREMIER CLASSIC WAFFLER 1800
Cost: $50
Thermostat: Manually adjusted
Design: Sleek chrome with black plastic handles. One of three machines with ready light that signals preheated grids as well as finished waffles.
Preheating Time: 4 minutes
Cooking Time[1]: 2 minutes
Waffle Capacity[2]: 38 sq in
Performance: Thick and heavenly waffles that are remarkably crisp on the outside and fluffy on the inside; in short, produces the ideal waffle using our batter. Very fast and very good.
Special Features: Can be stored on end to save space.

DAZEY SHORT ORDER CHEF DWG-300
Cost: $30
Thermostat: Manually adjusted
Design: Basic white plastic with black handles. Ready light goes off when grids are preheated. Awkward hinged top is unsteady and could tip over.
Preheating Time: 8½ minutes
Cooking Time[1]: 6½ minutes
Waffle Capacity[2]: 81 sq in
Performance: Excellent waffles that are crisp and light. First batch cooks more quickly than later ones. Good bet for quantity and quality although design won't win any awards. Note low price.
Special Features: Reversible grids with griddle on flip side.

BLACK & DECKER SWEET HEARTS WAFFLEBAKER G12
Cost: $45
Thermostat: Automatic
Design: Compact white plastic. Ready light goes off when unit reaches proper temperature; machine makes loud chirping when preheated or when waffles are done.
Preheating Time: 5 minutes
Cooking Time[1]: 3½ minutes
Waffle Capacity[2]: 42 sq in
Performance: Light, tender waffles are on the thin side. Steam beads on handle, which becomes hot during later batches.
Special Features: Can be stored on end to save space.

TOASTMASTER COOL-TOUCH WAFFLE BAKER 220
Cost: $45
Thermostat: Automatic
Design: Compact white plastic with full-perimeter channel to catch excess batter. Ready light signals preheated grids as well as finished waffles.
Preheating Time: 4 minutes
Cooking Time[1]: 3½ minutes
Waffle Capacity[2]: 38 sq in
Performance: Light, airy waffles with crisp exterior. Even cooking gives excellent results, although waffles quickly became soggy. Strong fourth place.
Special Features: Can be stored on end to save space.

OSTER DESIGNER WAFFLE MAKER 3871
Cost: $45
Thermostat: Automatic
Design: White plastic flying saucer. Ready light goes off when unit has reached proper temperature. Wide built-in drip ridge catches overflow and is easy to clean.
Preheating Time: 3½ minutes
Cooking Time[1]: 5 minutes
Waffle Capacity[2]: 38 sq in
Performance: Somewhat soggy waffles despite space-age design. Ease of use and cleaning are strong points.
Special Features: Automatic shut-off after one hour. Can be stored on end to save space.

PALMER ELECTRIC WAFFLE IRON 1300T
Cost: $60
Thermostat: Automatic
Design: Attractive chrome with black plastic handles. Lack of ready light makes it impossible to know when proper temperature is reached.
Preheating Time: 15 minutes
Cooking Time[1]: 3 minutes
Waffle Capacity[2]: 39 sq in
Performance: Light, crisp waffles are a bit thin. First batch cooks faster; machine then slows down but recovers on later attempts. Despite design gaffes, machine yields decent waffles.
Special Features: None

BROIL KING HURRY HOT WAFFLE BAKER 736
Cost: $40
Thermostat: Manually adjusted
Design: White plastic with black handles that become extremely hot during use. Ready light goes off when grids are preheated.
Preheating Time: 7½ minutes
Cooking Time[1]: 5 minutes (on high)
Waffle Capacity[2]: 100 sq in
Performance: Gigantic waffles with good quality. Medium heat takes too long (8 minutes), so use high for crisper, faster waffles. Scorching handles knock this model down several places.
Special Features: Reversible grids with griddle on flip side.

TOASTMASTER FAMILY SIZE WAFFLE BAKER 269
Cost: $87
Thermostat: Manually adjusted
Design: Retro 1950s chrome with clunky handles. Ready light goes off when grids are preheated.
Preheating Time: 7½ minutes
Cooking Time[1]: 4 minutes (on high)
Waffle Capacity[2]: 81 sq in
Performance: Waffles must be cooked on high, otherwise they take forever (10 minutes) on medium to brown. Rubbery and tough on either setting. Price is not a reflection of quality here.
Special Features: Reversible grids with griddle on flip side. Can be stored on end to save space.

1. Average from four batches. If cooking time varied greatly, it is noted under performance. **2.** Total surface area of waffle(s) from one batch.

ILLUSTRATIONS BY DAN KROVATIN

BEST WINE

Pricey Champagnes Fizzle in Tasting

BEST BUY

California sparklers have made great strides, but our tasting found that the best Champagnes are still made in France — and they don't cost a fortune.

BY MARK BITTMAN

Almost all good sparkling wine, whether from the Champagne region of France or the winemaking regions of California or Spain, is made using the *methode champenoise,* a dual fermentation that transforms grape juice not only into wine but into bubbly wine. Most sparklers are made from chardonnay and pinot noir grapes, although the proportions vary significantly and small amounts of other traditional Champagne grapes are also used. (Spanish sparklers — *cavas* — are the exception; they're produced with grapes indigenous to the Penedes, the Catalonian winemaking region.)

Although the prices of Champagne (the word is customarily used to refer only to wines from the same-named former province of Northern France) have fallen recently, California sparklers remain, on average, considerably less expensive. This is not because the California wines are less expensive to make — since West Coast operations are newer, their mortgages are higher and the opposite is likely to be true — but because the French wines have more cachet on the international marketplace. Are sparkling wines from France actually better? Sometimes, according to our tasting panel.

There are three major differences that traditionally have made relatively inexpensive Champagnes superior to sparklers from elsewhere. The first is the region's chalky subsoil, a major determinant in grape flavor. Secondly, French law limits the amount of grapes that can be grown on a given plot of land; lower yields, say winemakers, produce more intensely flavored grapes. Third, winemakers in Champagne may allow their wines to rest on the lees, the sediment "thrown" during fermentation, for three or even five years; this produces wines of greater complexity. In California, the final filtering is often done after only one year, although this practice is begining to change.

Generally, California sparkling wines improve with every vintage; our panel ranked two moderately priced California wines in the top five, one of which sells for less than two-thirds the price of the top-ranked Mumm Cordon Rouge.

Also surprising were the low showings of near-hundred-dollar-per-bottle super-premiums Dom Perignon (fourth place) and Krug Grande Cuvee (eighth place); the Krug was even beat out by an Aria, a *cava* which sells for less than one-tenth its price.

As in the previous *Cook's Illustrated* wine tastings, the tasting panel was made up of both wine professionals and amateur wine-lovers. The wines were tasted blind; their identities were revealed only after the poll of preferences was made. When scanning these results, note the precipitous drop-off in points from the first wine to the second, and from the group of wines from second through fifth place to those below. Generally, the wines finishing from sixth place on garnered only moderately positive to quite negative comments. ■

BLIND TASTING RESULTS

Wines are listed in order of preference. In the judging, seven points were awarded for each first-place vote; six for second; five for third; four for fourth; three for fifth; two for sixth; one for seventh. Prices are average retail in the Northeast; consumers on the West Coast can expect to pay somewhat less for wines from California, somewhat more for those from Europe.

1. Mumm Cordon Rouge (France, 57 points), $26. Ever-popular sparkler, described as "dry, full-bodied, and refreshing." Positive comments from nearly every taster.
2. Moet and Chandon White Star Extra Dry (France, 47 points), $22. Biggest selling wine of this major producer. Described by most tasters as "on the sweet side," a quality obviously enjoyed by many.
3. Roederer Estate Brut Anderson Valley (California, 45 points), $16. This relative newcomer has been on the market for less than 10 years; given its near-second-place finish (and the price of the wine just below), we've named it Best Buy.
4. 1983 Moet and Chandon Cuvee Dom Perignon (France, 43 points), $95. First of the super-prestigious wines to be marketed in this country, and the best-known. The quality is there ("rich and flavorful"), but what a price!
5. Schramsberg Blanc de Noirs (California, 37 points), $21. Some found this wine, from one of the more prestigious California producers, "fruity and meaty." Others were unimpressed.
6. Perrier Jouet Grand Brut (France, 26 points), $24. Note precipitous drop-off in points from above wine; some tasters enjoyed this wine, but others found "off-odors" and described it as "bitter."
7. Aria Brut Cuvee (Spain, 24 points), $9. From one of the larger producers of Spanish sparklers, this wine must be considered a bargain. One veteran taster summed it up: "Clean and properly made — no more." The sparkler for holiday parties with tight budgets.
8. Krug Grande Cuvee (France, 21 points), $95. From what is generally considered to be the most prestigious Champagne house. One taster called it "great," another "classic." But too many thought it "not special" or without much character.
9. Mumm Cuvee Napa Brut Prestige (California, 18 points), $15. The California offspring of our winning wine did not do nearly as well as its cousin, although some called it "full-bodied" and "pleasant."
10. Veuve Clicquot Ponsardin (France, 16 points), $30. Currently the darling of Champagnes sold in the United States; this tasting did not reveal why.
11. Freixenet Cordon Negro Brut (Spain, 14 points), $8. The black bottle, one of the great marketing tools in wine history, may have hidden the flaws of its contents. Tasted blind, the wine had few admirers.
12. Korbel Brut (California, 13 points), $11. The oldest continuously produced *methode champenoise* wine from California. Korbel's large production, however, does not seem to translate into great wine.
13. Chandon Brut Cuvee (California, 12 points), $14. Moet and Chandon was the first of the French houses to open in California, about 15 years ago. The consensus: nondistinct and lacking in finish.
14. Kriter Brut de Brut Blanc de Blancs (France, 7 points), $7.50. An inexpensive, strong-selling wine that is bottled in Burgundy. Few tasters had anything positive to say about this one.

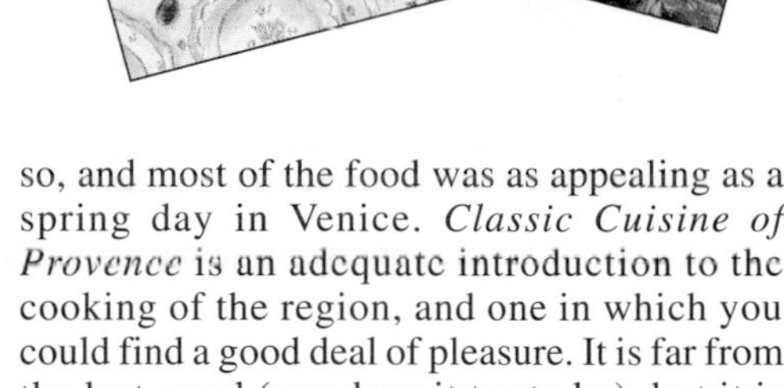

BOOK REVIEWS

BY PAM ANDERSON AND MARK BITTMAN

Provence the Beautiful Cookbook
Richard Olney
Collins Publishers San Francisco, $45.00

This book, the latest in a series that has covered France, China, Tuscany, Mexico, and more, has a secret weapon: Richard Olney. The author of *Simple French Food,* a classic that belongs in every cookbook library, Olney was also the brains behind the dated but once important Time-Life cooking series. In the 20 years since writing *Simple French Food,* he has lost none of his culinary sensibilities; rather he shows a remarkable ability to remain in touch with cooking trends and, it seems, to absorb the true spirit of any French cuisine with which he comes in contact.

Like the cooking of Tuscany, that of southern France is extremely simple, relying on basic combinations of essential flavors. This is regional cooking at its best, peasant food that is simply superb. Examples of this brilliance abound here: Lentils in Red Wine was easily the most delicious lentil dish we've ever tasted; it took less than an hour to prepare, and only about 10 minutes of that time was spent actively attending the pot. Spinach Gratin, no more than cleaned spinach baked — roasted, really — with salt, pepper, bread crumbs, and olive oil, was a revelation. Pork Cutlets with Tapenade, the region's marvelous olive paste, and Grilled Pork Chops with Piquant Sauce, a finely chopped mixture of typical local seasonings — shallots, garlic, parsley, mushrooms, vinegar, capers, anchovies, and *cornichons* — were each spectacular.

We differ in our overall opinion of the book. One of us loves the gorgeous layout and the fact that every single recipe is photographed in stunning color. The other begrudges the book's high price, finds its overall size absurd (10-by-14 inches, which, when open, takes up more counter space than your average microwave), and simply wishes that there were more Richard Olney recipes.

This could have been *the* book to define Provencal cuisine. Instead, it is a stunningly attractive work with more than two hundred wonderful recipes, a number of lovely photographs of the region, and a fair amount of unpretentious, serviceable, but not especially revealing text ("Tomatoes are in their glory in July and August").

As with the other cookbooks reviewed on this page, and so many others we have seen this year, it has a basic flaw: the recipes are not as precise as they might be, and give every indication that they might have benefited from another round of testing; one has too much stock, another produces enough sauce for three times the meat used, a third fails to suggest a substitute for an esoteric ingredient. These are hardly fatal flaws, but there are too many instances where the cook is left on his or her own to make a decision that is probably obvious to those who have already spent a number of years in the kitchen, but not so obvious to the novice who wants to pick up a book and be taught how to cook while absorbing a given cuisine. It is not impossible to create such a book; Olney's own *Simple French Food* is ample proof of that.

Classic Cuisine of Provence
Diane Holuigue
Ten Speed Press, $15.95

This book is entirely different from Olney's effort. Small, brightly illustrated (by Skye Rogers) in Provencal colors, and unambitious, it is a primer of sorts. And it is a limited success. Many of the recipes somehow lack the boldness and authentic feel of those of Olney; others, however, are right on the money. Some of our favorites: Baked Tomatoes Vinaigrette, a deceptively simple recipe that brings out all the lusciousness of good ripe tomatoes; Tuna Braised in Red Wine, a meaty treatment for this sturdy fish; and Spaghetti with Fresh Herbs, pasta tossed with a sauce of parsley, tarragon, basil, dill, chervil, and chives, along with butter and grainy mustard, for an unusual but delicious pesto-like effect.

Here, too, we found errant recipes. A stuffed cabbage was cooked for three hours, long enough that it fell apart (we did the natural thing — turned it into soup — and it was delicious). We were never told how to serve potatoes simmered in a saffron stock — swimming in liquid? with no garnish? — and, despite their precious ingredient, they were rather bland. So-called "naked ravioli" — little meatballs simmered in water — were topped with a bland tomato sauce, which also had meat in it; strange. These were the exceptions, however; most of the recipes were clear enough, if barely so, and most of the food was as appealing as a spring day in Venice. *Classic Cuisine of Provence* is an adequate introduction to the cooking of the region, and one in which you could find a good deal of pleasure. It is far from the last word (nor does it try to be), but it is nonetheless a worthwhile first step.

The Foods of Greece
Aglaia Kremezi
Stewart, Tabori & Chang, $50.00

Every year, a new Greek cookbook arrives on the scene, and every offering is a bit better than its predecessors. This is no exception; in our experience, it's the first time someone has at least attempted to define the real scope of this fascinating Mediterranean cuisine.

This is another large, lavishly photographed book, one which will sit more comfortably on your coffee table than in your kitchen. Many of the recipes lacked detail and were seriously flawed (in fairness, we were working from uncorrected proofs, and only hope that these rather serious defects will have been corrected by the time we — and the book — go to press).

But the food is delicious, and it makes you want to cook and eat. (Actually, it makes you want to cook and eat in Greece, a problem for most of us.) We relished Mashed Split Peas, an unusual appetizer salad the likes of which we have not seen before and will certainly make again; Zucchini Pie, a pizza-like creation; Veal in Eggplant Slices, little packets of meat and spices wrapped in eggplant; and Potato and Olive Stew in Tomato Sauce, a beautifully seasoned, attractive vegetarian dish that served 4 as a main course, or 8 to 10 as a side dish; and much more.

There were failures — Chicken in White Garlic Sauce was far too much work for a dish that was only so-so (and which produced enough sauce for four or five chickens), and Tomato Patties, an interesting combination of fresh and sun-dried tomatoes, parsley, mint, onions, garlic, and flour, which burned far too easily and became bitter — but these were far outnumbered by the spirited, interesting recipes. Again, we found errors of omission and a lack of precision; but if you're comfortable enough in the kitchen, *The Foods of Greece* could keep you busy — and happy — for a couple of months. ■

ADJUSTABLE ROASTING RACK

Adjustable V-shaped roasting racks raise fowl above the hot pan and allow air to circulate underneath. This promotes both even cooking (parts resting on hot pans tend to dry out) and browning. We prefer stainless-steel V-racks like those carried by La Cuisine Kitchenware (323 Cameron Street, Alexandria, VA 22314; 800-521-1176). Their large rack ($26) measures 14 inches and is best for turkey and roasting chickens. An 11-inch rack ($18) is fine for small chickens and game birds.

ITALIAN POTATO MASHER

Of all the potato mashers tested for the article on page 10, the *schiaccia-patate* (Italian for potato masher) was our clear favorite. This durable ricer can also handle everything from blanched broccoli (for timbales or soufflés) to fresh raspberries for a quick dessert sauce. The schiacciapatate costs $37.50 plus shipping and is available by mail from Bridge Kitchenware (214 E. 52nd Street, New York, NY 10022; 800-274-3435).

SHARP VEGETABLE PEELER

We found the Harp Peeler to be an especially useful kitchen tool. The extra-sharp blade is attached to a U-shaped handle for easy paring of potatoes, other root vegetables, cucumbers, or even asparagus. A side attachment effortlessly removes the eyes from a potato. Look for this handy device in kitchen supply shops or order it by mail from Bridge Kitchenware (*see* above). The price is just $2.60 plus shipping.

COUNTRY HAM

Susan McCreight Lindeborg, chef at the Morrison-Clark Inn in Washington, D.C., and subject of this issue's Master Class (*see* page 12), swears by the uncooked country hams from S. Wallace Edwards & Sons (P.O. Box 25, Surry, VA 23883; 800-222-4267). We found these meaty hams to have a pleasant smoky flavor (from hickory) and just the right amount of saltiness. What the company calls uncooked Virginia country ham comes in two sizes. The smaller version (11 to 12 pounds) costs $39; a larger (12- to 13-pound) ham costs $43. Both hams are shipped UPS at an additional cost of $6.

WAFFLE IRONS

The top-rated Vitantonio Premier Classic Waffler is available at Williams-Sonoma stores nationwide or from their catalog. To order by mail, call 800-541-2233. The price for this round iron is $50. Our best buy, the second-rated Dazey Short Order Chef, costs just $30 and is available at department and discount stores, including J.C. Penney, Wal-Mart, and Ace Hardware. The third-rated Black & Decker Sweet Hearts Wafflebaker is available by mail from the Service Merchandise catalog (800-473-7842) at a discounted price of $35. For information about the other waffle irons tested, telephone individual manufacturers: Toastmaster (314-445-8666), Oster (800-528-7713), Palmer (412-872-8200), and Broil King (201-589-6140).

ENGLISH CAKE WHISK

This handy device, which is also called an English cake maker, was developed more than one hundred years ago to aerate cake batters. Today, this flat, stainless-steel whisk can be used by cooks who don't have access to an electric mixer. (It's great for weekend cabins without fully stocked kitchens.) The King Arthur Flour Baker's Catalogue (P.O. Box 876, Norwich, VT 05055; 800-827-6836) carries an imported version for $14.25 plus shipping.

CAVIAR BY MAIL

Fresh Russian *malossol* caviar can be ordered by mail from the following importers and specialty stores that ship next-day air. Prices vary, so call, for the latest information. Caviar & Fine Foods (One Times Square Plaza, Suite A, New York, NY 10036; 212-581-7118; and 321 North Robertson Boulevard, West Hollywood, CA 90048; 310-271-6300) has a New York warehouse that will ship caviar to consumers at wholesale prices with 24 hours notice. The Los Angeles retail store fills phone orders at retail prices. Caviarteria (29 E. 60th Street, New York, NY 10022; 800-4-CAVIAR; and 158 S. Beverly Hills Drive, Beverly Hills, CA 90212; 800-287-9773) will fill mail orders from either location. In addition to the main store in New York which handles mail orders, Petrossian Delicacies Shop (182 West 58th Street, New York, NY 10019; 800-828-9241) operates caviar boutiques in Bloomingdale's stores in New York, Chicago, Boca Raton, Miami, and Palm Beach, and Neiman Marcus stores in Chicago, Dallas, and San Francisco. Other New York sources include Macy's (151 W. 34th Street, New York, NY 10001; 212-695-4400, ext. 2647), and Zabar's (2245 Broadway, New York, NY 10024; 212-496-1234), which accepts phone orders Monday through Friday, 9 A.M. to 4 P.M.

CITRUS OILS

Each bottle of Boyajian orange or lemon oil contains the essential oils from hundreds of fruits. Pure oils are cold-pressed from the rind and then bottled without adulteration. Much more powerful than liquid extracts or powdered flavorings, these oils give a potent lift to cookies, cakes, muffins, breads, sauces, vinaigrettes, and marinades. Use sparingly — the flavor is extremely intense. Both oils come in five-ounce bottles. Orange oil, which captures the essence of 220 orange rinds, costs $5. The lemon oil, which is even more potent and relies on the rinds of 350 fruit, costs $10. The oils are available at Williams-Sonoma stores nationwide or from the company's catalog. For more information, call 800-541-2233.

COOKIE CUTTERS

Holiday baking calls for cookie cutters and we have found several excellent mail-order sources. Fox Run Craftsmen (P.O. Box 2727, 1907 Stout Drive, Ivyland, PA 18974; 800-372-0700) carries hundreds of individual cutters as well as packaged sets organized around themes such as Christmas, Hanukkah, dinosaurs, bears, and the Pilgrims. Contact the company for a copy of their free catalog. Sur La Table (84 Pine Street, Pike Place Farmers' Market, Seattle, WA 98101; 800-243-0852) is importing a one-sheet cookie cutter. Simply place this large plastic sheet over rolled-out dough and press to shape about two dozen angels, hearts, moons, bells, and trees at one time. The cookie cutter comes with a large cookie sheet and costs just $9.95 plus shipping. Finally, La Cuisine Kitchenware (*see* above) carries almost 70 different metal cutters including shapes from traditional reindeer and holly leaves to helicopters, palm trees, and chile peppers.

COMMERCIAL PARCHMENT PAPER

Rolls of parchment paper can be expensive and difficult to locate in many supermarkets. You can now purchase flat sheets (they don't curl) from a commercial paper supply business. E. A. Dages (975 Bethlehem Pike, Montgomeryville, PA 18936; 800-732-4377) sells pieces of parchment paper that measure 24 inches by 36 inches. They will cut sheets to fit your baking sheets as well. The price is $2.70 per pound for uncut paper and $3.10 per pound for cut sheets. There is a five-pound minimum — enough parchment paper for numerous baking projects — on all mail orders.

EXOTIC PRODUCE BY MAIL

When it comes to unusual produce, Frieda's, Inc. lives up to their slogan: "We change the way America eats." Among other products, owner Frieda Caplan has helped introduce Americans to kiwis, Asian pears, spaghetti squash, and purple potatoes. By calling 800-241-1771 you can get a listing of available products that can be sent to you by mail, including everything from fresh habanero chile peppers to cactus pears to lotus root, as well as all of the hard squashes pictured on page 14. ■

BUTTERMILK WAFFLES
page 28

THE BEST PUMPKIN PIE
page 22

RECIPE INDEX

BREAKFAST
Almost-as-Good-as-Buttermilk Waffles.............28
The Best Buttermilk Waffles...........................28

MAIN DISHES
The Best Grill-Roasted Turkey.............................21
The Best Oven-Roasted Turkey with Giblet Pan Sauce.................................20
Country Ham Stuffed with Spicy Southern Greens.............................12

SIDE DISHES
Cream Biscuits with Herbs...............................13
Mashed Potatoes and Apples with Bacon and Browned Onions.............................11
Mashed Potatoes with Parmesan Cheese and Lemon...11
Mashed Potatoes with Poached Garlic and Olive Oil 11
Master Recipe for Dinner Rolls.......................15
Master Recipe for Mashed Potatoes.................11
Spiced Peaches..13

CONDIMENTS
Homemade Vanilla Extract 2
Whole-Egg Mayonnaise.................................3

DESSERTS AND COOKIES
The Best Pumpkin Pie.................................22
Chocolate Trinity Parfaits..................Back Cover

Cookie Doughs:
Chocolate Butter Cookie Dough.........................7
Citrus Butter Cookie Dough.............................7
Master Recipe for Holiday Butter Cookie Dough.......................................7
Nut Butter Cookie Dough...............................7
Spice Butter Cookie Dough.............................7

Finished Cookies:
Classic Cut-Outs 8
Linzers 9
Mincemeat or Jam Turnovers 8
Mock Thumbprints 8
Petticoat Tails 9
Pinwheels 8
Viennese Crescents 9

MASHED POTATOES AND APPLES WITH BACON AND BROWNED ONIONS
page 11

PHOTOGRAPH BY RENEE COMET

COUNTRY HAM STUFFED WITH SPICY SOUTHERN GREENS
page 12

ASSORTED HOLIDAY COOKIES
pages 7 to 9

THE BEST OVEN-ROASTED TURKEY WITH GIBLET PAN SAUCE page 20

ALL PHOTOGRAPHS BY ERIC ROTH

Chocolate Trinity Parfaits

In the chilled bowl of a mixer fitted with a whisk attachment, beat 1¼ cups heavy cream and 1 tablespoon sugar on high speed until it forms stiff peaks. Whisk ¼ of the whipped cream into 4 ounces of melted semisweet or dark chocolate. Fold this mixture back into the remaining whipped cream, transfer to a stainless steel bowl, cover with plastic wrap, and refrigerate. Beat 1 cup cream, ¼ cup sugar, 1 tablespoon cocoa, and ¼ teaspoon vanilla extract to stiff peaks over medium speed. Transfer to a stainless steel bowl, cover with plastic, and refrigerate. Beat a final cup of cream, 1 tablespoon sugar, and ¼ teaspoon vanilla on high to stiff peaks, then fold in 2 ounces of grated semisweet or dark chocolate. Transfer to a stainless steel bowl, cover with plastic, and refrigerate all the creams for at least 30 minutes before assembling the parfaits. Fill a pastry bag (without a tip) with the dark chocolate cream. Pipe a portion of this cream into each of 8, 6-ounce stemmed glasses. Repeat piping process with cocoa and speckled creams, cleaning pastry bag in between. (Can be covered and refrigerated up to 4 hours before serving.) Garnish with white or dark chocolate curls and raspberries, if desired. *Makes 8 parfaits.*